The Blackwell Companion
to Christian Spirituality

Blackwell Companions to Religion

The Blackwell Companions to Religion series presents a collection of the most recent scholarship and knowledge about world religions. Each volume draws together newly commissioned essays by distinguished authors in the field, and is presented in a style which is accessible to undergraduate students, as well as scholars and the interested general reader. These volumes approach the subject in a creative and forward-thinking style, providing a forum in which leading scholars in the field can make their views and research available to a wider audience.

Published

The Blackwell Companion to Judaism
Edited by Jacob Neusner and Alan J. Avery-Peck

The Blackwell Companion to Sociology of Religion
Edited by Richard K. Fenn

The Blackwell Companion to the Hebrew Bible
Edited by Leo G. Perdue

The Blackwell Companion to Postmodern Theology
Edited by Graham Ward

The Blackwell Companion to Hinduism
Edited by Gavin Flood

The Blackwell Companion to Political Theology
Edited by Peter Scott and William T. Cavanaugh

The Blackwell Companion to Protestantism
Edited by Alister E. McGrath and Darren C. Marks

The Blackwell Companion to Modern Theology
Edited by Gareth Jones

The Blackwell Companion to Christian Ethics
Edited by Stanley Hauerwas and Samuel Wells

The Blackwell Companion to Religious Ethics
Edited by William Schweiker

The Blackwell Companion to Christian Spirituality
Edited by Arthur Holder

Forthcoming

The Blackwell Companion to the Study of Religion
Edited by Robert A. Segal

The Blackwell Companion to the Qur'ān
Edited by Andrew Rippin

The Blackwell Companion to the Bible and Culture
Edited by John Sawyer

The Blackwell Companion to Contemporary Islamic Thought
Edited by Ibrahim Abu-Rabi

The Blackwell Companion to Christian Spirituality

Edited by

Arthur Holder

BLACKWELL PUBLISHING
350 Main Street, Malden, MA 02148-5020, USA
9600 Garsington Road, Oxford OX4 2DQ, UK
550 Swanston Street, Carlton, Victoria 3053, Australia

First published 2005 by Blackwell Publishing Ltd

1 2005

Library of Congress Cataloging-in-Publication Data

The Blackwell companion to Christian spirituality / edited by Arthur Holder.
     p.   cm. — (Blackwell companions to religion)
  Includes bibliographical references and index.
  ISBN-13: 978-1-4051-0247-6 (hardback : alk. paper)
  ISBN-10: 1-4051-0247-0 (hardback : alk. paper)
  1. Spirituality I. Holder, Arthur. II. Series.
  BV4501.3 .B535 2005
  248—dc22

                             2004029753

A catalogue record for this title is available from the British Library.

Set in 10 on 12.5pt Photina
by SNP Best-set Typesetter Ltd, Hong Kong
Printed and bound in India
by Replika Press Pvt Ltd, Kundli

For further information on
Blackwell Publishing, visit our website:
www.blackwellpublishing.com

Contents

Notes on Contributors

Michael Barnes, SJ, teaches theology and religious studies at Heythrop College, University of London, where he is also co-director of the Centre for Christianity and Inter-religious Dialogue. He has written various books and articles on inter-religious relations, most recently *Theology and the Dialogue of Religions* (2002). He also runs the De Nobili Centre for Dialogue in Southall, a strongly multicultural and multi-faith area of West London.

Diana Butler Bass is Senior Research Fellow and Director of the Project on Congregations of Intentional Practice, a Lilly Endowment-funded research study of contemporary mainline Protestantism at the Virginia Theological Seminary in Alexandria, Virginia. She is the author of four books on American Christianity, including *Strength for the Journey: A Pilgrimage of Faith in Community* (2002) and *The Practicing Congregation: Imagining A New Old Church* (2004). In addition to teaching and writing, she has served on a number of national committees of the Episcopal Church (USA) and on the staff of an Episcopal congregation as director of adult education.

Michael Battle is Associate Dean of Academic Affairs at the Virginia Theological Seminary in Alexandria, Virginia. He previously taught at Duke University Divinity School and the School of Theology at the University of the South (Sewanee). He has also worked as an inner-city chaplain with Tony Campolo Ministries, and in Uganda and Kenya with the Plowshares Institute. He holds certification in spiritual direction from the Shalem Institute. He also is vice-chairman of the board of the Ghandi Institute. He is the author of *Reconciliation: The Ubuntu Theology of Desmond Tutu* (1997) and *Blessed are the Peacemakers: A Christian Spirituality of Nonviolence* (2004).

Douglas Burton-Christie is Professor of Christian Spirituality in the Department of Theological Studies at Loyola Marymount University, Los Angeles. He is author of *The Word in the Desert: Scripture and the Quest for Holiness in Early Christian Monasticism* (1993) and editor of the journal *Spiritus*, the official journal of the Society for the Study of Christian Spirituality.

John A. Coleman, SJ, is the Casassa Professor of Social Values at Loyola Marymount University, Los Angeles. For twenty-three years he was Professor of Religion and Society at the Graduate Theological Union, Berkeley. His most recent book, co-edited with William Ryan, is *Globalization and Catholic Social Thought: Peril or Promise?* (2005). He is currently working on issues of globalization, ethics and religion, and ecology and the common good.

Philip Endean, SJ, teaches theology at the University of Oxford, and is editor of *The Way*, the journal of contemporary spirituality published by the British Jesuits. He is a co-editor and translator of *Saint Ignatius of Loyola: Personal Writings* in the Penguin Classics series, and is the author of *Karl Rahner and Ignatian Spirituality* (2001).

Alejandro García-Rivera is Associate Professor of Systematic Theology at the Jesuit School of Theology at Berkeley and the Graduate Theological Union. He is the author of numerous articles and books, including *The Community of the Beautiful: A Theological Aesthetics* (1999; 2000 Catholic Press Award) and *A Wounded Innocence: Sketches for a Theology of Art* (2003). He is past president of the Academy of Catholic Hispanic Theologians in the United States, and recipient of the 2003 Virgilio Elizondo award for distinguished achievement in theology.

Barbara Green, OP, is Professor of Biblical Studies at the Dominican School of Philosophy and Theology in the Graduate Theological Union in Berkeley, California. She is author of *How Are the Mighty Fallen? A Dialogical Study of Saul in 1 Samuel* (2003) and *Jonah's Journeys* (2005). She is general editor of Liturgical Press's "Interfaces" series on biblical characters.

David Hay is Honorary Senior Research Fellow in the Department of Divinity and Religious Studies at the University of Aberdeen and Visiting Professor at the Institute for the Study of Religion of the University of Cracow in Poland. He is a zoologist by profession and a Roman Catholic layman. He worked for some years at the Religious Experience Research Unit in Oxford, becoming its director in 1985. Subsequently, he was appointed Reader in Spiritual Education at Nottingham University, a post from which he retired in 2000. His books include *Exploring Inner Space: Scientists and Religious Experience* (1982) and, with Rebecca Nye, *The Spirit of the Child* (1998).

Arthur Holder is Dean, Vice President for Academic Affairs, and Professor of Christian Spirituality at the Graduate Theological Union in Berkeley, California. A priest of the Episcopal Church, he is the translator of *Bede: On the Tabernacle* (1994) and co-translator of *Bede: A Biblical Miscellany* (1998). He is co-chair of the Christian Spirituality Group of the American Academy of Religion, and serves on the governing board of the Society for the Study of Christian Spirituality and the editorial board of the society's journal *Spiritus*.

Amy Hollywood is Professor of the History of Christianity and Theology at the University of Chicago Divinity School. She is the author of *The Soul as Virgin Wife: Mechthild of Magdeburg, Marguerite Porete, and Meister Eckhart* (1995) and *Sensible Ecstasy: Mysticism, Sexual Difference, and the Demands of History* (2002).

Robert Davis Hughes III is Norma and Olan Mills Professor of Divinity and Professor of Systematic Theology at the School of Theology of the University of the South (Sewanee). A priest of the Episcopal Church, he is a Fellow of the Episcopal Church Foundation, a member of the Society for the Study of Christian Spirituality, and past president of the Society of Anglican and Lutheran Theologians. He publishes regularly in *Sewanee Theological Review* and *Anglican Theological Review*, maintains a private practice in spiritual direction, and is president of the board of the GOAL project, a mission society promoting twelve-step recovery worldwide.

Kwok Pui-Lan is William F. Cole Professor of Christian Theology and Spirituality at the Episcopal Divinity School, Cambridge, Massachusetts. She has published extensively in Asian feminist theology, biblical hermeneutics, and postcolonial criticism. Her recent books include *Introducing Asian Feminist Theology* (2000) and *Postcolonial Imagination and Feminist Theology* (2005). She co-edited *Beyond Colonial Anglicanism: The Anglican Communion in the Twenty-first Century* (2001).

Elizabeth Liebert, SNJM, is Professor of Spiritual Life at San Francisco Theological Seminary and a member of the faculty of the doctoral program in Christian spirituality at the Graduate Theological Union. A past president of the Society for the Study of Christian Spirituality, she is co-author of *The Spiritual Exercises Reclaimed: Uncovering Liberating Possibilities for Women* (2001) and *A Retreat with the Psalms: Resources for Personal and Communal Prayer* (2001) and author of *Changing Life Patterns: Adult Development in Spiritual Direction* (1992, 2000).

Ann Loades is Emeritus Professor of Divinity at the University of Durham, England, where she was the first woman to receive a personal chair. She is currently President of the Society for the Study of Theology (2005–6). One of the first two lay members of Durham Cathedral Chapter, she is also its first woman member. She was recently appointed Commander of the Order of the British Empire. Her publications include work on such diverse figures as Kant, Coleridge, C. S. Lewis, Evelyn Underhill, and Austin Farrer. Her most recent monograph is *Feminist Theology: Voices from the Past* (2001) on Mary Wollstonecraft, Josephine Butler, and Dorothy L. Sayers.

David Lonsdale teaches in the graduate Christian spirituality program at Heythrop College, University of London, and played a large part in creating that program. He was also co-editor of *The Way*, a journal of Christian spirituality, from 1984 to 1993. His books *Listening to the Music of the Spirit: The Art of Discernment* (1992) and *Eyes to See, Ears to Hear: An Introduction to Ignatian Spirituality* (2nd edn, 2000) are widely used in teaching and have been translated into several languages.

John A. McGuckin is a priest of the (Romanian) Orthodox Church. He is Professor of Early Church History at the Union Theological Seminary in New York, and Professor of Byzantine Christian Studies at Columbia University. He has written extensively on early Christian and New Testament literature. Recent publications include *St Gregory of Nazianzus: An Intellectual Biography* (2001) and *The Westminster Handbook to Patristic Theology* (2003). He is a Fellow of the Royal Historical Society. Current projects include a translation of Origen and a popular edition of the largely unknown treasures of Ethiopian religious poetry.

Mark A. McIntosh, Associate Professor of Theology at Loyola University of Chicago, is also currently serving as a chaplain to the House of Bishops of the Episcopal Church and as Canon Theologian to the Presiding Bishop and Primate of the Episcopal Church, USA. An Episcopal priest, he holds degrees in history and in theology from Yale, Oxford, and the University of Chicago. In addition to his most recent work, *Discernment and Truth: Meditations on the Christian Life of Contemplation and Practice* (2004), he is the author of *Mystical Theology: The Integrity of Spirituality and Theology* (1998) and two other monographs considering the relationship between theology and spirituality.

David B. Perrin, OMI, is Professor of Spirituality and Ethics at Saint Paul University, Ottawa, Canada. Most recently, he authored *The Sacrament of Reconciliation: An Existential Approach* (1998) and he is the editor of *Women Christian Mystics Speak to our Times* (2001). His research interest in mysticism centers on the mysticism of John of the Cross. Former Dean of the Faculty of Theology at Saint Paul University and past co-chair of the Mysticism Group of the American Academy of Religion, he currently serves on the governing board of the Society for the Study of Christian Spirituality.

Jill Raitt is Professor Emerita of Religious Studies and founder and Senior Research Fellow of the Center for Religion, the Professions, and the Public at the University of Missouri-Columbia. A past president of the American Academy of Religion, she has served as a senior editor of and contributor to the *Oxford Encyclopedia of the Reformation* and as primary editor of and contributor to *Christian Spirituality: High Middle Ages and Reformation* (1987), vol. 17 in *World Spirituality: An Encyclopedic History of the Religious Quest*.

Janet K. Ruffing, RSM, is Professor of Spirituality and Spiritual Direction at Fordham University, Bronx, New York. She is the author of numerous articles and of *Spiritual Direction: Beyond the Beginnings* (2000). In addition, she edited *Mysticism and Social Transformation* (2001) and prepared the critical introduction and translations for *Elisabeth Leseur: Selected Writings* (2005). She is one of the founding Coordinating Council members of Spiritual Directors International.

Robert John Russell is Professor of Theology and Science in Residence at the Graduate Theological Union, and Founder and Director of the Center for Theology and the Natural Sciences (CTNS). He co-edited the five-volume CTNS/Vatican Observatory series, "Scientific Perspectives on Divine Action." He helped lead the CTNS Science and the Spiritual Quest and Science and Religion course programs. He co-edits the new journal, *Theology and Science*. He is ordained in the United Church of Christ. His research includes eschatology and cosmology, quantum physics and divine action, and time, eternity and relativity theory.

Sandra M. Schneiders, IHM, is Professor of New Testament Studies and Christian Spirituality at the Jesuit School of Theology in the Graduate Theological Union, Berkeley, California. She is author of *Women and the Word* (1986), *The Revelatory Text* (1999), *Written That You May Believe* (2003), and two volumes on Roman Catholic religious life (2000, 2001). She has served on the editorial boards of *Spiritus*, *New Testament Studies*, *Catholic Biblical Quarterly*, and *Horizons*, and on the governing board of the Society for the Study of Christian Spirituality, of which she was president in 1997.

Philip F. Sheldrake is William Leech Professor of Applied Theology at the University of Durham, England. He is the author of several books, including *Spirituality and History* (1995) and *Spaces for the Sacred: Place, Memory, Identity* (2001). His current research and writing focuses on spirituality and theological method, and the spirituality/ethics of place and the meaning of cities. He is regularly a visiting professor in North America and is a past president of the Society for the Study of Christian Spirituality.

William C. Spohn is Augustine Cardinal Bea, SJ, Distinguished Professor of Theology and Director of the Bannan Center for Jesuit Education at Santa Clara University. He is the author of *What Are They Saying about Scripture and Ethics?* (2nd edn, 1995) and *Go and Do Likewise: Jesus and Ethics* (1999). He serves as Project Director for Discover (the Santa Clara program for reflection on vocation) and is a member of the Medical Board of California Ethics Task Force.

Columba Stewart, OSB, is a monk of Saint John's Abbey in Collegeville, Minnesota. He is Professor of Monastic Studies at the Saint John's School of Theology and Executive Director of the Institute for the Book, Art, and Religious Culture and the Hill Monastic Manuscript Library at Saint John's University. He is the author of *Cassian the Monk* (1992) and *Prayer and Community* (1998), and is currently at work on a study of early monastic prayer.

Joseph Stewart-Sicking is the Project Associate for the Project on Congregations of Intentional Practice, a Lilly Endowment-funded research study of vital mainline Protestant churches at the Virginia Theological Seminary in Alexandria, Virginia. An Episcopal layperson, his work focuses on the inter-relationships among Christian practices, Christian traditions, and congregational vitality in contemporary society.

William Thompson-Uberuaga is Professor of Systematic Theology at Duquesne University in Pittsburgh, Pennsylvania. A former president of the Catholic Theological Society of America, his published books include *Christology and Spirituality* (1991) and *The Struggle for Theology's Soul* (1996). He specializes in the dialogue between spirituality, theology, and philosophy (especially political theory).

Bonnie Thurston was an academic for thirty years. She now lives as a solitary in West Virginia, USA. An ordained minister in the Christian Church (Disciples of Christ), she was William F. Orr Professor of New Testament at Pittsburgh Theological Seminary and has authored many books including *Spiritual Life in the Early Church* (1993), *Reading Colossians, Ephesians, and II Thessalonians* (1995), *Women in the New Testament* (1998), *To Everything a Season: A Spirituality of Time* (1999), *Preaching Mark* (2002), the Sacra Pagina volume on Philippians (2004), and two books of poetry.

Susan J. White is Alberta H. and Harold L. Lunger Professor of Spiritual Resources and Disciplines and Associate Dean of Academic Affairs at Brite Divinity School, Texas Christian University. She received her PhD from the University of Notre Dame and was previously on the faculty of the Cambridge Federation of Theological Colleges, Cambridge, England and a member of the Faculty of Divinity of the University of Cambridge. Her recent books include *Christian Worship and Technological Change* (1997), *The Spirit of Worship: The Liturgical Tradition* (2000), and *A History of Women in Christian Worship* (2003).

Ulrike Wiethaus holds an interdisciplinary appointment as Professor of the Humanities at Wake Forest University. She combines her interest in medieval women's spirituality with cross-cultural and interdisciplinary work on the arts, film, and cultural representations of the sacred. She is the author of numerous articles and books on medieval Christian mysticism and spirituality, including *Ecstatic Transformation* (1995), and, most recently, a translation of the visions of a medieval holy woman, *Agnes Blannbekin, Viennese Beguine: Life and Revelations* (2002).

Richard Fox Young is Timby Associate Professor of the History of Religions at Princeton Theological Seminary. He served for some years as a Presbyterian Church (USA) mission worker with churches and Christian institutions in Asia. His major publications – *Resistant Hinduism* (1981), *The Bible Trembled* (1995), *Vain Debates* (1996), and *The Carpenter-Heretic* (1998) – use the indigenous literatures of South Asia to historically reconstruct the encounter of Hindus and Buddhists with Christianity and to reflect theologically on contemporary problems of pluralism, dialogue, and witness.

Acknowledgments

The editor and publisher gratefully acknowledge the permission granted to reproduce the copyright material in this book:

Bridgeman Art Library, for permission to reproduce the painting *Jonah and the Whale*, *c.*1988 (oil on canvas) by Albert Herbert (b.1925), from a private collection.

Sandra M. Schneiders, for permission to use excerpts from her unpublished work, "Seriously, Jonah!"

The Johns Hopkins University Press, for permission to reproduce a revised version of an article entitled "The role of practice in the study of Christian spirituality" from *Spiritus: A Journal of Christian Spirituality* 2: 1 (2002), 30–49. © The Johns Hopkins University Press.

Every effort has been made to trace copyright holders and to obtain their permission for the use of copyright material. The publisher apologizes for any errors or omissions in the above list and would be grateful if notified of any corrections that should be incorporated in future reprints or editions of this book.

Introduction

Arthur Holder

The Blackwell Companion to Christian Spirituality offers a comprehensive introduction to Christian spirituality, which has in recent years emerged as a distinct academic discipline in universities, colleges, and theological schools throughout the English-speaking world. The *Companion* is intended to be thoroughly interdisciplinary, broadly ecumenical, and representative of the most significant recent developments in the field. Without attempting to impose a single definition of Christian spirituality upon the contributors, as editor I have invited them to reflect on "the lived experience of Christian faith and discipleship." The six parts of the volume deal with approaches to the study of Christian spirituality, biblical foundations, historical developments, theological perspectives, interdisciplinary dialogue partners, and selected special topics in contemporary Christian spirituality. My hope is that *The Blackwell Companion to Christian Spirituality* will be of use to scholars in the field and in other related disciplines, to undergraduate and graduate students in theology and religious studies who desire a more accessible entry point to Christianity than might be provided by books dealing solely with doctrinal issues or institutional developments, and to Christians of all denominations and traditions who desire to learn more about the practice of their faith.

Defining Christian Spirituality

"For all who are led by the Spirit of God are children of God . . . When we cry, 'Abba! Father!' it is that very Spirit bearing witness with our spirit that we are children of God" (Rom. 8: 14–16). Although the apostle Paul never uses the word "spirituality," this earnest confession of faith suggests that any Christian understanding of that term must necessarily refer to the intimate loving relationship between God's Holy Spirit and the spirit (animating life force) of believers – a relationship that can be characterized both as kinship and as communion. The Christian life is always "life in the Spirit" (cf. Gal. 5: 25), in all its variety and unpredictability. The Spirit of God is one, but it manifests itself in diverse ways. As members of the human race, we all share in a common human spirit, but that spirit takes a distinct and particular form in each one of us. The phenomenon that has come to be known as "Christian spirituality" is thus a complex subject that can only be understood and appreciated when approached from a variety of perspectives, and with careful attention to its particular manifestations in an infinite range of historical and cultural contexts.

The word "spirituality" does not have a very long history in English, at least not in its current sense. As a term referring to lived Christian experience, its recent popularity in English seems to have been derived by way of translation from French Catholic authors in the early years of the twentieth century (Principe 1993: 931; Sheldrake 1995: 42–4). Readers of this volume will find frequent discussions of matters of definition, the details of which may be best appreciated in the context of the individual essays. Here it seems appropriate simply to indicate some issues about which the contributors are in general agreement, and some on which they disagree (or at least offer significantly different emphases).

Contemporary scholars of Christian spirituality, including the contributors to this volume, have readily accepted Walter Principe's demarcation of three different but related levels of spirituality: (a) the "real or existential level," (b) "the formulation of teaching about the lived reality" as constructed by influential spiritual leaders, traditions, or schools, and (c) "the study by scholars of the first and especially of the second levels of spirituality" (2000: 47–8). Which of these three senses is operative in a particular discourse can usually be determined from the context, just as speakers of English are accustomed to thinking of "history" as referring sometimes to past events, at other times to a narrative account of those events, and at still other times to the academic discipline that studies both past events and the accounts of them subsequently provided by later writers. (But note that in the academic discipline of Christian spirituality, as in that of history, postmodern theorists often question whether we ever have direct access to the first "existential" level for anyone except ourselves; if not, then these disciplines are in truth able to study only the discourses and artifacts that appear on the second level, and any inferences they draw about the first level are necessarily provisional or perhaps even illusory.)

All of the contributors to this volume seem also to hold that the study of spirituality appropriately involves a focus on "experience." Although there is no final consensus on what "experience" means or on how it can best be studied, these scholars do agree that the experience studied in the field of Christian spirituality is not limited to extraordinary moments of ecstasy or insight, or to explicitly devotional experiences such as prayer and meditation. Certainly the experience to which the discipline of Christian spirituality attends is not "spiritual" as opposed to "material" or "embodied"; these scholars are very much aware that in Pauline terminology "spiritual" (*pneumatikos*) means "under the influence of the Holy Spirit" and is contrasted not with the realm of the "body" (*soma*) but with that of the "flesh" (*sarx*) and its selfish desires. Thus these scholars want to avoid all suggestions of dualism and to insist that spirituality properly includes the whole of life: politics, economics, art, sexuality, and science, as well as whatever is explicitly religious. A difficulty, of course, is that many (perhaps most!) Christian "spiritual" writers and practitioners of previous eras have not shared this wholehearted aversion to dualism, so that these contemporary scholars must frankly acknowledge that their own convictions and interests are often at odds with the tendencies of the material they seek to study.

Finally, the contributors to this *Companion* agree that the study of Christian spirituality is inherently interdisciplinary. Although their own academic training came in a wide range of academic disciplines (including biblical studies, history, theology, sociology, psychology, physics, and biology), I believe that all of them would now identify themselves, at least on a part-time basis, as scholars of Christian spirituality – not in distinction from their original disciplinary identities, but as an enhancement or focusing of those identities. For some of them, Christian spirituality has become their primary academic discipline; others continue to see another discipline as the home base from which they venture forth into Christian spirituality from time to time; still others probably see themselves as having a foot in both camps, without feeling a particular need to distinguish when they are operating within one or the other. But surely none of them would claim that his or her approach to the subject is exhaustive or self-sufficient. Indeed, I believe that readers of this volume will be able to discern that all of these scholars, despite their disparate disciplinary locations, are engaged in a common conversation about a topic (Christian spirituality) that holds fascination for them in its expansive totality, not just in relation to their particular subfields of expertise.

Even with all these significant agreements, the contributors to this volume hold various points of view in relation to some critical questions of definition that engage all scholars in the field of Christian spirituality today. Perhaps foremost among these is a question about which element in the term "Christian spirituality" ought to be taken as primary. Some scholars, often but not always those who come from the disciplinary perspectives of biblical studies, history, or theology, begin (not always explicitly) with Christianity as a concrete historical phenomenon, and then go on to ask: "What is it within Christianity that we can identify specifically as 'spirituality,' as distinct from ethics or doctrine or institutional structures, or perhaps as a conjoining of those features of the Christian phenomenon?" Here the academic discipline of Christian spirituality is in effect a specialization within the broader field of Christian studies, or within a more narrowly defined field such as biblical studies, church history, or systematic theology. Other scholars (often but not always those who approach their work from the standpoint of the social or natural sciences, or who want to engage in conversation with scholars in those disciplines) seek to begin with spirituality as a universal human phenomenon (for example, "the capacity for self-transcendence"), and then go on to ask how Christians specify and thematize this common human experience in ways that are distinctive to their particular traditions.

Closely related to the question about which element ("Christian" or "spirituality") comes first is the often-heated debate about the relationship between spirituality and theology. Is the study of Christian spirituality inherently and irreducibly theological, simply because we cannot hope to understand any aspect of Christianity without reference to God and human discourse about God? Or is the academic discipline of Christian spirituality better seen as a form of religious studies, to which theology makes its distinctive contribution but only as one auxiliary discipline among many? There are, of course, many variations and subtle shadings of both views, often dependent upon how the protagonists are defining "theology." Is it equivalent to "doctrine," in which case spirituality scholars must take care to avoid letting intellectually or ecclesially preconceived conceptions of what Christians "ought" to feel and believe distract them from what those Christians actually experience in life? Or is "theology" rather to be understood as "faith seeking understanding" or simply as "knowing God," in which case it might again become (as it has always been in the Christian East) a virtual synonym for spirituality?

The debate around these and other such questions is conditioned by previous developments in the history of Western theology since the twelfth century, the time most often identified as marking a "split" between theology and spirituality, or between the reasoned expression of faith and its lived experience. The ascendancy of critical reason, the devotion to scientific methods, and the Enlightenment ideal of "objective" scholarship all come into play on both sides of the equation, along with the postmodern critiques of them that have emerged in the academy in recent years. Much of the current debate finds expression in arguments about the proper institutional location of Christian spirituality as an academic discipline. If it is a subdiscipline of theology, or an inherently theological enterprise, then perhaps it can only be carried out in the context of a believing community such as that found in a denominational seminary or a church-related college. (This view is more frequently encountered in the United States than in Britain or Canada, where theology is more easily afforded a place in the curriculum of secular universities.) But if Christian spirituality is really a descriptive discipline rather than a normative one, then (perhaps somewhat paradoxically) it is probably best pursued in an environment in which research and reflection are conducted apart from any authoritative shared faith commitment.

Obviously related to the question of the proper environment for research in Christian spirituality are the issues of practice and participation. If scholars of Christian spirituality seek to reflect on religious experience, is it appropriate for them at the same time to foster and shape the experiences of other people by serving as their spiritual guides? To what extent, and by what means, is it appropriate for those scholars to reflect upon their own experience? Is Christian spirituality best understood as a "theoretical" discipline like mathematics, or an "applied" discipline like engineering? Is growth in faith and holiness the true and proper aim of study in this field, or merely a happy but inessential byproduct? Can the study of Christian spirituality be undertaken by those of other religious traditions, or none? If so, are they doing the same thing as Christian scholars in the field, or is their study necessarily something different because they study as outsiders rather than as insiders? Is it ever truly possible for an insider to a particular spiritual tradition to adopt the posture of an outsider, and vice versa? If possible, is it desirable? Only a few of the essays here tackle these questions directly, but all of them provide at least implicit answers indicated by the author's choice of tone, style, and perspective. The reader who wants to identify each contributor's distinctive approach should pay close attention to the use of the first person (both singular and plural). Contemporary scholarship in the field of Christian spirituality moves along a spectrum from confessional autobiography to the presentation of an apparently "authorless" text. None of the essays in this volume goes to the extreme in either direction, but the contributions do represent a considerable range of points in between.

A final question that fascinates (and often puzzles) scholars of Christian spirituality has to do with the relationship between spirituality and religion. There are those who would argue that the two terms are synonymous, or at least that the distinctions commonly made between them inevitably end up reducing "spirituality" to something that is ahistorical, individualistic, disembodied, and utterly privatized – in short, not at all the sort of thing that interests scholars like the contributors to this volume, and hardly deserving of the name "Christian." Others might want to argue that spirituality is the individual's appropriation of a received religious tradition. (But how then can we speak meaningfully of the spirituality of the Baptists or the Armenian Orthodox, as though such groups had a distinctive corporate spirituality, and not merely a common religion?) Some suggest that spirituality is the universal human experience of transcendence that becomes particularized, and inevitably reified, in the forms and structures of any specific religion – thereby transferring to spirituality Schleiermacher's famous definition of religion as "the feeling of absolute dependence." For several of the authors whose work appears here, the contemporary tendency to set "spirituality" in opposition to "religion" (as in the phrase "spiritual but not religious") is a phenomenon deserving scholarly attention in itself, regardless of whether or not this oppositional definition is "correct." In other words, we need to listen carefully to what people are trying to say when they contrast the two terms with one another. We may not learn much about "spirituality" or "religion" as abstract concepts, but we will learn a great deal about the experience of the people who use the words in this way.

As previously stated, the working definition that I offered the contributors to this *Companion* was of Christian spirituality as "the lived experience of Christian faith and discipleship." None of the authors appears to have rejected this definition outright or found it especially problematic, although several say that it needs to be given further specificity or put in relation to the spirituality of people outside the bounds of Christianity. It is worth noting that the words "faith" and "discipleship" are unambiguously Christian terms, full of scriptural and theological resonance. It is hard to think of any serious Christian author across the centuries who did not use those words or their cognates with some regularity, or any Christian group that has not invoked them in both teaching and worship. So this working definition is clearly more emic to Christianity (that is, expressed in terms intrinsic to its self-understanding) than etic (expressed in terms derived from outside the phenomenon under analysis). Like any definition of a scholarly subject, this one has its advantages as well as its limitations. Ultimately, the value of any such definition must be judged by its heuristic quality: does it stimulate research, foster insight, and raise interesting questions to be debated and explored? By that important measure, and on the evidence of the essays in this volume, my working definition of Christian spirituality seems to have done its job.

An Introduction to the Essays

The structure of this *Companion to Christian Spirituality* is neither haphazard nor original to me. As my colleagues at the Graduate Theological Union in Berkeley will quickly recognize, the six component parts of the volume correspond closely to the protocol of our doctoral program in Christian spirituality, and to the syllabus of the introductory area seminar in which I have been privileged to participate on several occasions. (A prime motivation for editing this volume was the knowledge that now we will at last have a suitable textbook for this graduate-level course.) Thus we move from questions of definition and method to the foundations of Christian spirituality in Scripture and history, and then to engagement with theological perspectives; thus far, we are dealing with materials and questions that must be considered and (at least at a general level) mastered by all scholars in the field, regardless of the nature of their research projects. Then we come to consider a selection of interdisciplinary dialogue partners, any one or more of which a scholar might want to engage in relation to a particular research topic; and, finally, to some examples of topics in contemporary Christian spirituality that seem to be of special interest to many of those working in the field today. I gratefully acknowledge the help and inspiration provided over the years by students and faculty at the Graduate Theological Union, who have served as my mentors and guides in this exciting and ever-changing discipline.

Part I (*What is Christian Spirituality?*) contains a single essay by Sandra M. Schneiders, who has been perhaps the most articulate and prolific English-speaking scholar writing on the definitions and methodologies appropriate to this relatively new academic discipline. Here she explicates and refines her well-known definition of spirituality as "the experience of conscious involvement in the project of life-integration through self-transcendence toward the horizon of ultimate value one perceives" before going on to describe three approaches (historical, theological, and anthropological) to the study of Christian spirituality, with generous appreciation of the promise of each approach and insightful cautions about each approach's potential pitfalls. Finally, Schneiders offers her own nuanced perspective on the controversial issues of practice and participation in the study of Christian spirituality.

Both of the essays in Part II (*Scripture and Christian Spirituality*) combine historical research with issues of contemporary application, but the first essay deals primarily with the spiritualities that the Bible has helped produce, while the second essay concentrates more on the ancient spiritualities that produced the Bible. To a certain extent, these differing approaches reflect the most obvious difference between the Old Testament and the New (namely, that the latter was written by Christians but the former by Jews); however, they also represent two different approaches to "biblical spirituality." In the first essay, Barbara Green traces the history of Christian exegesis of the Book of Jonah in order to show how the Old Testament has been both formative and transformative for Christians; in conclusion, she identifies five perennial issues in the Christian appropriation of Old Testament texts. The second essay, by Bonnie Thurston, reminds us that the New Testament reflects a plurality of spiritualities, each of which arose from the religious experience of disciples in community, and all of which need to be studied in recognition that the first-century world was not the same as ours, even though Christians then and now claim experience of the same risen Christ.

The six essays in Part III (*Christian Spirituality in History*) provide an overview of some of the most significant themes, movements, and developments. Without attempting to be encyclopedic or exhaustive, each essay introduces the reader to selected persons, institutions, practices, and events that serve as illustrative cases. The approach here differs somewhat from many previous treatments of the history of Christian spirituality in that the authors have tried to present more synthetic accounts that avoid treating various "schools" of spirituality in isolation from one another. As a result, the reader may hope to gain some sense of the unity of Christianity, as well as its unquestionable diversity. In the first historical essay, Columba Stewart characterizes Christianity during the Roman empire (100–600) as searching for unity and forming a spiritual culture through practices of liturgy, devotion, and public witness (most notably, martyrdom, asceticism, and monasticism). John A. McGuckin carries the story in the Eastern church forward to 1700 by concentrating on some of the most remarkable Byzantine and Syrian writers in a variety of genres, including hymnody, doctrinal treatises, spiritual guidance, hagiography, and polemic. In the medieval West to the eve of the Reformation, Ulrike Wiethaus sees the emergence of a multicultural synthesis that has bequeathed legacies both positive (expanded roles for women, mystical literature, ideals of radical poverty, heroic acceptance of suffering) and negative (religious intolerance, fear of diversity, and an over-reliance on texts). Jill Raitt analyses European reformations of all sorts (Protestant, Catholic, Anglican, Anabaptist, Quaker) in the tumultuous period 1450–1700 as diverse ways in which spiritual practice left the cloister in order to reach out to lay people in their shops and homes. Co-authors Diana Butler Bass and Joseph Stewart-Sicking picture Christian spirituality in modern North America and Europe since 1700 as a changing mosaic of spiritual options exercised by creative individuals both within and beyond the churches in the aftermath of the Enlightenment and the breakdown of institutional authority. Especially welcome in this volume because it covers ground that will be unfamiliar to many readers is the essay by Richard Fox Young, who employs literature along with more conventional sources to examine spirituality in Africa, Asia, Latin America, and Oceania from the perspective of a new historiography that shifts the emphasis from Western transmission of the gospel to non-Western appropriation, and from the missionaries to the converts.

In Part IV (*Theology and Christian Spirituality*), we turn to theology's constructive engagement with lived Christian experience. Mark A. McIntosh draws on theologians as diverse as Maximus the Confessor, Aquinas, Traherne, and John of the Cross to root Christian spirituality in the divine generosity of self-giving at the heart of the Trinity. Suggesting that Christology's role in spirituality is analogous to the role of theological reason in the life of faith, William Thompson-Uberuaga argues that both fideist and rationalist Christologies lead to diminished spiritualities, while combinative forms offer better prospects in the face of both globalization and postmodern thought. Taking up the question of the Holy Spirit (often strangely neglected in talk of spirituality), Robert Davis Hughes III explores the Spirit's trinitarian mission as the source of a threefold pattern of conversion, transfiguration, and perfection in the spiritual life. Challenging Sandra Schneiders's view of the discipline of theology as being too restrictive, Philip Endean advocates a mystagogical theology that at its best and most imaginative is very close to what is today called "spirituality"; he then goes on to identify three contributions that the study of the doctrinal tradition regarding the human person (which is by no means the whole of what he means by "theology") can make to spirituality: articulation of context, concern with truth, and extension of sympathy. In his essay on the church as context for spirituality, David Lonsdale describes the church as a school of the affections and desires that forms disciples in discernment primarily through liturgy, which is its proper and distinctive activity. Liturgy naturally figures also in an essay on sacramentality by Ann Loades, but she points us not in the first instance to services of worship in churches but to the worldly sacraments of nature, creativity, procreation and parenting, work, music and dance, stillness and silence, and finally to Christ incarnate in our midst. Part IV concludes with William C. Spohn's rendering (based in virtue ethics) of spiritual practices such as fidelity in marriage, hymn singing, and liturgical prayer as the primary means by which the affections of Christian believers are shaped for moral character and action.

The essays in Part V (*Interdisciplinary Dialogue Partners for the Study of Christian Spirituality*) explore both the promises and the challenges for Christian spirituality in entering into dialogue with various academic disciplines, all of which have already been in prior conversation with other forms of theological and religious studies. In the first essay, John A. Coleman surveys recent sociological literature dealing with the vast array of spiritualities and religious movements in the United States at the turn of the twenty-first century, noting that while the categories "spiritual" and "religious" are often defined in opposition to one another, many people identify themselves as both (good news for churches that emphasize spiritual growth). Next, Janet K. Ruffing provides an overview of some major schools of psychology (psychoanalytic, cognitive, analytic, transpersonal) that are particularly relevant to spirituality studies, even though, as Ruffing cautions, their understanding of spirituality is often independent of religious communities, privatized, and inattentive to societal issues of justice and compassion that are critical in Christian spirituality. The possibilities for dialogue with the natural sciences (especially physics and biology) are explored by Robert John Russell, who directs our attention to the spiritual implications of scientific discussions about things as old as the Big Bang and as new as artificial intelligence, as small as a DNA molecule and as vast as the stars. Alejandro García-Rivera traces the historical development of aesthetics from Plato and Aristotle through the early church and the Middle Ages to Kant, Hegel, and von Balthasar, suggesting that the human ability to appreciate and create beauty is an intrinsic aspect of our experience of the divine. Amy Hollywood's essay shows that feminist readings of medieval spirituality, as carried out by Caroline Walker Bynum and other recent scholars, have revealed previously hidden aspects of that historical period, while raising complex methodological and theoretical issues that are pertinent to the study of Christian spirituality in any context. Susan J. White's essay on the dialogue with ritual studies incorporates concepts and investigative tools from anthropology, ethnography, and performance studies that will be useful to many spirituality scholars, especially in light of the current interest in religious practices, and liturgical practices in particular (as noted above with reference to several of the theological essays in Part IV). And if Christian spirituality is a form of *religious* experience, then we can hardly talk about it without some consideration of the other great world religions. In the final essay of Part V, Michael Barnes presents what he calls a "theology of dialogue" that seeks to go beyond the "history of religions" or "religious studies" models of understanding the religious "other."

If space had permitted, the final part, Part VI (*Special Topics in Contemporary Christian Spirituality*), could have been expanded to include many more topics. But the seven topics chosen represent some of those that have garnered the most scholarly attention in recent years, and promise to do so for some time to come. David Hay's essay on religious or spiritual experience provides both philosophical reflection and empirical data concerning this fundamental aspect of Christian spirituality, which has often been challenged as illusion or neurosis but continues to stimulate research by biologists, psychologists, sociologists, and many others. Defining mysticism as "[t]he experience of *oneness or intimacy with some absolute divine reality*," David B. Perrin investigates the relationship of mysticism to "ordinary" religious experience, to language and text, to body and soul, and to the prophetic and charismatic dimensions of Christian faith. In an essay that can fruitfully be read in conjunction with the historical essays in Part III – indeed, in relation to all efforts at finding meaning in the "classical texts" (written and otherwise) of Christian spirituality – Philip F. Sheldrake considers the task of interpretation: how can communities of Christian readers find wisdom in what they read? A fine example of just this sort of interpretation is provided by Douglas Burton-Christie in an essay reflecting on contemporary writing on the spiritual significance of nature, and especially the experience of loss on both personal and cosmic scales, in what has been described as an "age of extinction." Returning to the notion of "practice" and its role in the study of Christian spirituality, Elizabeth Liebert appeals to parallels with the field of pastoral theology and insights from educational theory to advocate practice in the classroom as an aid to scholarship, as well as a means of spiritual growth. Michael Battle asks what a Christian spirituality of liberation might look like if based on relationality and inclusion instead of identity politics, with Desmond Tutu as a contemporary example of a theologian and activist who represents both confirmation and critique of the perspectives of liberation theology. Finally, Kwok Pui-Lan brings the volume to a close with an essay in which she engages the increasingly pressing issues of interfaith worship and multiple religious identity, at the same time reminding us that interfaith encounter (with its attendant charges of "syncreticism") is as old as Christianity itself.

The Present, Past, and Future of a Discipline

This *Companion* can with justification claim to represent the current "state of the art" in the academic discipline of Christian spirituality. It should be noted that a number of important topics that do not appear in the table of contents are nevertheless dealt with in some of the essays collected here. For example, there are substantial treatments of "culture" as a category for Christian spirituality in the essays of Young, White, and Sheldrake. Readers who regret the omission of literary studies from the list of interdisciplinary dialogue partners are invited to look at the essays of Young, Hollywood, and Burton-Christie to find excellent examples of fruitful engagement with literature and literary theory. And the complex and contested relationship between spirituality and religion is explored from various angles by Bass and Stewart-Sicking, Coleman, Hay, Burton-Christie, and Kwok, while gender issues are treated not only in Hollywood's essay on feminist studies, but also in the essays of Wiethaus, Loades, and Kwok.

Although this volume focuses on the present state of the discipline, there is ample material here for readers who wish to get a sense of its past. Schneiders and Endean, as well as Hughes, Perrin, and Sheldrake, discuss aspects of earlier scholarly approaches to the subject, and the bibliographies they provide will guide readers toward other helpful sources. But perhaps the most effective testimony to the progress that has been made in the development of Christian spirituality as an academic discipline is simply the cohesiveness (which is not to say uniformity or unanimity) of the essays in this *Companion*. Notice how often contributors coming from very different perspectives and writing on quite disparate topics cite many of the same sources, including one another. Judith Klein has written: "The term *discipline* signifies the tools, methods, procedures, exempla, concepts, and theories that account coherently for a set of objects or subjects. Over time they are shaped and reshaped by external contingencies and internal intellectual demands. In this manner a discipline comes to organize and concentrate experience into a particular 'world view'" (1990: 104). If this is the case, then there is abundant evidence here that Christian spirituality is no longer merely "emerging" as a discipline, but has clearly arrived.

Klein's primary interest, however, is not in the establishment of disciplines but in the creative interstitial work of interdisciplinarity that goes on between and among disciplines. Thus she makes us aware that any discipline inevitably loses sight of whatever it chooses not to notice, and is unable to study whatever does not respond to its tools and methods. Scholars of Christian spirituality hope to minimize such disciplinary losses when they claim that theirs is an inherently interdisciplinary field. Will this "interdiscipline" or "field-encompassing field" be able to maintain its characteristic energy, its expansive vision, and its eclectic yet ordered approach to research? I believe that it will – that we as spirituality scholars and practitioners will do so – as long as we keep our focus on the lived experience of Christian faith and discipleship.

Much of the appeal of Christian spirituality as an academic discipline lies in what is often referred to as its peculiarly "self-implicating" character. Many students of spirituality have a profound stake in their studies because they are themselves pursuing the same "life in the Spirit" as the historical and contemporary Christians whose experience they seek to understand. For others, the study of Christian spirituality is perhaps not the study of a faith they call their own, but it is nonetheless self-implicating for them in the way that every great human intellectual endeavor invites – even compels – us to engage questions of authenticity and meaning, of purpose and commitment. But all of this does not mean that the study of Christian spirituality is necessarily "serious" (in the sense of being somber or grave). Readers of this book can expect to discover afresh the truth of Simone Weil's insight that in academic study it is desire, not willpower, that produces the best and most enduring work:

> The intelligence can only be led by desire. For there to be desire, there must be pleasure and joy in the work. The intelligence only grows and bears fruit in joy . . . It is the part played by joy in our studies that makes of them a preparation for spiritual life, for desire directed toward God is the only power capable of raising the soul. Or rather, it is God alone who comes down and possesses the soul, but desire alone draws God down. (1951: 110–11)

A good deal of pleasure, joy, and desire has gone into the contributors' writing of these essays and my editing of them. We hope that our readers will find their own desire for truth, beauty, goodness, and love kindled by what they read in this *Companion to Christian Spirituality*.

References

Klein, J. T. 1990: *Interdisciplinarity: History, Theory, and Practice*. Detroit: Wayne State University Press.

Principe, W. 1993: Spirituality, Christian. In M. Downey (ed.), *The New Dictionary of Catholic Spirituality*, pp. 931–8. Collegeville, MN: Liturgical Press.

——2000: Toward defining spirituality. In K. J. Collins (ed.), *Exploring Christian Spirituality: An Ecumenical Reader*, pp. 43–59. Grand Rapids, MI: Baker Books.

Sheldrake, P. F. 1995: *Spirituality and History: Questions of Interpretation and Method*, rev. edn. Maryknoll, NY: Orbis.

Weil, S. 1951: Reflections on the right use of school studies with a view to the love of God. In *Waiting for God*, trans. E. Craufurd, pp. 105–16. New York: Harper and Row.

PART I
What is Christian Spirituality?

CHAPTER 1

Approaches to the Study of Christian Spirituality

Sandra M. Schneiders

Spirituality as an *academic field* is the study of spirituality as an *existential phenomenon* (the material object) under a formality (the formal object) which distinguishes it from theology, on the one hand, and religious studies, on the other. This requires, if not a definition, at least an identification of the phenomenon being studied and a description of the specific formality under which it is being studied. This task will be briefly addressed in the first part of this essay.

The second part will deal with the major topic of this essay: basic contemporary approaches to the academic study of spirituality. By approaches, I mean orienting frameworks within which specific methodologies are developed for the study of particular phenomena within the field of spirituality. Approaches reflect primarily the types of knowledge (or skills) the student seeks to attain which reflect the aspects of spirituality that she or he finds most interesting or important. Methodologies are articulated complexes of procedures (methods) which are developed to investigate what is of interest. Methods do not, or at least should not, dictate either what can be studied or how it should be studied. Rather, methods are systematic attempts to ensure the validity and fruitfulness of the research. Our concern in this essay is with approaches rather than with methodologies or specific methods.

The third part of the essay will address a specific issue in the academic field of spirituality, namely, how the self-implicating character of the study of the human search for God influences work in the field.

The reader should bear in mind that spirituality is studied in a variety of academic contexts and the objectives pursued in these diverse settings significantly influence what is studied and how it is studied. In this respect, spirituality is analogous to some other humanistic fields of study, such as psychology. A freshman in college may study psychology primarily to gain some understanding of her or himself or to determine whether this field might become her or his major. A master's student may wish to acquire the necessary knowledge and skills to become a secondary school counselor. A physician may be doing a clinical specialization to become a psychiatrist. Or a PhD student may be primarily interested in theoretical research in the field. Any or all of these objectives might be simultaneously operative and mutually influencing in the work of any particular student. Analogously, some students of spirituality, especially those in formation programs and students taking their first courses in religion, are often primarily concerned with their own spiritual development. Some, especially those in seminary-type programs, are primarily concerned with learning how to mediate the riches of Christian spirituality to others and how to discern and deal with the spiritual concerns of those in their pastoral care. Others, particularly those in doctoral-level programs in spirituality, are primarily concerned with the qualitative and quantitative expansion of knowledge in the field and becoming equipped to contribute to the field by their own research and teaching in the future. However, while it is important to distinguish these objectives and attend to the differences they introduce into the approaches to the study of spirituality, it would be artificial to pretend that researchers have no interest in their own spiritual lives or in assisting others in theirs or that pastors have no need of theoretical knowledge of the spiritual life. In short, although the *field* of spirituality is a broad terrain in which personal, practical, and theoretical projects are pursued and interact, the *academic discipline* of spirituality is primarily the research discipline whose specific objective is the expansion of our knowledge and understanding of the God–human relationship.

Finally, while spirituality as such is not necessarily religious, denominational, or confessional, this volume is concerned with Christian spirituality. Therefore, unless otherwise specified, spirituality in this essay means Christian spirituality.

Spirituality as a Field of Study

The material object: spirituality as existential phenomenon

Christian spirituality as an academic discipline studies the lived experience of Christian faith, the subjective appropriation of faith and living of discipleship in their individual and corporate actualization(s). Because this definition is so general as to be open to misinterpretation, I would prefer to situate Christian spirituality as existential phenomenon within a more nuanced definition of spirituality in general and then specify it as Christian. Spirituality is the actualization of the basic human capacity for transcendence and will be defined for the purposes of this essay as the experience of conscious involvement in the project of life-integration through self-transcendence toward the horizon of ultimate value one perceives. Each element of the definition helps to specify what we are discussing.

First, spirituality is not simply spontaneous experience, however elevating or illuminating, but a conscious and deliberate way of living. It is an ongoing project, not merely a collection of experiences or episodes. Thus, lived spirituality is often referred to as one's "spiritual life," a term I will use occasionally in what follows. Second, the project is not self-enclosed but orients the subject beyond purely private satisfaction toward the ultimate good, the highest value, that the person recognizes, which may be God but might also be something other than God, for example, the full personhood of all humans, world peace, enlightenment, or the good of the cosmos. Third, the ultimate value functions as a horizon luring the person toward growth. Hence, the spiritual life is intrinsically dynamic. Finally, this definition allows us to disqualify as spirituality negative life-organizations such as addictions (no matter how all-consuming they might be), exploitative or aggressive projects that seek the good of the individual at the expense of others or the rest of creation (no matter how energizing such a project might be), or venal concerns with money, power, or pleasure.

Christian spirituality as Christian specifies the horizon of ultimate value as the triune God revealed in Jesus Christ to whom Scripture normatively witnesses and whose life is communicated to the believer by the Holy Spirit making her or him a child of God. This new life, which Paul calls "life in the Spirit" (cf. Rom. 7: 6; 8: 2, 6, 10–11; Gal. 6: 8) is celebrated sacramentally within the believing community of the church and lived in the world as mission in and to the coming reign of God. This life of faith and discipleship constitutes the existential phenomenon that Christian spirituality as a discipline studies.

The contemporary discipline of spirituality, aware that the human subject and its context are immensely more complex than was once thought, attends to topics that, in the past, were considered peripheral or irrelevant to the spiritual life. Today we recognize that the subject of Christian spirituality is the human being as a whole: spirit, mind, and body; individual and social; culturally conditioned and ecologically intertwined with all of creation; economically and politically responsible. The Christian's spirituality, although individually unique and intensely personal, is not a private or purely "interior" affair concerned exclusively with prayer and the practice of virtue. It is, as Peter Van Ness (1996: 5) described spirituality in general, the relation of the whole of oneself to reality as a whole. In the field of Christian spirituality, both "self" and "reality" are defined by Christian faith.

The formal object: spirituality as religious experience

All Christian theology studies Christian faith: God, Christ, Scripture, sacraments, church, morality, and so on. And the locus in which these realities appear is, ultimately, the experience of the church in its members throughout its history. In other words, all theology is an investigation of experientially rooted *faith*. The distinguishing characteristic, or formal object, of spirituality as a field of study is its specific focus on Christian faith as the *experience* of the concrete believing subject(s). In other words, spirituality studies not simply Christian faith but the lived experience of Christian faith.

Experience, religious or otherwise, is notoriously difficult to define. We might begin by saying that to experience is to be "subjectively aware" and that experience is always "experience of." First, experience is by definition subjective and, as such, incommunicable. My pain cannot be felt by you even though, because you have experienced pain, you can empathize, by entering analogically into my experience, and thus understand it. Experience, including spirituality as existential phenomenon, can only be communicated by articulation in "texts": verbal, literary, artistic, behavioral, and so on (cf.

Ricoeur 1976: 16, 30–1). Second, since experience is always "experience of," there is an object, "something" to articulate and to be understood. Thus, even in the case of mystical experience, which is the most ineffable of religious experiences, the subject can and does say something intended to allow the reader/listener access to "something." This articulated "something," precisely as experience, is the object of spirituality as a field of study, what the researcher wants to understand.

Since religious experience as experience can only be accessed in its articulations, the student of spirituality is always dealing with "texts." Again, the analogy with psychology is illuminating. The psychologist is not studying anxiety as such or in general but the particular experience of anxiety of this individual or group. Verbalization, texts, drawings, dreams, behaviors, and other such articulations of the anxiety are the psychologist's access to the particular experience of anxiety. In attempting to understand this particular experience, the psychologist draws on the large body of theoretical knowledge about anxiety as well as on his or her own direct or vicarious experiences of anxiety or related states. But neither the general theory nor the therapist's experience is the focus of study in this case. The material object of the therapist's attention is anxiety, but the formal object is anxiety as lived experience.

Similarly, the student of spirituality is not studying prayer as such but, for example, the prayer of Teresa of Avila as it is articulated in *The Interior Castle* and is manifest in her life which, itself, is mediated by her autobiography. The researcher presumably has considerable theoretical knowledge of prayer both through theological and psychological study and through personal and/or vicarious experience. But the focus of study is neither the theology of prayer nor the researcher's experience of prayer, but specifically the prayer of Teresa of Avila.

Spirituality, in other words, is an instance of what Paul Ricoeur (1976: 78–9) calls "the science of the individual." Studies in spirituality do not aim to develop a second-order theoretical language about the spiritual life which can be verified in all authentic Christian spirituality, but to investigate the spiritual life as it is and has been concretely lived. Spirituality is related to theology as the study of Hamlet, or even the Shakespearean corpus, is to the study of literary theory. The "individuals" that spirituality studies may be specific persons like Teresa, or specific movements like Benedictine monasticism, or themes like "the world," or practices like centering prayer, spiritual direction, or religious pacifism. Although there is constant interplay between the knowledge of the particular individual(s) which enriches theoretical knowledge of the spiritual life and the theoretical knowledge which helps illuminate the interpretation of the individual, the focus/object of spirituality as a field of study is the experience of the spiritual life *as* experience. Consequently, unlike theology, whose analyses and conclusions intend applicability to all instances in the class in question (for example, an adequate theology of grace should be applicable to all the baptized), spirituality studies unique experiences of the living of Christian faith which, in their very uniqueness, can encourage, challenge, warn, illuminate, confirm, expand, subvert, or otherwise interact with both general theological theory, on the one hand, and other specific experiences of faith, on the other. Dorothy Day's pacifist spirituality, for example, ran counter to the official theology of the US Catholic bishops during World War II and could not be fully appropriated by her (presumably very holy) contemporary, Thomas Merton.

Day's pacifism can be theologically related to, but not fully contained within, the Catholic just-war theory and studied within the context of moral theology. But the discipline of spirituality studies Day's pacifism as the existential encounter with the Beatitudes that shaped the unique faith experience and lived discipleship of this particular woman and both challenged and expanded our understanding of Christian faith and life (Krupa 1997).

Although three different approaches to the study of spirituality will be discussed below, it is important to realize that they interact continuously in most real research projects and that all three, influenced by the postmodernity that has emerged in the academy since the mid-twentieth century, are marked by the linguistic-hermeneutical turn that has undermined the scientistic positivism of the modern period.

Three Approaches to the Study of Christian Spirituality

The three approaches to spirituality as an academic discipline that will be discussed in this section – the historical, the theological, and the anthropological – are derived from reading, discussions, and observations in the field over the past thirty to forty years. In other words, this is not a *de jure* prescriptive classification but a *de facto* heuristic taxonomy.

The historical approach

The least controversial approach to the study of spirituality is the historical approach. This is due largely to the fact that history as a modern academic discipline has always admitted subject matter specializations, such as the history of Western Europe, the Enlightenment, the papacy, Baroque music, women's dress, or medieval penal methods. As long as something happened or existed, it is legitimate within the discipline of history to study it historically. Consequently, an interest in studying religious experience or some aspect of it as an historical reality does not need any particular justification, even if "locating" and identifying the object is problematic.

Many scholars approaching spirituality historically, both in the past and today, are actually primarily historians *of* spirituality rather than scholars of spirituality whose approach is primarily historical. The former are scholars who approach the phenomena of spirituality as trained historians, differing from their religious studies colleagues in religious or church history, not in terms of their understanding of historiography, historical methods, or the desired outcomes of research in terms of historical analyses or interpretations, but in regard to what they are interested in studying, namely, Christian religious experience. Many secular historians have done excellent work on Christian religious life, figures, literature, and movements (for example, Bynum 1987; Brown 1988; Ranft 1996). What seems to differentiate the historian of spirituality (for example, McGinn 1991–8) from the religious studies historian of religion is an interest in interpreting what is being studied as Christian faith experience within the context of Christian theology.

Historical spirituality scholars, on the other hand, are scholars of spirituality (not of history) who find the historical approach particularly useful for their projects (for example, Bynum 1982; Short 1999; McGinn 2001). Thus a researcher interested in the tradition of "nuptial spirituality" (mystical experience understood and expressed through the metaphor of "marriage to Christ") may decide to study its expression in the spirituality of the thirteenth-century beguines (Murk-Jansen 1998) or through the commentaries on the biblical Song of Songs in the works of Origen, Bernard of Clairvaux, Mechthild of Magdeburg, and Edward Taylor in the historical context of their respective lives and practice. The historical approach and its methodology are in the service of understanding nuptial spirituality rather than the construction of a history of nuptial spirituality or of interpretation of the Song of Songs as a text that nourished mystical experience in different periods. As the authors referenced above exemplify, the same scholar may function at different times, or even in the same work, as an historian of spirituality primarily interested in the development of some facet of spirituality and at other times as a spirituality scholar primarily interested in some aspect of spirituality studied within its historical context.

Prior to the mid-twentieth century, historians of spirituality shared with other historians, including most biblical scholars, a modernist understanding of history itself and of its methods and results. The modern historian was preoccupied with "what really happened" as that could be determined by the use of historical critical methods. And what "mattered" historically was the activity of major figures (almost always hegemonic Western males) and major movements (almost always those of the historical winners). Economic, political, military, and religious events dominated the concerns of modernist historians, biblical, social, cultural, and religious. Historiography was largely the attempt to construct uni-directional, periodized, cause-and-effect metanarratives that explained how and why things came to be and to be a certain way. Furthermore, historians tended to see this diachronic analysis of "the past" as genetic and the genetic as sufficient explanation, at least on the human level, of whatever took place in space and time. This is the context in which the modern study of the history of spirituality began in centers such as Paris and Rome, and the histories of spirituality that emerged (for example, Pourrat 1953–5; Cognet 1959; Leclercq et al. 1968) bore the imprint of this type of historical work. Until relatively recently, historians of spirituality tended to equate spirituality as a discipline with the history of spirituality, wondering aloud what else there might be to study except what has actually occurred as mediated through historical "texts," broadly understood. Today, they, as well as scholars of spirituality who take an historical approach to their subject matter, are aware that history is one access, among others, to phenomena that are indeed historical but have other equally interesting dimensions (for example, Norris 1996; Lane 2002).

In the final quarter of the twentieth century, all historical study began to feel the effects of the emergence of postmodernism in scholarship. Historians themselves began to question the basic assumptions of the historical critical method: that something objective "really happened" and had a kind of free-standing existence "in the past" that was accessible by proper methods; that the "real story" could be unearthed and told by the objective scholar who had no personal (and therefore distorting) role in that story;

that something like the "whole story" could be told; that causes could be determined which could only have produced what in fact happened, and so on. Revisionist history, history written from the underside and the margins, the stories of the historical losers and victims, the aspects and dimensions of the past that once seemed unimportant or uninteresting, began to emerge into the concerns of historians who increasingly acknowledged that they were not studying or writing "history" pure and simple but offering one of many possible constructions of the admittedly partial available data whose authority as evidence was, in the last analysis, conferred by the historian rather than discovered as objective and self-evident (Sheldrake 1992).

All of these currents are still very much in their developmental phases, but they are influencing all historical work (Burnett 2000), including the history of spirituality. Historians of spirituality are still concerned with establishing reliable texts, accessing the available data of past Christian experience, discerning connections, patterns, and influences (causal and otherwise), but they are also interested in analyses and criticisms that are not exclusively concerned with the uncovering or establishment of "the facts" but with the interpretation of whatever can be known. And they are very aware that interpretation is a function of the identity, social location, and presuppositions of the interpreter and the power arrangements that affect and are affected by interpretation. In other words, postmodernism in general, and the linguistic-hermeneutical turn in particular, are profoundly affecting historical work.

The historical approach to the study of spirituality is still primarily the work of professional historians whose interest centers on the lived experience of the faith which they share either actually or empathetically with their subjects, but whose methods tend to be those of the increasingly hermeneutical historical disciplines augmented by theological expertise. Increasingly, the methodologies of history are also being used by spirituality scholars who are not professional historians but find historical approaches most useful for their work. The results of historical studies in spirituality are not only valuable in themselves as investigations of Christian religious experience throughout the ages, but also are essential to any valid study in the field of spirituality because they supply the context for and/or constitute the positive data upon which other approaches exercise their inquiries. Spirituality as lived experience takes place only in time and space, within particular cultural contexts, in interaction with the other persons and forces operative in the same context, and influenced by what and who has preceded it. In this sense, all study in the field of spirituality is historical whether the purpose is to provide a history of a given phenomenon (history of spirituality) or to understand the phenomenon itself by means of historical approaches to the subject matter (historical spirituality).

The challenge for those approaching spirituality historically is to avoid either reducing spirituality to an account of "what happened" or accounting for "what happened" in purely genetic terms as what can be discerned by historical methods, and to recognize that even phenomena of the past can and must be studied by a variety of methods if the experience is to be understood as experience. Theology, psychology, gender, art, rhetoric, science, and so on must complement history to give access to religious experience in its uniqueness.

The theological approach

The contemporary theological approach to the study of spirituality has a complex history which must be taken into account in attempting to understand what scholars who take this approach today are doing. The Orthodox, Protestant, Anglican, and Catholic developments have been quite diverse. While the Orthodox have attempted to maintain the synthesis of theology and spirituality that characterized the pre-medieval common tradition, the split between theology and spirituality that occurred in the High Middle Ages has been variously handled by the other three branches. In the wake of the Reformation, Protestant orthodoxy was suspicious of "mysticism," insofar as the term suggested elitism or paranormal experience that was not rooted in Scripture and open to all believers, and of "spirituality" which suggested a works-righteousness approach to the life of faith. Protestants preferred to speak of "piety," a daily discipline of Scripture reading and prayer, both personal and familial, which was promoted by both theoretical and exhortatory literature from figures such as Martin Luther, John Calvin, Jonathan Edwards, Jeremy Taylor, and others.

Anglicans preferred the term "devotion" to that of piety, but also spoke of the "inner life" and the "life of perfection" which had affinities with Catholic approaches. Anglican spirituality was deeply rooted in the *Book of Common Prayer* and thus had a distinctively liturgical shape and content. Out of this tradition, the Anglicans, especially the English, also developed a voluminous literature on the spiritual life that was both practical (for example, Law 1978) and theoretical (for example, Underhill 1942) and which continues to bear the stamp of this sensibility (for example, Jones et al. 1986). Distinctive to the Catholic tradition was the incorporation of the study of spirituality into the university curriculum as a subdiscipline within theology. It is this Catholic academic development that is particularly significant for understanding the current development of spirituality as a discipline within the academy.

From the time of Dionysius (probably sixth century) through the Middle Ages (cf. Thomas Aquinas, *Summa Theologiae* II: 2.45.2) and into modern times in the writings of authors such as John of the Cross, "mystical theology" referred not to an object of study or a body of speculative or practical knowledge attained by the theologian but to an experiential knowledge of God infused into the soul by God in/as contemplation. John of the Cross says: "The sweet and living knowledge that she [the soul] says he [God] taught her is mystical theology, the secret knowledge of God that spiritual persons call contemplation" (*The Spiritual Canticle* 27: 5). Once theology came to be understood not so much as rumination on Scripture but primarily as a philosophically elaborated academic specialization in the university curriculum (thirteenth century and beyond), spiritual theology gradually came to be thought of not as the noetic effect of spiritual experience but as a subdiscipline of theology (dogmatic and moral) which could be studied and mastered as other subjects were. The question then became not how to dispose the spirit through reading and meditation for the free inflow of God's wisdom in contemplation, but what subject matter was to be studied and how, in order to understand the content and dynamics of the spiritual life. Spiritual theology emerged in the academy as a distinct subject in the seventeenth century as theologians and spiritual guides tried to systematize the available knowledge of the spiritual life in terms of the reigning scholastic theologies (for example, Scaramelli 1917; Tanquerey 1932; Garrigou-Lagrange 1950; Aumann 1980).

From the seventeenth century into the mid-twentieth century spiritual theology was understood (in Catholic academic circles which is where it was elaborated and pursued) as the theoretical study of "the life of perfection," meaning the interior life of persons (usually monks, nuns, and mystics) who attempted to live their Christian calling more intensely than so-called "ordinary Christians" whose spiritual life was characterized by vocal prayer, moral rectitude, and the faithful observance of the duties of their state in life (Saudreau 1926). This "science of perfection" drew its principles from theology, of which it remained a subdiscipline, and was eminently practical in intent, namely, to equip the spiritual director of those "seeking perfection" to guide these special souls in their three-stage journey through purification (the way of beginners) and illumination (the way of proficients) to mystical union (the way of perfection). Spiritual theology was divided into two parts: ascetical theology, which studied the "active life" (the stages of the spiritual life in which the activity of the subject in vocal and mental prayer, the practice of virtue, asceticism, and so on, was possible and effective), and mystical theology or the "passive life" (the stage of the spiritual life in which the activity of the Holy Spirit replaces that of the human subject who cannot effect the mystical union with God which is characteristic of this final stage). Note the change in meaning of the term "mystical theology" from the experiential knowledge of God directly produced in the soul by infused contemplation to the study of mystical experience as an object. Spiritual theology, then, was the field of study whose object was the whole spiritual life, and mystical theology was one of the two subdivisions of that field.

By the mid-twentieth century this classical theological subdiscipline had, for various reasons, come under serious question not only from Protestants but from within Catholicism itself. The three-stage understanding of the spiritual life, which can be traced back into the patristic period, seemed to have been systematized beyond recognition. The biblical basis of this rigid and somewhat artificial systematization was highly doubtful. But the major theological objections were that the approach was elitist, divisive, and seemed to deny the universal call of the baptized to the fullness of the spiritual life since not all, according to this schema, were called to the third stage (mystical union) in this life; it subverted the unity of the spiritual life in which, as the great spiritual guides of the past had always recognized, purification, illumination, and union are simultaneous and overlapping even when one or the other predominates at a particular stage of spiritual development; it seriously restricted the role of the Holy Spirit in the spiritual life by assigning the full operation of the gifts and fruits of the Spirit (which, according to traditional theology, are received in the sacraments of initiation) to the final stage of the spiritual life to which relatively few are called. These texts tended to over-emphasize paranormal experience – something which all the great mystics greatly relativized and even cautioned contemplatives against – as a distinguishing feature of the final stage of the spiritual life.

The primary practical objections to the classical spiritual theology paradigm were that it over-systematized and therefore fragmented the spiritual life which is much more organic and developmental; it was too restrictively concerned with the "interior life" (meaning prayer and the practice of virtue), whereas advances in psychology were making people much more aware of the complexity of the human subject and the involvement of all dimensions of the person in the spiritual life; it was highly prescriptive (even mechanistic), taking too little account of personal individuality; it paid little attention to the "ordinary Christian" who was, presumably, not "seeking perfection" even though experience suggested that there were many real saints among these non-cloistered God-seekers "in the world."

By the time of the Second Vatican Council, which reaffirmed the universality of the call to one and the same holiness (*Lumen gentium* 5), classical modern "spiritual theology" was giving way to what many modern believers found much more interesting, namely, "spirituality." This term gained currency throughout the second half of the twentieth century, gradually being adopted by Jews and Muslims as well as Christians across the denominational spectrum, Buddhists, Hindus, primal peoples, and adherents of other non-Christian traditions, and even by non-religious seekers such as some feminists, ecologists, New Agers, and eclectic practitioners who denied any interest in religion (Van Ness 1996). Paulist Press, in its influential series "Classics of Western Spirituality," included non-Christian spiritual texts (for example, Jewish and Islamic). The Crossroad *Encyclopedia of World Spiritualities* gave a non-restrictive description of spirituality as the existence and the dynamics of "the spirit" understood as the "deepest center of the person" (Cousins 1985: xiii) and devoted only three of its projected twenty-five volumes to Christian spirituality.

This very rapid extension of the referent of "spirituality" beyond its original Christian meaning (cf. Schneiders 1989, for a history of the term) raised the question, for scholars in the field of Christian spirituality, about the distinctiveness of their discipline. Clearly, the distinguishing mark of Christian spirituality as Christian is its rootedness in the Christian religious tradition which, for Protestants, Anglicans, Catholics, and Orthodox, has tended to be expressed and systematized in the theological tradition (dogmatic and moral, biblical, liturgical, and historical). In other words, Christian spirituality is Christian because of its relationship to the creed, code, and cult of the church's tradition. Those scholars, often working in confessional academic contexts such as seminaries and formation programs, who are less interested in interaction with non-Christian spiritualities than with Christian spirituality as such, tend therefore to focus on the theological identity of the latter (for example, Leech 1985; Senn 1986; Hanson 2000). While recognizing the importance of the history of spirituality and acknowledging the breadth of interest in the field outside the Christian sphere, these scholars choose to focus on spirituality from a specifically Christian, therefore theological, perspective.

I would suggest, in order to distinguish what these contemporary scholars in the field are doing from the classical "spiritual theology" described above, that it would be better to refer to the former as "theological spirituality" rather than "spiritual theology." The *focus* of these scholars is not on theology as such but on spirituality. It is their *approach* that is theological in that they work primarily within the framework established by Scripture, theology, and sacramental practice. They are not primarily interested in establishing a theory of the spiritual life (theology as second-order discourse such as classical spiritual theology attempted) applicable to all Christians or prescribing the practice of the spiritual life (an ascetical or moral program for spiritual development). Like other scholars in the field, they start with religious experience rather than with premises or propositions. They are certainly not exclusively focused on the "interior life," but very aware of the holistic character of the human subject and her or his religious experience. Furthermore, they recognize that all Christians are called to mature in the spiritual life and that they share this calling with non-Christians. Finally, although they use the basic coordinates of Christian theology to organize their work and accord these coordinates a normative role in their analyses and criticism of spiritual experience, they do not deduce the content or dynamics of the spiritual life of the individual or the community from inarguable theological premises. For example, the contemporary scholar studying faith as religious experience within a theological approach does not start with the definition of faith as theological virtue, its character as gift of the Spirit, or the moral obligations it entails, but with questions such as how human beings come to faith and how human faith is related to religious faith, developmental patterns of growth in faith, the effect on faith of the super-ego, superstition, projection, and so on, the variety of expressions of faith, and the relation of faith to religious practice. The theological character of faith is operative in the definition of the sphere of investigation, in the analyses of the related experiences, in the evaluation of the data surfaced in the investigation, in the appropriation of the results of the study. But it does not function purely deductively (to supply the "right" answers) or prescriptively (to disallow seemingly incompatible experience or enforce attitudes or behaviors deemed compatible with theological answers). In other words, what distinguishes the contemporary theological approach to spirituality is its emphasis on the specifically Christian character of the subject matter (religious experience) and the constitutive role of Christian theology in the methodologies developed to study that subject matter.

All Christian spirituality is Christian because of its rootedness in the normative texts and the communal experience of the church. It is, by definition, the living of Christian faith, not some vague concern with the "more" in life or some eclectic amalgam of practices or beliefs (Rolheiser 1999; Ranson 2002; Schneiders 2003). The contribution of the theological approach to spirituality is that it keeps the specifically Christian character of the discipline in focus and reminds everyone in the field, whatever their preferred approach, that Christianity is a specific faith tradition that has content and dynamics it does not share with other traditions, even those with analogous concerns.

The challenge for those who take a theological approach to the study of Christian spirituality is to remember that there is more to Christian spirituality than theologically articulated faith. The subject of Christian spirituality is a complex human being participating in a plurality of communities and whose multiple dimensions and involvements particularize the appropriation and expression of faith, often in ways that the general theory of the faith (theology) cannot or has not yet comprehended or articulated. In the first instance, spirituality gives rise to theology rather than the other way around. And theology never fully comprehends the experience it seeks to understand. Lived spirituality will always involve elements and aspects which can only be investigated adequately by the use of other disciplines, such as psychology, sociology, art, rhetoric, or science. The interdisciplinary character of the contemporary field of spirituality is not simply a trendy postmodern methodological choice but a response to the nature of religious experience and human knowledge in the contemporary context.

The anthropological approach

The third approach to the study of Christian spirituality, the anthropological, is the most recent development in the field and is most clearly influenced by postmodernity, both cultural and academic. This approach is rooted in the recognition that spirituality is an anthropological constant, a constitutive dimension of the *humanum* (Breton 1990). Human beings are characterized by a capacity for self-transcendence toward ultimate value, whether or not they nurture this capacity or do so in religious or non-religious ways. Consequently, spirituality as a feature of humanity as such is existentially (though not always experientially) prior to any particular actualization of spirituality as Christian, Buddhist, ecological, and so on. Christian spirituality is a particular experiential actualization of this human capacity and the discipline of Christian spirituality studies this particular actualization, but it can never abstract completely from the realization that Christianity shares both the experience we call spirituality and the field which studies such experience with other religious traditions and even non-religious movements. Such an awareness could not have emerged prior to the kinds of interactions, cultural and religious, that characterized the late twentieth century.

The anthropological approach to Christian spirituality, while taking seriously the historical and theological dimensions of the subject matter of the field, is also explicitly concerned with dimensions of spirituality that are accessible only to non-theological disciplines, such as the aesthetic, linguistic, psychological, or cosmological; with the "edges" where the field of spirituality is influenced by important aspects of contemporary experience that are not intrinsic to Christianity itself, such as the meaning of experience, ecological concerns, and gender issues; with the analogies with, challenges to, and affirmations of Christian experience coming from the spiritualities of other religious traditions or the spiritualities of contemporary seekers who repudiate or ignore institutional religion (Conn 1989, 1996; Liebert 1992; Burton-Christie 1994; Kline 2002; Saliers 2002). The anthropological approach to Christian spirituality, therefore, has much in common with contemporary theology done in the context of a theology of religions. It starts with the premise that Christian spirituality is first human and then Christian, that spirituality is ontologically prior to its specification by history and theology. And this opens it *a priori* to all that surrounds it. If nothing human is foreign to the Christian, then nothing spiritual is foreign to Christian spirituality.

Like postmodern research in general, anthropologically oriented studies in Christian spirituality tend to emphasize hermeneutical methodology. The primary focus of research is interpretation of the subject matter of the field in order to broaden and deepen our understanding of Christian spirituality as an instance of the human search for transcendence and ultimate meaning. Hermeneutics has a double focus: understanding and explanation (i.e., the expansion of knowledge), on the one hand, and appropriation (i.e., the expansion of subjectivity), on the other (Ricoeur 1976: 71–95). In the field of spirituality, the first focus leads the researcher to investigate the phenomena of Christian faith experience within the widest and richest available frame of reference in order to understand it as deeply as possible, thus expanding, qualitatively and quantitatively, our knowledge of the Christian spiritual life. The second focus is the widening of the horizon of the interpreter, which involves an expansion or deepening of subjectivity, of the self. In other words, personal transformation of the researcher (with implications for the world including the church) is integral to this approach. But this transformation is not so much in terms of better practice of the Christian faith (though this is not excluded) as in terms of an expansion of one's humanity, especially through encounter with the "other," whether personal, cultural, religious, intellectual, or through active participation in transformative praxis. The researcher is not so much learning what to do or how to do it better or how to help others in the spiritual life. She or he is becoming a spiritually richer and deeper person.

This new approach to spirituality, clearly a response to the increasingly diverse inter-actions among scholars from a variety of religious traditions and scholarly disciplines, has drawn many scholars in the field of Christian spirituality beyond exclusively Christian and strictly confessional boundaries. They recognize that spirituality is a universal human concern that is significant for the human enterprise as a whole. The question that was once posed as how Christianity could propagate itself and its gospel message for the salvation of the world has been recast as how Christian spirituality is related to other versions of the human quest for ultimate meaning and value, what Christians can learn from others as well as offer to others in terms of the spiritual life, and how all those interested in the future of the human race and the planet can mobil-ize the resources of their respective traditions to transform the lives of their own adher-ents for the ultimate good of all. In short, Christian spirituality anthropologically approached has become public discourse, both culturally and academically, and is learning to participate in a conversation it does not totally control, without losing or diminishing its specifically Christian identity.

The anthropological approach to spirituality manifests unmistakably postmodern sensibilities. It is wary of metanarratives, substantialism, and absolutisms of all kinds, even those emerging from heretofore unquestioned theological premises. It is especially aware of the mutually determining relationship between spirituality as experience and religion as tradition or institution, with the consequent relativizing of the latter's heretofore unquestioned priority. The postmodern sense of universal relativity encour-ages an ever-widening definition of religious experience, on the one hand, and a sharpened sense of the irreducible "otherness" of experiences that are not one's own (Fredericks 2003), on the other. Consequently, not only a complexification of the holis-tic approach to the human subject of religious experience but a heightened awareness of the dimensions and influence of "place" and "space" (both inner and outer), globalization, ecological crisis, the validity of religious experience outside one's own tradition, scientific developments, and cultural currents are characteristic of the anthropological approach.

The anthropological approach to the study of spirituality focuses characteristically on the interpretation of Christian religious experience in the most adequate framework for generating responses to contemporary questions rather than historical or theo-logical ones. For example, the scholar would probably be less interested in the history or theology of mysticism in relation to social change than in how mystical experience interacted with political involvement in the non-violent teaching and practice of Martin Luther King, Jr, and how black preaching as rhetoric inaugurated ordinary oppressed people into that mystical-prophetic dynamic. In other words, was the Civil Rights Movement essentially a spiritual phenomenon, and, if so, how is it to be understood? Is the Christian character of King's non-violence essentially different from that of Ghandi? What do the answers to such questions imply about real social change?

Methodologies within an anthropological approach are virtually always interdisciplinary (not merely pluri-disciplinary), with different disciplines taking the leading role in different research projects depending on the researcher's primary question (Klein 1990). Whereas historical and theological approaches frame the questions raised about complex spiritual phenomena from the standpoint of those particular disciplines, the anthropological approach addresses the phenomenon in terms of what the researcher wants to know about religious experience, which may not be primarily historical or theological. Thus, for example, if the primary question is about the role of Martin Luther King, Jr's spirituality in his leadership of the Civil Rights Movement, the point of entry may be his rhetorical appropriation in black preaching of Old Testament themes, and those themes might then become the framework for the analysis of the phenomenon.

The most congenial setting for the anthropological approach is the graduate research institution which allows and fosters but does not prescribe particular religious commitments and is not charged with the religious formation of individuals in a particular tradition or for particular ministries. Such a setting is particularly hospitable to this approach's interest in non-conventional questions, "marginal" phenomena, and the interaction of Christian spirituality with such contemporary concerns as feminism, cosmology, ecology, peace and justice studies, cultural developments, and so on.

The obvious contributions of this approach are its openness to investigating the widest possible range of questions, problems, and issues in the field of spirituality, its insistence on and ability to keep spirituality in the realm of public discourse, and its natural affinity with the postmodern agenda and sensibility. The challenge for those who approach the study of spirituality from the more anthropological perspective is to keep the specifically Christian character of the discipline in focus and to resist the postmodern lure of universal relativism, nihilistic deconstructionism, rejection of all tradition and authority, and suspicion of personal commitment.

Interaction of the approaches

Experience strongly suggests that these three approaches are not mutually exclusive or competing. Because all Christian religious experience is human and thus related to the spiritual enterprise of the human race, historically situated in a particular socio-cultural and temporal setting, and rooted in the theological tradition of Christianity, all three approaches are necessary in respect to almost any question in the field. The approaches differ in the point of entry into a study, the specific interests that are paramount, the most appropriate methodologies, and the natural proclivities of the researchers. And, as already mentioned, different approaches tend to flourish better in different academic environments. Historical approaches are probably most at home in the secular university setting; theological approaches in denominational settings concerned with ministerial preparation and formation; anthropological approaches in inter-religious graduate research settings. But the contemporary study of Christian spirituality is interdisciplinary by nature and fundamentally inductive and hermeneutical in methodology.

The Issue of Self-implication

The modernist conviction that research is an impersonal activity whose validity demands an objectivity equivalent to the "death of the researcher" is rejected today by most scholars, scientific or humanistic. Students fascinated by the human adventure with God need not disown their personal investment in their desire to study spirituality. And, as noted above, one's own spirituality provides empathic access to the phenomena spirituality studies. Spirituality, in other words, is intrinsically self-implicating. The question today among scholars in the field is not *whether* the personal religious experience of students plays a role in their work but *how* it can be appropriately integrated. This question has three foci. How can the student's experience function productively in research? What is the appropriate role of constructed experiences in understanding what one is studying? What is the experiential fruit of the study of spirituality?

The critical use of experience

Because spirituality is the study of experience which, by definition, is incommunicable as such, the analogous experience of the researcher is virtually necessary for understanding. Just as a psychologist who has never experienced fear, anxiety, or love will find it very difficult to understand emotional experience in her or his clients or in the literature of the field, so a person who has never experienced religious awe, temptation, prayer, or social commitment will have difficulty understanding (or even believing) the articulations of such experience in the "texts" (personal or literary) of spirituality. But just as one does not have to be schizophrenic to understand mental illness, one does not have to be a mystic to understand John of the Cross. In other words, it would seem that a person has to *have* a spiritual life to *understand* the spiritual life, and the deeper one's experience the more "understanding" one can be of the religious experience of others.

On the other hand, a researcher's personal involvement with the subject matter can be so intense that it can subvert the research. There is a certain kind of "objectivity" which must be methodologically cultivated to allow all the relevant data to be heard, weighed, and incorporated. For example, a homosexual person in a Catholic religious order studying the role of same-sex attraction in religious vocation would have to carefully control the desire to find such attraction virtually universal and spiritually superior to any other motivation for entering religious life. Indeed, such a finding would lead to the suspicion that the researcher rather than the research has become the focus of the project. The desire to understand one's own religious experience can lend passion and focus to a research project, but research is the effort to understand what is really "there," not a projection of one's own agenda or the legitimation of one's own experience. The task of mentors is to help students to develop methodologies that will allow and validate personal involvement (i.e., the exercise and enhancement of subjectivity) but rigorously control the type of subjectivism that skews research.

Personal experience as data

The second question concerns the introduction of experiential material into the classroom study of spirituality. In a class on Christian prayer, is it legitimate or desirable to lead students in, or to assign exercises in, praying, or to require students to report on their personal prayer experience? Some maintain that such experience is integral to the praxis model which is most appropriate for studying spirituality (Liebert 2002). Others would encourage students to experiment, actually or vicariously, with what they are studying but would hesitate to require personal practice (as opposed to observation) and self-revelation which could encourage resistance or dissimulation. Still others believe that such experiences are artificial at best and manipulative at worst and have no place in the classroom.

There is probably no "one right answer" to this question. Some experience can be a form of research, that is, a practicum, such as attending liturgical events in order to understand worship as an experience, or dialoguing in spiritual counseling with different people about their experience of God. Such experiences may well affect students personally, but their primary purpose is access to otherwise unavailable data.

Students may also be motivated to certain experiences by their study. For example, studying meditation might move a student to make a retreat in order to experience directly what she or he is encountering in texts. The student's own experience then becomes an analogous "text" which increases empathic understanding of what is being studied.

Creating an experience so that students can study a topic through their own experience of it – for example, studying prayer by observing their own experience of praying – seems more problematic. There is no way to know that what students experience as prayer by following instructions supplies any significant data about prayer, even their own, and believing that it does may not be helpful to the student in understanding prayer in the Christian tradition. On the other hand, a carefully constructed experience might help students understand better the dimensions and contours of what they are studying and raise useful questions that engage the students more existentially in the subject matter (Frohlich 2001).

Again, context affects the answer to this question. Students in a Christian ministerial formation program may well expect and be willing to engage in exercises that increase their experiential base for dealing with others and foster their own spiritual life. College students with little or no experience of spirituality may find experiments with some of the standard practices of religion exciting, and such experiments may facilitate their ability to talk about the subject. Students of various religious back-grounds (or none) participating in a graduate research seminar might find attempts to induce and/or structure their religious experience or require its revelation manipula-tive or even violent. As with any other subject in the curriculum, teachers must make prudential decisions about what, when, and how experiential material or methods should be introduced into a course in spirituality (Taves 2003).

The transformative potential of the study of spirituality

Finally, there is the question of the experiential impact of studying spirituality. Any serious personal engagement with "the other," whether social or intellectual, changes the subject. Real study, in other words, is transformative by nature (Weil 1951). Stu-dents who choose to study spirituality are usually personally involved in the search for God. What goes on in the seminar room and the library, in preparing examinations and writing a dissertation, is often profoundly transformative. Faith is stimulated, voca-tions are renegotiated, self-knowledge is deepened, appreciation of other traditions is broadened, commitment to service is consolidated. The quiet or dramatic interaction between study and personal growth is probably the most important aspect of the self-implicating character of the field of spirituality. As Socrates knew, one cannot wrestle with ultimate truth without becoming a different person. This is not a problem to be solved or a danger to be avoided but an effect to be celebrated.

References

Aumann, J. 1980: *Spiritual Theology*. London: Sheed and Ward.

Breton, J-C. 1990: *Approche contemporaine de la vie spirituelle*. Montreal: Bellarmin.

Brown, P. 1988: *The Body and Society: Men, Women and Sexual Renunciation in Early Christianity*. New York: Columbia University Press.

Burnett, F. W. 2000: Historiography. In A. K. M. Adam (ed.), *Handbook of Postmodern Biblical Inter-pretation*, pp. 106–12. St Louis: Chalice Press.

Burton-Christie, D. 1994: Mapping the sacred landscape: spirituality and the contemporary lit-erature of nature. *Horizons* 21, 22–47.

Bynum, C. W. 1982: *Jesus as Mother: Studies in the Spirituality of the High Middle Ages*. Berkeley, CA: University of California Press.

——1987: *Holy Feast and Holy Fast: The Religious Significance of Food to Medieval Women*. Berkeley, CA: University of California Press.

Cognet, L. 1959: *Post-Reformation Spirituality*, trans. P. H. Scott. New York: Hawthorne.

Conn, J. W. 1989: *Spirituality and Personal Maturity*. New York: University Press of America.

——(ed.) 1996: *Women's Spirituality: Resources for Christian Development*, 2nd edn. New York: Paulist Press.

Cousins, E. 1985: Preface to the series. In B. McGinn and J. Meyendorff (eds), *Christian Spiritual-ity: Origins to the Twelfth Century*, pp. xi–xiv. New York: Crossroad.

Fredericks, J. 2003: Masao Abe: a spiritual friendship. *Spiritus* 3, 219–30.

Frohlich, M. 2001: Spiritual discipline, discipline of spirituality: revisiting questions of definition and method. *Spiritus* 1, 65–78.

Garrigou-Lagrange, R. 1950: *The Three Ways of the Spiritual Life*. Westminster, MD: Newman.

Hanson, B. 2000: *A Graceful Life: Lutheran Spirituality for Today*. Minneapolis, MN: Augsburg.

John of the Cross 1973: *The Collected Works of St John of the Cross*, trans. K. Kavanaugh and O. Rodriguez. Washington, DC: Institute of Carmelite Studies.

Jones, C., Wainwright, G., and Yarnold, E. 1986: *The Study of Spirituality*. Oxford: Oxford University Press.

Klein, J. T. 1990: *Interdisciplinarity: History, Theory, and Practice*. Detroit: Wayne State University Press.

Kline, F. 2002: Artistic performance and ascetic practice. *Spiritus* 2, 173–9.

Krupa, S. 1997: Dorothy Day and the spirituality of nonviolence, 2 vols. Unpublished PhD dissertation, Graduate Theological Union, Berkeley, California.

Lane, B. C. 2002: *Landscapes of the Sacred: Geography and Narrative in American Spirituality*. Baltimore, MD: The Johns Hopkins University Press.

Law, W. 1978: *A Serious Call to a Devout and Holy Life: The Spirit of Love*, ed. P. G. Stanwood. New York: Paulist Press.

Leclercq, J., Vandenbroucke, F., and Bouyer, L. 1968: *Spirituality of the Middle Ages*, vol. 2 of *The History of Christian Spirituality*. New York: Desclée.

Leech, K. 1985: *Experiencing God: Theology as Spirituality*. San Francisco: Harper and Row.

Liebert, E. 1992: *Changing Life Patterns: Adult Development in Spiritual Direction*. New York: Paulist Press.

——2002: The role of practice in the study of Christian spirituality. *Spiritus* 2, 30–49. (A revised version of this article appears in Part VI of this volume.)

McGinn, B. 1991–8: *The Presence of God: A History of Western Christian Mysticism*, 3 vols to date. New York: Crossroad.

——2001: *The Mystical Thought of Meister Eckhart: The Man from Whom God Hid Nothing*. New York: Crossroad.

Murk-Jansen, S. 1998: *Brides in the Desert: The Spirituality of the Beguines*. Maryknoll, NY: Orbis.

Norris, K. 1996: *The Cloister Walk*. New York: Riverhead Books.

Pourrat, P. 1953–5: *Christian Spirituality*, 4 vols, trans. W. H. Mitchell et al. Westminster, MD: Newman.

Ranft, P. 1996: *Women and the Religious Life in Premodern Europe*. New York: St Martin's Press.

Ranson, D. 2002: *Across the Great Divide: Bridging Spirituality and Religion Today*. Strathfield, NSW: St Paul's Publications.

Ricoeur, P. 1976: *Interpretation Theory: Discourse and the Surplus of Meaning*. Fort Worth: Texas Christian University Press.

Rolheiser, R. 1999: *The Holy Longing: The Search for a Christian Spirituality*. New York: Doubleday.

Saliers, D. E. 2002: Beauty and terror. *Spiritus* 2, 181–91.

Saudreau, A. 1926: *The Degrees of the Spiritual Life: A Method of Directing Souls According to their Progress in Virtue*, trans. B. Camm. London: Burns, Oates and Washbourne.

Scaramelli, G. B. 1917: *The Directorium Asceticum, or, Guide to the Spiritual Life*, trans. Members of St Beuno's College, North Wales. London: R. and T. Washbourne.

Schneiders, S. M. 1989: Spirituality in the academy. *Theological Studies* 50, 676–97.

——2003: Religion vs. spirituality: a contemporary conundrum. *Spiritus* 3, 163–85.

Senn, F. C. (ed.) 1986: *Protestant Spiritual Traditions*. New York: Paulist Press.

Sheldrake, P. F. 1992: *Spirituality and History: Questions of Interpretation and Method*. New York: Crossroad.

Short, W. J. 1999: *Poverty and Joy: The Franciscan Tradition*. Maryknoll, NY: Orbis.

Tanquerey, A. 1932: *The Spiritual Life: A Treatise on Ascetical and Mystical Theology*, trans. H. Branderis. Tournai, Belgium: Desclée/Society of St John the Evangelist.

Taves, A. 2003: Detachment and engagement in the study of "lived experience." *Spiritus* 3, 186–208.

Underhill, E. 1942: *Mysticism: The Development of Humankind's Spiritual Consciousness*, 14th edn. London: Bracken Books.

Van Ness, P. H. 1996: Introduction: spirituality and the secular quest. In P. H. Van Ness (ed.), *Spirituality and the Secular Quest*, pp. 1–17. New York: Crossroad.

Weil, S. 1951: Reflections on the right use of school studies with a view to the love of God. In *Waiting for God*, trans. E. Craufurd, pp. 105–16. New York: Harper and Row.

PART II
Scripture and Christian Spirituality

CHAPTER 2

The Old Testament in Christian Spirituality

Barbara Green

In what legitimate, respectful, and fruitful ways do Christians appropriate what Jews call the *Tanakh*/Hebrew Bible and Christians more properly for them call the Old Testament? Christians have drawn eagerly on the Old Testament for two millennia in various ways, and the purpose of this essay is to provide an orderly, though necessarily partial, track through that process and to suggest the way forward.

Christian spirituality is both a more focused and a wider term than Christian Old Testament studies. Some biblical study falls outside Christian spirituality, and spirituality enfolds wider practice than Christian appropriation of the Old Testament. Two scholar-practitioners will help us to understand Christian spirituality. Sandra Schneiders defines spirituality as the "experience of conscious involvement in the project of life-integration through self-transcendence toward the ultimate value one perceives," which for Christians is the triune God revealed in Jesus, approached via the paschal mystery and the church community and lived through the gift of the Holy Spirit. Her understanding implies the radical capacity of the human spirit to engage God's Spirit and the importance of Scripture to mediate the foundational revelation and to supply the basic symbol system into which each individual and communal Christian story is integrated (Schneiders 1998: 1, 3). Christian spirituality begins as Jesus, steeped in the rich Jewish tradition of divine self-disclosure, interacts with those who respond to him; and that experience is converted into language and shared with others.

Contemplative art historian Wendy Beckett, discussing more inductively how art mediates the sacred, is also useful in this discussion of Hebrew Bible texts that are not explicitly Christocentric. Great art (including literature) involves a deep yearning for what is sensed but not yet present. Art makes tangible for our engagement the most profound needs and desires of the human heart: love, death, joy, pain, all of which are for Christians places for the encounter of the human spirit with God's. We engage by bringing our deepest attention to what is represented before us, and, in the process, move beyond what would otherwise limit us. The gain is a deepening of our awareness of what most matters, which for Beckett and many others is belonging to God as wholly as is possible: the process and endpoint of Christian spirituality. She shows a way of "getting perspective," of recognizing ourselves with clarity and reaching more authentically toward the community of God and other creatures where we long to live (Johnson 1997: 42–8).

Since the Old Testament is varied and complex, I will focus primarily on one representative text: the small book bearing the name of Jonah. In Jonah, we have a taut narrative, access to challenges associated with biblical prophecy, and a genre offering the mysteries of biblical wisdom. In spare summary: a prophet is commissioned to preach repentance to wicked Ninevites, but he flees, boarding a ship which on his account is whipped by a fierce storm. The crew, learning from him that he is fleeing from God, reluctantly jettisons him (chapter 1). But God has appointed a large fish to rescue him, and from within its innards Jonah cries to God (chapter 2). Delivered, he proceeds to Nineveh and preaches a single sentence which produces conversion from all who hear, and God, responsive, calls off what had been threatened (chapter 3). The last chapter (4) is taken up by discussions between prophet and deity about what has transpired.

Had the choice fallen on the more famous but less typical Song of Songs, on Genesis creation materials, or on the sprawling book of Psalms, the outcome would be in certain ways different. But Jonah will suit well. We will look at interpreters from four major chronological/cultural periods, alert to each era's social factors, focusing explicitly upon the governing hermeneutical assumptions and relevant moves as well as foregrounding textual interpretations. The exemplars chosen struggle to render the Old Testament useful for transformation and present us with a range of theories – explicit to implicit – for how it happens. They allow us access to a spectrum of possibilities and assist us to see the basic problematic as resident in the act of interpreting, not in content *per se*. My choices are idiosyncratic, prompting readers to their own researches. I sought serious engagement between text and interpreter's experience: responsible, relevant, reliable access to existential meaning via the Old Testament. All rely on something analogical between the text's world and their/our own. Our challenge is to draw appreciatively from the riches of the past and read well ourselves, conscious of what our forebears may not have seen, grateful for the best they have bequeathed to us, open to fresh possibilities.

Antiquity (First to Sixth Centuries)

The struggle of the earliest Christians to read Scripture was grounded in their sense of God's coherent purposes over time, the Christ-event deeply implicated with God's dealings as narrated in the Jewish Scriptures/Old Testament. Central for these early readers was a sense of God as authoring Scripture with care for each word. The human quest involved making sense of the divine communication, using various rationales and methods. The sense of Jesus as key to all of Scripture involved a minimizing of the original Old Testament situations for events later in time. Without much explicit discussion, the ancients appear to have assumed that events presented in the Old Testament had happened, though "happenedness" was hardly their greatest significance. Emerging from within the Hebrew tradition, Jesus makes three references to Jonah: Matthew 12:

38–42 ends a section where Jesus debates with some who ask for a sign. Responding that none will be given but the sign of Jonah, Jesus specifies the three days and nights in the belly of the fish, similar to what he will experience in the earth. In Luke 11: 29–32, Jesus chides those not responsive to his preaching: remarking that the Ninevites repented at Jonah's proclamation, Jesus characterizes his own presence as greater – hence his audience as so much the less responsive. Each saying makes its point with adequate though not utter clarity, moving via detail from the lesser Jonah to the greater Jesus, from "then" to a more urgent "now." A final allusion (Matt. 16: 4) has Jesus refer more ambiguously and enigmatically to the sign of Jonah, leaving his precise point to be inferred.

The comments of the earliest post-biblical interpreters seem informal and ad hoc, as though meaning were easy to access. Irenaeus of Lyons (c.130–200) explains various points from the Jonah narrative: Jonah's flight from God's first command as similar to Adam's fall; Jonah's prayer as salutary for his own situation; God's care for the state of Jonah's body while in the fish's digestive tract foreshadowing Jesus's resurrection (*Against Heresies* 3.20.1; 5.5.2). Irenaeus is doing two things: first, he allegorizes, drawing significance not from the story's most obvious sense but discerning a deeper meaning to illuminate the Christian reader's context. And he makes a typological comment, where a Christ-event helps an earlier significance to be seen. Though these are standard biblical moves, we will explore them in later interpreters, where they proliferate.

One of the most influential of the early interpreters was Origen of Alexandria (185–254), who names multiple senses of Scripture: the literal/historical meaning of the text is sought and retained, though gone beyond, if possible, to the more crucial level or set of levels, called by Origen the allegorical (or spiritual), the moral (tropolog-ical), and the heavenly (anagogical). The spiritual, moral and heavenly levels – accessed ordinarily via the literal – are where divine mysteries about God with human beings become available to those alert to them. Key for Origen is that the action made avail-able within Scripture is that of the Logos (Jesus the Christ) instructing the soul, teach-ing all readers the gifts of salvation: contemplation, divinization. The process described allows a reader to participate in the divine *paideia*/formation which the text mediates. Hence the referent of the biblical text is not its historical "happenedness" but the urgings of the Logos made available via the biblical text. Origen does not so much husk the literal level to get to the fruit of the spiritual as count on a process of transposition via a simpler level toward something ever-more profound. The spiritual sense re-enacts the transcript of the literal, not as an end in itself but parabolically. What is rendered present for the contemporary reader is the saving activity of God. The process of dis-cerning the spiritual meaning through the other senses is for Origen surely a matter of study but primarily of holiness and discernment (*On First Principles* 4.1–3).

In Antioch, interpreters proceeded a bit differently, as we can see from the Jonah scholarship of Theodore of Mopsuestia (350–428), monk and bishop. Antiochene typology envisions one meaning, distinct from Alexandrian allegory's several. Propo-nents of typology understand the author, assisted by an intuition called *theoria*, to envi-sion a single inspired meaning with two moments of completion. The Old Testament person, event, or teaching (called a type) manifests a fuller and future significance when a person, event, or teaching – involving Jesus (the antitype) – allows the type to be seen in its most salient particularities. In typological interpretation there is a more precise analogy linking the two situations than is the case with allegory, and a greater sense that the Old Testament type remains crucial for optimal participation in the New Testament antitype. The Antiochenes remain more committed to the originating circumstances of Old Testament narratives than do those who work with multiple levels of a text. In his *Commentary on Jonah*, Theodore spends considerable time construing the reactions of "the blessed Jonah": Jonah understood that the implied contrast between responsive Ninevites and recalcitrant Israelites would be disadvantageous for the Jews and suffered accordingly. Also Jonah anticipated that "the same" Assyrians would bring calamity upon Israel. Jonah's angry reactions were also accounted for by his feeling a fraud in the eyes of the Ninevites for having threatened what did not ultimately come to pass. Theodore also anticipates a later tendency to think that the prayer from within the fish does not match the narrative circumstances aptly, adding words to Jonah's prayer to contextualize it more precisely.

Jerome (346–419) utilizes both Alexandrian allegory and Antiochene typology. Beginning with the historical/literal level, Jerome situates Jonah in the eighth century BCE and then names other biblical books where he occurs: his young life saved by Elijah (1 Kings 17: 8–24, a rabbinic reading), which reminds Jerome to tell us there are two places where Jonah's tomb can be visited; a ministry under Jeroboam II (2 Kings 14: 23–5); Tobit 14: 3–4 is linked to the relapse of the Ninevites, since Tobit urges his family to flee Assyria before it is (finally) overthrown in the late seventh century BCE. Jerome draws on knowledge of languages and of local flora to offer a controversial translation for Jonah's leafy shelter: a fast-growing plant Jerome represents as "ivy." Finally, acknowledging what ought to have happened to a small man in the intestines of a large fish, Jerome insists that Jonah is neither the first nor the last to escape danger miraculously.

At what can be called the moral/tropological level, Jerome suggests that human flight from God is typical of our species; he warns readers against thinking that the use of lots was condoned by the sailors' effective use of them and offers a similar admonition against imitation when Jonah sounds suicidal. Finally, when the sinful Ninevites repent effectively, if temporarily, Jerome talks about whether saints and ex-sinners ought in fact to end up together.

And Jerome allegorizes: Jonah's flight from God is akin to human refusal; his sleep in the ship's hold resembles human stupefaction before God; the sailors' reluctance to jettison their passenger contrasts with the crowds calling for the crucifixion of Jesus; the boat is like the human race or the church, buffeted by false and confusing dogma; the whale recalls both the bosom of hell and the paunch of God (Bowers 1971: 25). Jonah's three-day journey across Nineveh and his single prophetic utterance resonate nicely, for Jerome, with the Trinity.

Jerome lavishly and with certain ingenuity sees Jonah as a type for Jesus: his flight from God resembles the incarnation, his three days in the fish the death and subsequent resurrection – that event prefigured pointedly when the whale spits Jonah forth; Jonah's sadness/anger is a type of Jesus's grief over Jerusalem's refusal to repent; Jonah's prayer in distress anticipates Jesus's prayer, and Jonah's ministry to Nineveh prefigures that of

Jesus to various gentiles (*Letters* 3.5; 16.1; 39.3; 77.4; 107.6; 108.8; 133.12; *Against Jovinian* 2.15; *Against the Pelagians* 3.6).

Augustine, eventually bishop of Hippo (354–430), is a giant in all fields of Christian spirituality. His most apt achievement for our purposes was the integration of neo-Platonist philosophy with Christian Scripture and his articulation of the relationship between life experience and biblical texts. Lacking the modern sense of the Bible as a collection of books authored at various times, Augustine inclines toward seeing it as a single vast puzzle, comprising in minute detail the story – even process – of God's salvific deeds, in which human beings participate by seeking coherent meaning within an intricate code. The challenge of interpretation is to grasp the significance of the myriad patterns and details. Augustine does not see literal and spiritual meanings as inevitably opposed, though his Platonic categories and sensitivity to humanity's fallen condition incline him toward the allegorical senses of Scripture as most suitable (*On Christian Doctrine*).

A Jonah sampling may be assembled from his writings. In Jonah's flight from and resistance to God, Augustine sees the classic human move of his own youth: to abandon our basic goal and chase a shadow (*Confessions* 2.6.14). Augustine derives from the whale God's successful utilization of animals, whether whales or worms (*The Literal Meaning of Genesis* 9.14.25). Commenting on Psalm 130, Augustine makes a lovely reflective comment on Jonah within the whale:

> "Out of the deep I have called unto Thee, O Lord: Lord, hear my voice" (v. 1). Jonas cried from the deep; from the whale's belly. He was not only beneath the waves, but also in the entrails of the beast; nevertheless, those waves and that body prevented not his prayer from reaching God, and that beast's belly could not contain the voice of his prayer. It penetrated all things, it burst through all things, it reached the ears of God: if indeed we ought to say that, bursting through all things, it reached the ears of God, since the ears of God were in the heart of him who prayed. (Augustine 1994: vol. 8, p. 613)

The repentance of the Ninevites prompts from Augustine two comments: that God provides opportunities for all kinds of people to repent, and that the Ninevites repent without total confidence that mercy is available to them. When discussing whether the Ninevites were advised that they had three or forty days for conversion, Augustine urges that the point is deeper than the literal number, since both numbers offer a more profound key to the passage in the life of Jesus. Finally, when corresponding with Jerome, Augustine alludes to the controversy stirred up by Jerome's non-traditional translation of the plant; Augustine chides Jerome for unnecessary perturbation of the faithful and urges the possibility of consulting Jews about such things (*Confessions* 2.6–7; *City of God* 18.44; *On Catechizing the Unlearned* 19.32; *Expositions on the Psalms* 51.11).

Those who fled their homelands seeking a deeper relatededness with God through intensive self-knowledge engaged Scripture even more existentially. The Egyptian desert monastics fed hungrily on God's authoritative word as daily food and drink, seeking to be transformed by Scripture into women and men of deep relatedness with God. The Bible was a dialogue partner, not simply interpreted but searched so as to be embodied.

The key question for the early monks – for all our interpreters – was how to derive particular and present meaning from ancient texts. Scripture was to be learned "by heart," ruminated upon – aloud – and engaged as addressed. A sample appropriation: early Christians worried over whether their sins could be forgiven. A story is told of a query made to an Abba by a soldier: the monk asked him if, when his cloak was torn, he threw it away; the soldier replied that of course he mended it and used it again. The teacher, drawing upon Jonah 4: 10, replied, "If you are so careful about your cloak, will not God be equally careful about his creature?" (Burton-Christie 1993: 276).

The itinerant Irish monks managed interpretation even more imaginatively, entering biblical narratives distinctively. The adventures of Brendan of Clonfert (c.483–577) are shaped around a whale – Jasconius – who assists Brendan's crew in their travels (Simms: 1989: 40–54). The better known Columcille (521–97, also called Columba) left Ireland as well, landing on the island of Iona (whose name is bound up with Jonah wordplay: "dove" in Hebrew is *yonah* and in Latin *columba*); there he founded a monastery. According to Columcille's biographer Adomnan, the monastic community shaped its life around the Old Testament in several ways. Besides a constant rumination on the Scriptures and liturgical celebration centered on psalms, the community – famously Columcille himself – constantly copied biblical texts into beautiful and serviceable manuscripts, thus both absorbing and transmitting the word. Adomnan worked Columcille's life-deeds right into biblical stories, smudging the line between narratives by making Columcille a Moses: covenant mediator, intimate of God, snake-handler, water-splitter, prescient about his death. For both the "sailor monks" and their desert counterparts, learning was less intellectual than practical, as much moral and spiritual as cognitive. To discern Scripture's meaning was a wisdom quest, reliant upon the Holy Spirit and upon holiness (O'Reilly 1997: 80–106; 1999: 159–85).

The Middle Ages (Twelfth to Fourteenth Centuries)

From a longer period we will sample three sets of interpreters who show substantial continuity with antiquity, while also shifting toward positions characteristic of the future. Indeed, if the medieval period maintains earlier emphasis on the Bible as primarily God's word, on the unity of sanctity and study, and on the multiple layers of meaning in Scripture, it also takes more seriously the human shaping of the Bible, the role of the young universities in directing its study, and the impact scholastic philosophy will have on the interpretation of Christian spirituality.

First, basic continuity is carried by scholars like Benedictine Rupert of Deutz (c.1070–1135) and Dominican Hugh of St Cher (1190–1263). Rupert articulates the close link between the liturgy and biblical study, considering it self-evident that Scripture should be dealt with in the context of worship. Rupert sees Jonah as a type of the savior for the gentiles, the great storm anticipating commotions occasioned by Jesus in Judea; the sailors' fear recalls that of the apostles when preaching in foreign lands. Jonah asleep in the ship's hold suggests Jesus's patience, while the worm appointed to gnaw at the sheltering plant is likened to the destructive rule of Rome (Bowers 1971: 47–8).

Hugh's Dominican Order was animated by a fresh blend of the basic elements of Christian spirituality: learning and love, prayer and preaching, contemplation of God and action on behalf of the neighbor. Simon Tugwell (1987: 26–7) says that "the intellectual life, undertaken with full seriousness, can itself be a genuine form of piety, provided it is motivated by charity, and especially if it is also motivated by a desire to communicate truth to people." Hugh's work on Jonah is rather a mix of elements. Jonah is a figure of Christ, though Hugh warns against pressing every detail to fit the pattern. Jonah's prayers from the whale are reminiscent of Jesus's cries to God while still among the dead, and Hugh envisions the whale as similar to the Red Sea: safe access for God's people on a three-day schedule. Hugh notes resonances between Jonah's prayer and Psalms 15 and 87. More fancifully, he finds Jonah's vine as Israel, shading the prophet as he awaits the conversion of the gentiles. Hugh exonerates Jonah of misconduct, likening the prophet's anger to that of Jesus crucified – surely a stretch, and an indication that words themselves remain the central comparative factor (Bowers 1971: 46–58).

A second and distinctive trajectory emerges from the School of St Victor in Paris, represented by Hugh (d. 1141) and his student Andrew (d. 1175). The Victorines diverge somewhat from other medievals, reading deeply and broadly rather than reducing their comments to ever-smaller texts; and they insist on interpreting biblical material itself rather than commenting on the scholarly glosses now surrounding texts. Assuming that *lectio divina* rose from and contributed to study and sanctity, Hugh insists, as had Augustine, that theological study be a prerequisite for biblical interpreters. The Victorines tend to see three basic senses of Scripture, folding the anagogical in with the spiritual so as to concentrate on the literal, the moral, and the spiritual. But they distinctively maintain the primacy of the literal sense, placed by God's Holy Spirit; to disregard it was to miscue about subtle and deep mysteries. In a point established by the end of the period, Hugh suggests that the letter signifies twice: first its historical referent and then a spiritual one; and he, as others before and since, affirms that texts whose literal meaning was problematic challenge creativity rather than representing an absurdity.

Discussing Jonah, Andrew relies substantially on Jerome, in appreciative conversation with contemporary Hebrew scholars as Jerome had been as well. Andrew does not so much theologize from the text as discuss its plain meaning when possible. For example, he speculates on the personas behind the various biblical prophets, evincing interest in details presumed by the books. Andrew wonders how Jeremiah can have understood God's knowing him in the womb (Jer. 1: 5); he opines that the baby mentioned in Isaiah 7 was an eighth-century child, born to the prophet and his wife; and he names the dynastic heir referred to in 2 Samuel 7 as Solomon. Christological meanings were later understandings (Smalley 1983: 83–195).

Third is a pivotal thinker, also Dominican: Thomas Aquinas (1225–74). Scholastic thought did not begin with Thomas or reach its fullest utilization in his writings, but his bringing of Aristotelian philosophy into sustained contact with biblical revelation was momentous, reinforced by Thomas's prominence in the history of theology. Ultimately Aristotelian categories had an effect of flattening Hebrew Bible appropriation, of distancing its interpretation from spirituality. But for Thomas the goal of "doing

Scripture" – whether in *lectio* and prayer, in writing and teaching, or in preaching – was always for love of God and neighbor. For him, faith was foundational for Scripture and theology, and Thomas's own life betrays no hint of the split that eventually comes between theology and spirituality, however much his writings may have abetted others along that path.

The basically Platonist understanding of innate senses of Scripture, underlying much of what we have examined so far, is challenged by Thomas's Aristotelian structures. Thomas sees God's revealed word as analogous to the human person, a composite of the physical/literal and spiritual. Just as there is no peeling back the body to find the soul, so the Old Testament literal sense is not detachable from the spiritual sense. Thomas theorized that Scripture's divine author intended many meanings and used things as well as words for signification. The human writer's words signified in a unified way, though referencing doubly. The first sense was the literal, including everything that the human author intended, less but not other than the divine author wished. Whether the human writer spoke plainly or used imagery, all comprised the literal meaning. A second referent, called the spiritual and including the moral, allegorical, and anagogical aspects, might also be indicated by the words. The particular relation between the first Christian referent and the second (Hebrew Bible) one was for Thomas the key to Scripture's meaning. The spiritual meaning, intended by God's spirit, was in no sense a merely human achievement; God acting in Jesus gives spiritual significance to earlier events, persons, and things (Weisheipl 1974: 106–10; Smalley 1983: 292–308; Valkenberg 2000: 9–53).

Thomas has done several important things by this newly articulated division. First, he has made the human author more significant than before and given greater importance to the meaning intended by that writer: the grammatical, historical, literary aspects; from this move will eventually come renewed interest in Hebrew Bible studies. Second, he has demoted the spiritual meaning of the Old Testament, though without denying its capacity to order humans toward God. Third, Thomas has resolved intractable problems rooted in seeing imagery as allegorical or spiritual instead of belonging at the historical or literal level. Fourth, Thomas insists that theological truth must rise from the literal sense (thus disqualifying certain points of his predecessors). When Thomas mentions Jonah, it is primarily to explain the resurrection of Jesus. Discussing its necessity and timing, Thomas makes Jonah's three days in the belly of the whale a tiny part of larger argumentation: the Old Testament is not simply a proof but used to illustrate, confirm, and provide insight into theological argumentation.

Renaissance and Reformations (Fifteenth to Seventeenth Centuries)

A third period for our consideration hosts three overlapping "events": the Renaissance (with its return to the classics and its fresh ways of seeing reality), the Protestant reform (with its repudiation of various excesses and its zeal to inhabit the early vitality of Christian experience), and the Catholic response to that reform (with its determined retrenchment and its concomitant re-commitment to the spiritual life and contemplative prayer). The period's crucial factors are generally known: the positioning of the human being at the center of consideration; a fresh awareness of history; better tools and methods for inquiring into familiar subjects; and a radical questioning of authority. The issue of how to appropriate the Old Testament in particular declines as a topic in its own right, taking its place among other subjects of inquiry. Issues of history and science – Scriptural reliability and veracity – begin to overshadow former concerns. Discussions form along confessional lines, with the Renaissance and Protestant Reformers tending to dispute and disregard the scholasticism which takes deeper root among certain of those within the Counter-Reform. A fledgling critical spirit also increases, barely discernible in this period, though about to sweep the field in the next.

Renaissance interpreters like John Fisher (1469–1535) were typically wise as well as learned, socially engaged as well as personally committed, fired with zeal for the classics and opposed to desiccated, abstract, arcane scholastic theology. Solid philology, textual principles, historical awareness, and literary sensitivity would clarify the meaning of the text. The result was often more moral than theological, aimed to illuminate human rather than divine life. Objecting to both crass literalism and arbitrary allegorizing, Renaissance scholars continued to reach for the key analogue between biblical texts and contemporary need. Fisher had a particular interest in God's mercy to sinners, a theme explored in a piece integrating Psalm 130 with the story of Jonah, the better to explore human alienation from God. He demonstrates Jonah's fall into sin by seven steps: fleeing God, hiring a ship, boarding it, going below to sleep, being cast into the sea, being taken into the "lowest part of a great whale's belly." Perhaps needing to complete the biblical seven steps down, Fisher names bluntly what nearly happens: had Jonah not repented, "he would have been digested & voyded out from hym [i.e. the whale] in a manner of dunge" (Bowers 1971: 73). Having identified the prophet's journey to alienation, Fisher shows the psalm tracing the same trajectory: consent of the mind, followed by a search for the opportunity to commit the wrong. Next comes a fuller consent to the evil, an active commitment to the deed envisioned. Such a situation hardens into habit, giving way to boasting in the wrong done. In another step, the sinner justifies the fault as virtuous, wrong as right. Finally, analogous to Jonah's timely rescue by God, the sinner must somehow survive despair and call for help. Key for both texts is the sinner's crying out to God and God's eager response – in fact, God's anticipation of such a cry (Fisher 1998: 204–37).

Martin Luther (1483–1546), Augustinian monk and university master, relates his struggles with a God who seemed to demand a near-impossible perfection. Luther's question emerged: how is any human being justified before God? His insight: God does not expect humans to earn their salvation; rather, it is given freely. Luther argues for the possibility and necessity of a relationship of deep trust and interdependence between God and humans rather than one based on threat and fearful effort. Luther held that the Bible, God's word, was spoken with clarity, on the whole, comprising one simple solid sense. The Bible was to be read by all, studied, expounded in knowledgeable preaching, and, of course, experienced. Luther opposed a number of things in regard to Scripture: mystical appropriations, allegorizing interpretations not expressly demanded by the text itself, scholastic excesses. He questioned the privileged respect granted to patristic commentary, which Luther felt had too paralyzing a grip on meaning. The Bible's authority was rooted neither in its traditional interpretation nor in any ecclesiastical institution. Luther's own readings of Scripture emerge as prophetic or moral, and always deeply Christocentric. As we have seen quite consistently, any sense of Old Testament events as important in themselves interested him little. The Hebrew Scriptures anticipated Jesus, Luther held, and were important primarily in that regard.

Luther preached and wrote on the book of Jonah, its central character functioning as an exemplum of a sinner – fearful before God and determined to flee, but able to be brought back as well and to acknowledge his own unworthiness. Jonah learned. Luther also considers Jonah a powerful preacher, delivering an effective word – more effective than Jesus, Luther hazards! The small prophetic book also shows God eager and active to effect the salvation of all peoples. In a preface, Luther takes up certain questions about who Jonah was, accepting some data (an eighth-century ministry) and refusing others (that Jonah was the boy raised from the dead by Elijah). Luther also critiques the Jews' refusal to turn to God as it appeared (to Christians) they ought to have done long since. Luther comments comparatively extensively on Jonah's reasons for flight: unwillingness to leave family and homeland; fear or dislike of Nineveh's king; anxiety both that his words would come true and that they would not; the perception that God was concerned only with Jews. Luther also speculates that Jonah must, with his bad conscience, have dreaded the fall of the lots. Was Jonah's flight a sin, Luther inquires? And he answers in the affirmative; Jonah did not deserve to be saved, but God cared for him nonetheless. Discussing the whale, Luther wonders whether the prophet expected to be consumed in the great digestive system. The three-day sojourn evokes for Luther not the reference to Christ in the tomb but rather the need to rely utterly upon God and the value of prayer. Luther exclaims while discussing the passage: "That must have been a strange voyage. Who would believe this story and not regard it as a lie and a fairy tale if it were not recorded in Scripture?" (1974: 68). The Ninevites' fasting occasions a discussion of works and grace, since some of his "sophist-like opponents" have used the moment against him. Luther points out that works were demanded neither by prophet nor deity, who sees the heart.

Teresa of Avila (1515–82), Roman Catholic contemplative, founder-reformer, writer, poet, and teacher, was most interested in how God works in the human soul, the project of transformation by which humans enter as deeply as possible the life and love of God. Though complex, her thought can be summarized: God is constantly present to us, and our challenge is to become more aware of it and to allow it increasingly to transform our lives. *The Interior Castle*, produced near the end of her life, describing the journey of the soul toward the King who dwells at its center, exemplifies her appropriation of Old Testament texts for broader purposes. When she draws on the Old Testament, Teresa tends to refer in short images to various places in Scripture. Her references are both allusive and elusive, in that she counts on her audience to know what a given image was and where it comes from (even if she forgets!). She does not talk theoretically about the interpretation process, and, in a sense, the images and phrases she borrows seem ancillary, compared with the work of those writing biblical commentaries. And yet Scripture thoroughly grounds her experience and her writings, and even her excerpts never seem detached from the whole. In the discussion of the fifth and sixth dwelling places, elaborated primarily by the Song of Songs, Teresa mentions Jonah, offering the image of the silkworm's transformation into a small butterfly. Teresa describes the work of worms, who feed on mulberry leaves and then spin the cocoons in which they die (metamorphose), so that what emerges is a creature transformed. It is a stunning – and non-biblical – image for the journey of the human toward God. But Teresa "converts" it with a brief reference to other such creatures, such as the worm in Jonah 4, which under cover of night gnaws its way through Jonah's leafy protection. Allegorically and somewhat a-contextually, she speaks of the worm: virtues can be destroyed by the "worms" of self-love, self-esteem, a judgmental spirit, lack of love.

Modernity and Early Postmodernity (Seventeenth to Twenty-first Centuries)

As Antiquity shaded into the Middle Ages, refining rather than contesting many of the earlier claims, so the Renaissance/Reformation era seeded issues of modernism, to be pursued in more developed and faster-moving configurations. The modern period has been characterized by historicism, scientism, and a certain "methodism," as well as by a quest for objectivity and resolute verifiability, by confidence in "assured results." But countering these strong forces has been, especially in recent decades, a (re)discovery of the significance of human language, a turn to the subject in ways the Renaissance had not imagined, and a profound awareness of the constructedness of all reality. These latter insights are only beginning to be appropriated. Our particular practitioners of Christian spirituality will be clustered at the era's beginning and end, the better to show aspects of contemporary use of the Old Testament for Christian transformation.

Though Pentateuchal studies were the seed-bed for modern biblical criticism, for our purposes the more general reflections of Congregationalist minister Jonathan Edwards (1703–58), associated with North America's Great Awakening, offer the framework we need. Though interestedly conversant with the modern period's issues, Edwards remained committed to a classical vision of biblical matters. Showing what now appears as mainly a rear-guard action on behalf of ideas whose time had passed, Edwards's erudition, honesty, and powerful articulation illuminate the struggle of the modern period with its antecedents. Edwards himself had a conversion experience as a young man, and his life project was to communicate the possibility and urgency of experiencing a glorious Divine Being whose purposes unfolded harmoniously with those of all creation. He wrestled with the biblical implications of how humans know. That the Old Testament was not understood with a naïve immediacy did not mean it was completely unreliable. Edwards labored to show the Bible historically respectable. Are manuscripts and consequent readings reliable? How can certain matters in the Bible be shown congruent with rational thought and science? How is faith linked with scholarship, revelation with epistemology? The truth of any narrative, including the Bible, was now closely bound up with its historicity. Could biblical scholarship show that the named authors were in fact the writers or reliable authorities, or were such works forgeries? Were the said authors in a position to know the things about which they wrote from experience, claiming the rights of eyewitnesses? Or had they, perhaps, worked with reliable archival material or empirical evidence of some sort – and could later scholars have access to it also? Could biblical works be corroborated from elsewhere? What correlations between ancient religions and the Bible strengthened its claims? Could the narratives themselves sustain the sort of incipiently rigorous scrutiny which was the lot of all documents, ancient ones in particular? (Brown 2002: 91, 114 and passim).

The implications of contested issues such as these may be seen in the Jonah commentary of Oxford scholar E. B. Pusey (1800–86), who writes with pained awareness of them. Pusey begins by verifying Jonah's eighth-century context and his links with other biblical characters whom he resembles. He talks briefly about the natural religion of the sailors, a topic of interest in the intellectual center of the British Empire. He argues for Jonah's authorship of the book, noting that all biblical prophets referred to themselves in the third person. Pusey praises the form and language of the book, and he opines that no one "beyond [historical-criticism's] babyhood" would be bothered by its issues. The miracles in the book are reliable – so the survival of Jonah within the fish – because they were narrated at the time by an eyewitness: the prophet himself. Were they not true, they would not have been included. Allowing that the eighth-century Hebrews were simple folk who knew little of maritime things or of the ways of large fish, Pusey adduces a newspaper article published in 1758 narrating how a large fish almost devoured a human being – lest any find the biblical tale incredible. The prophetic book also advances historical knowledge, which is presented realistically: tired from a hard journey, Jonah would go down below deck for a nap, and once overboard and swallowed, Jonah would easily and authentically articulate the psalm-like prayer, knowing the Hebrew psalter. Pusey amplifies what Jonah omitted, providing details about Nineveh available from the historical researches of later times. The commentary contains a map of Nineveh, information on the Assyrians, including plausible names of the responsive king, a sketch of Jonah's shrub and its proper name (*Ricinus communis*). Pusey misses Jonah's explanations of his own anger with God, which the Englishman supposes rises from the prophet's knowledge of both God's ultimate plan and the Assyrians' eventual destructive impact on Israel by the century's end. Presenting the deity as powerful and providential, appointing as needed a storm, a fish, a plant, a wind, Pusey cites Western classics – Ovid's *Metamorphoses* – with similar motifs; but, he breaks off, none of these reaches is necessary, since the psalms themselves (Pss. 18, 42, 124) testify to such phenomena. That Jesus quotes the book enhances its reliability and the confidence all ought to have in God's protective presence (Pusey 1860: 247–87).

Closer to our time, we find Jonah useful in political and social contexts. Jacques Ellul (1912–94), a French Protestant trained in social science and law, was a courageous resister of totalitarianism and suspicious of certain modernist assumptions: the inevitability of progress, the value of creeping secularism, the dominance of technology, the spread of urbanism. He wrote a reflective work on Jonah to suggest an alternative vision. This he shapes around prophecy – not Hebrew practice but Christian. Ellul describes God's choosing Jonah and his resistance, highlighting both the prophet's flawed refusal but also his eventual willingness to be a martyr and witness (by storm's end), if not yet a preacher. Gentile sailors are converted by their encounter with Jonah, whose willingness to suffer an ignominious task makes visible Jesus's incarnation, ministry, and death. Jonah's struggles in the whale occasion a second prophetic point. More than most, Ellul stresses the dangers represented by the water monster, suggesting as it does biblical encounters with watery death and separation from God. Jonah's near-death and his praising God from the other side of it proleptically draw Jesus's escape from death, to the benefit of others. Ellul's final comments are on Jonah's Nineveh experience, where he pursues not what happened to the Ninevites but what occupies Jonah and God. Ellul defends the authenticity of Jonah's first change of heart and God's active patience and inexhaustible fidelity. Jonah's role foreshadows what the Ninevites must experience: conversion to God's love (Ellul 1971: 9–103).

Rosemary Radford Ruether (b.1936), Christian feminist theologian, has spent her professional life writing, speaking, and working on the several challenges of liberation: civil rights, feminism, non-violence, Jewish causes, and, most recently, ecology. With her husband, she named a book after our prophet, which sorts Israeli and Palestinian claims in that torn and troubled land. Asking what kind of repentance within and between peoples is called for, she suggests it is "repentance and mutual acceptance between nations, as peoples equally created and loved by God" (Ruether and Ruether 2002: xix). Each side needs to abandon its innocence claim and grow beyond a solipsism that occludes the genuine suffering of the other. Ruether's Jonah is characterized as "a reluctant, angry, and resentful prophet," who directs his anger at a God who called him to a task that makes tangible God's mercy available for all (2002: xix–xx). With perhaps a bit more certitude than is advisable, the prophetic book is synopsized, the analogy implied: "Jonah does not want God to be a universal God, slow to wrath and bountiful in mercy toward all nations. Rather, Jonah wants God to be a punitive and partisan God who punishes the enemies of Israel" (2002: xx). Ruether locates the book's production as fourth century BCE, characterized by self-righteous Jewish religious exclusivism. She presents Jonah as disgusted at the repentance of the Ninevites and desirous of vengeance against them – a narrowing down of motivations which, as we have seen in this essay, the story does not quite condone. Critics argue not so much about whether a Christian has a right to object to Israeli policies, or if it is appropriate for words from the Hebrew Bible to be used "against" the heirs to that tradition, but whether Ruether has read the book with justly provocative implications or unfairly brought reductive categories to it.

Wendy Beckett (b. c.1930) has already been introduced in this essay, her context set. Offering a short meditation on Jonah, she says, "Prayer is God's taking possession of us. We expose to Him what we are, and He gazes on us with the creative eye of Holy Love. His gaze is transforming: He does not leave us in our poverty but draws into being all we are meant to become" (Beckett, 1993: 9). But, she goes on, the gift implies that we need to cooperate in some way, making the process reciprocal. How that is to be done drives her short comment on Jonah. She enlivens her reflection with reference to contemporary artist Albert Herbert's *Jonah and the Whale* (figure 2.1). Both the narrative and the painting evoke a story with deep meaning for those seeking God. Beckett sees Jonah as the archetypal figure who says no to God: "God in His desperate love makes [Jonah] taste the meaning of his no, and he is swallowed by the whale" (1993: 106). Herbert represents the moment when Jonah faces again the question of his calling and the fullness of his human gifts. Beckett asks, "Will he accept and step out of the safety

Figure 2.1   *Jonah and the Whale*, c.1988 (oil on canvas) by Albert Herbert (b.1925) Private Collection/Bridgeman Art Library.
Source: Courtesy England and Co., London

of his cetacean haven?" And she continues reading the picture: "poor, naked, frightened Jonah and the world of responsibility and maturity that awaits him." His choices: ease and safety and self-love, as opposed to work and risk and self-giving. But, she concludes, "Jonah's dilemma is in his own mind. God's love awaits him on every side" (1993: 106).

Sandra Schneiders (b. 1936), also previously introduced, is our last commentator on Jonah, in the informal genre of a college commencement address. We can disidentify if we so choose with this prophet who attempts to flee "the God of the universe in a wooden boat" (1993: 1). But Jonah is not the last to suppose that flight from God is possible, and Schneiders hints at other crafts familiar to us which have been put to the same futile use. Like many before her, she asks why Jonah is so resistant and then sketches him as a sort of spoiled favorite child who has tattled on a sibling with gleeful anticipation of the parental wrath to descend. Again, we may laugh at the child, but Schneiders redirects us to ourselves, to get perspective: "This story, we suddenly realize, is not about an ancient prophet but about the Jonah in our hearts whom we need to understand and to challenge to conversion. Jonah in the story is laughable but the Jonah in our hearts is quite serious" (1993: 3). And she details the pattern we can see in Jonah as he deals with Nineveh: first to refuse contact, then to attempt to dominate, to grow more angry, and then will to destroy those who are other to ourselves. Why do we do this?, she asks:

> Perhaps it is because accepting the other as truly other makes us experience, and challenges us to accept, our own essential limitation. If black or brown or red or yellow is accepted as an equal way to be and I am white then, obviously, being white is not the only good way to be and there is something valuable that I am not . . . Accepting the other as truly other and truly equal, as much a loved child of God as I am, means accepting my own real but limited goodness in the very act and fact of accepting the real but limited goodness of the other. This alone will enable us to freely share this earth as brothers and sisters, children of the one Holy Mystery, called to one common destiny. (1993: 3)

Calling attention to the significance of Jonah's shrub as a place to face our ecological selfishness, Schneiders rearticulates the basic question from God: "'Are you right to be angry because I have made such diversity and because I love everything that I have made and desire all to be happy, all to be saved? Should you not rather rejoice to be my prophet, to announce my love and care and saving intent to all of creation and especially to my daughters and sons whom I have made so diverse in so many ways and whose diversity redounds to my glory?' The story of Jonah ends without telling us what becomes of the stubborn prophet because, in fact, the story is still going on" (1993: 4).

Conclusion

As we have worked a path through the appropriation of the Old Testament in Christian spirituality, five perennial issues suggest their relevance for us. First, the *general challenge*: from biblical times and extending into the present there is a quest to understand and articulate how appropriation works in its various dimensions, though the "how" of it is not the whole project. Insights of one era are useful for the reflection of later interpreters, though a critical sorting needs to occur; even classic insights need fresh evaluation. The exact nature of the appropriation has yet to be articulated and must continue to be sought.

Second, the *nature of the project*: the Old Testament becomes a central place to seek, find, and make meaning that is responsible, accessible, reliable, valuable, apt and authorized; the meaning is sought personally and individually though not outside a social and ecclesial context. The quest is not carried out objectively but always in a way that is experiential, participative, committed, self-implicating. The profound relevance sought is constituted at least partially as self-knowledge and insight about the workings of God with creatures. The interpretive appropriation in Christian spirituality is shaped and driven by, originates and culminates in, an ongoing transformation into the life of the triune God within the ecclesial community. To engage with Scripture's capacity to shape identity is a never-ending life work for individuals and for the Christian church; riches remain available.

Third, the *canonical factor*: the commitment to the biblical canon implies that a set of ancient and classical texts remains privileged, normative, and identified as a primary place where God's self-disclosure with believers and believers' self-integration with God are experienced. A perennial issue is the matter of how the Old Testament/New Testament relationship works: the fact that the Christian Bible includes texts which originated within and are still shared by the Jewish community is massively significant. For Christians, the Christ-event is focal but must not denigrate the identity of the earlier tradition and is best developed in a trinitarian (rather than simply Christological) direction. The Christian appropriation of the Hebrew Bible/Old Testament suffers chronically from various forms of anti-Judaism and is only recently exploring and perhaps owning these stances, an agenda which will remain prominent in the interpretive task of the future. Related to a Christian commitment to canon is the Bible's "dual authorship." Christians acknowledge God's communication derived from the Bible, while also recognizing in detail the human production of the texts. This complex origin resists easy negotiation.

Fourth, and closely related to what has preceded, is *discourse around the nature of biblical language*. The process of talking about how Scripture signifies has always included the sense that the "literal" meaning of the text (which over time has included the lexical meaning, the historical referents, the intention of the author[s], the cultural contexts of early readers/producers, linguistic techniques, the canonical matrix) is not exhausted by those facets. Meaning reaches "more deeply" from what is most consistently called the spiritual level, rooting in analogy between textual experience and the lives of later readers. To polarize or dichotomize these factors, even to stack them as layers, is not useful. A better analogy is a web. The experience and categories of reader-interpreters have come to be seen as constitutive of meaning; meaning is not so much mined as discerned and constructed dialogically. The ground where transformative engagement is to be sought is experience, human experience with God and others – not simply the biblical words or their referents *per se* – though those remain part of the participation in and expression of experience. Deep experience with God is what is represented in Scripture and what is to be continuously and imaginatively re-presented by interpreters and practitioners who "Scripture."

Fifth, the *current challenge*: the project of appropriation needs to be compatible with and in relation to the broad intellectual and cultural currents of the era; those cannot be unknown or disregarded out of a false respect for the past. If in the past the originating context seemed dispensable to interpreters, that is clearly no longer the case; but neither do the historical factors exhaust the quest. Some knowledge of such things is necessary to prevent arbitrary and radically flawed constructions of significance. And "more-than-literal" meanings need to be in basic continuity with what can be learned from critical study – historical, literary, and ideological. Though there has been much of it in the past, the Old Testament is not at its best when asked to buttress dogma, to proof text, to contribute simplistic examples, in short, to do anything that reduces the Old Testament's depth. To resist its complexity is not helpful in the long run, though it may be tempting and seem effective in the shorter term. The point is to choose effectively what is needed in the wonderful life-project of drawing into deeper relationship with God.

References

Augustine of Hippo 1982: *St Augustine: The Literal Meaning of Genesis*, 2 vols, trans. J. H. Taylor, Jr. New York: Newman Press.

——1984: *Selected Writings*, trans. M. T. Clark. New York: Paulist Press.

——1994: *Selected Works*. In P. Schaff (ed.), *Nicene and Post-Nicene Fathers*, 1st series, vol. 1: *The Confessions and Letters*; vol. 2: *City of God; Christian Doctrine*; vol. 3: *On the Holy Trinity; Doctrinal Treatises; Moral Treatises*; vol. 8: *Expositions on the Book of Psalms*. Peabody, MA: Hendrickson.

Barron, W. R. J. and Burgess, G. S. (eds) 2002: *The Voyage of Saint Brendan: Representative Versions of the Legend in English Translation*. Exeter: University of Exeter Press.

Beckett, W. 1993: *The Gaze of Love: Meditations on Art and Spiritual Transformation*. New York: HarperCollins.

Ben Zvi, E. 2003: *Signs of Jonah: Reading and Rereading in Ancient Yehud*. Sheffield: Sheffield Academic Press.

Bowers, R. H. 1971: *The Legend of Jonah*. The Hague: Martinus Nijhoff.

Brown, D. 1992: *Vir Trilinguis: A Study in the Biblical Exegesis of Saint Jerome*. Kampen, The Netherlands: Kok Pharos.

Brown, P. 2000: *Augustine of Hippo: A Biography*. Berkeley, CA: University of California Press.

Brown, R. E. 2002: *Jonathan Edwards and the Bible*. Bloomington, IN: Indiana University Press.

——and Schneiders, S. M. 1990: Hermeneutics. In R. E. Brown, J. A. Fitzmyer, and R. E. Murphy (eds), *The New Jerome Biblical Commentary*, pp. 1146–65. Englewood Cliffs, NJ: Prentice Hall.

Burton-Christie, D. 1993: *The Word in the Desert: Scripture and the Quest for Holiness in Early Christian Monasticism*. Oxford: Oxford University Press.

Chase, S. 2003: *Contemplation and Compassion: The Victorine Tradition*. Maryknoll, NY: Orbis.

Donovan, M. A. 1997: *One Right Reading? A Guide to Irenaeus*. Collegeville, MN: Liturgical Press.

Ellul, J. 1971: *The Judgment of Jonah*, trans. G. W. Bromiley. Grand Rapids, MI: W. B. Eerdmans.

Fisher, J. 1998: *Exposition of the Seven Penitential Psalms*, trans. A. B. Gardiner. San Francisco: Ignatius Press.

Grant, R. M. with Tracy, D. 1984: *A Short History of the Interpretation of the Bible*, 2nd edn. Philadelphia: Fortress Press.

Hanson, R. P. C. 2002: *Allegory and Event: A Study of the Sources and Significance of Origen's Interpretation of Scripture*. Louisville, KY: Westminster John Knox.

Irenaeus of Lyons 1996: *Against Heresies*. In A. Roberts and J. Donaldson (eds), *Ante-Nicene Fathers*, vol. 1: *The Apostolic Fathers with Justin Martyr and Irenaeus*. Grand Rapids, MI: W. B. Eerdmans.

Jerome 1994: *Letters and Selected Works*. In P. Schaff and H. Wace (eds), *Nicene and Post-Nicene Fathers*, 2nd series, vol. 6. Peabody, MA: Hendrickson.

Johnson, K. (ed.) 1997: *Sister Wendy in Conversation with Bill Moyers*. Boston: WGBH Educational Foundation.

Lampe, G. W. H. (ed.) 1969: *The Cambridge History of the Bible*, vol. 2: *The West from the Fathers to the Reformation*. Cambridge: Cambridge University Press.

Luther, Martin 1974: *Lectures on Jonah*. In H. C. Oswald (ed.), *Luther's Works*, vol. 19: *Lectures on the Minor Prophets II: Jonah, Habakkuk*. St Louis: Concordia.

McGinn, B. and Meyendorff, J., with Leclercq, J. (eds) 1985: *Christian Spirituality: Origins to the Twelfth Century*. New York: Crossroad.

Marsden, G. M. 2003: *Jonathan Edwards: A Life*. New Haven, CT: Yale University Press.

Mursell, G. (ed.) 2001: *The Story of Christian Spirituality: Two Thousand Years, from East to West*. Minneapolis, MN: Fortress Press.

O'Reilly, J. 1997: Reading the Scriptures in the life of Columba. In C. Bourke (ed.), *Studies in the Cult of Saint Columba*, pp. 80–106. Dublin: Four Courts Press.

—— 1999: The wisdom of the scribe and the fear of the Lord. In D. Broun and T. O. Clancy (eds), *Spes Scotorum / Hope of Scots: Saint Columba, Iona and Scotland*, pp. 159–211. Edinburgh: T. and T. Clark.

Origen 1966: *On First Principles*, trans. G. W. Butterworth. New York: Harper and Row.

Pusey, E. B. 1860: *The Minor Prophets*. Oxford: J. H. and J. Parker.

Raitt, J., with McGinn, B. and Meyendorff, J. (eds) 1997: *Christian Spirituality: High Middle Ages and Reformation*. New York: Crossroad.

Ruether, R. R. and Ruether, H. J. 2002: *The Wrath of Jonah: The Crisis of Religious Nationalism in the Israeli–Palestinian Conflict*, 2nd edn. Minneapolis, MN: Fortress Press.

Ryan, T. F. 2000: *Thomas Aquinas as Reader of the Psalms*. Notre Dame, IN: University of Notre Dame Press.

Schneiders, S. M. 1993: Seriously, Jonah! Unpublished manuscript.

—— 1998: The study of Christian spirituality: contours and dynamics of a discipline. *Christian Spirituality Bulletin* 6 (1), 1, 3–12.

—— 2002: Biblical spirituality. *Interpretation* 56, 133–42.

Sherwood, Y. K. 2000: *A Biblical Text and its Afterlives: The Survival of Jonah in Western Culture*. Cambridge: Cambridge University Press.

Simms, G. O. 1989: *Brendan the Navigator: Exploring the Ancient World*. Dublin: O'Brien Press.

Smalley, B. 1983: *The Study of the Bible in the Middle Ages*, 3rd edn. Oxford: Basil Blackwell.

Stein, S. J. (ed.) 1998: *Jonathan Edwards: Notes on Scripture*. New Haven, CT: Yale University Press.

Teresa of Avila 1979: *The Interior Castle*, trans. K. Kavanaugh. New York: Paulist Press.

Theodore of Mopsuestia 2004: *Commentary on the Twelve Prophets*, trans. R. C. Hill. Washington, DC: Catholic University of America Press.

Torjeson, K. J. 1986: *Hermeneutical Procedure and Theological Method in Origen's Exegesis*. Berlin: Walter de Gruyter.

Trigg, J. 1983: *Origen: The Bible and Philosophy in the Third-century Church*. Atlanta: John Knox Press.

—— 1998: *Origen*. London: Routledge.

Tugwell, S. 1987: The mendicants: the spirituality of the Dominicans. In J. Raitt (ed.), *Christian Spirituality: High Middle Ages and Reformation*, pp. 15–31. New York: Crossroad.

Valkenberg, W. G. R. M. 2000: *Words of the Living God: Place and Function of Holy Scripture in the Theology of St Thomas Aquinas*. Leuven: Peeters.

Van Engen, J. H. 1983: *Rupert of Deutz*. Berkeley, CA: University of California Press.

Weisheipl, J. A. 1974: *Friar Thomas D'Aquino: His Life, Thought, and Work*. New York: Doubleday.

Winter, S. C. 1999: A fifth-century Christian commentary on Jonah. In S. L. Cook and S. C. Winter (eds), *On the Way to Nineveh: Studies in Honor of George M. Landes*, pp. 238–56. Atlanta: Scholars Press.

Zaharopoulos, D. Z. 1989: *Theodore of Mopsuestia on the Bible: A Study of his Old Testament Exegesis*. New York: Paulist Press.

CHAPTER 3

The New Testament in Christian Spirituality

Bonnie Thurston

Cosmology

The first point to be made in considering New Testament spirituality is that the New Testament is more than a document of the first century. Since the nineteenth century, New Testament scholarship has been dominated by approaches that view the text exclusively as text, without reference to the experiences that gave rise to it. Such scholarship emphasizes lexical and grammatical studies, form, redaction, and source criticisms, and historical and sociological analyses of the text. The unspoken assumption is that the New Testament is an artifact of history. Little attempt is made to understand the experience of those who produced it or the influence it continues to exert on those who view it as authoritative. As Luke Timothy Johnson observed in *Religious Experience in Earliest Christianity* (1998: 3), such a bias in favor of the "textually defined and the theologically correct" has led scholars to ignore the very thing that the earliest Christian texts talk about.

What the New Testament "talks about" is the human experience of God mediated by the person of Jesus of Nazareth. Any study of New Testament spirituality must begin with the fact that the texts are a record of human experience. In any age, but especially at its origins, Christianity revolves around the distinctive experience of the person of Jesus Christ, and any study of the New Testament without reference to the experience of Jesus that generated it is inadequate. The New Testament is the early church's considered reflection on the experience of meeting Jesus, the "historical Jesus" of Nazareth and/or the risen Jesus Christ. Put differently, the New Testament is a record of human beings' experience of communication between themselves and God in and through the person of Jesus Christ. The New Testament, in short, records spiritual experience. This presumes that "spiritual experience" is "real."

The reality of spiritual experience assumes a worldview no longer common in the West. Most modern Westerners are shaped by a culture with a secularized and one-dimensional understanding of reality and are taught that what is "real" is the material, visible, measurable, and quantifiable world perceived by the five physical senses. But the New Testament worldview was multi-dimensional. The early Christians who wrote the New Testament lived in a dual world, a world of matter and of spirit, a world of created things and their creator. For them, the spiritual world, though unseen, was "real," and it exerted power and influence on the seen, material world. For them, the world was not only, in the words of Gerard Manley Hopkins, "charged with the grandeur of God;" it was shadowed by evil forces capable of tearing at the fabric of human life.

This is exemplified in Mark's Gospel, the first to be written. In Mark, Jesus's first public act of ministry, after calling four fishermen to be his disciples (1: 16–20), is an encounter in the synagogue at Capernaum with "a man with an unclean spirit" which Jesus exorcizes (1: 21–8). When the spirit sees Jesus, it cries out: "What have you to do with us, Jesus of Nazareth? Have you come to destroy us? I know who you are, the Holy One of God" (1: 24). This encounter assumes a "spirit world" which contains malevolent forces (unclean spirits) and benevolent forces (here represented by "the Holy One of God"), each of which has influence over human life. The unclean spirits recognize Jesus as supreme representative of the "good" forces in the unseen universe. On one level, the New Testament is a record of the great struggle between these two forces in which the resurrection of Jesus is proof that the power behind the universe is neither malevolent nor neutral, but benevolent, "for us."

Similarly, the apostle Paul writes that "ever since the creation of the world [God's] eternal power and divine nature, invisible though they are, have been understood and seen through the things he has made" (Rom. 1: 20). What is unseen is "perceived" by means of what is seen. Paul speaks of things "not taught by human wisdom but taught by the Spirit, interpreting spiritual things to those who are spiritual" (1 Cor. 2: 13). The Pauline church knew its struggle was "not against enemies of blood and flesh, but against the rulers, against the authorities, against the cosmic powers of this present darkness, against the spiritual forces of evil in the heavenly places" (Eph. 6: 12). The early church spoke naturally (if awe-fully) of "the ruler of the power of the air" (Eph. 2: 2), of "elemental spirits of the universe" (Col. 2: 8), of "things visible and invisible, whether thrones or dominions or rulers or powers" (Col. 1: 16).

Christianity developed in a world of demons and angels, dreams and visions, a permeable world in which what was visible was but the veil over a divine truth. Many of the parables of Jesus work on this assumption: common, ordinary things (bread, salt, lost sheep) and relationships (parents to children) reveal divine, extraordinary truths about the Kingdom of God. This multi-dimensional reality is the "way it is" for the New Testament writers who recorded their experiences of and with Jesus.

Having established that the early Christians and writers of the New Testament lived with a worldview that assumed a spiritual as well as a physical universe, the next task is to define what we mean by "spirituality" in the New Testament context.

Definition

In his work on Second Temple Judaism, Jacob Neusner (1984, 1995, 2002) has taught us that we ought properly to speak of the Judaisms (plural) of the period. There was no monolithic Judaism, no one way to be a Jew in, say, Roman Palestine. Likewise, there is no *single* New Testament spirituality, but many and varied New Testament spiritualities. Whether one began one's Christian life as a Judean Jew or as a pagan from Ephesus clearly influenced how one lived out that life. We see, for example, in Acts 15 and in Galatians 1–2 the church working on the question of whether it was necessary to become a Jew before one could be fully Christian. One's cultural context (Jewish, Roman, Greek, for example), social status (free, slave, wealthy, poor), gender, and many other factors affected *how* one experienced one's allegiance to Jesus Christ. Furthermore, the New Testament is a collection of different kinds or genres of texts and represents writing and writers over a period of as much as a hundred years. Who wrote a book and for whom and when and where all influence the material it contains and thus the spirituality it exhibits. It is, therefore, important always to keep the lovely variousness of New Testament spiritualities in view.

That said, I open the discussion of the definition of New Testament spiritualities by altering slightly Sandra Schneiders's definition of "biblical spirituality": New Testament spirituality refers to the spiritualities that come to expression in the New Testament (2002: 134). Over the past twenty-five years, as spirituality has emerged as an academic discipline in the North American context, significant effort has been expended to define the field. Early on, Jon Alexander (1980) wrote an article entitled "What Do Recent Writers Mean by Spirituality?" in which he made a clear distinction between Roman Catholic ascetical theology and spirituality in a more "generic and experiential sense." After surveying definitions by Carolyn Osiek, Matthew Fox, Joseph Bernardin, Raymundo Panikkar, and Hans Urs von Balthasar, Alexander concluded that the various definitions had in common a concern for how people live out their faith, how they integrate "ultimate concerns and unrestricted values in concrete life" (1980: 253). Spirituality, in short, refers to affective and personally integrated religion.

Similarly, Sandra Schneiders defines spirituality as "the experience of consciously striving to integrate one's life in terms not of isolation and self-absorption but of self-transcendence toward the ultimate value one perceives" (1989: 684). A New Testament scholar, Schneiders provides a definition that both encompasses the integrative aspect of more general definitions and adds the distinctively New Testament (or Christian) feature of *koinonia* or community ("not of isolation"). Likewise, Luke Timothy Johnson argues for a phenomenological approach to the New Testament, an "embodied" approach. He quotes Joachim Wach's definition of religious experience (following Rudolf Otto) as "a response to that which is perceived as ultimate, involving the whole person, characterized by a peculiar intensity, and issuing in action" (1998: 60). Johnson posits that early Christians experienced a power that came "from outside those touched by it" which was "transmitted to them from another, to whom it properly belongs" (1998: 7). That "power" demanded a response, and the observable responses ("seen" in phenomena like initiation/baptism, glossolalia and communal meals/Lord's Supper) are the "stuff" of Christian spirituality. He concludes his study by observing that the early Christians "considered themselves caught up by, defined by, a power not in their control but rather controlling them, a power that derived from the crucified and raised Messiah Jesus . . . Christianity came to birth because certain people were convinced that they had experienced God's transforming power through the resurrection of Jesus" (1998: 184–5).

The New Testament, then, premises an invitation from an initiatory power which calls for a response. Something, indeed, *someone* from outside the finite and human initiates a relationship with individuals by means of a manifestation of power. The response is a life turned toward that power; how that response is lived out is "spirituality." Insofar as it has an "affective" quality, spirituality encompasses not only the will that decides to respond, but also the emotions. Insofar as it seeks to integrate faith and action, spirituality has an ethical component. Insofar as it is done in the company of others, it is communal.

In the New Testament, God issues an invitation to people in the person of Jesus of Nazareth. The power of God is clearly manifested in the life, death, and resurrection of Jesus, and it calls for a response. People's responses to what God was doing in Jesus the Christ *is* New Testament spirituality. As I have suggested elsewhere, spirituality is "what the early Christians did to put into practice what they believed. It was what they did to respond to a world filled with the presence of God and the risen Christ" (Thurston 1993: 3). A distinctive feature of New Testament spirituality is that it is communal. While individuals must, as individuals, respond to God's invitation in Jesus, "accepting the invitation" involves being initiated into a community in which one works out one's spirituality. To confess Jesus Christ as Lord, to be "in Christ" to use Paul's phrase, is to take one's place alongside others who have made the same confession, to become part of a community with all the joys and struggles communal life entails.

In defining New Testament spiritualities, one final word is important: "phenomenal," by which I mean "known through the text and not intuited, concerned with what the text reports rather than with hypotheses." As Johnson (1998: 57) notes, the "task of phenomenology . . . is to observe and describe behavior and its discernible functions." This is to say that New Testament spirituality is circumscribed by what the New Testament actually reports. The data can only be what the text says – for example, its descriptions of early Christian prayers and rituals – or what the characters and authors actually report about what they did and/or experienced. Students of New Testament spiritualities are still exegetes (those who draw out the meaning that is *in* the text) and not eisegetes (those who read *into* the text what might or might not be there). New Testament spirituality is bound by the text: that record of the early Christians' experience of the power of God manifested in the person of Jesus.

Methodology

Where in the New Testament texts does one look for its spiritualities? What are the means of approach or methods? A variety of answers suggest themselves. One might examine the spirituality of a particular person or writer (Jesus, St Mary of Magdala, St Mark, St John, or St Paul). One might look for descriptive passages in which people speak of their spiritual experiences or which depict various practices or record prayer texts. One might seek out prescriptive passages, texts which teach "how to" perform a ritual or how to pray, or texts which warn about what *not* to do. One is struck, again, by the variety exhibited in the New Testament texts. Before examining these three approaches, which I call the personal, the descriptive, and the prescriptive, in more detail, a note on historical context is in order.

In mining the text of the New Testament for its spiritualities, one must keep clearly in mind that it is a first-century document. The more one knows about the literary and historical context of the period, the more clearly one understands the spiritualities encountered. Serious study of the spiritualities represented in the texts of the New Testament, then, begins, as does any study of the New Testament, with knowledge of the Greco-Roman world and some facility with *koine* Greek. Familiarity with the requisite volumes of *The Cambridge Ancient History* is amply rewarded. Several recent scholarly series are helpful. Of particular interest is "The Library of Early Christianity," edited by Wayne A. Meeks, and "Studies of the New Testament and its World," edited by John Barclay et al. In the latter series, the volume by Hans-Josef Klauck, *The Religious Context of Early Christianity: A Guide to Graeco-Roman Religions* (2000) is particularly relevant. A more general introduction covering the same territory is Luther H. Martin's *Hellenistic Religions: An Introduction* (1987). Specifically helpful for the study of prayer is the collection of prayers edited by Mark Kiley et al., *Prayer from Alexander to Constantine: A Critical Anthology* (1997).

Spiritualities of the New Testament are the spiritualities of first-century people. Persons encountered in the New Testament are bound by the religious and spiritual choices, practices, and language of their age. It is well to remember (as I suggested at the outset) that their cosmology and concerns may not be ours. We must allow them to speak for themselves and in their own voice. As Schneiders asserts, "no one who is serious about biblical spirituality should be excused from the study requisite for a well-grounded understanding of biblical texts in their own historical-cultural contexts and according to their literary genres and theological categories" (2002: 142).

For example, if you wish to study prayer in the New Testament, you might begin with a summary of the Greek vocabulary for "prayer" with a special eye to how the various words are used in the parallel literature. Then you might undertake a review of the practice of prayer in Second Temple Judaism and/or in Greco-Roman religions. These background studies provide the context in which distinctively Christian prayer is to be understood. Or, if you wish to suggest that the Lord's Supper was the distinctive act of early Christian worship, an understanding of Passover, of Jewish dietary laws, and of the practice and meaning of table fellowship in the Greco-Roman world is requisite. There are other examples, but these suffice to make the point of the importance of knowing the context of New Testament spiritualities.

The first approach to New Testament spiritualities, then, is the personal, determining the spirituality of a particular person in the early church or of a writer of text(s). For example, one might study the prayer life of Jesus of Nazareth. This could be done in general, using all the texts of the New Testament that refer to it, but particularly the Gospels. Alternatively, one could study the prayer life of Jesus as recorded by a particular evangelist: Luke, for example, as there are more references to prayer in Luke than in the other Gospels. Available as textual evidence are the recorded prayers of Jesus, such as the "Lord's Prayer" in Matthew 6: 9–13 and Luke 11: 2–4 or the "High Priestly Prayer" of John 17 or short prayers of Jesus such as that from the cross in Mark 15:

34. The student would have to decide to what degree these texts are the *ipsissima vox Jesu* or the literary compositions of the evangelist. Also evident are examples of Jesus *at* prayer (Mark 1: 35, 6: 41, 6: 46, 8: 7, 14: 32–43) and the teachings of Jesus *about* prayer (Matt. 6: 5–15 or Luke 11: 1–13, 18: 1–14 or Mark 12: 40).

Similarly, one could study Pauline spirituality, either that of the apostle, which would be found in letters deemed by scholarship to be by Paul himself, or of his communities, represented by letters written by followers of Paul after his death to apply his ideas to their new situations. Since Paul, after Jesus, exerted the most influence on early Christianity, a brief excursus on his spirituality is in order. Schneiders (1986) notes that Paul first used the adjective "spiritual" for things under the influence of the Holy Spirit. For him, there was a distinction between the "spiritual person" and the "natural person" (see 1 Cor. 2 and Gal. 5: 16–18, 24–6).

Meye (1993) notes that critical to the formation of Pauline spirituality were his religious heritage as a Pharisaic Jew (Phil. 3: 4–6) and his encounter with the risen Christ on the Damascus road (Gal. 1–2; Acts 9, 22: 4–16, 26: 9–18). Saul of Tarsus understood himself to have been showered by God's grace through Jesus Christ in spite of his unworthiness as a persecutor of the church. This fact is the cornerstone of the spirituality that undergirds his two great theological principles: justification by faith through grace (Gal. 2: 16, 3: 24; Rom. 3: 28) and life "in Christ" (2 Cor. 5: 17; Col. 1: 27; and note the "in him" language of Col. 2: 6–15).

For Paul, the essence of spiritual life is trust in God, "faith." After experiencing the unearned love of God in his calling to apostleship (Gal. 2: 13–24), Paul does not abandon the ethical demands of the law, but he realizes it cannot empower. Empowerment for Christian life comes through faith in the risen Christ, which, itself, is gift. One enters into this life by an act of humility like that vividly exemplified in the "Christ Hymn" of Philippians 2: 6–11. The kenotic (emptying) action of humility is the movement that makes faith possible and initiates a continuing inner responsiveness to Christ who has, as Paul put it, "made me his own" (Phil. 3: 12). Paradoxically, by baptism one comes to live "in Christ," but continues to strive to be more fully "conformed to his likeness" (Phil. 3: 12–16). Since "we were all baptized into one body" (1 Cor. 14: 13) and "we do not live to ourselves, and we do not die to ourselves" (Rom. 14: 7), faith (and the resultant spirituality) is not a private matter in Paul's understanding. "Private" religious allegiances have consequences in public life. The Christian is no longer "conformed to this world" (Rom. 12: 2), but oriented toward God; as Paul puts it, his or her "citizenship is in heaven" (Phil. 3: 20). Again, Christian spirituality is understood to be communal, and this is evident in Paul's many instructions to communities.

For Paul, if faith is the seed from which Christian spirituality grows, then love is its finest fruit. The life of faith is ruled by the principle of love which fulfills any legal, ethical requirements and is the chief characteristic of life in Christ. "The one who loves," Paul writes, "has fulfilled the law," for "love does not wrong to a neighbor; therefore, love is the fulfilling of the law" (Rom. 13: 8, 10). "Love," as Paul uses the term, is intelligent, constructive goodwill, the honest desire to help, serve, and find fulfillment in service rather than in personal gain. Love is disinterested willing and working for the good of the other. It is the most important fruit of the spirit (Gal. 5: 22) and the one enduring virtue (1 Cor. 13: 8). Meye summarizes Paul's spirituality as "an expression of affirmation to God, a grateful 'Yes' from the heart of a believer which, in the power of the Spirit, is manifested in act and attitude" (1993: 906). Meye notes that Paul's "Israelite heritage" was shaped by the triad of prayer, Word of God, and community of faith (1993: 908). Each of these is manifestly evident in Paul's epistles.

Returning now to the matter of methodology, if one wishes to study Paul's spirituality, one might look at texts in which Paul describes his spiritual experiences (2 Cor. 10–13 or Gal. 1–2). One might examine his prayers, a particularly rich subject in Paul's letters since the structure of the Greco-Roman letter includes prayers of thanksgiving (1 Cor. 1: 4–9, for example), grace wishes (1 Cor. 1: 3, 16: 23), and blessings, benedictions, and doxologies (Rom. 16: 25–7). Each of these prayer forms can be isolated and compared among the letters. Additionally, one could study Paul's teaching about prayer (1 Thess. 5: 16–18 or Phil. 4: 6), or Paul's reports of his prayers for others. (For more on Pauline prayer, see Stendahl 1980; Hunter 1993; Longenecker 2001: ch. 10.) Pauline passages critical to both the descriptive and prescriptive approaches are cited below.

A final "personal" approach to New Testament spiritualities undertakes to uncover the spirituality of a particular writer in the New Testament. The issues involved in this endeavor for Paul have just been outlined. To discover the spirituality of a Gospel writer, one would begin by focusing on the passages in the Gospel that are either peculiar to that Gospel or redact (change or edit) its sources. If one wanted to study the spirituality of St Matthew, one would look for the distinctive ways in which that evangelist tells the Jesus story. For example, the fact that, at the outset, Matthew emphasizes parallels between Moses and Jesus and then organizes his Gospel around five discourses of Jesus, or that Matthew uses a "fulfillment formula" to show how Jesus fulfills Old Testament prophecies, suggests the "Jewishness" of his spirituality. One might ask which pericopae are only in Matthew? Do any of them record prayers or depict religious practices? When Matthew relates events in the life of Jesus, how does he diverge from the Marcan accounts of the same events? In other words, one would use the methods of synoptic comparison or redaction criticism while focusing on passages which deal with religious practices, prayers, teaching about prayer, and the like. (For examples of this sort of work, see Bouyer 1963: chs 2, 4, 5; Barton 1992; Minor 1996.)

A second approach to the spiritualities of the New Testament is the "descriptive," seeking out descriptions of the personal experiences of writers of New Testament books (Paul in 2 Cor. 11–12 or Gal. 1–2; the writer of 2 Pet. 1: 16–18 or of 1 John 1: 1–4) or of what the early Christians actually did to express or live out their faith in the risen Jesus. A cautionary remark is in order. When we read New Testament passages describing the spiritual practices of the early church we must be sure that they really *are* descriptive passages by keeping in view the question "who is telling the story and why?" We might ask "who benefits from relating the matter in this way?" There is always some tension in New Testament texts between "history" (what happened or what was done) and "theology" (the interpretation that the writer/recorder assigns to what happened). Textual study must reflect a more nuanced approach than the assumption that "what it says is exactly what happened" (see the reading of Acts 2: 42–7 below.) Why, for example, does Paul write as he does about the Lord's Supper in 1 Corinthians 11? Why would St Luke be especially interested in prayer? Why is the matter of food restriction important in 1 Corinthians, Romans, and Colossians? What is the "interface" between what those churches were actually doing, Pauline theology, and the "genuinely Christian"?

That caveat aside, one descriptive approach to New Testament spiritualities examines passages in which practices of the early Christians are described. Although this list is by no means exhaustive, I suggest that the following practices of the early Christians are representative (and I give an example or two of where such material is found): prayer (see discussions above); baptism (Mark 1: 9–11 and parallels; Rom. 6; Col. 2: 11–15); the Lord's Supper (Mark 14: 22–5 and parallels; 1 Cor. 11); fasting (Matt. 6: 16–18); singing of hymns (Mark 14: 26 and parallels; 1 Cor. 14: 26; Eph. 5: 19; Col. 3: 16; and note that the New Testament includes several hymns of the early church, for example Phil. 2: 5–11; Col. 1: 15–20; 1 Tim. 2: 11–13, 3: 16; the hymns in Rev.); healing (Acts 3: 1–10, 5: 12–16; Jas. 5: 13–18); almsgiving (Matt. 6: 1–4; 1 Cor. 16: 1–4; 2 Cor. 8–9); communal property (Acts 2: 44–5, 4: 32–5). A particularly interesting discussion of the spirituality of one early Christian community, which includes several of these elements, is found in 1 Corinthians 11–14.

That early Christian spirituality was communal is one of its distinctive features. As such, it included preaching and teaching. Preaching (kerygma) was proclamation of the gospel to those who were not yet followers of Jesus with the intent to bring them to belief. An example is Peter's sermon in Acts 2: 14–36. Many scholars think that 1 Corinthians 15: 3–11 summarizes the basic kerygmatic content: Jesus died for our sins according to the Scriptures; he was buried; he was raised on the third day according to the Scriptures; he appeared to many who had seen and known him before his death. Teaching (didache) was instruction for believers; it was intended to deepen their understanding of and commitment to Jesus. It is reflected in the third approach to New Testament spiritualities, the prescriptive.

Another source of information on the spiritualities of the New Testament is found in its explicit teaching material, the things that various writers commend and forbid. This prescriptive material is directed both to individuals and to communities. For example, Paul makes it clear that an individual's sexual attitudes and behaviors reflect his or her spirituality and affect the community (see 1 Cor. 5, 6: 12–20, 7). Or, the writer of Colossians warns that community against "philosophy and empty deceit" (2: 8) and against "human commandments" (2: 20–3), especially as they relate to food and festivals. Interestingly, outside the discourses in Matthew's Gospel, particularly the Sermon on the Mount, there is remarkably little explicitly prescriptive material in the teaching of Jesus. Jesus is more likely to suggest principles by which one might make decisions about action than to explicitly command or forbid them.

The apostle Paul is not so reticent. A difference between Jesus and Paul is that Jesus remained within the Jewish community which assumed the ethical parameters of the law. Paul, on the other hand, was engaged in the formation of a new community including both Jews and Gentiles. The Gentiles in the new Christian community might not have come from backgrounds that assumed the ethics of, say, the Decalogue. For them, more explicit directives were not only personally helpful, but communally necessary. Often in the second half of Paul's letters, one finds explicitly prescriptive material, technically called paraenesis. A particularly clear example of this is found in Romans 12: 1 – 15: 6. While these chapters read like a list of dos and don'ts (and they are that), the behaviors commended and forbidden are intended to lead to a life that demonstrates Christlikeness. Paul speaks of the believer's body as a "living sacrifice, holy and acceptable to God;" what is done in the body is the believer's "spiritual worship" (12: 1).

Interestingly, although he teaches that the believer's citizenship is in heaven (Phil. 3: 20) and that he or she is not to "be conformed to this world" (Rom. 12: 2), much of the *paraenetic* material in Paul's letters reflects behaviors and attitudes that would be received with approbation in the larger Greco-Roman environment. Scholars have noted points of correspondence between the ethical teaching of the Stoics and of Paul. Certainly, he uses Stoic teaching methods, perhaps most obviously the vice and virtue list (see Gal. 5: 19–23).

This suggests an interesting tension in early Christian spirituality. On the one hand, when they become followers of Jesus and are baptized, persons are "born from above," to use the phrase of the Johannine Jesus (John 3: 3). The center of life's focus shifts away from temporal concerns and toward eternal concerns. New creatures in Christ are to live very differently from the way in which they lived previously (see Eph. 4: 17 – 5: 20). But, on the other hand, Jesus himself affirms that believers are not to be taken out of the world (John 17: 15). Here is the great tension in early Christian spirituality: Christians were to live in the world as citizens of heaven, but do so in ways that were not so confrontational or counter-cultural or downright odd that they attracted the wrath of the authorities (either Jewish or, later, Roman). In an environment in which Roman authorities could persecute small Christian communities right out of existence, it is little wonder that the prescriptive material in Paul's letters suggested that Christians live in ways that would cast them in a favorable light. Indeed, this concern also shapes Luke's presentation of the early church in Jerusalem. The *paraenetic* material in New Testament books reflects their writers' attempts to shape the spirituality of the texts' recipients, sometimes (as in the case of the Household Codes in Col. 3: 18 – 4: 1; Eph. 5: 21 – 6: 9; 1 Pet. 2: 18 – 3: 7) in the direction of cultural and/or social acceptability and respectability.

To summarize to this point: the world of the New Testament had a lively awareness of, and interest in, both material and spiritual dynamics of life. There is no one "New Testament spirituality," but a variety of "spiritualities" reflecting both the many writers of the New Testament books and the many communities and cultures in which early Christians found themselves. To uncover these spiritualities, one studies persons encountered in the text and those who wrote them, texts that describe what the early Christians did and/or texts that prescribe or prohibit, texts that reflect the dos and don'ts of early Christian practice. In each instance, the inquiry is bound by the limits of the historical period and by what the texts themselves say, and is to be carried out using appropriate historical-critical methodology. The remainder of this essay models an approach in a brief examination of Acts 2: 42–7.

The Early Church in Jerusalem

The descriptive approach to New Testament spiritualities examines texts which describe what the early Christians did to express or live out their faith in the risen Jesus. As a means both of exemplifying this method and of introducing one pattern of New Testament spirituality, that of the early church in Jerusalem, I shall briefly discuss Acts 2: 42–7.

The Acts of the Apostles provides a particularly rich source of information on the spiritualities of early Christianity. It is the second half of a two-part work which begins with the Gospel of Luke. In Luke, the writer shows how Jesus moved from Galilee to Jerusalem, and in Acts how the church moved from Jerusalem (the center of Judaism) to Rome (the Gentile world-center). Of the writers of the New Testament, Luke bears the most resemblance to Hellenistic writers. Written about AD 85–90, Luke–Acts is classic apologetics, the presentation of material in a way that anticipates the doubts or objections of its readers. It uses the vocabulary and literary models of Greco-Roman writing (for example, literary prologues, the composition of speeches like those in Herodotus) as part of an attempt to demonstrate that Christianity was not a threat to the Empire with which it could live harmoniously.

In Acts, Luke provides several summaries of the life of the early Christian community in Jerusalem (2: 42–7, 4: 32–5, 5: 12–16). Although the followers of the risen Jesus are not called "church" (*ekklesia*) until 5: 11, when Luke writes of the early Jerusalem church he means the assembly of the believers in Jesus who continued to be devoted to the Temple and to participate in Jewish piety. "Church" is a congregation of the faithful, not a building. It had no official leadership or organization (no church orders appear in the New Testament until the late, pseudonymous letters of Paul which many take to be second-century documents), although the apostles exercised authority by virtue of their association with Jesus. These believers were clearly a community. Luke says "they all joined together constantly in prayer" (Acts 1: 14); the Greek word *homothumadon* (together or "one-minded") is an adjective Luke uses ten times in Acts.

Many scholars believe that the portrait Luke paints of the church is idealized. Holladay (1988: 1082) has pointed out that it emphasizes aspects of religious community valued in both Jewish and Greco-Roman society: daily devotion, respect in the presence of divine power, internal harmony and community solidarity expressed in concern for one another, and generosity. As F. F. Bruce (1985: 643) notes, "The picture of the church in Jerusalem in the first five chapters of Acts is that of a community of enthusiastic followers of Jesus, growing by leaps and bounds, and enjoying the good will of its neighbors." Luke records the "best face" of the church in order to commend it to his Greco-Roman readers. He highlights its connections with Judaism in order to indicate that Christianity is not an "upstart" or "new" religion, but part of an ancient plan of God, and thus, in Hellenistic terms, trustworthy.

While Luke should not be used uncritically as a source of information about early Christian spiritualities, the material can be taken with seriousness. Although the Lucan picture of the Jerusalem church may not be "objective," it provides much information about what the early Christians did. Acts 2: 42 summarizes the communal spiritual practices of the Jerusalem church: "They devoted themselves to the apostles' teaching and fellowship, to the breaking of bread and to the prayers." The text occurs at the end of Peter's Pentecost sermon (2: 14–40) with its rousing evangelistic call and fabulous success: three thousand were baptized (so baptism as an early Christian initiatory rite is introduced). The definite articles before the nouns in the Greek text of 2: 42 imply that "apostles' teaching and fellowship," "breaking of bread," and "prayers" are quasi-technical terms.

The "apostles' teaching" would have taken the forms of *kerygma* and *didache* mentioned in the discussion of descriptive methodology above. "Fellowship" (*koinonia*) meant not only the gathering of believers, but also implied a communal relatedness that was worked out economically. Acts 2: 44–5 and 4: 32–5 depict this experiment with communal possessions (which is exemplified positively and negatively in 4: 36 – 5: 11). As the "apostles' fellowship," the practice may have been a carryover from the ministry of Jesus when Judas kept the community's common purse (John 12: 6, 13: 29). Communal property also characterized the Essene community whose influence on early Christianity is becoming better known through work on the Dead Sea Scrolls. It should be noted that, since early Christians expected an immediate *parousia* (return of Christ), they were primarily concerned neither with promoting nor with changing the existing economic order. Concomitantly, the fact that Paul assumes the economic institution of slavery suggests that he was not a radical economic reformer. Early Christian spiritualities had implications for one's economic life, but did not prescribe a particular economic system (see also 1 Cor. 16: 1–4; 2 Cor. 8–9). The selling and division of property in the Jerusalem church was a voluntary expression of *koinonia*, of relatedness in Christ, not a universal rule of practice (see Acts 5: 4). Acts 4: 32 seems to fulfill Deuteronomy 15: 4ff ("There will . . . be no one in need among you, because the Lord is sure to bless you") and thus depicts the early Christians as perfect Jews. "The apostles' fellowship" suggested a community of profound connectedness. Communal property was but one expression of the fact that, in Paul's words, they who were many were one body in Christ and individually members one of another (Rom. 12: 5).

"The breaking of bread" (*te klasei tou artou*) was what has come to be known as the Lord's Supper or the Eucharist. Breaking bread was the characteristic act of Jesus, the action by which the early church recognized him (see Luke 24: 12–35, especially vv. 30–1, 35). The earliest celebrations of the church were probably not unlike the Jewish *chaburah* or fellowship meal of the teacher and disciples, although some scholars have suggested the pattern fits that of the Passover meal as described in the Mishnah, Pesahim 10. Breaking of bread was, as 1 Corinthians 11 makes clear, observed in the context of a real meal, a part of which was eaten as both remembrance of and thanksgiving for Jesus. Acts says that "breaking bread in their homes, they [the Jerusalem Christians] partook of food with glad and generous hearts" (4: 46). These meals were probably held in the evening to follow the precedent set by Jesus and by Jewish tradition and to allow slaves and laborers to gather with those in the Christian community of higher economic status. The focus of those meals was probably not the body and blood of Jesus experienced in bread and wine (associations which were terribly shocking for Jewish Christians as John 6 makes clear), but that Jesus, who had bid them farewell in the context of a meal (Mark 14: 12–26 and parallels), appeared to his friends after the resurrection in the same context (Luke 24: 36; John 21: 12ff). Cullmann (1953: 15) suggests that "the first Eucharistic feasts of the community look back to the Easter meals, in which the Messianic meal promised by Jesus at the Last Supper was already partly anticipated" (for further discussion, see Higgins 1952 and Jeremias 1955).

"The prayers" (*tais proseuchais*) refer to what many consider the heart of spiritual life. The root word for "prayer" here, *euche*, is one of the most commonly used words for prayer in the New Testament. It has the dual meaning of "prayer" and "vow." In classical usage, the term also connotes "a wish" or "an aspiration." In Hellenistic Greek, its verbal form, *euchomai*, means both "to pray to God" and "to wish." In Hellenistic Greek, the word means either "prayer addressed to God" or the derived meaning of a place set apart for prayer. It is the word translated into Latin and found in the Vulgate as *oratio*.

Luke was especially interested in prayer. For him, the disciples' "teach us how to pray" (Luke 11: 1) was the request for a distinguishing formula since religious groups were identified by their manner of prayer. In Acts 1–6 prayer sets the tone of the Jerusalem church. In the practice of their prayer the early Christians were greatly influenced by Jewish antecedents (Burns 1980; Beckwith 1984). Acts reports that "every day they continued to meet together in the temple courts" (Acts 2: 46). Early Christians prayed in the Temple where Malachi 3: 1 proclaimed that the Messiah would appear. Luke is subtly showing his Hellenistic audience how early Christians are the authentic extension of worshiping Israel.

The Jerusalem church also followed the Jewish hours of prayer. "Peter and John were going up to the temple at the hour of prayer" (Acts 3: 1). The standard pattern of first-century Jewish worship included use of the *Shema* (Deut. 6: 4–9) in the morning and evening and of the *Tephillah* (petitionary prayers) three times daily. The characteristic attitudes, in the sense of bodily posture, of prayer probably included standing (following Jewish custom) or kneeling (which might have included prostration). Standing with the arms outstretched and raised, palms upward, was the position of prayer described by the early Church Fathers and reflects their more Hellenized context (see 1 Clement [2003] 2: 29; Tertullian [2004] *On Prayer* 23).

Luke describes the Jerusalem church at prayer in many situations. They pray "constantly" (Acts 1: 14, 2: 42), when the need to choose leadership arises (1: 24–5, 6: 4) and to commission those leaders (6: 6, 13: 1–3). This commissioning is accompanied by the laying on of hands which also has Jewish roots. In Numbers 8: 10 the practice occurs in the mass commissioning of officers. The term *semihkha* (from "laying on," *samakh*) was used at the ordination of a rabbi and implied the passing on of power, physical or spiritual. The early Christians prayed in crisis (4: 23–31) and in celebration. Luke records at least one prayer text of the early church in Acts 4: 24–30; it exhibits both characteristically Jewish elements and Luke's own theological preoccupations (Thurston 1993: ch. 6). Finally, Luke is at considerable pains to depict the one-mindedness of the church's prayers (1: 12–14, 4: 24).

Another aspect of the spirituality of the early church in Jerusalem notable in Acts 2: 42–7 is "wonders and signs" (2: 43). Luke records that "many wonders and signs were done through the apostles" (2: 43), and "many signs and wonders were done among the people by the hands of the apostles" (5: 12). "Wonders" were nothing more than events which broke the natural order, and the Hellenistic world was full of wonder-workers. But, as in the prophetic sign-acts, "signs" pointed beyond themselves to the operative power of God. Primarily, the apostolic signs were miracles of healing (Acts 3: 1–10, 5: 13–16). These miracles parallel the life of Jesus. Luke wants to show that what

Jesus did the church can do too, precisely because the power of his Holy Spirit is at work among them.

Finally, although not specifically mentioned in Acts 2: 42–7, there are at least twenty significant references to "the name of Jesus" or "the name" in Acts 1–10. The name is described by Luke as the substance of early Christian proclamation (Acts 8: 12), the source of their power (3: 6, 16; 4: 7, 10, 30), the ownership by which they were claimed at baptism (2: 38; 8: 16; 10: 46), the means of their salvation (2: 21; 4: 12; 10: 42), and the reason for their persecution (5: 42). This is because, in the first century, "name" was more than a label for identification; it contained the essential nature (and power) of its bearer. In Acts, power and name are parallel concepts. Thus, in Acts 9: 34, Peter can say, "Aeneas, Jesus Christ heals you." The name of Jesus was powerful when faith in Jesus *to* heal was operative. The apostles had seen Jesus heal, and knowing he could do so, were able to mediate his power to heal. This concept of "the name" was an important link between the Jewish world of Jesus and the Hellenistic world of Luke's audience, and thus furthered Luke's apologetic (Thurston 1993: ch. 4).

In conclusion, then, bearing in mind that the picture drawn may be idealized, the early chapters of Luke's Acts of the Apostles, and in particular 2: 42–7, depict many aspects of the spirituality of the early Jerusalem Christians. Their activities were consonant with those of the larger Jewish community. Their spirituality was characterized by the instruction given by the apostles who had known Jesus, by the unity of the members of the community and their charity toward one another, by the breaking of bread and by prayer, both private and communal, and both in the Temple and in their own meetings. Their fellowship was radiant. They spent time together; they feasted with glad and generous hearts; they praised God. Other people saw this and wanted what they had. The rapid increase of numbers of those joining the fellowship ("the Lord added to their number day by day those who were being saved;" 2: 47) was intended by Luke to indicate the favor in which the church was viewed. They enjoyed "the favor of all the people" (2: 47) and "were highly regarded by the people" (5: 13). While we know from the crucifixion of Jesus that this was not the attitude of the Jewish authorities, Luke's apologetic purpose is clear here. If Christianity were not viewed as a threat in Jerusalem, the center of Judaism, why should it be so to Rome?

Writing in another context, Mary McKenna has called Acts 2: 42–7 a pivotal text, "the kernel of the long procession of Church Orders" (1967: 8). She characterizes the Jerusalem church as being close to the tradition of the Lord ("apostles' teaching"), centered in cult ("breaking of the bread"), and steadfast in prayer. Its strong sense of unity and community was evident in its "ceaseless service." While Acts evinces Lucan theological concerns, it also suggests that the spirituality of the Jerusalem church was essentially Jewish, was built around precedents from the life of Jesus (healing, prayer, fellowship meals), had wide-reaching or "wholistic" implications (for example, economic consequences), and was attractive to those outside the community. It clearly reflected what Luke Timothy Johnson called the experience of "God's transforming power through the resurrection of Jesus" (1998: 185), and observable responses to that experience in the lived, ethical implications of both experience and response for the Christian community into which it called those who believed.

Contemporary Application

The degree to which Christian traditions accept or reject the New Testament as normative for belief and practice forms a great "theological divide." Therefore, it is appropriate to reflect in closing on the pertinence of the New Testament for contemporary Christian spirituality.

Modern Christian experience is not unlike that which the New Testament chronicles. A personal Christian spirituality remains the experience of the relationship between an individual and God as mediated by the person of Jesus Christ, risen and alive. Now, that experience is counter-cultural to the degree that it assumes a non-modern cosmology, some version of the dual worldview of early Christianity. Christians cannot assume that what is visible, material, or measurable is "all there is." This is simply to highlight what the book of Hebrews and the Nicene Creed assert: "faith is . . . the conviction of things *not* seen" (Heb. 11: 1); "We believe in one God . . . maker of heaven and earth, of all that is, seen *and* unseen" (emphasis added).

Evelyn Underhill's famous metaphor that the spiritual life is amphibious, one of sense and spirit, is still accurate. This "dual nature" is everywhere evident in the New Testament, beginning with its language, which is multivalent, metaphorical, poetic. How else could the early Christians have spoken of the "mystery of religion" (1 Tim. 3: 16)? Similarly, the apostle Paul can assert that the human person is not only hopelessly corrupt (see Rom. 1: 18–31 or 1 Cor. 5: 1–13), but also potentially a "temple of the Holy Spirit" (1 Cor. 6: 19) whose "life is hid with Christ in God" (Col. 3: 3). Both are true. The struggle one encounters in the Christian *dramatis personae* of the New Testament to conform their likenesses to the divine image, to Christ "the image of the invisible God" (Col. 1: 15), is the same struggle in which the contemporary Christian is engaged.

But the point is not slavish conformity to first-century models. Indeed, there was no monolithic first-century Christianity to emulate. The practice of Christianity in Palestine and Rome in AD 50 would have been as culturally divergent as life is in the Middle East and Europe today. And yet God's transforming power in the resurrection of Jesus exerted (and exerts) its influence in each circumstance. This power of God at work to make all things new is the "norm" of New Testament spirituality, not the practices of early Christians (baptism or Eucharist or glossolalia, for example), not some particular way of carrying out a practice, and certainly not some set of "rules" for behavior which, in any case, many scholars suggest are non-existent in the text.

The pertinence of the New Testament texts for contemporary spirituality, then, is not in static norms set down for future generations to follow, but in the witness they give to a cosmic dynamic. This witness, for which so many early Christians were willing to die, was that, as Hebrew Scripture had intimated, God's love extended to all people. Its perfect vehicle is the life, death, and resurrection of Jesus. Its influence is continually exerted by the Holy Spirit. The Prime Mover of the universe is neither malevolent nor neutral, but actively in love with us, seeking us out, extending to us the divine embrace. As both the New Testament and Christian history attest, some Christians dance into it, some run, some stumble, some fall headlong. The journey there is as individuated as one's DNA. But then, as now, the basic movement of *Christian* spirituality is toward those extended, and wounded, arms. And it will ever be thus.

References

Alexander, J. 1980: What do recent writers mean by spirituality? *Spirituality Today* 32, 247–56.

Barton, S. C. 1992: *The Spirituality of the Gospels*. Peabody, MA: Hendrickson.

Beckwith, R. T. 1984: The daily and weekly worship of the primitive church in relation to its Jewish antecedents. *Evangelical Quarterly* 56, 65–80.

Bornkamm, G. 1969: *Early Christian Experience*. New York: Harper and Row.

Bouyer, L. 1963: *The Spirituality of the New Testament and the Fathers*. New York: Seabury.

Bowe, B. E. 2003: *Biblical Foundations of Spirituality: Touching a Finger to the Flame*. Lanham, MD: Rowman and Littlefield.

Bruce, F. F. 1985: The church of Jerusalem in the Acts of the Apostles. *Bulletin of the John Rylands University Library* 67, 641–61.

Burns, S. 1980: The roots of Christian prayer and spirituality in Judaism. In A. W. Sadler (ed.), *The Journey of Western Spirituality*, pp. 29–48. Chico, CA: Scholars Press.

Clement 2003: In B. D. Ehrman (ed. and trans.), *The Apostolic Fathers*. Cambridge, MA: Harvard University Press.

Cullmann, O. 1953: *Early Christian Worship*. London: SCM Press.

—— 1995: *Prayer in the New Testament*. Minneapolis, MN: Fortress Press.

Delling, G. 1962: *Worship in the New Testament*. Philadelphia: Westminster.

Fisher, F. L. 1964: *Prayer in the New Testament*. Philadelphia: Westminster.

Higgins, A. J. B. 1952: *The Lord's Supper in the New Testament*. Chicago: Henry Regnery .

Holladay, C. R. 1988: Acts. In J. L. Mays et al. (eds), *Harper's Bible Commentary*, pp. 1077–118. San Francisco: Harper and Row.

Hunter, W. B. 1993: Prayer. In G. F. Hawthorne et al. (eds), *Dictionary of Paul and his Letters*, pp. 725–34. Downer's Grove, IL: InterVarsity Press.

Jeremias, J. 1955: *The Eucharistic Words of Jesus*. Oxford: Blackwell.

Johnson, L. T. 1998: *Religious Experience in Earliest Christianity*. Minneapolis, MN: Fortress Press.

Kiley, Mark, et al. 1997: *Prayer from Alexander to Constantine: A Critical Anthology*. London: Routledge.

Klauck, H-J. 2000: *The Religious Context of Early Christianity: A Guide to Graeco-Roman Religions*. Edinburgh: T. and T. Clark.

Longenecker, R. N. (ed.) 2001: *Into God's Presence: Prayer in the New Testament*. Grand Rapids, MI: Eerdmans.

McKenna, M. L. 1967: *Women of the Church*. New York: P. J. Kenedy Press.

Martin, L. H. 1987: *Hellenistic Religions: An Introduction*. Oxford: Oxford University Press.

Meye, R. P. 1993: Spirituality. In G. F. Hawthorne et al. (eds), *Dictionary of Paul and his Letters*, pp. 906–16. Downer's Grove, IL: InterVarsity Press.

Miller, P. D. 1994: *They Cried to the Lord: The Form and Theology of Biblical Prayer*. Minneapolis, MN: Fortress Press.

Minor, M. 1996: *The Spirituality of Mark: Responding to God*. Louisville, KY: Westminster/John Knox.

Neusner, J. 1984: *The Messiah in Context*. Philadelphia: Fortress Press.

—— 1995: *Judaism in Late Antiquity*. Leiden: E. J. Brill.

—— 2002: *Judaism When Christianity Began*. Louisville, KY: Westminster/John Knox.

Schneiders, S. M. 1985: Scripture and spirituality. In B. McGinn and J. Meyendorff (eds), *Christian Spirituality: Origins to the Twelfth Century*, pp. 1–20. New York: Crossroad.

——1986: Theology and spirituality: strangers, rivals, or partners? *Horizons* 13, 253–74.

——1989: Spirituality in the academy. *Theological Studies* 50, 676–97.

——2002: Biblical spirituality. *Interpretation* 56, 133–42.

Stendahl, K. 1980: Paul at prayer. *Interpretation* 34, 240–9.

Tertullian 2004: *On Prayer*. In A. Stewart-Sykes (ed. and trans.), *On the Lord's Prayer: Tertullian, Cyprian, Origen*. Crestwood, NY: St Vladimir's Seminary Press.

Thurston, B. 1993: *Spiritual Life in the Early Church: The Witness of Acts and Ephesians*. Minneapolis, MN: Fortress Press.

——2000: The study of the New Testament and the study of Christian spirituality: some reflections. *Christian Spirituality Bulletin* 8 (2), 1, 3–6.

PART III

Christian Spirituality in History

CHAPTER 4

Christian Spirituality during the Roman Empire (100–600)

Columba Stewart

Searching for Unity in Faith

Early Christian spirituality is neither a single story, nor a linear development of ideas and practices. The story of Pentecost (Acts 2: 1–13) prefigures the array of Christian appropriations of Jewish and Hellenistic religious traditions in the first centuries of the church. Modern scholars have questioned whether there was, in fact, an identifiable, mainstream, tradition before the controversies of the third and later centuries. Irenaeus (c.130–200) presumed there was, and by the beginning of the second century some fundamental matters had already been determined by the emerging "Catholic" church.

The first theological challenge of Christianity was to explain itself in relation to its parent Judaism. This was an issue of biblical interpretation, demonstrating that Jesus, particularly in his death and resurrection, fulfilled prophecies in the Scriptures. The beginnings of this Christian reading of the Jewish Bible can be seen in the New Testament itself. In the second century, Marcion, a native of Pontus in Asia Minor with an international following, rejected the Old Testament with its depiction of a passionate and often wrathful God who related to human beings primarily through law, and claimed that Jesus taught the true God, a God of love. Marcion accepted Paul's letters, approving his polemics against the obligation to follow the Jewish law, and used an edited version of the Gospel of Luke. For mainstream Christians, however, the Old Testament was critical evidence for their claims about Jesus as the awaited Messiah, and witnessed to the involvement of God in the history of Israel, culminating in the incarnation.

Uneasiness about the physicality of the incarnation and resurrection lay behind some strands of Christian Gnosticism which maintained that Jesus's humanity and death were pedagogical devices, or even subterfuges, deliberately meant to obscure true teachings revealed only to Jesus's disciples and later to privileged initiates. Christian Gnosticism tapped into long-established dualistic worldviews, but seems to have varied widely in the degree of its syncretism of esoteric "wisdom" traditions with Christian teachings. The *Gospel of Thomas*, for example, contains some otherwise unknown sayings of Jesus that are probably genuine, alongside others that clearly show the influence of Gnostic thought. Other writings are wildly divergent from mainstream Christian literature. We know that Gnosticism was taken seriously as a major threat to fundamental Christian teachings as early as Ignatius of Antioch (d. early second century). Irenaeus of Lyons's late second-century *The Refutation and Overthrow of the Knowledge Falsely So Called* (more commonly known as *Against Heresies*) was directed against Gnostic interpretations of the Bible and of Christian doctrine. Irenaeus affirmed that the God who created the material world is the same as the trinitarian God of Christian faith, and emphasized the importance of an apostolic "rule of faith" as the criterion for assessing theological claims. Clement of Alexandria, in his *Stromateis* ("Miscellanies," early third century), responded to the Gnostic movements popular in Egypt by introducing an alternative ideal of "Christian Gnosis" founded upon Scripture and tradition, as understood with the help of Hellenistic philosophy.

The rejection by Marcion and others of commonly accepted Christian writings, as well as the circulation of many books of Gospels and Acts, required a clearer sense of which writings about Jesus and his followers were acceptable as part of a Christian "canon" (from the Greek for "norm" or "rule") of Scripture. Ignatius and Irenaeus had both emphasized the criterion of apostolicity for judging authentic teaching and, by extension, authentic Scripture. Various church councils produced lists of accepted books, with consensus settling upon the four Gospels of Matthew, Mark, Luke, and John; the Acts of the Apostles; and the letters attributed to apostles such as Paul, Peter, John, James, and Jude. Other letters, as well as the Apocalypse, or Book of Revelation, remained controversial in some churches, while works judged by most to be non-canonical (though perfectly orthodox), such as the *Shepherd of Hermas*, were reckoned by others to be inspired texts deserving of inclusion in the biblical canon. In Syriac-speaking churches, a harmonized version of the gospel (the *Diatessaron*), compiled from the four canonical Gospels in the mid-second century by the fiercely ascetic Tatian, was the standard version for three hundred years. Reaffirmation of the Christian reliance on the Jewish Bible did not settle disagreements over the precise contents of a Christian "Old Testament," though most accepted the books contained in the Greek Septuagint, the Hellenistic Jewish version of the Bible.

These developments raised the issue of doctrinal authority and leadership in the church. Ignatius of Antioch taught that the church is a community of believers gathered around a single local bishop, who is helped in his ministry by presbyters and deacons. The bishop or his delegate presided at the Eucharist, made authoritative judgments, and served as the recognizable sign of unity within the community: "Where the bishop is present, there let the congregation gather, just as where Jesus Christ is, there is the Catholic Church" (*Letter to the Smyrneans* 8.2). Ignatius' "monoepiscopate" and depiction of a threefold ordered ministry of bishop, presbyter (later "priest"), and deacon soon became the norm. This early ecclesiology, focused on the unity of the local church, was extended in the next century by Irenaeus to envision a communion of bishops who could all claim continuity with the teaching of the apostles. The criterion of apostolicity used to validate writings as Scripture was also used for church leaders: those who taught the apostolic faith, and were ordained to their ministry in the succession of apostolic teaching, were the legitimate and authoritative interpreters of the tradition. Irenaeus took the criterion of apostolicity one step further, locating the continuing source of apostolic authority in Rome, the city that had seen the martyrdom of the two greatest apostles, Peter and Paul (*Against Heresies* 3.2–5).

Creedal formulas developed for use in baptismal liturgies as well as for doctrinal instruction. Irenaeus' *Against Heresies* and the third-century *Apostolic Tradition* usually (and incorrectly) attributed to Hippolytus, a Roman theologian, both contain phrases that would become familiar in later texts such as the Apostles' Creed or the Nicene Creed. Baptismal creedal statements were trinitarian in structure, affirming the creation of the world by God the Father; the coming into the world of God the Son as a human being born of the Virgin Mary; his death and resurrection on the third day; and prophetic inspiration by the Holy Spirit. Christian interpretations of trinitarian faith shaped prayer and spiritual reflection. The early "Logos Christology" of Justin Martyr (c.100–c.165), developed further by Origen (c.185–c.254), preserved monotheism by emphasizing God the Father's primacy as the one who "speaks" the Word (*Logos*), the Son of God, who became flesh in Jesus Christ. Origen outlined a "grammar" of Christian prayer expressive of a trinitarian concept of God. He teaches that prayer should always be addressed *to* God the Father, *through* the Son, and *in* the Holy Spirit (*On Prayer* 15).

Liturgical custom was one spur to the development of Christology and pneumatology. Various "doxologies," or expressions of praise to God, were in use. Some followed Origen's model ("Glory to the Father, through the Son, in the Spirit"), while others were of a "coordinate" form addressed to Father, Son, and Spirit equally ("Glory to the Father, and to the Son, and to the Holy Spirit"). The Arian controversy of the fourth century focused attention on the relationship between God the Father and God the Son. Arius and his followers preferred Origen's traditional and more cautious Christology, but the Council of Nicea opted for a bolder assertion of the Son's full and equal divinity in the doctrine of the *homoousion*, the claim that the Son was of the same "being" (*ousios*) as the Father. Many perceived this teaching to be a dangerous innovation. The deacon Athanasius, later bishop of Alexandria, enthusiastically supported the council's affirmation of the fullest possible divinity of the Son lest salvation itself be in doubt. But Athanasius' famous dictum, "God became human so that humans might become God" (*On the Incarnation* 54), like the *homoousion*, only raised further questions. Was it now possible to speak in any meaningful way of the unique role of God the Father as being the source of both divine and human life? If Father and Son were of the same divine nature, was this not polytheism? And since liturgical formulas always included the Holy Spirit, how did the Spirit fit into the Godhead?

Two great Cappadocian theologians of the fourth century, Basil of Caesarea (c.330–79) and his friend Gregory of Nazianzus (c.330–90), expanded the questioning in a fully trinitarian manner. By basing distinction among the persons of the Trinity upon their relationships to each other, rather than upon any essential difference between them, Gregory managed to protect the unity of the Trinity (one God, indivisible) and the distinction of Father, Son, and Spirit within the Godhead (three Persons, unconfused). Because the Trinity is, by definition, relational, one cannot conceive of one divine person without the others: God the Father is Father because there is a Son,

God the Son is Son because there is a Father, God the Holy Spirit proceeds from the Father and was sent into the world by the Son. Origination is located in the Fatherhood of God, but it is not chronological priority. God has *always* been Father, Son, and Spirit: the relationships did not come into being at a point in time.

In the fifth century, theological and devotional reflection returned to Christology, focusing now on the relationship between the divine and human natures in Christ. Given that the incarnate Son was of the same divine nature as the Father, what room was there for genuine humanity? Were Jesus's actions to be divided between his human and divine natures? In practical terms, how to speak of and to him in prayer? It was in this context that devotion to Mary, Mother of Jesus, emerged as a significant aspect of Christian spirituality. Marian devotion arose from devotion to Christ as some began to attribute to her the title "Mother of God" (*Theotokos*).

To critics, such as Nestorius, a Syrian who became bishop of Constantinople, and Theodore, a theologian from Antioch who became bishop of Mopsuestia, the title of *Theotokos* confused the human and divine natures of Christ in a theologically irresponsible manner. Could the divine nature actually be subject to human birth? Their "Antiochene" Christology was intent on protecting the distinction between the two natures of Christ. To supporters of the title, such as Cyril, bishop of Alexandria, *Theotokos* suggested the fundamental unity of the human and divine in Christ. Their "Alexandrian" Christology spoke of Christ as becoming a single person *from* two natures, wary of any language that suggested a division between the divine and human natures of Christ.

The Council of Ephesus in 431, chaired by Cyril, affirmed the orthodoxy of the title *Theotokos*, inevitably engendering further dispute. A significant group of Syriac-speaking Christians rejected the Council of Ephesus and adhered to the Antiochene theology of Theodore. Intervention by Leo, bishop of Rome, in 449 laid the basis for the doctrine ratified in 451 by a Council at Chalcedon, near Constantinople, which elaborated a Christology of seemingly contradictory affirmations: Christ is "one person *in* two natures," which are united "without confusion, without change, without division, without separation."

Though this mix of Antiochene and Alexandrian formulas was acceptable to many, the compromise would eventually produce the worst schism in the church's first millennium. The majority of Christians in Egypt, Armenia, and much of Syria felt that the Council had moved too far from Cyril's position; the use of *in* two natures rather than *from* two natures was unacceptable to them. The formal separation between churches subsequent to these councils was a lengthy and complex process that met with much resistance from the Byzantine throne. The theological division of the church affected spirituality by ending the cross-fertilization of liturgical traditions that had characterized the earlier period, and meant that the interplay between doctrine and liturgical/spiritual practice would now occur within narrower geographical and cultural bounds. With Egypt, Armenia, and much of Syria no longer in communion with Constantinople and Rome, the Chalcedonian church was much more culturally homogeneous, becoming more and more a Byzantine imperial church. The political and religious consequences in the seventh century with the rise of Islam would be enormous, as the majority of Christians in the Middle East were ambivalent or hostile in their attitude toward the Christian Emperor in Constantinople, perceived by them as the defender of the Chalcedonian faith. The hard-won unity of faith of the first three Christian centuries was not lost, but from this time onwards differences became more pronounced.

Forming a Christian Spiritual Culture

Baptism and Eucharist: initiation into the community and nurture of faith

Christians made certain practices based upon Jewish purificatory and meal rituals central to their own religious identity. In Paul's letters (esp. Rom. 6), baptism had already acquired its fundamental meaning as incorporation into the death and resurrection of Jesus, granting forgiveness of sins. The normal form of baptism was a threefold immersion of the candidate with a verbal invocation of Father, Son, and Holy Spirit by the presiding minister. The *Apostolic Tradition* shows the development of baptismal ritual into its classical form, with a renunciation of sin, an exorcistic anointing with oil, interrogatory profession of faith, triple immersion, post-baptismal anointings, and Eucharist (*Apostolic Tradition* 10). Later theological development would interpret post-baptismal anointing and laying-on-of-hands by the bishop as a "seal" or "signing" with the Holy Spirit. After the legalization of Christian worship in the early fourth century, baptisteries could be built that often featured an image of Christ's baptism by John, providing clear visual reinforcement of the theological significance of the complex of ritual actions: participation in the new life given in Christ and the gift of the Holy Spirit.

Baptism allowed participation in the Christian sacred meal, the Eucharist, celebrated weekly in obedience to Jesus's command at the Last Supper to "Do this in memory of me" (Luke 22: 19). The Eucharist was associated particularly with Sunday, and became the typical form of Christian communal worship. Although originally celebrated within the context of a meal, the Eucharist soon became a distinct rite (see 1 Cor. 11: 20–2) consisting of biblical readings, a kiss of peace, prayers, and the sharing of blessed bread and wine. Early testimonies to the importance and manner of celebrating the Eucharist can be found in the late first-century Greek *Didache* ("Teaching"), probably of Syrian origin, the second-century account in Justin Martyr's *First Apology*, and the third-century text found in the *Apostolic Tradition*.

Early Christians regarded Eucharistic communion as a genuine reception of the body and blood of Christ under the outward forms of bread and wine: "We do not receive these things as ordinary bread and ordinary drink, but in the manner that our Savior Jesus Christ became incarnate through the Word of God and had flesh and blood for our salvation, thus also we have been taught that the food for which we give thanks through the Word of prayer from him . . . is the flesh and blood of that incarnate Jesus" (Justin, *First Apology* 66.2). This intimate participation in Jesus's life was focused on his passion, death, and resurrection, as was baptism.

Marking time through prayer and fasting

Christians inherited from Judaism the weekly pattern of a holy day, though shifted from the Jewish Sabbath to the first day of the week, Sunday, in remembrance of the resurrection of Jesus. Before the Emperor Constantine's promotion of Christianity, Sunday was a work day, and Christians gathered to celebrate the Eucharist during the night before or very early in the morning.

Easter, as the great celebration of the death and resurrection of Jesus, was the most propitious time for baptism into the paschal mystery. Prayer and fasting on the part of those to be baptized and their supporters was the origin of Lent, which by the fourth century was an extended penitential season of several weeks, culminating in the reconciliation of penitents, baptism of catechumens, and celebration of the Easter Eucharist. The days immediately before Easter became commemorations of events in Jesus's final days, though only in the medieval period was the liturgical program of "Holy" or "Great" Week completed. Its origins lay in the liturgies developed in Jerusalem in the fourth century and linked to sites associated with Jesus's passion, death, and resurrection. The fourth-century Spanish pilgrim Egeria recounted her visit to Jerusalem in the 380s in minute – and rather breathless – detail, describing a full array of services throughout the week preceding Easter. Liturgical celebration of the incarnation, the birth of Jesus, and of his baptism by John seem to have been third- or fourth-century creations linked to the developments in theological understanding of Christ's humanity and divinity.

The ascetical practice of fasting was closely associated with the Eucharist and the rhythms of the liturgy. In an echo of Jewish practice, the *Didache* calls for two fast days each week. As with the weekly holy day, there was a shift: because Jews fasted on Monday and Thursday, Christians were to fast on Wednesday and Friday (*Didache* 8.2). The Friday fast was associated with the crucifixion of Jesus and became a standard feature of Christian practice, as did fasting before receiving the Eucharist. Fasting was always linked to prayer, as in Jewish practice, by making one aware of weakness and dependence on God. It was also a form of self-denial for the sake of intense prayer for others, echoing Jesus's self-sacrifice, and could become a practical act of mercy by giving away the money that would have been spent on food.

Prayer at regular points in the day was another significant legacy of Judaism. In Christian circles, this practice soon became linked to Jesus's exhortations about persistence in prayer (Luke 18: 1–8) and Paul's exhortation to "pray without ceasing" (1 Thess. 5: 17). The *Didache* recommends prayer three times a day (using the Lord's Prayer, *Didache* 8.2–3), while later texts such as the *Apostolic Tradition* describe a more developed pattern of prayer at intervals throughout both night and day (midnight; cock crow; before work; third, sixth and ninth hours; bedtime: ch. 41). This practice is the origin of the Christian "Liturgy of the Hours" or "Divine Office," a formalized and typically communal kind of prayer which became normative in all early Christian traditions, though with regional variations of structure and content. Public celebration of morning and evening offices was common, as was the Saturday night vigil in preparation for Sunday.

The other "hours" of prayer would be practiced by ascetics or monastics, the clergy, and the particularly devout. In ascetic and monastic circles, the daily nocturnal vigil would become particularly important as a practice of watchful expectation of Christ's return like a "thief in the night" or a bridegroom arriving for the wedding celebration (Matt. 24: 36 – 25: 13).

Liturgical evolution

Before the fourth century, the development of liturgical, and particularly Eucharistic, ritual was gradual. Regionally, standard *forms* of Eucharistic praying emerged fairly early, though standard *texts* for the anaphora, or central Eucharistic prayer, were not typical until the third and fourth centuries. From that period we have early versions of the anaphoras that still distinguish the major Christian liturgical traditions. These texts show the influence of Jewish prayers (especially but not exclusively table prayers), emphasizing thanksgiving, blessing, and petition.

As a memorial of Christ's death and resurrection, the celebration of the Eucharist gradually acquired sacrificial language and symbolism. With sacrificial understandings of the celebration came a revisioning of liturgical ministry in terms of priestly mediation between God and people, and corresponding shifts in ritual practice to underscore the awe appropriate to such an exchange. The fourth century saw the adoption of imperial ceremonial, such as processions, incense, lights, stylized vesture, and so on. Freedom for public worship led to prominent and elaborately adorned church buildings. The crowds that filled them could no longer hear all of the words, and ritual had to convey more of the meaning of the liturgy.

Congregational singing at the liturgy was based almost entirely on the Psalms, although many liturgical hymns that would become important elements of devotional prayer date from the early centuries. These early formulas, such as the biblically inspired hymns "Glory to God in the Highest" and "Holy, holy, holy," as well as the acclamations "Lord have mercy" (*Kyrie eleison*) and "Holy God, Holy and Strong, Holy and Immortal, have mercy on us" (*Trisagion*), are found in both Eastern and Western traditions. Ecclesiastical (i.e., non-biblical) hymnody and liturgical poetry gradually became more and more prominent in the liturgies of the East, especially in the Liturgy of the Hours. The Syriac tradition of rhythmic homilies influenced the development of the Byzantine Greek *kontakion*, especially through the contributions of Syrian-born Romanos the Melodist (sixth century). Initial resistance to non-biblical hymnody gave way before the success of the genre, particularly in rivaling the hymnody of groups such as the Arians.

Personal prayer

The personal prayer of early Christians is accessible only through texts, which tend to provide theological reflection upon prayer or practical instructions. We know that the Psalms were central to Christian devotion, and became the mainstay of monastic prayer. Prayers preserved on papyri, potsherds, or inscriptions are largely memorial or intercessory in nature, tending toward a formalized style reflective of liturgical patterns. The Ur-prayer for Christians has always been the Lord's Prayer, which reflects Jewish prayer practice of Jesus's time. Prized because of its dominical origin, the Lord's Prayer also provided a model for prayer. Numerous commentaries on the Lord's Prayer survive from the second century onward. In presenting the Lord's Prayer as a devotional model, commentators note its combination of praise and petition. Origen, for example, notes that the ideal prayer should begin with praise of God, move to thanksgiving and confession of sins, and only then offer requests for oneself and for others, before concluding with more praise (*On Prayer* 33.1). He also presents a very traditional set of instructions on the posture for prayer. A Christian should pray standing, with arms raised and outstretched in the classic *orans* position which can be seen in early Christian iconography. For Origen, this posture was the means for the body to become an image (*eikon*) of the soul raised and stretched out toward God. One should also face east whenever possible, for the rising sun is the symbol of new life in the resurrection of Christ. Kneeling is appropriate when asking forgiveness of sins, but is not a normal posture for prayer (*On Prayer* 31.2–3).

Mystical prayer

Though Paul and other early Christian writers recorded visionary experiences, for many reasons, later theologians were more reticent. Some, like Clement, were nervous about claims of prophecy. For Origen, mysticism was an experience of the inner person and the spiritual senses, a deeper realization of the mind's capacities rather than an ecstatic surpassing of them. There were anxieties about any form of prayer that suggested affinities with non-Christian ecstatic possessions or frenzies. However, Origen left enough room for later theologians to develop the mystical dimensions of prayer more fully, especially in his approach to biblical interpretation, which encouraged personal and "spiritual" readings of the Bible.

Origen's influence is obvious in the work of Evagrius of Pontus (d. 399), a native of Asia Minor, student of Basil the Great and Gregory Nazianzen, and promising deacon in Constantinople who became a monk in Egypt in the aftermath of a personal crisis. Evagrius brought his great learning to the desert, where he wrote a series of ascetical texts integrating the practical teaching of the Egyptian monks with a cosmic theology based on Origen's speculative thought. Evagrius' emphasis on identifying distracting "thoughts" and his teaching on "pure" or imageless prayer brought Origen's spiritual theology into the monastic tradition in a powerful, though controversial, manner. Evagrius' teaching on imageless prayer was directed at those who thought that God could be pictured in the mind. By relying on literal interpretation of biblical theophanies or on imaginative depictions of Christ, Evagrius suggested, such people limited their prayer to an image of their own devising and made a fundamental mistake about who God truly is. Evagrius wrote that one might expect, however, an experience of the "light of the mind" or "light of the holy Trinity" illumining the mind when at prayer.

Evagrius' spiritual theology reads as emotionally cool, stressing the rational mind's self-realization in prayer.

A very different mode of spiritual theology was popularized by the writings of a mysterious late fourth-century figure usually named "Macarius" in the manuscript tradition, but today typically referred to as "Pseudo-Macarius" to avoid misleading attribution of his works to either of the two famous fourth-century Egyptian monks of that name. Though he wrote in Greek, Pseudo-Macarius seems to have been formed by Syriac Christian tradition. Pseudo-Macarius' work emphasizes the heart, and is emotionally "warm" when compared to Evagrius's. He frequently refers to the mind's "dwelling on high," "caught up" and "intoxicated" by desire for God. "Fire" and "light" figure in his work as descriptors of powerful experiences in prayer. Pseudo-Macarius works homiletically with biblical imagery, interpreting familiar figures and stories in terms of the ascetic struggle against sin and the need for help from God, who alone can drive sin out of the heart and replace it with the fullness of the Holy Spirit. Pseudo-Macarius stayed close to personal experience, and his subjective approach can seem to de-emphasize the role of church and sacraments in the Christian life. His sometimes stark opposition between the presence of sin or the Holy Spirit in the human heart, and the way in which he described spiritual "sensation" of the Spirit's presence, also drew criticism. Extracts from his writings were at the center of ecclesiastical condemnation of "Messalians," an ascetic group alleged to have placed unceasing personal prayer before all other spiritual practices (the name comes from the Syriac for "those who pray"). The homilies themselves, however, were never condemned, and became mainstays of Byzantine devotion.

Evagrius and Pseudo-Macarius were progenitors of later spiritual theologies that refused to choose between their two seemingly different approaches. In the fifth century, both John Cassian in the Latin West and Diadochus of Photike in Greece wrote of prayer in Evagrian terms as pure and imageless, but also intensely marked by tears, warmth, and fiery bursts of ecstatic experience. Cassian seems to have had some access to the Pseudo-Macarian tradition or something close to it, and certainly knew Evagrius' work. Diadochus clearly had the writings of both Pseudo-Macarius and Evagrius before him as he wrote. The ability to create a synthesis between two very different streams of spiritual reflection would prove to be of great importance. Cassian gave the West a repertoire of themes to complement the huge impact of his contemporary, Augustine of Hippo, and Diadochus' work foreshadowed the rich achievement of Isaac of Nineveh in the seventh century. In Isaac's writings, composed in Syriac but soon translated into Greek, Pseudo-Macarian and Evagrian theologies of prayer and spiritual experience found their fullest integration.

Gregory of Nyssa (c.330–c.395), younger brother of Basil of Caesarea, provided another opening to spiritual reflection. In his most famous mystical text, Gregory interpreted the life of Moses as an archetypal search for God. The account culminates at Mount Sinai. As Moses climbs through the cloud enshrouding the mountain, he discovers in the "luminous darkness" that, despite his approaches to the divine presence, God always remains beyond any human capacity to grasp or understand. The experience of God for Gregory consists precisely of that incapacity: "not to see is to see" (*Life of Moses* 2.163). Gregory then adds a dynamic element to his teaching. Even in the darkness of not seeing, Moses' desire for God continues to grow. In his own ever-increasing desire, Moses has an experiential echo of the divine infinity: "Never to find satisfaction of the desire is really to see God" (2.239).

Gregory's dynamic Christian Platonism was the starting-point for a line of spiritual thought in the Greek East that, during the next millennium, would continue to develop in theological precision and experiential depth. Its next stage of significant advance was the dense but fascinating work of the pseudonymous "Dionysius the Areopagite" (cf. Acts 17: 34), who wrote around 500, most likely in Syria. The spiritual theology of Pseudo-Dionysius is even more marked by Neoplatonism and its reliance on paradox than Gregory of Nyssa's. God is the One from whom all things proceed in ordered hier-archies (angels, sacraments, clergy, laity) which communicate the divine light. Pseudo-Dionysius understood the liturgy – for him fundamental and central – as a means of drawing Christians back into union with God since it manifests the hierarchies most fully. The rites become a rich field of symbols, with every action bearing hidden meaning keyed to the project of return to God. Pseudo-Dionysius' symbolic interpreta-tion of the liturgy begins a tradition of liturgical commentary of great significance in the Byzantine world. In other works, he engages with the paradox that, although God has many names in Scripture, indeed powerful and useful names, God is beyond all names or affirmations. Even if God is best describable through *negation* of attributes or affirmations, nonetheless God is ultimately beyond *both* affirmation and negation. Pseudo-Dionysius' systematic exposition of these two ways of knowing would have a great impact on the medieval Latin West. In the East, his Christian use of Neoplaton-ism and his liturgical orientation shaped the thought of Maximus the Confessor (d. 662), and through him the Byzantine mystical and theological traditions that culminated in the fourteenth-century spiritual theology of Gregory Palamas and the liturgical commentary of Nicholas Cabasilas.

The decisive influence of Platonism was felt in Latin Christianity as well, through its towering theologian of the early Christian period, Augustine of Hippo (354–430). His brilliance and eloquence so quickly dominated the Latin Christian world that by the time of his death he had reoriented Western theology and spirituality. Augustine would be by far the most significant figure in Western Christianity for at least the next thou-sand years. In his *Confessions*, Augustine left a highly personal – though rhetorically stylized – chronicle of his intellectual and spiritual development. Addressed to God as a long prayer of repentance and gratitude, its first-person stance sets it apart from all other early Christian spiritual texts. Augustine's story of conversion is two-track. He had to overcome his intellectual difficulties with Christian doctrine (and some intellec-tual snobbery). He also had to feel so helplessly trapped in the inveterate habits of his personal life that he would finally realize his absolute need for God's grace. His focus on sexual compulsion, which here as in his theology of Original Sin he employed as the most vivid, but not necessarily most significant, example of the fatal weakness of the human will, helped to put sexuality firmly at the center of Christian moral anxiety, espe-cially in the West. Augustine's spiritual theology was shaped by two principal themes: the primacy of charity, both divine and human, and the insights into God's nature and the human search for God that he found in Latin translations of Plotinus' Neoplatonism. His philosophical debt to Neoplatonism lay in accepting that God is not materially present throughout the universe and therefore discoverable "out there" somewhere. Instead, God's presence is spiritual, and can be sought by turning within the self to what is also immaterial and spiritual, the rational mind. Only the mind can move beyond visible things to see the unchanging light that is beyond even itself, a move that is possible only in love for the God who made it (*Confessions* 7.10.16; 7.17.23). Augustine's most famous description of mystical ascent takes him beyond all sensory mediation of God to "hear him unmediated, whom we love in all these things, hear him without them, as now we stretch out and in a flash of thought touch that eternal Wisdom who abides above all things" (*Confessions* 9.10.25).

Both themes helped to shape Augustine's trinitarian theology, which became the Western counterpart to the Cappadocian trinitarianism of the East. Augustine understood the dynamism of the Trinity in analogy to the intellectual faculties of recollection, contemplation, and love. The "image and likeness" of the trinitarian God is to be found in the movements of human reason. By interpreting the Holy Spirit as the love uniting Father and Son, Augustine followed the tendency of Latin theology to teach the "double procession of the Spirit," i.e., that the Holy Spirit proceeds from Father and Son, rather than only from the Father as declared in the Creed from the Council of Constantinople. In time, this difference from the Cappadocian doctrine that the Father is the single source of all divinity became the principal theological stumbling-block between East and West. In Augustine's thought, however, the mirroring of the Trinity in the human person was a vital link between trinitarian theology and spirituality. The Christian life, and especially participation in the sacraments, gradually restored the trinitarian image to its original perfection.

Ways of Christian Virtue and Perfection

Martyrdom

Apart from the Bible itself, the earliest form of popular Christian literature comprised the stories of the deaths of martyrs. Their experience of Christ's passion in their own bodies manifested Christian identification with the Paschal mystery in a uniquely vivid way. For Christians before the "Peace of the Church" in 313, stories of martyrdom prompted introspection about their own response to the possibility of martyrdom as well as admiration for the courage of the martyrs. Surviving "Acts" of martyrs range from highly literary creations to laconic recounting of the most basic facts, which can be even more powerful than the dramatized accounts. Persecutions were sporadic and localized, but even so their impact on the Christian imagination was enormous.

Some of the fundamental figures of pre-Constantinian theology were martyrs: Paul, Ignatius, Irenaeus, and Cyprian. As a boy, Origen witnessed his father's arrest and death, and as an old man he himself was arrested, tortured, and condemned to forced labor. Though released, he died soon thereafter from his injuries, earning the title of "confessor" of the faith. The church of Alexandria saw its bishop, Peter, killed in the very last wave of persecution, and entered the new era of freedom profoundly shaped by the suffering of the past. When we read the works of martyred theologians, we must keep in mind, as they must have, the potential cost of the faith they articulated. Their commitment was to more than a lifestyle or philosophy. The Acts of ordinary men and women demonstrate that it was the courage of faith, not theological sophistication, that gave martyrs the strength to choose death rather than apostasy. Accounts suggest that it often took some real determination to die for one's Christian beliefs. The outcome preferred by civil authorities was disavowal of Christian faith demonstrated by offering incense, a libation, or other act of acknowledgment before an image of the emperor depicted as a god (the official charge against Christians was typically that of atheism, i.e., not worshipping the true gods). Other options were handing over Christian scriptures or sacred vessels, or renunciation of the faith during a public trial. A martyr had to reject every such opportunity for escape. In the Acts, one can frequently see the reluctance of officials to impose the final penalty, and even their anger at what seemed to be pointless and foolish obstinacy.

A devotional consequence of persecution was the cult of the martyrs, which began in the form of honoring them in their burial places. In this practice lay the beginnings of Christian veneration of saints. The focus narrowed to the actual remains, which could be divided and transported in order to make the power that had come to be associated with the martyr's bones more widely accessible. The miraculous finding of the cross in Jerusalem in the early fourth century fueled interest in other relics, which became the basis of legends and intense devotion. Augustine describes the revelation to Ambrose in a dream of the burial place of two Milanese martyrs, Gervasius and Protasius, the recovery of whose bodies became a potent tool in Ambrose's political struggles (*Confessions* 9.7.16). Augustine's depiction of his own mother's devotion to the tombs of the martyrs is presented as a glimpse of an anachronistic practice (*Confessions* 6.2.2). The focus had shifted to the more mobile power of relics. Cities vied in their local cults, trying to outdraw their local rivals on feast days and to trump each other by the miracles performed by the saints whose relics they possessed.

Asceticism

Martyrdom certainly inspired other forms of powerful witness to Christian devotion. A life of asceticism, the sustained practice of physical and spiritual disciplines, was an option for those seeking an intense experience of Christian discipleship. The place of asceticism in the first three Christian centuries, however, was ambiguous and often controversial. Asceticism was a current in Christian practice from earliest times, reflecting the ascetical orientation of some Jewish groups. Even in the New Testament there are signs of approval for celibacy or virginity, or texts that have been interpreted as such (Matt. 19: 12; 1 Cor. 7: 12ff; 1 Tim. 3: 2, 12; Rev. 14: 1–5). Early Christian writers regard it as part of the Christian landscape (Ignatius, *Letter to Polycarp* 5.2; Justin, *First Apology* 15.6). The border between unusual piety and elitist sectarianism was not always clear, though some individuals and groups clearly set themselves apart from the larger church by their claims of perfection or adherence to "true" Christianity. The emphasis on strict fasts, mandatory celibacy, and charismatic leadership of second-century groups such as Tatian's "Encratites" (so-called from their *enkrateia* or discipline) or the prophecy-oriented Montanists clearly made them an alternative church rather than a movement within the church.

At the same time, the status of these movements varied in different parts of the world. Tatian enjoyed respect in his native Syria, and was the compiler of the *Diatessaron*, the Syriac harmony of the Gospels used liturgically until the mid-fifth century. Ecclesial asceticism was an early and distinctive feature of Syriac Christianity in the form of the "Sons and Daughters of the Covenant," who lived a celibate Christianity in service to the church. The two great Syriac theologians of the fourth century, Aphrahat and Ephrem, were Sons of the Covenant. Their emphasis on "singleness" (Syr. *ihidayutha*) was based on a close identification with Christ, the "single one" (only-begotten), and found particular expression in celibacy. This movement may reflect an earlier stratum of Syriac Christianity that limited baptism to those willing to make a commitment to sexual renunciation, whether before or within marriage. The Montanists had success in North Africa, even recruiting Tertullian, the first notable Latin theologian. Roman Africa was known for its rigorous interpretation of Christian morals and for hard-line attitudes about the pastoral response to those who had denied the faith but then repented and sought to return to the church. The non-Christian dualistic Manicheans intrigued the young Augustine, who was an "auditor" of their teaching for a brief time.

The usual trip-wire for earning the opprobrium of ecclesiastical authorities was ascetical disdain of marriage, which was perceived as a threat both to a biblically sanctioned way of life and to a bulwark of the social order. Another point of contention could be seeming disregard for the sacramental life of the church or for its leaders. It can be difficult to sift the controversial literature for real information about ascetic groups amidst the ecclesiastical paranoia and fear. We know enough of some ascetically oriented Gnostic movements, of the Manicheans, and of other groups to know that they were significant players in the religious marketplace. More difficult for the church to handle were groups like the Encratites, who embraced Christian doctrine while insisting on a much more rigorous program of fasting and sexual renunciation than did the Christian mainstream. The problem of integrating the ascetic impulse into the larger church was resolved only in the fourth century with the emergence of formalized monasticism and practices such as episcopal consecration of virgins.

The apocryphal Acts and Gospels provide some of our best access to early Christian asceticism, and also illustrate the affinities between asceticism and martyrdom which foreshadow some of the formative themes of monasticism. One of the most widely circulated was the *Acts of Paul and Thecla*, a work dating from the second century that was frequently quoted by early Christian authors. The heroine, a young woman named Thecla, overhears Paul's preaching on his visit to Iconium. Paul teaches "the word of God about self-control and resurrection" and "virginity and prayer": "Blessed are they that have kept the flesh chaste, for they shall become a temple of God; blessed are they that control themselves, for God shall speak with them; . . . blessed are the bodies of virgins, for they shall be pleasing to God and shall not lose the reward for their chastity." Thecla is so moved that she resolves to break her engagement and remain a virgin, to the consternation of fiancé, family, and townsfolk. She attaches herself to Paul to learn more. Her mother urges that she be burned for refusing to marry, but she survives the flames unscathed. Another man falls in love with her but turns her over to the civil authorities when she resists his advances. Condemned to death, she is taken to the arena, where she throws herself into a ditch of water in an act of self-baptism. The wild beasts will not approach her, and she confesses her faith before the governor, who marvels and decides to release her. She then becomes a cave-dwelling ascetic for the rest of her ninety years. This story is archetypal in many ways: the emphasis on virginity, self-determination by a young woman even in the face of rejection by family and friends, amazement at her constancy. The unusual element is Thecla's retreat into solitary asceticism. In the period preceding the emergence of "monasticism" as an identifiable, approved form of Christian asceticism on the margins of normal church life, figures like Thecla inspired imitation, particularly by young women, who remained in their family homes or gathered together in the towns to live as lifelong virgins among other Christians, not in solitude. Thecla's story clearly puts her ascetic witness on a par with conventional martyrdom, for she is spared death twice for the sake of her commitment to virginity.

Monasticism

The monastic movements of the fourth century find their context in the array of asceticisms within and outside the church. The traditional honor paid to Antony the Great (251–356) as the "founder" of monasticism needs to be nuanced in the light of ascetic traditions of long standing. Indeed, according to Athanasius' *Life of Antony*, he was able to place his sister in a community of virgins when he determined to leave behind all possessions and family ties. He found an ascetic mentor who had been living in solitude on the outskirts of the village for many years. Antony's innovation was heading into the desert, definitively breaking the conventional ties with village and cultivated land that sustained life in Egypt. By doing so, he repositioned asceticism as a movement on the margin of church and society but very much enmeshed in both. Antony was depicted as fiercely loyal to the Nicene bishops and in no way a critic of normal ways of Christian life. He healed and counseled laity in addition to teaching those pursuing the monastic life. Antony becomes the prototypical monk, renouncing an ordinary relationship with the world for the sake of another kind of relationship, and setting the normal issues of human existence against the backdrop of eternity and the vastness of the desert. Antony withdraws both geographically and psychologically, his ever-greater physical withdrawal echoing his deeper and deeper confrontation with himself and the "demons" that oppress him. Antony's teaching on the psychodynamics of temptation echoes the tradition of discernment of spirits found as early as the *Shepherd of Hermas* and developed by Origen in book 3 of *On First Principles*.

The desert school of spirituality that arises in fourth-century Egypt emphasizes rigorous self-examination in order to move past the internal and external forces that subvert human focus on God. Evagrius of Pontus systematizes the tradition into a scheme of "eight principal thoughts" that packages the teaching of Origen, Antony, and their successors into a brilliantly simple yet profound form. The system passed to the West in the writings of John Cassian, and from him to Gregory the Great, who transformed it into the list of "seven capital sins" beloved of medieval moral treatises. In the monastic environment, however, the goal was not so much moral regulation as freedom from emotional and psychological disturbances for the sake of unceasing prayer and love of both God and neighbor. This non-judgmental perspective is evident in the remarkable collections of "sayings" (*apophthegmata*) of the desert fathers and mothers.

Antony's form of monastic life caught the imagination of the late antique world in both East and West, but was only one kind of the developed form of asceticism that can be called "monasticism." Another Egyptian, Pachomius, abandoned solitude for the sake of forming a community of monks that prayed, worked, and ate together in a highly ordered and very cloistered ascetic society. The two models of solitary (anchoritic) and communal (cenobitic) life found many imitators and some hybrid forms in loose associations of hermits gathered around a spiritual guide. The phenomenal growth of monasticism among both men and women in the fourth and fifth centuries has been explained in many ways, perhaps most frequently as a reaction to the Constantinian church's assimilation to conventional society. There is little question that monasticism was a form of witness and self-dedication for a Christian church that no longer lived under the threat of martyrdom. Monasticism would, in many ways, especially in the East, become "typical Christianity," dominating spiritual theology and liturgical development.

Monasticism appeared later in the West, largely inspired by contact with Eastern monastic movements. There had been a tradition in the Latin church of consecrated virginity, beginning in Africa and spreading to Italy, especially under the leadership of Ambrose in Milan. The self-determination of the young women who made this choice threatened parental (and especially paternal) control of daughters, and required the full persuasive powers of church leaders to defend it. The evolution from domestic virgins to communities of consecrated women was natural and inevitable.

There are fourth-century records of male hermits in Italy, but the most famous Western monk of the period was Martin, who became bishop of Tours (*c*.315 or 336–97). Martin was a miracle-worker and battler of pagans. His style of rough-and-ready monasticism was critiqued by John Cassian, who came to Gaul from the East and sought to introduce the monastic traditions of the East as a corrective to what he perceived to be unformed local ascetic traditions. Meanwhile, a cenobium had been started on the island of Lérins, off the southern coast of Gaul, in the early fifth century. These traditions would inspire the cenobitic movement in Italy which ultimately produced the *Rule of Benedict* (*c*.540). This compendium of monastic and practical wisdom was destined for a great future, but at the time of its composition was just one among many efforts in the West to codify monastic life for the sake of stability and continuity.

Conclusion

The first centuries of Christianity established the basis for both unity in faith and difference in doctrine. The cultural diversity that enriched Christian liturgy and literature also created tensions as political conflicts and clashing worldviews opened fissures that only grew wider over the next several hundred years. By 600, the intellectual sophistication and spiritual depth of Christianity had prepared the churches of East and West for their remarkable but divergent paths. What they shared far outweighed any real differences among them, but Christian spirituality is always finally the story of human beings who remain fully human even as they are caught up in the things of God.

References

Acts of Paul and Thecla 1886: trans. A. Walker in *Ante-Nicene Fathers*, vol. 8. Buffalo, NY: Christian Literature (numerous modern rpts).

Apophthegmata patrum 1975: trans. B. Ward in *The Sayings of the Desert Fathers: The Alphabetical Collection*. Oxford: Mowbray.

Apostolic Tradition 2001: trans. A. Stewart-Sykes. Crestwood, NY: St Vladimir's Seminary Press.

Athanasius 1954: *On the Incarnation of the Word*. In E. R. Hardy (ed. and trans.), *Christology of the Later Fathers*. Philadelphia: Westminster Press.

——1980: *The Life of Antony*, trans. R. C. Gregg. New York: Paulist Press.

Augustine of Hippo 1963: *The Trinity*, trans. S. McKenna. Washington, DC: Catholic University of America Press.

——1991: *Confessions*, trans. H. Chadwick. Oxford: Oxford University Press.

Basil of Caesarea 1980: *On the Holy Spirit*, trans. D. Anderson. Crestwood, NY: St Vladimir's Seminary Press.

Benedict of Nursia 1981: *Rule for Monasteries*. In T. Fry (ed.), *RB 1980: The Rule of St Benedict in Latin and English with Notes*. Collegeville, MN: Liturgical Press.

Brock, S. 1992: *The Luminous Eye: The Spiritual World Vision of St Ephrem*. Kalamazoo, MI: Cistercian Publications.

Bunge, G. 2002: *Earthen Vessels: The Practice of Personal Prayer According to the Patristic Tradition*. San Francisco: Ignatius.

Clément, O. 1993: *The Roots of Christian Mysticism*. London: New City.

Clement of Alexandria 1887: *Stromateis*, trans. W. Wilson in *Ante-Nicene Fathers*, vol. 2. Buffalo, NY: Christian Literature (numerous modern rpts).

Diadochus of Photike 1979: *Chapters on Knowledge*. In G. E. H. Palmer, P. Sherrard, and K. Ware (trans.), *The Philokalia*, vol. 1. London: Faber and Faber.

DiBernardino, A. (ed.) 1992: *Encyclopedia of the Early Church*. New York: Oxford University Press.

Ephrem of Nisibis 1983a: *Hymns*. In S. P. Brock (ed.), *The Harp of the Spirit*. London: Fellowship of St Alban and St Sergius.

——1983b: *Hymns*, trans. K. E. McVey. New York: Paulist Press.

Evagrius of Pontus 2003: *Praktikos* and *Chapters on Prayer*. In R. E. Sinkewicz (trans.), *Evagrius of Pontus: The Greek Ascetic Corpus*. Oxford: Oxford University Press.

Frend, W. H. C. and Stevenson, J. 1987: *A New Eusebius: Documents Illustrating the History of the Church to AD 337*, rev. edn. London: SPCK.

Gospel of Thomas 1998: In S. J. Patterson, H-G. Bethge, and J. M. Robinson (eds), *The Fifth Gospel: The Gospel of Thomas Comes of Age*. Harrisburg, PA: Trinity Press International.

Gregory of Nazianzus 1954: *Theological Orations*. In E. R. Hardy (ed. and trans.), *Christology of the Later Fathers*. Philadelphia: Westminster Press.

Gregory of Nyssa 1978: *The Life of Moses*, trans. A. Malherbe and E. Ferguson. New York: Paulist Press.

Hermas 1964: *The Shepherd.* In K. Lake (ed. and trans.), *The Apostolic Fathers*, vol. 2. Loeb Classical Library. Cambridge, MA: Harvard University Press.

Ignatius of Antioch 1970: *Letters.* In C. C. Richardson (ed. and trans.), *Early Christian Fathers.* New York: Macmillan.

Irenaeus of Lyons 1970: *Against Heresies.* Selections in C. C. Richardson (ed. and trans.), *Early Christian Fathers.* New York: Macmillan.

Jasper, R. C. D. and Cuming, G. J. (eds) 1990: *Prayers of the Eucharist Early and Reformed*, 3rd rev. edn. Collegeville, MN: Liturgical Press.

John Cassian 1997: *Conferences*, trans. B. Ramsey. New York: Newman Press.

——2000: *Institutes*, trans. B. Ramsey. New York: Newman Press.

Justin Martyr 1966: *The First and Second Apologies*, trans. L. W. Bernard. New York: Paulist Press.

McGinn, B. 1991: *The Presence of God: A History of Western Mysticism*, vol. 1: *The Foundations of Mysticism.* New York: Crossroad.

Murray, R. 1975: *Symbols of Church and Kingdom.* Cambridge: Cambridge University Press.

Pelikan, J. and Hotchkiss, V. (eds) 2003: *Creeds and Confessions of Faith in the Christian Tradition*, vol. 1. New Haven, CT: Yale University Press.

Pseudo-Dionysius 1987: *The Complete Works*, trans. C. Luibhéid. New York: Paulist Press.

Pseudo-Macarius 1992: *Spiritual Homilies*, trans. G. A. Maloney. New York: Paulist Press.

Origen 1966: *On First Principles*, trans. G. W. Butterworth. New York: Harper Torchbooks.

——1979: *On Prayer.* In R. A. Greer (ed. and trans.), *Origen: An Exhortation to Martyrdom, On Prayer and Selected Works.* New York: Paulist Press.

Stevenson, J. (ed.), rev. Frend, W. H. C. 1989: *Creeds, Councils and Controversies: Documents Illustrating the History of the Church* AD *337–461.* London: SPCK.

Stewart, C. 1992: *Cassian the Monk.* New York: Oxford University Press.

Young, F. 1983: *From Nicaea to Chalcedon: A Guide to the Literature and its Background.* Philadelphia: Fortress Press.

——1997: *Biblical Exegesis and the Formation of Christian Culture.* Cambridge: Cambridge University Press.

CHAPTER 5

Christian Spirituality in Byzantium and the East (600–1700)

John A. McGuckin

Signs of the Times

The sixth century of the Christian era witnessed a sea-change in the nature of life in the Roman empire. It is commonly said to have coincided with the rule of the emperor Justinian (r. 527–65), though most of the subjects of the empire in that period might not have known it, for all the signs were that Justinian was a great restorer (his military campaigns pushed back the boundaries of Rome which had been progressively weakened in the years before him, and his building works were monumental, such as can still be seen in the church of Hagia Sophia in Istanbul); nevertheless, his reign was the last time for many centuries to come that Christian affairs would progress with the ease and remarkable success that had seemed to characterize their ascent in the previous three centuries. Two important social factors in this were, first, the rise of Islam, which almost from its birth began a military expansion westwards into traditional Roman territory in Palestine, Egypt, and Syria, and, secondly, the long-term social effects of the massed migration of tribes from the vast steppes of Asia that had begun in the previous century and a half. The event is known in the consciousness of Western history as the invasions of the "barbarians." The names of the tribes (Vandals, Huns, Goths, chief among them) still live in the Western collective memory. These great socio-political factors led to the ever-increasing division of the Christian church and empire in West and East. The disruption to social and ecclesiastical life which the barbarian invasions caused in the Western provinces led to great disaffection with the emperors who still ruled in Byzantium (Constantinople), and the papacy (a move prefigured under Gregory the Great, 590–604) began to be seen more and more as an alternative center of cohesion, but in a socio-political vision now imagined as rising from out of a patchwork of smaller nation-states. So began the ascent of Western Europe, on a very different trajectory from that of Byzantium, which continued with the older vision of a single multi-national empire, bonded together by a common (Greek) Christian faith, and the single rule of a God-beloved emperor. These great changes to the structure of the old Christian empire, and its two halves, the Latin and the Greek, were inevitably reflected in the patterns of its theological and spiritual writings.

By the sixth century it was rare for any Western Christian intellectual to have command of the Greek language, and just as rare for a Greek to be able to work in Latin. Perhaps even more effectively than barbarian invasions, or political collapse, this divorce of the linguistic culture set a wedge between the churches in East and West, and gave rise to distinctive new differences in the spiritual reflections of the monks and theologians who were the chief writers of the early medieval period. This time is known, rather misleadingly, as the "Dark Ages" in the West. The term signifies the discontinuity as Western Christianity tried to refashion itself out of the ruins of Roman imperial stability. In Byzantium, during the same period, the church never had to deal with an intellectual discontinuity of the same order. There is, of course, a marked decline in the financial and political affairs of the Christian empire from the seventh to the tenth centuries, and this is clearly witnessed in the social, financial, and political annals, but in no sense was there any of the intellectual or cultural collapse (or, we should say more accurately, cultural discontinuities) that often marked the West. Even with the shrinking of Byzantine territory, and the destruction of Christian centers of learning that went hand in hand with this (the loss of Alexandria in Egypt, Damascus, Antioch, and Jerusalem in Roman Syria, for example, were bitter blows to Christianity), there was always a counter-movement where scholars and manuscripts came flowing into Constantinople as a natural center and bulwark of Christian life. The greater the external pressures, the more Constantinople seemed to shine, and in its turn shone out back over the Eastern Christian world, an image of the beauty of the Christian witness.

Byzantine spirituality in this period develops in a smooth flow from its foundations in the earlier imperial ages (the so-called "patristic" era) and demonstrates new intellectual confidence in the manner in which it is more open to a synthesis of gospel truths in philosophical forms. The continuing role of Constantinople, the "Great City," which served as a magnet for all the talent of the Eastern Christian world, and as a great influence to be emulated whenever possible in the provinces, ensured that while Byzantium was a vast and complex union of cultures and races, it nevertheless had a common and coherent intellectual and spiritual tradition. This is why, to this day, there is a common spirit and a recognizable ethos in almost all forms of Eastern Christianity, even among those that have been ecumenically separated for centuries by theological controversies.

The main characteristic of spiritual theology in the period after Justinian can be said to be that of creative synthesis. Many earlier writers have concluded from this that (in contrast to the earliest Christian centuries) Byzantium was a "dead hand" on intellectual life. Such a view can no longer be sustained from close encounter with the original texts. There is a profound drive to be seen to be within the tradition of the earlier fathers and teachers, to be sure, but also dynamic impetus is at work among the later Byzantines to make a synthesis of the earlier tradition; and since that legacy contained disparate elements that added up to a very variegated spiritual heritage (the Semitic biblical idioms, the speculations of Greek Logos theology and philosophy, the Egyptian and Syrian stress on asceticism and psychic awareness) the early Byzantine period had much to "blend" and did so with a commendable intelligence and sensitivity. From bib-lical, Greek philosophical, and monastic elements there arose a distinctive Eastern Christian spiritual heritage that was both rich and complex, and destined to have a long endurance, ultimately outliving the Christian empire that nurtured it, and surviving into the present, still as the common ethos of the Eastern Christian churches.

The Twilight of Classicism (CE 600–900)

Those living in the Age of Justinian understood Constantinople to be the New Rome, and described themselves as "the Romans" (*Romaioi*). They were, and for the next thou-sand years would remain, puzzled at the way in which the rest of Europe described them as "the Greeks." Justinian himself saw his reign as an unbroken part of a long line of classical Roman values. This is witnessed, not least, in his attempt to stabilize and codify Roman law, and in his great legal reforms that had such an impact on the medieval era to follow. In the domain of spiritual theology, the chief writers of this period show similar presuppositions. They are the last voices of the classical imperial past. They tend to sum up and harmonize different elements, but their voice and style of dress is "antique" in cast. One of the aspects of this late imperial antiquity is its international character. Syrians are disseminated in Greek modalities, ancient styles of scriptural interpretation and commentary are propagated through liturgical hymns that are sung as far afield as Antioch, Jerusalem, and Alexandria. Ancient philosophical speculation, once conducted in the schools, is now taken on the road by itinerant monks and mystics. It is classicism, certainly, but all set in a new and exciting motion. Only some of the main writers can be highlighted in what follows, but in their own way they each show the marks of the dynamic recapitulation that Byzantine theology in this period was manifesting.

Romanos the Melodist

Romanos is perhaps the greatest of the Byzantine religious poets of antiquity. His works entered the fabric of the liturgy of the Greek-speaking church and set the tone for the visual and mental "imagery" of what the Christian mysteries evoked and involved. His work is iconic and foundational in this regard. Most later Orthodox painted icons actu-ally derive the specifics of their imagistic vocabulary from lines of Romanos' poetry. Romanos (active *c*.540, died after 555) was a Syrian by birth, possibly a Jewish convert to Christianity. He was ordained deacon at Beirut and came to Constantinople *c*.515, at the end of the reign of the emperor Anastasius. He was the most famous musician and poet of the age of Justinian. His specialty was the *Kontakion* (the term means "a sermon on a roll"), which was basically a long biblical hymn. This was a standard element of liturgical style in his day, and was itself a throw-back to ancient Semitic liturgical practice. It would "roll on" for a long time (his poems are generally epic in length) but was later reduced in size and significance as the liturgy evolved. The *Kon-*

takion still has a (much smaller) place in the liturgical offices of the Eastern Church, something like the collect prayers of the Western liturgy today.

Romanos represents a Syrian Semitic style in his poetic renderings of the biblical narratives, a form of storytelling, that is, that plays on the drama of the events he is poetically and paraphrastically retelling. He delights in using heightened contrasts and paradoxes to convey the sense of wonder and mystery of the story of salvation. Just as in the inner structure of the Bible itself, his poetic passages often aimed at telling the story of salvation afresh. They re-presented it as a story of salvation for the hearer. Usually the biblical tale was told again in an elaborately embellished form, with asides added from the narrator who explained the story for his own audience, and interpreted its spiritual significance, often by adding dialogue to the characters in the scene, which made the events fill out with lively exchanges. In his *Christmas Hymn* (this and his *Hymn of the Virgin's Lament* are both still used today in the Orthodox Church's liturgical celebrations of Christmas and Great Friday of Holy Week), the Virgin is given a dramatic monologue in which she wonders who the Magi are, and why they bring her such strange gifts. By singing out the Gospel texts, and stretching them to the undulating Byzantine music that so lent itself to the proclamation of the leading cantors (who occupied facing pulpits in the church as they led the people who were expected to sing the antiphonal refrains), a new and dynamic way was found to preach the gospel in sound and image. This poetic style of appropriating Christian doctrine proved so popular with the Byzantines that it remained a standard element of most Eastern spirituality ever after. To this day, there are few "said services" in Eastern Christianity, as almost all church worship is sung.

One factor that impressed itself on spiritual thought-patterns because of this was the Syrian style of poetic rhetoric. This, of course, was something that was native to Romanos, not peculiar to him, but part of an old tradition that went back to Bar Daysan and Ephrem the Syrian, great third- and fourth-century Syrian poets. In the Syrian poetic tradition points were made by means of strong polarities of ideas. The polarities were stacked up in a cascade of images. It was not expected that a doctrine should be "proved" by a logical linear method; rather, that it should be circled around in poetry and music, until such time as the heart of the performer and hearer had been "seduced" into an apprehension of the mysteries that were depicted in the narrative. This "entering into" the mystery could only be done by empathy and affectivity, not by will or mental effort. The music and the poem had to do its work. As a result, many of the ancient Syrian hymns, and the Byzantine liturgical poems that derived from them, are apparently repetitious to the Western mindset, as they keep coming back to a central point by means of many different perspectives on the same idea. This Syro-Byzantine rhetoric especially advanced two kinds of polarities: that of dissonance and that of complementarity. In the style of dissonance, pairs of biblical types would be found, such as Mary and Eve, or Christ and Adam. Eve, for example, would be said to be "foolish" for not asking questions of the serpent, and gullibly taking its word that the apple represented a good thing. On the contrary, Mary asks "wise questions" of the angel Gabriel. The first shows herself a foolish opener of the gate of destruction, while the other shows herself to be the wise opener of the gate of salvation. The juxtaposing of the opposites was an old rhetorical ploy to make the listener mentally offer his or her own contribution to the debate that the poem had initiated. This involvement was exactly what the poem had sought from its hearers, and the poem usually concludes by inviting the audience to join in praising the Lord or the Mother of God who acted with such wisdom and mercy in the plan of salvation.

The pairing of complementarities is also heavily used. The Tree of Life, written about in terms of the family of Jesse, for example, is fulfilled in the Tree of Life that is the cross of Jesse's descendant, Jesus. Such images are used in cascades, in such a way that the Jesus story is told in a rich weave of biblical symbols. People listening to the hymns learned much about the whole panoply of Scripture, but in a profoundly Christocentric and soteriologically focused manner. This hymnic character became constitutive of most Byzantine theology to follow. It has not been a matter of great interest to many later commentators on Western theology, who have often used inappropriate categories of analysis, rendering hymnography as something distinct from theology or spirituality, but when these hymns entered, as they most certainly did, into the consciousness of whole peoples (they are commonly known in Greek and Russian folklore today), the liturgy itself can be said to have provided the basic syntax for a spirituality that set the image of a victorious salvation at the core of its understanding of Jesus and the gospel. The poems are deeply affective. The hymn of lamentation which Romanos wrote for Good Friday, for example, depicts Mary as a ewe-sheep bleating for the death of her lamb. It may be an odd image for a modern urbanite, but was strangely affecting for ancient subsistence farmers, such as populated most of the early Christian churches. In this hymn the Virgin invites the congregation to weep with her, as she grieves over the death of her only son. She laments that "he who hung the stars" upon the firmament of heaven is now "left to hang upon a cross." Playing on the deep affectivities of ancient men and women (who generally all joined in with the weeping at funerals, not leaving that to the immediate family alone, as at present), and on the deep sense of honor and shame that ordered most of Greek society, the poet invites empathy, making the congregation sense how Christ's death must not be "dishonored" by neglect, but has to enter into their own consciousness and be appropriated by them as a "familial" event. In this way, the sense of being bonded to Christ and the Virgin by being invited to share in the funeral feast forms a major part of the motive of the poet, and the innate spirituality of the hymn.

Without being too formalist, we might call this typical Byzantine aspect of liturgical style, a spirituality of "psychic appropriation," and it served as a profoundly deep source for generations of Byzantine Christians giving their loyalty to Christ over many subsequent centuries. Several of the Syrian spiritual writers argued that, unless the heart of the believer was moved (and felt to be moved), the Spirit could not make its home there, and without the Spirit's presence, prayer and worship were but dead formalities. The idea was not wholly endorsed by the later Byzantine tradition, but it was enthusiastically affirmed that the heart must indeed sing if prayer and praise were to be authentic in the eyes of God. There was a whole series of Byzantine poets after Romanos, such as the nun Cassiane, or Joseph the Hymnographer, Cosmas of Aitolos, or Andrew of Crete, but perhaps the most famous after Romanos was the eighth-century theologian and monk, John the Damascene.

John of Damascus

John of Damascus (Yanan ibn Mansur) was a member of a high-ranking Christian family, and followed his father in holding office at the court of the Islamic Caliph at Damascus. He resigned his post around 725, probably because of political pressures, and became a monk at Mar Saba monastery near Bethlehem, where he was ordained priest. During the first Byzantine iconoclastic crisis (726–30), when the validity of using iconic depictions of Christ and the saints in liturgical worship was being called into question, he wrote three *Discourses* in defense of the icons which became standard works on image veneration and sacramental representation. He was anathematized by the iconoclastic synod of 753, but Palestine was then out of the reach of the Byzantine court. The icon venerators (Iconodules), who were eventually victorious, posthumously hailed him as a heroic confessor at the Ecumenical Council of Nicaea II in 787. His correlation of the theology of icon to incarnational Christology was a notable aspect of his apologia. After John (and the triumph of the icons which he stood for) most Eastern Christian devotion and prayer would be indissolubly bound up with a colorful and heartfelt veneration of icons. His collection of texts relating to the ascetical life, the *Sacra parallela*, is now preserved only in fragments, but his compendium of theology (*On the Orthodox Faith*), which he wrote to be a systematic summation of all Christian doctrine, exerted a massive influence on later ages, and became a major source for St Thomas Aquinas in the West.

John's practice of hymn-writing (in company with his kinsman Cosmas) continued the example of Romanos, and many of his works are still used in the Eastern churches to this day. John's awareness of the Greek philosophical tradition, from Pseudo-Dionysius the Areopagite and Maximus the Confessor to his own day, his understanding of the many theological controversies that had rocked the church, as well as his own reflections on Christology and sacramental thought, made his poetry even more of a synthetic composite than that of his Syrian predecessor Romanos. John's poems on the incarnation celebrate the mingling together, in a new ontological harmony and interpenetration, of the natures of the created and the uncreated.

Using dynamic images similar to those of Romanos, he delights in juxtaposing the attributes of infinity and fragility in the same person of Jesus the God-Man, and suggesting that this act of incarnation was more than a once-for-all affair affecting Jesus, but was rather a cosmic mystery whereby the entire human race, bodily, as well as spiritually, and morally, was brought into communion with the divine. Human flesh, therefore, is itself a real vehicle of divine presence (as it was in the case of Jesus) and all of human life is thus brought into the light of the divine redemption. The icon is only one small example of how a material reality can be "transfigured" as Jesus's own flesh was on Thabor, so that it passes from mere materiality into being a vehicle of divine grace and presence. The very world in John's view was a sacrament of the glory of God, but nowhere was this more wonderfully so than in the heart of men and women, who were the dynamic and living images (icons) of God.

John's poetry represented how centrally the idea of the "dynamic transference" of the incarnation had come to stand at the heart of Byzantine spirituality; in other words, how the incarnation of God as a man was taken to be a paradigm of how, through the church's sacramental and mystical life, humanity itself was transfigured into divine presence. Athanasius the theologian had described this succinctly in the fourth century when he said in his treatise *De incarnatione* "[The Word] became man that we might become god," but John's work shows how deeply this axiom had been taken to heart. The Byzantine doctrine of *theosis* (deification by grace) runs throughout all his rhapsodic songs on the mercy of the incarnation.

Maximus the Confessor

Maximus was one of the most important Byzantine theologians of the seventh century. He was a masterful synthesizer, who once more combined all the traditional elements of the Syro-Byzantine theology of prayer that had gone before him with the theological orthodoxy of his day, which had passed through many fires of controversies from the fifth to the seventh centuries. Much of his insight is drawn from his three greatest theological heroes: Origen of Alexandria, Gregory of Nazianzus, and Pseudo-Dionysius the Areopagite. By the seventh century, all three were looked on as either theologically dubious, profoundly obscure, or both. Maximus set himself the task of weaving them together, explaining the difficulties, and, above all, bringing out the common values of all three thinkers, all of whom believed passionately that the highest vision of the mind as it approached God was synonymous with mystical vision that transcended rational thought and entered a higher state of knowing (*gnosis*).

Maximus was an aristocrat in the service of the emperor Heraclius. In 614 he abandoned his career and entered the monastic life at Chrysopolis, near Constantinople. The disruptions caused by the Persian war (626) caused him to move to Crete, Cyprus, and finally North Africa. In the middle of the seventh century, while he was resident in a Greek monastery at Carthage, he was drawn into a controversy that had risen over the interpretation of Christology. In order to resolve a long-running dispute between the Chalcedonian and non-Chalcedonian parts of the Eastern church (the so-called Monophysite dispute), the emperors had supported a compromise view that sidestepped the two-nature theology of the Council of Chalcedon (451) and instead described Jesus as divine-Man possessed of a single divine will. This unicity of psychological subject in Jesus, it was thought, could account for the singularity of Jesus's divine power and presence in the incarnate state far better than Chalcedon's clumsy creed, and also serve as the basis for an ecumenical reunion between the churches. This position was known as Monothelitism (one-will) and it was opposed by the Dyothelite party which taught there were two wills in Christ, one human and one divine, each corresponding to the two natures (human and divine), and each presiding over what was proper to its own remit. Maximus regarded the Monothelite position not only as a betrayal of Chalcedon in the (forlorn) hope of reconciling the Monophysites, but also as a dangerous heresy that implicitly evoked a less than fully human Savior, a Christ who was not possessed of a true human will. For Maximus, Monothelitism was a vision of the Savior's humanity that verged on the mechanical. His many works attacked the Monothelite Christology, advancing a powerful doctrine of the freedom of the human person which is assured by the incarnation of Christ. As he argued, if Christ lost his will to the approach of the divine person in the incarnation, then how could he be a model of the freedom which God offers to humanity? If Christ could not sustain a truly human life because of the "burden" of the divinity, what was the point of God making humans free at all? On the contrary, Maximus argued, human freedom is one of the most divine qualities God gave to the human race. Christ was not only consummately free as God, he also showed human beings the example of a man who was sublimely free, in his own psychic, emotional, and moral life. Both in his divinity and his humanity Christ, therefore, becomes a pattern for the church to follow.

Maximus' resounding words on the spiritual excellence of personal freedom had political repercussions, of course. For his defiance of the emperor, he was summoned to trial in 658 and again in 661. Tradition has it that his tongue and his right hand were cut off for his "impudence." He died soon afterwards from his wounds. This is why he was posthumously given the title "Confessor." In Maximus, high theology becomes merged with the deepest principles of spirituality and with the search for active motives for the moral and ascetic life. For him, all three find their resolution in the concept of the mystery of Christ, the God-Man. The incarnation, seen as the high point of all human history, is the dynamic method and means of the deification of the human race: a spiritual re-creation of human nature that allows individuals the freedom needed to practice virtue, since all humans were formerly enslaved by passions. Even in his most controversial theologizing, Maximus never fails to stress the essence of theology as being a mystical vision of the Christian life as an ever-deepening communion with God. Theological doctrines are simply the coded instructions of the mystical life, as far as he is concerned. His ascetical writings (*The Ascetic Life* and the *Chapters on Charity*) and his theological commentaries on difficult subjects (*The Ambigua, Questions to Thalassius*) are deep works of reflective speculation that have increasingly attracted attention in recent decades. His liturgical studies (*Mystagogia* and *Commentary on the Our Father*) show Maximus as a powerful intellectual who is also capable of writing lyrically on prayer.

Isaac the Syrian

Another highly significant writer who influenced and shaped Byzantine spirituality for centuries to come was the Syriac-speaking theologian Isaac of Nineveh. Isaac was a monk of the Chaldaean church from Beit Quatraye, possibly Qatar on the Persian Gulf. He was appointed bishop of Nineveh sometime before 680, but after a few months in the position resigned his charge and returned to the solitary life of a hermit. He is said to have become blind in later life from his scholarly labors. His spiritual authority and the beauty of his writings on prayer and mystical experience made his works cherished by both the rival Monophysite and Nestorian factions of the Persian church of his time. In the ninth century they were translated from the Syriac into Greek and Arabic versions, and came to Byzantium shortly after, where they had a great impact on the developing "Hesychastic" spiritual theology of the eleventh century and after.

Isaac was universally recognized by all the monks, of all parts of the Eastern church, as a master of spirituality who knew what he was talking about from personal experience. He himself stood within the age-old tradition of the Syriac spirituality "of the heart" which can be witnessed in most Syrian spiritual writers from the earliest times (such as Aphrahat, or Pseudo-Macarius of the fourth century). Like them, Isaac lays great stress on the sensibility of the grace of God in the heart. It is necessary, he teaches, to be able to feel the operations of the Holy Spirit, and to be able to discern them, if one is to grow in spiritual wisdom and mystical perception. For this, the advice of a wise spiritual guide is profoundly necessary. Much of later Byzantine spiritual writing will ever afterwards continue this emphasis on the need for a spiritual guide if one is serious about a life of prayer. Isaac writes as such a teacher and guide to a community of disciples who are all based in the monastic life. Most of his sermons and spiritual homilies presume this audience of experienced monastics. Isaac is one of the most mature and gentle authors on the spiritual life from Christian antiquity. In recent years, lost works have been rediscovered, and by virtue of new English translations he is once again becoming known as one of the great minds of early Christian spirituality.

Valuable as his works were in themselves, they took on an even greater significance when they were translated into Greek and disseminated as basic works of reference among the Byzantine monasteries of the Middle Ages. The pneumatology and spiritual affectivity that can be witnessed in Isaac became a leading characteristic of later Byzantine thought, and were responsible for a revival of monastic spirituality that later would become known as Hesychasm. In this early movement (it can be witnessed in Symeon the New Theologian, for example), the call for men and women to experience for themselves the charismatic workings of the Holy Spirit within the individual heart became a great rallying cry for the church to stand against the "dead hand" effects of official religiosity and bourgeois piety.

The Middle Byzantine Revival (CE 1000–1200)

The earliest form of the Hesychastic revival in spirituality corresponds with the rising fortunes of the Byzantine empire itself. Throughout its own "Dark Ages," the empire had been suffering centuries of decline and shrinkage before the advance of Islamic power. In the middle of the tenth century a series of vigorous emperors began to turn the tide, and reassert the power and independence of the Byzantine state and culture. Missions were undertaken in Bulgaria and Ukraine (ancient Rus) to great effect, and the Byzantine spiritual traditions were adopted in those countries along with the Eastern forms of liturgy. All of this soon became a common *lingua franca* of spirituality throughout the Greek and Slavic peoples.

Byzantine hagiographies

The Middle Byzantine period also saw a movement to popularize forms of devotion by means of saints' lives. These hagiographies, as they were called, were generally based upon much older patterns of saints' lives such as had been composed in the fourth and fifth centuries, celebrating the exploits of the desert fathers and mothers. A classic example of such was the *Life of Antony* by Athanasius of Alexandria. Others, such as the fifth-century Syrian bishop Theodoret, had written up the exploits of the great ascetics and pillar dwellers (*stylites*), and this type of literature had found an avid readership in the cities of the empire, such as Constantinople and Alexandria, from an early date. In the later Byzantine period, the lives of saints, as a genre, had continued to be popular but was constantly evolving. As the empire had shrunk in size from its earlier days, so its ideas of sanctity had become more domesticated, as it were. The great saints of the past were still regarded as having set the standard, but the Middle Era Byzantine saints were much more "local." Sanctity had taken on a small-town aspect, where the local folk expected their holy man (it was a predominantly male-oriented genre, though there are several lives of holy women) to be their speaker before God, their advocate, absolver, and healer. The form of "canonization" in the Eastern church demanded certain basic elements: a reputation for holiness, the demonstration of living and posthumous miracles (at the tomb of the saint), an incorrupt body (ideally) or at least a tomb cared for by monastics that could serve as a pilgrimage site, and, lastly, a formal *Vita* which could be read out to the pilgrims and used in the festal celebration of the new saint. Some of the later hagiographies show signs that they were being consciously used to correct social injustices. This is why (as in the *Life of St Mary the Younger* d. c.903) sometimes the heroine is a married woman (normally monastics or bishops are the main subjects of canonization). In the case of Mary the Younger she was a victim of domestic violence. The *Life* points out in no uncertain terms how her husband's boorish behavior (which was common in antiquity) was despicable and contrary to a Christian life, as well as being the occasion of Mary's "martyrdom." By means of the hagiography, her example of domestic prayer and charitable living was advocated as a common standard for all, and her canonization was advanced on the "extraordinary" grounds of her martyrdom in the act of Christian witness (she was beaten to death by her husband for giving away family wealth). As in the early days, the hagiographies were extraordinary literature, and read to us moderns in the style of lurid cartoons. Nevertheless, by means of this popular genre – religious romances, as it were – the ideas of monastic prayer and devotion were given a wide and popular audience in the Byzantine world. Monasticism always, and partly as a result of this, remained close to the hearts of the people in the Eastern church. The monks and nuns were regularly visited as spiritual confessors, in parallel to the ordinary clergy of the cities. This ensured that monastic spirituality predominated in the Byzantine world, whether in the monasteries or without. This is a characteristic of the Eastern church even to this day.

Symeon the New Theologian

One of those who passed with surprising speed from the secular sphere to the monastic life was Symeon the New Theologian (949–1022). He had begun life as an attendant at the imperial court, possibly as a courtier eunuch, as was common in those times, even among aristocrats such as Symeon. He describes himself in his writings as having led a dissolute life, but having been guided by a wise old monk, named Symeon Eulabes from the Stoudite monastery in Constantinople. The old man advised him to say some prayers regularly each night, and in the course of saying them he described how a remarkable visionary experience happened to him, such that he only came back to his senses as day dawned, and he realized he had spent the entire night in ecstasy. He described how he had seen a radiant light suffuse his room as he prayed. As his eyes grew accustomed to it, he realized that this great light was his spiritual father Symeon, who was engaged in the act of interceding for him before an even greater light (Christ), whom he had not been able to see at first. Through this experience he came to understand that he stood within a great chain of God's mercy, wrapped in the light of the divine presence which dissolved all sin, but was mediated only to open and repentant hearts, and normally only through the mediation of one disciple to another.

His political career suffered several traumatic shocks at this time, and he had to take refuge with the old monk, eventually deciding to renounce his political aspirations permanently in 976 when he had taken refuge once more in a monastery and had experienced another vision of Christ as Light. Symeon adopted the same monastic name as his spiritual father, and within three years was head of his own monastery. His spiritual doctrine stressed elements of the old Syrian tradition of Isaac of Nineveh, and he preached it to many of his community who had been monks for many years before him. His whole life and doctrine proved immensely controversial, and in the end he was exiled from Constantinople by the emperor and the patriarchal court. Even from exile he continued to write poems and discourses on the spiritual life. One collection of hymns, which he wrote for his new monastic foundation in exile (*The Hymns of Divine Love*), is among the most remarkable examples of all mystical literature. It celebrates Christ the Light in the style of love poetry. There is a most personal sense of the presence of God, quite different from all that is found in antique literature.

In many respects, Symeon anticipates the new sense of mystical closeness with Jesus that is seen more and more in the Middle Ages. All his writing denies that mystical union with God is exclusively reserved for the canonized saint of the hagiography, or reserved to the unusual times of life, but is rather like air and water for a living creature, the substantial meaning of all existence. For Symeon, the highest degree of mystical union comes about when the soul is deeply conscious of its sinfulness and its need. His writings were kept in manuscripts on Mount Athos and became the favored reading of many monks there. The passionate Jesus-centered devotion of Symeon made it seem to many Athonite monks in the fourteenth century that they, in their turn, had found a spiritual guide who had anticipated their Hesychastic revival, and anticipated them in stressing the elements of light-filled transfiguration and deeply personal affectivity as keys to spiritual renewal.

The Hesychastic Revival (CE 1300–1500)

Hesychasm was one of the last great movements to determine the ultimate shape of Byzantine spirituality. It too occurred at a time when the affairs of the empire were experiencing a veritable revival in all forms of politics, art, and culture, in the so-called Palaeologan renaissance. The word derives from *hesychia* which means "stillness," but it was also a synonym at that time for a form of monastic life lived in retirement (the two things seem synonymous today but in Byzantium many monks lived in the busy cities working as civil servants).

Hesychasm began on Mount Athos, the colony of hermitages and communities on the Halkidiki peninsula in Greece, which is still occupied today by many monasteries. Here there was a spiritual renewal movement that called out for monastics to return to their primary focus in recollected lives of prayer. The writers claim that in their time the spiritual life of the monasteries was dominated by oral prayers extensively repeated and that little was known about interior recollection of spirit. Several of the leading monks on Athos, especially Gregory of Sinai (1258–1346) and Gregory Palamas (1296–1359), had advocated methods of psychic focus such as the "Jesus Prayer" (the slow repetition of the simple phrase: "Lord Jesus Christ Son of God have mercy on me"), as well as a spirituality centered around the idea of being "transfigured" by the divine light of deification (using the symbol of Jesus's radiance on Mount Thabor) and methods of quietening the heart and imagining the heart as the center of the psychic "vision" of God.

These trends were in no way "new" to Eastern Christian spiritual thought, but once again the Byzantine tradition showed a genius for renewal by returning to old sources and making a new synthesis from them. The Egyptian monastic tradition, associated with Evagrius of Pontus, had long taught that in order to see and hear God, who is beyond all thought and all imagery, the mind has to become still and void of images. The Syrian monastic tradition, as we have seen, taught that the presence of God had to be experientially felt in the heart of the believer, with a passionate devotion. God would only dwell in a warm and devoted heart, and when the indwelling occurred, the eyes of the heart would be able to see and feel the presence.

Both streams of monastic spirituality were powerfully brought together in the Hesychastic school, which really served as a powerful renewal movement in the late Byzantine church. In returning to its spiritual sources, this movement within monasticism began a series of deeper theological controversies. It was happening at a similar time to the Western renaissance in scholastic theology. Many Byzantines were impressed by Western forms of theological analysis that had been based on the authority of Aristotle. To the Aristotelians in theological circles, a strict division had to be preserved between the uncreated and the created orders of existence. When the Hesychast theologians claimed that the vision of God was possible with the very eyes of the soul and heart, they were ridiculed by theologians who thought that they were more sophisticated, and pointed out to the monks that if the eyes of a creature saw God, it could only be a manifestation of God which was not actually God, since the deity transcended all material forms. The Hesychasts refused to allow the syllogism to stand. While God was transcendent, they argued back, the gift of a direct and authentic perception of the divine had indeed been given as a possibility to the soul of the mystic. The vision of God was a direct encounter between the energies of God (divine in themselves) and the human soul, and this encounter was the ultimate destiny of the human race (as symbolized in the moment of perfection represented in the incarnation). To deny that a real and direct encounter, or vision, was possible between God and a human being was, for the Hesychasts, a major dereliction of the Christian faith in redemption. Battle lines were soon drawn up between the Hesychasts and their opponents, and this is why we have such knowledge of the Hesychastic school. In the end, they triumphed over their adversaries, and their theology – that a veritable vision of God was a call for the whole church, and neither impossible nor reserved for a few extraordinary souls – was endorsed as the official doctrine of the Greek Orthodox Church.

After the Collapse: Byzantino-Slavic Spirituality (CE 1500–1700)

By the fourteenth century, when Gregory Palamas was issuing a last magnificent flourish of spiritual theology and advocating the Hesychastic synthesis of the themes of luminous vision, quietness of heart, and the awareness of the presence of the Spirit within the heart, the ancient Byzantine empire was drawing toward its tragic end. In May of 1453 the Ottoman armies of Mehmet II blasted through the walls of Constantinople and the last of the Roman emperors died defending his city. After that date, the Christians of the ancient Eastern provinces of Rome experienced the status of a subjugated nation (*Milet*), and although they were allowed to retain some of their churches, for payment of a tax, the oppression was experienced as a bitter one, a yoke under which the church groaned. Christianity was not allowed to evangelize openly, or proclaim its faith except under the most strictly controlled conditions. In this environment, Christian culture became an act of resistance, and at the center of the nexus of all Christian organization in the East there stood the monastery. The monastic communities were the lighthouses of culture and spirituality, and the centers for the teaching and transmission of the faith. In the aftermath of the collapse of Byzantium, the Russian Tsars assumed the fallen mantle of leadership of the Christian peoples, and the wider commonwealth of Byzantine cultures endured, even when it was under the rule of the Ottomans. In many instances, the Ottoman Sultans appointed Greek Christian rulers (*Voivodes*) over Christian peoples in their control, such as the Romanians. Monasteries in the Balkans and the Slavic lands, and also on Mount Athos, which had negotiated its continuing independence, continued to serve as Christian centers of learning. Most of what was produced, at least in the theological domain, were editions of past works. In the course of this time a great collection was begun of all the monastic writings from the past which favored and illuminated Hesychastic principles of spirituality. It was the brainchild of two Athonite monks, Makarios of Corinth and Nicodemus the Hagiorite, and was meant to be a library of spiritual reading. They called their collection the *Philokalia* (*For Those who Love Beautiful Things*) and it contained the ancient classics from such as Evagrius and Dorotheos of Gaza, but also ranged into medieval sources such as Symeon and the two Gregorys ("of Sinai" and "Palamas"). The *Philokalia* was a veritable reference library for Hesychasts, and in one collection (of several volumes) it provided Orthodox monasteries with a picture of the whole spiritual tradition.

The issuing of the *Philokalia* became an impetus that lit the fire of enthusiasm once again, and its fame spread through all the subjugated Byzantine commonwealth. For the first time, Hesychasm started to become a "standard" of Byzantine spirituality, and whole monasteries began to adopt it as the guide to all their spiritual practices. In Romania and Russia the monastic St Paisy Velichovsky circulated the *Philokalia* in a

Slavonic edition and it grew to have an immense influence also on Orthodoxy outside Greece. From the eighteenth century to the present, this Philokalic renewal has set the tone of Orthodox spiritual reflection and practice, often with the Jesus Prayer being the outward practical sign of the whole inner philosophy. In recent times, as Eastern Christian spirituality has become more available in the form of written descriptions and commentaries, the practice of the Jesus Prayer, obedience to spiritual elders, and study of the *Philokalia* have increasingly come to mark the spiritual life of many Orthodox lay people. Texts such as *The Way of the Pilgrim* (written in the nineteenth century by a Russian monk, though alleging to be the record of a Russian peasant who dedicates himself to Hesychastic spirituality) have also brought the tradition of quietness and heart-centered concentration to the attention of a large readership in the West.

References

Brown, P. 1988: *The Body and Society: Men, Women, and Sexual Renunciation in Early Christianity.* New York: Columbia University Press.

Browning, R. 1980: *The Byzantine Empire.* New York: Scribner.

Bryer, A. and Cunningham, M. 1996: *Mount Athos and Byzantine Monasticism.* Aldershot: Variorum.

——and Herrin, J. 1977: *Iconoclasm.* Birmingham: University of Birmingham, Centre for Byzantine Studies.

Bulgakov, S. 1988: *The Orthodox Church.* Crestwood, NY: St Vladimir's Seminary Press.

Chitty, D. 1966: *The Desert a City: An Introduction to the Study of Egyptian and Palestinian Monasticism under the Christian Empire.* Oxford: Blackwell.

Clément, O. 1995: *The Roots of Christian Mysticism.* London: New City.

Constantelos, D. 1968: *Byzantine Philanthropy and Social Welfare.* New Brunswick, NJ: Rutgers University Press.

Cyril of Scythopolis 1990: *Lives of the Monks of Palestine*, trans. R. M. Price. Kalamazoo, MI: Cistercian Publications.

Daley, B. (trans.) 1998: *On the Dormition of Mary.* Crestwood, NY: St Vladimir's Seminary Press.

Dawes, E. and Baynes, N. 1977: *Three Byzantine Saints.* London: Mowbrays.

Frend, W. H. C. 1972: *The Rise of the Monophysite Movement.* Cambridge: Cambridge University Press.

Geanakoplos, D. J. 1984: *Byzantium: Church, Society, and Civilization through Contemporary Eyes.* Chicago: University of Chicago Press.

Gregory of Nazianzus 2000: *The Theological Poetry*, trans. P. Gilbert. Crestwood, NY: St Vladimir's Seminary Press.

Gregory Palamas 1983: *The Triads*, trans. N. Gendle. New York: Paulist Press.

Hackel, S. (ed.) 1981: *The Byzantine Saint.* London: Fellowship of St Alban and St Sergius.

Hussey, J. M. 1986: *The Orthodox Church in the Byzantine Empire.* Oxford: Clarendon Press.

Kadloubovsky, E. and Palmer, G. (trans.) 1992: *Writings from the Philokalia on Prayer of the Heart.* London: Faber and Faber.

Kazhdan, A. P. (ed.) 1991: *The Oxford Dictionary of Byzantium*, 3 vols. Oxford: Oxford University Press.

Lossky, V. 1957: *The Mystical Theology of the Eastern Church.* London: J. Clarke.

——1975: *In the Image and Likeness of God.* London: Mowbrays.

Louth, A. 1981: *The Origins of the Christian Mystical Tradition: From Plato to Denys*. Oxford: Oxford University Press.

McGuckin, J. A. 1994: *St Cyril of Alexandria and the Christological Controversy*. Leiden: E. J. Brill.

——2001a: *St Gregory of Nazianzus: An Intellectual Biography*. Crestwood, NY: St Vladimir's Seminary Press.

——2001b: *Standing in God's Holy Fire: The Byzantine Tradition*. London: Darton, Longman, and Todd.

——2003: The legacy of the thirteenth apostle: origins of the Eastern Christian conceptions of church–state relation. *St Vladimir's Theological Quarterly* 47, 251–88.

Maguire, H. 1995: *Byzantine Magic*. Washington, DC: Dumbarton Oaks Research Library and Collection.

Mango, C. 1976: *Byzantine Architecture*. New York: H. N. Abrams.

——1980: *Byzantium: The Empire of the New Rome*. London: Weidenfeld and Nicolson.

——1984: *Byzantium and its Image*. London: Variorum.

——1986: *The Art of the Byzantine Empire 312–1453*. Toronto: University of Toronto Press.

——(ed.) 2002: *The Oxford History of Byzantium*. Oxford: Oxford University Press.

Meyendorff, J. 1975: *Byzantine Theology*. New York: Fordham University Press.

——1989: *Imperial Unity and Christian Divisions: The Church 450–680*. Crestwood, NY: St Vladimir's Seminary Press.

Nichol, D. M. 1994: *The Byzantine Lady: Ten Portraits 1250–1500*. Cambridge: Cambridge University Press.

Nichols, A. 1993: *Byzantine Gospel: Maximus the Confessor in Modern Scholarship*. Edinburgh: T. and T. Clark.

Ostrogorsky, G. 1980: *History of the Byzantine State*. Oxford: Oxford University Press.

Ouspensky, L. 1992: *Theology of the Icon*, 2 vols. Crestwood, NY: St Vladimir's Seminary Press.

Palmer, G., Sherrard, P., and Ware, K. (trans.) 1995: *The Philokalia*, 4 vols. London: Faber and Faber.

Pelikan, J. 1977: *The Christian Tradition: A History of the Development of Doctrine*, vol. 2: *The Spirit of Eastern Christendom: 600–1700*. Chicago: University of Chicago Press.

Quasten, J. 1975: *Patrology*, vol. 3: *The Golden Age of Greek Patristic Literature: From the Council of Nicaea to Chalcedon 451*. Utrecht: Spectrum.

Rodley, L. 1994: *Byzantine Art and Architecture: An Introduction*. Cambridge: Cambridge University Press.

Romanos Melodos 1995: *On the Life of Christ: Kontakia*, trans. E. Lash. San Francisco: HarperCollins.

Runciman, S. 1990: *Byzantine Style and Civilisation*. Harmondsworth: Penguin.

Sharf, A. 1991: *Byzantine Jewry from Justinian to the Fourth Crusade*. London: Routledge and Kegan Paul.

Slaatte, H. A. 1980: *The Seven Ecumenical Councils*. Lanham, MD: University Press of America.

Smith, W. and Wace, H. (eds) 1887–8: *Dictionary of Christian Biography*, 4 vols. London: John Murray.

Speake, G. (ed.) 2000: *The Encyclopedia of Greece and the Hellenic Tradition*, 2 vols. Chicago: Fitzroy Dearborn.

Spidlik, T. 1986: *The Spirituality of the Christian East*. Kalamazoo, MI: Cistercian Publications.

Symeon the New Theologian 1976: *The Hymns of Divine Love*, trans. G. Maloney. Denville, NJ: Dimension Books.

Talbot, A. M. 1996: *Holy Women of Byzantium: Ten Saints Lives in English*. Washington, DC: Dumbarton Oaks Research Library and Collection.

Thomas, J. and Hero, A. C. (eds) 2001: *Byzantine Monastic Foundation Documents: A Complete Translation of the Surviving Founders' Typika and Testaments*, 5 vols, trans. R. Allison et al. Washington, DC: Dumbarton Oaks Research Library and Collection.

Trypanis, C. (ed.) 1971: *The Penguin Book of Greek Verse*. Harmondsworth: Penguin.

Wybrew, H. 1989: *The Orthodox Liturgy: The Development of the Eucharistic Liturgy in the Byzantine Rite*. London: SPCK.

CHAPTER 6

Christian Spirituality in the Medieval West (600–1450)

Ulrike Wiethaus

The impact and character of a millennium of medieval spirituality will remain open to debate as long as new questions and perspectives arise in our own search for an authentic and committed religious life. No matter how one wishes to compute Western civilization's medieval inheritance, however, it is indisputable that the centuries between 600 and 1450 were decisive for the formation of much of Christian spirituality today. Spanning close to a thousand years, the medieval millennium witnessed the transformation of European tribal cultures into class-based societies, the unprecedented spread of religious literacy, the rise of the Roman Church as a multi-tiered and multinational institution, the phenomenal growth of monasticism, and the invention of a money economy that irreversibly changed all human relationships. Improved knowledge of African, Asian, and Middle Eastern cultures led to hard questions about the sacred origins and trajectory of human history and religious belief systems.

Given such complexity, even the rubric of "spirituality" is somewhat misleading for the span of time between the fall of the Roman empire and the rise of Italian city states, since medieval people preferred a different terminology. More uncompromising than many of their contemporary counterparts, medieval Christians sought after holiness, defined as purified lives lived in a radically critical distance from a world under siege by military conflicts, corruption, and decay. Our medieval ancestors were acutely aware of the vulnerability of life, the passing of time, the weight of history. Their efforts to live a life of Christian integrity often entailed either a determined return to apostolic beginnings or passionate preparations for the end of the world as much as for their own death. Their era, many felt, was worn out and grown old without much hope for regeneration. For Christians, then, the medieval millennium constituted the final, not the middle, ages. Concepts related to the term "spirituality," such as contemplation, devotion, mysticism, and asceticism all point to the same intense trajectory toward holiness, characterized by compassion for those who suffered as much as by committed teaching and preaching and experiences of visions and ecstasy.

More inclined than perhaps most of us today to sever secular ties, individuals as much as groups were determined to emulate exemplary holy women and men who had put their lives at risk in search of uncompromised virtue, penance, and prayer, whether in a community of like-minded seekers or in the hoped-for but rarely found solitude of a hermitage. Skeptical or merely more sanguine medieval Christians viewed holy people with some doubt. Suspicions of hypocrisy, or worse, heresy, devil worship, or mental illness could increase to such a degree that more reputable mystics could be asked to "test" the authenticity of claims to holiness. The letters of encouragement by the German visionary genius Hildegard of Bingen (1098–1187) to a younger, more insecure Benedictine nun, St Elisabeth of Schönau (c.1129–64) are an early example of such professional supervision. Yet even skeptical Christians engaged in religious practices that would strike us today as intensely spiritual. These included pilgrimages; emotionally extravagant praying sessions at shrines and less formal sites of holiness; the regular use of charms and incantations for protection, good health, and matters of the heart; the possession and circulation of prized relics; and encounters with a host of supernatural beings, whether benevolently, malevolently, or indifferently inclined toward humans. For the educated classes, whether religious or laity, the rigorous engagement with all dimensions of holiness generated devotional texts, architecture, art, music, and theological explorations conducted under the continuous threat of ecclesiastical censorship. Medieval spiritual culture remains challenging even today.

Environmental, political, and economic changes necessarily influenced the course of medieval spirituality as well, as did encounters with other cultures and religions through trade or warfare. Inescapable and unpredictable turns of history were met with a tremendous effort to keep faith with a respected past and to embrace innovations cautiously and with measured deliberation. Sacred narratives such as the life of Christ were examined closely to provide comfort and guidance through changing times.

With hardly any exception, the medieval remains from which we can reconstruct our view of Christian spirituality comprise artifacts and texts from the educated classes; the spiritual lives of the great majority of medieval Christians, impoverished and illiterate, thus remain silent in their depth and nuance. Besides sacred architecture, art, and music, our sources include liturgical rites that measured sacred time; genres of religious writing such as letters, poems, penitential codes, sermons, saints' lives, and the theological and pedagogical treatises composed by mystics and spiritual teachers. Although much has been lost to the ravages of time, the legacies of medieval spirituality have remained a vital part of contemporary Christianity. Orders founded in the medieval period still exist across continents; European sites and relics of saints and miracle workers still attract contemporary pilgrims in search of healing; chants and other liturgical music are performed for appreciative audiences; monastic buildings still host spiritual retreats; and mystical writings continue to be published in numerous world languages. High social regard for the contributions of medieval women mystics has persisted despite a consistently patriarchal theological tradition and leadership in the medieval church.

To appreciate the uniqueness of medieval devotion during these turbulent centuries, a few differences with contemporary spirituality must be pointed out, if only briefly. Medieval spirituality in the West developed in tandem with the expanding pastoral, administrative, and political reach of the Roman Church. Contemporary spirituality, in contrast, is much less dependent on institutional approval; spiritual Christians might even resent ecclesiastical interference and anything resembling censorship. Collective belonging in the strongest sense possible, rather than an individualistic journey of the spirit, was what counted most for medieval Christians; even hermits lived out their lives under the watchful eyes of a community. Supernatural realms were always described as densely populated, whether heaven, purgatory, or hell; even a dying saint was believed to be surrounded by crowds of angels and devils. The communal institution of monasticism formed the stable core of medieval spirituality, concentrating on the textual production and reproduction of spiritual ideals, fostering pilgrimage sites and the cult of relics, nurturing mystical impulses through liturgical routine and continuous community support, and amplifying creative spiritual insights through its exegetical and liturgical resources.

Medieval spirituality was generally public rather than private, and tied to a wider range of issues than the desire for personal growth, a modern Western concept that would not have made much sense to a medieval Christian. To be recognized in their role, holy women or men were expected to act as "living sermons," that is, to exteriorize mystical insights gained through visions and ecstasies in intentionally provocative public ways. One very typical example of medieval spiritual performativity is the story of St Francis (c.1181–1226) stripping naked in the marketplace of Assisi to express his desire for poverty. Another, less spectacular category of spiritual performance, however, the daily liturgical recitations of nuns and monks, could only be fully explored and developed by those freed from the labor demands of an agrarian, family-based economy, that is, the celibate religious class and the nobility – a very small elite indeed, who worked hidden from view of the public.

Most of what has remained of medieval spirituality derives from the disciplined and steady productivity of religious specialists. In the majority, these specialists were celibate men trained in the use of Latin and as a group accustomed to wielding unexamined patriarchal authority over illiterate and non-Latinate Christians. Whereas contemporary Christian spirituality tends to insist on democratic values such as equality and freedom of thought, full access to spiritual instruction for everyone, and non-hierarchical and non-discriminatory student–teacher relationships, medieval spirituality unfolded in a very different social environment, one shaped by deep divisions in social rank, gender status, and wealth, and with a concentration of power and knowledge in the hands of a few. Holiness was expressed and recognized through pastoral care of others, whether through preaching, spiritual direction, charitable acts, prophesying, or healing, but also through a disciplined life of prayer, consent and loyalty to ecclesiastical authority, asceticism, and the meticulous keeping of liturgical hours. Unlike today, only a few medieval authors were able to articulate a critique of religious anti-Judaism, sexism, and homophobia, and the violence endorsed in crusades and the persecution of heretics.

It is also necessary to grasp how deeply medieval anthropological and cosmological views differed from contemporary definitions. Once recognized as fully human (this category was frequently up for debate in regard to peasants, slaves, foreigners, Jews, and women), a person was generally defined as a spirit being who, unlike ghosts and angels, inhabited a body with an entirely separate and distinct will. The soul would enter into this semi-autonomous "body being" at some point during a pregnancy, leave it intermittently during sleep or states of altered consciousness, and abandon it permanently at death. The body would, however, absorb the holiness of a perceived saint much like a sponge and preserve some of it as a form of energy even after the soul's departure – hence the healing power of a saint's relics and grave site.

It was believed that the souls of good Christians would be given a second, eternally incorruptible body entity at the end of time. The soul possessed sense organs much like the body itself, enjoyed its own mobility, and could experience supernatural scents, colors, and sounds. The seat of human intelligence and insight was not the brain, but the heart. It was believed that other major organs carried out psychological and cognitive tasks as well; blood in particular was regarded as a potent substance that could be put to manifold spiritual and magical uses. The paramount medieval example of a belief in the efficacy of blood is Eucharistic piety, which also triggered, in a parallel psycho-social development, the paranoid fear of a Jewish need for Christian blood.

For many mystics, heaven, purgatory, and hell could be visited with greater ease than neighboring countries. From the eighth-century Anglo-Saxon historian Bede the Venerable to the early fourteenth-century Italian poet Dante Alighieri, descriptions of otherworldly journeys peppered the spiritual maps of medieval Christians. As in other areas of religious belief, European Christianity incorporated and in the process transformed Old Norse, Celtic, and Germanic traditions of visionary journeys to the land of the dead and the hidden world of spirit beings. Perhaps because so much change was beyond the control of individuals, the flow of time was perceived with some ambivalence. The conditions and contexts of spiritual experiences were fashioned by communities who resisted fast-paced change rather than embraced novelty. One time-stabilizing spiritual habit was the celebration of the predictable cycles of ancient festivals and holidays that syncopated day and night, the flow of seasons and of human life. Even life was defined by its most predictable aspect: from its inception, it would be shaped by the desire for a good death.

The following survey divides the medieval search for a holy life into three developmental phases. Aspects of each stage naturally continued in subsequent centuries, thus adding ever more complexity and depth. Risking the danger of oversimplification, early medieval spirituality (sixth through eleventh centuries) may be characterized by a gradual European synthesis of indigenous religious practices and Roman administrative structures. Emblematic of the second phase of medieval spirituality (eleventh through thirteenth centuries) is the extraordinary proliferation of literacy, the far-reaching circulation and reproduction of texts by renowned authors and their pious imitators, and the growing popularity of textually based spiritual practices. If mystical knowledge should only be taught to those who were carefully prepared and supervised, as was the concern of many medieval Christians, would widespread religious literacy not cause more harm than good? The much-criticized heresy trials and inquisitorial procedures, violent and politically motivated as they often were, nonetheless also expressed a distinctly medieval anxiety to preserve and to protect the integrity of esteemed traditions and teachings. Eventually, the increasing dependency on texts resulted in spiritual lives measured against textually fixed rules and ideas rather than the needs of the moment. A canon of devotional manuals gradually absorbed and replaced oral traditions and discarded works deemed too audacious; the tightly cir- cumscribed act of reading became the most common and acceptable contemplative practice, and special books were designed to facilitate this type of meditation. Perhaps not surprisingly, supernatural phenomena – all rooted in the body and sensory experi- ences – became associated more with the uneducated than the educated classes, and more so with women than with men.

The late medieval period (mid-thirteenth through early fifteenth centuries), cali- brated by devastating epidemics and climatic changes, witnessed the rise of popular spiritual movements, often led by charismatic teachers, both male and female, who openly voiced criticism of institutionalized religion. Rightly or wrongly, numerous medieval Christians felt betrayed and abandoned by religious institutions in their strug- gle to cope with the horrors of the plague, of famines, and of seemingly endless polit- ical strife inside and outside the church. In an effort to preserve Christian unity, we find the ecclesiastical repression of nonconformist religious views and an even greater rejec- tion of mystical experiences, which could include prophetic criticism of the church hierarchy, as hallucinations and the devil's deception. The thirteenth century marks another medieval legacy barely recognized for its roots, the social attitudes learned during what some scholars have described as the formation of a persecuting society (Moore 1987): an intensification of anti-Judaism and the increasingly forceful rejec- tion of marginal social groups, whether lepers, prostitutes, or homosexual men and women. European Jewish communities thus became the first victims of crusading militias on their way to Jerusalem, their violence fuelled by sermons and military propaganda.

Early Medieval Spirituality (Sixth to Eleventh Centuries): Indigenous Traditions, Biblical Teachings, and Roman Administrative Skill

Perhaps surprisingly so, the early medieval period struggled with some of the same issues confronting us today. Medieval responses thus offer opportunities for reflection and fresh insight. European forebears from the sixth to the eleventh centuries had to resolve the challenge of their particular version of multiculturalism and the resulting "cultural seepage" (Wood 2001) of diverse if not contradictory spiritual traditions. Two equally formidable religious and cultural trajectories gradually fused to create stability and a certain measure of comfort during the tumultuous beginnings of a common European identity: the adaptation of Roman administrative structures by the Roman Church and by European secular rulers, on the one hand, and the steady flow of indige- nous practices into Christian spirituality, on the other. Both legacies, so radically dif- ferent from each other but yet in the end complementary in productive and fascinating ways, culminated in the creation of an enduring and still-evolving style of communal living devoted to spiritual excellence, Western monasticism, and an institution that grew to span the globe, the Roman Catholic Church.

Despite popular images of heroic missionaries facing down blood-thirsty heathens, Christianity in many cases spread gradually and without much resistance along trading routes and through the quotidian encounters and exchanges made possible by the expanse of the Roman empire and the mobility of indigenous European peoples. If indigenous military leaders aspired to rise to prominence within the boundaries of the former Roman empire, they would more often than not choose pragmatically to convert together with their tribes as part of acquiring the "Roman prestige package." Marrying a Christian woman could also prove advantageous if she would not insist too strongly on a monogamous relationship. Notable exceptions to this conversion pattern were the culturally separatist Vikings, Mongols, and Saxons, who still suffer from the false perception of having been more "savage" and ruthless than their Christianized neighboring tribes. The rule of cultural and spiritual pragmatism would also work in reverse: if a Christian military leader such as Charlemagne (742–814) wished to legitimize the invasion and conquest of non-Christian or "heretical" European tribal groups, he could ride under the banner of a Christian missionary mandate. This, too, is a legacy of the medieval millennium that extends into the present.

For better or worse, Christendom adopted Latin as its official language, as well as an ecclesiastical structure and even church architecture modeled after Roman patterns. These organizational features replaced or fused with local systems; their implementation, however, always depended upon the cooperation of local ruling elites. Although some indigenous European societies before the spread of Christianity appear to have supported a separate class of priests and/or priestesses and to have constructed distinctive religious buildings, others did not. In either case, the challenges to building a long-term institutional presence in foreign cultures were extraordinary. Nothing less than a gradual transformation of host cultures would suffice.

Two religious leaders of sixth-century Italy epitomize the organizational and multi-cultural genius of early medieval spirituality: St Benedict of Nursia (480–555/60), the founding father of Benedictine monasticism and mysticism, and Pope St Gregory the Great (c.540–604), a prolific author and admirably gifted administrator and pastoral counselor. St Gregory's social pedigree was significantly more prominent than Benedict's, whose limited education and "simplicity" were noted early on. Both men, however, were able to integrate Roman and local traditions and laid the groundwork for the growth of a commonly shared medieval spirituality.

Although many religious leaders before and after St Benedict contributed to monasticism, nobody proved to have greater influence than St Benedict. He left us a monastic institution that shaped European art and religion, education, and society. His profoundly humanistic rule of monastic conduct – demanding nothing too harsh, nothing too burdensome – still functions as a spiritual guide and inspiration today. Our only source for his life is found in an influential collection of hagiographies by St Gregory the Great, called *Dialogues*. St Gregory tells us that, after a long period of struggle to find a lifestyle wholly dedicated to the divine, St Benedict finally created a synthesis of previous monastic and eremitical traditions and rules that appealed through its common sense, balance, and humanity. It took some time to find a congenial group of supporters. According to St Gregory, disgruntled monks made at least two attempts to murder St Benedict.

The prologue to the rule likens the monastery to a school in which men can train to become warriors for the gain of eternal life. "This message of mine is for you, then," St Benedict wrote, "if you are ready to give up your own will, once and for all, and armed with the strong and noble weapons of obedience to do battle for the true King, Christ the Lord" (1998: 3). The core of St Benedict's teachings is contained in the famous "Twelve Steps of Humility" in the seventh chapter of the rule. Geared toward the harmonious cooperation of the monastic community and the liberation of the human spirit from the infantilizing push and pull of human "sins and vices" (1998: 17), the twelve steps of humility paradoxically invert the image of a fierce warrior in stressing absolute mastery over the self and its passions. The steps include fear of God, doing God's will at all times, obeying the abbot (as long as the abbot fulfills his responsibilities), patient endurance of suffering, regular confession, ungrudging acceptance of menial work, regarding oneself as lesser than all other monks, following the rule with attentiveness, embracing silence, avoiding laughter, and speaking only with gentleness; in short, conducting oneself with humility at all times.

St Gregory also recounted the life of St Scholastica, St Benedict's sister and a member of a community of pious women who lived close to St Benedict's monastery. It is likely that St Benedict and his monks administered to the spiritual needs of the women according to the values of the Benedictine rule. To stress her extraordinary holiness, St Gregory describes numerous miraculous events surrounding Scholastica's person. These accounts are significant for two reasons: the inclusion of St Scholastica's biography, no matter how apocryphal it may be, affirms the importance of a feminine branch of Benedictine monasticism from its beginnings, even though women are not mentioned in the rule itself. Secondly, her hagiography preserves elements of an indigenous pattern of female sanctity not found in the Christian Bible. St Scholastica leads a spiritual community of women; she can foresee the future and influence the weather through her prayers – all characteristics of indigenous priestesses and seers.

Extraordinary lives do not tell us much about the daily spiritual practices of ordinary Christian women, but we know from penitential manuals that charms and magical formulas were widely used to help in matters of fertility and childbirth, illness, and love. Other textual records of women saints from the time period stress leadership skills and noble women's traditional roles as peacemakers and mothers to the people. A paradigmatic holy woman of this type is St Radegund (c.525–87), the Thuringian-Frankish "queen saint" who left a polygamous marriage and founded a royal monastery at Poitiers, which became richly endowed and known for its support of the arts and education. Educated and strong-willed, St Radegund has also been celebrated as a severe ascetic, healer, and miracle worker, and is still revered as the patron saint of Poitiers. Other encloistered holy women of the early medieval period are the famous leader of a double monastery at Whitby, St Hilda (614–80), and the remarkable women in the circle of St Boniface (680–754), such as the writer Hugeburc of Heidenheim, and the abbesses Leoba and St Walburga.

"Family values" seems to epitomize gendered spirituality for many Christians today, but the historical truth is that early medieval Christianity proved to be disruptive if not harmful to indigenous (and indeed biblical) family structures organized around clan solidarity and polygamy. Among the noble class, the insistence on Christian monogamy made infertile or otherwise undesirable wives more vulnerable to male violence, even murder, undermined the social status and thus security of concubines and second or third wives and their offspring, and blocked polygamy as a peaceful means of building a network of alliances among potential enemies. Widows, female slaves, orphans, and captives could not be integrated into an extended family network through marriage and thus became even more marginalized in early medieval warrior societies. The founding of monasteries as a haven for unmarriageable or unwanted women thus was a dire social necessity. It sometimes proved to be an opportunity for exercising female independence and education if freely chosen or willingly embraced, but not all women placed into a monastery went willingly. Noble families worked hard to keep their connections to cloistered kin alive and adapted monastic houses to their own needs as residences and administrative centers.

If St Benedict created the stable foundation of medieval monasticism, St Gregory the Great must be credited with bridging biblical and European cultures and forging the parameters of the multicultural encounter that defined early medieval spirituality. His colorful compendium of idealized local traditions of sanctity and multicultural encounters entitled *Dialogues*, composed in the stylistic format of philosophical dialogues from earlier Greek and Roman sources, attempted nothing less than to demonstrate that the Italy of his own era was a second Holy Land filled with remarkable wonder-workers evoking the patriarchs and prophets of the Bible. Most of the contemporary saints selected for inclusion in the *Dialogues* were men of the church – bishops, abbots, or priests. St Gregory was a strong promoter of St Benedict's monastic initiative, arguing that it brought into the present the apostolic life of Christ and his disciples, and that it encapsulated the force and power of biblical patriarchs and prophets. The fourth book of the *Dialogues* contains stories exemplifying teachings on the human soul, on death and the afterlife. All four books offer paradigmatic Christian encounters with indigenous religious practices in narrative form and include a famous conversion story of an unnamed Jew, no doubt intended as models for missionary efforts and Christian–Jewish relationships. Convinced of Christian superiority and the "blindness" of the Jews, St Gregory promoted gentle persuasion and faith in supernatural intervention on behalf of Christian missionary endeavors. The *Dialogues* were widely read and excerpted throughout the medieval millennium. Other popular works by St Gregory include his guidelines for pastoral care and his extensive exegesis of the Books of Job and Ezekiel, which contain his mystical teachings. Mirroring his own active life, St Gregory stressed the complementary function of action and contemplation. He taught that prayer and the meditative reading of Scripture eventually allow the soul to experience divine presence, which in turn prepares and strengthens the soul for the active life. During his papacy, St Gregory promoted missions across Europe and encouraged the integration of sacred sites and festivals into Christian practice.

The biographies and concerns of spiritual leaders such as St Benedict and St Gregory exemplify the fact that indigenous traditions contributed several features to medieval spirituality, some of which have survived until today. They comprise the role and prestige of the female seer and healer, sacred sites distinguished by prominent natural characteristics, and a sacred calendar of communal festivities in tune with seasonal cycles, such as solstices or harvesting and planting seasons, which eventually became more differentiated in the liturgical year. Following indigenous practices, Christian holy days were established in accordance with astronomical knowledge (for example, the Twelve Days of Christmas) in order to strengthen the fabric of social life, whether to honor ancestors (All Saints' and All Souls' Days) or to minimize social tensions (feast days of status inversions and carnivals). Other contributions include the cult of the dead (ancestors), a belief in the separation of mortal body and immortal soul and in the ability of the soul to engage in supernatural travel, and, finally, a belief in the sacred qualities of a political or military leader.

A study of the approximately five thousand active pilgrimage sites in Europe today reveals that at least 4 percent still can be traced directly to pre-Christian cultic activity (Park 1994). The characteristics of many other sites fit indigenous religious prefer- ences. Almost half of the shrines incorporate sacred natural elements, such as moun- tains, water, trees, stones and caves, as well as animals and plants. Many shrines continue a cult of the dead, now venerated as saints or the Virgin Mary. The strongest continuation of indigenous spiritual usage of natural sites occurs in Ireland, where approximately 92 percent of pilgrimage sites feature sacred stones, wells, springs, and so on, and about 9 percent of the sites (some sites have double spiritual references) are characterized by veneration of the dead (Park 1994).

Early generations of medieval saints tended to be members of the nobility; because of their prominence, their burial sites ensured a growing cult that could anchor Christianity in a particular region and continued the regional dominance of certain families. If we can trust penitential handbooks, written for confessors, a Christianized use of such practices coexisted with the survival of pagan gods and goddesses in shrines and cultic practices for many centuries.

High Middle Ages (Eleventh to Thirteenth Centuries): A Universe of Texts, Readers, and Authors

With comparatively stable regional boundaries, safer transportation and travel routes, and the gradual emergence of centralized royal power and its legislative and executive privileges, cultural and spiritual productivity was able to flourish in unprecedented ways. Due to the demands of an increasingly urban and educated European popula- tion, the need for religious literacy and instruction increased dramatically, accompa- nied by anxieties about Christian unity and integrity and the unchecked proliferation of new texts and thus new ideas. Historians estimate that an early medieval European population grew from about 12 million in 600 to 24 million in the year 1000, and more than doubled again by the early fourteenth century (Schuler 1992).

Driven by its own set of rhetorical rules, medieval literacy, whether secular or religious, collapsed temporal, geographical, and cultural distances for a population increasingly dependent on long-distance trade, transportation, and travel. Whereas early medieval spirituality might be best understood in terms of forging common ground from diverse regional spiritual traditions, the eleventh through thirteenth cen- turies are distinguished by an immensely analytical attentiveness to processes of contemplative reading, writing, and textual exegesis. A growing spirituality of the written word necessitated a counter-movement intended to slow unchecked growth. This effort, whether expressed through censorship, public book-burnings, or the persecution and even execution of an author as a heretic, was in no small part caused by an intense anxiety over betraying and cutting ties with the Christian past and losing a much cherished unity. One of the foremost figures of medieval spirituality, the Castilian nobleman and priest St Dominic de Guzman (c.1170–1221), thus is poignantly depicted as supervising the public burning of books.

Contemplative text-driven spirituality came into its own first in monastic institutions, where it had been practiced even before the eleventh century. Monastic textual spirituality was fuelled by an intensified need for the reform of Benedictine houses and a return to a simpler apostolic life. The most successful and respected reformed wing of the Benedictine family was the Cistercian order, shaped by the forceful and tireless guidance of St Bernard of Clairvaux (1090/91–1153), a mystic and spiritual author of extraordinary influence. It was St Bernard who popularized love or bridal mysticism, especially through his unfinished series of sermons on the Song of Songs. Devotional writings were motivated by the desire to explain the mystical meaning of biblical sources, but the exegetical explanations took on a life of their own and created new psycho-spiritual maps for the relationship between the divine, especially Christ, and a tiered community of believers. The erotic playfulness of courtly love poetry influenced much of the language of love mysticism, but it also drew from earlier Greek and Syrian traditions of so-called apophatic and cataphatic mysticism.

Textually centered spirituality expanded beyond the monasteries to cathedral schools and newly founded universities. The so-called Victorine school of contemplative thought includes numerous renowned teachers of contemplation, including Hugh of St Victor (c.1100–1141) and his student Richard of St Victor (d. 1173). Victorine efforts consisted of systematizing and classifying religious experiences in light of the books of the Bible, with divine and human love at the center of creation. Two fascinating representatives of academically driven spirituality are the philosopher and theologian Peter Abelard (1079–1142), and his highly educated wife Heloise (c.1102–64). Both charted unknown waters in their attempt to reconcile the institutional demands of marriage, university life, and the cloister with personal ambitions, passionate love, and an authentically lived religious life. Their difficult struggles were as much shaped by lofty ideals pronounced in philosophical, biblical, and literary writings as through the public and private exchange of exquisite letters and autobiographical reflections and confessions. Reflecting on her life as a well-regarded abbess and her passion for Abelard, Heloise thus could write to her spouse:

Men call me chaste; they do not know the hypocrite I am . . . I am judged religious at a time when there is little in religion which is not hypocrisy, when whoever does not offend the opinions of men receives the highest praise . . . In my case, the pleasures of lovers which we shared have been too sweet . . . Even during the celebration of the Mass, when our prayers should be purer, lewd visions of those pleasures take such a hold upon my unhappy soul that my thoughts are on their wantonness instead of on prayers. (Heloise 1981: 133)

In a third wave, text-driven spirituality entered the world of the laity. The growth of textual devotion from monastic center to lay periphery also involved a linguistic change: whereas monastic and academic text-based devotion developed in Latin, spiritual lay authors employed vernacular languages, and in the process created new and sophisticated vocabularies in their mother tongues. Scholars are still trying to rediscover the ways in which Jewish and Muslim traditions of scriptural exegesis and a "mysticism of the text," such as the Jewish *kabbalah*, influenced Christian authors. Women, although always a minority in the realm of textual spirituality, were active users and producers of texts both in monastic and lay settings, but barred from access to the world of university learning, a medieval restriction that remained in place until the late nineteenth century and beyond. Nonetheless, women's revelations and prophesies were frequently accepted as authentic.

Whereas Cistercians were committed to a cloistered lifestyle, two additional orders, known as mendicants, stressed an itinerant way of life of preaching for their male branches. These are the Franciscan order, founded by St Francis of Assisi (c.1181–1226); and the Dominican order, founded by St Dominic de Guzman (d. 1221). Dominican and Cistercian female houses were initiated without prominent founding mothers such as St Scholastica. Although generally less well endowed than male houses, the female or second orders could nonetheless vastly outnumber male houses in certain regions.

The biographies and teachings of St Bernard of Clairvaux and St Francis of Assisi illustrate the range of monastic innovation. Both St Bernard and St Francis came from respected, but not very prominent, families. Both made efforts to extend the reach of Christendom, St Francis and his followers through intensive missionary activities in Muslim countries, St Bernard through preaching the Crusades and in recruiting militias across Western Europe. As the founder of an order dedicated to charity and compassion for the poor, St Francis modeled an uncompromising return to apostolic simplicity and devotion. The Franciscan ideal has been to follow Christ perfectly, given symbolic expression in the stigmata that St Francis received in 1224 during a prolonged ecstatic experience on the La Verna Mountain. Although St Francis personally composed only a comparatively small number of spiritual works, his charisma and radical life inspired a prodigious body of spiritual literature intended to lead others to the same mystical heights as achieved by St Francis. The Franciscan order also furthered devotion to the Virgin Mary, who was worshiped as the order's protector. St Francis composed a prayer addressed to the Virgin, in which she is identified with the church, and "in whom there was and is / all the fullness of grace and every good" (1982: 149).

In a collaboration similar to that between St Scholastica and St Benedict, St Francis worked with a close female companion, St Clare of Assisi (1194–1253), who founded and guided the female branch of the order. From their inception, however, and against their will, the Poor Clares had to accept more restrictions than the male order, which were rationalized by women's greater vulnerability in a world of sexual violence.

Other contemporary spiritual movements, such as the Waldensians and the Cathars, were equally dedicated to the *imitatio Christi* and believed themselves to be as authentically Christian as, for example, the Franciscans. The church, however, decided otherwise, in the final analysis, because St Francis, and most Franciscans after him, professed loyalty and complete submission to Rome, whereas groups labeled "heretical" maintained a critical distance from the church hierarchy and developed alternative, independent leadership structures.

Monastic orders attracted loosely organized lay associations. These so-called "third orders" eventually produced extraordinary spiritual teachers who taught through personal example, as well as through oral and written instructions. Side by side with these church-approved communal efforts, which benefited from a pan-European ecclesiastical network, spirituality flourished in countless smaller movements organized around one or more charismatic teachers and miracle-workers. Even in light of the scarcity of surviving records, the variety of belief systems and the number of sects and teachers are astounding, and constitute a veritable "New Age" movement in medieval garb. Several church councils, beginning with the Fourth Lateran Council in 1215, and the training and dispatch of a host of papal inquisitors across Europe were intended to curb the proliferation of autonomous spiritual movements. Reforms of the clergy, improved education, and a stronger emphasis on church rites, especially the Eucharist, were also implemented in the effort to create a unified Christian spirituality. Especially in the area of biblical interpretations of the meaning of human life and in the mystical exploration of courtly love, cross-cultural influences from the monotheistic systems of Judaism and Islam came to bear upon Christian spirituality. Christian anxieties about conversions increased as knowledge about the depth of Jewish and Muslim spiritualities became more widespread. Joined with crusader rhetoric, the fear of conversion added to the rise of anti-Islamic and anti-Judaic polemic.

In response to a growing urban class of the destitute and chronically ill, Christian lay organizations founded hospices, orphanages, and houses for reformed prostitutes. Women's groups, such as the beguines, specially took on the burdens of caring for the sick and dying, and both lay men and women organized spiritual networks to care for leper colonies; saints such as Elizabeth of Thuringia (1207–31) became renowned for their extravagant generosity and compassion. "Beguine" is a loosely defined term for religious lay communities of women in Northern Europe, who shared their incomes and adhered to a common rule of life, yet without supervision by an established order.

The life and writings of the beguine Mechthild of Magdeburg (c.1212–84) illustrate the uneasy balance between loyalty to the church, a critique of social ills, and an emphasis on individually received revelations. Mechthild's poems, mystical dialogues, and self-confident commentaries on religious issues of the day were compiled in a book entitled *The Flowing Light of the Godhead*. As she tells us, she was repeatedly warned by clerics that her book should be burned. Despite such troubles, she was a strong supporter of the Dominican order and likely received much of her theological knowledge from Dominican teachers. Dominican houses circulated her book after her death as authentic spiritual literature intended to strengthen the faith of all who would read the book seven times. Especially in the first half of *The Flowing Light of the Godhead*, themes of bridal mysticism are developed in a collection of songs, poems, and dialogues between Christ as bridegroom and the soul as bride. The second half of the book focuses more strongly on apocalyptic interpretations and church reform, but always returns to authoritative commentaries on the relationship between body and soul, and soul and the divine. Mechthild spent the end of her life in a Cistercian house at Helfta. The Helfta nuns regarded Mechthild as a holy woman and integrated some of her teachings into their own spiritual writings.

Late Middle Ages (Thirteenth to Fifteenth Centuries): Widening Rifts and Radical Responses

Challenged by devastating outbreaks of the plague, famine-inducing climatic changes, the Hundred Years War, and a deep institutional crisis of the papacy, late medieval Christians reacted with a spectrum of spiritual responses, ranging from the extreme to the level-headed. Scholars have traced the impact of the "Little Ice Age," beginning in the early fourteenth century, and the terrifying "Great Famine," which lasted from 1315 to 1321. The effects of these crises shook the foundations of European culture and society. Across France alone, for example, historians estimate that at least 3,000 villages were abandoned during the fourteenth century. Between the fourteenth and the fifteenth century, the English population declined to about half of its size. As a result of the famine, populations were driven to move eastward, and many communities experienced additional social stresses through an increase in petty crimes such as thefts and marauding groups of beggars.

Penitential and apocalyptic themes dominated the spiritual landscape from the late thirteenth century onwards, enhanced through the visions and raptures of spiritual leaders who tended to be well-to-do urban rather than struggling rural men and women. At its most excessive, the desire to repent for catastrophes generally perceived to have been caused by human corruption was channeled into the flagellant movement and gruesome individual acts of self-immolation. The first wave of the flagellant movement originated in Umbria in the 1260s and quickly spread north, propelled by a sense of impending social and economic doom. The second wave began in 1348 as a response to the plague epidemic, but was outlawed by the church within a year and eventually declared heretical. Flagellants endorsed the anti-Judaic stereotype that Jewish communities caused the plague epidemic by poisoning the wells of Christians, a hysterical polemic that led to widespread mob violence against Jewish communities. Existential dread and collective trauma were mirrored in the artistic preference for hyper-realistic images of a tortured Christ on the cross and paintings and re-enactments of the so-called Dance of Death, in which a skeleton leads a group of victims from all walks of life in a round dance. Somber devotional treatises on the "Art of Dying" (ars moriendi) were popular among the laity. English communities developed liturgical plays with a focus on Christ's suffering and the Last Judgment. The anchoress and theologian Julian of Norwich (c.1343 until after 1416) developed a profound spirituality of hope and love based on a near-death vision of the bleeding and torn Christ on the cross.

Less dramatic, but perhaps more influential in the long run, the trend to systematize the spiritual experiences of previous generations of mystics continued to grow, but it drove the divisions between the laity and the university-trained scholars ever deeper. The pithy comment of the Dominican theologian and mystic Meister Eckhart (c.1260–1328), that he would even preach to wooden posts if nobody else would understand him, is symptomatic of this rift. Meister Eckhart was eventually accused of heresy. Even well-trained colleagues were not able to fully grasp the enormous sophistication and subtlety of his ideas. Shifting from Cologne, where Meister Eckhart preached, to Oxford, we find another type of radicalization among university-trained Franciscans. The Franciscan theologian William of Ockham (c.1285–1350), among others, was strongly supportive of the radical wing of the Franciscan order, whose proponents attacked the primacy and privileges of the papacy. Censured by Pope John XXII, William was forced to seek refuge with the anti-papal German king, Louis of Bavaria. The persecution of spiritual Franciscans began in earnest with the papal condemnation of their views of apostolic poverty in 1322 and made a decline of the Franciscan order inevitable.

The tensions inherent in an exclusively academic approach to spiritual matters find their most poignant expression in the biography of Jean Charlier de Gerson (1363–1429). A gifted administrator, Gerson rose quickly to the post of chancellor of the University of Paris, an institution which owes its ascent to prominence to the charisma of Peter Abelard. By all accounts, Gerson enjoyed a stellar career as an administrator. As a productive spiritual and theological author, he voiced his opinions without compromising personal standards of integrity. One can find him involved in all the major religious issues of his time, whether evaluating the authority of church councils vis-à-vis the papacy, judging the experiences of male and female visionaries (he wrote in defense of Jeanne d'Arc), writing opinions on heresy trials and accusations of necromancy, or commenting on literary satires poking fun at religion.

In a remarkable letter addressed to his colleagues in Paris, however, Gerson deplored the general state of theology and contemplative thought, fields to which he made important contributions. Despite his best efforts to infuse academic life with spirituality, he laments,

> I am afraid . . . that I will enter into the same vice of which I vehemently accuse others. And what is this, you ask? There are those who by all kinds of trifles and clumsy novelties clutter up parchment and the minds of listeners . . . We do write, but our sentences have no weight, our words no number or measure. For all that we write is flabby, mean, slack. We do not write what is new. Instead we repeat what is old but treat and transmit it in a new way. (Jean Gerson 1998: 178)

Frustrated and disillusioned, Jean Gerson finally quit university life and spent the last ten years of his life in contemplative seclusion.

Less extravagant than the flagellants, lay spiritual groups with greater institutional stability emphasized the values of the emerging urban burgher class, best perhaps represented in the popular *Devotio Moderna* movement. The spirituality of the *Devotio Moderna*, measured and sober, suspicious of mysticism and theologically articulate, was developed through collaboration between lay people and clergy. It found its strongest voice in the works and ministry of the wealthy burgher Gerhard Groote (1340–84), who was born in Deventer and educated in Paris. Before the plague cut short his life, he served a large male and female congregation through sermons and pastoral care, and wrote numerous treatises outlining his exacting program of church reforms and disciplined piety. His ideal was that of the *vita ambidextera*, a holy life lived in search of a vision of the divine and in helping those in need.

All of the previous themes finally come full circle in the life and death of the visionary and military leader, Jeanne d'Arc (*c.*1412–31), burned at the stake as a lapsed heretic as a result of the most shockingly corrupt religious trial of the medieval era. As a young uneducated woman of peasant background, her comet-like life was guided by a spirituality grounded in mystical experiences and folk stories without the support of theological training or ecclesiastical approval. Transcripts of her heresy trial prove that her wit and understanding of Christian theology were none the weaker because of it. In choosing to don men's clothing and bear arms in a military mission without precedent, Jeanne d'Arc boldly transcended rigid gender roles that would last for another five hundred years. Her brave pursuit of holiness in a time of war and famine made her the patron saint of modern France and an emblem of medieval spirituality worldwide.

Conclusion

The medieval millennium marks the creation of a common European spiritual tradition. Its genius lay in its ability to produce a multicultural synthesis and the creative reinterpretation of biblical and patristic sources. Medieval spirituality gradually absorbed and reinterpreted vastly different belief systems from various indigenous European traditions, Judaism, and the cultures of the Mediterranean basin. Its development was propelled by an ecclesiastical institution shaped to assert political influence and to unite Christian communities, on the one hand, and the bold impulses of spiritual movements and leaders in search of a life of holiness, on the other. Medieval spirituality still offers relevant resources and challenges today. Positively speaking, these include the leadership roles of medieval women as visionaries and abbesses, the wide spectrum of recorded mystical experiences, the ideals of radical poverty, and a profound acceptance of death and suffering. More disturbing and challenging is the medieval legacy of religious intolerance, especially in the form of anti-Judaism, the fear of diversity within and outside the church, and a disproportionate reliance on texts to the neglect of an embodied, sensual, and orally communicated spirituality that incorporates a reverence for the sacredness of place, space, and sound.

References

Aers, D. and Staley, L. 1996: *The Powers of the Holy: Religion, Politics, and Gender in Late Medieval English Culture*. University Park, PA: Pennsylvania State University Press.

Benedict of Nursia 1998: *The Rule of St Benedict: In English*, trans. T. Fry. New York: Vintage.

Bynum, C. W. 1987: *Holy Feast and Holy Fast: The Religious Significance of Food to Medieval Women*. Berkeley, CA: University of California Press.

Cantor, N. F. 2001: *In the Wake of the Plague: The Black Death and the World It Made*. New York: HarperCollins.

Cavadini, J. C. (ed.) 1995: *Gregory the Great: A Symposium*. Notre Dame, IN: University of Notre Dame Press.

Devotio Moderna 1988: *Basic Writings*, trans. J. van Engen. New York: Paulist Press.

Francis of Assisi 1982: *Francis and Clare: The Complete Works*, trans. R. J. Armstrong and I. C. Brady. New York: Paulist Press.

Gregory the Great 1959: *Dialogues*, trans. O. J. Zimmerman. New York: Fathers of the Church.

Gurevich, A. 1988: *Medieval Popular Culture: Problems of Belief and Perception*. Cambridge: Cambridge University Press.

Heloise 1981: *The Letters of Abelard and Heloise*, trans. B. Radice. New York: Penguin.

Jean Gerson 1998: *Early Works*, trans. B. P. McGuire. New York: Paulist Press.

Kieckhefer, R. 1984: *Unquiet Souls: Fourteenth-century Saints and their Religious Milieu*. Chicago: University of Chicago Press.

McGinn, B. 2001: *The Mystical Thought of Meister Eckhart: The Man from Whom God Hid Nothing*. New York: Herder and Herder.

——, Meyendorff, J., and Leclerq, J. (eds) 1987: *Christian Spirituality: Origins to the Twelfth Century*. New York: Crossroad.

McNamara, J. A. K. 1996: *Sisters in Arms: Catholic Nuns through Two Millennia*. Cambridge, MA: Harvard University Press.

——and Halborg, J. E., with Whatley, E. G. 1992: *Sainted Women of the Dark Ages*. Durham, NC: Duke University Press.

Mechthild of Magdeburg 1998: *The Flowing Light of the Godhead*, trans. F. Tobin. New York: Paulist Press.

Moore, R. I. 1987: *The Formation of a Persecuting Society*. Oxford: Blackwell.

Park, C. C. 1994: *Sacred Worlds: An Introduction to Geography and Religion*. London: Routledge.

Partner, P. 1997: *God of Battles: Holy Wars of Christianity and Islam*. Princeton, NJ: Princeton University Press.

Raitt, J., with McGinn, B. and Meyendorff, J. (eds) 1989: *Christian Spirituality: High Middle Ages and Reformation*. New York: Crossroad.

Schuler, P. 1992: Bevölkerungszahl. In P. Dinzelbacher (ed.), *Sachwörterbuch der Mediävistik*, pp. 95–6. Stuttgart: Alfred Kröner Verlag.

Sullivan, K. 1999: *The Interrogation of Joan of Arc*. Minneapolis, MN: University of Minnesota Press.

Szarmach, P. (ed.) 1984: *An Introduction to the Medieval Mystics of Europe*. Albany, NY: State University of New York Press.

Vauchez, A. 1993: *The Laity in the Middle Ages: Religious Beliefs and Devotional Practices*. Notre Dame, IN: University of Notre Dame Press.

Wakefield, W. L. and Evans, A. P. (trans.) 1991: *Heresies of the High Middle Ages*, 2nd edn. New York: Columbia University Press.

Wood, I. 2001: *The Missionary Life: Saints and the Evangelisation of Europe 400–1050*. London: Longman.

CHAPTER 7

European Reformations of Christian Spirituality (1450–1700)

Jill Raitt

The story of European Christian spirituality from 1450 to 1700 begins within a larger cultural history of urban development, the spreading Italian Renaissance, the European invention of the printing press, the growth of national consciousness, the stabilization of national languages, and the development of navigational tools that would send Europeans around the world. By 1450, Christendom had survived the Black Death and the scandal of three claimants to the papal crown, but was still enmeshed in the clash of imperial versus papal claims. Voices within and without the church clamored for reform, and one major reform effort, conciliarism, had yielded to a victorious Pope Eugene IV. In 1439 Eugene IV had welcomed emissaries from an embattled Constantinople that would fall to Turkish armies in 1453.

The Fifteenth Century

Fifteenth-century spirituality was marked primarily by efforts to reform church government and by a return to observance of their original rules by some of the religious orders whose regulations had been mitigated during the previous century due largely to the Black Death. It was also a time when those with pastoral concerns tried to heal the growing split between theology and spirituality, especially in the major universities where future ecclesiastical leaders were trained.

It is appropriate therefore to begin with Nicholas of Cusa (1401–64), a mathematician, a theologian, a conciliarist, and a reformer who left the raucous Council of Basel to follow Eugene IV to Florence and was then sent to Constantinople as the pope's emissary. Cusa, a deeply spiritual, highly intellectual theologian, represents in his own person both conciliarism and its defeat and then, as papal legate to the imperial diets (1438–49), the pope's cause in his dispute with the emperor. Appointed bishop of the diocese of Brixen, Cusa instituted reforms there from 1450 to 1460, and, in 1459, began reforming Rome itself as vicar-general for the humanist Pope Pius II. Cusa's theological inquiry led him to teach, sixty years before Luther, a doctrine of justification by faith through grace and the sole mediation of Christ (Jedin 1993: 338–9).

His early and best-known treatise, *On Learned Ignorance* (*De docta ignorantia*, 1440), used mathematics to explain a theological method, the coincidence of opposites (*coincidentia oppositorum*). Cusa admitted that *The Mystical Theology* of Pseudo-Dionysius had influenced him, but his theory, he wrote, was not derived from it, but rather from reflection on his own experience. The primary model of coincidence is Christ in whom the human and divine natures coincide. Other instances are the plurality and unity of the Trinity, and learned ignorance itself. Beyond all of these is God whom Cusa came to call simply "What" (*Quid*). Twenty-four years later, when he was a cardinal, Cusa's spiritual life, together with his theological explorations, led him beyond God as *Quid* to God as Possibility Itself (*Posse ipsum*), and so discernible everywhere as the verb "can" behind every actuality (Jedin 1993: 6–9; 56–70). This discovery, explained in his *On the Summit of Contemplation* (1464), gave him great joy a few months before his death.

During the Middle Ages and into the fifteenth century, lay people continued to seek ways to follow Christ without becoming members of religious orders. Typical of such movements were the beguines, women who gathered in one house, pooled their resources, prayed together, and served the poor. Because they were not cloistered nor easily brought under close ecclesiastical supervision, they were increasingly suspected of heretical ideas and practices and in the late fourteenth and fifteenth centuries were severely repressed. By 1500, they were practically destroyed. Lay men also gathered in similar arrangements, but they were even more suspect and fared less well than the women. In the late fifteenth century, the Sisters of the Common Life adopted the rule of the third order of St Francis. The Common Life movement, known also as the *Devotio Moderna*, spread through their educational institutions and through the popular little book of spiritual direction by Thomas à Kempis (1380–1471), *The Imitation of Christ*, the most frequently published book after the Bible from the sixteenth into the twentieth century. While the Brothers preferred true devotion over learning divorced from God, they were hardly anti-intellectual themselves, although later centuries would so interpret their teaching. From the Brothers' school at Windesheim came Desiderius Erasmus (*c.*1466–1536), a great scholar and one of the most influential humanists of the sixteenth century. Erasmus wrote a handbook of Christian behavior, the *Manual of the Christian Knight* (1504), for a learned elite able to read the New Testament and the Fathers of the Church so that they could follow Christ based on their interior prayer guided by the Holy Spirit.

For most Christians in the late Middle Ages, however, such reading was not possible and their spirituality took the form of pious devotions. While vernacular devotional and spiritual literature was becoming more available, preaching remained the primary means of cultivating popular devotion. From the twelfth century on, devotion grew to the humanity of Christ (especially as exhibited in his passion), to Mary and the saints, and to the Eucharist. The corpus on crucifixes became more twisted and bloody, while Mary stood below or swooned in the arms of the apostle John. Pilgrims to saints' shrines and to relic collections carried rosaries and sang such Marian hymns as *Ave maris stella* and *Salve Regina*. The feast of Corpus Christi grew more elaborate and, during the terrible Black Death, processions wound through the streets of towns and villages with the Eucharist carried in a golden monstrance accompanied by incense and the ringing of bells. Lay confraternities and craft-related sodalities met in churches dedicated to their patron saints. There they attended mass, listened to sermons, fasted, went together on pilgrimages, sponsored elaborate funerals for their members, and provided care for their members' widows and orphans.

The Sixteenth Century

The reform efforts of the fifteenth century were not strong enough to forestall the splintering of Christendom that led to the century-long wars of religion. Martin Luther's doctrine of "justification by faith alone" characterized the Protestant churches that then divided over other doctrines and practices such as the sacraments of the Lord's Supper and baptism. The invention of the printing press had made books readily available by the early sixteenth century. Books and often comically illustrated pamphlets flew from the presses. Through this new medium, ideas flowed even faster. The reformation caught on, was sponsored by political leaders, and hastened by lively civic debate. The Tridentine answer, slow in coming, answered the Protestant challenge and set the Roman Catholic Church on a track that held firm until Vatican II in the twentieth century. The latter part of the sixteenth century was marked by the development of denominational confessions, interdenominational warfare, and the development of new kinds of religious orders and spiritualities.

At the beginning of the sixteenth century, demands for reform grew louder. The response was Lateran V (1512–17), which proposed solid improvements. It is unlikely that Pope Leo X would have carried out these reforms, but reform was about to be forced upon him and his successors. As Lateran V ended in 1517, a concerned Augustinian monk and professor of Scripture at the University of Wittenberg posted ninety-five theses for debate. Chief among his points was the illegitimacy of the sale of indulgences, a clear case of the sin of simony, the sale of spiritual goods. Martin Luther (1483–1545) sought to reform the church, sure that the pope would agree. But, instead, Pope Leo X wished only that the pesky monk would be silenced. Luther taught that grace is free and cannot be "earned" by works or merits since Christ on the cross had merited all the grace needed for the justification of sinners. Christ was offered once and for all, said Luther, so that the mass cannot be a sacrifice; no priest can offer Christ again. Christians can only trust in God's promise of justification and respond in gratitude to God by helping their neighbors. Christians are at once sinners and justified by the grace of Christ through which also they share in the priesthood of all believers that allows a layperson to speak of Christ's promise, that is, to apply the gospel to an anxious neighbor.

For Luther, spirituality consists in a heartfelt trust in Christ's work "for me" and in generous service to the neighbor. Celibacy, Luther taught, is a work and contrary to the order of God to increase and multiply. Luther himself married a former nun and urged other religious to follow his example. He denounced meditation as a work by which monks think to gain heaven. For prayer, Luther recommended the petitions of the Our

Father and the use of the Psalms to ask for help and to express praise and gratitude. One should not pray to the Virgin Mary, who, although she is the Mother of God, is unable to answer prayer, a power reserved to Christ, the sole mediator. Still less can saints respond to prayer. Nor are masses or prayer efficacious for the dead. Because Christ covers all sin, the dying Christian who trusts in Christ goes immediately to heaven; there is no purgatory. Pilgrimages, shrines, relics, all smack of works-righteousness and so, taught Luther, are anathema. Contrary to the practice of the Roman Catholic Church, Luther gave the cup to the people at mass because the Lord said "Take this, all of you, and drink of it." Scripture is God's Word and the only guide to faith and doctrine, so the Bible should be in the hands of every Christian in languages everyone can understand. Luther himself translated Erasmus's Greek New Testament into German.

At the same time that Luther began his reform in Wittenberg, Huldrych Zwingli (1484–1531), a parish priest near Zurich, Switzerland, came to a more radical version of justification by faith alone. His reforms resembled Luther's in many ways, but Zwingli went further. While Luther taught that whatever is not forbidden by Scripture is allowable, Zwingli taught that only what Scripture permits is allowable, a much narrower method of applying Scripture to social and personal life. Zwingli denied the real presence of Christ in the Lord's Supper, whitewashed the walls of the churches, and nailed shut their organs. He and Luther met in 1529 to try to resolve their doctrinal difference regarding the Lord's Supper. Luther held fast to a real presence of Christ "in, with, or under" the bread and wine which, nevertheless, are not "transubstantiated" into the body and blood of Christ. Zwingli, trained as a humanist, found irrational Luther's insistence that bread is body. Rather, taught Zwingli, the words "This is my body" should be understood to mean "This signifies my body." Luther insisted that "is" means "is," so the body and blood of Christ are given with the bread and the wine. The two reformers could not be reconciled.

Zwingli's Eucharistic theology emphasized the worshiping community which comes in faith, and therefore in grace, to offer thanks to God. By that action, the members of the community are more and more transformed into the body of Christ. It is the community, not the bread and the wine, that is transformed by the action of the Holy Spirit. The Lord's Supper is a service of remembering, of gratitude, and of joy, a necessary symbol of the union of believers (Raitt 1987: 300–17). "Prophets," in the original meaning of the word, formed the people of Zurich. Prophets speak for God and may, therefore, on occasion be given predictions of things to come, but primarily prophets are God's spokespersons. The Zurich *Prophezai* was a seminary in which future pastors learned the biblical languages and how to preach from the Bible. Zwingli, and after him Heinrich Bullinger (1504–75), set the pattern for the tradition of learned clergy in the Reformed churches, a tradition furthered by the work of John Calvin (1509–64) and his colleague and successor in Geneva, Theodore Beza (1519–1605). Reformed theology is strongly pneumatological. The doctrine of the Holy Spirit permeates every aspect of Reformed doctrine but in a manner that enhances the sole mediation of Christ.

Zurich, and later Geneva, became Christian states in which politics and religion coalesced under the sovereignty of God. Sinners require laws and the people require justice;

hence the discipline of magistrates was part of the covenant between God and all believers, wherever and whenever they live or lived. Because the Holy Spirit is not bound, for Zwingli, even the good pagans who lived before Christ could have been justified. Christian teaching and moral expectation reached into all aspects of life, public and private. Law and gospel joined hands in Zwingli's theology.

It was in Zurich that the first Anabaptists were put to death by drowning for challenging the validity of infant baptism. They taught a believer's baptism that followed an experience of conversion to faith in Christ and to amendment of life. Since they were justified by faith, baptism, as an ordinance of the Lord, was performed to declare the mutual commitment of the congregation and the newly baptized. Backsliders, those who failed to maintain a virtuous life after the example of Christ, were banned, cut off from further contact with the community until they repented. Among the Anabaptists, the Lord's Supper was a memorial service that gathered the community in a home or other plain building to remember Christ's passion with gratitude. Anyone could say the words of institution and the bread and wine were served in common dishes. According to George H. Williams (1962), the Anabaptists were one of three groups belonging to the "Radical Reformation." The most radical were the "Spiritual" Anabaptists who relied on the interior working of the Holy Spirit to the extent that they denied the necessity of the Scriptures. These neo-Docetists denied the reality of the incarnation and the bodily resurrection of Christ, who possessed only a "spiritual body," a doctrine that affected their conception of the sacraments. Thus Caspar Schwenckfeld "conceived of the Eucharist as an inward feeding on the 'heavenly flesh' of Christ" (George 1987: 337). The third and smaller arm of the Radical Reformation was the Evangelical Rationalists. Michael Servetus was an Evangelical Rationalist who rejected everything not explicable by reason, for example, the doctrine of the Trinity. This early Unitarian met his death in Geneva although he was under a sentence of death elsewhere as well.

The Anabaptists were outlawed almost as soon as they began. In 1529 the imperial diet at Speyer legitimized Justinian's law concerning the Donatists. Anyone who rebaptized was subject to execution without trial. Anabaptists – a designation that in the sixteenth century included the other two radical groups – were persecuted all over Europe throughout the sixteenth century. It is no wonder that they developed a theology of martyrdom that carried their imitation of Christ to the point of offering themselves as sacrifices in union with Christ's sacrifice for all people and indeed for all creation that still groans under the burden of human sinfulness. In this they earned Luther's scorn; he accused them of works-righteousness akin to that of the Roman Catholics. To prepare for martyrdom, the Anabaptists drew again upon late medieval Rhineland mystics, especially Joannes Tauler's doctrine of abandonment to the will of God (*Gelassenheit*). The handing over of one's will to God in patience and faith came from the conviction that God asks only for loving surrender and so coerces no one, either by irresistible grace or by its corollary, double predestination. Nor would Menno Simons (1496–1561) allow his followers to coerce anyone, hence the pacifism of the Mennonites. He urged complete conformity with the will of God and with the passion of Christ. He told his followers: "The thorny crown must pierce your head and the nails your hands and feet. Your body must be scourged and your face spit upon. On Golgotha you must pause and bring your own sacrifice" (George 1987: 342). In 1660, more than a century after the decree of 1529, there appeared in Dutch *The Bloody Theater or Martyrs' Mirror of the Defenseless Christians Who Baptized Only Upon Confession of Faith, and Who Suffered and Died for the Testimony of Jesus their Savior* (George 1987: 343). The hefty folio volume of 1,290 pages recounted martyrdoms from the early church through the middle of the seventeenth century. Forms of prayer among the Radicals varied from something similar to modern Pentecostalism to Mennonite silent prayer on one's knees following a simple service.

The Anabaptists anticipated the Puritans in their demand that membership in their community required an experience of being reborn. The reduction of spirituality to emotional experience brings with it a number of problems, as the Puritans of the Massachusetts Bay Colony were to discover a century later. Unlike the Puritans who sought freedom to establish their own religion, many Radicals taught complete freedom of conscience and an end to all religious persecution. Some Radical groups, rejecting double predestination and a permanent hell, taught universal salvation, even of the fallen angels. Many groups shared their goods and were egalitarian to the point that: "Women served as protectors, patrons, prophets, apostles, preachers, deacons, and hymn writers" (George 1987: 365).

The major splits not only between Catholics and Protestants but among Protestants themselves had already occurred when a young Frenchman, converted to "Lutheranism," fled Paris. John Calvin (1509–64), while passing through Geneva on his way to a scholar's life in Strasbourg, was persuaded by William Farel to assist with the reformation of Geneva. Calvin, trained as a lawyer, had read deeply in the Fathers of the Church. He was influenced as well by Martin Bucer, the Lutheran pastor of Strasbourg, during Calvin's stay there after the Genevans sent Farel and Calvin packing. Recalled to Geneva, Calvin remained there for the rest of his life, developing a theology enshrined in his *Institutes of the Christian Religion*, commentaries on Scripture, and theological treatises. Calvin's spirituality was based on gratitude for all that God had done in Christ. Prayer of praise, gratitude, and petition found its voice in the Psalms, set to appropriate music for use in churches, especially by Claude Goudimel (*c.*1514–72), Geneva's great composer. Calvin defended infant baptism and taught a theology of the Lord's Supper that affirmed a true, rather than a real, presence of Christ offered through the power of the Holy Spirit to the faithful who were then united substantially to Christ in heaven where he sits at the right hand of God. The elements of bread and wine are used instrumentally during the Lord's Supper, but they retain no special character after the service is over and may be consumed as common bread and wine. Calvin therefore differed from both Luther and Henry Bullinger, Zwingli's successor in Zurich who would not allow any talk of substance with regard to the Body of Christ in or through the Lord's Supper. The Company of Pastors and the Consistory, made up of magistrates and church elders, urged the citizens of Geneva to live godly lives. In Geneva, as in Zurich, citizenship in the Republic required membership in the church, an idea carried into the Massachusetts Bay Colony by the Puritans in the seventeenth century.

During the 1530s the Roman Catholic Church began to mobilize against the now serious threat posed by the Protestant Reformation. Pope and curia began to respond to cries within the church and challenges outside it, and at last, in 1545, the first session of the Council of Trent began. Its three sessions (December 1545–March 1547,

May 1551–April 1552, and January 1562–December 1563) were interrupted by plague and by war, but its accomplishments were to last, with few revisions, until Vatican II. Trent reaffirmed not only the efficacy of faith informed by love and that grace is not coerced by works, but also an optimistic idea of human nature that allowed for freedom, and therefore cooperation, with God's always prevenient grace. God's action is always primary and the Christian's cooperation is secondary, a response to God. Trent provided for far-reaching reforms that included seminaries for the training of priests and requirements that bishops live in their dioceses and assume their proper duties overseeing the teaching of doctrine and the administration of the sacraments. Wary of further divisive movements, Rome centralized the work and oversight of the church as much as possible. It developed catechisms and other modes of educating the laity. The post-Tridentine church replaced purely local saints with a calendar of saints for the universal church. Canonization of saints became the prerogative of Rome, which drew up lists of universal feasts, replacing local feast days. While the Council of Trent and acts such as these strengthened the Roman Catholic Church, it also formalized structures that became less and less pliant and able to respond to changes in the fast-moving European political and cultural worlds.

Throughout the sixteenth century, there arose new orders dedicated to the education of clergy and of laity, such as the Ursulines (1544) for women and the Jesuits (1540) for men. But, like the third orders of the medieval mendicant orders, these new orders created ways to draw laity into their spiritual life and activities, primarily through confraternities and sodalities. The strongest of these were the Marian sodalities that were gathered by Pope Gregory XIII under the headship of the Superior General of the Jesuits. The rule for these sodalities required members to pray daily, attend daily mass, confess weekly, and receive communion at least once a month. They were also to dedicate themselves to the works of mercy such as care for the sick and imprisoned, teaching catechism, and assisting the poor. While priests were assigned as directors, officers within confraternities were elected by their members. Networks of confraternity members spread across Europe and began to affect not only the charitable and religious life of the towns, but their political life as well. Priests of the new and older orders found themselves busy with spiritual direction as the pious life of the faithful grew more robust and more lay people engaged in meditation and contemplation.

Two of the most important spiritual developments of the sixteenth century began in Spain. The first was the writing of *The Spiritual Exercises* by Ignatius of Loyola (1490/1–1556) who used them to form the men who would become the Society of Jesus. The Jesuits used the *Exercises* to convert lay men and women to a closer following of Jesus through retreats that typically last from six to thirty days and require three to five daily periods of prayerful meditation. The first "week" of the *Exercises* considers the work of God the creator for humankind. By this means, one is drawn to a generous return of self to God. The second week follows the life of Christ and contains several key meditations designed to draw the exercitant into the generous service of "so good a Lord." During the third week, one meditates on Christ's passion and ends again with prayer to follow generously the Christ who died "for me." Meditation during the fourth week is on Christ's resurrection and on heaven, ending with the prayer, "Take and receive," a dedication of one's whole self to the service of Christ. A pattern is set by the *Spiritual Exercises*, but the manner in which one follows the exercises is not rigid. Ignatius stressed that the primary job of the spiritual director is to "help souls" by setting the stage and then stepping aside so as not to come between God's direct action in the soul of the exercitant.

The second spiritual development to arise in Spain was the reform of the mendicant Carmelite order by St Teresa of Avila (1515–82) and St John of the Cross (1542–91). They not only reformed the order of Our Lady of Mount Carmel but also gave to the world spiritual works that still inspire their readers. Both have been declared doctors of the universal church for the extraordinary power and effectiveness of their spiritual writing and direction. Teresa wrote down-to-earth directions for her nuns such as *The Way of Perfection* and *The Interior Castle* and an autobiography that describes her far-from-smooth path to a life of union with God. Teresa's mysticism was firmly Christo-centric, eschewing any suggestion that she might seek, or counsel others to seek, a God who transcended either the Trinity or the incarnation. Teresa envisioned the soul as a diamond that is also a castle with seven dwelling places. The soul enters through the door of prayer. Its progress from the recognition of its sinfulness to the spiritual espousals is not linear, but involves returns to the first dwelling place and sudden glimpses of its goal, continual union with God in Christ. Teresa illustrates her directions and exhortations with metaphors drawn from common experience such as watering a garden. The beginner may have to draw water from a well and lug heavy buckets to the garden. A more advanced person may have only to tend an irrigation system, while the experienced gardener may have only to watch God's good rain water the garden for her. Teresa was a practical as well as a wise guide. If a sister claimed visionary experiences, Teresa might suggest that the sister be given a more substantial diet, a warm bath, and extra rest. For Teresa, the test of progress was not visions but a constant, gentle charity toward all and fidelity to a daily life of prayer and work.

John of the Cross was a man of many skills and great insight. He was an artist, an architect, a trained theologian, and extraordinary poet. His works are more difficult to understand than Teresa's, but were also translated and influential beyond Spain and beyond the sixteenth century. His way of all and nothing (*todo y nada*) asks for a strip-ping away of everything to which a person might cling and recognition of one's own nothingness; that is the *nada*. The purpose of such self-emptying is to be filled with God to whom one wishes to belong totally, the *todo*. John's burning poetry and commen-taries, strongly influenced by the Song of Songs, are an original synthesis of earlier spir-itual traditions. The two Carmelites make clear their passion for God and their paths from beginner to enjoyment of "spiritual marriage" or continual union with God in Christ. Both Spanish mystics were also active, crisscrossing Spain to found new houses of the Discalced (shoeless) Carmelites. Their reform, like the reforms that took place earlier in many of the older orders, consisted of a return to observance of the unmiti-gated rule of the first European Carmelites.

During and following the Council of Trent, concern for reform of the clergy marked Italian spirituality. Philip Neri (1515–94) founded the Italian Oratory and, with the

Spanish Ignatius of Loyola, led the reforming movement in Rome. Equally concerned with clerical reform was Charles Borromeo (1538–84), a model reforming bishop. His reforms are his major contribution since he wrote very little that has survived. It is Catherine of Genoa (1447–1510), whose works began to be published in 1551, who had a remarkable influence on the spirituality of Italy, Spain, and France in the sixteenth and seventeenth centuries, and more widely still into the twentieth century. Catherine did not write herself; her confessors and her disciple Battista Vernazza are responsible for capturing the saint's teachings and ecstatic utterances. Catherine of Genoa spoke of spiritual union, through Jesus Christ, with the divine essence itself. Catherine aimed at pure love, a perfectly disinterested charity that loves God for God alone to the complete forgetfulness of self. Her *Treatise on Purgatory* is her best-known work. In it, she compares the condition of the souls in purgatory to the trials she herself underwent as a woman of deep prayer. In the presence of God, she became intensely aware of her sinfulness and her burning desire to be cleansed so that she could be united with God in pure love.

During the sixteenth and seventeenth centuries, England went through its own long process of reformation that stretched through the reigns of Henry VIII (1509–47), his young son Edward VI (1547–53) under the regency of the Protestant Edward Seymour (Edward VI's uncle), and Henry's daughters, the Roman Catholic Queen Mary (1553–8) and the Protestant Queen Elizabeth I (1558–1603). As Henry VIII began challenging the legitimacy of his marriage to Catherine of Aragon, he was opposed by his chancellor, Sir Thomas More, a layman, a humanist, and friend of Desiderius Erasmus, and by Bishop John Fisher. Both cultivated a deep but hidden spirituality that sustained them through their martyrdom. Meanwhile, the reformation had taken hold through the "White Horse Men" at Cambridge who met to discuss the works of Luther, among others. The movement became dominant during the reign of Edward VI, allowing Thomas Cranmer, then Archbishop of Canterbury, to produce a remarkable document, *The Book of Common Prayer* (1549, 1552). Under Queen Mary, Cranmer died a martyr and the Protestant clergy who had emerged in Edward's reign fled from England to Freiberg, Zurich, and Geneva. When Elizabeth became queen in 1558, they returned, demanding that she accept the reformed liturgies and theologies they had learned in Europe. But Elizabeth, a true daughter of Henry VIII, maintained both the Act of Supremacy, which declared England's sovereign to be head of the Church of England, and Henry's preference for Catholic theology. The Elizabethan Settlement resolved the dispute between the two forms of English Protestantism in England, but not in Scotland. One of the Marian exiles was the Scot John Knox (1505–72) who became a convinced Calvinist during his stay in Geneva. He returned to Scotland in 1559, and in 1560, Scotland, by a new law, declared its allegiance to the Reformed faith. Meanwhile in England, people watched the royal alternation of Roman Catholic and Protestant with consternation. During Mary Tudor's reign, Protestants gathered secretly to study doctrine, while English Anabaptists suffered under a continual ban, as did their European counterparts. Catholics hid priests like the Jesuit poet Edmund Campion who risked their lives to provide the sacraments. Campion's poems bespeak a tender love of Jesus that was strong enough to carry him to a martyr's death. Heroic testimonies poured forth from both Protestant and Catholic presses.

The Seventeenth Century

During the seventeenth century, England continued to struggle over how far its form of the reformation would go, and found that it would go as far as regicide. On the continent, the wars of religion raged until peace, of sorts, returned in 1648 with the Peace of Westphalia. Meanwhile, confessionalism in the Protestant churches, and scholasticism in both Protestant and Catholic seminaries, became increasingly rigid and sparked a reaction in Germany and France of pious groups seeking a biblically based interior life encouraged by gatherings in homes. Reaction to scholasticism took a different turn in 1650 when René Descartes published his Meditations, separating philosophy from theology and setting reason on an autonomous course toward the Enlightenment of the following century.

At the end of the sixteenth century, a deadening form of scholasticism dominated in both Protestant and Catholic seminary education. Handbooks reduced the powerful theologies of Luther and Calvin to scholastic formulas. From the University of Salamanca in Spain emanated a revival of Thomistic scholasticism that had been strong and fruitful in the sixteenth century, but was succeeded in the seventeenth century by an emphasis on doctrine and polemical hair-splitting. The scholastic mode of seminary teaching and insistence on doctrinal conformity resulted in two movements. In Catholic France, the rejection of Catholic scholasticism in favor of the philosophy of René Descartes led to modern rationalism, while in the Lutheran areas of those lands that would become Germany, reaction to Lutheran scholasticism resulted in the phenomenon of Jacob Boehme and his followers and in the more enduring Pietist movement.

Bridging the sixteenth and seventeenth centuries, and, in his unique fashion, taking elements from both Lutheran piety and Catholic mysticism, was Jacob Boehme (1575–1624), who with his disciples spread his ideas through German-speaking lands and in translation into England in 1660 where they were known to John Milton (1608–74) and Isaac Newton (1642–1727). Boehme was a shoemaker and a married householder with four sons, living in the town of Alt Seidenberg near Görlitz. In Görlitz, Boehme came to know followers of the spiritualist Caspar Schwenckfeld von Ossig (1489–1551) and Valentine Weigel (1533–88), a nature mystic, who introduced Boehme to the works of Paracelsus (Theophrastus Bombastus von Hohenheim, 1493–1541) and to Jewish *kabbalah*, a mystical tradition that originated in Spain in the late twelfth century.

As was the case with Boehme's less controversial contemporary, Johann Arndt (1555–1621), who also drew on Catholic piety and mysticism, the explorations of the Görlitz Lutherans were a reaction to the rigidity of Protestant scholasticism and a search for true piety and a more personal life of devotion and holiness. Boehme's most influential work, *The Way to Christ*, was published in 1624. Before and after its publication, orthodox Lutherans attacked Boehme and drove him from his home. He returned to Görlitz, was reconciled, and died there. The love of God was the center of his experience, expressed in the marriage of his soul with the Virgin Sophia who reveals "what God is in his depth. Wisdom is God's revelation and the Holy Spirit's corporeality; the body of the Holy Trinity" (Boehme, *Antistiefelius* 2.253, quoted in the introduction to 1978: 9). The complexity of Boehme's thought cannot be reduced to a simple summary; it challenges even a devoted reader.

The German Pietist movement brought together Calvinist and Lutheran ideas with the Catholic devotional movements of the late Middle Ages. It began with Philipp Jakob Spener (1635–1705) who in 1675 published a preface to Johann Arndt's *Postills on the Gospels* (1615–16). Spener's *Pia Desideria: or Heartfelt Desires for a God-pleasing Improvement of the true Protestant Church*, became the seminal text for German Pietism. A. H. Francke (1663–1727) made Halle a center of Pietism, and Nicholas Lewis, Count Zinzendorf (1700–60) founded the Herrnhut Brotherhood in 1722 and there welcomed refugees from Moravia. The Moravian community provided settlers for the colony of Georgia. It was during his sojourn there that the Anglican clergyman John Wesley (1703–91) met some of the Moravian brethren. Their influence converted Wesley who, once he had returned to England, established the pious groups known as Methodists. Spener's plea to end inter-Protestant polemics influenced also the Pietist professor at the University of Berlin, Friedrich Schleiermacher (1768–1834), who, in the nineteenth century, was instrumental in uniting the Reformed and Lutheran churches of Germany. Among other major works, Schleiermacher wrote *On Religion: Speeches to its Cultured Despisers* (1799), a theological work based on Pietist experience crystallized as a "feeling of absolute dependence."

During the reign of Elizabeth I, her English subjects could enjoy the plays of Jonson and Shakespeare. In the early seventeenth century, the King James Bible was published whose splendid English, together with the rhythm and language of the *Book of Common Prayer*, became the language of English spirituality. But England's religious leaders continued to oppose one another until war erupted and ended with the short triumph of Oliver Cromwell, under whose rule Ireland was laid waste and subjugated and King Charles I beheaded. Cromwell's Latin secretary was John Milton (1608–74), whose Puritan austerity conflicted with his enjoyment of a life of culture, including the arts proscribed by the Puritans, but whose *Paradise Lost* (1667) remains the apogee of Puritan literature. During this tumultuous century, England produced the "metaphysical poets" who wrote perceptively and feelingly of their own spiritual struggles as Anglicans. John Donne (1572–1631), George Herbert (1593–1633), Henry Vaughn (1622–95), and Thomas Traherne (1637–74), grounded in a solidly incarnational theology, wrote of spiritual struggle and profound joy.

Donne grew up in a staunchly recusant family. Two of his cousins became Jesuit priests; one of them was captured and committed to the Tower of London in 1584. Donne's brother, Henry, was captured with a Roman Catholic priest and died in prison in 1593. Donne began a serious examination of the controversy between Roman Catholicism and the Church of England. In the end, he took the Oath of Supremacy. After a difficult time trying to support his growing family, Donne was ordained to the Anglican priesthood in 1615. In 1621 he became Dean of St Paul's and at last was free of financial concerns. Donne's spirituality developed through his priestly duties. He moved from doubt and cynicism to hope. Like St Augustine, whose works he read, Donne steadily sought for truth, journeying sometimes in the consciousness of God's love and sometimes in bitter darkness. Awareness of his sinfulness was assuaged only by a growing trust in God's mercy, best summed up in "A Hymne to God the Father."

George Herbert's contemporaries considered him a saintly parson whose poems, sermons, and essays were reflections on the life of a dedicated Anglican divine. Both of his long works, *The Country Parson* and *The Temple*, celebrate Christian life faithfully and conscientiously lived within the Anglican Church. Editor John N. Wall, Jr sums up Herbert's passion, which was to "devote all his energies, all his skills with language, all his persuasive powers, to move his congregation toward that ideal of community which the Church taught was the goal of human life on earth" (Herbert 1981: 25). Herbert lived the humble life of a country parson but with the rich understanding of a man nurtured in Elizabethan culture, with firm determination to preach as much by example as by word. The poem called "Love III" is anthologized for its poetic beauty, but it also appears in collections meant to help readers live more deeply spiritual lives.

Henry Vaughn admired George Herbert, to whom Vaughn gave credit for his conversion. Vaughn's poetry draws upon nature, and his poetry is thought to have had an influence on William Wordsworth (1770–1850). Thomas Traherne, the last born of the metaphysical poets, is perhaps most deeply indebted to the best of the long Western mystical tradition from Plato, Plotinus, Augustine, and Pseudo-Dionysius to the medieval writers, Richard of St Victor, St Bonaventure, Meister Eckhart, Henry Suso, and Jan van Ruusbroec. He is also indebted to the great English mystics, the author of the *Cloud of Unknowing*, and Julian of Norwich. Even the works of Jacob Boehme appear to have influenced Traherne.

Puritan spirituality was far less at home in Anglican England. Having warred, won, and lost, the Puritans became a small minority when the cavaliers prevailed in 1660. Many Puritans left England; in 1620 some of them founded the Massachusetts Bay Colony, which they hoped would become an exemplary Puritan outpost.

In 1652, George Fox (1624–91) founded the Religious Society of Friends in Lancashire. The Friends sought a deeply interior experience of continuing conversion like that described by Fox. They also sought a simple form of worship and found it in the silence of their meetings in which they sat together until one was moved to speak. Their experience bound them into a community that sought only to practice peaceably their newfound fellowship in the Holy Spirit who leads to Christ. But such a radical break with the established church and even with the worship of Cromwell's Commonwealth reaped persecution. In 1681, the Quaker William Penn negotiated for land in America, which he called Pennsylvania after his father. It was Penn's dream to help Quakers leave the persecution that he and others had suffered to undertake "a Holy Experiment." In 1682 he drafted Pennsylvania's constitution, which established principles of basic human rights in the colony, and under which it was governed until 1756.

On the Continent, most of the streams of Catholic spirituality flowed together into Paris at the beginning of the seventeenth century. From Italy came the translated works of Catherine of Genoa and from Spain the translated works of Teresa of Avila and later of John of the Cross. In 1609, there appeared *Règle de perfection réduite au seul point de la volonté divine*, by an English emigré, William Finch, whose Capuchin name was Benet Canfield or Benoît de Canfield (1562–1610). Canfield's abstract mysticism required one to bypass the incarnation to reach perfect conformity of one's will with the divine and so to achieve union and transformation into God. Images and discursive meditation belong to the first steps of contemplation and should be discarded so that one is annihilated by God's uniting action. Canfield's works had profound influence in France for the whole of the seventeenth century, and even survived being placed on the Index of Forbidden Books in 1689 during the "Quietism" problem.

All of these currents came to a focus in the salon of a remarkable woman and gifted mystic, Barbe Acarie (1565–1618). Gathered around her were men and women of spiritual and intellectual genius. In 1601 her salon was the meeting place of, among others, Pierre de Bérulle, Benet Canfield, Pierre Coton, SJ, confessor to King Henry IV, Francis de Sales, and Dom Beaucousin, a Carthusian who had translated Jan van Ruusbroec's (1293–1381) *Spiritual Espousals* into French. In 1604 Mme Acarie brought to Paris two Carmelite nuns who had been trained by St Teresa of Avila herself. The type of spiritual life her circle encouraged in its earliest years was "abstract mysticism," which sought to transcend all ideas and images, even the humanity of Christ, something the Carmelite nuns, following St Teresa of Avila, declared to be wrong-headed. Under their influence and through a retreat directed by his former teachers the Jesuits, Bérulle (1575–1629) underwent a conversion to incarnational theology. Bérulle is recognized as the father of the "French School" of spirituality whose members included Bérulle's confidante and adviser Madeleine de Saint-Joseph, Jean-Jacques Olier, and John Eudes.

In the French School, the Dionysian, Neoplatonic cycle of exit and return was wedded to the incarnation in a theological spirituality that asked its followers to enter the life of the Trinity through the incarnate Second Person, whose own journey into the depths of humiliation makes possible both his and the Christian's entrance into the glory of God, one and triune. Thus Bérulle's spirituality continued to emphasize the obliteration of self (*anéantissment*) in adoration before the ineffable otherness of God, but christened it, so to speak, by making Jesus Christ its prime example. At the same time, Bérulle and his successors shared the post-Tridentine concern for pastoral renewal. In 1611, Bérulle founded the French Oratory. His goal was to reunite what he considered necessary for priestly ministry: "authority, holiness, and doctrine." Without holiness and doctrine, the ecclesiastical state was "an unlearned, spiritless shell of authoritarian power." Olier and Eudes shared Bérulle's pastoral goal. Olier founded the Company of St Sulpice (the Sulpicians) who became a model of seminary education. Eudes founded the Congregation of Jesus and Mary for the same purpose, which was not to draw diocesan clergy into religious orders but to prepare them to be the kind of holy, learned clergy who could demand the respect their calling required to be effective.

Jean-Jacques Olier (1608–57) was a friend of Francis de Sales and Vincent de Paul. His work and writings reflect, with greater simplicity than Bérulle's, the latter's spirituality and pastoral concerns. John Eudes (1601–80) knew both Bérulle and Olier. He was schooled by the Jesuits and then entered the Oratory (1623) and was ordained in 1625. The congregation he founded was devoted to missions and the education of the French clergy. He also founded the Religious of Notre Dame of Charity to work with young women who needed refuge. The order eventually became two: Our Lady of Charity of Refuge, and Our Lady of Charity of the Good Shepherd. Eudes concentrated the spirituality of the French School in the symbol of the Sacred Hearts of Jesus and Mary.

Although a Savoyard, Francis de Sales (1567–1622) was educated by the Jesuits in Paris. After his ordination, de Sales participated in the *milieu dévot* that gathered around

Mme Acarie, but his spirituality developed differently from that of the French School. *Introduction to a Devout Life* is a manual for Christians, lay, clerical, or religious. Its language is simple and direct, as is its message: God's great love for all creation, but especially for human souls, who should never doubt God's infinite desire to forgive anyone who, with a penitent heart, seeks reconciliation. Francis de Sales was closer to the desire of the Jesuits to reassure people of God's universal love and their freedom to respond to that gift, and so he was at the opposite pole from the predestinarian rigorism of the Jansenists of Port Royal (see below). De Sales's political orientation was also quite different from the Parisians, whether Bérullian or Jansenist. In 1592 he was ordained and became Provost of the Church of St Peter in Geneva. But Catholics were not permitted in Calvinist Geneva, a republic constantly on the edge of war with Catholic Savoy. It became de Sales's dream to return Catholicism to Geneva through love and a learned, pious clergy rather than by force, as the Duke of Savoy attempted more than once. His dream was never realized, and he lived south of Geneva in the Savoyard town of Annecy where he became bishop of Geneva in 1602. He encouraged lay people to seek spiritual direction, and it was for a lay woman, Mme de Charmoisy, that he wrote *Introduction to a Devout Life*, which rapidly won a wide readership throughout France.

In 1604, de Sales met Jane Frances Frémyot, Baroness de Chantal, who heard him preach in Dijon. Like Mère Madeleine and Bérulle, de Chantal and de Sales influenced one another's growing spirituality as de Chantal flourished under his direction and he through her letters and advice. Together they founded the Visitation of Holy Mary, an order for women seeking a monastic life of prayer combined with service to the poor. Because women could not take solemn vows without being cloistered, the new religious order had to give up visitation of the poor and sick in their homes and practice their love of neighbor within the confines of their convent. Visitandine houses multiplied until by de Chantal's death in 1641 there were eighty in France. St Francis de Sales died in 1622, but not before he had learned from de Chantal to overcome his distaste for mysticism. De Sales studied the great contemplative authors, and his *Treatise on the Love of God* (1616) included his carefully studied and deep appreciation of the contemplative tradition. The book became nearly as popular as the *Introduction to a Devout Life*; both remain spiritual classics.

A younger friend of Francis de Sales was Vincent de Paul (1580–1660), who with Louise de Marillac (1591–1660) founded the Daughters of Charity in 1633 to minister to the poor in their homes and in hospitals. When faced with the choice of solemn vows and the cloister or their fundamental vocation to the poor, they chose their vocation. They could not, therefore, take solemn vows or wear a veil; instead, they took simple annual vows and wore caps. The spirituality of the Daughters of Charity reflects the teachings and practices of both de Paul, called the Apostle of Charity, and de Marillac who was, like Jane de Chantal, first married and a mother, before the death of her husband in 1625 allowed her to devote herself entirely to God and the service of the poor. The man who helped her to find the way to do so was de Paul, a priest dedicated to missions among the populace as a major means of conversion and spiritual development. De Paul found his way to God in the active life of service to the poor, which led him to deeper prayer and made of him a reformer, a founder, and gifted spiritual director. In the mission of the Word, de Paul found the mission of Jesus, the model of his own ministry and of the Congregation of the Mission that he founded in 1617. With St Francis de Sales, de Paul shared also the conviction that God is found in the present moment and that love is both the way and the end of one's actions, prayer, and life.

Some of the greatest spiritual leaders in seventeenth-century France were schooled by the Jesuits; for example, Pierre de Bérulle and St Francis de Sales. Blaise Pascal (1623–62), also Jesuit trained, turned against his former teachers when he fell under the influence of the Arnaulds of Port Royal, Angélique (1591–1661), abbess of the Cistercian Abbey of Port Royal, and her youngest brother, Antoine, dubbed "the Great Arnauld." The Arnaulds were drawn not only to contemplation, but also to a kind of learned spirituality that found expression in a work whose short title is *Augustinus*, by Cornelius Jansen (1585–1638). The movement that adopted *Augustinus* predated its publication. Called Jansenists, they rejected the scholasticism of the theological schools and attempted to respond to the controversy then raging between Jesuits and Dominicans concerning free will and grace. Against the condemned "laxism" of Jesuit "probabilism," the Jansenists of Port Royal taught limited atonement, predestination of the elect, and a severe penitential system. It is understandable why Jansenists were accused of being Calvinists, even though the scholars of Port Royal wrote not only against the Jesuits, as did Blaise Pascal in his *Provincial Letters*, but also to convert the Huguenot minority in France.

Quietism is the name given to a late seventeenth-century movement led by Mme de Guyon, also known as Jeanne-Marie Bouvier de la Motte (1648–1717). She urged others to share her understanding and practice of mysticism, which she called "prayer of the heart." She published in 1685 her *Short and Easy Method for Prayer*. The mystic is lost in God in an indistinct and objectless contemplation that is a return to the abstract mysticism of Canfield, whose works were put on the Index of Forbidden Books with Mme Guyon's in 1686. The young Abbé de Fénelon met Mme Guyon and was won over by her direction. Fénelon, who had become bishop of Cambrai, tried to defend Guyon against the powerful Jacques-Benigne Bossuet (1627–1704), who in 1695 obtained an official condemnation of Mme Guyon. By 1699, Fénelon had submitted, Mme Guyon was labeled a Quietist, and the movement subsided. The abstract mysticism with which the century had begun ended in the triumph of the anti-mystic party led by Bossuet.

Conclusion

Between the mid-fifteenth century and the end of the seventeenth century, spiritual practices left the cloister. Inspired religious leaders understood that the increasingly literate populace needed not only instruction but also intentional spiritual methods that they could incorporate into their lives as lay people. From the beguines to St Ignatius to St Vincent de Paul, retreats, spiritual direction, and books helped Catholic laity to follow spiritual paths. The Reformation encouraged Protestants to take up their Bibles and to apply the gospel to their lives as individuals and, increasingly, in small groups, most notably among the Pietists of the seventeenth century.

But by 1600, the intellectual formation of ministers and priests reflected the unimaginative scholasticism that reigned in the seminaries. While conformity and confessionalism satisfied only the most conservative, the dissatisfaction of others took two opposed directions. Some, like the German Pietists who emphasized spiritual experience, sought to deepen their spirituality through small gatherings – a tendency whose reverberations reached into the nineteenth-century Romantic Movement. The more intellectual French spiritual circles moved in a different direction. At one extreme were the Arnaulds of Port Royal and, at the other, the philosophy of René Descartes. Even though Descartes wanted to remain a practicing Catholic and wrote a theology of the Eucharist based on his philosophical insights, his method of reasoned doubt and his *cogito ergo sum* encouraged philosophy to break its link to theology. Autonomous reason was the foundation of the Enlightenment of the eighteenth century.

References

Arndt, J. 1979: *True Christianity*, trans. P. Erb. New York: Paulist Press.

Bérulle, P. de, et al. 1989: *Bérulle and the French School: Selected Writings*, ed. W. M. Thompson, trans. L. M. Glendon. New York: Paulist Press.

Boehme, J. 1978: *The Way to Christ*, trans. P. Erb. New York: Paulist Press.

Büsser, F. 1987: The spirituality of Zwingli and Bullinger. In J. Raitt, with B. McGinn and J. Meyendorff (eds), *Christian Spirituality: High Middle Ages and Reformation*, pp. 300–17. New York: Crossroad.

Bynum, C. W. 1987: Religious women in the later Middle Ages. In J. Raitt, with B. McGinn and J. Meyendorff (eds), *Christian Spirituality: High Middle Ages and Reformation*, pp. 121–39. New York: Crossroad.

Clements, A. L. 1969: *The Mystical Poetry of Thomas Traherne*. Cambridge, MA: Harvard University Press.

Cognet, L. 1959: *Post-Reformation Spirituality*, trans. P. H. Scott. New York: Hawthorn Books.

Dupré, L. and Saliers, D. (eds) 1989: *Christian Spirituality: Post-Reformation and Modern*. New York: Crossroad.

The Early Kabbalah 1986: ed. J. Dan, trans. R. C. Kiener. New York: Paulist Press.

George, T. 1987: The spirituality of the Radical Reformation. In J. Raitt, with B. McGinn and J. Meyendorff (eds), *Christian Spirituality: High Middle Ages and Reformation*, pp. 334–71. New York: Crossroad.

Herbert, G. 1981: *The Country Parson; The Temple*, ed. J. N. Wall, Jr. New York: Paulist Press.

Ignatius of Loyola 1991: *Spiritual Exercises and Selected Works*, trans. G. Ganss. New York: Paulist Press.

Jedin, H. 1993: *The Medieval and Reformation Church: An Abridgement of the History of the Church*, vols 4–6, ed. and trans. J. Dolan. New York: Crossroad.

John of the Cross 1987: *Selected Writings*, trans. K. Kavanaugh. New York: Paulist Press.

Kieckhefer, R. 1987: Major currents of late medieval devotion. In J. Raitt, with B. McGinn and J. Meyendorff (eds), *Christian Spirituality: High Middle Ages and Reformation*, pp. 75–108. New York: Crossroad.

Nicholas of Cusa 1997: *Selected Spiritual Writings*, trans. H. L. Bond. New York: Paulist Press.

Raitt, J., with McGinn, B. and Meyendorff, J. (eds) 1987: *Christian Spirituality: High Middle Ages and Reformation*. New York: Crossroad.

Sales, Francis de and Chantal, Jane de 1988: *Letters of Spiritual Direction*, trans. P. M. Thibert. New York: Paulist Press.

Sedgewick, A. 1977: *Jansenism in Seventeenth Century France*. Charlottesville: University of Virginia Press.

Teresa of Avila 1979: *The Interior Castle*, trans. K. Kavanaugh and O. Rodriguez. New York: Paulist Press.

Williams, G. H. 1962: *The Radical Reformation*. Philadelphia: Westminster Press.

Zohar: The Book of Enlightenment 1983: trans. D. C. Matt. New York: Paulist Press.

CHAPTER 8

Christian Spirituality in Europe and North America since 1700

Diana Butler Bass and
Joseph Stewart-Sicking

The Challenges of Modernity

During the past three centuries, Christians in Europe and North America faced enormous challenges regarding the ways in which they experienced God. Throughout the
West, in the societies that once understood themselves as the guardians of faith, Christian tradition became increasingly less tenable in the wake of massive philosophical,
scientific, political, and social change. These cultural movements profoundly influenced
the practice of the spiritual life for Europeans, Americans, and Canadians, regardless
of their denomination or theology. Often, these changes have been viewed as negative,
a decline of the great spiritual traditions of Western Christianity from their zenith in
the Middle Ages. Certainly, the cultural circumstances of modern Europe and North
America have undermined many traditional spiritual practices. Yet, the picture is more
nuanced than a simple fracturing and decline. In many ways, modern Western Christian spirituality can be cast in Dickensian terms: "It was the best of times; it was the
worst of times." The conditions that unhinged traditional spirituality in the West also
have opened the way for new forms and creative renderings of Christian spiritual practice. In the modern period, Western Christian spirituality both responded to and reacted
against massive cultural change. The processes of adaptation and resistance gave rise
to enormously varied patterns of spirituality, which, in themselves, defy conventional
categories of understanding the Christian life.

For much of the twentieth century, scholars posited nearly all the changes in
Western culture under the rubric of "secularization," an unfolding of historical movements whereby secular forces and social organization displaced religious belief and
institutions. Accordingly, scholars argued that the world became "disenchanted" as the
"sacred canopy" of meaning eroded and God was banished from everyday life (Weber
1946: 139 ff; Berger 1990). In more recent decades, however, observers have become
increasingly skeptical about secularization as a guiding principle for understanding religion in the West. While traditional religion, especially institutional Christianity and

formal dogmas, fell on hard times in Europe and North America, people on both continents experienced a new interest in and expression of spirituality in their lives. By the new millennium, after three hundred years of "secular" modernity and the diminishment of belief, much of Western society still possesses a vital sense of the sacred, including the particular Christian understanding of the sacred. If modernity did not completely banish the experience of God from Western society, what happened in the past three centuries?

Increasingly, scholars of Christian spirituality have identified the roots of modernity in the intellectual changes of the fourteenth century (von Balthasar 1991; Dupré 1993). During this period, John Duns Scotus and his followers began to promote nominalist philosophy. Nominalism emphasized God's inscrutable otherness and contended that it is impossible to speak about God's reality using analogies from the natural world. As a result, philosophy and science came to be considered independent of theology and faith. When nominalism combined with an emerging humanist strain of thought that stressed human creativity, a new, modern style of thinking emerged (Dupré 1993).

This uncoupling meant that, for the first time in a millennium, it became possible to engage science and philosophy without reference to theology – the supernatural ordering of the universe and the human being. Since the ways of God were deemed unfathomable, purely human projects became the focus of science and philosophy. Creation as cosmos became nature, the human being as microcosmos became the subject, and redemption as deified nature became redemption by supernatural grace (Dupré 1993). The parting of science and religion, and the new rivalry between the two, formed the basis of modernity, along with the equally contentious rivalries of reason versus revelation, fact versus feeling. Spirituality, once a kind of metaphysical science of the soul's approach to God, was increasingly consigned to irrational and emotive categories.

The separation of science and faith into two arenas has often been identified as the process of secularization. Yet contemporary cultural theory suggests that, instead of secularization, the term "de-traditionalization" better describes the interplay of forces that have reconfigured religious practice in the Western modernity. De-traditionalization does not necessarily imply that religious belief has disappeared. Rather, as Paul Heelas states, "de-traditionalization involves a shift of authority from 'without' to 'within'" whereby "individual subjects are themselves called upon to exercise authority" and "'voice' is displaced from established sources, coming to rest with the self" (1996: 2). De-traditionalization is a set of processes by which societies that were once shaped by univocal ("of one voice") authority become multivocal ("of many voices") cultures in which authority shifts to individual persons. Traditions are eroded or eradicated under the weight of contending options and personal choice. In a situation of multivocality, individuals must choose which belief systems, social practices, or religious traditions to embrace and follow, thus making personal autonomy the sole arbiter of what is true, good, or beautiful.

Most historians agree that, in the West, both late medieval theology and the Protestant Reformation set the processes of de-traditionalization in motion when traditional conceptions of Christendom and its authority were questioned by both new theological options and the emergence of the idea of freedom of individual religious conscience.

De-traditionalization increased in its scope and reach during the Enlightenment, finding political expression in the American and French Revolutions and enlarged religious toleration in other European countries. The displacement of traditional religious authority by individual autonomy reached its peak in the 1960s and 1970s, thus constituting a near complete break with preceding constructions of society, meaning, identity, and tradition (Hammond 1992).

Although scholars argue about the extent of de-traditionalization and its ramifications for Christianity, there is no disagreement that it has occurred. While medieval Christendom and Reformation church–state arrangements created the cultural conditions for certain kinds of Christian spirituality to flourish, the ever-increasing sense of personal autonomy and individual choice in the modern – and postmodern – West has fostered different patterns of spiritual life and attendant practices. Through the past three centuries, the displacement of external authorities has nurtured a profound sense of the self in relation to God, allowed for an enlarged vision of human community and creation, and prompted serious re-engagement, re-appropriation, and re-working of Christian traditions.

This essay argues that, in modern and postmodern Europe and North America, these intellectual, political, and cultural conditions provide the most fruitful way to explore Christian spirituality. The rubric of de-traditionalization, with its attendant uncoupling of once-interlaced categories, helps unpack the otherwise complex diversity of spiritualities that have emerged in the period. Therefore, this essay is not arranged primarily by geography, schools, or theologies. Rather, it attempts to track the movements of Christian spirituality in relation to the growth of personal autonomy; the decline of formal structures of Christian organization, belief, and practice; and the tension between science and religion.

By approaching the subject in this way, modern Christian spirituality can be seen as a kind of vast project that moves between the poles of mind and heart, of rationalism and mysticism, of certainty and doubt, of exclusion and toleration, of violence and peacemaking, that places the sacred self in lifelong quest for meaning and purpose against an ever-growing fear that God is absent and may well have died.

Where is God? (1700–1820)

Although Western Christians in the early modern period struggled with many questions, the overarching one was surprisingly clear: "Where is God?" The fracturing of the Catholic tradition into rival Protestant groups meant that no one church could claim religious authority without question. The agony of wars between Christians unhinged questions of suffering and violence that opened the way for massive doubt and unbelief. New conceptions of science suggested that God and the angels did not specifically direct nature; rather, a distant God established a pattern of natural laws by which the universe operated. Experiments in democracy, religious toleration, and building nation-states reorganized traditional ideas of the divine origin of personhood, family, and community identity. Although many early modern Christians were relatively optimistic about human capacities and nature, they were often surprisingly pessimistic about God's being, presence, and work in the world. Across the West, it was increasingly obvious that God had moved. Perhaps God had abandoned the world – or God had even vanished. Christians needed to find new ways to experience God, to hear God, and to discern God's will.

As classical mysticism was negatively relegated to "enthusiasm" – a kind of irrational type of inward experience belonging to the spiritual elite – many Christians began to borrow from new cultural emphases on reason, tolerance, harmony, order, providence, and morality in order to understand and reconceptualize their experience of God. Thus, while some traditional Christians (particularly Roman Catholics) retained an interest in classical mysticism and devotional practices, others developed spiritualities that reflected the temper of the times. The early modern period was a Janus-like era, with styles that both reached back toward the Middle Ages and reached forward to later modern concerns. Toward whatever direction Christians reached, however, the early modern period was an era of great innovation and change, suggesting answers to the question "Where is God?" that remain as lively options even today.

Jeanne-Marie Bouvier de la Motte Guyon (1648–1717) provides an example of those who attempted to find God by returning to the mysticism of the ancient and medieval church. But given the changes to the path of return, her journey back takes a characteristically modern turn. Since scholastic doctrine and mechanistic natural science seemed to silence God's word, the mystic turned her attention to the possibility of God acting through her interior experiences. Hence, the early modern period birthed a new literary form – autobiographical mysticism – that sought to create within the self a space for God to speak (de Certeau 2000).

Guyon's autobiographical writings show a soul seeking God within with an unprecedented psychological transparency. Her spirituality is reminiscent of the Rhineland mystics, but it also integrates the optimistic humanism of St Francis de Sales and his desire to tutor every Christian in the love of God. At its heart is the "internal exercise of love" (Guyon 2002: 9) whereby the soul increasingly abandons its own desires and surrenders wholly to God. Given over to God's purposes, the soul becomes indifferent to its own ends and acts as an instrument of God's providential will. For Guyon, prayer presupposes the opposition of head and heart and of external and internal. Prayer is an internal matter, concerned with reforming the heart. She averred that were the church to recognize that true sanctity comes from internal and not external change, efforts at cultivating holiness would be much more successful.

While Guyon based much of her spirituality upon the Catholic doctrine of *apatheia* or indifference, she developed this concept in controversial ways. Like many Christians of her age, Guyon distrusted human desire. Thus, she stressed the radical transformation of the soul solely by God's grace. Prayer should be characterized not by exertion but rather by patience and openness. Likewise, virtue cannot be developed through external exercises but only by the sovereign action of God residing in the soul. The soul's only role is to give itself over to the annihilating power of divine love.

The openness with which Guyon expressed these doctrines proved controversial. Given the Jansenist–Quietist conflict of her time, such daring was bound to incur scrutiny, especially from a woman. Guyon's case shows how mysticism and scholastic theology were sundered in modernity, and how mystics were outsiders to the church.

French authorities imprisoned Guyon for seven years and banned her writings. Yet her influence persisted. Given a more orthodox form by Jean-Pierre de Caussade, her beliefs would influence Catholics through the next three centuries. And, outside Catholicism, they would be widely influential among Protestants, especially those in the Wesleyan tradition.

Like Guyon, the American theologian Jonathan Edwards (1703–58) struggled with issues of human agency and divine will. Edwards solved the problems by linking the Calvinist doctrine of predestination and Enlightenment philosophical impulses with God's saving activity. As a theologian who dabbled in science, Edwards embodied the rationalist ideal of the early modern period. As heir to the Puritans, however, he did not allow reason to undercut his belief in revelation and mystical experience. He posited that in addition to a faculty of human reason, God had also created a faculty of affection that operated according to predictable natural laws.

Edwards believed that humankind could employ reason to know about God and God's universe, but must employ the affections to know God. For Edwards, as with other reformed Protestants, the affections were not operable until "turned on" by God's divine agency. Only when God instilled the soul with a "divine and supernatural light" could the justified comprehend God's beauty and respond to it through growth in holiness. Although Edwards remained fully committed to scientific inquiry, he nevertheless believed that the fullness of human knowing came through a lively experience of divine beauty. Other eighteenth-century Protestants, notably John Wesley and George Whitefield, developed Edwards's insights and initiated a popular trans-continental revival movement which emphasized the emotive aspects of faith through a felt experience of being "born again." A Christian spirituality thus seated in the heart – rather than in the head – would eventually shape much of Anglo-American evangelical Protestantism.

Some Enlightenment Christians were disturbed by what they understood as a rebirth of "enthusiasm" in evangelical religion. One such person was Thomas Jefferson (1743–1826), writer of the American Declaration of Independence and president of the United States. Few scholars of Christian spirituality take Jefferson seriously as a representative figure. Yet Jefferson ranks with two other American presidents – Abraham Lincoln and Jimmy Carter – as thoughtfully engaged with theology, morality, and Christian practice. Despite Jefferson's many personal shortcomings, historian Martin Marty cites him as a "reverent" thinker who represents the religious impulse of the Anglo-American Enlightenment and who believed that "religion was a major grounding for, or instrument of, virtue and morality" (Sheridan 1998: 9).

Unlike Jonathan Edwards, whose vision depended on a powerful sense of the Augustinian God, Jefferson's vision of God derived from nature and was revealed through reason and morality. Although his political opponents branded him as an infidel, Jefferson always considered himself a reasonable Christian and was deeply influenced by the Unitarian Joseph Priestly. Convinced that Jesus was not divine, Jefferson thought him a great moral teacher whose life exemplified the principles whereby humanity would be improved through the spread of Christian charity. By enlarging the sphere of benevolence, Jefferson argued that republican government would flourish and social harmony – a kind of reasonable Christian utopia – would result.

Thus, Jefferson crafted a vision of Christianity that was reasonable, natural, and orderly – ideals all reflected in his estate in Virginia – and a type of spirituality that extolled the "genuine precepts of Jesus." While rejecting the devotional excesses of medieval Christianity, Jefferson sought to restore the purity of New Testament Christianity, a simple set of Jesus's ethical teachings. Although Jefferson's particular arrangement of these teachings and his deism would not prove a strong tradition in America, his attempt to return to primitive Christianity by interpreting Scripture for himself, exercising free theological inquiry, and affirming doubt as an expression of religious experience would provide a powerful model for liberal Christian spirituality for generations to follow.

By linking Christian teachings with the moral foundation of the Republic, Jefferson suggested that religion could play an important role in public life without granting any one church the privileges of establishment. Jefferson summed up his own radically republican faith by saying, "I am a sect by myself, as far as I know" (Sheridan 1998: 69). And therein he expressed the complete revolution of religious authority and spiritual experience of early modernity, and opened some provocative ways of answering the questions raised by that revolution.

Many more traditional Christians were uncomfortable with Jefferson's brand of primitive faith and were equally uncomfortable with the displacement of tradition in favor of nature, reason, and individual autonomy. Such Christians resisted the radical relocation of authority and experience to the reasonable self or moral political community. An example of this discomfort is found in the life of Elizabeth Bayley Seton (1774–1821) who, after a privileged life as a New York Episcopalian and the death of her socially prominent husband, embraced Roman Catholicism and would eventually be canonized as the first American-born saint.

Seton's case illustrates several aspects of early modern spirituality. Like Guyon, she found God through a return to medieval Christian spirituality. During a pilgrimage to Italy, she was overwhelmed by a mystical experience during the mass and converted to Roman Catholicism upon her return to the United States. Seton founded a religious order (of which she became the superior) and a school for girls. Throughout, hers was a spirituality of loss, poverty, and suffering as she embraced trials and persecution on behalf of spreading her faith on the Western frontier of the early Republic. And, also like Guyon, she dutifully recorded her spiritual insights in autobiography which reveals both deep personal devotion and crisp theological intelligence.

Unlike Guyon, however, Seton submitted to the male authorities above her. This often put her in great personal anguish and risk. However, she saw the conflict as suffering for the sake of faith, and she eventually died because of lack of support and poor judgment on the part of her superiors. Ultimately, Seton's story is a kind of ironic reversal of Thomas Jefferson's spirituality. Like him, and countless modern people, she rejects her familial religion and chooses her own faith, but she chooses to embrace hierarchical authority, mystical prayer, the supernatural, and submission to tradition.

At the hinge between this period of early modernity and high modernity stands the Prussian philosopher Immanuel Kant (1724–1804). Just as the spirituality of reason and experience was flourishing, Kant sought to cut it off at its roots. In his *Critique of Pure Reason*, Kant provided a devastating attack against metaphysical types of religion.

According to Kant, the mind apprehends the universe through the categories of reason; the phenomena which appear to the mind are not the things in themselves. Thus, it is impossible to know God or any transcendent reality through any ideas, observations, or experiences; one cannot transcend experience through concepts derived from experience. The only transcendental thought that is admissible is morality, since as things-in-themselves human beings could be free. Kant carries the modern separation of natural science and religion to its logical conclusion.

God with Us (1820–1915)

Kant's critique of both the reasonable God "out there" and mystical experience of God "in here" in favor of moral duty and action seems to place him outside the scope of Christian spirituality. However, the move Kant made toward identifying God's reign with human goodness represented a profound shift in the West's experience of God. Ironically, as Kant undermined the basis for traditional spiritual practices and dismissed the possibility of knowing God through reason, he opened the way for God to be known and experienced through human history, human morality, human happiness, and human culture. In high modernity, God moved again as Christians increasingly answered the question "Where is God?" with "God is with us." The deist God, the rational God, gave way to the immanent God known through the romantic beauties of human experience and the dutiful human activity of building God's kingdom. As a result of their interest in humanity, Christians appropriated the new science of history for spiritual ends as they identified human history (and, ironically, practices and traditions rejected in the early modern period) as the primary arena of experiencing God in their lives.

In England, the best example of this impulse is the Oxford Movement, whose leading proponent, John Henry Newman (1801–90), has been long criticized by scholars of Christian spirituality for his lack of "contemplative rapture" (Wakefield 1991: 278). Typically, Edward Pusey (1800–82) was called the "doctor mysticus" of the movement. However weak Newman's spiritual expressiveness, his intense concern to recover the catholicity of Anglicanism and holiness through the church's sacraments was an important contribution to modern Christian spirituality. Through this, and through his theological exposition of doctrinal development, Newman illustrates the high modern attention to history as an arena of God's activity in the world as he makes historical questions key to vital spirituality and practice. Finally, Newman was motivated by political issues in protecting the English church against parliament's theological meddling, thus making the Oxford Movement a kind of spirituality of protest against political establishment. When he eventually converted to Roman Catholicism, Newman both fulfilled his quest to find the historical church and found a way out of the political problems of religious establishment in the modern world.

Those who followed Newman – whether they remained Anglican or converted to Roman Catholicism – would further make God immanent as they developed an intense interest in serving the poor and working in urban missions. Many would eventually blend the spirituality of the past (Catholic practices) with spiritual concerns that addressed the present, urging society toward a better future by becoming Christian Socialists or proponents of the Social Gospel movement.

Another contrasting example of Roman Catholic spirituality in this period is St Thérèse of Lisieux (1873–97). Born Thérèse Martin in Alençon, France, she died only twenty-four years later of tuberculosis, having lived since the age of fifteen as a sister of the Carmel at Lisieux. St Thérèse was in many ways a typical young woman of her times, and her unique spiritual depth shone precisely through her unremarkable surroundings rather than eclipsing them – indeed, her greatest insight was that sanctity and grace flow through the littlest aspects of life.

St Thérèse was one of nine children of devout middle-class parents, and, like four of her siblings, she entered the cloister. Like many novices, St Thérèse had first been convinced that she was called to heroic virtue, but as she examined her piety and interactions with others, she found herself lacking. Turning to St Paul, she realized that "all is grace." This fundamental insight developed into her doctrine of spiritual childhood, outlined in St Thérèse's autobiography, *The History of a Soul*. The doctrine of spiritual childhood begins by considering how God's love reaches out to the least and littlest. In light of God's mercy and love, Christians are called to approach God as a child with empty hands, abandoning themselves to God's purposes and mercy to direct and crown their acts. A child does not want to control her parent's gift; the parent looks with love on the child and fondly lifts her up. St Thérèse teaches that love ennobles any act, no matter how small. All Christians are called to live in the littleness of love and to strew as fragile petals before the Father every aspect of their daily lives and relationships, no matter how mundane.

Like many Catholics of her era, St Thérèse exhibited the polarities of modernity. Her experiential and self-referential piety seems quintessentially modern, yet she was also profoundly rooted in tradition, immersing herself in Scripture and the writings of the saints. Her theology is profound (even possibly a Catholic response to Luther), and yet it is a "little way" that outmaneuvers any and all of the grand ideas of modernity and in classically Catholic fashion reintegrates the natural, even the banal, with the supernatural gifts of God.

Among Protestants, Friedrich Schleiermacher (1768–1834) provides a key example of the liberal response to de-traditionalization and modern science. Throughout his writings, he sought to provide a compelling vision of the Christian faith to "cultured despisers" who were likely to believe religion and its traditions to be superstitious and repressive. Schleiermacher's response was an ingenious synthesis of Christian spirituality and modern philosophy that took shape through exploring the religious consciousness.

One part of this synthesis is familiar. Schleiermacher (1999) identified the essence of religion with the *Gefühl* (feeling/intimation/experience/consciousness) of absolute dependence upon that "whence of our being" over whom we can have no power. However, Schleiermacher intended this general observation to be the root of a very practical and deeply Christian piety in which, by the grace of Christ's influence, the believer seeks to live in a state where every impulse that enters the mind is conjoined to the God-consciousness. The grace of Christ is the capacity to encounter God in every experience. And, counter to many modern impulses, Schleiermacher maintained that the believer cannot encounter this grace alone. It is rather an experience transmitted through language by evangelism and rekindled in community.

Schleiermacher also sought to maintain traditional orthodox doctrine while radically reinterpreting it to match his notion of piety focused on consciousness. For instance, sin for Schleiermacher (1999) really is turning away from God and a hindrance to life, not because it is a transgression against God's honor, but because it is failing to live each moment in light of the God-consciousness. Schleiermacher's great synthesis provided the model for a liberal theology: traditional doctrines must be translated into terms consistent with modern science and philosophy, and this model continued to have influence throughout the following century.

Like Schleiermacher, the American William James (1842–1910) also sought to be an apologist for religious experience to its cultured despisers. But, unlike Schleiermacher, James felt no compunction about jettisoning doctrine in order to do so. His conception of religious experience as the universal and pure essence of religion stands at the hinge point between centuries, summarizing the romantic impulses of the former and foreshadowing the de-institutionalization of religion in the next.

At first glance, it might seem odd to include William James in a discussion of Christian spirituality. James was a psychologist and philosopher, not a theologian. He was a secular Harvard professor who did not believe in organized religion. And, by his own assessment (James 1997), he seemed to have a temperament that made him unable to enjoy the very religious experiences he studied. Yet he admits that he could not escape the nagging of a "mystical germ" that told him that "thither lies the truth" (James 1920: 135). Thus, he sought to be an apologist for the reality and value of religion in a positivistic and secular period which tended to regard religion as useless fantasy.

James's view of spirituality is presented in *The Varieties of Religious Experience*, delivered as the Gifford Lectures for 1900. In these lectures, James sought to understand the value and nature of religion from a scientific perspective. From the beginning of his exploration, James differentiated religious experience, which is fundamental, from "ecclesiasticism." According to James, established religions both feed off the extraordinary experience of their founders and add the "historic incrustations" or "over-beliefs" of doctrine to that purely spiritual experience. Thus, individual religious experience should be considered the heart of the spiritual life, and creed, code, and cult are all secondary detractions. James defined religion as "*the feelings, acts, and experiences of individual men in their solitude, so far as they apprehend themselves to stand in relation to whatever they may consider to be divine*" (1997: 42). Thus the essence of religion is to be found through studying those extraordinary individuals who have such experiences.

Yet, these feelings are no hallucinations; they are quite real, and they show the marks of genius. In exploring spiritual virtuosi, James concluded that religious experience is unlike other experience and therefore must reside at the fringes of consciousness. Moreover, the positive influence of the saints convinced him that spiritual aptitude is an adaptive capacity of the human species. Thus, while religion is absolutely natural, it is also absolutely real, since its effects are real.

James is the quintessential example of those who sought to mediate the chasm between the reductionist view that religious experiences were totally natural and thus false and the traditional evangelical view that religious experiences were supernatural and thus true (Taves 1999). James's solution, that religious experiences are both natural and true, is both creative and appealing. Yet it is also very modern, taking for granted the separation of the natural and supernatural. James's mystical and anti-ecclesial stance would cast a long shadow over those strands of twentieth-century Christian spirituality that increasingly see themselves as "spiritual, but not religious."

Is God? (1915–1980)

The late modern period was one fraught with irony. Christians had dodged Kant's two-pronged attack on Enlightenment spiritualities by reasserting God's immanence in history and the human psyche. By 1900, however, God was removed from the equation. If God was so enmeshed in human experience, what need is there of God? Many political, social, and philosophical movements of the early twentieth century kept basic Christian ideals while ignoring – or even rejecting – the God who was once at the center of such passions. Medicine, Marxism, and psychology offered solutions to human problems without reference to God. The early part of the twentieth century would be the great age of ideologies in the West, some of them contending that God could not be discovered in all human acts. Other ideologies would claim God's blessing, while committing heinous crimes against humankind. Some of human experience, Western Christians would learn, might be more closely related to evil than divine beauty. Instead of wondering where God was, Western Christians began to wonder if God even existed.

Perhaps no other writer better captures the essence of late modernity than the Anglican C. S. Lewis (1898–1963) whose essays placed "God in the dock," thus pitting the Christian faith against all secular ideologies. Lewis, a skeptical and agnostic Oxford don, embraced Christianity after a lengthy philosophical struggle over claims to Jesus's divinity. His work, especially *Mere Christianity*, breathed new life into the venerable practice of Christian apologetics. He popularized proofs for God based on evidence, logic, intellectual rigor, and poetics.

Joining Lewis in this academic and artistic defense of Christianity were J. R. R. Tolkien, Dorothy Sayers, and Charles Williams, a group of English writers collectively known as the Inklings. Not mystics, they best exemplify a strain of spirituality of the mind as they tackled the defense of Christian faith against painful questions raised by modern worldviews and, at the height of their careers, the violence of fascism and war. Lewis and his associates drew stark contrasts in essays, plays, poetry, and novels between good and evil, depicting the world in a tragically heroic struggle between God and the Devil. God, Lewis assured, would always win, but victory would only come through faithful courage, lively orthodoxy, and supernatural assistance. However difficult the trials of faith, Lewis insisted that Christianity was a life of joy that offered the seeking soul spiritual assurance through an embrace of truth.

The power of Lewis's artistic apologetics is evident in its extraordinary continued popularity. Arguably, the Inklings, especially Lewis and Tolkien, have influenced more people across the globe with the Christian message than anyone else in the twentieth century. And their tradition of poetic apologetics was carried on by other writers such as the British journalist Malcolm Muggeridge and the American Madeleine L'Engle.

Dorothy Day (1897–1980) was also a convert to Christianity. Her passage to faith went through the Marxist and anarcho-syndicalist critique of modernism. Born in Brooklyn, Day had a childhood which reflected the rapid de-traditionalization of late modernity. As she notes in her autobiography, *The Long Loneliness*, her parents were raised without church, and churchgoing was only a sporadic part of her own upbringing. Day's early exposure to Christianity was limited to trips with friends to the local Episcopal church and reading Dostoevsky as she devoured literature. While Christianity interested her, her spiritual longing came to be satisfied through her encounters at university with the radical thought of Marxists, anarchists, and unionists.

Day became an activist in the early labor movement, writing for a radical newspaper and enduring jail for her beliefs. She found herself at the core of the movement during heady times, meeting luminaries like Trotsky. She fell in love and had a child with her anarchist common-law husband. And, along the way, she encountered Catholicism. Day increasingly realized that Christianity seemed able to address those shortcomings she had felt in the revolutionary movement, and, during her pregnancy, she decided that she would leave her partner, join the church, and have her child baptized. Later, Day met Peter Maurin, a French expatriate and a "modern Saint Francis," and together they founded the Catholic Worker movement.

The spirituality of the Catholic Worker movement transformed the Marxist critique of capitalism and its emphasis on praxis by reading it through the lens of Scripture and the tradition of the church. Rather than fomenting revolution, the Catholic Worker movement provided prophetic social witness through its houses of hospitality which offered unconditional love to the marginalized. Catholic workers embraced pacifism and voluntary poverty, and they lived in lay communities following a rule of life focused on the Eucharist and the monastic hours. While Marxism and other radical movements may have identified the alienation and loneliness that is endemic to modern society, Dorothy Day believed that only Christianity and its notions of agapic love and radically inclusive community were able to provide the solution: "We have all known the long loneliness and we have learned that the only solution is love and that love comes with community" (Day 1952: 286).

Another American mystic who emphasized community, justice, and love was Howard Thurman (1900–81), the first black dean of the chapel at Boston University. Against the backdrop of American segregation, violence, and oppression, Thurman constructed a spirituality of wholeness that both comforted the oppressed and challenged the prevailing social (and white Christian) norms of race. Borrowing from ancient streams of African memory of communion with nature, Thurman explored the essential unity of all living things. This unity expanded to a hopeful vision of community in which respect, responsibility, and justice would be practiced. Thus, "Thurman's ideal of community was the wholeness, integration, and harmony of creation" (Bridges 2001: 128). Sin was lost harmony that could only be restored by individuals shaped by Christian practices of meditation and suffering. Through the struggles of prayer, protest, persecution, and martyrdom, believers encounter a loving God who empowers them to embody the essential unity and harmony of creation in wider human community. Thurman thus answered the question "Is God?" in the context of African-American Christian community. Yes, God is. For God, according to Thurman, was embodied in the radical wholeness of the blessed community in worship, prayer, and social action. Thurman's spirituality of community shaped the vision of his younger friend and colleague, Martin Luther King, Jr.

At the border between late modern and postmodern trends in spirituality stands the Trappist monk Thomas Merton (1915–68). Indeed, he straddled many borders: a sometimes-hermit with the vocation of being a writer, a worldly intellectual who discovered a call to be a monk, a Christian mystical theologian who wrote on Zen. As a monk, he was steeped in the pre-modern Christian tradition, and yet he also had a keenly modern ability to examine his own psyche. Both of these talents were combined in his writings, which recovered classic Christian spirituality (for example, the desert dwellers, apophatic theology, the monastic tradition) and presented it in a way that was compelling to a late modern audience. Merton's writings showed his readers that living faithfully to a tradition is both possible and compelling in contemporary culture.

Merton also began to reintegrate those strains of thought that were sundered in modernity: natural and supernatural, science and religion, tradition and progress, philosophy and theology, contemplation and action. For instance, his writings often took modern psychological insights about self-deception and angst and reframed them in the traditional Christian terms of humility and faith. Rather than relying on psychoanalysis or science to reveal the true self, Merton suggested that we discover our true selves in silent contemplation and naked encounter with God. For Merton, modern concerns and insights were seen as important pointers to their fuller explanation in classic Christian doctrines. In the age of anxiety following World War II, people losing confidence in modern progress found in Merton's exposition of the Christian tradition a living way of life – one more complete and less deceitful than any that secular philosophy and science had to offer.

Merton's influence continues to be felt through the works of his fellow Trappists, Thomas Keating and Basil Pennington. Like Merton, they too have been concerned with presenting classic Christian contemplative practices in a way that is compelling to a modern audience steeped in psychology, skepticism, and religious pluralism. Through their writings on the practices of *lectio divina* and centering prayer, Keating and Pennington have introduced new generations to ancient practices and have revived interest in the Christian contemplative tradition.

Another hinge figure is Dietrich Bonhoeffer (1906–45), the German Lutheran pastor and theologian executed by the Nazis for his participation in the plot to assassinate Adolf Hitler. Much of Bonhoeffer's spirituality resembles that of Dorothy Day in his critique of institutional religion and his optimism for secular sources of action and knowledge. In his last writings from prison, Bonhoeffer called for a "religionless Christianity" and urged the church to embrace the secular world of both beauty and suffering. In the midst of the Nazi horror, Bonhoeffer experienced the power of grace and genuine faith in unexpected and unpredictable places, while the church surrendered to the state and Hitler claimed their God on his side.

In addition to answering the modern question "Is God?" Bonhoeffer would also reach toward concerns that would become more acute in the last years of the twentieth century. While his "religionless Christianity" seemed outmoded after the "God is Dead" movement of the 1960s, Bonhoeffer's deep passion for Christian tradition – in his case, the original theological insights of Martin Luther – and commitment to communal Christian practices would energize the first postmodern generation some fifty years after his death. Bonhoeffer's authentic Christianity – demonstrated in the alternative community of those who resisted Nazi control of the state church – anticipated the coming answer to the question "Is God?" As high modernity waned, Christians began to side-step the philosophical questions that puzzled Lewis, Day, Thurman, and Merton and, instead, simply *acted as if* God does, indeed, exist. And then that God placed the faithful in a line of belief and practice that proved worthy of imitation – and provided surprising meaning in creating a healing way of life – in a new age.

God is . . . Maybe (1980–Present)

In some ways, the spirituality of the turn of the millennium is a distillate of the century that preceded it. In the advanced capitalist societies of Europe and North America, every aspect of life has come to be commodified (Jameson 1991). Spiritual experience – that modern invention that William James considered a talent confined to mystical prodigies – now comes packaged and marketed for consumption by the masses. And with globalization and the increased religious pluralism in Western societies, spiritual seekers are able to peruse an ever-widening selection of religious wares. Postmodern individuals would seem to be presented with the possibility of becoming nomads (Deleuze and Guattari 1987), no longer tied to any particular place or community, free to celebrate the flux of their undulating spiritual experiences.

But there are also many ways in which the turn of the millennium is truly post-modern, representing a departure from modern patterns of thought. As the French philosopher Jean-François Lyotard (1984) puts it, the postmodern condition is characterized by the demise of the grand narratives of modernity, those self-legitimating theories that sought to explain the entirety of reality. In postmodernity, Westerners have begun to realize that science and philosophy cannot be the self-appointed arbiters of ultimate truth that they had been throughout the modern period.

Many Christian theologians (for example, Milbank 2003) believe that this new openness constitutes an opportunity for Christian spirituality to redress the de-traditionalization and uncoupling of science and religion at the heart of modernity. And contemporary Christian theology is beginning to bear the fruit of the past thirty-five years' effort to come up with ways around those two characteristically modern theological impasses. Influenced by the philosophies of Ludwig Wittgenstein and Alasdair MacIntyre, Protestant theology has moved beyond the liberal strategy of translating theology out of its traditional idiom to see theology as the unique language of the Christian community which is necessarily transmitted through tradition (Lindbeck 1984). Roman Catholic theology has seen the rise of integralist theology (for example, de Lubac, Rahner, von Balthasar), which seeks to undo the modern uncoupling of philosophy and theology by maintaining that there is no such thing as pure nature, untouched by grace, which can be the subject of natural philosophy. Moreover, both Catholic and Protestant theologians are beginning to reflect the influence of Eastern Orthodox and global theologies which have never been affected by the characteristically Western patterns of modern thought. And, with a postmodern sense of bricolage, they are placing these ancient traditions in conversation with non-Christian religions as well as with contemporary Western theological explorations in liberation, feminist, and queer spiritualities. The result is both a recovery of historic traditions and a dramatic interplay of spiritual practices across once unbreachable theological boundaries.

In light of these emerging patterns, contemporary Christian spirituality is beginning to be marked by an attitude one theologian describes as "metanarrative realism" (Milbank 1993: 385 ff): seeing the truth as dependent upon the stories one tells about reality, and living one's life as a participant in the particular story of God's action through Israel, Christ, and the church. While the postmodern condition may decrease the credibility of grand human narratives, it allows for human beings to see themselves and the world again as participants in a divine narrative. Stressing the interpenetration of grace and nature, and maintaining that knowledge of God is mediated by narrative, community, and tradition, postmodern Christian spirituality transforms the nomad into a pilgrim (Bass 2004).

Archbishop of Canterbury Rowan Williams (1950–) is a good example of the emerging postmodern style of theology and spirituality. As a scholar, Williams uses the entire gamut of Christian theology: ancient, medieval, modern, postmodern, Western, Eastern, Catholic, Protestant. His writings show a similar breadth: Christian social criticism, devotional works, historical studies of doctrine and mystics. Nonetheless, they are united through their concern for recovering ways of thinking that have been lost and weaving them into a way of life that reintegrates theology and spirituality.

Williams's spirituality moves beyond modern categories. He has been associated with the progressive Anglo-Catholic movement, which has combined traditional Christian practices and liturgy with a progressive social ethic. Yet, as seen in his leadership during the controversy in the Anglican Communion over the ordination of a gay bishop, he has also held his own comfort with gay ordination together with a broader theological desire to recover the notion of interdependence and communion in the face of modern autonomy.

American Matthew Fox (1940–) takes many of the same themes and combines them with a different effect. A former Dominican (who was dismissed from the order), and now an Episcopal priest, Fox founded the University of Creation Spirituality in Oakland, California, based on the teaching explored in his controversial book, *Original Blessing* (1983). Creation spirituality "integrates the wisdom of western spirituality and global indigenous cultures with the emerging postmodern scientific understanding of the university and the awakening artistic passion for creativity" (University of Creation Spirituality 2002). Fox draws from an incredible breadth of Christian spirituality – from the New Testament to contemporary poets and theologians – but is grounded in Meister Eckhart, Hildegard of Bingen, and St Francis of Assisi. While integrating a host of sources from classical spirituality, Fox uses the "creation-centered" mystical tradition to challenge some fundamental points of Christian theology and church authority (in ways not unlike Madame Guyon). His system of creation spirituality argues that the universe is inherently good and that salvation is best understood as "preserving the good." Accordingly, Fox believes that everyone is a mystic, a prophet, and an artist, whose spiritual journey involves a fourfold path of delight, darkness, creativity, and compassion. Fox integrates this blessing-mysticism with feminist, gay, and eco-theologies defining God as male and female, seeking full inclusion for all peoples in the work of God, and encouraging panentheism as a way of healing creation.

Another American, theologian Stanley Hauerwas (1940–) of Duke University, has also sought to recover a more integrated approach to Christian theology and practice. Hauerwas's work reflects an unlikely constellation of influences: the Thomist virtue ethics of Alasdair MacIntyre, the Anabaptist radicalism and pacifism of John Howard Yoder, the spirituality of conversion and holiness of John Wesley, the narrative theology of Karl Barth, and the high ecclesiology of Pope John Paul II. Hauerwas seeks to offer a Christian alternative to the modern story that we have no story, and its fiction that human beings are independent of one another.

In countering modern ethics, Hauerwas attacks the liberal Protestant attempt to accommodate the strange language and practices of Christianity to the least common denominator of secular discourse. Instead, Hauerwas suggests that Christianity is indeed about a strange community, formed by the story of God's action in Christ, which anticipates the Kingdom of God by practicing peacemaking. Christianity is an adventure in discipleship that forms people in character through practicing a way of life in community that has been handed down through the church's traditions and narratives.

This focus on Christian practices seems to have captured the attention of a new generation of North American authors. American Nora Gallagher (1949–), raised in a secular home, writes eloquently about discovering faith through the spirituality of the church year. She intertwines themes of pilgrimage and practice by drawing from a wide range of Christian tradition (Gallagher 1998). Similar themes are found in the works of other American women, all born between 1945 and 1965, such as Kathleen Norris, Anne Lamott, Debra Farrington, and Diana Butler Bass. The young Southern American author, Lauren Winner (1977–), examines how Christians could learn from the practices of orthodox Judaism, the religion from which she converted (Winner 2004). Winner notes that as Christians are reconnecting with the practices of their faith, they could benefit from examining the practical wisdom they have inherited from Israel. While Christians are not bound by *halakhah*, they are called with St Paul to see how Christian practice fulfils the law in a new way. Winner shows evidence of an attempt to recover not only the practices of the patristic and medieval church, but also the practices of Judaism as transformed in the apostolic era.

Conclusion: The Modern Mosaic of Christian Spirituality

Christian spirituality in the modern period is often seen as characterized by a decline in the mystical tradition and the spiritual disciplines and devotional practices of Christendom. This essay suggests that modern Christian spirituality is not in decline, but it has changed. Throughout the past three centuries, the Christian spiritual impulse has been continuously dislocated and relocated, disoriented and reoriented, undermined and reorganized by a series of intellectual, political, social, and moral challenges. With each successive wave, creative thinkers have gathered up the longings of Christian people to connect with their God and find meaning in a conflicted world through the resources of an ancient faith. As such, no one pattern can rightly claim to be the sole form of Christian spirituality in modernity. Rather, the pathways outlined above touch on the multitude of spiritualities that Christians have explored in the past three hundred years.

This plethora of spiritual options need not be defined as a decline. Rather, this mosaic of Christian spirituality pictures one of the fundamental realities of the modern experience: the shift away from univocality to multivocality brought about by the inclusion of previously excluded voices. Much of the traditional Christian spirituality passed down to modern people was that of the "approved" sort; only rarely did outside voices of challenge sneak through institutional structures. Throughout Christian history, the most creative voices were often those of mystics and spiritual leaders. When institutional Christianity recognized them, it was usually because the institution failed to understand their power or was in awe of their holiness.

With the fracturing of institutional unity at the beginning of modern Europe, these spiritual visionaries – artists, activists, doubters, questioners, and practitioners – began to press against the formal structures of religion and offer their own conceptions of God, meaning, and community in an ever-shifting culture. The creative response of Christian people to construct spiritualities able to answer the challenges of modernity has never been lacking. Perhaps all that has been lacking is the imaginative vision of observers to notice and offer definitions of contemporary Christian spirituality that match its creative experimentation in practice.

References

von Balthasar, H. U. 1991: *The Glory of the Lord: A Theological Aesthetics*, vol. 5: *The Realm of Metaphysics in the Modern Age*. San Francisco: Ignatius.

Bass, D. B. 2004: *The Practicing Congregation: Imagining a New Old Church*. Herndon, VA: Alban Institute.

Berger, P. L. 1990: *The Sacred Canopy: Elements of a Sociological Theory of Religion*. Garden City, NY: Anchor.

Bridges, F. W. 2001: *Resurrection Song: African-American Spirituality*. Maryknoll, NY: Orbis.

de Certeau, M. 2000: Mystic speech. In G. Ward (ed.), *The Certeau Reader*, pp. 188–206. Malden, MA: Blackwell.

Day, D. 1952: *The Long Loneliness*. New York: Harper and Row.

Deleuze, G. and Guattari, F. 1987: *A Thousand Plateaus: Capitalism and Schizophrenia*, trans. B. Massumi. Minneapolis, MN: University of Minnesota Press.

Dupré, L. K. 1993: *Passage to Modernity: An Essay in the Hermeneutics of Culture*. New Haven, CT: Yale University Press.

Fox, M. 1983: *Original Blessing*. Santa Fe, NM: Bear and Company.

Gallagher, N. 1998: *Things Seen and Unseen: A Year Lived in Faith*. New York: Knopf.

Guyon, J-M. B. de la Motte 2002: *A Short and Easy Method of Prayer*. Grand Rapids, MI: Christian Classics Ethereal Library (available at www.ccel.org, accessed August 4, 2004).

Hammond, P. 1992: *Religion and Personal Autonomy: The Third Disestablishment in America*. Columbia, SC: University of South Carolina Press.

Heelas, P. 1996: Introduction: detraditionalization and its rivals. In P. Heelas, S. Lash, and P. Morris (eds.), *Detraditionalization*, pp. 1–20. Malden, MA: Blackwell.

James, H. 1920: *The Letters of William James*, 2 vols. Boston: Little, Brown. Quoted in D. M. Wulff, *Psychology of Religion: Classic and Contemporary*, 2nd edn. New York: Wiley.

James, W. 1997: *The Varieties of Religious Experience: A Study in Human Nature*. New York: Touchstone.

Jameson, F. 1991: *Postmodernism: Or, the Cultural Logic of Late Capitalism*. Durham, NC: Duke University Press.

Kant, I. 1965: *Critique of Pure Reason*, trans. N. K. Smith. New York: St Martin's Press.

Lewis, C. S. 1991: *Mere Christianity*. San Francisco: Harper.

Lindbeck, G. A. 1984: *The Nature of Doctrine: Religion and Theology in a Postliberal Age*. Louisville, KY: Westminster John Knox Press.

Lyotard, J-F. 1984: *The Postmodern Condition: A Report on Knowledge*, trans. G. Bennington and B. Massumi. Minneapolis, MN: University of Minnesota Press.

Milbank, J. 1993: *Theology and Social Theory: Beyond Secular Reason*. Malden, MA: Blackwell.

—— 2003: *Being Reconciled: Ontology and Pardon*. New York: Routledge.

Schleiermacher, F. 1999: *The Christian Faith*, ed. H. R. Mackintosh and J. S. Stewart. Edinburgh: T. and T. Clark.

Sheridan, E. 1998: *Jefferson and Religion*. Charlottesville, VA: Thomas Jefferson Memorial Foundation.

Taves, A. 1999: *Fits, Trances and Visions: Experiencing Religion and Explaining Experience from Wesley to James*. Princeton, NJ: Princeton University Press.

Thérèse of Lisieux, 1996: *Story of a Soul*, 3rd edn, trans. J. Clarke. Washington, DC: ICS Publications.

University of Creation Spirituality 2002: About us (available at www.creationspirituality.com, accessed 4 August, 2004).

Wakefield, G. S. 1991: Anglican spirituality. In L. Dupré and D. Saliers (eds), *Christian Spirituality III: Post-Reformation and Modern*, pp. 257–93. New York: Crossroad.

Weber, M. 1946: Science as a vocation. In H. H. Gerth and C. W. Mills (trans. and eds), *Max Weber: Essays in Sociology*, pp. 129–56. New York: Oxford University Press.

Winner, L. 2004: *Mudhouse Sabbath*. Orleans, MA: Paraclete Press.

CHAPTER 9

Christian Spirituality in Africa, Asia, Latin America, and Oceania

Richard Fox Young

Whether the context is Western or non-Western, literature is a useful resource for revealing the multi-faceted nature of Christian spirituality. Since Africa has created more literature of this sort than any other region outside the world of Europe (Killam and Rowe 2000: 240–9), I begin with a citation from *Ethiopia Unbound* (1911: 1–10, passim) by the Ghanaian Methodist Joseph Ephraïm Casely-Hayford (1866–1930), one of West Africa's first writers of English fiction. Though longish, it evokes themes I address, among them the relationship between indigenous languages, cultures, and religions and the Christian spiritualities that have found expression around the globe, primarily in non-Western milieux. I leave aside the references to Ethiopianism, today and since his time a thread in the tapestry of African Christianity. Keep in mind, however, that Casely-Hayford was an advocate of Christianity's re-Africanization. Ethiopia, as an ancient center of the faith, became a pan-African symbol (Hastings 1994: 479) for Christians who believed that Christianity was African in origin and essence and in need of liberation from Europe to become African again.

Strange and Wonderful Names of God

In late Victorian London, two friends walk along Tottenham Court Road. One is from the Gold Coast, Kwamankra, who studies law; the other is from England, Silas Whitely, who studies theology. Though he harbors doubts about Jesus's divinity, Whitely is to be ordained in the Anglican Church. Kwamankra, an adherent of one of West Africa's traditional religions, finds Whitely's perplexity puzzling. At his Russell Square rooms, Kwamankra tries to help Whitely resolve his doubts:

> "Jesus Christ, man or God?" he repeated slowly and musingly unto himself – then turning somewhat suddenly to his friend, he said, "You know, Whitely, since I learnt your language . . . I have been trying to get at the root idea of the word 'God'; and so far as my researches

have gone, it is an Anglo-Saxon word, the Teutonic form being *Gutha*, which is said to be quite distinct from 'good.' Whence, then, one may ask, come your ideas, as associated with the fountain of all good, of omnipresence, omniscience, omnipotence? Of course they are borrowed from the Romans, who were pagans like ourselves, and who, indeed, had much to learn from the Ethiopians through the Greeks."

Kwamankra, whose real interests are linguistics and religion, has devoted himself to a project involving both, a lexicon of Fanti (Akan), his mother-tongue, and English. Turning to the letter "N," Kwamankra picks up the thread of his earlier discourse:

. "[Y]ou remember a while ago my taking you to task over the feebleness of the idea of God in the Anglo-Saxon language. I have just got the corresponding word here in Fanti. It is a big word, so big that you can hardly imagine it:" –
NYIAKROPON
. . . "Breaking up the word into its component parts, as I have done, we have:" –
Nyia nuku ara oye pon. That is,
He who alone is great.

Lest Whitely think Fanti has merely one such word, Kwamankra treats him to another, *Nyami:*

"Broken up, it stands in bold relief thus:" –
Nyia oye emi. That is,
He who is I am.
"Now compare the Hebrew 'I am hath sent me,' and you have it. Nor is this a fanciful play upon roots, for our people sing unto this day:"
Wana so onyi Nyami se?
Dasayi wo ho inde, okina na onyi,
Nyami firi tsitsi kaisi odumankuma.
"meaning:"
Who says he is equal with God?
Man is to-day, tomorrow he is not,
I am is from eternity to eternity.
"You can now understand . . . why your difficulty [about Jesus's divinity] surprised me. But now that I come to think of it, it may be due to the limitations of your language."

Unaccustomed to thinking of God by other names, Whitely is no match for Kwamankra, who now poses a question for which Whitely's studies have been no help:

[*Kwamankra*]: "Supposing Jesus Christ had been born of an Ethiopian woman instead of Mary of the line of David, do you think it would have made any difference in the way he influenced mankind?"
[*Whitely*]: "What a strange question." . . .
[*Kwamankra*]: "Yes, it is strange . . . But, tell me, what is there extraordinary in the idea?"
[*Whitely*]: "Oh, I don't know. Habits of thought, convention, and all that sort of thing, I suppose."

To jump to the end, Whitely's theological doubts remain unresolved and he winds up on the Gold Coast, a tragi-comical colonial chaplain.

Spirituality and the New Historiography of World Christianity

One of the most noteworthy changes in the historiography of world Christianity (Shenk 2002) is the shift in emphasis from Western transmission of the gospel to non-Western appropriation, from missionaries to converts, and from mission to church. The Silas Whitelys are receding into the background, while the Christians of Africa, Asia, Latin America, and Oceania, who metabolize Christianity in contrastive ways involving language, culture, and religion, now occupy the foreground more than ever before, reinvested with an agency of their own. Historiographers have always recognized that indigenous peoples adapt what they adopt; the difference between earlier scholarship and today's is the difference between Eurocentricity and polycentricity: because there is no standard-issue Christianity, adaptation tells us that the cross-cultural process is working the way it should, not the way it shouldn't.

The impetus behind the new historiography, which derives primarily from Andrew Walls (1996, 2002a) and his former students Lamin Sanneh (1989) and Kwame Bediako (1995), is essentially biblical and theological. As in most new developments, the premise is less surprising than the application. The *point d'appui* is the familiar passage from John's Gospel, "the Word became flesh and dwelt among us" (1: 14). Above all else, the language of linguistics distinguishes the new historiography from the old. For Walls and others, incarnation implies translation, not into generic humanity or generic language – such things do not exist – but into specifiable particularity. In this view, incarnation as translation entails, enables, and endorses Christian pluriformity: "Christian diversity," according to a Wallsian dictum (1996: 28), "is the necessary product of the Incarnation." Even though Walls hastens to add that all subsequent translations of Christianity remain contingent upon the original, the model is one of radical de-normatization.

Experientially, the new historiography is decidedly subversive. In this respect, poor Whitely may not be so atypical after all. What the new historiography subverts is "habits of thought, convention, and all that sort of thing," the sort of thing that limits one's horizon of awareness to the world of Europe, or – since Eurocentricity has its reactionary, non-Western counterparts (exemplified by Kwamankra) – to that of Africa, Asia, Latin America, or Oceania. In short, the study of Christianity's multiple transformations is potentially transformative. To those who know the literature, Wallsian perspectives engender an ecumenicity and spirituality all their own. Against those who argue that translation is tainted by compromise, hybridity, and caricature, Walls and the Wallsians envision in world Christianity new possibilities for expanding and enriching the church's understanding of the incarnation of the Word.

Being situated on the edges between languages, cultures, and religions is nothing new for Christianity, which was non-Western before it became anything else; it remains so, for Christians of the Middle East, their counterparts scattered across Asia (the Syro-Malabar churches of South India especially), and much of North Africa, including

Ethiopia. Since Christianity has been polycentric almost from its very inception, thinking of Lagos or Seoul or São Paulo or Port Moresby as pulsating centers of a vibrant Christianity, like Jerusalem, Antioch, Rome, and Canterbury, should not be so great an effort. But the edges between Christianity and the religions that traditionally establish the locus of Christendom no longer lie where they did. One has a great deal of catching up to do, so rapidly is Christianity being re-centered; a few remarks on the shift in Christianity's center of gravity from the North to the South are therefore in order. "At the beginning of the third millennium," Wilbert Shenk observes (2002: xii; cf. Barrett et al. 2000; Jenkins 2002), "the impact of this historical shift is clear: 60 percent of all Christians live outside the traditional Western heartland." In the eighteenth century, the non-Western cohort in the total population of world Christianity was only a third of its present numbers; that cohort did not even begin to cross the halfway mark until the 1970s. Studies on Christian spirituality need to keep in step with this dramatic shift, to which the new historiography is itself an *ex post facto* response.

Against this background, one must be wary of reductionism. Spirituality is not a singular form that pervades entire continents and peoples. While it would be delightful to speak of an Oceanic Christian spirituality, which sounds especially nice, one cannot, not only because spirituality cannot be confined geographically, but also because the whole orientation of the new historiography resists generalizations across cultures and within cultures, without appropriate adjustments. To speak of spirituality generically would be to transgress the translation principle (namely, the specifiable particularity of the incarnational process). That being said, I should add that I do not bring an interiorist bias to my interpretation of spirituality. To me, spirituality encompasses (i.e., includes but is not limited to) the religious ethos and consciousness engendered by the cross-cultural transmission and appropriation of Christian faith.

Catholic Spirituality on the Borders between Cultures (pre-1700)

While the Christian missionary movement is primarily a phenomenon of the eighteenth century and later, earlier centuries were hardly times of idleness in the Middle East, Africa, or Asia. Nestorians were inveterate travelers and by the eighth century had already reached China. Small communities lingered on; traces were evident nearly a thousand years later, to the surprise of Catholic missionaries who supposed that they were the ones who came first. Nestorians may have found their way to Anuradhapura (an ancient center of Sri Lankan Buddhism) even earlier than the eighth century, and to kingdoms on the maritime routes through Southeast Asia. In Central Asia, Nestorians were found among the Mongol clans of the steppes; Catholic envoys to the Khans in the thirteenth century found themselves in a more Christian environment than they expected. Now a power to be reckoned with, the Mongols were making the transition to a more expansive, inclusivistic religion, one that would allow their traditional religion to remain intact. For a purpose like this, Nestorianism and Catholicism seemed less suitable than Buddhism. While Nestorian Mongols adapted the terminology of local traditional religion (for example, *tengri* for "God," the term for supranaturals), sources on the inculturation of Mongol Christianity are meager. One feels a sense of loss at knowing little about a vanished church (Moffett 1998; Tang 2002).

Of more permanent duration was Iberian Catholic expansion, which began before the voyages of Columbus. Secular priests accompanied Portuguese fleets around the coast of West Africa, establishing churches in enclaves such as São Tomé, mainly for pastoral care of their compatriots. Missionary zeal, however, was not lacking; within years, the kingdom of Kongo on the River Zaïre saw its sovereign, Nzinga Nkuvu, baptized as João I (1491), the first-fruit of transplanted Catholicism. This was Catholicism with an affinity for African traditional religion in seeing the cosmos as a battlefield of powers, malign and benign. Under João I's successors, Kongo Catholicism would struggle, but its first years saw the displacement of indigenous religious functionaries, the *nganga*, by priests of the church; though called *nganga* too, they were perceived as giving access to considerably greater supranormal powers (Hastings 1994: 73–86). One sees in this extraordinary fusion of worldviews, the Iberian and the African, a pattern that would be replicated elsewhere along the coast from Angola to Mozambique. Less often, however, would this happen in South, Southeast, and East Asia. The church established itself at Goa (on India's southwest coast), Mylapore (on its southeast coast), Kotte (on Sri Lanka's southwest coast), Malacca (on the Malay peninsula), and Macao (on China's Pearl River estuary), but all such enclaves sat on the margins, not the centers, of major civilizations and world religions. Signs of interest in Christianity were few. An early example is this stanza from Chinese (Zhang 1997: 144) by a poet of the late seventeenth century, Liang Di, who found the sound of an organ at a Macanese cathedral mesmeric:

> From the top of St Paul's, music rises
> That can be heard far and wide.
> It is as soft as scissors cutting silk,
> As clear as a goose yelling,
> As melodious as a swallow singing,
> As saddening as a monkey yelping.

One must keep in mind that Portugal's far-flung empire was a maritime one based on mercantile opportunism and the vagaries of regional politics more than conquest. When Portugal occupied the Sri Lankan littoral, its dominance crowned by the baptism of Dharmapala, king of Kotte (1557), Buddhists who resisted Christianization took refuge in the Central Highlands. One still finds in Catholic villages along the coast north and south of Colombo occasional performances of *nadagama* (Sinhalacized, Iberian-style passion-plays; Goonatilleka 1984). In earlier times, *nadagama* were an effective means of evangelization and a helpful inducement to keeping the evangelized on the coast under pastoral supervision. Only in Goa, wrested from the Marathas and a center of ecclesiastical control for the whole of Asia, was a policy of Christianization (the Rigor of Mercy) enforced; all a Goanese Hindu had to do to flout it, however, was to walk a few miles to the temples inland.

Catholicism's infrastructure was nowhere more vulnerable than in Japan. Though the mission there, founded by Francis Xavier (1506–52) in 1549 (Higashibaba 2001), was financed by the Macao silk trade, Portuguese naval power proved of no avail less than half a century later when the Shogun Hideyoshi saw Christian teachings as a threat to the post-mortem deification (as a Shinto *kami*) he believed would be his just deserts. Though initially received with enthusiasm by Kyushu's feudal lords (many were under the impression that Christianity was a variant of Buddhism), and even though the mission was preserved from many a mishap by the deft oversight of Alessandro Valignano (1539–1606), the Jesuit architect of a comprehensive policy of cultural accommodation, Catholicism was nonetheless perceived as foreign (the operative term being *batakusai*, "smelling of rancid butter," a reference to European culinary habits). Simply put, Catholicism was the religion of *Deus* (Japan Jesuits were better at accommodating culture than language; Elison, 1973). When Shogun Tokugawa Iyesau delivered the *coup de grâce* in the early seventeenth century, Christianity went underground. Japan's hidden (*kakure*) Christians – with images of Mary disguised as Kannon, a parish system based on village models, and syncretized sacred texts – effected a more inculturated Christianity than Valignano envisioned (Harrington 1993).

To really understand Catholicism's extraordinary encounter with Asia, one looks to localities distant from Portuguese influence: to Beijing in China, where Italian Jesuit Matteo Ricci (1552–1610) mingled with Confucian mandarins (Kim 2001); to Madurai in South India, where Roberto de Nobili (1577–1656), another Italian Jesuit, preached wisdom to the wise (Amaladass and Clooney 2000); and to Tonkin and Cochinchina, where French Jesuit Alexandre de Rhodes (1593–1660) immersed himself in all Vietnamese religions (Phan 1998). All three were remarkable inculturationists. Not only would they reject *Deus* (Ricci rendered "God" as *Shangti*, Lord on High; de Nobili as *Saruveshvaran*, Lord of All; de Rhodes as *Duc Chua Troi Dat*, Noble Lord of Heaven and Earth), they were also outwardly acculturated (Ricci robed himself in Confucian literati garb; de Nobili resembled a world-renouncer; de Rhodes could have been mistaken for a Vietnamese in traditional hat and Confucian gown). Ricci and de Rhodes regarded ancestor veneration as civil rather than religious; papal interference in the Chinese Rites Controversy of the early eighteenth century, however, nullified the practice. The same controversy swept aside the Malabar Rites, as de Nobili's innovations were called. Latinization had always been a potent force; already in 1599, at the Synod of Diamper, Catholic authorities began interfering with the spiritual traditions of Kerala's Syro-Malabar churches (Thottakara 1990).

The tendency to replicate Iberian Catholicism is likewise evident throughout Christianity's early history in Latin America, the Caribbean, the Philippines (Marzal 1993), and even Oceania (Garrett 1982). By the eighteenth century, the infrastructure would remain much the same until Vatican II (1962–5) shook the church to its Iberian foundations (Hastings 1999). The appalling violence of Catholic evangelism in the early post-Columbian period, when Aztec, Maya, Inca, and other ethno-linguistic peoples succumbed to brute force, is well documented (Rivera 1992). Despite voices of protest (Bartolomé de las Casas) and great scholars of Nahuatl and other languages (Bernardino de Sahagún), the region produced few inculturationists of Ricci's, de Nobili's, or de Rhodes's stature. Instead, one finds behind-the-scenes resistance to Iberianization (Klor de Alva 1993) and occasional rebellion (in the Andes especially; Szeminski 1993). Indigenous Christians themselves took the lead in unsanctioned inculturation, such as resulted from the Nahua Juan Diego's vision in 1531 of the Virgin Mary, which neatly fused Iberian traditions with those of a pre-existing Aztec cult to become Our Lady of Guadalupe (Burkhart 1993). Iberian folk Catholicism's considerable blandishments, however, were evident almost from the start. Adrian Hastings tells us (1999: 334) that in Mexico people "begged to be allowed to build churches and flogged one another remorselessly in the penitential processions of Good Friday." As in New Spain, so in New France: austerities among Iroquoian and Algonquian converts, women especially, could be alarmingly severe. In a 1680s' report from a mission on the St Lawrence River, Jesuit Claude Chauchetière related the following (Greer 2000: 150–1): "some of them learned, I know not how, of the pious practices followed by the nuns of the Montreal hospital. They heard of disciplines, of iron girdles, and of hair shirts. The religious life appealed to them, and so three of them formed an association in order to set up some sort of convent, but we stopped them, because we did not think the time had yet come for this." One of the three, Kateri Tekakwitha, a Mohawk, proved unstoppable. Adding an indigenous touch to the usual rigors, she exposed herself to the Canadian snows, perished, and attained sainthood. On the whole, however, Christianity looked decidedly less saintly to the marginalized peoples of the New World (Axtell 1985; Tinker 1994; Treat 1996).

The Upsurge of Protestant Spirituality on the Borders between Cultures (1700s)

While Catholicism held its ground in the New World, its existence in the African interior depended on the success of Portuguese commercial activity along the exterior; most of all, slavery compromised the church and cast a pall over it (Hastings 1994: 127). The eighteenth century was not particularly good for overseas Catholicism. Its severest trial may have been the Jesuit suppression starting in the 1770s, which meant the loss of the church's most progressive inculturationists. In China, where certain Catholic practices resembled those of millenarian secret societies such as the White Lotus, magistrates took it upon themselves to suppress potentially subversive activities. Secret societies were generally vegetarian, and so it happened in the 1750s in Sichuan that Christians were arrested simply because the word for "fasting" (*zhai*) was used by sectarians too (Entenmann 1996). Once the papal decision on the Chinese Rites Controversy reached Emperor Kangxi, the Jesuits, long-esteemed at court, found it harder to hold on. But they did, and because they did, a Korean, Hong Yu-han, was able around 1770 to get hold of Catholic literature from Beijing. Reading it with wonderment, Hong devised a regimen of worship according to the lunar calendar and then retreated to the mountains in good Confucian-Taoist fashion for a life of solitary contemplation. Ricci's *The True Meaning of the Lord of Heaven* attracted other Confucian literati; in this bastion of family values, they met in clandestine study groups. On being told by Beijing church authorities that ancestral rites (*chesa*) were disallowed, some were martyred in the late eighteenth century, violations of filial piety being abhorrent to the state (Grayson 1985: 70–7; Chung 2001). Until the Jesuit suppression, Indian Catholicism fared better, as we will see. All things considered, however, the change in centuries from the seventeenth to the eighteenth is characterized by a remarkable upsurge of Protestant momentum overseas.

Where Portugal went, other nations followed; first Holland, which in the second half of the seventeenth century established the Dutch East Indies Company and the Dutch Reformed Church in a swath of territory from Capetown to Colombo to Batavia. As such, however, mission was disallowed in Dutch domains; that restriction remained until the mid-nineteenth century. By the end of the eighteenth century, however, Moravians, whose humble occupations made them seem innocuous, worked among the Bushmen ("Hottentots") of the Cape (Hastings 1994: 197–205). The Reformed Church in Sri Lanka included vast numbers of "civil-rite" Hindus and Buddhists, virtually the entire population under Company control; seeing baptism as the best safeguard for their civil rights, these were "public" Christians who continued their traditional observances in private. Few *Predikants* preached outside the routine circuit. Phillipus Baldeus, who ministered in Jaffna in the northern peninsula of Sri Lanka in the later seventeenth century, was one who did. To his great surprise (and ours) Baldeus encountered Christian brahmans who traced their origins to the six sons of Abraham and his third wife/concubine Keturah (Gen. 25: 1–6; 1 Chr. 1: 32–3; Hudson 2000: 5–9). While Sri Lanka is a good deal farther east of the Arabian "incense route" along which this community is said to have settled, and while the real origins of Jaffna's Christian brahmans will probably remain obscure, it was to be the case that almost everywhere Protestants went, some form of Christianity – pre-adapted – was already there.

While English historiography tends toward the view that Protestantism in India began at Serampore (on the Ganges near Calcutta) with the Baptist missionary William Carey at the end of the eighteenth century, German historiography is quick to say "*Es begann in Tranquebar*" (Lehmann 1956) nearly a century earlier. The latter is correct; a Danish enclave in the Kingdom of Tanjore on India's southeast coast, Tranquebar became the epicenter of Lutheran Pietism in 1706. Bartolomaeus Ziegenbalg (1683–1719), the mission founder, though a German product of the Pietist establishment at Halle, had been commissioned by the Danish throne to bring the Augsburg Confession and the Lutheran Church to the Tamil people. In the whole of early Protestant mission history, no individual was more committed to amicable interaction with Hinduism than Ziegenbalg; by the same token, rarely were so many Hindus willing to be constructively engaged. Conversions, however, were rare; many of the first parishioners were former Catholics of the dominant Vellala (cultivator) community, or from the underside of the caste hierarchy. The New Jerusalem Church, where all such folk worshiped, was, of course, severely aniconic, unlike Catholic churches. That, in the indigenous view, could not be helped; the seating arrangements, however, were their affair. One sees here that indigenous Christians invested themselves with their own agency. The floor was covered with mats, but with a space between; Vellalas sat on one side, social inferiors on the other. Physical separation outside the church seemed right and proper inside the church. The point is disputed, but communion (as was customary in some German churches) was evidently served with two chalices for the sake of the Vellalas; their purity would have been polluted by the saliva (*eccil*, one of the worst bodily impurities) of lower-status Christians. Though this was tolerated in Ziegenbalg's time, later missionaries insisted that all partake from a single chalice; those who refused were excommunicated in a frenzied purge. The issues, of course, were seriously theological, not least to the Tamils involved, who in defense argued for a specifically Vellala Christian praxis. In effect, Vellalas were saying that spirituality is non-generic (Jeyaraj 1996; Hudson 2000, esp.).

Among Catholics, inculturation proceeded apace, but along two different lines, one Sanskritic and literary, effected by de Nobili's successors, the other, effected by the laity, was vernacular and communal. A classic instance of the first is the *Ezour Veda*. So thoroughly imbued with the flavor of Hindu literary works was this masterpiece that many in Europe who came to know of it, including Voltaire, denounced it as a Jesuitical forgery foisted on the Hindus to make them think they were reading the *Yajur Veda*, one of their ancient sacred texts, whose title it resembled. There was, in fact, no deceit: *Ezour* = Jesus. The author was a French-speaking Jesuit whose pronunciation of "Jesus" became "*Ezour*" due to the rules of phonetic combination in Sanskrit (i.e., the "s" followed by "v" becomes "r"; *veda* denotes a sacred text, Hindu or otherwise). In the tradition of preaching wisdom to the wise, a corpus of similar texts came into circulation. A representative stanza turns the terminology of non-dualism (Advaita) to the praise of God: "Him, who is without qualities [*nirguna*], who never varies, the Lord, him I worship with joined hands" (Amaladass and Young 1995: 13). When Vedanta was better understood, Jesuit Sanskritists would incline toward a more theistic idiom and declare that God abounds in all good qualities. Still, there remained a Vedantic twist in that God was said to be *all* attribute (i.e., devoid of substance-accident distinctions, as in "God *is* love"). To this end, *sat* (being), *chit* (consciousness), and *ananda* (bliss) found a place in the Catholic vocabulary. All was not rarified philosophical theology, however. Jean Calmette (1693–1740) of the Carnatic mission translated the breviary into Sanskrit and added prayers of his own. The most remarkable is one for the investiture (*upanayana*) of a Christian with the sacred thread emblematic of brahmanhood. As in de Nobili's day, caste was still regarded as a social status (Amaladass and Young 1995: 192–5). All such traditions, and along with them the literature, fell into desuetude following the Jesuit suppression. Left to their own devices, Indian Catholics became their own inculturationists; vernacular, communal manifestations of piety could astound the missionaries who remained. One of them, the Abbé J. A. Dubois (1770–1848), thought the unsanctioned festivities of his flock more than a little excessive (1823: 69–70):

> Accompanied with hundreds of tom-toms, trumpets, and all the discordant noisy music of the country; with numberless torches, and fire-works; the statue of the saint placed on a [cart] is charged with garlands of flowers, and other gaudy ornaments, according to the taste of the country, – the [cart] slowly dragged by a multitude shouting all along the march – the congregation surrounding the [cart] in confusion, several among them dancing . . . some wrestling, some playing the fool; all shouting, or conversing with each other, without any one exhibiting the least sign of respect or devotion.

Compare this account with modern social anthropological studies of Christian festivals in South India (Dempsey 2001; Younger 2002), and the main change is that the church now sanctions such festivities.

Protestantization beyond Europe (1800s)

Dubois' Eurocentric snootiness was not uncommon; indigenous agency in the inculturation of spirituality was of perpetual concern almost everywhere. As we have seen, some individuals were more empathetic than others; in the main, the models were European, though sometimes draped in the vestments of local high culture. Though the nineteenth century started on a similar footing, missionary models would be increasingly contested. The opposite is ordinarily assumed, given the fact that this century springs to mind – for good historical reasons – when one thinks of missionary "triumph." Though remarkable endeavors were happening on the Cape, where Johannes Van der Kemp of the London Missionary Society arrived in 1799 to labor among the Xhosa, some of the action most worth watching was still occurring in South Asia.

William Carey (1761–1837) arrived in 1793, the first missionary of the Baptist Missionary Society. Carey's eminence is difficult to exaggerate because he exemplifies the most quintessential of Protestant endeavors: vernacular Bible translation. What this effected, however, was more important for what it prompted others outside India to do. Scholars who do not read Indian languages overlook the fact that Carey was an inveterate, if inadvertent, Sanskritizer; Serampore translations tended toward the highbrow. The ramifications for the vocabulary of Christian faith have been enormous. Ironically, behind the Sanskritization, one finds an anti-Catholic bias, no more than was common, but one that prejudiced Carey against all things brahmanical, including Sanskrit, which to him was India's Latin. Ordinary folk did not understand it, hence the need for vernacular translations (*the* Protestant imperative). Even before the Bengali Bible was finished, however, Carey set to work on the Sanskrit, determined to substitute biblical content for the "pebbles and trash" of Hindu literature. Desacralization by resacralization imbued the entire project with an oddly brahmanical character (Amaladass and Young 1995: 31–9).

Fount of an unacknowledged Sanskritization within Indian Protestantism by virtue of being the Ur-translation, Carey's Bible turned out to be unreadable because of the awkward syntax, which deviated hardly a whit from the King James Bible. The same Sanskritizing tendency was evident among Carey's Anglican contemporaries in Calcutta, though without the anti-Catholic bias. William Hodge Mill (1792–1853), a High Church patristics scholar with the Society for the Propagation of the Gospel in Calcutta during the 1820s, knew the *Ezour Veda*, admired it, and attempted to replicate it with a work of his own. Mill did not translate the Bible as such; instead, he composed an epic in mellifluous verse, the *Shrikhrishtasangita* (*Hymn to the Blessed Christ*; Amaladass and Young 1995: 197–327). It begins as follows:

> May the Holy One receive my simple offering,
> Given by me at the feet of the Golden One.
> May he accept my supplication at the feet of the One,
> Who is of jasmine-like fragrance and pure body.

Mill's work was well received by brahmans who appreciated belletristic literature; to Christians who mostly came from marginal communities, it was impossibly erudite.

Nonetheless, the *Hymn to the Blessed Christ* resonated with Anglo-Catholic worship in Calcutta's "Tractarian Gothic" churches, where instead of the communion tables and massive pulpits of the "Evangelical Colonial" churches, one found altars, crosses, candlesticks, and incense (Clark 1977: 183). By the late eighteenth century, Sanskrit was being heard in Catholic circles again. Though Latinization was still the prescribed model, Brahmabandhav (Theophilus) Upadhyay (1861–1907), the most ardent Sanskritizer since the seventeenth century, composed *The Hymn to the Blessed Trinity*, which many Catholics sing throughout India today. Redolent of Vedanta, it begins (Gispert-Sauch 1972: 60): "I adore you, O *Sacchidananda* [Being-Consciousness-Bliss], Highest Goal, scorned by the worldly, yearned for by the saintly."

Inculturation, by Sanskritization or otherwise, was not only a natural process – though sometimes it seemed artificial – but also a response to the objection that Christianity was the religion of uncultured Europeans. Converts might protest, as one from the *tondaman* caste in South India did (Hutteman 1765: 93): "By becoming a Christian, I did not turn an *Englishman*; I am yet a *Tondaman*!" Still, in many respects, Christians were changing in ways that Sanskritic embellishments belie. In the Protestant view, the first commandment prescribed an exclusivistic religious behavior: converts were expected to declare their conversions, as proof of the transformed heart. Many, however, being bi-polar or multi-polar in orientation, were not ready ("adhesion" rather than "conversion" would be the better word for such an orientation). Ram Ram Basu, Carey's Bengali pandit, was a classic case. Even before Carey arrived in India, Ram Ram heard the gospel from a Baptist layman and composed lyrics in praise of Jesus Christ; these became "The Hindoo's Hymn" and were sung in English churches before Carey went out to India. Upon their acquaintance, Carey found Ram Ram a person in-between Hinduism and Christianity. The pressure was on, Ram Ram wavered, and was dismissed. Habits of the heart die hard, but to be Protestant one not only had to avoid festivals like the one Dubois described, one had to consciously engender a religiosity centered more on belief – and the confession of belief – than praxis, unlike Hinduism and other religions.

Over time, as belief attained a more sharply defined profile, the changes Protestantization effected within Christians transformed praxis in a variety of ways more consequential than merely staying at home when Catholics processed in the streets. One sees this toward the end of the nineteenth century in Japan where the prohibition of Christianity had been rescinded and where, to give the populace of this modernizing nation a sense of unity in the midst of change, the Meiji oligarchs constructed a new civil religion in the form of state Shinto, based on emperor-system ideology. An incident of *lese-majesté* occurred in 1891, which to this day continues to mark Protestant Christianity as quintessentially a religion of conscience – and of pertinacity. Uchimura Kanzo (1861–1930), a graduate of Amherst and a teacher in an elite Tokyo school, declined to bow before the scroll of the Imperial Rescript on Education, as public servants were required to do. Vilified and accused of being un-Japanese, Uchimura was, of course, practicing the first commandment in a costly, public manner (Miura 1996). But as for being un-Japanese, Uchimura himself founded in 1901 a distinctively Japanese ecclesiology, *Mukyokai* (Nonchurch Christianity), a lay-led Bible-study circle which shunned ordained clergy and decried Western denominationalism (Mullins 1998: 55–67).

By the century's end, further indications of indigenous initiative across the Christian world would be seen, as Christians of all persuasions took the Bible – an "autonomous instrument of Christianization" (Hastings 1994: 243; Ndung'u 2000) – into their own hands and read it through their own eyes. Independence, however, encountered formidable countervailing forces, not least of all from Europeans who controlled the younger churches and endeavored to suppress all such extra-ecclesial inculturation. A symptomatic instance comes from the remote Brantas River region of East Java in the mid-nineteenth century where C. L. Coolen, of mixed European and Javanese descent, established a flourishing Christian colony. The unordained Coolen "peppered his sermons with Javanese mystical terms," Robert Hefner writes (1993: 104), "incorporated references to *Dewi Sri* (the popular Javanist rice goddess) into his prayers, employed Sufi-style *dzikir* chanting for the Christian confession of faith, and sponsored such esteemed Javanese arts as *gamelan* music and *wayang* shadow theater, usually just after the Sabbath worship." A moral community was in formation here – gambling and opium-smoking, endemic in the area, were on the wane – but the worship smacked of syncretism. The Reformed Church intervened, imposing on the Coolen community a lifestyle one might describe as Christianity in European "trousers," one of the main issues having been the matter of clothing, which was Javanese and emblematic of resistance. Exceptions can be adduced, but mainly from places where missionaries were scarce. In Buganda in the later nineteenth century, for example, where a large-scale, locally initiated movement into the churches transformed the kingdom into one of East Africa's Christian heartlands, converts dressed as usual in the local *kanzu*, like everyone else (Hastings 1994: 477).

Such was not the case in Freetown and elsewhere in West Africa, where the returned Nova Scotian, Jamaican, and other "Black European" Africans were being resettled after the British prohibition of slavery and where Christian communities of the New World were being replicated. Among those resettled was a former Yoruba slave, Samuel Adjayi Crowther (1807–91), who was made Bishop of the Niger Diocese in 1864, a landmark event in African church history. Crowther's case is instructive because his elevation to the episcopate signaled a victory for mission administrators such as Henry Venn of the Church Missionary Society, whose policy for mission was "euthanasia" by Africanization. Although we saw that indigenous agency in Christian inculturation was of concern whenever it was found outside the church, in Crowther's case there was cause for celebration: here was an African to lead the church the way an English bishop would. In this respect, Crowther, a capable administrator, was a resounding success in difficult circumstances where infrastructure was anything but strong. Under him, the Igbo, neighbors of the Yoruba, were reached, which signaled the commencement of mission by Africans to Africans – another of Venn's Africanizing ambitions. Once again, however, "White European" mission personnel mustered countervailing forces and, on Crowther's death, forced the appointment of a European successor. The overall failure of sanctioned inculturation within the European-initiated churches underscores the significance of independence, which becomes the most dynamic force in African Christianity as the twentieth century approached. There had, of course, been inculturationists among the missionaries, people like Johannes Van der Kemp, mentioned earlier, who labored on the Cape earlier in the century. About him, it is said that he had the following exchange with a Xhosa elder (Hastings 1994: 273; 338–71):

> [*Van der Kemp*]: "What do you say about the creation of all things?"
> [*Xhosa elder*]: "We call him who made all things Utikxo."
> [*Van der Kemp*]: "Very well, I bring you that very one."

Casely-Hayford's Whitely seems a sad caricature when one knows of missionaries like Van der Kemp, who sought out and respected God's African names. The closer one gets to the twentieth century, the more it will matter that Africans share these names with other Africans – lifting them up, but not leaving their original sense behind.

New Spiritualities and Old (1900s and beyond)

Only in the early twentieth century can one put names to African Christians who proclaimed the gospel at their own initiative. The Liberian "Prophet" William Wadé Harris had been close to "Black European" Christians and was acculturated to their ways. Called in a dream to take off his shoes, get up and walk, he left the settlements in 1912 and journeyed into Bishop Crowther's old domain, the Niger Delta, singing and healing along the way until stopped by colonial authorities. Harris did not encourage a following, though he spoke of himself as a new Elijah; those whom he moved, he encouraged to be whatever variety of Protestant was locally available. Prophets remained on the margins of their churches, unless, as was the case with the Zaïrian Baptist Simon Kimbangu (1899–1951), the movement took on a life of its own. Not unlike the Harris story, a dream was involved and gifts of healing, neither of which sat well with the Baptists, the Catholic Church, or the Belgian colonial administration. We have seen before how countervailing forces kick in: Kimbangu was arrested, tried, imprisoned, and thus made emblematic of European Christianity's rejection. Anthropologist Johannes Fabian's *Remembering the Present* reproduces a Zaïrian street-artist's illustration of Kimbangu's trial (1996: 54–5): the accused, other courtroom figures, and Monseigneur de Hemptinne, the official Catholic representative, are depicted. Not seeing through African eyes, nothing leaped out of the picture until I was told: de Hemptinne has his legs casually crossed and the heel of his shoe slightly tilted toward Kimbangu. Interpreting that posture for Fabian, the artist explained that the Monseigneur was thinking: "How dare he found a religion? Am I not the one who brings the religion of the white man? We cannot have a black man preaching religion." As the twentieth century progresses, it no longer matters that the established churches looked askance at extra-ecclesial inculturation. Simon Kimbangu's prophet's staff passed into the hands of his sons, signaling the routinization of the father's charisma (to use Weberian terms); under new management, the movement became a church (a member of the World Council of Churches, no less).

African-initiated churches (AICs) like the Kimbanguist have become, since the 1950s, a pan-African phenomenon. No longer marginal, they are now the dominant churches of black South Africans; churches of European initiation no longer constitute the Protestant mainstream (Anderson 2000: 306, 318). Like the Kimbanguists, AICs do not remain perpetually "younger" churches; as older ones denominationalize, others flash into existence, responding in Protestant ways to reading the Bible in one's own vernacular. And, just as the world over, Pentecostal/Charismatic Christianity flourishes in the interstices between the established African churches and the AICs (Martin 2002). Some trace their origins to the Los Angeles Azusa Street Revival of the early 1900s, others to revivals in Lagos, Nairobi, or Soweto. To inventory all such developments around the 1950s, one could manage with a fairly uncomplicated AIC nomenclature (Hastings 1979: 67–85). Now, along with the burgeoning field of Pentecostal/Charismatic studies (Caplan 1987, on India; Martin 1990, on Latin America; Rubinstein 1996, on Taiwan), we have Allan Anderson's (2000) nuanced typologies of the newer-wave South African Zionist/Apostolic churches. To evoke the overall ethos, I turn again to literature and cite from Nigerian writer Timothy Mofolorunso Aluko's *Kinsman and Foreman* (1966: 70–2), which tells of Titus Oti, an Anglican, and how he was drawn to a hole-in-the-wall church (fictitiously called the Prophets of Iban) in a Lagos backstreet. Elder Matthew, who wears a white *kaftan*, welcomes Titus. And then

> A woman's voice raised a popular song in Yoruba, in which the whole congregation joined, accompanied by a band of three drums and an empty beer bottle from which a little boy produced an excellent rhythm with a four-inch nail.
>
> > "I am a son of God, Allelujah . . .
> > "The Devil can do nothing with me for
> > "I am a son of God, Allelujah." . . .

The effect on Titus was tremendous. This was a religious song with a difference. It produced in him a completely different effect from the prayers and responses at the services at All Souls which were sung in a tediously monotonous manner. It was entirely different from the effect produced on him by Pastor Morakinyo singing in a single musical note the three prayers after the creed. This was worship in a true African setting. And mechanically he removed his own shoes and joined in the singing and clapping of hands.

Besides being a community of the dispossessed rural poor, torn from ancestral ties to village, clan, and family, who eke out their existence in urban anonymity, Elder Matthew's Lagos church manifests the hallmarks of inculturation from below – *kaftan* instead of cassock, Yoruba instead of English, songs of spiritual warfare instead of sung liturgies. Of humble origins, Titus is now an engineer riding the sociological escalator of the upwardly mobile; as such, he is emblematic of Christians who feel the drag of the past, aspire to free themselves of it, and see in African traditional religions no possibility of an underlying rapport. Titus is a person in-between, but the world he lives in is not unlike the Bible's, which is nothing if not "comprehensively supernaturalistic" (Hastings 1994: 458) when seen through eyes like his.

Appropriate adjustments considered, Titus feels drawn to the Prophets of Iban for some of the same reasons that other Christians outside the world of Europe (not necessarily Pentecostal/Charismatic Christians) feel drawn to churches everywhere that regard the ancestors and other supranaturals with awe and dread instead of post-Enlightenment disdain (as was the case at Pastor Morakinyo's All Souls). Some see themselves as being in need of proper safeguards *against* them, as Titus does; others see themselves as being in need of proper communion *with* them. Few imagine, however, that ancestors and other supranaturals are anything but actually existing entities or that they have no bearing on salvation.

But what might a proper orientation of either description toward the trans-empirical realm of traditional religion actually entail? Among the Nagas of India's northeast highlands, missionized by American Baptists, it might mean, when latent anxieties about the wellbeing of the dead are aroused, that one turns to the "Holy Spirit People" (*tanula akuter*). Like traditional shamans, they give voice to the dead, although that voice is now the Holy Spirit's. Even though the church's pastors provide doctrinal assurance that the dead are safe in God's care, one needs tangible evidence. In Christianity of the made-in-Japan variety, it might mean that the ancestors' well-being is assured through vicarious baptism. On such occasions, indigenously initiated churches such as Murai Jun's Spirit of Jesus Church (founded 1941) use ritual hymns (Mullins 1998: 151–2) redolent of Buddhist imagery such as crossing to the farther shore:

> The ship that goes out knows no bottom,
> Sinking deeper and deeper in the depths.
> Still now the salvation of our ancestors is closed,
> Eternal spirits anguishing ceaselessly.
> [. . .]
> Oh, the cries of joy reverberate!
> Our ancestors have been saved!
> The light of grace shines all around,
> The songs of the angels thunder throughout heaven and earth.

A hymn like this would not be sung at Elder Matthew's church. "The Devil can do nothing against me" speaks of liberation from *all* supranaturals, including ancestors and even Olorun, the name of God in Yoruba. To this congregation, far from being strange and wonderful, Olorun is too familiar, too dreadful to invoke in worship (unlike the practice in the established African churches, on which see Paris 1995: 29 and Walls 1996: 94–7). The vagaries of inculturation from below resist sweeping generalizations across cultures and within cultures. One can turn *from* the ancestors to Christ, and one can turn the ancestors *toward* Christ; whichever way one goes, "no conversion is complete without the conversion of the past" (Walls 1996: 53).

The allelujahs sung at Elder Matthew's service have been sung, of course, since Christian antiquity. Aluko's Titus Oti may have felt that he experienced "worship in a true African setting" there, but the allelujahs, whether sung in Yoruba accents or others, form a bond between Christians everywhere and the worship traditions of Israel; they also prompt a turning of the pre-Christian past toward another sacred history. Inculturation from above, sanctioned by established churches (Catholic especially, because of the creative ferment engendered by Vatican II vernacularization directives, but Protestant too), tends to regard the relationship between pre-Christian past and Christian present as one of fundamental rapport awaiting (re)discovery and (re)assimilation. To some, the pre-Christian/Christian dichotomy no longer seems tenable theologically; to others, the rapport is rendered fundamental by a process of Christianizing reconciliation.

Yet other orientations have emerged. At one end of a continuum, one might put Christians who look to vernacular "little traditions" for rapport with the past; developments in contemporary Meso-America are especially interesting in this regard (Cook 1997). At the other, one might put Christians who look to non-vernacular "great traditions." Of the latter, especially evident in Asia, the Catholic contemplative tradition is emblematic. Thanks to being the preferred inculturational model of Europeans who write for Western audiences (Raguin 1997), the idea of a Catholic Vedanta (Le Saux 1974) or Catholic Zen (Johnston 1971) no longer elicits much surprise. Although this end of the continuum tends toward the highbrow, its influence over indigenous worship is considerable. Founded by Fr D. S. Amalorpavadass, India's prestigious National Biblical Catechetical and Liturgical Center (NBCLC, Bangalore) continues to perpetuate the same Sanskritizing tendencies we noted in the seventeenth century. The NBCLC's chants for the Indian Eucharistic celebration include the following:

> *Om shuddhaaya namaha* (Praise to the most holy),
> *Om pavanaaya namaha* (Praise to the sanctifier),
> *Om vishva jeevanaaya namaha* (And praise to the vivifier of the universe).

To anyone who appreciates Sanskrit, the language is at once exquisitely Upanishadic and yet, in the context of Christian worship, somehow *un*-Upanishadic. For Dalit and tribal Christians, however, who come from marginalized communities and who are by far the major cohort in India's Christian population, Sanskritization signifies the "tyranny of the sacred word of the Hindus" (Clarke 1998: 123) from which they seek liberation for having been excluded from the past it represents. Countervailing forces of an indigenous variety are in the making.

The eighteenth century through the twentieth century into the present testifies to the premise of non-generity on which I started: we do not study Christian spirituality if we only study our own. "No single place or culture," runs a final Wallsian dictum (2002b: 19), "owns the Christian faith or permanently dominates its expression."

References

Aluko, T. M. 1966: *Kinsman and Foreman*. London: Heinemann.

Amaladass, A. and Clooney, F. X. 2000: *Preaching Wisdom to the Wise: Three Treatises by Roberto de Nobili, SJ, Missionary and Scholar in 17th Century India*. St Louis: Institute of Jesuit Sources.

——and Young, R. F. 1995: *The Indian Christiad: A Concise Anthology of Didactic and Devotional Literature in Early Church Sanskrit*. Anand, Gujarat (India): Gujarat Sahitya Prakash.

Anderson, A. 2000: *Zion and Pentecost: The Spirituality and Experience of Pentecostal and Zionist/Apostolic Churches in South Africa*. Pretoria: University of South Africa Press.

Axtell, J. 1985: *The Invasion Within: The Context of Cultures in Colonial North America*. Oxford: Oxford University Press.

Barrett, D. B., Kurian, G. T., and Johnson, T. M. (eds) 2000: *World Christian Encyclopedia*. Oxford: Oxford University Press.

Bediako, K. 1995: *Christianity in Africa: The Renewal of a Non-Western Religion*. Maryknoll, NY: Orbis.

Burkhart, L. M. 1993: The Cult of the Virgin of Guadaloupe in Mexico. In G. H. Gossen (ed.), *South and Meso-American Native Spirituality: From the Cult of the Feathered Serpent to the Theology of Liberation*, pp. 198–227. New York: Crossroad.

Caplan, L. 1987: *Class and Culture in Urban India: Fundamentalism in a Christian Community*. Oxford: Oxford University Press.

Casely-Hayford, J. E. 1911: *Ethiopia Unbound: Studies in Race Emancipation*. London: C. M. Phillips.

Chung, D. 2001: *Syncretism: The Religious Context of Christian Beginnings in Korea*. Albany, NY: State University of New York Press.

Clark, I. D. 1977: The Tractarian movement in the Anglican Church in India in the nineteenth century. *Indian Church History Review* 11, 182–203.

Clarke, S. 1998: *Dalits and Christianity: Subaltern Religion and Liberation Theology in India*. Delhi: Oxford University Press.

Cook, G. (ed.) 1997: *Crosscurrents in Indigenous Spirituality: Interface of Maya, Catholic and Protestant Worldviews*. Leiden: E. J. Brill.

Dempsey, C. G. 2001: *Kerala Christian Sainthood: Collisions of Culture and Worldview in South India*. New York: Oxford University Press.

Dubois, J. A. 1823: *Letters on the State of Christianity in India; in Which the Conversion of the Hindoos is Considered as Impracticable*. London: Longman, Hurst, Rees, Orme, Brown, and Green.

Elison, G. 1973: *Deus Destroyed: The Image of Christianity in Early Modern Japan*. Cambridge, MA: Harvard University Press.

Entenmann, R. E. 1996: Catholics and society in eighteenth-century Sichuan. In D. H. Bays (ed.), *Christianity in China: From the Eighteenth Century to the Present*, pp. 8–23. Stanford: Stanford University Press.

Fabian, J. 1996: *Remembering the Present: Painting and Popular History in Zaire*. Berkeley, CA: University of California Press.

Garrett, J. 1982: *To Live among the Stars: Christian Origins in Oceania*. Geneva: World Council of Churches.

Gispert-Sauch, G. 1972: The Sanskrit hymns of Brahmabandhav Upadhyay. *Religion and Society* 19 (4), 60–79.

Goonatilleka, M. H. 1984: *Nadagama: The First Sri Lankan Theatre*. Delhi: Sri Satguru Publications.

Grayson, J. H. 1985: *Early Buddhism and Christianity in Korea: A Study in the Emplantation of Religion*. Leiden: E. J. Brill.

Greer, A. 2000: *The Jesuit Relations: Natives and Missionaries in Seventeenth-century North America*. New York: St Martin's Press.

Harrington, A. M. 1993: *Japan's Hidden Christians*. Chicago: Loyola University Press.

Hastings, A. 1979: *A History of African Christianity, 1950–1975*. Cambridge: Cambridge University Press.

——1994: *The Church in Africa, 1450–1950*. Oxford: Clarendon Press.

——1999: Latin America. In A. Hastings (ed.), *A World History of Christianity*, pp. 328–68. Grand Rapids, MI: W. B. Eerdmans.

Hefner, R. W. 1993: Of faith and commitment: Christian conversion in Muslim Java. In R. W. Hefner (ed.), *Conversion to Christianity: Historical and Anthropological Perspectives on a Great Transformation*, pp. 99–125. Berkeley, CA: University of California Press.

Higashibaba, I. 2001: *Christianity in Early Modern Japan: Kirishitan Belief and Practice*. Leiden: E. J. Brill.

Hudson, D. D. 2000: *Protestant Origins in India: Tamil Evangelical Christians, 1706–1835*. Grand Rapids, MI: W. B. Eerdmans.

Hutteman, J. 1765: The life of a pandaram, a fierce convert to Christianity at Cudulore. In *An Account of the Society for Promoting Christian Knowledge*, pp. 89–93. London: J. and W. Oliver.

Jenkins, P. 2002: *The Next Christendom: The Coming of Global Christianity*. New York: Oxford University Press.

Jeyaraj, D. 1996: *Inkulturation in Tranquebar: Der Beitrag der Frühen danisch-halleschen Mission zum Werden einer indisch-einheimischen Kirche, 1706–1730*. Verlag der Ev.-Luth. Erlangen: Mission.

Johnston, W. 1971: *Christian Zen*. New York: Harper and Row.

Killam, D. and Rowe, R. (eds) 2000: *Companion to African Literatures*. Bloomington, IN: Indiana University Press.

Kim, S. 2001: Strange names of God: the missionary translation of the divine name and the Chinese responses to Matteo Ricci's *Shangti* in late Ming China, 1583–1644. Unpublished PhD dissertation, Princeton Theological Seminary.

Klor de Alva, J. J. 1993: Aztec spirituality and Nahuatized Christianity. In G. H. Gossen (ed.), *South and Meso-American Native Spirituality: From the Cult of the Feathered Serpent to the Theology of Liberation*, pp. 173–97. New York: Crossroad.

Le Saux, H. [Abhishiktananda] 1974: *Saccidananda: A Christian Approach to Advaitic Experience*. Delhi: ISPCK.

Lehmann, A. 1956: *Es begann in Tranquebar: Die Geschichte der ersten evangelischen Kirche in Indien*. Berlin: Evangelische Verlagsanstalt.

Martin, D. 1990: *Tongues of Fire: The Explosion of Protestantism in Latin America*. Oxford: Blackwell.

—— 2002: *Pentecostalism: The World their Parish*. Oxford: Blackwell.

Marzal, M. M. 1993: Transplanted Spanish Catholicism. In G. H. Gossen (ed.), *South and Meso-American Native Spirituality: From the Cult of the Feathered Serpent to the Theology of Liberation*, pp. 14–69. New York: Crossroad.

Miura, H. 1996: *The Life and Thought of Kanzo Uchimura, 1861–1930*. Grand Rapids, MI: W. B. Eerdmans.

Moffett, S. H. 1998: *A History of Christianity in Asia*, vol. 1: *Beginnings to 1500*. Maryknoll, NY: Orbis.

Mullins, M. R. 1998: *Christianity Made in Japan: A Study of Indigenous Movements*. Honolulu: University of Hawai'i Press.

Ndung'u, N. W. 2000: The role of the Bible in the rise of African instituted churches: the case of the Akurinu churches in Kenya. In G. O. West and M. W. Dube (eds), *The Bible in Africa: Transactions, Trajectories and Trends*, pp. 236–47. Leiden: E. J. Brill.

Paris, P. 1995: *The Spirituality of African Peoples: The Search for a Common Moral Discourse*. Minneapolis, MN: Augsburg/Fortress Press.

Phan, P. C. 1998: *Mission and Catechesis: Alexandre de Rhodes and Inculturation in Seventeenth-century Vietnam*. Maryknoll, NY: Orbis.

Raguin, Y. 1997: *Ways of Contemplation East and West*, 3 vols. Taipei, Taiwan: Ricci Institute for Chinese Studies.

Rivera, L. N. 1992: *A Violent Evangelism: The Political and Religious Conquest of the Americas*. Louisville, KY: Westminster/John Knox.

Rubinstein, M. A. 1996: Holy Spirit Taiwan: Pentecostal and Charismatic Christianity in the Republic of China. In D. H. Bays (ed.), *Christianity in China: From the Eighteenth Century to the Present*, pp. 353–66. Stanford: Stanford University Press.

Sanneh, L. 1989: *Translating the Message: The Missionary Impact on Culture*. Maryknoll, NY: Orbis.

Shenk, W. R. (ed.) 2002: *Enlarging the Story: Perspectives on Writing World Christian History.* Maryknoll, NY: Orbis.

Szeminski, J. 1993: The last time the Inca came back: messianism and nationalism in the Great Rebellion of 1780–1783. In G. H. Gossen (ed.), *South and Meso-American Native Spirituality: From the Cult of the Feathered Serpent to the Theology of Liberation,* pp. 279–99. New York: Cross-road.

Tang, L. 2002: *A Study of the History of Nestorian Christianity in China and its Literature in Chinese, together with a New English Translation of the Dunhuang Nestorian Documents.* New York: Peter Lang.

Thottakara, A. (ed.) 1990: *East Syrian Spirituality.* Rome: Centre for Indian and Inter-religious Studies.

Tinker, G. 1994: Spirituality and Native American personhood: sovereignty and solidarity. In K. C. Abraham and B. Mbuy-Beya (eds), *Spirituality of the Third World,* pp. 119–32. Maryknoll, NY: Orbis.

Treat, J. (ed.) 1996: *Native and Christian: Indigenous Voices on Religious Identity in the United States and Canada.* New York: Routledge.

Walls, A. F. 1996: *The Missionary Movement in Christian History: Studies in the Transmission of Faith.* Maryknoll, NY: Orbis.

—— 2002a: *The Cross-cultural Process in Christian History: Studies in the Transmission and Appropriation of Faith.* Maryknoll, NY: Orbis.

—— 2002b: Eusebius tries again: the task of reconceiving and re-visioning the study of Christian history. In W. R. Shenk (ed.), *Enlarging the Story: Perspectives on Writing World Christian History,* pp. 1–21. Maryknoll, NY: Orbis.

Younger, P. 2002: *Playing Host to Deity: Festival Religion in the South Indian Tradition.* Oxford: Oxford University Press.

Zhang W. 1997: Catholicism in the poetry of Macao during the Qing Dynasty. *Review of Culture* (Macao) 30 (2nd series), 141–66.

PART IV

Theology and Christian Spirituality

CHAPTER 10

Trinitarian Perspectives on Christian Spirituality

Mark A. McIntosh

Jesus of Nazareth regularly induced moments of startled wonder and dawning new perception among his followers. These experiences often seem to have involved, in some form, the sudden appearance of merciful reversals and surprising abundance. Kings lavish outrageous plenty on uninvited guests in parables; the hungry poor receive food beyond all imagining in the wilderness; the dead are raised to life; and, as if in perfect fulfillment of all this, Jesus himself appears alive from the dead among his betrayers, offering them forgiveness and peace and a share in his own new risen life. Christian spiritualities are all rooted in and unfurl as branches of this unfathomable divine generosity made visible, Christians believe, in Jesus.

The Gospel according to John especially invokes this mysterious generosity – as an invitation to journey into an ever-greater intimacy with God. Jesus tells his followers that he must leave them as they presently encounter him, but adds, "I will come again and will take you to myself, so that where I am, there you may be also" (John 14: 3). Where he is turns out to be "in the Father," a location only discoverable by the way-faring of self-sharing love. And the disciples' journey into this self-giving life is not only bidden by Christ, but inspired and consummated by yet another voice of divine generosity, the Holy Spirit: "I still have many things to say to you, but you cannot bear them now. When the Spirit of truth comes, he will guide you into all the truth . . . He will glorify me, because he will take what is mine and declare it to you. All that the Father has is mine" (John 16: 12–15). The Spirit of truth guides Jesus's followers by conducting them farther and farther, beyond their present capacities, into the fullness of the Father's life, which is given away to Jesus and through Jesus to the world, all by the power of this same Spirit. In all this lies the origin of both Christian faith in God as Trinity and of Christian spirituality as a participation in that trinitarian life.

In what follows, I want to explore three dimensions of the *relationship* between God's life as Trinity and Christian spirituality. First, we should unfold a little further what might be meant by this idea of a trinitarian source for spirituality – and what is *not* meant. And then, in the second and third sections of this essay, we will consider, as examples, what this trinitarian perspective brings to light in two central themes of Christian spirituality: the paschal mystery and humanity's vocation in creation.

Unfathomably Giving Life: The Trinitarian Rhythm of Christian Spirituality

The ever-greater giving away of life in Jesus, painted as luminous icon in the passages from John above, is unfathomably mysterious. Most of ordinary human experience is fenced around by limit, necessity, and the constraints of scarcity – all of which reach into life from the inescapable shadows of death itself. Because death so profoundly shapes human perception, Jesus's abandonment of himself to it is deeply mysterious. But while inexplicable, it seems nonetheless to have evoked in his followers an immeasurable sense of being loved by him: "Having loved his own who were in the world, he loved them to the end [*telos*]" (John 13: 1). Their experience is of Jesus's passover into dereliction and death as a *telos*, a consummation, of giving love that points beyond itself to the one whom Jesus himself experiences as his own source, as the one who loves him and shares with him beyond all limits. James Alison (commenting on John 14 and following) explains this transforming impact of Jesus's dying and rising upon believers:

> Jesus *is going* [to the Father] in order to prepare for us a place: it is his going to death which opens up for us the possibility of a place with the Father. It is his *going* which constitutes the only way to the Father, since apart from the creative and deliberate self-giving up to death of Jesus, there is no access, no way for us to begin to have our imaginations re-formed by the vivaciousness of God, and thus begin to share actively in his life, *because we cannot, as we are, imagine beyond, or outside, our formation within death*. It is only by knowing Jesus and his self-giving that we begin to have any knowledge of the Father. (Alison 1996: 62; emphasis in original)

Alison shows how Jesus's destiny not only makes the abundant life of God mysteriously present to the disciples, but that this giving life also brings the disciples into a new landscape, no longer bounded by death but open to the boundlessness of God's life. This inbreaking of inconceivable generosity pries open minds and hearts conformed to the fear of death, and pours out within them a new Spirit, an Advocate and Giver of a share in that very same sharing life of the one to whom Jesus entrusts himself. Another witness from the early Christian era puts it this way: "Since, therefore, the children share flesh and blood, he himself likewise shared the same things, so that through death he might destroy the one who has the power of death, that is, the devil, and free those who all their lives were held in slavery by the fear of death" (Heb. 2: 14–15).

In a real sense, the whole of Christian life might well be said to spring from this new and transforming access to a divinely sharing life that frees us from the dominion of death. But especially we could say that this is the source of all Christian prayer and that journey into ever-greater intimacy with God we sometimes call "spirituality." Herbert McCabe analyzes this self-sharing availability of Jesus as the ground of prayer:

[Jesus] is not first of all an individual person who then prays to the Father, his prayer to the Father is what constitutes him as who he is. He is not just one who prays, not even one who prays best, he is sheer prayer. In other words, the crucifixion/resurrection of Jesus is simply the showing forth, the visibility in human terms, in human history, of the relationship to the Father which constitutes the person who is Jesus. The prayer of Jesus which is his crucifixion, his absolute renunciation of himself in love to the Father, is the eternal relationship of Father and Son made available as part of our history . . . For us to pray is for us to be taken over, possessed by the Holy Spirit which is the life of love between Father and Son. (McCabe 1987: 220)

So I am suggesting in all this that the yearning desire that beckons toward the spiritual journey is, in its most authentic depths, God the Holy Spirit: the same Holy Spirit who beckons the divine Source or Father yearningly towards Another, and the same Holy Spirit who impels this Other, the Word and Wisdom of God, to give voice to the loving source from within the utter alterity of creation, and even human alienation from God, in the suffering and loving of Jesus. God the Holy Spirit may thus be identified as fostering Christian spirituality by pouring out within believers a beginning of that transforming state of existence that opens up toward the infinitely sharing life of God: Father sharing all in love and freedom with Son, who does not count equality with God a thing to be grasped but also equally and eternally shares divine life, and Holy Spirit whose very yearning and power of sharing both eternally unite and infinitely diversify the Trinity.

I do not mean by this that all Christian spirituality is inevitably self-consciously trinitarian, nor do I mean that all Christian spirituality must be fully analyzable into trinitarian terms. The trinitarian rhythm of self-sharing abundance is far more deeply and graciously operative within Christian spirituality than can always be discerned. I do sense, however, that many common marks of Christian spiritualities become especially intelligible and luminous when considered in terms of a journey in the Spirit into the ever-greater freedom, love, and generosity of Jesus's relationship with the one he called Abba. Let me identify three such common marks of Christian spirituality in particular: self-transcendence, a deepening love for others, a growing sense of freedom and agency.

Now there is an interestingly characteristic paradox inherent in these three features: they crop up in various forms of Christian spirituality with fair regularity in spite of the fact that, in the normal economy of human existence, they are each highly susceptible to a negative form that renders them pretty well inimical to each other – or else makes them covert confederates in a self-defeating downward spiral. And yet when they grow in healthy ways within Christian spiritual journeys they do not undermine each other but seem strangely to exchange an unhindered mutual vitality. Take self-transcendence, which is all too easily infected by cultural propensities toward narcissism. Steady relinquishment of the present self in openness toward a greater reality can almost imperceptibly slide into egoistic self-preoccupation with one's own development, *or* be taken hold of by unacknowledged hurts and compulsions toward self-punishment. In either of these shadow forms, self-transcendence would become nearly toxic to any authentic love for others, distorting it into self-aggrandizement in one case or an exhausting self-negation in the other. And, once again, either form would also undermine any growth in genuine freedom and agency.

If, however, we were to look for each of these three features (self-transcendence, love for others, freedom and agency) in, say, Catherine of Siena or Ignatius of Loyola, we would find them all present together – not siphoning energy away from each other but growing stronger from each other's strength. Think of Catherine's conviction in the *Dialogue* (for example, chs 3–8) that the self who emerges transformed from the cell of self-knowledge is the only one who can really serve its neighbors. Or think of Ignatius's teaching (*Spiritual Exercises* nos 165ff) that the one who has accepted the deepest humiliations in serving God and neighbor is most free at last, clearest in his or her sense of calling and missioned with a joyous sense of agency that is intimately sensitive to God's working in all things.

At the heart of these paradoxes of the Christian spiritual life seems to lie the same paradox announced in the Gospels: "Those who want to save their life will lose it, and those who lose their life for my sake, and for the sake of the gospel, will save it" (Mark 8: 35). What I have been suggesting, then, is that the ground of all this is the constitutive dynamic of trinitarian life itself, that is, life in which each One *is* by giving way to the Other, in which the personhood of each is not diminished but eternally realized by sharing the whole of divine life with each. Trinitarian relational life, in other words, is the deep structure of spiritual growth, illuminating the human spiritual journey with eternal significance – a journey in which human beings are consummated by an ecstatic journey of love beyond the selves given them by biology or culture, in which they are not depleted but free and authoritative in their life for and with others, including the divine Others.

Trinitarian *belief*, unfolded within the community's continuing participation in the trinitarian life of God, is not an artificial set of formulas by which to regulate Christian spirituality. Rather, trinitarian belief is an itinerary, a call beckoning believers to a shared journey into mystery. So the point of thinking "trinitarianly" about Christian spirituality is to become enlightened and empowered by the real life of God, to which (Christians believe), the doctrine of the Trinity directs us. As Thomas Aquinas puts it, the human spiritual act of faith does not reach its goal in a statement of belief but in the divine reality itself (*Summa theologiae* 2–2, 1.2, reply 2). Or, in the words of Evelyn Underhill:

> The Creed is no mere academic document, no mere list of "dogmas." It is an account of that which *is*; and every word it contains has a meaning at once universal, practical, and spiritual within the particular experience of each soul. It irradiates and harmonizes every level of our life . . . Since the life of prayer consists in an ever-deepening communion with a Reality beyond ourselves, which is truly there, and touches, calls, attracts us, what we believe about that Reality will rule our relation to it. We do not approach a friend and a machine in the same way . . . We pray first because we believe something; perhaps at that stage a very crude or vague something. And with the deepening of prayer, its patient cultivation, there comes – perhaps slowly, perhaps suddenly – the enrichment and enlargement of belief, as we enter into a first-hand communion with the Reality who is the object of our faith. (Underhill 1991: 5–7)

Underhill points to a crucial reciprocity here: the belief (in this case, in God's trinitarian life) orients the spiritual seeker to a set of basic way-marks for encountering the divine reality. But those are only a guide, like a grammar book; the intent of them is to foster a deeper and truer conversation and meeting. And, reciprocally, trinitarian understanding of God is itself the expression of the community's ongoing spiritual life, its encounter with God through Christ in the Holy Spirit.

William of St Thierry observes that the Trinity comes graciously to inhabit the spiritual seeking of the one who is reflecting on the Trinity: "Immediately the memory becomes wisdom and tastes with relish the good things of the Lord . . . The understanding of the one thinking becomes the contemplation of one loving" (1971: 92). In this way, Christian spirituality contributes to the deepening understanding and development of Christian doctrine – perhaps even more than doctrine, however needful, contributes to spirituality. I think what William is describing here (in a letter intended for those very much intent on practicing the spiritual life) gets to the core of this reciprocity between trinitarian faith and spirituality. It is perhaps conceivable as the transition from speaking of God by means of terms and concepts to speaking to God by means of deepening desire; one discovers that the terms and concepts have come to life as names by which one is enabled to call out to God and be addressed in response, and the ideas begin to be animated no longer by one's own thinking of them but by God's own knowing and loving of God-self. "The understanding of the one thinking becomes the contemplation of one loving," as William puts it. "When the object of thought is God and the things which relate to God, and the will reaches the stage at which it becomes love, the Holy Spirit, the Spirit of life, at once infuses himself by way of love and gives life to everything" (1971: 92).

Living within the Trinitarian Dimension of the Paschal Mystery

All of this is to say that even if trinitarian thought is not explicit in a particular feature of spirituality, it will probably allow certain elements to grow luminous and meaningful – perhaps even opening the doors of perception to deeper awareness of the one who animates the spiritual journey as a whole. Few acts could be more central to Christian spirituality than sharing in Christ's dying and rising. What light can trinitarian reflection shed on this fundamental companionship with Christ? In simplest terms, it awakens a sense of the mystery of the Father to whom Christ goes, and of the burning love of the Spirit hidden in the passion of Jesus. Obviously, entire volumes could be devoted to the subject of passion mysticism and spirituality (see Cousins 1987 for a good brief introduction and bibliography), so my aim here is simply to note two significant trinitarian perspectives.

In the remarkable closing lines of his *The Journey of the Mind to God*, Bonaventure radically transforms the classical contemplative ascent of the mind: he recontextualizes it within the paschal mystery. The ultimate goal of the mind's journey is not simply a silent beholding of truth, but a passing over from this life to a wholly other existence by way of the cross. It would, unfortunately, be easy enough to find examples in the history of Christian spirituality of passion mysticism gone awry, either grown self-involved, mesmerized by covert dramas of self-despising, or grown into the manipulative tool of the powerful over the marginalized, endlessly legitimizing their suffering and enforcing their oppression.

Bonaventure, by contrast, sees the passion as deliverance and transition into the unimaginable reality of God, into the liberating truth of endless goodness endlessly bestowed. In the spiritual journey, says Bonaventure, the mind can advance through many degrees, but its final stage is not simply a yet more costly moment of "advance" by suffering, a self-annihilation which somehow wins a more refined vision of truth. No, the mind must "transcend and pass over, not only this visible world, but even itself" (Bonaventure 1993, 7.1, p. 37). Bonaventure does not admonish the soul to attempt a more rigorous suffering in imitation of the suffering Jesus; rather, he advocates that one should gaze upon the mystery of the Father's love hidden in Jesus on the cross, and, beholding this unutterable mercy, be set free; "such a one celebrates the Pasch, that is, the Passover, with Him. Thus, using the rod of the Cross, he may pass over the Red Sea, going from Egypt into the desert, where it is given to him to taste the hidden manna" (1993, 7.2, p. 38). What is the goal of this journey from slavery into new life? "With Christ crucified, let us pass out of this world to the Father, so that, when the Father is shown to us, we may say with Philip: It is enough for us" (1993, 7.6, p. 39).

Bonaventure's trinitarian vision of the passion allows him to hold Christ's suffering open to the mystery of the Father. In so doing, he restores to Christian spirituality the deep relational grammar of Christ's passion, and sets spirituality free from temptations to solipsistic self-absorption. Also, because he emphasizes this trinitarian dimension, he undercuts a toxic counter-spirituality of self-denigration or oppression; the cross is not a brutal constraint, forever immuring suffering persons or groups into their status, for it is the rod and staff of the free pilgrim who is called to journey on into immeasurable bounty, to the hidden manna of true life and the liberty of the ever-greater Father.

Bonaventure also emphasized the role of the Holy Spirit in passion mysticism. Indeed, the Seraphic Doctor ascribes to the Holy Spirit that intense stirring of love that he so prizes in contemplating the passion. The Spirit is the true agent who effects within the believer the passover to the Source which Christ accomplishes on the cross. No one receives this "mystical and most secret" transformation into divine life "except him who desires it, and no one desires it except he who is penetrated to the marrow by the fire of the Holy Spirit" (1993, 7.4, p. 38). Later, Bonaventure remarks that God *is* this fire and that "Christ enkindles it in the white flame of His most burning Passion" (1993, 7.6, p. 39). Christ's passionate desire to do the will of the one who sent him bursts into full flame on the cross, and Bonaventure reveals the secret name of this fire to be the Holy Spirit. In making this identification, the Franciscan again brings to light the fully trinitarian nature of the passion *and* its consequent capacity to enkindle the same fire within the believing community. This trinitarian ground for passion mysticism delivers it from any tendency toward a privatizing individualism or emotionalism; for the yearning of those who contemplate the cross is never simply their own feeling, their own possession, but rather the communal, relational passion of the Holy Spirit at work throughout time and space.

Not only does the Holy Spirit open a spirituality of the passion to an ever-fuller relational and communal depth; the Spirit also awakens new voice and agency within those drawn into the mystery of Christ's incarnation and passion. In other words, this trinitarian dimension within spirituality preserves it from collapsing inward – either into a divine monism in which the soul is simply annihilated (with all the dangerous potentials for quietism, passivity, or even the legitimizing of an abusive condition) or into a peculiar form of idealism in which the "divine" metamorphoses into a mere cipher for the most exalted forms of human narcissism. Recovering the agency of the Holy Spirit in passion mysticism reveals in a gracious light the "space," the room for alterity and authentic human agency, even in that most intimate union of self-giving marked by sharing in the cross. John of the Cross explores this theme most keenly, perhaps especially in *The Spiritual Canticle* (for excellent considerations on agency in John, see Howells 2002 and Williams 2002). After observing how Christ communicates to the soul the "sweet mysteries of his Incarnation and of the ways of the redemption" (John of the Cross 1979, 23.1, p. 499), John says that from this "espousal made on the cross" (23.6, p. 500) the soul's relationship with Christ the bridegroom grows gradually onward toward an unimaginable depth.

As John unfolds the mysteriousness of this growing union, he brings to light the important sense in which the soul is gifted with the desire of the Spirit – not so as to take the place of the soul but rather to strengthen it for real agency of its own within the infinite self-sharing of divine existence. "The soul's aim is a love equal to God's. She always desired this equality, naturally and supernaturally, for a lover cannot be satisfied if he fails to feel that he loves as much as he is loved" (1979, 38.3, p. 553). Significantly, John envisions a new identity and voice for the soul, an identity no longer conceivable in terms of either subordination or rivalry but of equality, a relational identity whose selfhood and agency is constituted by receiving all from and giving all freely to the other. And, of course, for John, this developing identity of the soul springs directly from the trinitarian pattern of life in which it is increasingly participating. This means that the soul will know and love God by sharing in God's knowing and loving of God, and yet, precisely because of the trinitarian space for genuine otherness in God, this knowing and loving in which the soul participates will also be truly the soul's own.

> As her intellect will be the intellect of God, her will then will be God's will, and thus her love will be God's love. The soul's will is not destroyed there, but it is so firmly united with the strength of God's will, with which He loves her, that her love for Him is as strong and perfect as His love for her . . . This strength lies in the Holy Spirit, in Whom the soul is there transformed. (1979, 38.3, p. 554)

John interestingly highlights both the soul's own desire and the need for the soul to have a strength of its own so as to love God as much as the soul desires. We might think here of the role ascribed to the Spirit in the Gospels, sending Jesus into the wilderness to discover yet more deeply the authenticity and truth of his desire to do the will of the one who sent him.

Interpreting passion spirituality in this trinitarian light points to a healthy form of spiritual self-surrender, a self-sharing enacted out of a growing freedom and authority to love with a strength (given by the Spirit) that is both beyond oneself and yet increasingly one's own. John emphasizes that God does not simply *give* the soul the divine love, but that "He will show her how to love Him as perfectly as she desires . . . As if he were to put an instrument in her hands and show her how it works by operating it jointly with her, He shows her how to love and gives her the ability to do so" (1979, 38.4, p.

554). The soul's apprenticeship does not infantilize but empowers a voice fully enfranchised by the trinitarian making space for the other. Discerning the fully trinitarian role of the Holy Spirit holds spirituality open to this paradoxical freedom. (On the question of the Spirit and agency from a feminist perspective, see the insightful arguments of Coakley 2002.)

Trinitarian Illumination and the Human Calling in Creation

Now we can turn to another example in which a trinitarian perspective sheds helpful light on an important theme in Christian spirituality. Few subjects have witnessed a greater renaissance (and more ambiguity) in recent decades than the question of spirituality and creation. My aim is not to rehearse the perplexing history of interpretation regarding Genesis 1: 28, the prodigious growth of creation spiritualities in a lavish variety of forms, or the important links with ecological concerns. (Wallace 1996 offers a creative and incisive analysis of the intersection of creation life-centered theology, spirituality, and pneumatology.) Instead, I want to point to an important elucidation of trinitarian theology: the understanding of creation as radiant with intelligibility and truth, and of humanity as called to serve and facilitate the creation's consummation in glory (further on this, see McIntosh 2004).

A fairly central thread in Christian theology has been the idea that all the creatures have been known and loved eternally within the knowing and loving that is God's trinitarian life. In Origen's *On First Principles* (1.2–3), Augustine's *Lectures on the Gospel according to St John* (1.17), and Maximus' *Chapters on Knowledge* (1.42ff), to name only three particular instances, we can find various expressions of this theme. The idea is that the fullness and joy of the eternal trinitarian processions include, as a dimension of their relational self-sharing, the ideas of all the ways in which God can share this giving life with the other, not only the divine Others (i.e., the three divine Persons) but with *completely* other others (i.e., the creatures)! Indeed, it is part of the divine delight and freedom that God's life can choose to give itself in the creation and consummation of these others. For the remarkable seventeenth-century theologian and poet Thomas Traherne, we could even go so far as to say (with echoes of Dionysius, Eriugena, and Eckhart) that this love for the creatures is entirely one with the loving yearning of the Spirit who animates Father and Son, and with the conceiving by which God knows the Other in God, namely the eternal begetting of the Son. This Person, says Traherne, "as He is the Wisdom of the Father, so is He the Love of the Father . . . And this Person did God by loving us, beget, that He might be the means of all our glory" (Traherne 1985, 2.43, p. 77; for an excellent brief introduction to Traherne, see Inge 2002). On this view, the secret depth of every creature radiates the divine self-knowing, called forth by love, and this deep structure of every creature is the reason why it *is* itself, and *as* itself is knowable, *intelligible*. For every creature has the quality of a word, and not just any word but an expressivity of infinite love.

We find the same view expressed in Thomas Aquinas. In his *Commentary on the Gospel of St John* (2.91), Aquinas says that all the creatures-to-be exist as eternal archetypes in the mind of God, as the plan of an artisan has an intellectual existence apart from the actual chest or table that comes to be made of wood. It is important for Aquinas that the creatures come forth from this knowing of the Father in the Son. Why? Because this trinitarian relationality *is* the "truthing" that is Truth itself, the eternal and infinite correspondence in joy of the divine Persons one to another. And because creatures spring from this eternal event of truth-making *they* are veritable themselves, they have a truth that is intelligible to other creatures capable of apprehending and delighting in it, as an earthly echoing of the trinitarian celebration from which all things flow. "Since God by understanding Himself understands all other things . . . the Word conceived in God by His understanding of Himself must also be the Word of all things" (Aquinas 1975, 4.13.6, p. 94). Noteworthy here is the fact that all things are produced within and from this eternal act of divine self-knowing and loving; the Word who is this self-knowing is therefore, as Aquinas puts it, "the perfect existing intelligibility" (1975, 4.13.6, pp. 94–5). So knowing the creatures in their full significance is going to entail an encounter with the Word who speaks them all; and the desire to understand them and rejoice in them properly, according to their own truth, can only be kindled by the Holy Spirit who inspires the production of their eternal archetypal form in the mutual loving of the Trinity.

In and of themselves, then, all creatures are miracles of divine delight; they exist as events of pure gratuity and freely self-giving love between the divine Persons. So whatever biological constraints each creature may be under, whatever cultural constructions may come to shape creaturely meaning, all creatures have, as it were, a true voice and beauty that only become radiantly apparent as the creatures are heard and seen in their divine truthfulness. But how *are* the creatures to be appreciated in this way, discovered in their true giftedness and freedom, recognized and cherished for what they are, namely, expressions of eternal joy and desire to be with and for one another eternally? For this alone is to perceive their true sign-fullness of the trinitarian life which originates them. In the deepest sense, the truth of the creation is only accomplished through the historical missions of the Word and Holy Spirit, reaching consummation in Christ's death and resurrection and the sending of the Spirit at Pentecost.

As Maximus argues (see Louth 1996 for a perceptive analysis), the incarnation of the Word means the taking up of various dimensions of the creation into their proper speaking. This is not simply a matter of the *logoi* (the rationale and truth) of human bone, blood, muscle, and hair being freed into their true resonance in expressing (as Jesus) the *Logos* in whom and through whom they exist. That certainly is the case, but Jesus also extends the same incorporation of the creation into the life of the Word more widely: the earth itself becomes fruitful with a mysterious abundance and hidden treasure in his parables; the broken relations among humankind become exposed in their sterility and drawn into the healing relationship he creates among his followers. The incarnation extends to include more and more of creation, restoring to it a true voice as it shares again in the speaking of the Word. At Pentecost the secret work of the Spirit is revealed, moving the creation through a burning desire – the heart of creation is set free to know and its mouth to speak the truth in a manner that surpasses all earthly divisions of nature or culture.

The risen Christ, according to Maximus, "in rising on a pure mind manifests both [himself] and the principles (*logoi*) which have been and will be brought to existence by it" (Maximus 1985, 1.95, p. 45). The power of the resurrection working within humanity through the Holy Spirit continues to accomplish this liberation and truth-faring of all the creatures. But, in keeping with the incarnational momentum, this is an activity in which the creatures themselves take part. Especially the intelligent creatures have a role to play, for they not only can be taken up into a more radiant earthly sign of the trinitarian joy which is their source (as in the elements of the Eucharist), but they can also freely choose to draw the other creatures into this offering: in the hands of the human community, says Maximus in the *Mystagogia*, the bare stuff of creation (usually subjected to bitter division and quarreling) can be made into bread and wine, and offered again into the loving hands of the creator, and so be received back again all glorious in its true light, become not just biologically nutritious but life itself.

None of this form of creation spirituality would be possible apart from a deeply trinitarian grammar, a deep structure to the creation that echoes and resounds with the joy of the divine Persons. Indeed, one might even argue that whenever humanity has grown deaf to this deep trinitarian resonance, the living gratuity and freedom of the creatures have been trampled; creation itself is rendered into a silent mute object, an essence, a bare nature to be investigated and if possible exploited, rather than an expression of trinitarian personal freedom and relationality – an expression given created existence precisely so as to permit an analogously free and loving response from the creation. Humankind is one element within creation (among others) capable through grace of expressing this journey from bare natural and biological necessity up into personal relationship, freedom, and love. And, along with other intelligent creatures, humans have the capacity, as empowered by the Holy Spirit, to participate in the Word's restoration of voice and communal, flowing life to all creatures. Even the most glorious flower may become yet immeasurably more resonant, more sign-full, when taken into the hand of a child and given away to a hurting friend, for then its flowery nature is expanded infinitely by participating in an act of loving fellowship and compassion, echoing the trinitarian friendship that conceived the flower from all eternity.

Few theologians or spiritual teachers, in my judgment, have equaled Thomas Traherne in exploring this intrinsic giftedness of creation – God's desire to give life to all through all – and humanity's vocation to share in this celebration. Humanity is called to discern this deeper truth of all things, to hear and respond to the divine giving in them all. The question is whether humanity will operate like visionary angels or more like greedy pigs in this regard:

> The services of things and their excellencies are spiritual: being objects not of the eye, but of the mind: and you more spiritual by how much you esteem them. Pigs eat acorns, but neither consider the sun that gave them life, nor the influences of the heavens by which they were nourished, nor the very root of the tree from whence they came. This being the work of Angels, who in a wide and clear light see even the sea that gave them moisture: And feed upon that acorn spiritually while they know the ends for which it was created, and feast upon all these as upon a World of Joys within it: while to the ignorant swine that eat the shell, it is an empty husk of no taste nor delightful savour. (Traherne 1985, 1.26, p. 13)

Angelic knowledge here opens onto a vision of sublime charity and abundance of limitless extent, and, more importantly, includes a real sense of the *joy* intrinsic to each creature as a sign of the trinitarian delight that gave being to it. Swinish perception, by contrast (and I would venture Traherne has human grubbing more in mind than any porcine variety), is dimmed down to a dull snuffling up of whatever lies immediately at hand, grabbing it for oneself before anyone else can consume it.

In Traherne's view, the trinitarian vision of creation leads to a serious critique of social wrongs. Instead of being freed into the limitless bounty of divine giving, humankind has developed a distinctly swinish appetite for the quickly grasped and consumed; and this translates into human relations, so that people want to possess each other and invent schemes of false self-presentation and a whole simulated realm of appearances designed to get the better of each other:

> You would not think how these barbarous inventions spoil your knowledge. They put grubs and worms into men's heads that are enemies to all pure and true apprehensions, and eat out all their happiness. They make it impossible for them, in whom they reign, to believe there is any excellency in the Works of God, or to taste any sweetness in the nobility of Nature, or to prize any common, though never so great a blessing. They alienate men from the Life of God, and at last make them to live without God in the World. (1985, 3.13, pp. 116–17)

For humanity to fulfill its potential as the generous knowers and celebrants of creation's truth, a very different eye will be needed. What Traherne seeks to awaken is a new vision of the trinitarian generosity that grounds all creation, a recognition that this is "the highest reason in all things" (1985, 3.18, p. 119).

In one of his most famous passages, Traherne imagines this revolution in the human perception of creation:

> You never enjoy the world aright, till you see how a sand exhibiteth the wisdom and power of God: And prize in everything the service which they do you, by manifesting His glory and goodness to your Soul, far more than the visible beauty on their surface, or the material services they can do your body. Wine by its moisture quencheth my thirst, whether I consider it or no: but to see it flowing from His love who gave it unto man, quencheth the thirst even of the Holy Angels. To consider it is to drink it spiritually. To rejoice in its diffusion is to be of a public mind. And to take pleasure in all the benefits it doth to all is Heavenly, for so they do in Heaven. To do so, is to be divine and good, and to imitate our Infinite and Eternal Father. (1985, 1.27, pp. 13–14)

Traherne signals a trajectory inherent within this deeper seeing and appreciating of all creatures: it leads not just to an enjoyment of God's generosity *per se*, but to an awareness of the very roots of that generosity in the "public mind" of heaven itself, the self-diffusive bounty of the Trinity.

As humanity comes to participate more deeply in this trinitarian knowing and loving of all things, it becomes more able to see the divine purpose in all things: a desire to delight the other, to give joy, and to share together in the happiness of mutual life. Because all creatures are in fact expressions of this divine intent, they are only brought to their consummate state as they are themselves appreciated and offered by thanks-giving to the giver, echoing within the created order the trinitarian giving and receiv-ing. "What are the cattle upon a thousand hills," asks Traherne, "but carcases, without creatures that can rejoice in God and enjoy them?" (1985, 3.82, p. 155). In a crucial sense, Traherne argues, intelligent creatures, who are capable of knowing the full truth of creation by receiving it in gratitude and thanking God for it, may help each creature into its consummate state, precisely as an event of sharing:

> Praises are the breathings of interior love, the marks and symptoms of a happy life, over-flowing gratitude, returning benefits, an oblation of the soul, and the heart ascending upon the wings of divine affection to the Throne of God. God is a Spirit and cannot feed upon carcases: but He can be delighted with thanksgivings, and is infinitely pleased with the emanations of our joy. (1985, 3.82, p. 155)

The trinitarian undertones in this passage are evocative of the mutual "breathing" described by John of the Cross. We should note here that in calling on humanity to bear creation into the trinitarian life, Traherne is not somehow denigrating the material cre-ation: *spirit*, in his theology, is not so much set in opposition to *matter* as to *isolation* and bare essence, the muting of creatures' inherent relationality so that they become mere "nature." So when Traherne speaks of the human vocation to think the creatures back into a state of thankfulness and praise, he is not intending (I would argue) to extricate them from matter; he is suggesting that their "matter" is inherently far more relational, an event of communication, than our usual treatment of creation suggests (perhaps Traherne is in this sense saying something not far from recent thought in quantum physics; see Polkinghorne 1996 on the relational energy of sub-atomic reality).

In this trinitarian perspective on creation, then, we not only recover a new and blessed generosity in every creature, but rediscover also a role for humankind more con-ducive to creation's praise and consummation than its exploitation. Traherne envisages humanity not as reducing creation to useful, consumable form, but in fact extending creation into its intended fullness and resonance, precisely by appreciating it in praise:

> The world within you [i.e., as intelligible, as thought] is an offering returned, which is infi-nitely more acceptable to God Almighty, since it came from Him, that it might return unto Him. Wherein the mystery is great. For God hath made you able to create worlds in your own mind which are more precious to Him than those which He created; and to give and offer up the world unto Him, which is very delightful in flowing from Him, but much more in returning to Him. (1985, 2.90, p. 99)

The greater delight and enhancement of creation, as taken into the celebration of praise, does not imply a denigration of its sheer createdness *per se*. It is precisely so that the creatures may have the freedom and opportunity to choose in love a responsive friendship with the creator that they receive created existence. Not all the creatures are, perhaps, capable of making this free act of oblation, this willing sharing in the trini-tarian *perichoresis* (mutual presence), but God has given some of the creatures the capacity to accomplish this, as is most meet, through a communal relationship among themselves. As the intelligent creatures unite together to lift up their fellow creatures in the act of praise, they translate them, as it were, back into their native heavenly tongue; they facilitate their expressivity in the language of eternal giving and receiving love.

References

Alison, J. 1996: *Raising Abel: The Recovery of the Eschatological Imagination*. New York: Crossroad.

Aquinas, Thomas 1975: *Summa contra Gentiles*, Book Four: *Salvation*, trans. C. J. O'Neill. Notre Dame, IN: University of Notre Dame Press.

Bonaventure 1993: *The Journey to the Mind of God*, trans. P. Boehner. Indianapolis, IN: Hackett.

Coakley, S. 2002: *Powers and Submissions: Spirituality, Philosophy, and Gender*. Oxford: Blackwell.

Cousins, E. 1987: The humanity and the passion of Christ. In J. Raitt, with B. McGinn and J. Meyendorff (eds), *Christian Spirituality: High Middle Ages and Reformation*, pp. 375–91. New York: Crossroad.

Howells, E. 2002: *John of the Cross and Teresa of Avila: Mystical Knowing and Selfhood*. New York: Crossroad (esp. on trinitarian and human agency in John, see chs 2 and 3).

Inge, D. (ed.) 2002: *Thomas Traherne: Poetry and Prose*. London: SPCK.

John of the Cross 1979: *The Spiritual Canticle*. In K. Kavanagh and O. Rodriguez (trans.), *The Collected Works of St John of the Cross*. Washington, DC: Institute of Carmelite Studies.

Louth, A. 1996: *Maximus the Confessor*. London: Routledge.

McCabe, H. 1987: *God Matters*. London: Geoffrey Chapman.

McIntosh, M. A. 2004: *Discernment and Truth: Meditations on the Christian Life of Contemplation and Practice*. New York: Crossroad (esp. on creation and illumination, see chs 8 and 9).

Maximus the Confessor 1985: *The Four Hundred Chapters on Love*. In G. C. Berthold (trans.), *Maximus Confessor: Selected Writings*. New York: Paulist Press.

Polkinghorne, J. 1996: *The Faith of a Physicist: Reflections of a Bottom-up Thinker*. The Gifford Lectures, 1993–4. Minneapolis, MN: Fortress Press.

Traherne, T. 1985: *Centuries*. Oxford: A. R. Mowbray.

Underhill, E. 1991: *The School of Charity: Meditations on the Christian Creed*. Wilton, CT: Morehouse.

Wallace, M. I. 1996: *Fragments of the Spirit: Nature, Violence, and the Renewal of Creation*. New York: Continuum.

William of St Thierry 1971: *The Golden Epistle: A Letter to the Brethren at Mont Dieu*, trans. T. Berkeley. Kalamazoo, MI: Cistercian Publications.

Williams, Rowan 2002: The deflections of desire: negative theology in trinitarian disclosure. In O. Davies and D. Turner (eds), *Silence and the Word: Negative Theology and the Incarnation*, pp. 115–35. Cambridge: Cambridge University Press.

CHAPTER 11

Christology in Christian Spirituality

William Thompson-Uberuaga

That Christology's role in Christian spirituality is analogous to theology's role in the life of Christian faith forms the guiding axiom of the thought experiment to follow. Expressed in a brief formula: Christian spirituality is to Christology as faith is to reason. But since faith and reason come from somewhere rather than nowhere (Jantzen 1999: 205), we need to add the historical and social coordinates within and by which they take shape. History and society, furthermore, are characterized, among other things, by time and space; freedom and necessity; progress and regress; good and evil; the planned and accidental; a receding past, an ungraspable present, and an inrushing future; a mysterious beginning and a transcendent beyond. To speak, then, of "the" faith and reason relationship or "the" spirituality and Christology relationship is to speak in the terms of model thinking for the sake of gaining clarity on positions whose concrete borders are very leaky indeed.

We will begin with the generic, rather widespread definitions of Christian spirituality as the lived experience of Christian discipleship (Senn 1986: 1–7; Downey 1997: 30–52), and Christology as the *logos* (word, reflection, discourse, dialogue) concerning Jesus as the *christos*. Christology, then, may be understood more widely as any serious reflection upon the person of Jesus and why it is that the Christian community confesses him the Christ, or more narrowly as a scholarly enterprise engaged in the same reflection, but now with the skills and methods of the scholarly tradition. These wider and narrower uses roughly correspond to the distinction between a pre-scientific and scientific form of Christology, as long as "scientific" is not confined to academic institutions. Christology in the narrower sense existed long before universities emerged, and it continues to exist among thinkers and groups not necessarily affiliated with such academic institutions; for example, monasteries, reformist groups, and more spontaneously organized intellectual circles. In modern times, for example, Cardinal Newman, Baron Friedrich von Hügel, Evelyn Underhill, and Hans Urs von Balthasar were not university professors, yet each produced rather significant contributions to "scientific" theology and Christology.

Historical and Social Coordinates

We will consider the biblical, classical-medieval, modern, postmodern, and global inheritances to be five crucial transitions in human history that have shaped and continue to shape Christian spirituality and theology. We will follow the view that the Reformation is a mixed genre, exhibiting both significant continuity with the earlier biblical, and especially classical-medieval transitions, as well as anticipations of the modern age to follow (along with the Renaissance).

In the more comprehensive sense, the "historical" encompasses the socio-cultural, the latter being one of its dimensions. It is not that we are "here" and history is "there," as if we must construct bridges from one to the other. We are "here" in our socio-cultural and geographic somewhere rather than nowhere. But that somewhere is a particular wave of the earlier transitions as they intersect concrete persons and societies. The social and cultural forms of Christian spirituality in relationship with Christology are simply a current phase of the flowing movement of the historical process. We are within this flow, and while a study like this might give the impression of occupying an imperial perch from which to survey the totality of history, common sense warns us that in fact no such totalistic perspective exists.

Christian Spirituality and Christology in Opposition

This subheading has a ring of the paradoxical and perhaps even the irrational about it. How can a spirituality proclaiming itself Christian be opposed to a serious *logos* about why Jesus is the Christ? Or, correspondingly, why would such a serious *logos* be opposed to the lived experience of discipleship under the same Jesus it purports to follow? In what follows we will be building upon and adapting the analysis of the faith and reason relationships proposed by Robert Monk and Joseph Stamey (1984: 128–57; Thompson 2001; Thompson-Uberuaga 2002).

"What has Athens [reason, in other words] to do with Jerusalem [or faith]? What harmony can there be between the Academy and the Church?" Or yet again: "The Son of God died; it must needs be believed because it is absurd. He was buried and rose again; it is certain because it is impossible." These celebrated declarations put forth by the third-century Tertullian (*The Prescription of Heretics* 7; *The Flesh of Christ* 5) have become the signature expressions, somewhat unfairly, of fideism, the rejection of reason for the sake of faith (Bettenson 1956: 14). Tertullian's struggle against the hyper-rationalism of his gnostic adversaries, and his own extensive use of and even endorsement of *logos* (reason) in the service of the faith, would seem to make the stereotypical equation of this ecclesiastical writer with fideism unfair. Thus, we are invoking these declarations as poignant expressions of the fideist position, without necessarily embroiling all of Tertullian's considerable theological labor under the category.

At its extreme edge, a fideistic spirituality regards human reason as corrupting. Moving along the continuum of possibilities, such a spirituality would at least regard reason with intense suspicion, thinking it prone to distortion in matters of Christian life. Whether we are thinking of Christology in its wider or narrower senses, the dimension of reason that makes Christology a reasoned (*logos*-using) reflection upon Jesus as the Christ is under suspicion or thought to be a corrupting influence.

Whether anyone can actually sustain the most extreme forms of such fideistic spirituality, at least in practice, is questionable. Tertullian may have had his fideistic moments, but in fact few have had the terminological influence over doctrinal and academic Christology that he had and has. His formulas of the "one person [*persona*]" and "two natures [*substantiae*]" anticipated and likely shaped the eventual creedal teaching on the hypostatic union of Christ (Studer 1993: 69). Cleary a highly refined and creative use of *logos* was at work in Tertullian's effort. When he endeavored to defend the teaching of Jesus's sonship as the divine *Logos* put forth by the Father, he appealed to everyone's inner *logos*: "reason is found expressed in discourse at every moment of thought, at every stirring of consciousness. Your every thought is speech; your every consciousness is reason" (*Against Praxeas*, 5; Bettenson 1956: 119). If we follow Tertullian, then, even the avowed fideist is at every conscious moment employing *logos*!

Tertullian became a Montanist, an adherent of an early pneumatic movement of several shades in Phrygia, Rome, and North Africa. His own form embraced some of the rigorous teachings advocated by Montanists, "inspired" by the fuller understanding of the apostles made possible by the Spirit for the pneumatic, namely, no second marriages, frequent fasts, the Spirit as always prompting one toward martyrdom, excluding public roles for women in the church, and so on (Heine 1992: 898–902). Such a Montanist spirituality offers us some idea of the type of spirituality fostered by heavy doses of a suspicion of reason in matters of faith. The awareness of the pneumatic dimension sounds appealing, but when severed from *logos* it can land one in a biblical and dogmatic literalism, both aspects fairly noted in Tertullian's work (Kearsley 1998: 60–5).

Tertullian offers some insight into contemporary fundamentalist spiritualities. Creationists remind one of the combination of the most extreme forms of biblical literalism and rather esoteric uses of scientific rationalism in simultaneous operation. Reason may be corrupting and untrustworthy, but it can be "plundered" by the person of faith to out-reason the reasoners, and in that sense it can be thought to be purified and set straight. Others simply in *a priori* fashion dismiss "reason" when it raises intellectual challenges to the assertions of faith. It would not be difficult to note touches of this strategy in the history of modern US Protestant fundamentalism and Roman Catholic stereotyping of the so-called modernists.

Latter-day fideist spiritualities distrust and/or eschew the *logos* of theology and Christology in favor of faith, but faith needs its human carrier, and so, if reason is unworthy, perhaps feelings, emotions, or actions will fill the void. One or another of the means available to the human person, through which faith needs to express itself, will need to stand in. Adherence to Jesus the Christ will not necessarily be absent in these spiritualities. But that adherence will lack the challenge of reflective *logos* made possible by the cumulative labors of the intellectual tradition of the church and the academy. The result is likely to be a Christian piety expressed too narrowly in emotional devotions and/or actions (good works) of various sorts, from the inner-churchly to the social. Churches with a doctrinal tradition will continue to exercise some formative influence here (Tertullian was formed by "the rule of faith"), shaping the emotions and actions in certain Christ-directed ways, but the danger will be the problem of doctrinal rigidity and literalism that comes with an undeveloped tradition of theological *logos*. Today's postmodern pluralism, along with the tensions of an increasingly global clash of cultures and worldviews, is just the kind of socio-cultural context calculated to foster an even greater retreat from the vagaries of a shifting reason to the certainties of faith. The *logos* is not just humbled but ruthlessly attacked as a chimera.

Now let us reverse perspectives. We have sketched a fideist spirituality eschewing a reflective Christology, analogous to a faith eschewing reason. Fideist spiritualities prefer fideist "Christologies," which are really Christologies with the suffix "-ology" diminished or truncated. If you will, such Christologies and spiritualities are Apollinarian, recalling Apollinaris's denial of the human reason in the person of Jesus. As reason might eschew faith, so analogously a rationalistic posture eschewing spirituality would form the reverse alternative. This would likewise be a form of spirituality, so to speak, but one in which the prefix "spirit-" in "spirit-uality" is more or less equated with the human *ratio* and more and more distanced from a human spirit echoing in some way the divine Spirit.

Do fideisms foster rationalisms? Or vice versa? The history of late medieval nominalism (a fideism of various stripes) and the roughly simultaneous emergence of the humanistic wing of the Renaissance incline one to an affirmative answer to both (Walsh 1999: 55–9, 67–110). By the way, the late medieval period of nominalism has been thought to be the critical period of the "separation" of spirituality from theology, echoing the "separation" of faith from reason (Vandenbroucke 1950). If our analysis here is on the mark, the "separation" is rather more of a regular occurrence throughout Christian history. At the same time, paradoxically, "separation" may not be the most accurate term to use, for what seems to occur is either a fideizing or rationalizing of spirituality.

We do not need to wait until modernity to be able to encounter rationalistic Christologies/spiritualities. Whenever the *logos* overreaches itself, there we have an incipient rationalism, the harbinger of what today's postmodern thinkers rightly name "totalization." We have already noted Tertullian's struggles with the gnostics. We do not often think of them as rationalists, and in the light of today's revisionist study of the gnostics, it is well to be cautious in generalizations. But likely Tertullian, and clearly Irenaeus, thought of them as people "in the know" ("gnosis"). Irenaeus even characterized those he was arguing against as people claiming to be able to read God like a book, with such intimate knowledge of the divine emanations that one would think they assisted at the divine *Logos*'s birth (*Against Heresies* 2.28.7 and 6). Some of the gnostics characterized their gnosis as a form of faith, to be sure, but it was a strangely semi-rationalized mythology which typically went along with a strong alienation from the human body. Hence Tertullian's exclamations: "in loving man [Christ] loved the process of birth also, and his flesh." "Was not God really crucified? Did he not really die after real crucifixion? Did he not really rise again, after real death?" (*The Flesh of Christ*, 4–5; Bettenson 1956: 125). We owe to Tertullian one of the most "stunning aphorisms" of the Christian faith, formulated in opposition to gnosticizing rationalism: *caro salutis est cardo* ("The flesh is the hinge of salvation"; *On the Resurrection* 8.1; Studer

1993: 67). The female sex, because of its association with bodiliness, also might not fare too well in the gnostic antibodily cosmos. Hence the Gospel of Thomas's infamous assertion that "every female (element) that makes itself male will enter the kingdom of heavens" (*Gospel according to Thomas* 114; Layton 1987: 399).

It is not so much that a rationalistic Christology allows no infusions from Christian spirituality. As long as the "Christ" in "Christ-ology" remains, if but with a "trace," such would seem nearly impossible. More likely the spirituality will be subtly rationalized (as with the gnostics), according to the prevailing understanding of *ratio* at the moment. (Such rationalizing may well have been a key factor in Arius' inability to accord full divinity to the *Logos* as well, given what seems like his rather Hellenistic view of divine transcendence.) The deistic rewriting of the Gospels by Thomas Jefferson accompanied his deistic spirituality (Adams 1983). Today's Jesus Seminar Christologies are in the Jeffersonian tradition by and large (Brown 1997: 819–30), but the definitions of the hegemonic "reason" have shifted along the lines of late- and post-modernity. Accompanying these are the New Age spiritualities of today's gnostics, some avowed (Bloom 1996), others not. Adherence to Jesus, however, brings subtle moderating influences upon such rationalizing, and within churches with strong biblical and doctrinal traditions, the moderating influences can even be stronger. So we need to imagine enormous shades of rationalism. In concrete history, consistency is not always evident. Tertullian could write eloquently of Christ's flesh as the hinge of our salvation, yet he could derail into Montanist rigorism and the inferiorization of women.

Brief Interlude: Border-living-and-thinking as Harbinger

Living on the edges, while often lonely and painful, indicates some form of alienation from prevailing orthodoxies. Those orthodoxies have broken down, or are in advanced stages of breakdown, as far as the one alienated from them is concerned. Likewise, some forms of alienation are signs of health. Alienation can be the creative dark night of greater purification portending the breakthrough to a more wholesome alternative. Spiritual writers frequently note a dark night–illumination dialectic, and it will not be inappropriate to refer to it here in these reflections upon the role of Christology in Christian spirituality.

Let us consider Kierkegaard. Typically, his writing is associated with an existentialist irrationalism, concentrated in the formula of the "leap of faith." As such he becomes the quintessential modern fideist. His celebrated stages, from the aesthetic, to the ethical, and on to the stage of faith, are marked by "leaps" of the will, culminating in the final one of faith. What is one leaping over? – life oriented around the axis of the satisfaction of the senses, however refined (the aesthetic), and around that of abstract, universal reason (the ethical). Kierkegaard typically associates Socrates with the ethical standpoint, but his understanding of it is more avowedly directed against his understanding of Hegel. Hegel universalizes the incarnation, on Kierkegaard's reading. It is not a person but a principle, expressing the relationship between spirit and matter present in everyone. Kierkegaard's standpoint of faith is a protest against such abstractionism, an attempt to re-find one's way to the concrete and personal (Gardiner 1988:

40–64). It is also a protest against the greatly diluted state Christianity of nineteenth-century Denmark, which, in his view, was "a polite moral humanism with a modicum of religious beliefs calculated not to offend the susceptibilities of the educated" (Copleston 1963: 339).

The truth which an incarnate God offers comes by way of a double paradox. On the one hand, the incarnation itself paradoxically unites the eternal with the temporal, and by so doing makes it possible for the human person to offer a response to the Infinite, who has now become personally available. This is accompanied by another paradox, namely the miracle of the leap of faith. Such faith must be our own authentic choice, but paradoxically it must also be the gift of grace (Kierkegaard 1962: 81; Gardiner 1988: 65–102).

We might almost say that Kierkegaard chooses to be a fideist if the only alternative is to be a Hegelian (as he understands this). From this perspective, faith's object is "the absurd," entailing a "crucifixion of the understanding" (Kierkegaard 1941: 189; Gardiner 1988: 101–2). We may also, alternatively, say that he is seeking to rehabilitate the role of the personal and existential (existing through the leap), as well as seeking to heighten awareness of the pull toward the inauthentic (the problem of dread and sin) in human existence. Abstract reason has forgotten these essential conditions of the Truth which the absolute paradox of the incarnation reveals (Copleston 1963: 345–51; Webb 1988: 226–83, 302–17). In this latter perspective, his work is a significant contribution toward a more balanced Christian spirituality and a more adequate Christology. His contribution functions as a cautionary tale of how a more full-bodied faith might well challenge and enrich a reason grown rather abstract, hypostatized, and severed from its experiential matrix.

Kierkegaard thus anticipates some postmodern styles of theology and Christology. "Postmodern" would indicate the search for a "soft" and more modest kind of *logos*, which avoids the hypostatized and totalistic thinking called "ontotheology" since Kant (Caputo 2002: 1). Whether one has to give up the *logos* entirely in order to accomplish this remains one of the most contentious issues in today's academic theology. This is not unrelated to Christology as well, inasmuch as the divine *Logos* of Jesus is the traditional symbol of God's personal disclosure to humanity. What would the dissolution or deconstruction of the *logos* mean for both Christology and Christian living? The *logos* grounds human community and communication, and divine and human community through the *Logos* become flesh. The question of the *logos* entails high stakes indeed.

Combinative Approaches

Throughout Christian history, faith and reason, and, analogously, spirituality and theology/Christology, have existed in various forms of more or less congenial, if at times challenging, combination. One might almost say that the capacity of Christianity to achieve, however fragmentarily, such a congenial combination of various shadings is the foundation for the building up of a Christian culture and civilization. Medieval culture is the typically classical example of this cultural combination, but today's potential combinations are obviously much more pluralistic. Let us, for purposes of heightened clarity, distinguish between a softer and a harder form of dialogical combination between spirituality and Christology. By "softer," we mean the view that just as there are areas of potentially fruitful collaboration or overlap between faith and reason, so too between Christian spirituality and Christology/theology. "Harder" forms of combinative thinking, on the other hand, argue for a tighter connection between them, an "intrinsically necessary" one, rather than occasional connections. We will work with each of these forms in turn.

First, let us recall some examples. The New Testament fused original Jewish Christianity and Hellenistic culture. The Jerusalem Council of Acts 15 represents a dramatic example. The various tongues of Pentecost in Acts 2 celebrate a new era of collaboration between all the nations made possible by the outpouring of the Spirit. Now Athens and Jerusalem should be able to work with one another. Eastern and Western patristic theologies/Christologies are largely the result of creative collaboration between forms of Platonism, Stoicism, and Aristotelianism, on the one hand, and the biblical inheritance, on the other. The medieval period achieves even more spectacular syntheses, culminating in the likes of John Damascene in the East and Bonaventure and Thomas Aquinas in the West. The Protestant wing of the later Reformation (and to some extent the Roman through, namely, Erasmus) largely represents a new form of collaboration between the biblical inheritance and the newer Renaissance schools of rhetoric and philology. Neo-Thomisms of various kinds, the Neoplatonizing forms of Eastern Christian theology, and the nearly endless forms of collaboration between faith and traditions of philosophy and the other humane and social sciences in modern and postmodern times, along with the newer but tentative collaboration between Christian faith and the other religious traditions of the world, are but further examples and continuations.

Underlying any combinative perspective is probably some attempt to carry out the missionary mandate of the gospel, which minimally implies the universally saving relevance of Jesus (Matt. 28: 19–20). In the effort to achieve this, one seeks points of connection between gospel and culture. At times, the relationship brings a clarifying and confirmation, but often it is a challenging and a purifying. One thinks of the slow emergence of human rights, of the overcoming of slavery, of the grudging acceptance of an evolutionary view of the universe, of the equal dignity of women, and so on. All of these insights of the humane and philosophical traditions were slowly assimilated by faith and eventually seen as articulations of faith's deeper meaning.

Analogously with this to-and-fro interchange between faith and reason, Christian spirituality has sought and found enrichment (either by way of confirming validation, clarification, or critical purification) from the critically reasoned reflection of theology and Christology. It is as if a certain faith "instinct" is at work, leading lived Christian experience to the recognition that it needs elucidation (a sort of inner exegesis) and/or challenging for its own health. And inasmuch as Jesus the Christ is the source and center of any recognizably "Christian" spirituality, there is a special orientation toward Christological reflection guiding it. One might think of the emergence of the Christological doctrines, worked out in the first seven ecumenical councils, as central examples of "non-scientific" Christology, guiding the church's spirituality, shaping it in a Christoform manner, helping it avoid excessive subjectivism or emotionalism. These would then also work to promote greater social and ecclesial cohesion, slowly but effectively building up the *corpus Christi*. Behind this creedal, "non-scientific" Christology was the more scientific Christology and lexical armory of the Fathers (and presumably some of the Mothers, such as the younger Macrina; Pelikan 1993: 8–9), who greatly benefited from the insights of Hellenistic and Latin philosophy.

Soft combinative approaches are especially concerned to protect the relative autonomy of spirituality and critical reflection. Christian discipleship would, then, not be able to smother critical thought, nor would critical reflection smother spirituality, severing it from its experiential roots. This is thought to foster the equality of both. Such is, in some ways, something new, the result of modernity's increasing differentiation of the human sciences and their separation from ecclesial controls in the modern liberal democracies. However, the semi-autonomous atmosphere of the monastic setting of medieval theology *vis-à-vis* the greater church, and then again that of the medieval universities *vis-à-vis* the greater church, seems somewhat anticipatory.

Soft combinations of spirituality and Christology foster spiritualities and Christologies of a more Antiochene orientation. "Antiochene" denotes the tradition stressing the fullness of the duality of Jesus the Christ: as divine and human, albeit united somehow in one being. Theodore of Mopsuestia (392–428), one of the Antiochene "North Stars," expressed this concern forthrightly:

> Let the character of the natures stand without confusion, and let the person be acknowledged as undivided – the former in virtue of the characteristic property of the nature, since the one assumed is distinct from the One who assumes him, and the latter in virtue of the personal union, since the One who assumes and the nature of the one assumed are included in the denotation of a single name. (*On the Incarnation* 5; Norris 1980: 113)

Theodore and his successor Nestorius had not yet achieved the precisions of the Council of Chalcedon on the most acceptable way to express the union of the two natures, but their stress upon the need to affirm the fullness of the two natures is the special contribution of the Antiochene tradition (Young 1983: 199–240).

As faith honors the Godward dimension of Christian discipleship, so reason honors the human dimension. Faith and reason in combination would honor both, and so, too, analogously, would a spirituality in combination with reflective theology and Christology. The dimension of spirituality would challenge the theological and Christological *logos* not to outreach itself. *Logomania* would be averted. The dimension of reason/*logos* would challenge the spirituality to remain humble, human, historical, and self-critical. *Logophobia* would be averted.

The hard combinative view is likewise a "conspiracy of faith and reason" (Voegelin 2001: 514), but the conspiration between them is thought to be tighter and intrinsic; that is, faith is viewed as the ground of reason. "Ground" hearkens back to the way in which *Grund/t* is used in the German mystical tradition (Eckhart, for example; see McGinn 1986: 402), namely, as originating source. Consequently, faith somehow engenders reason; spirates it, if you will. Likewise, reason, as an outgrowth of faith, enables faith to remain itself. A faith that inhibits the critical *logos* is a faith *manqué*. Pursuing our analogy, then, Christian spirituality becomes, on this view, the ground of theology, Christology, and all other applications of reflective *logos*. Faith and reason, in fact, are but epistemological dimensions of the ampler "engendering experience" of spirituality in the process of becoming luminous for itself through its own intrinsic exegesis (Voegelin 1990b: 173–232). On this view, obviously, it is not simply a matter of potential areas of overlap between spirituality and the-(and Christ-)ologies, or faith and reason; nor is it simply a matter of occasional dialogues. It is a matter of the very integrity of each that they be related as ground to inner emanation. All forms of Christian theology (Christo-, anthropo-, ecclesio-, and so on) are potentially forms of spirituality, spirituality in its form of becoming luminous for itself.

The tradition sometimes distinguishes between the faith by which one believes (*fides qua creditur*) and the faith in those truths that are revealed (*fides quae creditur*). The former helpfully initiates us into the notion of faith in the ampler sense of trusting fidelity to the divine Ground disclosing itself in human experience. This graced fidelity arouses our questing, and as it does so, thus emerges the reflective process of the *logos*. It is like falling in love; lovers are desirous of knowing one another. The mutual love grounds and arouses the lovers' questing (cf. Tallon 1997: 137–54, 221–49, 289–92). Somehow, if the love does not go astray, the knowledge sought remains this side of an invasive curiosity. Analogously, then, spirituality, as the fuller experiential matrix of faith, is the full-bodied unfolding of graced fidelity to the divine disclosure through Jesus the Christ. One of the dimensions of the flow of this fidelity is the lovers' being drawn toward knowing, toward *logos*. Love in the process of exegeting itself is something of a description of this theological *logos*. Incidentally, this transposition into spirituality of faith as seeking understanding re-sensitizes us to the traditional connection between faith, hope, and love. This famed triad owes much of its authority to Paul, surely (1 Cor. 13: 13), but a logic surfaces in their connectivity in this perspective of spirituality. Fidelity is rooted in the outgoing flow of a love energized by hope.

Spirituality becomes on this view a highly differentiated phenomenon. On a more comprehensive level, it refers to the full complex of our lived experience of Christian discipleship, in all its potential dimensions. The loving and hopeful fidelity to the flow of this experience arouses, among other features, our questing *logos* as it seeks to participate in Jesus and in his salvific movement of shared discipleship. We might borrow the categories from liturgical theology of primary and secondary theology (*theologia prima* and *theologia secunda*; Kavanagh 1992: index, s.vv. "Theology, primary, secondary"). Inasmuch as a pre-scientific *logos* is always a dimension of spirituality, the latter is always a primary theology. At times it also becomes a theology at a further level of scientific reflection (*theologia secunda*). Secondary theology is just that: second, originating in, in service to, only a partial articulation of, and always in need of returning to the much fuller manifold of first theology.

This style of spirituality and theology in "hard" combination recalls Augustine (*The Master* 11.37; Rist 1994: 56–63) and Anselm ("faith seeking understanding": *Proslogion*, prologue and ch. 1). Yet our modern and now postmodern and global frameworks have generated a new modulation, beyond that of traditionally narrowing "faith" to an explicitly Christian faith (think of Karl Barth or Hans Urs von Balthasar, for example), to that of viewing "faith" more widely as the graced experience of fidelity to the pull of the divine Ground offered to all (think, for example, of Karl Rahner, and perhaps of Schleiermacher earlier). If you will, faith in this wider sense, and so spirituality, is at work beyond the explicitly Christian orbit, in the endeavors of all. Grounding any form of knowing is its faith moment. Such a view, which I share, anticipates the postmodern recognition that "pure" forms of scientific knowing transcending all faith/belief perspectives are chimeras. At the same time, from a Christian perspective, this faith, even if it is not explicitly Christian at all times, is somehow connected with Christ inasmuch as Christ remains inseparable from the divine Ground.

As the soft combinative form is more Antiochene in its Christological orientation, so this harder form is more Chalcedonian, even tending toward a more "extreme" Alexandrine orientation. What does this mean? As Jesus's divinity and humanity are distinct but not separate (the Chalcedonian pattern; Hunsinger 1991: 185–8, 201–18), so analogously Christian spirituality and theology/Christology will follow the same pattern. Christian spirituality is a polyvalent reality of several inner differentiations, echoing the one "person" of the divine–human Jesus. "Unity in distinction" is another abbreviated formula of the Chalcedonian pattern. A Chalcedonian incarnational spirituality will always exhibit this rather tight unity in distinction.

We are employing the term "Alexandrine" to evoke the stress of that Christological tradition upon the divine *Logos* as the grounding foundation of the divine–human distinctions (Norris 1980: 26–31; Young 1983: 240–65). Cyril is Alexandria's counterpart to Antioch's Theodore of Mopsuestia. Cyril's often-noted formula for the incarnation, "one incarnate *hypostasis* of the Word" (*Third Letter to Nestorius* 8), expressed this unifying and differentiating grounding of the *Logos*. This concern to preserve the unity of the two natures found a more acceptable formulation, for the Antiochenes, in Chalcedon's teaching of the hypostatic union, in which "the distinctive character of each nature [is] preserved, and [each] combining in one Person and *hypostasis* – not divided or separated into two Persons, but one and the same Son and only-begotten God, Word, Lord Jesus Christ . . ." (Hardy 1954: 352, 372).

The smothering of human nature by the "power" of the divine *Logos*, namely, the derailment into monophysitism, remains nearby. Chalcedon, especially in its Alexandrine reading, takes us to the very edge. Pope Leo expressed its best intentions, namely, that in the incarnation, what God "did was to enhance humanity not diminish deity" (*Letter to Flavian* ["Leo's Tome"]; Norris 1980: 148). Leo's words implicitly acknowledge the danger of humanity's diminishment. Correspondingly, the human, incarnational, and so reason-dimension of spirituality, while highly celebrated and "enhanced" through its deification, is just this side of the fall into diminishment.

Combinative spiritualities reflect the unity in distinction of Jesus the Christ, but they do so in the soft and hard forms just noted. The softer, like the synoptic Gospels, tends to maximize the distinctions (divinity and humanity, faith and reason); the harder, like Paul and the Gospel of John, tends to maximize the union. But these are likely not simply intellectual options open in a neutral way to interested observers. The tension between them seems to reflect the tension of an incarnational faith and spirituality. Incarnation means vulnerability. The very tension itself, an in-between moving back and forth and finding oneself on one edge or the other rather frequently, might well be a signature feature of such incarnational spiritualities.

New Oscillations

Modernity has brought new oscillations to these incarnationally combinative spiritualities. Its earlier Enlightenment form sought to mediate in the growing fissure between fideist and rationalist spiritualities. The so-called anthropocentric turn, miming the modern turn toward the empirical, brought with it a widened view of experience, and a heightened appreciation of its role, as a site of the encounter with God. Spirituality could and should be rational without being rationalistic. This also meant a rediscovery of the affective dimension of experience (the Pietists, Schleiermacher, some of the Roman Catholic modernists). If you will, the Romantic phase of the Enlightenment brought with it an "affectional transposition" of doctrine and experience (Pelikan 1989: 118–73).

Softer combinative forms always run the danger of accommodationism; that is, surrendering to the prevailing philosophical or cultural orthodoxy of the time and place. A certain cognitive instability characterizes a rather free-floating toing and froing between spirituality and theo-/Christology. This is why liberal brands of Christianity tend to foster their corrective, in the form of the so-called "Neo-Orthodox" brands (Tracy 1975: 27). Harder combinative spiritualities, on the other hand, because of the hegemonic role played by faith, seem less susceptible to accommodationism, although, as noted, they run the monophysite's danger of the slide toward avoiding the real challenge of experience and history. The aim of all of these was not to replace the traditional sources of Christian spirituality, namely Scripture and the sacramental means of grace within the church, but to recover the experiential roots of the latter. But "experience" is a notoriously contentious term, as the previous comments already indicate.

The late phase of the Enlightenment increased its contentiousness, for it recalled the distorting influences of personal (Freud) and social (Marx and the sociologists) pathologies (Hughes 1958). This also brought a certain rehabilitation of the traditional teaching on personal and "original" sin, something the Neo-Orthodox spiritualities endeavored to express. The reality of pathology and its corresponding need for therapy heightened the significance of the soteriological dimension of Christology and its corresponding role in spirituality. At the same time, the dialogue with the sociologists breathed new significance into the socio-cultural dimension of Christian living, thus balancing an early Enlightenment tendency toward an over-emphatically individualistic form of piety and biblical reading. Today's liberationist, feminist, womanist, political, and even now ecological spiritualities are direct heirs of this sociological turn. And, again, accommodationism and socio-political quietism are the dangers, respectively, of the soft and hard forms of combinative spiritualities.

The historical dimension of Christian spirituality and its traditional sources (the Bible and the sacramental means of grace within the church) received increasing consideration in the modern period, as the latter grew more historically conscious. The late Enlightenment's sociological turn was a sociological extension of the earlier application of philosophical and historical methods to the sources of Christian faith. Christology is not just about Jesus as an isolated person. Such a view of the "person" is a distortion, ignoring the formative role of others and of culture in general in the constitution of the person. Christology, then, is about Jesus's "movement," his friends, disciples, and supporters, even his opponents. Each mutually "shaped" the other. Perhaps, if the historical quest for Jesus were to think of Jesus in more socio-cultural terms, then it would not so quickly view the Scriptures as impediments to recovering his "person," but rather as the record of a movement in which Jesus and his companions are inextricably one (Soelle and Schottroff 2002: 35). Likewise, Christian discipleship should bear the marks of this biblically informed personhood-in-relationship. The ecclesial, socio-cultural, ecological, and even geographic dimensions of spirituality likewise receive new attention from this vantage point. All of this also gives new meaning to the inextricable connection between Christology and soteriology.

The postmodern transition at a minimum both intensifies and challenges these various "turns." The prefix "post-," in "postmodern," indicates a dissatisfaction with the modern project in all of its forms; at the same time, the suffix "-modern" indicates the inability to completely sever ties with that project. A frustrating dialectic between the modern and its deficits characterizes postmodern strategies. If modern historical methods will reconstruct the narrative of history, the postmodern will deconstruct. Narratives are never final, closed, heeding all voices, or able to transcend history's flux (time) and spatial location (geography). The archaeological approach to history of the modern project gives way to a Nietzschean, genealogical approach. The genealogist recognizes that we only confront the past by largely reconfiguring it from the perspectives of our own will to power, our own interests. "The project is to traverse with quite novel questions, and as though with new eyes, the enormous, distant, and so well hidden land of morality – of morality that has actually existed, actually been lived; and does this not mean virtually to *discover* this land for the first time?" The historian-genealogist challenges the pretensions of modern history and philosophy, with their confidence in "the truth" of reality, metaphysical or historical. The genealogist's favorite color, wrote the Nietzsche just cited, is gray! (Nietzsche 1967: 21; Ansell-Pearson 1994: 121–46).

What, then? Is Christian spirituality "gray," that is, simply an endless play of signifiers, always deferring commitment, supplementing itself through a seemingly endless series of self-interested wills to power? Are the traditional sources of its discipleship, Bible, sacraments, and other ecclesial practices, gray as well? Is the *kerygma* of Jesus as the Christ the gray side of the true Jesus, resulting from the will to power of an alienated group of Jesus's followers seeking vindication, or of Hellenized Christians seeking to impose their Hellenistic metaphysics onto Jesus? Is the Christian tradition an endless graying of the originating sources?

Intriguingly, Nietzsche seems to have recognized, or at least seems to have implied the recognition of, the parasitical nature of his own enterprise. For, indeed, how does one recognize the naked will to power in Nietzsche's sense? Does this not entail some contrast with an "unnaked power," if you will, a beneficent power, an *Omnipotens* which is also *benefaciens*, not "naked" but a meaningful *logos*? "In reality there has been only one Christian, and he died on the cross," he wrote (*The Anti-Christ*, 39; Nietzsche 1990: 163; Walsh 1999: 113–14). Likewise, but more willingly, combinative spiritualities, like the combinative Christologies upon which they are centered, live in the tension of this contrast. They should, however, thank Nietzsche for helping them to attend to it. The Antiochene trend will lean toward the humanward and hence gray side of the tension, to be sure, while the Alexandrine side will lean in hope toward the transfiguring deification of that gray into the blue. "Blue" is used here to evoke the divinizing oceanic depths of the divine found on Russian icons, as, for example, in the three figures of Rublev's famed Trinity icon. Blue was precisely the color that Nietzsche opposed to his genealogist's favorite color gray (Nietzsche 1967: 21).

Finally, today's global turn further complexifies the transitions already noted, and combinative spiritualities by their very nature do not seek to dodge but to participate in the complexification. Will this be simply the clash of civilizations or their transfiguration? Increasing tribalism or human solidarity? Ethnic "cleansing" or ethnic integration? Obviously, combinative spiritualities and Christologies believe in combinations rather than separations.

The Jerusalem Council of Acts 15, Pentecost, and Paul's teaching of justification by faith are all examples of combining, which always brings a transformation of the elements combined. The Jerusalem Council brought an accommodation between Jewish and Gentile Christianity. Pentecost affirmed the goodness of the many cultures and languages making up a truly Spirit-endowed faith. Paul's teaching of justification relativized, rather than negated, the customs of Jewish Christianity *vis-à-vis* the Gentiles; gracious faith was the key to salvation. Grace cannot be tied to one culture or set of religio-cultural practices. These are all forms of crossing over, analogous to the crossing over of the Word into the flesh (Dunne 1972; Schreiter 1997; Küster 2001). Pope Leo long ago articulated the general orientation that undergirds the shape of the globalizing hoped for by combinative spiritualities: divinity is not diminished but humanity is enhanced. But if the broad framework is glimpsed in hope, the concretely specific contours of the globalizing process are more gray and ambiguous. Such is where we are now, in the darker night before the clearer dawn. One is reminded of Hans Urs von Balthasar's emphasis upon Holy Saturday, Jesus's tomb experience (von Balthasar 1990: 148–88). Globalization seems in some ways a Holy Saturday experience, neither simply death nor simply resurrection, but in-between. Will it be more of a clash and struggle (Balthasar's rather Antiochene interpretation), or will it be more deification and victory (the more Alexandrine view)?

Is Jesus obstacle or solution to the challenges of globalization? A fideist might be tempted to say "I believe, even if it seems absurd," echoing Tertullian, thus falling back upon the traditional claims for the sole saving work of Jesus the Christ. Jesus as the saving Lord heals our sinful divisions and is the foundation of our reconciliation with one another, even if we cannot grasp how this makes sense of the other religious traditions of the world: "through him God was pleased to reconcile to himself all things, whether on earth or in heaven, by making peace through the blood of his cross" (Col. 1: 20). The rationalist, in good Jeffersonian fashion, might be tempted in the other direction; namely, our times teach us that any number of moral personalities are available to us, worldwide, to enable us to heal our divisions and achieve a harmony among peoples. Jesus, in other words, is one among many representatives of the Lord God.

Somewhere between those positions are the Antiochene and Chalcedonian-Alexandrine spiritualities. The Antiochene stress on honoring the diversity and distinctiveness of natures presses toward a greater honoring of religious diversity. At least, this is its logic, inasmuch as it seeks to honor the full amplitude of the humanity Jesus came to embrace. This would traditionally occur within the overall context of the specialness of the incarnation, which, as we have seen, is also a characteristic of the Antiochene style of Christological spirituality. Just what this specialness consists in will need to be negotiated over and over again. It is a question of faith and reason in perpetual dialogue and struggle, and this calls for much theological patience and tolerance. As long as Christology is united with spirituality, we have reason to hope that these virtues, so needed in a global time, will be forthcoming. Patience and tolerance would seem to be virtues rather appropriate to an incarnational spirituality. In "becoming" human, God seems to be practicing heavy doses of each.

The Chalcedonian pattern, which accommodated Antioch's concerns, should also be able to accommodate the globalizing extension of its tradition. At the same time, the Alexandrine element within the Chalcedonian perspective presses toward a greater emphasis upon the new and unique oneness between God and humanity in the one person of the Savior. The hypostatic union, the oneness in personal being of Jesus the Christ, is the assurance that God is at work one-ing the divine Self with all, but only because that one-ing has reached its fullest expression in the incarnation. "But when the fullness of time had come . . ." (Gal. 4: 4). That the one-ing of God and humanity in Jesus utterly honors and preserves his human distinctiveness grounds our hope that all human distinctiveness has room for it within the divine Ground. The "natures" are not diminished, as, analogously, reason is not diminished by being grounded in faith understood as the hopeful and loving fidelity to the divine Ground.

Christology and trinitarian theology developed simultaneously, and, as one went, so went the other. The unity in distinction of combinative spiritualities imaged a divine Ground of unity in distinction. Correspondingly, both Gregory Nazianzus (*Third Theological Oration* 2) and Gregory of Nyssa (*Address on Religious Instruction* 3) wrote of the Trinity as a mean between the Hellenistic diversity of gods and Jewish monotheism (Hardy 1954: 160–1, 273–4). In a global age this diversity is known to be even greater, and yet the need for oneness remains, if we are not to be locked into isolated enclaves. Somehow the old problem of the one and the many persists. Intriguingly, the trinitarian teaching seems to put both on an equal level, and this offers us hope that somehow our human future can move beyond a clash of civilizations and learn to honor diversity in unity.

The incarnation was the event that enabled and really "forced" Christianity to articulate in a more differentiated manner the divine as a mysterious unity of shared diversity. God is "Giver, Given, Gift/ing" (Downey 2000: 55–9) in one helpful formulation. The divine Source (Giver) offers us the possibility of union/community through the communication of the incarnate Word/Wisdom (Given), and that possibility is affirmed by us and effected in us as it indwells our beings and brings us all to richly diverse modes of participative response to it (Gift/ing). In a global age the Gift/ing of the Spirit in the richly diverse cultures and religions of the world will perhaps lead us to a greater honoring of the "other." The work of the Spirit is not subordinate or inferior to the work of the Son, even while they are one. Each is in *perichoresis* (mutual coinherence). Global tolerance and patience are perhaps the humble beginnings of this.

Issues of Evaluation?

Glancing back, how might each of our perspectives handle the "truth" issue? Combinative spiritualities recognize that they arise from the "somewhere" of the in-between space of faith and reason, or of spirituality as "first" and "second" theology. Their geography, then, does not lift them onto a privileged perch ("the Archimedean perspective"; Voegelin 1990a: 177) beyond the faith–reason tension. "Truth" is then not precisely a "thing" to be locked up in a piggy bank of simple propositions to be committed to memory, but the luminosity emerging from participation in this to-and-fro exchange between faith and its *logos*. In Christological terms, it is the luminosity found through following along the "way" opened up by faithfully living the "life" of discipleship (John 14: 6).

The "hard" combinative form seeks to avoid the cognitive instability of the softer style, which waffles between faith and reason and may too easily make itself conform to the orthodoxies of the moment. At the same time, the hard style's danger is the too-easy slide into a cramped faith posture which refuses to open itself to the challenges coming from its own reflective *logos* in the context of society and history. The rootedness of faith and reason within the matrix of spirituality also challenges us to recognize that the faith and reason interchange can only remain healthy through spiritual practices, disciplines, and virtues within the context of the traditional "means" of grace (church community, sacraments, and the Bible). However, combinative spiritualities are optimistic by fundamental orientation, inasmuch as they arise from a posture of faith in the divine Ground. The Ground is luring us in ways calculated to promote our flourishing, and in the light of this, we find ourselves enabled to diagnose spiritual pathologies.

Fideistic and rationalistic spiritualities, on the other hand, while they might well be symptomatic of the struggling emergence of new "settlements" between faith and reason, tend rather to imply that Archimedean perch beyond the tension between faith and reason: either a faith perched beyond needing reason's challenges, or a reason perched beyond the need for faith. Their "somewheres" seem to pretend to a location in the "nowhere" of an unhistorical geography. On the other hand, combinative spiritualities might well display a critically cautious solidarity with all these options and their various modulations, and seek to learn from them. After all, the lived experience of a faith following along the path of its own reflective *logos* knows many dark nights (back steps, sidesteps, stalls) on the way to the illuminations of the forward steps. People do not move to the extreme edges, like fideism and rationalism, unless something is driving them there. Best to attend to what it may be.

"Be still, deadening north wind; south wind, come, you that waken love, breathe through my garden . . ." (*Spiritual Canticle*, v. 17; John of the Cross 1991: 473).

References

Adams, D. W. (ed.) 1983: *Jefferson's Extracts from the Gospels: "The Philosophy of Jesus" and "The Life and Morals of Jesus"*. Princeton, NJ: Princeton University Press.

Ansell-Pearson, K. 1994: *An Introduction to Nietzsche as Political Thinker: The Perfect Nihilist.* Cambridge: Cambridge University Press.

Anselm 2001: *Prosologion,* trans. T. Williams. Indianapolis, IN: Hackett.

von Balthasar, H. U. 1990: *Mysterium Paschale: The Mystery of Easter,* trans. A. Nichols. Edinburgh: T. and T. Clark.

Bettenson, H. (ed. and trans.) 1956: *The Early Christian Fathers: A Selection from the Writings of the Fathers from St Clement of Rome to St Athanasius.* Oxford: Oxford University Press.

Bloom, H. 1996: *Omens of the Millennium.* New York: Riverhead.

Brown, R. E. 1997: *An Introduction to the New Testament.* New York: Doubleday.

Caputo, J. D. (ed.) 2002: *The Religious.* Malden, MA: Blackwell.

Copleston, F. 1963: *A History of Philosophy,* vol. 7: *Modern Philosophy: From the Post-Kantian Idealists to Marx, Kierkegaard, and Nietzsche.* New York: Doubleday.

Cyril of Alexandria 1983: *Third Letter to Nestorius,* ed. and trans. L. R. Wickham in *Cyril of Alexandria: Select Letters,* pp. 12–33. Oxford: Clarendon Press.

Downey, M. 1997: *Understanding Christian Spirituality.* New York: Paulist Press.

——2000: *Altogether Gift: A Trinitarian Spirituality.* Maryknoll, NY: Orbis.

Dunne, J. 1972: *The Way of All the Earth.* New York: Macmillan.

Gardiner, P. 1988: *Kierkegaard.* Oxford: Oxford University Press.

Hardy, E. R. (ed.) 1954: *Christology of the Later Fathers.* Philadelphia: Westminster.

Heine, R. E. 1992: Montanus, Montanism. In D. N. Freedman (ed.), *Anchor Bible Dictionary,* vol. 4, pp. 898–902. New York: Doubleday.

Hughes, H. S. 1958: *Consciousness and Society: The Reorientation of European Social Thought: 1890–1930.* New York: Vintage.

Hunsinger, G. 1991: *How to Read Karl Barth: The Shape of his Theology.* New York: Oxford University Press.

Irenaeus of Lyons 1996: *Against Heresies.* In A. Roberts and J. Donaldson (eds), *Ante-Nicene Fathers,* vol. 1: *The Apostolic Fathers with Justin Martyr and Irenaeus.* Grand Rapids: W. B. Eerdmans.

Jantzen, G. M. 1999: *Becoming Divine: Towards a Feminist Philosophy of Religion.* Bloomington, IN: Indiana University Press.

John of the Cross 1991: *The Collected Works of St John of the Cross,* trans. K. Kavanaugh and O. Rodriguez. Washington, DC: Institute of Carmelite Studies.

Kavanagh, A. 1992: *On Liturgical Theology.* Collegeville, MN: Liturgical Press.

Kearsley, R. 1998: Tertullian. In D. K. McKim (ed.), *Historical Handbook of Major Biblical Interpreters,* pp. 60–5. Downer's Grove, IL: InterVarsity Press.

Kierkegaard, S. 1941: *Concluding Unscientific Postscript,* ed. and trans. D. F. Swenson and W. Lowrie. Princeton, NJ: Princeton University Press.

——1962: *Philosophical Fragments,* ed. and trans. D. F. Swenson and W. Lowrie. New York: Harper and Row.

Küster, V. 2001: *The Many Faces of Jesus Christ: Intercultural Christology.* Maryknoll, NY: Orbis.

Layton, B. (ed. and trans.) 1987: *The Gnostic Scriptures.* New York: Doubleday.

McGinn, B. (ed. and trans.) 1986: *Meister Eckhart: Teacher and Preacher.* New York: Paulist Press.

Monk, R. C. and Stamey, J. D. 1984: *Exploring Christianity: An Introduction,* 2nd edn. Englewood Cliffs, NJ: Prentice Hall.

Nietzsche, F. 1967: *On the Genealogy of Morals and Ecce Homo,* ed. and trans. W. Kaufmann. New York: Vintage.

——1990: *Twilight of the Idols/The Anti-Christ,* trans. R. J. Hollingdale. London: Penguin.

Norris, R. A., Jr (trans. and ed.) 1980: *The Christological Controversy.* Philadelphia: Fortress Press.

Pelikan, J. 1989: *The Christian Tradition: A History of the Development of Doctrine*, vol. 5: *Christian Doctrine and Modern Culture (since 1700)*. Chicago: University of Chicago Press.

—— 1993: *Christianity and Classical Culture: The Metamorphosis of Natural Theology in the Christian Encounter with Hellenism*. New Haven, CT: Yale University Press.

Rahner, K. 1978: *Foundations of Christian Faith: An Introduction to the Idea of Christianity*, trans. W. V. Dych. New York: Seabury.

Rist, J. M. 1994: *Augustine: Ancient Thought Baptized*. Cambridge: Cambridge University Press.

Schreiter, R. J. 1997: *The New Catholicity: Theology between the Global and the Local*. Maryknoll, NY: Orbis.

Senn, F. C. (ed.) 1986: *Protestant Spiritual Traditions*. New York: Paulist Press.

Soelle, D. and Schottroff, L. 2002: *Jesus of Nazareth*. Louisville: Westminster/John Knox.

Studer, B. 1993: *Trinity and Incarnation: The Faith of the Early Church*, ed. A. Louth. Collegeville, MN: Liturgical Press.

Tallon, A. 1997: *Head and Heart: Affection, Cognition, Volition as Triune Consciousness*. New York: Fordham University Press.

Thompson, W. M. 2001: Spirituality's challenges to today's theology. *Josephinum Journal of Theology* 8, 54–73.

Thompson-Uberuaga, W. 2002: New christologies: state of the question. *Liturgical Ministry* 11, 1–12.

Tracy, D. 1975: *Blessed Rage for Order: The New Pluralism in Theology*. New York: Seabury.

Vandenbroucke, F. 1950: Le divorce entre théologie et mystique. *Nouvelle Revue Théologique* 72, 372–89.

Voegelin, E. 1990a: *Collected Works*, vol. 12: *Published Essays 1966–1985*, ed. E. Sandoz. Baton Rouge: Louisiana State University Press.

—— 1990b: *Collected Works*, vol. 28: *What is History? and Other Unpublished Writings*, ed. T. A. Hollweck and P. Caringella. Baton Rouge: Louisiana State University Press.

—— 2001: *Collected Works*, vol. 14: *Order and History, vol. 1: Israel and Revelation*. ed. M. P. Hogan. Columbia: University of Missouri Press.

Walsh, D. 1999: *The Third Millennium: Reflections on Faith and Reason*. Washington, DC: Georgetown University Press.

Webb, E. 1988: *Philosophers of Consciousness: Polanyi, Lonergan, Voegelin, Ricoeur, Girard, Kierkegaard*. Seattle: University of Washington Press.

Young, F. M. 1983: *From Nicea to Chalcedon: A Guide to the Literature and its Background*. Philadelphia: Fortress Press.

CHAPTER 12

The Holy Spirit in Christian Spirituality

Robert Davis Hughes III

"The Holy Spirit is central to Christian spirituality and to any understanding of it. In fact, the word *spirituality* reflects the realization that the Christian life is led in the power and under the guidance of the Holy Spirit; it does not primarily designate this life as dealing with the 'spiritual,' in the sense of 'immaterial' " (Farrelly 1993: 492b). So M. John Farrelly, OSB begins his excellent article on the Holy Spirit. Indeed, from the standpoint of a growing theological consensus, spirituality is simply about the Holy Spirit and her (Farrelly 1993: 493a, 502b; Johnson 1996: 42–60) impact on the total lives of human beings. Spiritual theology as a theology of the spiritual life has the Holy Spirit for its primary subject, and, I have argued, should be part of a doctrinal locus on the Holy Spirit related to teaching on the person of the Spirit as soteriology is related to Christology (Hughes 2001b). As such, Christian spirituality is not about something immaterial; indeed, as we shall see, the indwelling of the Holy Spirit has a strongly physical, even bodily, and hence ecclesial and social, dimension. Nor is it about the development of some ghostly or "inner" property of human nature as such; rather, it is a description in concrete terms of what it means to be indwelt by the Holy Spirit and hence to be immanent in the flesh of Christ and the paschal mystery.

This emphasis reflects the data on spirituality in the documents of Christian origins. In Scripture and earliest tradition, spirituality simply is pneumatology. While there are biblical materials that could be gathered later to support other topics, and patristic treatises such as Origin's *On Prayer*, most of what the Bible and the early Fathers have to say about spirituality is simply a working out of the doctrine of the Holy Spirit and her relationship to the Christian believer and community. Dunn (1983), Bermejo (1989), Farrelly (1993: 493–6), and Callen (2001, biblical section of each chapter) have complete and thorough analyses of the biblical materials. Good analyses of this material can also be found in major contemporary works on pneumatology (Tillich 1963; Congar 1983, vol. 1: 3–62; Herron 1983: 3–60; Johnson 1996: 76–103; Kärkkäinen 2002: 23–36). In the Eastern part of the undivided church, many of the foundational texts for later spirituality arose directly from the controversies about the divinity of the

Holy Spirit as the third person of the Holy Trinity. Basil of Caesarea's *On the Holy Spirit* is the *locus classicus*, along with many of the writings of Gregory Nazianzus, but the tradition of a strong pneumatology continues in the Eastern Church through Simeon the New Theologian and Gregory Palamas, right through to the present day (Lossky 1974, 1976, for example).

The Decline of Pneumatology in the West

Things were not so fortunate in the Western Church, where a number of factors led to a decline in pneumatology (Lossky 1974, 1976: see the commentary on Lossky by Jenson 1997, 1999 at several points; Bermejo 1989: 160–7; Farrelly 1993: 492b). While the Eastern claim that all the blame lies at the door of Augustine's doctrine of the Holy Spirit's double procession as the *vinculum caritatis* (bond of love) between the Father and the Son (*On the Trinity* 15.27–31) may be too harsh a judgment on him, it is not entirely wrong either (Bermejo 1989: 160ff). There are indeed strengths to the Western position, as Macquarrie notes (1977: 331): a close link between Spirit and Word, and hence between the mystical and the prophetic/ethical. A strong role for the humanity of Christ emerges in Western spirituality, especially with the mendicants in the thirteenth century. The Eastern tradition also has its own disastrous errors, notably too great a distinction between the divine essence and the trinitarian relations (Jenson 1997: 149–53). Nevertheless, almost as an unintended consequence of Augustine's doctrine of double predestination and his use of the term "grace" in the anti-Pelagian writings as something not quite the Holy Spirit herself, an increasing lack of explicit pneumatology developed in Western theology; this resulted in a number of problems and flaws in later theology of the spiritual life (Congar 1983, vol. 1: 159–66; Bermejo 1989: 160–7 and passim).

First, in the traditional list of theological *loci* or topics of the *exitus-reditus* scheme codified by the scholastics, there is no specific locus for the Holy Spirit. This not only requires us to shoehorn the Spirit into some other locus (usually the *De trinitate* portion of the locus on God), but the economic scheme of the *exitus-reditus* pattern is also damaged by having no way to account structurally for the Spirit's ecclesial, sacramental, and eschatological role, despite the fact that all three realities are clearly attributed as works of the Spirit in the third paragraph of the classic creeds.

The Western tendency to treat the Holy Spirit as *only* the *vinculum caritatis* between the Father and the Son has over-emphasized the Spirit's proper nature and name as Love, to the exclusion of a role in the other theological virtues (Bermejo 1989: 176–8) and has also caused us in the West to lose sight of the Spirit's communal and eschatological dynamism (Rahner 1979, vol. 2; Farrelly 1993: 496–9). Most particularly in the realm of the economy of God's actions in the world and history, there has been an over-emphasis on Augustine's rule of *monarche*: that the external acts of the Trinity are undivided (*On the Trinity* 15.5). This has caused a failure to appreciate the rigorous trinitarian rhythms of the economy, while turning the doctrine of the Trinity into a mere abstract speculation on the inner nature of God (LaCugna 1991). Indeed, in Western theology the treatise *De Deo uno* has wrongly held primacy of place in the locus on God (Thomas and Wondra 2002: 67ff is a deliberate exception), further isolating the Trinity and hence the Spirit from the economy and the Christian life. Eastern theologians would and do add that this also leads to treating the God-head or *Divinitas* itself as a kind of fourth thing that the three have in common, instead of seeing the Father as the source and fount of all being, including that of the other persons of the Trinity. Perhaps the most elegant solution in contemporary Western theology to this excessive *monarche* is Robert Jenson's assertion that the external or economic works of the blessed Trinity are indeed undivided, but not therefore indistinguishable (Jenson 1997: 110–14). This allows him to make the trinitarian structure of the economy the principal organizing feature of all that follows in his systematics (Jenson 1999).

The fact that these systematic considerations are likely to be seen by Western Christians as abstract and dimly related to Christian spiritual life is itself testimony to the problem, as the Holy Spirit virtually disappears from thinking about the Christian life in the West (Bermejo 1989: 167–8; Jenson 1997: 156ff). What results is a kind of binitarianism: functions that Scripture and Eastern tradition ascribe to the Holy Spirit become appropriated to Christ (and, in later Protestantism, to the human Jesus *per se*) or to grace used as an impersonal term, a kind of quasi-substance separate from the person and work of the Holy Spirit herself (Herron 1983: 94). Jenson's critique of Barth's binitarianism, in spite of Barth's own best intentions, is brilliant and telling (1997: 153–6). Despite corrective tendencies since the Charismatic movement and Vatican II (Congar 1983, vol. 1: 167–73; Farrelly 1983: 502–3), a recent and important work on the spiritual life, such as William Johnston's *Mystical Theology: The Science of Love*, has no chapter or index item for the Holy Spirit, though the Spirit is mentioned in passing (Johnston 1995: 91). As the tradition of spiritual theologies proper began to develop in the seventeenth century, the Spirit either disappeared into Christology, or was depersonalized by making either the God-head an impersonal fourth thing or grace a quasi-substance. Thus, these theologies became a discussion of Christian perfection or human spiritual development, not theologies of the Holy Spirit's impact on Christian lives (Hughes 2001b: 87–91).

Further unfortunate consequences follow, even as we seek to recover language to praise the Spirit's role in our lives and experience, especially gender-inclusive language. "Sustainer," often used as a substitute for Holy Spirit in inclusive language attempts to name the Trinity, has no eschatological dimension and little sense of dynamism. "Sanctifier" has a better theological pedigree, but given the rampant privatism of the West tends to be interpreted only individualistically, with no sense of the Spirit's ecclesial or cosmic mission. Indeed, in most Western theology until recently, eschatology in general was reduced to the fate of the individual (heaven, purgatory, hell), with little or no discussion of the Holy Spirit's sacramental consecration of the universal *pleroma* (fullness). Jenson, in particular, writes eloquently of the disaster that follows from this failure to recognize the Spirit as the future of God in both immanent and economic relations (1997: 157). In liberal theologies (Lampe 1977 is a *locus classicus*; Tillich 1963 comes close), Spirit becomes "spirit" and even "human spirit," losing any sense of the distinctiveness of the third person of the Trinity and also leaving the human body behind; indeed, following its Manichean infections, Western spirituality frequently becomes antithetical to body/matter. We will return to this theme in the next section.

The Western tendency, then, is to collapse trinitarianism to a bipolarity at best, by assigning the economic tasks of the Holy Spirit to Christ or a depersonalized concept of "grace" treated as a kind of quasi-substance. Christic monism, modalism, and Manicheanism lurk in the background, and possibly Nestorianism as well (Jenson 1997: 127–33, 188). The proper emphasis – that what Christians call "spirituality" results *from* being in Christ and results *in* the imitation of Christ – is wounded by a neglect of an important fact: it is only through the indwelling of the Holy Spirit that we can be either in Christ or imitative of him. The specific damage is the over-emphasis in Western spirituality on sharing in the *missio Christi*, while ignoring our call to participate in the *missio Spiritus*, which remains ill defined. The Wesleyan/Pentecostal/Charismatic tradition is perhaps the one exception. Their ongoing fight with Calvinist evangelicals shows exactly this problem on the Protestant side, as does the tendency of the Calvinists to ignore the teaching of Calvin on the role of the testimony of the Holy Spirit in rendering the Scriptures as the Word of God (Calvin, *Institutes* 3.2.34).

The "flip side" has been that when "Spirit-spiritualities" do erupt in the West (Manicheanism, Montanism, the collection of phenomena grouped under "the Brethren of the Free Spirit," *The Mirror of Simple Souls*, the Spiritual Franciscans, the Quakers, Freemasonry, and so on), they often bypass the discipline and suffering of the *missio Christi*, render the body and matter as evil or illusory, and seek to escape from the ecclesial structures of the Body of Christ as an incarnated, socio-historical institution. This is one reason why they are so often and unfortunately persecuted by that institution in the West, which developed a deep suspicion of "enthusiasm." Henry More (1662) provides a classic text. The more recent Charismatic movement in the mainline churches has brought the Holy Spirit to the foreground of consciousness again, and has had many empowering effects, but also some of the problems typical of such movements in the West (Congar 1983, vol. 1: 134–212; Bermejo 1989: 326–87; Callen 2001, written throughout from this perspective).

The Spirit/Body Paradox

A little-noticed paradox is that the stronger the doctrine of the Holy Spirit, the more significance is given to flesh and body in spirituality. Indeed, this was the very matter at issue between Barlaam and Gregory Palamas at the end of the Byzantine imperial era. Barlaam, representing a typical Western and scholastic point of view, applied the terms of spirituality only to the soul, and hence attacked the physical, almost yoga-like practices of the Eastern monks, known as Hesychasm. The slander of calling such persons "navel gazers" stemmed from their practice of the prayer of Jesus as a breath prayer, increasingly popular in our own time through the dissemination of the Russian "Pilgrim's Tale" and similar works. Indeed, these practices constitute, as far as I know, the only positive physical spiritual praxis in Christianity (Gregory Palamas 1983: Meyendorff's Introduction: 1–10). Otherwise, and in the West especially, all physical praxis is penitential, repressive, and often alarmingly punitive.

I have already noted the generally stronger doctrine of the Holy Spirit in the very Eastern circles that also gave rise to this positive physical praxis. Once one understands fully the theology, the connection is not surprising. Bermejo presents a particularly strong account of the physicality of Christian spirituality, in harmony, he argues, with both St Paul and the Eastern Fathers. There are two dimensions to this physicality. First, the link between us and Jesus is primarily a physical link of flesh to flesh. Our immanence in Jesus, crucified, transfigured, risen, and glorified, is through the body of Jesus as the focus of the Spirit. By the sacraments, our flesh is linked to his, and hence our human nature to his, and thus to the paschal mystery which is the history of that flesh, and even to divine nature because of the hypostatic union in him. Our immanence in Christ, branches to vine, is primarily or at least strongly physical, and ecclesial (Bermejo 1989: 37–121). Hence, as Gregory Palamas argues, since our sanctification flows directly from his transfiguration, the body is not left out of our own transfiguration, but is part of it. It is on this ground that he defends the Hesychastic practices of the monks of Mount Athos (Gregory Palamas 1983: 15–16, 41–55).

The second dimension of physicality in Christian spirituality is the fact that the indwelling of the Holy Spirit is also not in our souls alone, or a link to our human spirit. Rather, the Holy Spirit, as Bermejo (1989: 83ff) reminds us Paul teaches, dwells in our bodies as a temple, just as YHWH tabernacled in the Jerusalem Temple. It is this indwelling, initiated in baptism and nourished in Eucharist and spiritual praxis (including physical), that links our flesh to that of Jesus, and hence, through the hypostatic union, leads to *theosis* ("divinization") (Gregory Palamas 1983: 57–69).

The failure of the West to understand this ground of *theosis* in flesh leads to the typical Western fears of deification/divinization language. If we do not understand that our growth into God depends on the Holy Spirit indwelling our bodies, linking our flesh to the crucified, transfigured, resurrected, and glorified flesh of Jesus, and hence a share in his hypostatic union, all claims to divinization appear to be about the disincarnating development of natural properties of the human soul or spirit in its own right. The fear, rightly held, is that this will lead to a disparaging of the institutional (i.e., incarnate) church and the sacraments. It is probably another long-distant echo of the sad heritage of Manicheanism in the West. Both the fear and the proper object of that fear, the various "free spirit" movements, are based on a kind of docetism which understands the role neither of Jesus's flesh nor ours in the economy of salvation, nor the indwelling of the Holy Spirit in our bodies.

Where a healthier view has begun to rise in the West, however, it often corrects two disincarnating tendencies found even in the thought of the Eastern Fathers. First, the Platonic doctrine of an inherently immortal soul is slowly being replaced by a recovered biblical doctrine of the resurrection of the body as the terminal image for the fate of the Christian believer in the communion of saints (Moltmann 1967: 208–16; Jenson 1999: 354–68). We are reminded in the literature of this recovery that the resurrection of the body is a work of the Holy Spirit, as is obvious from its place in the third paragraph of the creeds. As such, it is a new act of grace, and again not the playing out of some inherently natural human property. Second, and here Tillich is the giant, there is a renewed sense of how the Holy Spirit (Tillich's "Spiritual Presence") is always incarnated in ongoing history, resolving its ambiguities (Tillich 1963, passim), and making Christians responsible for the culture in which they live, including the "higher" culture of literature, art, and music (Tillich 1959). In both these trends we see again the paradox that the stronger the understanding of the role of the Holy Spirit in Christian spiritual life, the better the understanding of the place of flesh in the divine economy and the importance given to all incarnating trends that oppose the notion of "spiritual" as primarily "immaterial" or even primarily "inner" (Thomas 2000).

Constructive Proposals

The Holy Spirit is the Spirit of Christ, and supports the *Logos/Sophia* in the *missio Christi* (even as both support and serve the creative mission of the Father/Mother). But the Spirit has her own mission, building upon and completing the *missio Christi* by making it universal and cosmic in scope, in space and time. This is what John's Gospel means by calling the Holy Spirit a second Paraclete/Advocate/Comforter (14: 16; Brown 1970: 1137–44). Jesus himself is clearly the primary paraclete. The Spirit neither replaces the primary advocate, nor merely links us to him, but has her own role to play as well. Indeed, as Herron points out perhaps better than anyone else, in the economy of the incarnation and its history there is already and from the beginning a complex interweaving of the missions of the second and third persons, as Jesus is incarnate by the Holy Spirit, filled and commissioned with the Spirit at his baptism, and empowered by the Spirit in teaching and works throughout his ministry (Herron 1983: 155–79). Jesus also yields the Spirit at his death, and then is raised in the power of the Spirit, to become the one who bestows the Spirit as supreme gift on his followers.

The Spirit's work is never apart from the mystery of Christ, but has its own content and integrity. Without some attention to the Spirit's mission, indeed, we cripple the climax of the *missio Christi* by ignoring the ascended and glorified Christ as the Spirit-sender, and by reducing the second coming to merely mythical status, with little or no connection to the Spirit-guided history lying between the Ascension and the Parousia. As Jenson has shown, we also deprive the Spirit of her own proper personal vantage point as God's future as well as our future in God (Jenson 1997: 156–61).

I offer three constructive proposals to remedy this situation as it applies to Christian spirituality. In doing so, I am following clues in the three great pneumatologies of our time – Tillich (1963), Congar (1983), and Johnson (1996) – and the magnificent trinitarian systematics of Jenson (1997, 1999). Specific pointers to the right path have also come from Bermejo (1989) and Callen (2001). While I will indicate the sources of some major points, the dependence of what follows on those primary texts could not be fully documented without unbearable tedium. I take full responsibility for any errors in shaping these seminal ideas into the following three constructive proposals.

A theological locus for the Holy Spirit

The Holy Spirit should have her own theological locus, coming between Christ and church in the classic list as now modified by Rahner (1963), with the church now preceding the sacraments. (I am indebted to Herbert W. Richardson for my understanding of the systematic implications.) In addition to a proper discussion of the person of the Holy Spirit, and the interplay of the Spirit with the other persons of the immanent Trinity, this locus would include a newly configured section on the work of the Spirit which could appropriately be labeled "spiritual theology." That is, pneumatology is to spiritual theology as Christology is to soteriology. Spiritual theology, as the theological ground for Christian spirituality, must be reconfigured as a theology of the work of the Holy Spirit in the Christian life as a whole, in personal/private and public/corporate and even cosmic dimensions. As such, rather than spiritual theology being subordinate to moral theology, moral theology becomes a part of this larger account which derives from the *missio Spiritus* and its trinitarian shape. That is, spiritual theology will include a discussion of the Spirit's role in the missions of the other two persons, and then of the Spirit's own proper mission. The impact of each on individual, community, and cosmos will be at the core of the subject matter (Hughes, 2001b). The three great pneumatologies mentioned above, plus Jenson's systematics and Bermejo, are the closest we have yet come to envisioning and executing such a project, as far as I know.

The Spirit's threefold mission as source of the "threeness" of our spiritual life

This trinitarian shape of the Spirit's mission can now be seen as the source of what has seemed to be three stages in human spiritual development. Since it first appeared in the writings of Pseudo-Dionysius (1987), this notion of three stages in the spiritual life has become a virtually omnipresent concept in theologies of the Christian life, from Bonaventure's *De triplica via*, for example, through Protestant accounts of the *ordo salutis* as justification, sanctification, perfection (see Hughes 2001a; Jenson 2001). Rahner has given a devastating critique of reading this three-foldness as a law-like description of human development, especially of linking the three classic stages of purgation, illumination, and union to beginners, proficient, and perfect (Rahner 1967; Hughes 2001b: 91, 96–7). Yet there does seem to be some truth in this sense of "threeness" in the spiritual life. What I have proposed is that this threeness is a resonance in us of the Spirit's threefold mission, which is not sequential, but concurrent. That is, the trinitarian structure of the Spirit's mission impacts us as three concurrent currents, much as a pilot or a scuba diver must contend with pitch, roll, and yaw in dealing with currents in three dimensions. At any given moment, one or more of these currents may predominate in an individual life, but none is ever completely absent. This allows us to account, for example, for the ongoing need of repentance and confession in stages of life dominated by illumination or union.

The three currents: conversion, transfiguration, perfection

The first current of the impact of the Spirit's mission on us I have called "conversion." It is the story of the Spirit's work in the Father/Mother's own proper *missio*, if the Father/Mother can be said to have a mission, being only sender and not sent. All theological language is at best analogy, of course, and I do believe it is proper to speak of "mission senders" as also missionaries. In one sense, it is all the Father/Mother's mission, carried out by the Word/Wisdom and Spirit. But, in another sense, it is "appropriate" to see as the immediate purpose and hence mission of the Father/Mother the great biblical acts of creation, covenant, and call to reconciliation, to return, re-turn and hence con-vert. Both Word/Wisdom and Spirit have their proper but subordinate roles to play in these three great acts. They have been well spelled out in their trinitarian fullness by Jenson (1999). The details are more than can be traced here. The Spirit's essential role throughout is liberation, first within the immanent divine life itself, as the Spirit frees the Father and the Son from each other, and hence for each other as the third who constitutes the relation between them (Jenson 1997: 159–61). Similarly, in creation it is the Spirit who frees the creator Father "from retaining all being in himself" and gives the creatures as such their ontological and moral freedom (Jenson 1999: 26). It is this very freedom given by the Spirit that, at the moment of its deepest realization in creation, distinguishes organic from inorganic, and the human from other animals, as those created to be conscious, in conversation with God, and hence in the image of God who is also conversation. It is in this primary sense that the Spirit is life-giver within her work in the Father/Mother's own creative mission.

Similarly, covenant is the establishing of social relations, between God and a people, and the members of a people with one another. This is also constituted by the Spirit's gift of freedom as God's future and ours. God the Father/Mother is freed to be in a free and covenanted relationship with God's own creatures, as the creatures are themselves liberated to be in this relationship freely, with the obedience of faithfulness, not servility, and for this freedom also to be the defining characteristic of relations with one another. To be in the Spirit is to be part of a people called and formed by God.

When sin intervenes (and it would be impossible speculation in one sense for us to imagine the story as if it had not), the Spirit frees the Father/Mother from the demands of retributive justice to issue the great *shuv*, the great call to re-turn, to conversion, just as the Spirit frees the human creatures from the bondage of sin so that they may make a free and graced response to that call. As many great Christian authors have recognized, the first act of this gift of restored freedom is "conviction of sin." The first real reassertion of freedom by the sinner is precisely the confession, "I have sinned" (as David to Nathan, 2 Sam. 12: 13). For Christians, of course, the role of the Word/Wisdom as incarnate and crucified is crucial in establishing this possibility. But it is an essentially trinitarian experience: "identified with the Son and filled with the Spirit, one cries out: 'Abba, Father!'" (Johnston 1995: 206; Rom. 8: 15; Gal. 4: 6). The final completion of the *missio* of the Father/Mother, reconciliation of all things with God-self, however much accomplished by the atoning work of the incarnate Word/Wisdom, is crowned by the prayerful cry of the Spirit dwelling within those liberated to make the cry.

The themes of the classical stage of the *via purgativa* can then find their proper place in the current raised by this *missio*. (For an excellent, brief description of the *via purgativa* as conversion of the heart, see Johnston 1995: 192–210.) The first work of the Spirit, then, is to bring us to life in the Father/Mother, establish the covenant relationship between us, and, when it becomes necessary, to reconcile us to the Father/Mother.

As previously noted, the Spirit dances with the Word in a complex series of steps in this process. It is the image of Life that dominates our experience of the Spirit as the freedom of the future in God, and the theological virtue evoked in us by the Spirit as a sympathetic response is faith. Calvin (*Institutes* 3.2) gives an excellent exposition of the role of the Holy Spirit in human faith. Faith in this sense is belief in the divine acts themselves, trust in their good purpose, and obedient faithfulness in freedom to the relationship which ensues. The Vatican II definition of faith as trustful and surrendered obedience in *Dei verbum* 1.5 is most helpful here, especially in its clear delineation of the work of the Spirit (Johnston 1995: 176–8). (For the use and definition of the theological virtues and their order and relationship to the other themes, I am heavily dependent on Rahner 1984.)

In David Tracy's sense, the mode of theological discourse defined by this current is "proclamation" – the great telling of the mighty acts of creation and salvation (Tracy 1981: 386–9). The resulting *style* of spirituality, as I have called it, the form taken by our self-transcendence in response to God's self-transcendence addressing us in this current, is self-denial (Hughes 2002: 119–20, following Tracy 1981: 421–35). This is not a denial of the true self, but rather a denial or renunciation of all the forces of evil that imprison the true self from finding its liberty and life in the Spirit. Sometimes this calls for the classical disciplines usually called "self-denial" or "abnegation" or even "mortification," where these are a correction of habits turning the self aside from its true destiny. Sometimes it is a revolutionary renunciation against forces that deny true selfhood to an individual. In our time, these two often come together in the struggle with various forms of addictive disease, the sacred illness of our time (May 1988, 1992: 160). Sometimes it is a long process of therapy and healing from traumas that have deeply wounded and distorted the true self. For most of us, I suppose, it is some mixture of all of these, as true repentance means turning away from all that is not our destiny in God and toward that destiny that is the life and freedom of the Spirit. In whichever mode of "return" it may appear, this turning and healing work is at bottom a consequence of the indwelling Spirit. As Farrelly (1993: 500a) says: "The Spirit has a certain precedence within this gift of grace, because it is by the Father and Son pouring the Spirit into the human person that he or she is given the Spirit's relation to the Father through the Son, and the capacity for the life of a disciple that reflects this gift."

There is no logical reason, as far as I know, why the Christian life at this point could not be a simple transition from dominance of the first trinitarian current of the Spirit's *missio* to the second (at least so it is in most lives, though even the order is not uniformly necessary; see John of the Cross, *Dark Night* 1.14.5; Johnston 1995: 219). One can only say that the tradition teaches that, in our fallen existential circumstances, there is a dark interlude in the midst of the transition, which calls for a second conversion and a deeper renunciation. This is the tradition of the classic "Dark Nights" of John of the Cross, helpfully described for us in this developmental context by William Johnston (1995: 211–34). The enthusiasm of initial conversion and birthing into the life of the faith by the Spirit usually begins to cool, and we can make the tragic errors of trying to reignite it or replicate it in ourselves. When this fails, as it always does, even Christians of long standing and great faith can be surprised by the desolation that follows, especially when there is no teaching in the community that this is to be expected, and is the birth of a deeper intimacy with God (Jones 1985: 159–84). We are usually brought face to face at this time with the ways in which we have not lived up to our new calling, and discouraged by our ongoing battles with the demons of possessiveness and despair. This crisis initiates in us what St John of the Cross called "the dark night of the senses." It is both a last gasp of the style of self-denial, and also our initial letting go of it, as we face the deepest layers of our own self-betrayal.

At a much deeper level – that which is usually called the passive purgation of the senses – this is not an act on our part at all, but a deeper upwelling of the Spirit in her indwelling. "This dark night is an inflow of God into the soul which purges it" (John of the Cross, *Dark Night* 2.5.1; Johnston 1995: 220). Johnston also likens this first dark night to the experience, in Jungian terms, of beginning to come to grips with our own shadow (Johnston 1995: 218). God is no longer teaching us indirectly through the exterior senses, but directly through the upwelling of the Spirit. God the Mother is weaning us from the milk of children that we may begin to walk on our own in her presence (John of the Cross, *Dark Night* 1.1.2; Johnston 1995: 216–17).

It is only after some initial purgation in the desert or the dark night of the senses, only with some relief from possessiveness, control needs, addiction, trauma, or oppression, that we can begin to see the world and our own selves as illuminated and transfigured by the light of divine glory, the Tabor light which is the uncreated energies according to Gregory Palamas, and hence come to love the world in God, and thus, oddly enough, for the first time for its own sake. Only when we have learned, usually through pain and suffering, some loving detachment from the world, can we receive it back as a gift (see John of the Cross's *Sketch of Mt Carmel*, and Johnston 1995: 230). Faith is being reborn as loving knowledge at this gateway to the second current, which I have called "transfiguration," and includes all the themes of the classical *via illuminativa*. But the very fact that this current lies, as it were, between the two dark nights (Johnston 1995: 218–20) reminds us again that a purely developmental step-theory will not do. The current of conversion is always present even when others dominate, and there is always more purification to come. Also, the journey is never as neat as the map, however informative the map may be. The crucial point holds, however: the desert and dark nights are not the absence of God, though they feel that way, but a further upwelling of the indwelling Spirit, the living water, making more room for herself.

The second great current of the Spirit's *missio* results from her role in the proper *missio* of the second person of the Trinity, the Word/Wisdom, especially incarnate as Jesus. In particular, the second work of the Spirit is to produce the concrete fact of our immanence in Christ, thus fulfilling the *missio* of the Word/Wisdom (Bermejo 1989: 37–70). Viewed from the other side, Jesus's own *missio* culminates in the outpouring of "another advocate" (John 14: 16; Brown 1970: 1135–44). Indeed, the Word/Wisdom and Spirit have been in a complex dance together throughout the events of the incarnation, from the conception of Jesus by the Holy Spirit right through to his sending the Spirit. These economic relations reflect the complexity of the immanent relations within God's own life. Alasdair Herron (1983: 39–60, 157–79) has portrayed this as clearly as anyone. Baptism is the great sacrament of our immanence in Christ and his death and resurrection, the full reality of immanence in vine and branches. It is also the seal of the Holy Spirit and her indwelling. Rather than being two effects of baptism, it is best to see these as a single effect: to be in the Spirit is to be in Christ, and vice versa. The presence of Christ in the Eucharist we understand today to be crowned through Eucharistic epiclesis – the invocation of the Spirit. Indeed, this is the way all the sacraments work. *Koinonia*, the relationship of fellowship and communion formed into a common life of a priestly people, is the fundamental sacramental reality as the Holy Spirit forms the church as the body of Christ through bonds of *communio*. Hence, to be in Christ and the Spirit is also to be in the church, his body and bride. The great sacraments of initiation also bring to each individual a commission to mission, to share first in Christ's mission and offer to all other peoples a like opportunity to be immanent in him.

The dominant images for the Spirit in this current are light and truth. Historically, baptism was called "the illumination." It is also the beginning of our transfiguration, the name I have given this current, following the Eastern terminology. Through word and sacrament the Spirit leads us into all truth, so that in our own transfiguring we also see the world illumined by God's glory – not altered, but seen for the first time as it truly is. The theological virtue raised in us by the Spirit's transfiguring current is love. As we shine forth in our own true nature, we are enabled to love God, neighbor, and the world truly for the first time (see Rahner 1984: 133–51; for a brilliant exposition of love at this point, see Simone Weil's essays on the "Forms of the Implicit Love of God," in Weil 1973: 137–215.) The theological mode appropriate to this current in Tracy's terminology is "manifestation" – the recognition and celebration of God's glory in ourselves and all the world (Tracy 1981: 376–85). The style of spirituality or self-transcendence is self-fulfillment, but limited and formed by love of neighbor and of God (Hughes 2002: 120–3).

Perfect love casts out fear (1 John 4: 18), both in our relationship with God, as we have another advocate who acquits and equips us, and with our neighbor, as love ends enmity and breaks down barriers. This changes the character of ongoing conversion. The emphasis is not so much on "conversion from what" as "conversion to whom." All of ordinary life, especially the demand of charity, is consecrated as a means of grace, a path to further sanctification and even perfection. Hence, questions of vocation and "states of life" as works of the Spirit belong here, as they revolve around recognizing the structures of ordinary life as means of grace and manifestations of God's glory. This includes marriage, consecrated celibacy, and worldly work, as well as other paths of sanctification, and each needs a theology of the Spirit's role. The "inspiration" of art, music, literature, dance, scholarship, science and all pursuit of truth, even (or perhaps most especially) politics at its best, also manifests the transfiguring work of the Spirit. The Western Augustinian emphasis on the Spirit as the *vinculum caritatis* is accurate for this part of the Spirit's *missio*. So is the criterion for discernment of spirits and of spiritual growth of "the dominion of charity" (which Bermejo strangely underplays). The mistake is not including the Spirit-images and criteria of the other two currents. The vast majority of mature Christians probably lead most of their lives with this as the dominant current. Its peak is the experience called in the tradition "the spiritual betrothal," which bears, I think, some correspondence to the Wesleyan "faith of assurance" (Callen 2001: 183–206).

This image of the spiritual betrothal points to the second dark night, which lies between it and the consummation of the spiritual marriage in the final current of glory and union. In an age when so few endure the unfulfilled desire that all once knew between commitment and consummation in human mating, the image may have lost some of its power; but the poetry of the *Spiritual Canticle*, both the original biblical poem and its many uses in the tradition of Christian spirituality, not least that of John of the Cross, still speaks to us (Johnston 1995: 257–77). It is this prayer of intense desire for one who is now fully beloved but seems absent that is the positive side of this night. The closer we actually get to God our beloved, the more intense is the pain caused by whatever still separates us. The more negative side is the refiner's fire, the desire of the soul to be purified from even the smallest imperfections which obstruct or lessen in any degree the promised union. It is the desire of the espoused to be at their best for each other. Needless to say, this night is also a further upwelling of the Spirit, who gives us the inarticulate groans of longing (Rom. 8: 26), and is herself the refining fire of love. Despite this more positive description of the second night, those who have undergone it report an even deeper desolation; and it seems as a matter of fact that many turn back and few in this life actually persevere to go on to sanctified lives dominated by the third current, even though it is the destiny of all believers.

The third work of the Holy Spirit, the Spirit's own proper *missio*, is our own sanctification and perfection as part of the sacramental consecration of the whole material universe, the *pleroma*. Again, Jenson's pneumatology makes it clear precisely why the Spirit's own proper *missio* has this unifying and eschatological function of fulfillment, both ours and God's (Jenson 1997: 156ff; 1999: 309 ff, esp. p. 319). Sacramental consecration of the *pleroma*, perfect fulfillment, bringing to destined end, kingdom of God, beatific vision, *theosis*, are all differing perspectives on one overwhelming reality, the consummation of the Spirit's indwelling (Bermejo 1989: 113–21; Johnston 1995: 206; Jenson 1999: 338–69; Callen 2001: 95, 244, n. 26). This current has been present from the beginning, primarily through the bodily indwelling of the Spirit as *sperma theou*, seed of God growing towards perfection.

The primary image for the Spirit is "Love" as a consuming and purifying fire or flame. That is, the refiner's fire now burns more gently as the passion of love. John of the Cross gives this as the description: "The ninth step of love causes the soul to burn gently. It is the step of the perfect who burn gently in God. The Holy Spirit produces the gentle and delightful ardor by reason of the soul's union with God" (*Dark Night* 2.20.4; Johnston 1995: 225). Beyond lies only the tenth step of beatific vision or *theosis*, fully realized only in eternal life (*Dark Night* 2. 20.5). Other sanjuanist images help grasp this reality, which most of us experience only buried deep within the other two currents. This is the spiritual marriage longed for since the betrothal, celebrated in the *Spiritual Canticle*. It culminates in *theosis*, and while the bridegroom is Christ, the Word/Wisdom, it is also a union of the human spirit with the Holy Spirit, who is the bond of love in this marriage, as in earthly ones (*Spiritual Canticle* 22.3). The role of the Spirit in this mystery of union in glory is most intensely celebrated by St John in *The Living Flame of Love*.

Daily growth of both individual and universe includes the moral life, the imitation of Christ, the ascetical, plus the mystical as either infused contemplation and/or prophetic liberating praxis. Much more frequently than is often assumed, these last two are found in the same persons and can be seen as two sides of a single reality, even if our age is likely to stress the prophetic, liberating praxis (Johnston 1995 is very good on this, esp. pp. 326–65). The theological virtue raised in us by this current of glorifying union is hope. This may seem strange, as one would think that, in the consummation, there is nothing left to hope for. But several theologians, from Gregory of Nyssa through Wesley to Rahner, have provided a deeper analysis, in which we come to understand even the consummation in perfection as further journey (Wesley 1964: 31; Gregory of Nyssa 1978; Rahner 1984: 253–7; Jenson 1999: 321). That is, this hope which does not pass away is an inevitable outcome of personal love, which always hopes for still more. As we encounter the Holy Spirit in her proper name and nature as Love, we hope for greater love in ourselves, deeper penetration by Love itself into our own being, being drawn ever more deeply as beloveds into the essence of Love itself, the mystery of the trinitarian *perichoresis* (mutual coinherence). In this life, and perhaps even in the next, there is always a deep longing to and for love, which requires both humility and hope. The very disappearance of hope in theological thought is a symptom of the binitarianism which does not see this as all the work of the person of the Holy Spirit, because it is the depersonalization and abstraction of love that makes it hopeless, as if it could be satisfied.

The theological mode of this current, in Tracy's terms, is "prophecy" (Tracy 1981: 390–404). While prophecy is not fortune-telling but theological analysis of the present, it is nonetheless eschatological, with an eye on the future, which, as God's future, *is* the Holy Spirit. It requires hope, for it is a preaching in the present of the hopeful future Love requires. I have named the style of self-transcendence in this current self-criticism (Hughes 2002: 118–19, 123–6; this naming of the third style is one of the principal proposals of the article). This is not the gross housecleaning of the *via purgativa*, but the birth of true humility, the mother of hope. Through the final purgation of the second dark night we experience the deeper repentance and even despair of the saints, hope of the hopeless and helpless, as every flaw which keeps us from perfect union becomes painful. It is prophetic because it must now confront the various forms of false consciousness of our own social location, gender, race, class, as dross to be consumed if prophecy and liberating praxis are to be true. Prophecy inspired by the Spirit must be as free of all our own agendas as possible, suffused with the will of God.

The end is *theosis*, union, full participation in the inner life of the Trinity in a perfect reign of justice and peace, a vision of God characterized by loving knowledge. This is an end, a *telos*, for which we have no natural capacity, a desire we have no hope of our own of ever having satisfied. It does, in the end, come to us as a gift, as inclusion in the consecrated perfection of the *pleroma*, coinherence in the trinitarian life itself through the hypostatic union by the power of the Spirit. We and all things are illumined by the light of Glory, which is only God's energies, but is nonetheless divine and divinizing according to Gregory Palamas (1983: 71–111). If Jenson is right, to set up these energies as a barrier to God's essential life is the final error even of Palamite Orthodoxy (1997: 152–3). Gregory Palamas is right, however, that we shall see God with our own bodily eyes, which cannot by nature behold God, through "the communion of saints, the resurrection of the dead, and the life everlasting" (Jenson 1997: 229–30; 1999: 338–69). That is the mystery of our fulfillment and the world's – a destined end for which we have no natural capacity (Hughes 2002: 130), but which the Spirit gives us as the consequence of the gift of herself.

The *missio Spiritus* is also what drives all three currents in us toward true self-transcendence as the proper style of each (Hughes 2002: 126–32). That is, because the role of the Holy Spirit lies on a continuum from "in your face" to sacramental indwelling; from the gift of life to the supernatural existential as the universal resonance in our existence of God's self-transcendence as the source of ours; on to the indwelling of the *sperma theou* as the source of mystical union in infused contemplation and the resultant harmony with God's will which leads to prophetic liberating action, the Holy Spirit is also the Spirit who constantly and finally renews the face of the earth in justice and peace, and consecrates the entire *pleroma*. The whole is trinitarian, of course, but the Spirit gets, as it were, the last word, as the future which is ours and God's together.

The three currents come together at any given moment in our lives as we grow toward union with the Father/Mother by sharing in the coinherence of Word/Wisdom and Spirit. Because our flesh is united to the flesh of Jesus as the Spirit makes us immanent in him, we grow in Christlikeness even to sharing in the hypostatic union. This reality is crowned by the indwelling of the Holy Spirit as immanent in us, in our bodies as her temple, adorning us with virtues for the marriage and filling us with the divine *zoe*, the inner life of the Trinity itself. As no one of the Three is any less than all taken together (Augustine, *On the Trinity* 8.15.5), because of the Spirit's indwelling, it is also proper to speak of the indwelling in us of the whole Trinity, as of us in the whole Trinity (Bermejo 1989: 113–17). From this perspective, then, "spirituality" as experienced by Christians is shaped, root and branch, stages (or currents) and dark interludes, by the Holy Spirit and the impact of her trinitarian *missio* on the human person and community.

The Gifts of the Spirit

A final word on the *charismata*, the traditional gifts of the Spirit, whether from the list in Isaiah 11, the Beatitudes, or the Pauline lists, especially 1 Cor. 12–14, is in order. The Pentecostal/Charismatic movement, with its roots in the Wesleyan Holiness movement, has probably done more to recover an active doctrine of the Holy Spirit in the West than any other force. From the perspective taken here, the individual spiritual gifts are not separate packages delivered willy-nilly. There is one supreme spiritual gift, the indwelling Spirit herself; individual gifts are the impact on individuals of this supreme gift, and occur across the trinitarian spectrum of the Spirit's *missio*. Some, such as the theological virtues, and the beatitudes, as well as the fruits of the Spirit, seem to be the common inheritance of all the Spirit-filled, into which we all grow at various paces. These gifts can be for the individual and her adornment, but they also shape each of us into fit ornaments in the communion of saints and the Kingdom of God.

In both Scripture and tradition, however, it is plain that the Pauline *charismata*, both prayer and ministerial gifts, can be given at any time, and are not primarily for the individual. Instead, these are given for assisting the Spirit in her economic work, especially the building up of the body of Christ as the instrument of mission in the world (Bermejo 1989: 326–72; Callen 2001: 116–88 and passim; Congar 1983, vol. 1: 3–64 is the *locus classicus* for the ecclesial dimension of the Spirit's work). Placing the question of the gifts in the larger scheme of the Spirit's trinitarian *missio* affords an opportunity to reinsert missing themes in the mainstream of Western Christian spirituality, as well as to correct some false tendencies in the Free Spirit/Wesleyan/Pentecostal side. This allows us to see again that, from the standpoint of Christian theology, spirituality simply *is* a description of the indwelling Spirit at work in the saints, fulfilling the trinitarian *missio* in us and the world as we all move toward the destined sacramental *pleroma*.

References

Augustine 1991: *On the Trinity*, trans. E. Hill. Brooklyn: New City Press.

Bermejo, L. M. 1989: *The Spirit of Life: The Holy Spirit in the Life of the Christian*. Chicago: Loyola University Press.

Brown, R. E. 1970: *The Gospel According to John*, vol. 2. Garden City, NY: Doubleday.

Bulgakov, S. 2004: *The Comforter*, trans. B. Jakim. Grand Rapids, MI: Eerdmans.

Callen, B. L. 2001: *Authentic Spirituality: Moving beyond Mere Religion*. Grand Rapids, MI: Baker Academic.

Calvin, John 1960: *Institutes of the Christian Religion*, ed. J. T. McNeill, trans. F. L. Battles. Philadelphia: Westminster Press.

Chan, S. 1998: *Spiritual Theology: A Systematic Study of the Christian Life*. Downer's Grove, IL: InterVarsity Press.

Congar, Y. 1983: *I Believe in the Holy Spirit*, 3 vols, trans. D. Smith. New York: Crossroad Herder.

Dunn, J. D. G. 1983: Spirit, Holy. In G. S. Wakefield (ed.), *The Westminster Dictionary of Christian Spirituality*, pp. 357–8. Philadelphia: Westminster.

Farrelly, M. J. 1993: Holy Spirit. In M. Downey (ed.), *The New Dictionary of Catholic Spirituality*, pp. 492–503. Collegeville, MN: Liturgical Press.

Gregory of Nyssa 1978: *The Life of Moses*, trans. A. J. Malherbe and E. Ferguson. New York: Paulist Press.

Gregory Palamas 1983: *The Triads*, trans. N. Gendle (intro. J. Meyendorff). New York: Paulist Press.

Herron, A. I. C. 1983: *The Holy Spirit: The Holy Spirit in the Bible, the History of Christian Thought, and Recent Theology*. Philadelphia: Westminster.

Hughes, R. D., III 2001a: Retrieving and reconstructing "justification by grace through faith": some disturbing questions. *Sewanee Theological Review* 45 (1), 51–71.

——2001b: Starting over: the Holy Spirit as subject and locus of spiritual theology. In R. B. Slocum (ed.), *Engaging the Spirit: Essays on the Life and Theology of the Holy Spirit*, pp. 85–102. New York: Church Publishing (orig. pub. in *Anglican Theological Review* [2001] 83, 455–72).

——2002: A critical note on two aspects of self-transcendence. *Sewanee Theological Review* 46 (1), 112–32.

Jenson, R. W. 1997: *Systematic Theology*, vol. 1: *The Triune God*. Oxford: Oxford University Press.

——1999: *Systematic Theology*, vol. 2: *The Works of God*. Oxford: Oxford University Press.

——2001: Reply to Robert Hughes. *Sewanee Theological Review* 45 (1), 72–4.

Johnson, E. A. 1996: *She Who Is: The Mystery of God in Feminist Theological Discourse*. New York: Crossroad.

Johnston, W. 1995: *Mystical Theology: The Science of Love*. London: HarperCollins.

Jones, A. W. 1985: *Soul-making: The Desert Way of Spirituality*. San Francisco: Harper and Row.

Kärkkäinen, V.-M. 2002: *Pneumatology: The Holy Spirit in Ecumenical, International, and Contextual Perspective*. Grand Rapids, MI: Baker Academic.

LaCugna, C. M. 1991: *God for Us: The Trinity and Christian Life*. San Francisco: Harper.

Lampe, G. W. H. 1977: *God as Spirit*. Oxford: Oxford University Press.

Lossky, V. 1974: *In the Image and Likeness of God*. Crestwood, NY: St Vladimir's Seminary Press.

——1976: *The Mystical Theology of the Eastern Church*. Crestwood, NY: St Vladimir's Seminary Press.

McDonnell, K. 2003: *The Other Hand of God: The Holy Spirit as the Universal Touch and Goal*. Collegeville, MN: Liturgical Press.

McIntosh, M. A. 1998: *Mystical Theology: The Integrity of Spirituality and Theology*. Oxford: Blackwell.

Macquarrie, J. 1977: *Principles of Christian Theology*, 2nd edn. New York: Charles Scribner's Sons.

May, G. G. 1988: *Addiction and Grace*. San Francisco: Harper and Row.

——1992: *Care of Mind, Care of Spirit: A Psychiatrist Explores Spiritual Direction*. San Francisco: Harper.

——2004: *The Dark Night of the Soul: A Psychiatrist Explores the Connection between Darkness and Spiritual Growth*. San Francisco: Harper.

Moltmann, J. 1967: *Theology of Hope: On the Ground and the Implications of a Christian Eschatology*, trans. J. W. Leitch. New York: Harper and Row.

More, H. 1662: *Enthusiasmus triumphatus*, repr. edn 1966. Los Angeles: William Andrews Clark Memorial Library, University of California.

Pseudo-Dionysius the Areopagite 1987. *Works*, trans. C. Luibheid. New York: Paulist Press.

Rahner, K. 1963: *The Church and the Sacraments*. New York: Herder and Herder.

——1967: Reflections on the problem of the gradual ascent to Christian perfection. In *Theological Investigations III: Theology of the Spiritual Life*. London: Darton, Longman, and Todd.

——1979: *The Spirit in the Church*, vol. 1: *Experiencing the Spirit*, trans. J. Griffiths; vol. 2: *The Charismatic [Dynamic] Element in the Church*, trans. W. J. O'Hara. London: Sheed and Ward.

——1984: *The Practice of Faith: A Handbook of Contemporary Spirituality*, ed. K. Lehman and A. Raffelt. New York: Crossroad.

Sheldrake, P. 1998: *Spirituality and Theology: Christian Living and the Doctrine of God*. London: Darton, Longman, and Todd.

Taylor, J. V. 1972: *The Go-between God: The Holy Spirit, The Church, Eschatology*. London: SCM Press.

Thomas, O. C. 2000: Problems in contemporary Christian spirituality. *Anglican Theological Review* 82, 267–81.

——and Wondra, E. K. 2002: *Introduction to Theology*, 3rd edn. Harrisburg, PA: Morehouse.

Tillich, P. 1959: *Theology of Culture*, ed. R. C. Kimball. New York: Oxford University Press.

——1963: *Systematic Theology*, vol. 3. Chicago: University of Chicago Press.

Tracy, D. 1981: *The Analogical Imagination: Christian Theology and the Culture of Pluralism*. New York: Crossroad.

Weil, S. 1973: *Waiting for God*. New York: Harper and Row.

Wesley, J. 1964: *John Wesley*, ed. A. C. Outler. New York: Oxford University Press.

CHAPTER 13

Christian Spirituality and the Theology of the Human Person

Philip Endean

The gospel, if we hear it aright, subverts us. It changes our ideas, our sense of ourselves; it makes us wonder, in both senses of the word, about what it is to be human. Perhaps no one has put it better than Samuel Crossman in the seventeenth century:

> My song is love unknown,
> My Savior's love to me
> Love to the loveless shown
> That they might lovely be
> O who am I,
> That for my sake
> My Lord should take frail flesh and die

Editors, and indeed compilers of hymnals, have to take a decision about the punctuation at the end of this stanza. It could be a question mark – Christ's incarnation and death making us wonder *about* who we are. It could also be an exclamation mark – we wonder *at* who we must be for the wondrous exchange to have taken place. The one thing the sentence cannot be is a simple statement, ending with a normal full stop.

The literary issue here reflects a theological point of great significance about the nature of theological truth – one which, I submit, we must recognize and allow for fully if we are to consider sensibly any question about how spirituality and theology relate. Theologians often make a pious apophatic gesture in preambles, asides, or perorations, but few allow the sense of wonder, the recognition that they are writing about realities they cannot control, systematically to influence the way in which they conduct their business. The primary form of theological truth is not the informative statement. Theology holds us open to a mystery about which we exclaim and ask questions. The informational truth it delivers is genuine but secondary: an assurance that what calls forth our response of wonder is real.

What is being said here applies, obviously, far beyond what theologians quaintly call "Christian anthropology" – far beyond the theology of grace and sin, of human origins and fulfillment, of body and soul, of individual and community. Similar things must also be said about the Trinity, about Christology, and about the church. "Who am I?" is not the only question that Christianity poses. Who is God, who can be at once creator and sustainer of all that will ever exist, and yet also be present, in person, within the creation? Who is Jesus Christ, at one with the Father, and also fully human, accepting even death, death on a cross? What is the church, at once a temple of the Holy Spirit and an all-too-fallible, shoddy human agglomeration? Christianity's truth lies less in the explanations it offers than in the questions it generates (Vass 1968: 130; Lash 1973: 177). Its assurance lies not simply in creedal declarations, but in a conviction that the questions lying behind those truths are meaningful and sensible ones. How can death lead to life? How can a revelation focused in one particular place be of decisive significance for the whole cosmos? How can an infinite creator God keep in being creatures who transgress God's will?

It is significant in this context that the climax of Ignatius of Loyola's presentation of sin lies precisely in "an exclamation of wonder with deep feeling":

> going through all creatures, how they have left me in life and preserved me in it; the angels, how, though they are the sword of the divine justice, they have endured me, and guarded me and prayed for me; the saints, how they have been engaged in interceding and praying for me; and the heavens, sun, moon, stars, and elements, fruits, birds, fishes and animals – and the earth, how it has not opened to swallow me up, creating new hells for me to suffer in forever. (Ignatius of Loyola 1996, no. 60)

The point is not that the statements of Christian truth are wrong, or unsatisfactory. Rather, they are misleading if presented on their own simply as facts, without any sense of the questions and struggles from which they emerge. I once knew an elderly lady addicted to popular romances. I lent her Jane Austen's *Mansfield Park*. After she finished chapter 1, she said to me conspiratorially, "I think I know what happens already – Fanny's going to marry Edmund, isn't she?" Simply to focus on the factual claims of Christianity, without reference to the human processes behind them, is like reading a great classic love story simply in terms of who marries whom at the end. The truth may be told, but the fashion of its telling falsifies it.

Karl Rahner made the point more technically in the essay he wrote as a prologue to his collected essays (in English, *Theological Investigations*). Complaining about the sterility of what then passed for conventional theology, of a concern simply with exact formulas, Rahner pleaded for a more empathetic approach to the history of theology, approaching the past,

> closely enough to hear it with all the overtones with which it once resounded, overtones which at that time were not perhaps the explicit formulations of an academic theology, but rather the echoes of preaching, faith and Christian life . . . The historian must . . . in company with the theologians from the past (and of course listening to what they are saying) fix their gaze on the reality itself – not chronicle past theology, but actually *do* theology in company with it . . . [The] lecture-room method puts everything on the same level; it is incapable of being sensitive to the hidden energies of an old theology, it fails to discover that which has remained implicit, that which (precisely because of its being

implicit) is most influential there, the covert reality taken for granted. It overlooks the opposition or the gap which may sometimes be present between what is said and what is meant, between the perhaps over-facile solution of a particular problem and the fundamental principle; it has the parts but not the spirit which holds them all together. (Rahner 1954: 17–18)

Much, evidently, turns on just what we mean, not only by "spirituality" but also by "theology." Before we can speak sensibly about the role of the Christian theology of the human person in the study of Christian spirituality, therefore, we need to explore the presuppositions underlying the very question – and the greater part of what follows will be given over to that task. I shall be putting forward a position on what it means to teach and study the Christian theology of the human person (and indeed describing my own practice). Why do we still engage with classic theological texts such as Luther's *The Freedom of a Christian*, the Council of Trent's Decree on Justification, and the anti-Pelagian writings of Augustine? What are we hoping to achieve when we look again at standard theological problems such as those of original sin or the resurrection of the body? I then want respectfully to suggest that many current discussions of the relationship between theology and spirituality are predicated on a more narrow, impoverished view of theological learning than the one I will have sketched – one that may be influential in the theological academy as it currently conducts its business, but one that can also be cogently criticized on grounds *internal* to theology. On this basis, I shall suggest that the interest in "spirituality" is best understood as pointing, not to the need for some theory of God and humanity somehow inaccessible to "theology" (a claim which, when put in those terms, involves a contradiction), but rather to the need for renewal in the standard procedures of theology – a need that is certainly a sore one at present, and may well, in the nature of things, be permanent. Talk of "spirituality" is best understood as a reminder to theologians of their responsibility, precisely as theologians, to learn from humanity's ongoing relationship with God, and to write and teach in such a way as to promote and foster that relationship.

Only when those points are securely established are we in a position to approach the question of how doctrinal reflection on grace might contribute to the study of spirituality. I shall suggest three major roles: that of *specifying a context*; that of *raising questions about truth*; and that of *broadening vision*.

Theology and Being Human

"My song is love unknown." What does it mean for the human person to be confronted by an unknown, lovely power that transforms us into its own loveliness? Christianity begins with an experience of Christ's salvation, of liberation, and hence with doctrines of grace, justification, and sanctification. These doctrines, however, inevitably push us back, to accounts of what the human person was before the transformation occurred: to doctrines of sin, both original and actual, and indeed to accounts of God's purpose in the original creation of the human race. The Christian experience of life in Christ here and now also raises questions about our future. What does it mean to grow in the new life of grace? How should we understand our ultimate destiny if our life now is like this?

When Ezekiel talks of our being given a new heart and a new spirit (Ezek. 36: 26), when Paul speaks of a new creation (2 Cor. 5: 17), the familiarity of the language and its devotional power mask a conceptual problem. Either the new creation is in some kind of continuity with the old one, in which case it is not really "new"; or it is not, in which case the gospel ceases to be good news for us and degenerates into a report about what will happen to some other creatures – creatures who might perhaps resemble us, but who are nevertheless different from us, in some sense no longer human. Christian theology involves us in the struggle with this dilemma. Christian language of Christ somehow living in us, of our being in Christ, poses in more radical form the question of how divine and human agency relate. Hence Christianity must live with questions of grace and freedom, and also with the question of how what God does in Christ relates to God's initial creation (the problem of nature and grace). The solutions to the grace and freedom issue vary between strong doctrines of the bondage of the will and more or less coherent attempts to articulate a real sense in which we remain free under grace. For its part, the question about salvation and creation provokes a spectrum of responses varying from a heavy stress on God's action in Christ somehow supplanting the initial creation to optimistic assertions of an original blessing given within the creation from the beginning. More generally, the issue then arises of the relationship between theological accounts of reality and those yielded by other sciences. Does theology represent an alternative explanation of reality, standing in competition with what is delivered by, say, psychology or palaeontology? Or can we develop a vision in which theology and secular science are somehow compatible, complementary?

Moreover, questions about redemption and creation obviously raise issues about sin. That people experience Christ as "savior" suggests that we need to be saved from something; and if Christ's saving role extends universally, the sin in question must be aboriginal, universal – hence the tendency in the tradition toward pessimistic accounts of the human condition at large. A Christian theology of the human person has to consider the relationship between what it wants or needs to say about the origins of the human race and more scientifically informed accounts. There are some who believe that evolutionary theory discredits the notion of original sin; there are others who adopt various strategies toward a reconciliation.

The experience of new life in Christ, however, raises speculative issues not only about the creature's past but also about its future. The spiritual classics have a proper place within systematic theology as accounts of how the creature is changed, how it grows into the likeness of Christ. Moreover, we also need to reflect on the statements Christianity makes about human beings and their ultimate future, specifically about life after death. On what basis can we talk about a reality which, in any obvious sense, is inaccessible to us? What do we make of the famous four last things: death, judgment, heaven, and hell? Is the concept of purgatory defensible?

The main issues in a Christian account of the human person in large part reflect discussions conducted within Western culture more generally. Quite apart from questions of freedom and determinism, there are other questions about what it is to be human that certainly shape any particular theological vision but on which there is no definitive Christian teaching. One of these questions is the mind–body problem. Christianity's belief in some kind of life after death, as well as other doctrines mentioning "the soul," feed into long-standing, inconclusive philosophical discussions regarding the nature of human consciousness and its possible independence of our bodies, discussions that have recently taken a new turn with the development of neuroscience and of artificial intelligence. Equally contested is the relationship between the individual and society. Much classical Christian theology couches its discussion in terms of the individual and his or her salvation. But a good case can be made for saying that we can only be human in relationship with others. In that case, salvation is either collective or it does not exist at all. More recently, we have become more sensitive to the role of gender, and have learned to ask questions about ideological distortion. Arguably, the mainstream theological tradition has been shaped almost exclusively by men, indeed privileged men, with the result that it does not incorporate the wisdom that can be learnt only from the experience of the marginalized. Perhaps our theological categories require thoroughgoing reform.

Neither Western culture in general, nor the Christian churches in particular, have come to any stable consensus on such issues as these. Hence the Christian theology of the human person is inevitably pluralist, more so than, say, Christology or the doctrine of the Trinity. It is perhaps in the area of eschatology that the options become most apparent: projecting our commitments onto the future displays their implications. Questions about freedom become radicalized in discussions about predestination; questions about the soul start to matter when we consider what life after death might be like, and whether there could ever be a human soul in separation from the body. The current debates about universal salvation depend both on issues about how far and in what sense a creature can go against the creator's will, and also about how far human identity is relational (for if one human being is definitively raised to the life of God, then a consistently relational account of the human person will maintain that all of us, in God's good time, will join him, and hence lead us to a form of universalism).

Beyond Deductive Arguments

At the risk of causing the reader irritation, this account of the Christian theology of the human person has been cast largely in interrogative terms. Following the quotation from Karl Rahner's programmatic essay, I want to hold that the study of theology consists principally in keeping alive certain questions. Its most proper fruit is not the "measurable outcome" beloved of educational bureaucrats, nor the commitment to any particular set of beliefs striven for by a fundamentalist catechetics, but rather a growth in familiarity with the questions that Christian revelation leaves unresolved, an evermore educated ignorance.

The study of theology is therefore not simply a matter of acquiring "right" answers, but an initiation into permanently insoluble questions. If we are to consider sensibly the relationship between theology and the new academic discipline of "spirituality," we need to move beyond the impasses which arise when theology is presented as a source from which spirituality may – or may not – draw "conclusions" or "implications." Too often, "theology" is presented as if it were an experimental science, delivering findings about God and God's dealings with creation in the same way that biology provides us with facts about living organisms, or that sociology yields truths about the dynamics of human life in society. The issue about spirituality and theology then appears as a dilemma: either the study of Christian spirituality is simply a subdivision within this version of Christian theology (which seems in various ways to impoverish spirituality quite intolerably); or else the study of spirituality is something other than a theological discipline (which calls into question its Christian identity or its intellectual seriousness or both). But if the facts delivered by Christian theology are there only to hold us open to wonderment, then we can approach this question of spirituality's identity in other ways.

Spirituality, at least as it is understood in the present volume, is a nascent discipline, and is still working toward establishing its identity. Its antecedents are complex. Within Roman and other Catholic traditions, there has been since at least the beginning of the twentieth century a practice of studying texts centered on prayer, written by elite figures coming from various forms of consecrated life. Inspired by the renewal of Vatican II, and especially by the idea developed in *Lumen gentium* of the "universal call to holiness," this style of study broadened. It was always the case that careful reading of a Teresa or an Ignatius or a Julian revealed that they were not simply offering treatises on consecrated life or on one particular set of Christian activities called "prayer," but rather visions of the Christian life as a whole: they were putting forward, even if in unconventional and unsystematic genres, theological accounts of what it was to be human. Vatican II empowered people really to recognize this point. Moreover, the general sense of boundaries being opened up, provoked by the Council, led to new ecumenical and interfaith contacts, and sanction was implicitly given to the thought that a more experiential approach to academic reflection on God might lead us beyond the inconvenient conflicts arising from differences in conventional theology. Protestant traditions, which had been all but founded on a rejection of the elitism implicit in older approaches to "spirituality" (Allik 1993: 784), thus came in contact with enthusiastic and energetic Catholic programs of spiritual renewal, and seem to have found in them some form of liberation from an arid intellectualism. Institutionally, programs in spirituality have developed in some autonomy from those in theology, focusing on "the study of religious experience as experience": what had been a relatively minor subdiscipline of theology somewhere in the moral and pastoral area, cultivated largely by members of religious orders, has become a field of study in its own right.

The most sustained and influential statement of the rationale behind such a vision of spirituality and theology has come from the feminist biblical scholar, Sandra M. Schneiders, in a series of important articles from the mid-1980s onwards. Schneiders, who is a leading figure in the program developed at the Graduate Theological Union in Berkeley, California, has developed her position as the conversations have continued, but she has consistently and resolutely held out for the relative independence of spirituality from theology: "I find most convincing and clarifying the position that regards spirituality as an autonomous discipline which functions in partnership and mutuality with theology" (Schneiders 1989: 689). A theological approach:

rules out, or at least prescinds from, the study of some of the most interesting phenomena on the current spirituality scene, such as the integration into Christian spirituality of elements from non-Christian sources, e.g., native spiritualities, the other world religions, or feminism, in a way that goes well beyond classical ecumenical or inter-religious dialogue. (Schneiders 1994: 11–12)

It also has a tendency, she says, to impose norms and criteria of what is to count as authentic spirituality "in a way I consider far too restrictive given the enormous variety and latitude of contemporary Christian spirituality" (1994: 12). Schneiders is evidently worried about any approach which presents "spirituality" as somehow under theology's control. What is lost in such an approach is:

> all the rest of spirituality as lived experience, all that is not susceptible of theological analysis such as the psychological, sociological, artistic, scientific, and so on. Grace, for example, is not theologically different in John of the Cross and Hildegard of Bingen. The difference in their spiritualities arises from such factors as their gender, temperaments, ages, experiential backgrounds, historical settings, and so on. These are features not amenable to theological analysis and are thus factored out in a purely theological study of these spiritualities. (Schneiders 1998: 5)

Schneiders seems to be advocating some kind of pluralist vision of the academy, in which some people would study Teresa of Avila's mystical prayer in terms of a theology of grace, whereas others – the real students of spirituality – would be asking about her mystical experience "from psychological, psychosomatic, artistic, cultural, and literary, as well as theological angles" (Schneiders 1998: 6).

The question of theology's role in the study of spirituality here appears in terms of theology making a limited contribution to an intellectual activity that is somehow wider than the purely or merely theological. If we construe spirituality simply as a part of what theology says about the human person, then we are landed with a very impoverished, deductive account of what it is to study Christian spirituality – one which seems to present John of the Cross and Hildegard, or the Verdi and Fauré requiems, as effectively equivalent, which seems absurd. It follows that we have to consider the study of spirituality as somehow a wider, more inclusive activity than the pursuit of theology.

Schneiders wants to contrast theology and spirituality on three main counts: theology imposes more or less appropriate normative criteria in a way that spirituality does not; spirituality refers to a wider range of activity than theology; spirituality is an interdisciplinary study, whereas theology is much more unitary. None of these contrasts seems fair to theology when it is done as it should be.

Schneiders is certainly justified in criticizing theologians who conduct their business as if they had reliable purchase on the object they seek to articulate, and on that basis seek to impose restrictions not only on what believers say, but also on what the Holy Spirit does. If theology is understood as a matter of providing exact descriptions, and on that basis imposing norms and criteria, then of course there is scope for understanding spirituality as somehow emancipated. There are important and all too justifiable points just below the surface here – though the fact that they need making is shameful and lamentable – about the abusive practice of religious authority and the ideologies it develops to legitimate itself. As, however, I have tried to show already, there is no reason whatever to understand theology in these terms, and indeed a good case for not doing so. That Schneiders can speak in passing of theological "analysis" is perhaps significant. Analysis, the breaking down of reality into its component parts in order to explain how it operates, is not the only mode of cognition; and the concept of theological analysis is close to being a contradiction in terms. If theology behaves as though it analyzes the action of God among us, it is locked in hopeless contradiction between its method and its subject-matter. The relationship between theology and human experience does not have to be one of hegemony and deductive constraint. Rightly practiced, theology is a tentative, interrogative enquiry.

As for the range of theology's reference, Schneiders seems to be moving from an obvious and uncontroversial point about the limitations of systematic theological discourse to a much more problematic claim about things existing outside the range of theology. If theology is about God's dealings with the world, then it must have *something* to say about everything. Moreover, "theology" (even if we grant Schneiders's implicit claim that this term does not include biblical studies and the history of Christianity) is itself unthinkable unless we see it as employing intellectual methods – for example, linguistic analysis, philosophy, history, social sciences – which are not in themselves explicitly theological. "Theology" is always theology of *something* – something which inevitably allows and demands discussion in other terms. Of its nature, *theology* is eclectic and interdisciplinary. These epithets cannot helpfully be used in an account of what distinguishes the discipline of "spirituality."

The idea of spirituality as an interdisciplinary activity is best illustrated from one of Schneiders's own examples. She is surely right that there is little significant difference between John of the Cross and Hildegard of Bingen as far as their dogmatic commitments are concerned. Moreover, even were that not true, a study of these rich, complex authors couched simply in the idiom standard in dogmatic theology would be unlikely to be fruitful; and there are indeed spectacular examples of excessively cerebral theological readings of the spiritual classics. But the distinction at stake here is not between theology and something else; it is rather the distinction between theology done in inappropriate, pedestrian fashion and theology done well and imaginatively.

John and Hildegard wrote of their own experience of transformation, and hoped that others would follow. It is for this reason primarily that they are worth studying. Within more or less formal ministries of spiritual direction and accompaniment, it may become clear that a person will be helped by one of these great authors and not by another. Or – to take another example – musical settings of the same text, and conveying the same doctrinal content, might work in dramatically different ways. The Vaughan Williams processional written for Elizabeth II's coronation functions liturgically in ways quite different from the plain tone to which Joseph Gélineau sets Psalm 99, or from the two rather different rounds used for that text at Taizé, or from the settings of that psalm in many polyphonic Renaissance motets. What is at stake here is a set of judgments about what helps people respond to God. The judgments are not just arbitrary matters of taste; we can be and become more or less competent in making them. We may often make such judgments out of instinct; moreover, if we do articulate a rationale, the terms we use may be literary, psychological, or musicological (just as our disputes about the meaning of a biblical or dogmatic text might well turn on points of Greek grammar). Nevertheless, it seems strange to suggest that such judgments are not theological. These judgments, however they may be articulated, concern how people become more open to God. If that kind of judgment about the human person is not theological, then what is? Theology, theological interpretation, is essentially eclectic.

To think, therefore, in terms of theological reflection contributing to the study of Christian spirituality may itself be problematic. The very idea of a "contribution" suggests a narrower discipline (theology) playing a role within a broader one (spirituality). This may be already to trivialize the discipline and vocation of theology, however accurately it may reflect conventional bad practice. What the question requires is a sense of the theology of the human person as enabling rather than repressive, as informing the emancipation and creativity characteristic of the new discipline called "Christian spirituality" rather than setting limits on it. Can we understand the theology of grace as normative for the study of Christian spirituality, without insisting that any manifestation of spirituality must somehow be simply deducible from theological principles? It is to this task that we now turn.

Theology as Mystagogy

The idea of a restrictively controlling theology often appears in discussions of spirituality as a benightedness from which any sane person instinctively recoils, an unreconstructed attitude which no one in their right mind takes seriously. The trouble with such summary dismissals is that they are not radical enough. They fail to bring out that such a vision of theology is a self-contradictory illusion, an empty specter, and thus they contribute to its unholy perpetuation. The first task in this section is to exorcise this ghost.

No worldview, no "theory of everything," can be coherently presented as if it were an experimental claim in Newtonian physics, verified by neutral, objective observation and measurement. We may, by our very nature, have a sense of the meaning of life, of what makes things be – but such visions *ex hypothesi* incorporate us. We participate in them "from inside"; any account of reality as a whole, and any coherent discourse about God, will be self-implicating. It will be asserting – as stoutly as any postmodernist railing against grand narratives – that the ultimate principle of meaning and coherence lies not within the human mind but within a creative agency that is greater than the human mind. And it will, of its nature, avoid exhaustive definition, because – quite apart from any considerations about the transcendence of God – it refers to an activity that is not yet finished. Its language will be formal, interrogative, waiting to be filled out with content from ongoing experience. We may assert the ultimate realities, but only as realities permanently to be disclosed. Christian revelation, therefore, has to be understood not as a set of principles from which we deduce what our lives must be, but rather as a set of promises empowering us to deal with our lives' unpredictability in peace and trust: "The clarity and ultimate definitiveness of Christian truth is the inexorability of humanity's deliverance into the mystery, and not the clarity which comes from being able to see, and see beyond, a partial element of humanity and its world" (Rahner 1976: 183; English translation 1978: 181).

Moreover, if Christianity is about God-with-us, then any account of how we respond to God will be itself an aspect of the doctrine of God. As Karl Rahner has taught us, we cannot speak about God without speaking of humanity; nor can we speak of humanity without speaking of God (Rahner 1966: 43; English translation 1972: 28). One of Rahner's early prayers makes the point starkly:

> you, Father, have spoken your Word into my being through and through, the Word that was before all things, more real than they, the Word in which alone all reality and all life first comes to be . . . This Word, in which alone there is life, has become through your action, God of grace, my experience. (1938: 45, my translation)

At least on Christian assumptions (how far this point is *dependent* on Christian revelation is an interesting question that we must leave unexplored), there can be no disjunction between the doctrine of God and human experience. The reality of God happens in and through humanity; thus the doctrine of God is always and forever the doctrine of human experience, and vice versa.

Once we consider what must be the case about any coherent discourse regarding ultimate reality, conventional accounts of the relationship between spirituality and theology appear in a new light. The reason why spirituality is a self-implicating discipline, open to the contingencies and particularities of human experience, has nothing to do with spirituality being a special kind of theological discipline: such features will characterize *any* sensible discourse about the ultimate nature of things. The interrogative account of the theology of the human person offered above no longer appears as a form of apophatic special pleading, but simply falls into place: the problem has been the captivating hold of Newtonian physics on our sense of what counts as knowledge, and its tendency to see the declarative statement as the normative form of truth. Moreover, once we abandon the idea that empirical observation can serve as the paradigm for all knowledge, then we can also conceive the normative role of metaphysical discourse as something other than providing a source for deductions. It articulates, rather, the context of meaning within which the free and unpredictable, and therefore the manifestations of spirituality in the full sense, can occur.

The picture emerging is therefore one of a kind of duality in theological truth: regulative principle and particular, unpredictable manifestation (we might speak of the charismatic). Theology is not there to impose order on chaos, but rather to articulate, and thereby facilitate, a free and autonomous process. Theology cannot coherently proceed without being open to the concerns driving the study of spirituality: the object of theology is precisely the mystery to which human beings are still responding, in which human beings are still participating. Theology is a unity-in-distinction: an interplay of simple, generally valid theory and exuberant, unique expression; of biblical pattern in Jesus and indefinitely many and diverse continuations in the Spirit; of regulative principle and ongoing experience. To adapt, not very originally, a Kantian turn of phrase: doctrine without spirituality is empty; spirituality without doctrine is blind (Endean 2001: 246–51).

In an ideal world, no one would be speaking about bringing theology into closer contact with spirituality because both activities and both disciplines are concerned with the same reality: the mystery of God among us. The most we are talking about is a difference in emphasis. If much is being made of the distinction, then at least one of these intellectual activities, if not both, is being pursued dysfunctionally. The study of both theology and spirituality is a matter of mystagogy, of being led to appropriate, to understand, and on that basis to accept in freedom, the reality of our lives. Theological constructions stand in essential need of ongoing renewal through subversion – a renewal to which what is now being presented as a new discipline called "spirituality" can make important contributions. Such renewal may on occasion shock conventional piety, but it remains an eminently theological act. It is only because distorted and impoverished accounts of theology have taken hold that the study of spirituality has come to appear as something different in kind.

The Doctrines of Grace and the Study of Spirituality

We are now in a position directly to face the question about how the dogmatic theological reflection about grace can inform the study of spirituality. Perhaps the distinction to be made is not that between theology and spirituality – given the assumptions about theology developed here – but rather between doctrine and spirituality. Within the one intellectual process of mystagogy (let us call *that* "theology"), there is a place for a rough division between approaches to the one theological mystery of God's self-gift among us focusing primarily on regulative sources and principles on the one hand (let us use another word, namely "doctrine"), and, on the other, those which begin from ongoing experience (spirituality).

Informally and tentatively, I would identify three principal contributions which the study of the doctrinal tradition regarding the human person can make to the understanding of Christian spirituality: the *articulation of a context*, the *concern with truth*, and the *extension of sympathy*.

The first of these, the *articulation of a context*, can be named briefly. When Eckhart or Ruusbroec explores the union of the soul with God and uses the vocabulary of identity, when Julian writes about sin in ways that seem to challenge Augustinian convention, then a student will need to be aware of the standard doctrinal treatments of such topics in order even to recognize that something significant is being said. Conversely, and more critically, when the student of Ignatian spirituality comes across triumphalist talk of "finding God in all things" as a Jesuit invention, a broader theological awareness will remind him or her of biblical texts such as the promise of Matthew's Jesus that he will always be there when disciples are gathered in his name.

The question of the *concern with truth* may be nuanced and relativized in the light of what has been said earlier about the need to understand theological statements in their human context, but it is not fully removed. Expressions of spirituality make truth claims that can be argued about and evaluated. Gerard Manley Hopkins's masterpiece, "The Wreck of the Deutschland," expresses a sense of humanity being held by the providence of God amid disaster:

I admíre thee, máster of the tídes,
Of the Yóre-flood, of the yéar's fáll;
    The recúrb and the recóvery of the gúlf's sídes,
The gírth of it and the whárf of it and the wáll;
    Stánching, quénching ócean of a mótionable mínd;
Gróund of béing, and gránite of it: pást áll
    Grásp Gód, thróned behínd
Déath with a sóvereignty that héeds but hídes, bódes but abídes;

As such, it differs from the vision implicit in a work like Benjamin Britten's *War Requiem*, which juxtaposes the Requiem Mass with some poems of Wilfred Owen in a statement that seems far more ambiguous and agnostic. As Owen comes across a Calvary at a cross-roads in Flanders – and as Britten incorporates it into the *Agnus Dei* – we are reminded of Jesus's teaching, but the question of hope and providence is barely articulated:

One ever hangs where shelled roads part.
In this war He too lost a limb,
But His disciples hide apart;
And now the Soldiers bear with Him.

Near Golgotha strolls many a priest,
And in their faces there is pride
That they were flesh-marked by the Beast
By whom the gentle Christ's denied.

The scribes on all the people shove
And bawl allegiance to the state,
But they who love the greater love
Lay down their life; they do not hate.

In the imaginative world of the *War Requiem*, Christian hope is evoked but not affirmed. The question of Owen's "Futility" is left unanswered: "O what made fatuous sunbeams toil / To break earth's sleep at all?"

It would be harebrained to suggest that the question of which of these visions is true is a simple one, or that a study of these two expressions of spirituality should focus primarily on it. Both spiritual masterpieces can broaden our human sympathy and sensitivity, and enhance our feeling for language, music, and sound, in ways that remain valid whatever we make of the theological claims being made or implied. But there is nevertheless a theological issue here to be discussed, and one which will play at least a small part in any discussion of the spirituality expressed. Loosely, we might relate it to the discussion of the nature of justification during the Western Reformation. Is our confidence in the grace of Christ such that we can speak, despite all the immediate evidence to the contrary, of a goodness that is truly ours and that eradicates sin definitively? Or is our position more paradoxical, dialectical – a sense of being at one and the same time destroyed and whole? The point being made here is minimal: the doctrinal truth question is relevant to the study of spirituality. This is not to imply that the doctrinal disagreement can be definitively resolved, still less is it to deny the importance of setting any possible resolution of it in a richer human context. Moreover, the need remains to find creative ways of reformulating the doctrinal issue as a means toward overcoming the sense of impasse. The point is simply that truth claims – complex and irresoluble though they are – cannot simply be neglected in the process of education that is the study of spirituality.

The third role I want to identify is perhaps the most important: the study of doctrine as a way of *cultivating the range of human sympathy* that is an absolute requirement for the sensitive study of Christian spirituality. To repeat: the truths of doctrine are primarily matters of interrogation and admiration rather than of statement. The event of Christ complicates rather than simplifies our self-understanding: he reveals to us our involvement in an aboriginal calamity of sin which we must somehow struggle to integrate with what science tells us about the origins of the universe; he complicates our understanding of human identity by revealing its compatibility with divine identity, and hence opening up a hornet's nest of problems about freedom; he commits us to staying with, and not dismissing, what would otherwise be impossible dilemmas about the survival of death. The study of the doctrinal tradition has a regulative function in disciplining our tendency to settle for over-simple, over-tidy solutions to such questions.

Moreover, we theologize on the basis of Christianity, not Jesuanity – this Jesus is connected with the mystery creating and sustaining the whole universe. That principle generates a central theological task: the exploration and overcoming of how conventional understandings of divine action in our lives implicitly restrict it (to the explicitly Christian rather than the graced creation; the monastic or clerical rather than the whole people of God; the interior life rather than the messinesses of the political and sexual, and so on). Familiarity with the doctrinal tradition should enable us to extend it in new contexts, and respond to them in ways that are innovative, and as such, authentically traditional. When a feminist theologian appeals to "women's experience" in order to question prevailing conceptions of what counts as sin or as wholeness, she is professing theology, not abandoning it – and she is only in a position to do this because she has appropriated the tradition well enough to continue it rather than merely prate it or reject it. Given that the study of spirituality will tend to focus on areas where the tradition is being extended and renewed – thus in our own day on such topics as gender, interfaith relations, the links between theology, economics, and social systems – the study of the doctrinal tradition will be an important resource precisely as it shows that doctrines are not fixed entities, but rather expressions of an emancipatory dynamic. Hence fidelity consists in a continuing exploration, rather than in mere repetition.

The temptation when reading the tortuous formality of the treatment of grace in Thomas Aquinas's *Summa theologiae* is to translate its paradoxes into the idiom of testimony. What he means, we think, is more immediately expressed by evoking a statement such as Paul's "it is no longer I who live, but it is Christ who lives in me" (Gal. 2: 20). Yet there are important advantages in staying with the more austere, metaphysical idiom. It holds us open to the possibility that the reality it evokes might take place in ways unfamiliar to us, outside the conventional, beyond the range of our descriptive sympathy. Ignatius of Loyola was making this sort of point when he encouraged the one giving the Spiritual Exercises to be boring:

The second is that the person who gives to another the way and ordering of meditating and contemplating must narrate faithfully the story of the meditation or contemplation in question, just going over the points, with brief or summary development; for if the person who is contemplating takes the true foundation of the story, working on it and thinking about it on their own, and finds something which makes them understand or feel for the story a little more (whether this arises through their own thoughts or whether it is due to the understanding being enlightened by divine power), it is of more spiritual relish and fruit than if the one who gives the Exercises had explained and expanded the meaning of the story a great deal; for it is not the knowing of much that contents and satisfies the soul, but the feeling and relish for things from inside. (Ignatius of Loyola 1996, no. 2)

"From inside" – this translation of the Spanish *interior* brings out how Ignatius seeks to understand the Christian mystery as a participant, as one who is drawn up into its movement, a movement that we cannot comprehend and view from outside, but only take part in, following into the unknown where it leads us. In such a perspective, there is also value for a classical metaphysical idiom, precisely because of its dryness, its distinction between the underlying reality and the contingencies of its particular realization. For all the associations of the metaphysics with Dead White European Males, the result can be a holism and inclusiveness that makes much advocacy of such values appear provincial.

The "Christian" in "Christian Spirituality"

Central to this essay has been a deep dissatisfaction with the assumptions underlying much contemporary discussion about the relationship between theology and spirituality. In suggesting three roles which the study of the doctrinal tradition regarding grace and the human person plays in the study of Christian spirituality, I have insisted that the topic cannot properly be studied unless one develops a richer and more subtle account of what it is to do theology than those which scholars in spirituality often take for granted.

A major issue at stake here is the way in which the object of study conditions the method of study. One cannot simply transpose the model of knowledge appropriate to discussion of particular things in the world to discourse about a God who is not an object but rather the sustaining context of all that is – including our very act of knowing – and of the unknown future. Metaphysical considerations – quite apart from legitimate Barthian concerns regarding revelation – require us to develop a self-implicating "'theological' theology" (Webster 1998). It is because such a vision of theology is so rarely realized satisfactorily that the study of spirituality has developed in a healthy counter-reaction, a counter-reaction marked by ambivalence about its theological identity.

We might conclude by extending the point. The phrase "the study of Christian spirituality" is in fact ambiguous in its reference. The structure of the phrase suggests that "Christian" qualifies the *object* of a study which in its method is confessionally neutral. Were that vision to be pursued consistently, the result would be a descriptive discipline;

theological language would be subject to decoding in terms of some other, more fundamental category. Religious expressions are some kind of superstructure, and at least potentially a source of illusion. Christian scholars would establish their academic credentials and demonstrate their openness to learning by a willingness to set their Christianity methodologically aside, and to embrace a perspective that was somehow wider, more neutral and objective.

There are important and legitimate values in such a descriptive, religious-studies approach to the material, but the actual practice of contemporary scholars of Christian spirituality seems to me to be motivated rather differently. Minimally, few Christian scholars in practice wish to restrict their interest to expressions of spirituality developed by Christians. More generally, they are moving toward what we might term "the Christian study of spirituality," one in which "Christian" specifies the method and goal of interpretation, and where the range of objects is left unrestricted, as is only proper to any discipline about a God who creates all things. In this version of the study of spirituality, Christian theology provides the ultimate categories of understanding; and other forms of discourse – social-scientific, literary, the theologies of what Christians call "other religions" – are used in order to help us use the Christian terms properly. Thus we might use Freudian theory not to unmask the Christian illusion, but rather to distinguish adult Christian commitment from the slavery of the superego. We are not replacing Christian moral discourse with something more accurate, but rather drawing on the wisdom of other disciplines in order to deepen and purify an understanding of reality articulated principally in the categories of Christian theology. Moreover, the logical connection between the ultimate identity of things and their role in God's dealings with the creation generates an account of learning as transformative: the self-implicating nature of the discipline indicates not academic questionability but rather an ultimacy to which the sciences of disinterested neutrality are secondary. The freedom characteristic of the academy lies, not in the bracketing of Christianity, but rather in commitment to a maximally generous account of the Christian significance of all that exists. This will generate a permanent attitude of challenge to prevailing constructions of the religious; academic study will serve to challenge the all-too-human tendency toward idolatry, the tendency to restrict the holy to the familiar (a tendency notably present in many conventional Christologies and ecclesiologies). The study of spirituality, in this sense, is marked by a permanent openness to a God who is always greater than our constructions, and who is calling us, through our study, to transformation.

These two models of the study of spirituality are, of course, ideal abstractions. Neither exists anywhere in full purity, and inevitably scholars will be influenced by both. But it perhaps needs to be recognized that the two approaches are radically different; and we might speculate that the methodological questions about the identity of "Christian spirituality" as a discipline can be traced back to ambivalences about the different theoretical approaches they represent (Endean 1995). Though both models are coherent, this essay has been written in the spirit of the second: it has insisted that the categories of Christian theology in general, and of the Christian theology of the human person in particular, remain the foundational categories for the (Christian) study of spirituality. That second model, with its commitment to letting Christianity help define what counts as a discipline, has to live with the risks of fideism. It may stoutly criticize any particular exercise of Christian authority, but it cannot totally abandon the idea that God speaks within human history in ways to which we must simply surrender. It involves an act of trust in the value of a particular tradition, even if that trust takes the form only of a hope against hope. Breadth of mind, cross-cultural openness, imaginative sympathy are vital qualities for creative work in the field of Christian spirituality. But – to borrow from Karl Marx – it is not enough to interpret the world in various ways; the point is to change it. Only if the study of spirituality is pursued from within a theological and confessional tradition can it be transformative.

References

Allik, T. 1993: Protestant spiritualities. In M. Downey (ed.), *The New Dictionary of Catholic Spirituality*, pp. 784–90. Collegeville, MN: Liturgical Press.

Endean, P. 1995: Spirituality and the university. *The Way Supplement* 84, 87–99.

—— 2001: *Karl Rahner and Ignatian Spirituality*. Oxford: Oxford University Press.

Ignatius of Loyola 1996: *Spiritual Exercises*, trans. E. Mullan. In D. L. Fleming (ed.), *Draw Me into your Friendship: The Spiritual Exercises – A Literal Translation and a Contemporary Reading*. St Louis: Institute of Jesuit Sources.

Lash, N. 1973: *Change in Focus: A Study of Doctrinal Change in Continuity*. London: Sheed and Ward.

Rahner, K. 1938: *Worte ins Schweigen*. Innsbruck: Felizian Rauch.

—— 1954: Über den Versuch eines Aufrisses einer Dogmatik. In *Schriften zur Theologie*, vol. 1, pp. 9–28 (Einsiedeln: Benziger), trans. C. Ernst in *Theological Investigations*, vol. 1. London: Darton, Longman, and Todd.

—— 1966: Theologie und Anthropologie. In *Schriften zur Theologie*, vol. 8, pp. 43–65, trans. G. Harrison in *Theological Investigations*, vol. 9, pp. 28–45. London: Darton, Longman, and Todd, 1972.

—— 1976: *Grundkurs des Glaubens: Einführung in den Begriff des Christentums* (Freiburg: Herder), trans. W. V. Dych as *Foundations of Christian Faith: An Introduction to the Idea of Christianity*. London: Darton, Longman, and Todd, 1978.

Schneiders, S. M. 1989: Spirituality in the academy. *Theological Studies* 50, 676–97.

—— 1994: A hermeneutical approach to the study of Christian spirituality. *Christian Spirituality Bulletin* 2 (1), 9–14.

—— 1998: The study of Christian spirituality: contours and dynamics of a discipline. *Christian Spirituality Bulletin* 6 (1), 1–12.

Vass, G. 1968: On the historical structure of Christian truth. *Heythrop Journal* 9, 129–42, 274–89.

Webster, J. 1998. *Theological Theology*. Oxford: Clarendon Press.

CHAPTER 14

The Church as Context for Christian Spirituality

David Lonsdale

That the church *is* a context for Christian spirituality may seem obvious enough for anyone who knows anything about the church at all. After all, that is what religious communities and institutions do: they offer spiritual traditions and corporate settings which foster their own brand of "spirituality." But once one goes beyond that to ask *how in practice* the Christian church is a context for spirituality, and what "spirituality" in this context might mean, the matter becomes more complex. Several elements contribute to this complexity. One is the fact that "Christian spirituality" as a discipline using modern theological methods is still in its infancy (Sheldrake 1995: 32–55). Readers of this volume need to be aware that in this area, in comparison with other branches of theological study, only a small body of good contemporary scholarship exists. (My research for this essay has not unearthed any recently published book which addresses directly the topic of the church as context for spirituality.) In the Anglophone world, there is only one professional association (the Society for the Study of Christian Spirituality) for scholars and teachers in Christian spirituality. The younger teachers and scholars now getting into their academic stride are only the first generation to emerge from graduate school fully trained in the study of spirituality as a modern theological discipline. And the very few academic journals available, apart from those published by Roman Catholic religious orders, whose focus tends to be their own form of Christian spirituality, are relatively young. A second complicating factor is a certain conceptual vagueness about the meaning of the word "spirituality" in current usage, both popular and academic. Thirdly, it is now commonplace to refer to the contemporary world as one of religious and cultural plurality and diversity. This global diversity includes forms of belief and practice, both religious and non-religious "spiritualities" one might say, which are not only very varied but also, in some cases, in conflict with each other. Christianity likewise embraces a variety of churches, spiritual traditions, and patterns of belief and practice – some of which, on closer examination, reveal themselves as mutually contradictory and incompatible. The challenge, therefore, is how to speak of Christianity and spirituality in ways which, on the one hand, recognize and respect difference and, on the other, succeed in identifying what is distinctive about the church as setting for spirituality in a context marked by complex diversity.

This essay makes use of the notion of Christianity as a "school," proposed by Nicholas Lash (1988: 258). If that metaphor is valid, then it might be possible to identify some key aspects of the "pedagogy" – a way of both learning and teaching – that is characteristic of the church. "Teaching," in this case, does not primarily mean giving instruction or preaching, but rather a more profound process of formation of a community and of persons in a community. Lecturing, catechesis, sermons, encyclical letters may all be part of the church's pedagogy, but I want to suggest that the source of all that kind of activity, the heart of the church's learning and teaching precisely as church, lies elsewhere.

Speaking of Spirituality

One aspect of diversity which affects the subject of this essay is the slippery nature of the meaning of the word "spirituality." In the midst of considerable conceptual vagueness, it is possible to detect two different but related meanings in contemporary popular and academic discussions. More traditionally, "spirituality" in Christian contexts tends to refer to those patterns of worship and prayer, action and relationship that are characteristic of a particular faith community, together with the beliefs, doctrines, and attitudes from which they spring. "Spirituality" in this sense usually implies membership of a faith community or religious institution. It points to the experience and life of a community as it is ordered by its fundamental beliefs. In its traditional usage, then, "Christian spirituality" typically refers to the outworking of belief in the life of the church; in other words, life in the Spirit in fidelity to the Word to the glory of the Father.

Contemporary discussions of spirituality in faith communities tend to recognize that personal and communal identities are shaped over long periods of time through relationships. We become persons through being related and exist as persons only in and through such relationships. Being related to the physical environment, family, significant people, groups, communities, churches, and whole societies is not something added on to the personal identity of an individual previously shaped in isolation. They are the means by which individual identity is created. Identities do not come to be or continue to exist except in and through relationships. The spirituality of the members of a faith community is shaped over time by inhabiting both a particular religious landscape and those other interlocking non-religious landscapes in which their lives are partly spent.

This kind of spirituality, rooted in a faith community, often has clear ethical, social, and political dimensions. In the biblical world and through much of Christian history (as in Islam and Judaism), a separation of the "inner life" from speech and action in the "external" world, and the idea that faith could be isolated from social, political, and economic thought and action, would have been incomprehensible. In those times, on the contrary, it was clearly recognized that a community's faith makes certain ethical demands, in regard to social justice and the conduct of politics, both on the community as a whole and on its members individually. A separation of "inner" and "outer," "vertical" and "horizontal" dimensions of life and the restriction of spirituality to an "inner," "private" sphere are both comparatively modern and by no means universal in contemporary Christianity.

William Stringfellow noted a different meaning for the word "spirituality" as far back as 1984. He pointed to the vagueness and confusion of much contemporary talk on this topic by compiling a list of meanings of the word current in his time. These included: "stoic attitudes, occult phenomena, the practice of so-called mind control . . . interior journeys, an appreciation of eastern religions, multifarious pious exercises . . . assorted dietary regimens, meditation, jogging cults . . . contemplation, abstinence, hospitality, a vocation of poverty . . ." (quoted in Leech 1992: 3).

This use of the word "spirituality" has emerged relatively recently. Some of its characteristic features may be identified. First of all, "spirituality" of this kind is not necessarily linked with any particular set of religious beliefs or commitments, nor does it imply belonging to any faith community or institution. Indeed, some of its advocates view detachment from religious beliefs or community as its virtue and strength. Daniel Hardy recalls his daughter saying, "What I admire about Sheila is that she is spiritual but not religious" (2001: 95). Secondly, the usage reflects a widespread view of spirituality, not as a particular way of living in every sphere, but as referring to "the spiritual dimension," a realm of life in its own right. Thirdly, on this understanding, spirituality is widely regarded as belonging to the area of "private life," a matter of personal choice which is largely unconnected with spheres of social concern, politics, and economics. "Spirituality" in this sense, it may be argued, is rooted in and reinforces a type of individualism that pervades much of Western, and particularly American, culture.

This understanding of "spirituality" seems to claim moral neutrality for itself. It appears to rest on an assumption that there exists an elusive, generic something, which can be called "spirituality" and which may be embodied in the speech and actions of both religious and non-religious people, atheists as well as believers, Christians and people of other faiths, witches and Christian mystics. In this context, Adolf Hitler and Francis of Assisi may be cited as examples of "evil" spirituality and "good" spirituality, respectively.

It is difficult to avoid the thought that the key explanatory model at work here is that of the marketplace, the relationship between consumer and producer. "Spirituality" is marketed as a product. Consumers recognize that they have personal spiritual preferences and needs and are able to pick and choose the spiritual "product" that suits them. This suggests a picture of individuals, acting more or less in isolation from each other, choosing at will from a range of "spiritual" beliefs, attitudes, and practices. This also has a very "postmodern" ethos: a sense that personal identity, the self, has no more than a fleeting, insubstantial existence, and may be deconstructed and reconstructed relatively quickly and painlessly, by the adoption or rejection of certain "spiritual" practices.

Perhaps the most profound difference between these two approaches to an understanding of spirituality lies in their basic orientation. Certain faith communities, those of Judaism, Islam, and Christianity, for example, have always recognized what might be called the supremacy of God. Since God constitutes and sustains the universe and humanity within it, human beings are not their own master. In these traditions, "spirituality" is a human response to the mystery of God, one aspect of which is humanity's recognition of its own dependence. Communities and individual believers find "salvation," however that may be understood, by giving glory to God by word and action, in worship, prayer, and the ordering of life.

Moreover, much of the Christian spiritual tradition presents the journey of growth in God's truth and holiness as a matter of relinquishing all claims to self-sufficiency and of acknowledging that ultimately human wellbeing lies in surrendering in love to the embrace of a forgiving, reconciling, healing God, after the pattern of the life and death of Jesus. Paradoxically, in that surrender, we find ourselves, as Nicholas Lash puts it, "not slaves but sons and daughters, brothers and sisters" (1986: 192).

By contrast, it is hard to avoid the suspicion that the second type of spirituality discussed here is not so much a surrender in love as an instrument for control in the interests of individual wellbeing and personal fulfillment. It may be argued that therapeutic processes that see "spirituality" as a means toward self-fulfillment, recovery from addiction, or psychological growth run the risk of making relationship with God into a human instrument to be manipulated. If this is in fact the case, then there is a danger that "spirituality" becomes no more than yet another technology, another instance of instrumental reason seeking to control personal environment, "body, mind, spirit," health, and ultimately destiny. When this "spirituality" does profess belief in God, it runs the risk of instrumentalizing a God who, in any event, often seems to bear little resemblance to the unfathomable mystery of Judaism, Islam, or Christianity, the "Lord of life" who cannot be possessed or manipulated.

The emergence of spirituality as a distinct subject of study in the academy, in the United States and elsewhere, has prompted attempts to arrive at a generic definition of "spirituality" which seeks to encompass all supposed instances of it, Christian and non-Christian, religious and non-religious. The notion, however, that there is, as it were, an "essence" or " common core" of something which we might call "spirituality" and which is instantiated in different historical circumstances, both Christian and non-Christian, religious and not, is very questionable. For one thing, supposed examples of an "essential" spirituality often appear, on less superficial examination, to be very different, so that there is no possibility of a comparison of like with like. Any attempt to reduce all manifestations of a supposed "common core" of spirituality is also open to the ethical objection that it fails, in the end, to respect difference and to allow what is strange and other to be strange and other. It runs the risk of claiming that particularities are not in fact differences but only more of the same. Hence "strangers" find themselves diminished, patronized, and forbidden to be themselves, having been reduced to yet another instance of a common, "human spirituality."

Christian Diversity and Unity

The later decades of the twentieth century saw a shift in approaches to the theology and doctrine of the church. Nicholas M. Healy (2000) refers to more traditional ways of speaking about the church among theologians as "blueprint ecclesiology." This tends to focus on exploring the images of the church used by biblical writers. It stresses that the church is an "invisible" reality (a mystery) as well as a "visible" reality (a human community, society, or institution) and tends to be prescriptive, in that it starts from an ideal and moves from there to what the church ought to be. Dissatisfaction with this approach in terms of both method and content has led to calls for the theology of the church to focus on the actual historical reality of the church as the starting-point for theological reflection (Healy 2000; Hardy 2001).

It is impossible, in a short essay, to do justice to the richness and complexity of the different patterns of worship and prayer, thinking, feeling, and acting which go to make up the forms of spirituality inherited, fostered, and practiced in such a wide and varied range of churches and communities. So striking is the diversity that it is sometimes difficult to detect what they have in common. Theological differences between the churches and traditions are well documented (for example, Avis 2002). Theological and historical changes have also given rise to differences of ecclesial experience: what might the understanding and experience of "church" and "spirituality" of an Orthodox farm worker on the Russian steppe and a wealthy lawyer in a Pentecostal church in Hollywood or downtown Chicago possibly have in common? Whilst it is obviously true that all Christian churches are in some sense united by devotion to Jesus and reading the Bible, closer examination reveals profound differences in, for example, how Jesus is understood, how devotion to Jesus is conceived and lived out in practice, and how the Bible is read in the various churches. All of these are signs that different churches nourish significantly different forms of Christian spirituality, some of them mutually incompatible, and the nourishing itself takes different forms.

Within this diversity, however, it is possible to detect a common tradition. Rowan Williams (2000) has developed the idea that, in biblical accounts, "revelation" is an event that generates for a people or community new possibilities for human living, which they were not aware of before and which they attribute to an initiative on God's part. So, in the Exodus, God's action of liberation opens up for the freed community new possibilities for life in relationship with God. Likewise, the disciples of Jesus came to understand that the events they had witnessed had also disclosed new possibilities for human life. They came to believe that the possibilities generated were not for one community alone but were offered to the whole of humanity. The church, therefore, may be understood as the community that professes faith in the God who is the source of these possibilities and which, in response, witnesses to them and works to realize them both in its own life and in the wider world. The church is thus the people of the new creation. "So to come to be 'in Christ,' to belong with Jesus, involves a far-reaching reconstruction of one's humanity . . . a new identity in a community of reciprocal love and complementary service, whose potential horizons are universal" (Williams 2000: 134). Baptism initiates a person into this community.

In the beginning, the church understood itself as the continuation of God's people of Israel, the people whose corporate life is constituted by their covenant with God. The covenant comes to expression in their history, their common worship and Scriptures, and in the shaping of their social life. For Christians, it is in Christ, in the events of his life, death, and resurrection, and in the "sending of the Spirit," that the church is constituted as the new Israel, and God's further purposes for human society are disclosed: that all human beings and nations might be brought into unity.

Historically, therefore, the question of the spirituality proper to Christians begins with the people of God in the Old Testament covenant. While still the continuation of the covenant people of God, the church sees itself as owing its special character to the foundational events of this people in the life, death, and resurrection of Jesus Christ. The church has, therefore, an implicit trinitarian basis: it is constituted by God's Word and empowered and guided by God's Spirit.

Liturgy: The Pedagogy of the School of Spirituality

The next step in the argument of this essay is the exploration of two ideas: first, that the activity proper to the church is "liturgy," and, secondly, that this liturgy is the center and source of the church's formation as a school of discipleship. Michael Barnes reflects on these ideas extensively in the context of the dialogue of religions (2002: 133–56, 182–204), and this part of the present essay is especially indebted to his work. Etymologically, liturgy is "the work of the people" in worship and celebration. It is also important to note, however, that "before becoming a 'work' of worship and celebration, liturgy is *God's* work, what is accomplished *in* the community of faith before it is accomplished *by* it" (Barnes 2002: 199).

It is obvious that the forms of liturgy found along a spectrum of Christian churches and groups today differ considerably. Complex historical and theological factors through two millennia have brought about major differences of form and emphasis today between liturgies in different Christian communities. A distinction between "churches of the Eucharist" and "churches of the Word" and "churches of the Spirit" can be a help toward clarification, so long as it is not taken too rigidly. Some churches hold the celebration of the Eucharist, the Lord's Supper, as the center of the church's life and the source of its theology and activity. Other communities tend to view reading, studying, and reflection on the Bible, together with Bible-based preaching, as the heart of the church's life and spirituality. In a third group, it is rather recalling and renewing the work of the Spirit, as told in the stories of Pentecost and Acts, that is the heart of the church and source of its mission.

In spite of these differences, each Christian community, in some shape or form, gathers to recall and renew, celebrate and ponder its own foundation in the life, death, and resurrection of Jesus and the sending of the Spirit. This, whether it happens in the church as worship or elsewhere as study and explication, is liturgy, and it is the distinctive activity of the church. Christian liturgy means returning to the Christian story of the life, death, and resurrection of Jesus, remembering that story, retelling it (even reliving it), celebrating it with gratitude and praise, pondering it. The heart of the church's pedagogy, the means by which the church and its members are schooled in the beliefs, attitudes, and practices which constitute Christian identity and discipleship – in a word, Christian "spirituality" – lies here. This activity, "the work of the people," is the heart and source of the church's pedagogy as a "school," the center of its formation of persons through discipleship of Jesus from which all other catechesis and religious and theological education flow.

A School of the Affections and Desires

It is important to note that the formation offered by liturgy, especially in the celebration of the Eucharist, is not simply intellectual, a formation of the mind. Liturgy is a school for the whole person, the community as a whole. In particular, it offers a schooling of the affections and desires to remake a person in the image of Christ.

The church is always beset by the pressure of unruly affections and desires. Siren voices, both within and outside, appeal to propensities within the church that threaten its integrity, and the story of the church, both past and present, witnesses to its weakness, the ease with which unruly impulses may have their day. The trinitarian basis of the church and the trinitarian dynamic of the liturgy – giving glory to the Father in fidelity to the Word and in the power of the Spirit – offer a clue to sources of disorder in the church (as well as sources of good order). One impulse to disorder is that which moves the church to forget that its God is a welcoming, forgiving, reconciling, healing God, and to use its power, either toward its own members or those outside, in contradiction to this image of God. Another unruly desire would draw the church to forget its grounding in God's free, gratuitous self-gift in the Word and thus to claim self-sufficiency in its own speech, power, structures, and institutions. A third impulse is to forget that it is dependent upon the Spirit to be able to speak God's truth and draw people into God's holiness; to forget the need for openness to the Spirit in humility; to forget that it does not know the future and so needs to be receptive, willing to learn. There is, in addition, the lure for the church of ignoring its call to fidelity to the Word and so becoming attached to something other than the Word. This represents the attractiveness of being identified with the "world," to be no different from the societies and cultures in which it inevitably lives, insofar as they are in conflict with fidelity to the Word. This list does not exhaust the potential for disorder in the church; it does, however, illustrate that the potential is always present.

In these conditions the church has to allow itself, over and over again, to be schooled in its affections and desires by the mystery of the life, death, and resurrection of Jesus; in other words, formation in faith, hope, and love. By repeatedly recalling, celebrating, and pondering the Christian story, the church is formed in faith in a God of welcome and hospitality, forgiveness and healing. When it faithfully remembers Jesus's surrender of himself to God in the face of death, the church is schooled in hope against hope for the fulfillment of God's promises for humanity in an unknown future threatened by confusion and violence, loss and death. The God whom Christians worship is also the source of the love by which they wish to live. In the liturgy, Christians recall and renew the love of the welcoming, forgiving, and healing God and the real cost of love made evident in the life and death of Jesus. And, as Barnes (2002) also highlights, since the Last Supper of Jesus points forward to a meal which Jesus promises to share in the kingdom of the Father, Christian liturgy also points forward to the future "in anticipation of the abundance of God's self-giving." Liturgy "is not reducible to a human recollecting of Jesus; it is rather the process of continuing participation in the foundational event – the forming of Christ in the corporate and individual life of believers" (Williams 2000: 140).

In liturgy, therefore, the church's affections and desires are shaped and redirected through a formation in faith, hope, and love. This is the heart of the church and source of its knowledge, motivation, and energy as context for spirituality. Whatever else a church may do by way of instruction, catechesis, education, or formation in discipleship has its source here in retelling, celebrating, and pondering the Christian story.

Formation of a School of Discernment

What this amounts to is the formation of the church as a school of Christian discernment. The purpose of this discernment is to learn and live out, in the power of the Spirit, those forms of Christian discipleship that arise out of, on the one hand, the church's fidelity to the Word and, on the other, its understanding of the needs of the world. In order to carry this out, the church needs to be contemplative. By "contemplative," I understand an attentive engagement, a paying attention, which has both an active aspect, in the sense of being curious, speaking, asking questions, and also, and especially, a passive, receptive dimension, in the sense of being willing not to speak, allowing oneself to learn, to be schooled or shaped in a certain way. Moreover, in order to be true to itself and to its God, the church must turn its contemplative gaze in two directions. In the first place, the church needs to pay attention, day by day, year by year, both in its liturgy and in prayer, meditation, study, and so forth, to the mystery of God, wherever that mystery is present. To use a different sense, the church needs to have a disciple's ear in order to learn acquaintance with God and to be formed by the Word in the power of the Spirit. At the same time, if the church is to serve the world as well as witness to the Word, it needs to be acquainted with the world, in order to be able to create and live out daily, under the guidance of the Spirit, those forms of Christian discipleship which are appropriate to the needs of particular times and places, communities and persons. The church, therefore, needs to contemplate the world, and in so doing to draw on all forms of human enquiry that will deepen its understanding of the world in its particulars.

Disorderly impulses in the school of discernment

The church as school of discernment is not free from threats of sinful and ultimately destructive disorder, whether actual or potential, in relation to the Word and the Spirit. One impulse, in the face of a confusing, hostile, and dangerous world, is to attempt to meet the challenges of the present by simply repeating the tradition in the words of the tradition. "Tradition" in this context may mean the Bible or particular doctrinal formulas. Here is the same impulse as that which wants to make certain forms of ecclesial devotion, ritual, order, structure, or institution into something absolute and unchangeable. The difficulty with this is that, in terms of language, it seems to suggest that a particular form of human speech about God is not provisional, partial, and halting, but wholly adequate; that it has captured all that there is to say of the incomprehensible mystery of God. In terms of ecclesial structures and rituals, this position suggests that the "new creation" disclosed in the Word is already achieved; particular rituals or ecclesial structures are complete as mediations of the unfathomable mystery of God.

In fact, the church's speech about God is always provisional, stammering; the language of faith is always lame, halting, imprecise, open to change. Likewise, the possibilities for humanity disclosed by the Word, for which the church is witness and sign, are not known in advance. The church does not possess a plan of how God's promises are to work out in the future. It contemplates the mystery of God spoken in the Word and bears witness to what it finds there. And it contemplates the world in all its particularity. But it also recognizes that it does not know how God's hopes and intentions are going to be realized in particular conditions of time and place.

A second form of unruly impulse, both within and outside the church, which affects its effectiveness as a school of discernment, is the attraction of the antinomian charismatic tendency. This is the impulse to place uncritical trust in enthusiasm, the power or intoxication of certain religious experiences as self-evidently the voice of the Spirit of God.

The trinitarian "grammar" of Christian discernment

Both these disorderly trends lay themselves open to the criticism that they fail to respect and engage with the trinitarian basis of the church and the trinitarian dynamic of a Christian discernment that is grounded in a liturgy ordered toward giving glory to the Father in fidelity to the Word and in the creative, transforming power of the Spirit. In other words, the Word reveals (and conceals) the unknown God and the new possibilities for human life. It is the part of the Spirit to guide the church in acting in such a way that these possibilities may come to fruition both in its own life and in the world at large. The basic pattern of discernment, then, consists in: first, engagement, in liturgy, contemplation, and study, with the events of the life, death, and resurrection of Jesus; second, contemplative engagement with people and circumstances in the present in the world in all their awkward concreteness and particularity; third, openness to and trust in the Spirit as the self-gift of God who enables the church continuously to find what its foundational events mean in relation to particular situations here and now. The work of the Spirit is to bring the community to maturity by forming Christ in its members in all their particularity; to work for the transformation of human lives, structures, and institutions, within and outside the boundaries of the church, into the new creation of the kingdom of God.

The dynamic of Christian discernment, then, is to return over and over again to the foundational events (the Word), in order to engage in the struggle to realize their significance in terms of transformation and creative possibilities, within the church and outside, here and now (the work of the Spirit). To quote Williams again: "my thesis is that any puzzlement over 'what the church is meant to be' is the revelatory operation of God as 'Spirit' insofar as it keeps the Church engaged in the exploration of what its foundational events signify . . . The renewed human possibility of liberty or creative responsibility generated in Jesus is concretely and particularly generated in this or that aspect of the community's life, in all those things that provoke fresh engagement with Jesus" (2000: 145).

The Ethical Dimension

It is evident that there is an ethical dimension to God's truth and holiness and hence to the church's formation in Christian spirituality. Two main ethical questions arise in this context. The first has to do with the church's ordering of its own internal life; the second concerns what is usually referred to as the church's "mission" or, perhaps more accurately, the church's participation in God's mission, the "sending" of Son and Spirit from the heart of love to unite in transforming and healing the world. Crucial to this discussion is how the church uses power, both within the community and in relation to those outside.

Within the church community

The ethical task of the church as context for spirituality is that of learning and foster-ing the order within: forms of relationship and ministry, church order, patterns of thinking, feeling, and acting which are proper to its true identity and calling. Here, too, I would argue, the heart and source of the church's ethical formation – both its being formed and its shaping of its members – is its retelling, renewing, celebrating, and pon-dering the story of its foundational events.

As we have seen, the church is beset by mysterious attractions to the disorder of sin, whether as a present reality or a future possibility. The church and its members can and do become drawn into patterns of thinking, feeling, and acting, in the ordering of inter-nal personal and communal life, which are in conflict with the church's calling and purpose. In its ethical discernment, I would suggest, the church is open to temptation in relation to both the Word and the Spirit. The first consists in trying to escape the labor of continuing discernment and the provisional, risky, always revisable ethical conclusions that result from this by seeking the comfort of supposedly certain, eternal, unchanging, unrevisable ethical norms or laws. It matters little whether these eternal and universal norms are particular verses or precepts of the Bible, or supposedly unchallengeable, unchangeable norms established by ecclesial authority; they spring from the same impulse. A second ethical temptation – and it has to be said that it does not seem to bother the mainstream Christian churches much at present – is that of the Free Spirit, which, in its "pure" form, would reject any ethical limits on the freedom of the children of God. However, in the face of a violent, confusing world and the dark-ness of loss and death, the church's members are also not immune from losing faith in the continuing presence of God and hope in the Spirit's power to transform and heal.

Particularly damaging impulses to disorder in the church have to do with the use or abuse of power. At any given time, all individuals or groups in the church, both those who exercise authority and those who live under it, both men and women, rich and poor, clergy and laity, members of different ethnic or cultural groups, are likely to be drawn into relationships and patterns of behavior where questions arise about fidelity to the Word and openness to the transforming, healing Spirit in their use of power.

The primary ethical task of the church as context for spirituality is to learn, foster, and practice habits of Christian discernment by telling, celebrating, and pondering the story of Jesus Christ, in the light of its own receptive, contemplative understanding of the world, and living out the ethical consequences of that mystery in thought, feeling, speech, action, and the ordering of life in all its aspects, including especially perhaps the church's use of power. The church does not know in advance how the Spirit is going to lead it in its task of witnessing to and realizing, in the concrete particularities of time and place, the possibilities for human life and its transformation and healing. It can come to know and do this only by repeatedly returning to the mystery of Christ in order to find and follow, in the power of the Spirit, the ethical paths that truly give glory to God in fidelity to the Word.

Since the disorder of sin, however, is constantly in evidence, both within and outside the church, not only as a future threat but also as a present reality, this learning has constantly to be renewed. The dialectic between Word and Spirit is vital, as we have seen. The church returns repeatedly to its founding events in the life of Jesus in order to understand, by the gift of the Spirit, their meaning for its ethical ordering in the present of personal and corporate life.

In relation to the stranger

Religious and cultural diversity are defining features of the contemporary world. In practice, Christians live in both a religious landscape and several others whose contours are not defined in religious terms. They move daily in the cultures of workplaces that are not Christian or religious and may be hostile or apathetic toward Christianity or any kind of religious faith and practice. Christian communities and churches live in close and unavoidable relationship with the worlds and cultures of both religious and non-religious strangers, the challenge of whose presence, as Barnes (2002) points out, is always at hand, whether welcome or not. Moreover, Christian communities and individuals are inevitably to some degree formed by those relationships, given that relationships with others are not something added on to identities previously shaped in isolation, but are constitutive of both personal and communal identities. If some understanding and practice of "mission" is a constitutive element of Christian spirituality, then there is a question of some urgency as to what exactly "mission" might mean in the present context of religious diversity. In ethical terms, what, in a Christian perspective, constitutes a "right relationship" between Christians and the worlds of the stranger? In other words, the ethical dimension of mission has to do with questions about the use of power in relation to the stranger for a church that is committed to worshiping and proclaiming a God of welcome and hospitality and to faithfulness to the Word in the power of the Spirit.

Impulses toward the disorder of sin always threaten the church's relationship to the world. One option is for the church to seek to dominate, to act with violence toward the stranger. This may of course take different forms, and it is clear that Christian churches have often treated both those outside Christianity and members of other churches in this way, often on the assumption that the churches alone possess God's truth and holiness, and so to realize God's promises for humanity (to do God's will) means working to bring all into the same Christian fold. This provides motivation for such phenomena as sectarian hostility, aggressive evangelism, and religious persecution, but it is also present in much less obvious forms in other versions of Christian mission. As an approach it is open to the criticism that, in failing to respect what Jonathan Sacks (2002) calls the "dignity of difference," it attacks, demeans, or oppresses outsiders, and that its devotees presume to know in advance how the Spirit intends to realize God's promises for humanity's future. It is an attitude to the world which suggests that God's promises have already been realized in a particular section of humanity; the rest must conform to this or perish.

A second option is the "inclusive" one: the ethical treatment of the stranger which assumes that Christianity can legitimately lay claim to everything that is of truth or value possessed by the stranger. This too fails to recognize and honor difference and the diversity of God's creation. It claims that what appears different in the world of the stranger is in fact not really so, but only an inferior or deviant version of what is present either in Christianity as a whole or in a particular faith community. As regards "spirituality," this stance suggests that all spiritual gifts which appear to exist outside Christianity as a whole, or outside a particular form of it, are already possessed in fullness within. Any "spiritualities" claimed outside the church are really no more than inferior and "anonymous" forms of Christian spirituality, although their devotees, for some reason known only to God, are unable or unwilling to recognize that fact.

A third option, sometimes called "normative pluralism," holds that all forms of Christianity, and indeed on a broader canvas all forms of "spirituality," are equally valid and efficacious, relative to particular times, people, societies, and cultures. This view advocates mutually tolerant co-existence. A particular problem with it, however, is that it is difficult to see how one could maintain this position and still argue that the church shares in God's mission, unless that mission is simply to rejoice in "difference," to retreat inside one's own Christian ghetto, whether in fear or in benign tolerance toward all strangers. It is hard to see how this constitutes giving glory to God in fidelity to the Word in the power of the Spirit; how this can be a sharing in God's mission to transform and heal the world in the image of the kingdom of Christ. Moreover, in terms of spirituality, this approach rests on a version of relativism: all forms of spirituality are of equal value. The only important question is what suits the individual or her group.

The church is called by God to treat the stranger, whoever the stranger may be, with love guided by the Spirit in fidelity to the Word. It finds its source and model of love in the God of Jesus Christ who offers welcome, hospitality, and healing to all. The church witnesses to the abundance and richness of the gifts it has received and wishes to share those gifts with others in love. The church, as a school of faith, hope, and love, is formed, as we have seen, in repeatedly remembering, renewing, celebrating, and pondering the events of its foundation in the story of the life, death, and resurrection of Christ. It is here that the church learns how to love the stranger with "the mind of Christ."

It follows from the argument of this essay that the ethical forms in which this love for the stranger is expressed are a matter for continuous discernment. That is so, not only because the world is constantly changing, but also because a propensity to sin is always present. In other words, the church is never free from the siren voices, within and without, plausibly urging it to give glory to something other than God, to avoid the cost of love, or to trust in a power other than the Spirit. The purpose of this discernment is to learn and practice mission, the particular forms of love toward the stranger which flow from the church's engagement with the mystery of God in the Word, on the one hand, and, under the guidance of the Spirit, are fitted for the particular settings of time and place, in all their historical and cultural variety, in which the church and the stranger meet. The source of the church's formation as a school of discernment, and that which gives its ethical activity toward the stranger a peculiarly Christian shape and dynamic, is the celebration of the Christian story, in worship and prayer, reading and study. In both these activities, retelling the Christian story and learning its meaning over again in the light of concrete events and particular features of time, geography, and culture, the church seeks to respond to its call to give glory to God in faithfulness to the Son, and in openness to the guidance and energy of the Spirit.

Conversation

I would wish to argue that some version of conversation or dialogue provides a paradigm for right relationship, within the church and between the church and the religious and non-religious "stranger." Consequently, the church is true to itself as a school of spirituality when, in the light of these ethical questions, which are urgent in a context of religious diversity, it learns a form of conversation with the stranger which ultimately has its source in the church's relationship with the triune God. In particular, in its liturgy, the heart of formation in faith, the church celebrates a God who welcomes and is hospitable to all. It also contemplates the words and actions of the Word who discloses and initiates a "new creation," new possibilities, not just for one nation or community but also for the whole of humanity. In fidelity to the Word, the church also bears witness to and works to bring those new possibilities to fulfillment under the power and guidance of the Spirit. The purpose of this is not to try to bring all people into a particular religious institution. Nor does the church know how or where any conversation with religious or non-religious strangers will end. Conversation with the stranger is ethically responsible when it is truly consistent with Christian discipleship and giving glory to the Father in fidelity to the Son and in the power of the Spirit. Ethical responsibility implies neither treating the stranger with violence nor patronizing by reducing the other to really "one of us."

In an earlier part of this essay, I described two different usages of "spirituality" which, I argued, were based on radically different models, one embedded in religious traditions and communities, the other an inhabitant of the marketplace. My conclusion for this section is that such a conversation as I have tried to describe would be an appropriate form of relationship for the church to learn and adopt in approaching the world of that particular stranger.

Conclusion

At the center of the church as context for Christian spirituality, so this essay has argued, lies celebration. The activity proper to the church, which constitutes its pedagogy as a school of Christian discipleship, is liturgy, "the work of the people," in repeatedly retelling, renewing, celebrating, and pondering the story of the life, death, and resurrection of Jesus in response to a God who constitutes, transforms, and heals the world. This is the source from which all other catechesis and religious and theological formation flow. It is also the pedagogy that shapes the church as a school of Christian discernment, a formation that enables the church to discover and practice forms of discipleship which represent both its fidelity to the Word and its cooperation with the Spirit in relation to particularities of time and place. The church wishes to share the abundance of what it has received from God both with its own members and with the rest of humanity. By allowing itself to be schooled in discernment of the paths of true discipleship, the church is able to share what it has received, both in its ordering of its own life within the church and in its dealings with the world outside.

All of this, evidently, is trinitarian through and through. Every aspect of it reflects a relation to a creator who transforms and heals the world by means of the "sending" of the Word and the Spirit. The church is constituted in the events of the life, death, and resurrection of Jesus, the Word of God, and understands itself as committed to giving glory to the Father in fidelity to the Word and in the power of the Spirit. The church's liturgy, a celebration of God's self-gift to the world, follows the same movement: worship of the Father, in Christ, in the power of the Spirit in recognition of what God has given. So, too, the church's pedagogy as a school of Christian discernment follows the same pattern: its purpose is to enable the church to discover and live those forms of Christian spirituality by which, in the particular circumstances of time and place, under the gentle hand of the Spirit, it may give glory to God in fidelity to the Word. When the church is true to itself, the ways in which it orders its own life and ministry and regards and deals with the stranger reflect the same faithfulness to the Word and openness to the Spirit to the glory of the Father. In learning and fostering Christian spirituality, the church partakes of, reflects, celebrates, and shares with others the abundance of the self-gift to the world, in the Word and the Spirit, of the unknown God who offers welcome and healing to all.

References

Avis, P. (ed.) 2002: *The Christian Church: An Introduction to the Major Traditions*. London: SPCK.

Barnes, M. 2002: *Theology and the Dialogue of Religions*. Cambridge: Cambridge University Press.

Hardy, D. W. 2001: *Finding the Church: The Dynamic Truth of Anglicanism*. London: SCM.

Healy, N. M. 2000: *Church, World and the Christian Life: Practical-prophetic Ecclesiology*. Cambridge: Cambridge University Press.

Lash, N. 1986: Considering the Trinity. *Modern Theology* 2, 183–96.

—— 1988: *Easter in Ordinary*. London: SCM.

Leech, K. 1992: *The Eye of the Storm: Resources for a Spirituality of Justice*. London: Darton, Longman, and Todd.

Sacks, J. 2002: *The Dignity of Difference: How to Avoid the Clash of Civilizations*. London: Continuum.

Sheldrake, P. 1995: *Spirituality and History: Questions of Interpretation and Method*, 2nd rev. edn. · London: SPCK.

Williams, R. 2000: *On Christian Theology*. Oxford: Blackwell.

CHAPTER 15

Sacramentality and Christian Spirituality

Ann Loades

As a phrase, "sacramentality and spirituality" indicates a significant intersection of theological reflection and lively commitment to discipleship. Living as disciples at this intersection requires of us a certain courage to endure and embrace change. We know that we change as we involve ourselves with one another, as we must to become human persons. If we attend to God's search for us, which makes it possible for us to search for God in our turn, our perceptions of God may well change as well as our perceptions of ourselves and of others.

The conjunction of "sacramentality" and "spirituality" itself marks a notable shift in Christian sensibility about how that engagement with God may be discerned, at least in some Christian communions. For we find ourselves in a new era of understanding the inter-relationship of the human and non-human, and of religious diversity both Christian and non-Christian, though quite what we will make of it all we have yet to see. We can, however, identify in some churches major developments in reconceiving "sacramentality" in the course of the twentieth century, to which we will need to attend, though we do not here review the insights of the human sciences into how human beings become themselves in relation to God (spirituality). In principle, we need not exclude in advance knowledge from any source which will aid our search for understanding.

We can, of course, make some progress in looking in earlier publications under the headings of "sacrament" and "sacramental," and then at "spirituality" (each with subdivisions), but the particular conjunction of "sacramentality" and "spirituality" requires fresh thought, which we attempt here. That requires putting together what we already know, in one way or another, rather than making entirely novel suggestions, even should that be possible. It is more a matter of making imaginative juxtapositions of what may be familiar to us from other contexts, and of putting them together in different but illuminating ways. Some of the results will turn out to be mistaken, though not instantly recognizable as such. Many will be provisional and disposable. The capacity to discriminate between options is no longer, if it ever was, properly the task of some "specialists" – the ordained, who do, of course, have particular roles in their churches. It is the responsibility of the whole "people of God," of any one who is open to the promise of divine grace and God's transformative Spirit in human affairs (sacramentality). We are all offered the same aspirations – living in the light of Christ's resurrection to which we are called to witness – though how that will be lived out will be as variable as are human beings themselves.

We will begin by thinking through some of our presuppositions and our inherited resources, before attempting to identify the possible reconfiguration of those resources and the demands to be made of them in the circumstances in which we find ourselves at present, and in those we can reasonably anticipate. We will begin with "sacramentality" in its broadest possible range of meanings, having to do with life as a whole (that is, not just with ecclesiastical life). Sacramentality is fluid across the distinctions between "church" and "world." We need to think: "only connect." We shall conclude with sacramentality in connection with Christ himself as sacrament.

The Natural World

Human beings, female and male, of all ages, shapes, and sizes, in an astonishing variety of histories and cultures, discover and make themselves in intradependence with one another. We recognize "Abide in me as I in you" (John 15: 1–8) as true of the relationship of Christ with his disciples because we are sufficiently familiar with what it can mean in other human relationships. Intradependence is also essential in understanding sacramentality and spirituality, since both have to do with becoming fully human persons by participating in and being graced by life other than our own, beyond human resources, extraordinary though these undoubtedly are. We have a very large part to play in making one another who and what we are, and in what we may become. So finding one's own identity, one's "individuality," which is undoubtedly important in taking responsibility for ourselves, our intentions, actions, and their consequences, does not require "only-oneself-ism," but involves securing a sense of bounded identity. That boundary is, as it were, permeable, however, and that not only by and with human "others," but by interaction with those not of our own species. For human beings share much with other beings, as our imaginative sympathies and engagement with them exhibits. Human beings and all "others" are inter-adapted, co-evolved, endlessly capable of surprising and of being sources of wonder to one another. We can take clues here, for example, from the popularity of "wildlife" programs on the television (Noah's ark in modern form), the many ways in which we "anthropomorphize" animals, and the attentiveness of a theater audience to any animal on stage.

All beings are necessarily also vulnerable to one another, and capable of inflicting both accidental and deliberate damage on themselves and others and their environment. The human species in particular is undoubtedly capable of depths of malice beyond anything to be found in the non-human. Our perspective has nothing to do with sentimentality about who and what we are. Yet shame at the worst of which we are capable may not, on a Christian view, precipitate us into supposing either that the world is not our true home, or that the world is not created by the God who interacts with us.

Our conviction rather is that we cannot finally extricate ourselves from the hurts and harms we inflict on one another by our own efforts, graced though we may be to do what we can. Rather, we are companioned by God and not left to our own devices, and the creativity manifested in the world in which we find ourselves is supremely manifested in divine redemption, to which human beings respond with their plea for mercy, the Kyrie eleison, Christe eleison.

The first move in understanding ourselves begins with recognition of one another as "creatures." The context in which we find ourselves is not one of our self-making, but is deemed to be derived from an extraordinarily generous God. God is in no sense to be identified with it so that the world is mistakenly seen as "sacred." That would steer us in the direction of superstition and idolatry, mistakenly attributing to creatures power or powers they do not and should not possess or attempt to possess, and which may not be attributed to them. That creator and creatures are not to be identified is crucially important to understanding sacramentality and spirituality, which negotiates the differences, treading somewhat warily to avoid confusion. On the other hand, to claim that the world is derived from God does not mean that the world is bereft of God. On the contrary, it means that the life-giving resources of the divine life, identifiable as "God–Christ–Spirit" in Christian worship (in the Gloria in excelsis, for instance), grace and transfigure the world. It is entirely appropriate that imagery from nature is part and parcel of human language and the language of worship, and the use of natural things in worship.

Thus we may well enjoy sacramentality in its most "catholic" sense; that is, concerned with, directed to, and drawing on the whole that is our context. Such sensitivity may be learned by participation in the specially significant sacraments of Christian tradition which give us clues to the character of the richly "quasi-personal" presence we may discern in the limitlessly interesting world in which we find ourselves. We may also come to think that there may be much to be learned about sacramentality from some non-Christian religious traditions about which most of us know all too little. And we also note in passing that scientific discovery and construal of the world in all its immensity and microscopic energies and detail need not destroy our sense of wonder at it. On the contrary, the human capacity to discover, to imagine, and to make things of extraordinary sophistication may make us more, rather than less, alert to divine creativity, and the more willing to refer human creativity to its divine source if we are to safeguard ourselves from self-destructive pride. We may articulate our sense of wonder by means of such texts as Job 38 and 41, Psalm 104, the so-called "Hymn of Creation" from the Septuagint version of Daniel (the Benedicite or blessing of God sung from out of the burning fiery furnace), Francis of Assisi's "Canticle of the Creatures" (well known in William Draper's transposition of it into the hymn "All Creatures of our God and King"), Christopher Smart's *Rejoice in the Lamb*, or Gerard Manley Hopkins's poem, "God's Grandeur." Finally, the Sanctus of Isaiah 6, central to many, if not all, forms of the Christian Eucharist (thanksgiving), insistently reminds us of the fact that the world reveals divine authority and splendor to us (Brown and Fuller 1995: 1–18, "A Sacramental World").

Human beings turn readily to the "natural" world expressed in such texts as those suggested above for a sense of the divine presence, not least to seek glimpses of the unviolated and the unspoiled. They may all too quickly discover or rediscover that what appears to be natural is to some extent a matter of human creative contrivance. (The provision of clean running or "living" water is only one very important example.) In the shaping of a landscape, for instance, human "grace" cooperates with the given natural world to reconceive its possibilities. Painters of landscape, many of them no mere imitators of what they see, have played their part in such interaction, whether concentrating on order and harmony, or indicating a more hidden but discernible reality, as in the work of Cézanne. Landscape architects and gardeners also play their part, as have those who have defended wild places and their inhabitants by the creation of "national parks." The main point is that those who rejoice in the natural world are, as it were, responding to an invitation to celebrate the existence of creatures quite other than themselves. Some of them, such as whales and other creatures of deep water, clearly enjoy capacities beyond the human, adapted as they are to habitats inhospitable to humankind. In contemplation of such ocean-goers, human beings may well, like Job, find salutary reminders that the world is one which they share, but which they cannot finally control. Awe, as well as wonder, and its concomitants in deliberate effort not to manipulate or use other creatures to their harm, but to refrain from interference when- ever possible, in part may account for the popularity of "creation" spirituality and of so-called "Celtic" spirituality, the latter at least free of equivocation about the vulnera- bility of human beings to their environment without cooperative endeavor for the pro- vision of shelter and food.

Poiesis: The Realm of Human Making

If not to the actual or apparently natural, human beings turn to the realm of human making, to *poiesis*, for other clues to the discernment of divine presence. The extraor- dinary resources of human language, richly metaphorical and frequently corrigible, are undeniably important, particularly in the work of those who write poetry (one mode of *poiesis*). For poets make novel connections of words and phrases so that we see and think of ourselves not merely differently, but with greater clarity of insight, always open to new possibilities in the future. By metaphor, we simply mean the capacity to speak of one thing in terms of another, and by so doing, to gain some perception of that of which we cannot otherwise "speak." This is indeed fortunate, for there is the ever- present possibility of idolatry in language about God, not least in definably religious contexts, and we need at times to remember that the divine mystery finally evades our capture in words. This is one of the reasons why we need a multiplicity of ways of refer- ring to God – to remind us of the divine mystery. In worship, of course, we deploy "word" in prayers, hymns, and preaching, and all need constant attention if they are to mediate divine presence to us. Falsehood ever lurks around what matters most to us.

Religious texts apart, there is in principle much to be said for the confidence to claim religious significance for many other manifestations of *poiesis*, human creativity, without destroying their own proper integrity. It is not that believers already know all that there is to know about God, and that non-religious creativity is merely illustrative of a guaranteed, prior knowledge. In its very independence of religious use or relevance, *poiesis* may say "God-Spirit" and correct religious anthropomorphism and incipient idolatry by so doing. In the present era, both old and new forms of creativity proliferate side by side: drama, poetry and dance, carving and furniture-making, cinema, film and photography, advertising, gardening, engineering and architecture, sports, skating and gymnastics (sometimes at phenomenally high levels of competition), the artistry of the circus and of musicals, design, fashion and clothing, sculpture, metalwork, flower-arranging, running supermarkets and factories, airlines and transport, embroidery, public space, high levels of technological enterprise – and many more.

When we consider examples of *poiesis* we should perhaps be as wary of "good taste" as of idolatry. Only connect – and ignore nothing. Human beings and ecclesiastical congregations are irreducibly diverse. Sacramentality requires generous appreciation of and curiosity about the tastes of others, very different as they may hopefully be. Occasionally, we discern new "images" of grace (bearing in mind the definition of sacrament as "outward and visible sign of an inward and spiritual grace"), as it were, when attending for the first time to a realm of human making quite new to us. Consider, for instance, the invention of glass, apparently "fixed" when placed in a window, but even there subtly and almost indiscernibly mobile, capable of embodying and transmitting texture and color, at once impermeable and translucent. In particular, the discovery of glass-blowing inadvertently gave visible form to invisible breath as the glassblower produces a transparent globe from the energy of his or her own body. This is just one small example of how those concerned with sacramentality may quite accidentally find much to illuminate them in dimensions of life from which religious evaluation has been too long lacking, should they venture to do so (see Brown 2004). We also bear in mind that there is no reason whatsoever to rely solely on scientific discovery for the generation of such illumination, just as there is no reason whatsoever to ignore it, even when, like *poiesis* most broadly conceived, it is, for its own working purposes, most God-excluding. God can be hidden as well as made manifest. We briefly turn now to two other areas under-explored in relation to sacramentality but arguably important since we are looking for characteristics of intra-personal exchange which may illuminate moments of divine transformative presence. These two areas are human procreativity of our own kind, and creativity in certain modes of work.

Procreation and Parenting

It is commonly the case for many human beings, even if they are not themselves "genetic" parents, that being involved with the very young requires ingenuity to a remarkable degree, as is the case with rearing the young of other social creatures. We know that both genetic parents are co-procreators of new human life, and that this is now immensely complicated by the development of reproductive technology, the burdens of which fall especially on women. Such technology aside, in many parts of the world the life-giving capacity of women through pregnancy and childbirth threatens the very life of women themselves. They grace new life into being with their own flesh and blood, not merely by birth-giving but in rearing children. The feasts of the

"Annunciation," the "Visitation," and the "Nativity," or ceremonies such as the "Nine Lessons and Carols," resonate with some of the most important facets of human life and its transmission through new beginnings in the life of a community's newborn, even though we can make no assumptions whatsoever that women in particular will necessarily have access to or be readily given sufficient social and personal support to rear a child if "father" (with cash and other resources) is not immediately and consistently present. Implications for sacramentality, surely. What we also know is that the young may flourish where there is sufficient stability and care for them, and that some unusual and unconventional family groupings may provide "parents." If we see children as gifts to the human community and not simply to their genetic or "social" parents, parenting arguably brings human beings close to a sense of divine grace and generosity. "Made children by adoption and grace" is memorable here (Joseph in relation to Christ). "Parenting" is here a metaphor for the intergenerational care and concern that must be expected of extended and blended family groups not least in the highly mobile societies in which they are likely to be found. For every human person should receive at their most helpless the long-term nurture and protection they need not merely to enable them to survive, but, most promisingly, to flourish, and they should receive it from all adults, both male and female, in equitable relationships sharing the demands made by the young. They arouse in their parents the affections central to human wellbeing, and learn receptivity and intradependence as in the divine–human inter-relationships we explore via the notion of sacramentality.

This has nothing to do with being unrealistic about the young, or about the traumas of relationship with their parents that may occur. The young can be insatiably demanding, smelly, spotty, runny-nosed, crying, cross and sleepless, willful and argumentative and impossible to please. They are central to the lives of human communities, however, each of them "one-off," as the loss of a community's children in disaster all too terribly reveals – one of the points at which we discover the meaning of the "sanctity" of life. However exasperating children are at times, however, if healthy they may be spontaneous, eager and curious, enjoying play of all kinds, imitating, singing, dancing, making things for sheer pleasure – the sort of habits that may develop into the many human forms of creativity to which we have briefly attended. They are capable of eliciting the best from those around them, not least by way of time and attention, and sometimes their very presence can help relieve conflict, for it is in care for them that adults learn to soothe distress and anger, ask for help, help the helpless and show kindness, as well as to develop the patience which results in genuine respect for and tolerance of others.

What we know of the attitude of Christ to the young indicates his willingness to be identified with them in their "littleness," given the way in which they and their interests are so readily overlooked, as indeed lack of theological reflection and opportunities for worship may reveal, the occasional ceremony such as a "Christingle" service apart. They continuously represent before us vitally important characteristics of adult life and of life in engagement with God. For the care of the young requires those most fundamental acts of washing and feeding without which no child can survive, transformed as they are into the specific sacraments of baptism and Eucharist; and the constant "letting go" of mistakes that makes it possible to continue life with one another and to open up the human future, which the young bear with them as they edge toward maturity.

So much is shared with them before either we or they quite know what we are doing, which says much too for our relationship with God. Bearing this point in mind may help us not to make too much of whether in baptism something is done for us on our behalf or whether baptism has to do with our own personal declaration in faith, since all depends on the self-giving of God. And it is in the gratuitous sharing of food at home that we learn the basis of companionship and conviviality. We therefore recognize that the relationships the young have with those who care or do not care for them, and whether or not churches become the kinds of communities into which the young are welcomed, will certainly affect at profound levels of their being how they may experience and name God, and how important "parent" language for God will remain in Christian worship and prayer. This will also be affected by whether the young find women's full human dignity, irrespective of whether or not they are mothers, persuasively fostered in and by the church.

We have to bear two points in mind. The first is that whatever language we have used and continue to use of God, whether in public or private worship, a fundamental theological rule is that God transcends both sex and gender, and the roles associated with these in our societies. The second point is new to many, but surely follows from the first, and is connected with our thinking of our most formative relationships as sacramental. We have yet to ponder the full significance of thinking that, whilst all our language for God is finally inadequate, the words and deeds we associate with the female/feminine are as adequate or inadequate in speaking of God as those associated with the male/masculine, if, that is, women bear the "image" of God in as full and in as limited a way as do men (Johnson 1993). We turn from the importance of relationships with the young to our second under-explored area: the adult world of work which many of the young will join sooner or later.

The World of Work

For most adult human beings, the worlds of vocation in work, paid or unpaid, private or public, and the manifold forms of creativity that come to expression in social and political life, need to be thought of as possible realms of sacramentality. We know enough of the importance of the flair and problem-solving skills of the manager, the administrator, and the entrepreneur, the "mover and shaker," the "finisher," and the "fixer," to suspect that these may yield some insight into divine providential care if we choose to explore their achievements. Unless we grapple with the incipient chaos and muddle of life and the obscurity and confusion which arise from failure to give things proper attention in good time, it may well be difficult to think of divine providential care for us. We must, of course, be alert to the very considerable dangers of "sacralizing" human political power, but just as we need to reflect on ordinary life and its relationship to its ultimately divine author, so we need to reflect on what we may experience of God or not in the public, shared world, the *polis*. This would seem to follow from Christian commitment to liturgy, which is certainly and as always to be undertaken as "public service" by the church for the world. Liturgy has to do with *koinonia hagion* (commonly translated as Holy Communion, and too often limited in its meaning to one particular Christian ceremony, albeit the central one). The phrase has to do with the making common of the holy as well as with the sanctification of the common, with the permeability of the thin boundary between the religious and the non-religious, and it is to the "common," the ordinary, that one is dismissed at the end of each and every ceremony, with a blessing and grace.

This may lead us to live with a certain willingness to entertain and understand risks and difficulties with something of the panache seen in at least some entrepreneurs and politicians, and to dispense with the arrogance of assuming that Christian perception here must inevitably take the form of negative criticism and denunciation from the irresponsible sidelines rather than of constructive contribution. We may well suspect that we need ways of thinking and living in the *polis* which elicit from us new "fruits of the Spirit" if we are to negotiate what is likely to remain a very complex and mistake-ridden world. In other words, sacramentality and spirituality have far-reaching implications for the ways in which we manage our affairs, not least the ways in which we negotiate consensus and strive for peace. We have no reason to suppose that there is any aspect of life which is in principle bereft of the possibility of divine presence, such that we avoid entanglement in institutional and political life.

The Kyrie eleison and the creeds insistently remind us where our loyalty fundamentally is to lie, and that beyond church as well as state. Yet however cautious we may be about the expression of the divine presence, there can be no easy retreat to the narrowly construed "religious" at this point, with all the evasions that might entail, and however fascinating ecclesiastical politics may be for some. There can, of course, be good reasons for such apparent "retreat," however temporary that may be, not least the re-evaluation of resources, the recovery of energy in silent prayer, and simply awaiting in patience for apparently inexorable tides to turn. Retreat can also give us time and space to translate "training" from the gym and the health club into the discipline (*ascesis*) which will free us up to gain the forms of life that matter, to recover or discover the maturity of refusal, particularly of the temptation to assess who we are in terms of what we possess.

There is, as it were, more to fasting than the refusal of what one can put in one's mouth, and there are many well-tried, shareable practices appropriate to learning the capacity to refuse. Fasting can express gratitude to God, the preparation for feasting, penitence, and lining oneself up in protest with or on behalf of the unfortunate. From discipline may spring new vitality to face one's particular burden of problem-solving or innovation or some other contribution to the negotiation of the "common good," as bearers of hope and trust where these are absent or lacking. We may also have to bear the pain of discovering that we do not have the gifts that will be helpful in respect of a particular problem; or that we have gifts we did not suspect which will demand a great deal from us in their exercise. Conversation with trusted "soul-friends" may be helpful. We are at this stage simply trying to identify aspects of human life which in their creativity may engage us with God, and God is not necessarily to be found where we expect. What we can say is that we have no good reason to exclude our openness to divine presence from an aspect of life – work – which is of such central importance to many. We turn at this point to matters thought to have close connection with the discernment of divine presence in creativity – music and movement – work for some.

Music and Movement

We venture to suppose that one excellent example which illuminates divine creativity and therefore sacramentality may be found in music, powerfully dependent as it is on human modes of interaction with one another, but this time, often wordlessly – another clue we shall need to bear in mind in thinking about and experiencing sacramentality and spirituality (see Begbie 2000). In music, rich and complex harmony, non-identical repetition that both closes an "event" and yet provokes desire for further repetition, multiple layering and connection and the sheer inexhaustibility of musical creativity, especially in jazz and other forms of improvisation – all enable us to attend to the dynamism of temporality and divine engagement with human life within it. We experience the presence of God, if we do, in the transience of time. Playing or listening to jazz is one way of appreciating this, since the sheer alertness of the musicians, deploying skill and discipline and attentiveness to one another, makes it possible for them to take risks, change roles, and to experience extraordinary degrees of freedom together. Whether playing jazz or other musical forms, musicians above all know that music is the creation of human bodies. They interact with one another through faces – eyes, mouths and brows, heads rising and falling – with hands and breath, and the instruments which become integral to the musician's body, together becoming the "means of grace" which make possible the sounds in which listeners actively participate by attention and in patience. We can also learn much from the interaction of an orchestra about the ways in which a "corporate body" becomes one in shared endeavor, and re-think the relationship of president/leader, assistants, choir and soloists, instrumentalists, composers, lighting and sound experts in a religious ceremony.

Also, in listening to music we learn what it is to join in by "intention," so vital in participation in forms of worship in which we do not have a role other than that of silent participation. We recall the line from Psalm 40: 6, "ears thou hast dug for me," and its transposition via the Septuagint into Hebrews 10: 5 as "a body hast thou prepared me" when we attend to what we may learn from music about sacramentality. In addition, even when performing a musical "text," a score, music reminds us of the importance of valuing the transient, the fluid and fleeting when discerning divine engagement with creatures, wherever that may be. John Coltrane's jazz composition *A Love Supreme*, variations on a most simple theme, itself insists that God may not be confined within our too easily narrowed perspectives. Given the sheer contingency and finitude of life, there is every reason not to make the mistake of confusing sacramentality with the fixed and the frozen, and experience at some level of "live" music performance may be very important here.

To concentrate on music a little further, it is obvious that its sacramentality is not reducible to music for liturgy, sometimes referred to as "sacred" music. Music is more than a means to enrich liturgy, a particular mode of the worship of God, though it may, of course, so enrich it. It cannot in this context be reduced to the equivalent of background music in a shop, though to say that alerts us to the ways in which music can repel as well as attract us. We want to claim that music has to do with making worship possible (Col. 3: 16), and to worship God without music of any kind is as odd as worshiping God without words, though both may be necessary at certain points, as we shall see. It is impossible to prescribe in advance which music will be always helpful in particular circumstances, though some may well stand the test of time in particular communities. It need be neither complex nor performed by highly trained musicians, though sometimes it will need so to be. Much will depend upon how widespread participation in music is part and parcel of a particular culture. What is central is the care taken in its preparation and performance, and the conviction that those who listen are as important as those who perform; that listening itself is a skill and a contribution to the praise of God; and that each of these is as important as presidency at a ceremony, of preaching or leading prayers.

In any event, we need not be too ready to deplore the fact that some of the great texts from Christian liturgy may be performed in concert halls and theaters, beyond the confines of explicit acts of worship. Such performances at the very least sustain sacramentality in a wide variety of contexts, and different composers in any case illuminate the texts in quite astonishing ways. To take just one example, the stark simplicity of Kyrie eleison might seem to preclude difference of musical exploration, but nothing could be further from the case, even within the work of any one composer. The work of composers as different as Messiaen, Martin, and Pärt in response to biblical texts is also profoundly significant. Then, of all the "Requiem" settings of the twentieth century, Benjamin Britten's *War Requiem*, with its juxtaposition of liturgical texts and Wilfred Owen's poetry, illuminates the grief of war as does no other. Given the prevalence of war on the human agenda, it is perhaps not surprising that it is regularly performed outside an ecclesiastical setting, as are other arrangements of requiem texts. Together with, for example, the last movement of Shostakovich's Piano Trio No. 2 in E Minor, Opus 67 (which explores the horrors of the dances near-skeletons were forced to perform on the edges of their own graves in extermination camps), Britten's *War Requiem* cuts through any form of sacramentality which denies or avoids the world's tragedies. Another work written for concert performance in the first instance is James Macmillan's *Veni, Veni Emmanuel*, which in its "Coda" has a pulsing "heartbeat" for Christ risen beyond human horror. Written to celebrate Evelyn Glennie's gifts as a solo percussionist who sounds her body via her instruments, the work transcends her hearing disability. It has received several hundred performances within its first five years.

Moving in the other direction – from concert hall to liturgy – Duke Ellington composed in the last years of his life music for three "sacred concerts," regularly performed from the mid-1960s onward. Selections from these concerts have been incorporated into celebrations of the Eucharist, in which words, ceremony, and jazz combine and express sacramentality with exuberance and delight. Ellington's "David Danced before the Lord" has not only been played and sung, but jazz-tapped by Will Gaines, born in

Baltimore in 1928 but still able to "sound" his body through his feet. Perhaps only in "charismatic" worship may we have a comparable opportunity to delight in God, though there is much also to be learned from the supposedly secular world's interest in the figures that populate the Gospels, such as Tim Rice's lyrics for Andrew Lloyd Webber's *Jesus Christ Superstar*, which is excellent in its use of drama, dance, lighting, and staging to focus an audience's attention on some of the rich seams of the Christian tradition (Drane 2000).

As yet under-explored is renewed interest not just in music which happens to have been danced, as it were, but in dance itself, which both on-stage and off may convey a sense of transforming divine presence, and that not just in the performance of work on explicitly religious themes. There is no necessary connection whatsoever between dance and mere diversion or profanity. Just as human beings learn to share in music of greater or lesser complexity, so they gain from dancers the sense of exhilaration that comes from wordless but intensely physical experience of music, at the peak of vitality and bodily expressiveness. For some at least, this will provide clues to hitherto undreamt-of capacities of the human body, and its promised transformation. The very hard floors of ecclesiastical buildings present dancers with significant limitations, however, since such floors make it impossible to jump, and getting off the floor is part of the joy of many dance forms. The main point here is that music by itself is only part of the story of finding the sacramentality of the body, and of female bodies at that (Ross 1998; Beattie 2002).

One approximation to dance is the use of processions, which may integrate movement, word, and music in a way that is essential if we are not to muddle "spirituality" with the merely intellectual. For instance, an Epiphany procession which moves from the east, as did the Magi, pausing to offer incense at a crib as a sign of worship of divinity made helplessly vulnerable in the Christ-child, may then move westward to the font, refilled with living water to commemorate Christ's own baptism, and providing an opportunity for all to reaffirm baptismal vows. It may then return to the main sanctuary where the Eucharist is normally celebrated, to give thanks for the new creation manifest in the wine of Cana. The advice of dancers and actors would be invaluable whenever we move ourselves around or employ gestures, processions apart: stewarding visitors, using hands in blessing, making the sign of the cross, kneeling or standing for prayer, genuflecting or not, exchanging the "peace," reading Scripture, preaching, turning to the east to say the creed, carrying the Gospel into the church or down into the congregation for the Gospel reading, processing the Reserved Sacrament, carrying candles in a church flooded with hundreds of "tea lights" at the Feast of the Presentation of Christ in the Temple (Candlemas), footwashing, laying on hands in consecration, asperging people or a building, bowing, holding hands, prostrating oneself, singing and treading a labyrinth, smiting the breast, kissing the altar, a book, or an icon, folding the hands to pray, laying flowers at a shrine, lighting an Advent wreath. And the interplay of faces is essential here, the interplay that begins from the moment of birth. We do not need "make-up," but we do need to look alert and alive if we are to communicate what we say and sing. Gestures are meaningless unless human beings are able to look into one another's eyes, seek one another's faces in love and trust as we hope to be able to look into the face of Christ. The iconostasis in an Orthodox church is a kind of portrayal of faces, but one which summons us to a Christ beyond the one we can represent to ourselves, and who invites us to a life beyond anything we can presently imagine.

Stillness and Silence

We turn at this point to some theological reflections which caution us if we move too quickly to make claims about sacramentality and spirituality. One crucial difference between all our "makings" at their best (including any kind of "performance," whether or not performance of religious ceremony) and our response to God, is that we cannot in any sense elicit the divine presence by analogy with the way in which we can elicit the attention and applause of other human persons. Any attempt so to elicit divine presence reveals serious misunderstanding of how God may engage with us and how we may respond to God. We may believe, as in specifically Christian sacraments, that there are, as it were, reliable ceremonies in which, if we participate with true intention, we may be disposed to divine presence, but we need constantly to remind ourselves that we are attempting to be alert to God, not to precipitate God into the world which we may misperceive, cluttered as we may be by self-indulgent fantasies. Freedom from such clutter may come about in connection with or as the result of the worship of God, since its first and essential point is sheer adoration of the God whose world we delight in and wonder at.

We are dealing here with something integral to the fruition and fulfillment of what it is to become a fully human being (a "saint"), even though God is, in a sense, "unsayable" beyond even what we take to be true of God, insofar as we lay hold on whatever God reveals. Thinking through sacramentality and spirituality requires these negatives, these reminders of God's transcendence over our self-projections and delusions. The contemplation of abstract art may help to make the point – Rothko, Mondrian, Kandinsky. So we may, in the last analysis, find utter starkness and simplicity, stillness and silence, necessary at least for a time, and the point of such a manner of worship should not be lost on us. We might well sometimes think that our utter dependence on God and trust in divine immediacy to us is such that God needs no sacramental means by which to mediate divine presence to us. No ceremony of any kind may be required, and most emphatically none mediated by human beings of only one sex to the other with reciprocity denied. And what we may take from simplicity and silence back to ceremony, if it is to ceremony that we return, is acknowledgment of the importance of long enough silences for people to be still, and "collect" themselves together in re-focusing themselves on the matter in hand, the sheer adoration of God. We might also think that it is better to do nothing ceremonially than to do so little that the point of it is lost, but, in venturing beyond the minimal, realize that there is no immunity from making a mess of it. Certainly, from time to time, there will need to be some radical reassessment of what goes on. For instance, we may come to appreciate the importance of the color symbolism of a Salvation Army banner, while adamantly refusing to countenance one bearing a National Socialist swastika.

Christ as Sacrament

Let us now recall that we seek to engage with God because we believe God seeks us. We read Genesis 3: 9, in which God is portrayed as hunting and calling for his earth-creatures in his garden; or Christ's conversation with the Samaritan woman in John 4. Christian sacramentality essentially takes its rise from this conviction of being sought by God, though whether the Fourth Gospel intends the sacramental mediation of that seeking or is resolutely opposed to it in terms of specific ceremonies is far from clear. The words of John 4: 23 are concerned with finding God in Spirit and in truth, as indeed many a reformer down the centuries might wish to point out. We work, however, with the convictions that the "unsayable" God not only made all flesh but became Word-made-flesh directly expressed in a particular human being, Christ himself as sacrament, grace, and Spirit manifest to us. In the Fourth Gospel we may judge that Christ's own words and the imagery he employs, the actions he performs, alike reveal something of the evangelist's struggle, and perhaps Christ's own struggle, to lay hold on and to convey the mediation of divine presence in his life, death, and resurrection (Brown and Loades 1996). Then, in terms of developed Christian doctrine, Christ's "ascension" has to do with God's continuing commitment to the creatures he loves and redeems, for Christ himself in his glorified humanity continues to be sacrament above all particular sacraments.

Sacramentality embraces not simply our present context, but the life of the redeemed which we may find in recollection of the members of the *communio sanctorum*, the "communion of saints," the company of the sanctified, who share the conviviality, companionship, and exuberance of a repossessed Paradise. The Latin phrase is marvelously and perhaps deliberately ambiguous, for it may refer to those who are sanctified – "All Saints" – and/or to their enjoyment of "holy things," particularly those of the heavenly banquet with Christ as "Host."

Some of the saints may be especially important. For instance, we realize that what is true of Mary the mother of Jesus, which is celebrated in such feasts as the Dormition/Assumption mid-August, is true of all of us. This is, that throughout life we all of us depend upon divine gracious promise. The saints, however, are not just those personally celebrated in ecclesiastical tradition, but may well include the "nobodies" who have lived with utter fidelity to God in the courage of their living and dying, and whose martyrdoms in the twentieth century exceed those of earlier ages (Johnson 1998). Our response in worship to God's commitment takes us some way toward experiencing the exchange of generosity and love that is the divine life itself, as we learn to stammer "Trinity," blessing one another with the grace, love, and fellowship of one with another.

Furthermore, we worship God to be able to go on doing so, no matter what, in extremity if need be, for in so doing we align ourselves with God's defeat of evil overheard in Christ's utterances on the cross. Evil may encompass our own undoubted tragedies and those integral to war, terrorism, refugee and death camps across the world. For the ultimate defeat of evil we have to trust to the significance of the divine self-manifestation of Christ's risen and glorified person which embraces not only the humanity of the victims, but of those who betray and destroy others. Failure and betrayal are at the heart of the narratives of Christ's passion. As Psalm 68: 18 has it: "Thou art gone up on high, thou hast led captivity captive, and received gifts for men, yea, even for thine enemies, that the Lord God might dwell among them." The worship of God will necessarily require of us prayers of intercession for those who bring such evils about, admittedly an excruciatingly difficult task, but central to prayer for the life of the *polis* as of the church, never bound by the worst but courageous enough to choose the best. The creative discontinuity of forgiveness may enable the discovery of unexpected opportunity.

Apart from prayer, lament over evil keeps us open to the justice as well as the mercy that manifests divine presence, notwithstanding many difficulties in our lives concerned with establishing where justice may lie and what it may require of us to establish it (Ackermann 2003). The Kyrie eleison and the Sanctus already mentioned, and the central creeds of Christendom (the Apostles' Creed for baptism in churches of Western origin, the Nicene Creed in the Eastern, and the latter universally for the Eucharist) insistently remind us of where human loyalty is to lie, with the God who is the source of justice and mercy alike, and who does not leave us to our own resources, or so we trust and hope. Nor may we leave others bereft of such help as can be given to them (Isa. 58: 6–9; Matt. 25: 31–46; Tob. 1–2, for instance, and the tradition of corporal and spiritual works of mercy can be revisited here).

In Scripture and creed and the texts of liturgy, God becomes "sayable" as we focus on Christ as sacrament. The things we use, and how we use them, give expression to the words, and non-human, natural things become sacramental gift to us: incense, salt, fire, oil, ashes, flowers, grain and grape (and their analogates in some cultures). The key point to remember here is that these things need to be generally available or easily obtainable (holiness and commonality again). We may or may not dress up in certain ways in gowns and robes and headgear, put on preaching bands, embroidered chasubles and copes and stoles, using special cloths and cushions and hangings, books, chalices and patens and bells or whatever, but none of these things should preoccupy us overmuch, and nor should the controversies of the past, except insofar as we can learn from them so as to overcome division constructively, whilst delighting in difference where we can.

We know that sacraments (two at least – baptism and Eucharist – three or seven or more or less) are capable of bearing variant but coherent meaning, as they must if they are to be universally embraced by human beings to sustain them through all the changes of their lives from birth to death in very different circumstances. And we have to allow for variable cultural expression and ceremony for both baptism and Eucharist. The unity of the sacraments and our unity are to be found not in uniformity but in the intradependence of all on the Christ we receive. We become "body" of Christ by being sustained by his "body," to which we are joined in faith and embraced in love in both Eucharist and church.

References

Ackermann, D. M. 2003: *After the Locusts: Letters from a Landscape of Faith.* Grand Rapids, MI: Eerdmans.

Beattie, T. 2002: *God's Mother, Eve's Advocate: A Marian Narrative of Women's Salvation*. London: Continuum.

Begbie, J. 2000: *Theology, Music and Time*. Cambridge: Cambridge University Press.

Brown, D. 2004: *God and the Enchantment of Place*. Oxford: Oxford University Press.

——and Fuller, D. 1995: *Signs of Grace: Sacraments in Poetry and Prose*. London: Cassell.

——and Loades, A. 1996: Introduction: the divine poet. In D. Brown and A. Loades (eds), *Christ: The Sacramental Word. Incarnation, Sacrament and Poetry*, pp. 1–25. London: SPCK.

Drane, J. 2000: *The McDonaldization of the Church: Spirituality, Creativity and the Future of the Church*. London: Darton, Longman, and Todd.

Fink, P.E. (ed.) 1990: *The New Dictionary of Sacramental Worship*. Dublin: Gill and Macmillan.

Foley, E. 1991: *From Age to Age: How Christians Celebrated the Eucharist*. Chicago, IL: Liturgy Training Publications.

Ford, P. F. 1999: *By Flowing Waters: Chant for the Liturgy*. Collegeville, MN: Liturgical Press.

Hall, B. and Jasper, D. (eds) 2003: *Art and the Spiritual*. Sunderland: University of Sunderland Press.

Hastings, A., Mason, A., and Pyper, H. (eds) 2000: *The Oxford Companion to Christian Thought*. Oxford: Oxford University Press.

Johnson, E. A. 1993: *She Who Is: The Mystery of God in Feminist Theological Discourse*. New York: Crossroad.

——1998: *Friends of God and Prophets: A Feminist Theological Reading of the Communion of Saints*. London: SCM.

Luff, A., Dunstan, A., Ferguson, P. et al. (eds) 1997: *Sing His Glory: Hymns for the Three-year Lectionary*. Norwich: Canterbury Press.

MacGregor, N. 2000: *Seeing Salvation: Images of Christ in Art*. London: BBC Worldwide.

Pelikan, J. (1997): *The Illustrated Jesus through the Centuries*. New Haven, CT: Yale University Press.

Ross, S. A. 1998: *Extravagant Affections: A Feminist Sacramental Theology*. New York: Continuum.

Saint Gregory of Nyssa Episcopal Church 1999: *Music for Liturgy: A Book for All God's Friends*. San Francisco: St Gregory of Nyssa Episcopal Church.

CHAPTER 16

Christian Spirituality and Theological Ethics

William C. Spohn

Spirituality and ethics are both necessary ingredients of Christian discipleship. The Gospel narratives make clear that Jesus taught his followers both how to pray and how to act in a manner that fitted their new relation to God. The Gospels do not, however, provide a theoretical account of how spiritual experience leads to moral practice or why it often fails to do so. Part of the task of theological ethics is to reflect on that connection; part of the task of a critical Christian spirituality is to spell out the moral implications for action and character that come from religious commitment.

There is an ethical dimension intrinsic to the Christian life because the experience of following Jesus Christ includes elements that are not optional but obligatory. Humanity itself rules out certain forms of behavior and has an inner drive toward flourishing, however obscure that may be. The Scriptures have moral authority for Christians because the texts are believed to contain the normative self-revelation of God in Jesus Christ as well as the appropriate ways to respond to Christ. Christian discipleship is a particular way of life that is shaped by specific values and patterns of behavior. Minimally, the New Testament rules out certain dispositions and forms of behavior as incompatible with loving God. One cannot claim to love the invisible God while hating the all-too-visible neighbor (1 John 4: 20). Maximally, the example of Jesus, who laid down his life for his friends, sets a heroic standard since love leads the disciple to make the same ultimate gift that the master did. Central to all the New Testament writings is the inseparable connection between loving God and loving the neighbor (Luke 10: 27). Images like the good tree bearing good fruit (Matt. 7: 17) and the vine and branches (John 15: 1–8) indicate that the new life given by Christ has a natural dynamism to produce morally beneficial results. Ordinary service, from offering a cup of water to visiting the imprisoned, gains ultimate religious significance since it serves Christ, who identifies himself with those in need (Matt. 25: 31–46). Conversely, harming the neighbor has ultimate consequences.

At the same time, the Christian moral life is founded on spirituality, the experience of God in Christ. Theological ethics reflects on the life of faith, which is fundamentally a response to an actual experience of God's goodness in Christ: "We love because he first loved us" (1 John 4: 19). That love is shown in the person and actions of Jesus of Nazareth. It also must be evident in what the risen Christ does in the present as well. The gratitude and radical trust that respond to God are evoked by a personal reality that has become part of Christians' personal awareness. Christian discipleship flows from a present experience of being claimed, healed, and sent by the Spirit of God sustained by a community of faith. That believers are loved by God is not simply a fact or theory but an experience that calls for a response. While religious language and doctrine may interpret this mysterious engagement, they cannot produce it, any more than a theory of friendship could produce friends. For believers, God does not deal with the world wholesale, as a cosmic principle or general factor in history, but as an irreducibly personal power and gracious presence that knows individuals and calls them by name (John 10: 3). Faith trusts that this relationship persists even when it is felt more as absence than presence. That experience, guided by Scripture and doctrine, provides both the content of Christian ethics (its values and patterns of action) and also its motivation (the affective dynamics that move humans to become disciples and act accordingly).

Ethics and Spirituality Defined

Ethics refers to the critical study of morality, namely, the direct, lived experience of human values and obligations. Ethics stands to morality as theology stands to spirituality, the lived experience of faith. When treatises on Christian ethics abstract moral principles from the lived experience of the faith, they may give the impression that Christian ethics is primarily an intellectual position that stands on the authority of its own arguments. Scripture presents a very different picture, one much closer to the actual reasons why anyone comes to faith. The Christian moral life comes as a response to God's summons in Christ, not as the conclusion to an argument. Theological ethics serves that relation by attempting to deepen believers' understanding of the gospel's demands, critically refine their behavior, and make it intelligible to those who do not share their faith.

Although Christian discipleship necessarily includes moral commitment, the intellectual challenge is to provide an adequate account of how committed religious living influences, or ought to influence, moral character and action. I take Christian spirituality to be the practical, affective, and transformative dimension of authentic Christian faith. I will argue that spirituality becomes practical through inculcating affective dispositions that lead to the radical transformation of believers as their innermost identity gradually takes on the shape of Jesus's cross and resurrection.

The three aspects of spirituality progressively work to produce committed Christian moral life. They build on one another to bring forth the fruit that God's life engenders:

(1)   *Practical.* Discipleship involves the believer in intentional spiritual practices and leads to specific practical consequences. For example, the command to love your

enemies calls Christians to develop regular practices of mercy, that is, conscious, committed disciplines of forbearance and forgiveness that take actual steps toward reconciliation. Forgiveness is not confined to times of confrontation and suffering injury. Regular spiritual practices like self-examination, fraternal correction, and confession of sins should help Christians acknowledge their own need for forgiveness and increase their readiness to extend it to others. The practices should prepare them to meet opposition and injury with the distinctive attitude and disposition, the virtue of mercy (Jones 1995).

(2) *Affective*. These spiritual practices shape the "affections," the deep emotions that define "the heart," the biblical image for the cognitive-emotive center of personal reality. Affections are the person's operative values because they are dispositions, abiding inclinations to act in certain ways. Christians should be disposed to show mercy and understanding rather than act defensively and retaliate against those who wrong them. Like the spiritual practices, these dispositions are rooted in faith convictions about what God has done for humans in Christ. The conviction and experience that God has been unconditionally merciful ought to dispose and oblige believers to be merciful to others.

(3) *Transformative*. Under the power of the Holy Spirit, the various practices of ordinary Christian life work to transform the moral character of believers and their life together. "Trans-form" means to "change shape" in the sense that the fundamental patterns of character change from the defensive, anxious, and guilty dynamics of self-centered existence to patterns of trusting faith, persevering hope, and generous love. Acting on these new affective dispositions and in opposition to the dynamics of sin gradually helps the person take on "the mind of Christ" (1 Cor. 2: 16); that is, the same virtues and patterns of behavior that were made manifest in his life, death, and resurrection. Human choice and intention are not supplanted by divine activity, but they are given new shape and vitality by grace. The Spirit of Christ operates in the individual's heart and in the community of faith to produce this transformation or "sanctification." Gratitude to the one who laid down his life to reconcile humanity with God, therefore, should motivate a corresponding disposition to mercy and practice of forgiveness. The content of that practice will be distinctively shaped by memories of Jesus's table fellowship with outcasts and parables like the unforgiving servant (Mark 2: 13–17; Matt. 18: 21–35).

Since humans are radically relational creatures, who learn from and are inspired by others, the moral transformation of discipleship does not occur in isolation but in the actual human communities of the Body of Christ and the emerging social reality of the Reign of God. Believers learn spiritual practices in the community of faith as it worships, acknowledges its failings, and tries to serve the world. The wisdom of the community and its tradition inculcates and guides the practices of its members. All of the central spiritual practices aim to build up the Body of Christ in the world by carrying out Jesus's mission to create a community of saving solidarity. Consequently, spiritual practices should not focus on individual growth but on the gradual growth of the entire Body of Christ, which is meant to bring the world closer to the justice, love, and peace that is the Reign of God.

Virtue Ethics: The Heart of the Matter

Which type of ethics will be the most appropriate way to interpret Christian spirituality? Ethics is most commonly approached through principles, consequences, or virtues. Although principles and consequences play a role in Christian life, virtue ethics best captures the full dynamics of the life of discipleship. It focuses on the whole person rather than on individual actions, and on the heart, where convictions and emotions are joined. Virtue ethics has the scope and depth necessary to analyze the radical transformation envisaged in the New Testament. The other two approaches, by contrast, tend to omit important features of Christian moral experience.

An *ethics of principles* appreciates the importance of moral norms and obligations but misses the overall shape of discipleship. Karl Barth's theological ethics, for example, concentrates on the present "command of God" (Barth 1957). Although based on the paradigmatic mandates of Scripture, the divine command is always existentially new because God is radically sovereign and free to command new and surprising actions. The command is addressed to the believer in unique circumstances and apprehended by faithful obedience. Unfortunately, Barth gives the impression that Christian life is a series of radical decisions that lack continuity. He pays little attention to the emerging identity of the disciple and the abiding dispositions of the heart because he feared that doing so would reinforce sinful self-preoccupation. Since the moral life includes a sense of direction and continuing commitments, ethics must attend to more than occasions of obedience. Although a spirituality shaped by obedience to divine commands may appreciate God as Lord and Commander, it overlooks other aspects of the One revealed in Jesus Christ: Father, Creator, Judge, Healer, and Companion.

Scripture describes not only what God requires, but also how God empowers believers to act. In fact, the requirements are always responses to what God is doing. The Ten Commandments are preceded in Exodus 19 by a recital of Yahweh's gracious deliverance of Israel from slavery in Egypt and the promise of an everlasting covenant with them. For those who continue to respond to that promise, the moral question is not "What should I do?" but "What is God enabling and requiring me to do and become?" (Gustafson 1975). Virtue ethics looks to these sources of empowerment and to the continuities of life, to the sorts of people we ought to become and the communities we ought to build.

The second type is the *ethics of consequences*. The right action is the one that produces the most benefit for the agent or society as a whole. Certainly Scripture is concerned about consequences. The Old Testament often refers to blessings that come from following the Lord's ways and curses that come from abandoning them. Jesus preaches that present conduct leads to the ultimate consequence of eternal life or damnation. Many ethicists discount rewards and punishments as "pre-moral" since they appeal to self-interest. Such a prohibition on considering results does not accord with the command to love one's neighbor as oneself, which presumes an appropriately ordered self-love. When spiritualities concentrate too narrowly on results, as in achieving personal sanctity or acquiring inner peace, they risk reducing the life of faith to a means to satisfying human needs. Socially minded theologies have argued that, since Christ's overall aim was to bring to fruition the Kingdom of God, that should be the goal and measure of all Christian action.

An ethics of consequences, however, appreciates only a part of discipleship. Certainly Christians ought to produce good works and alleviate human suffering. Love of neighbor cannot be assessed without looking to consequences to determine whether the neighbor is actually benefiting. Yet Christians do not believe in order to be good or productive, but because God has first loved them and called them into a new relationship in Christ. The Mennonite theologian John Howard Yoder states that the crucifixion challenges any concern about results. God calls Christians to be faithful, not effective. It is God's business to bring about the kingdom, while it is the duty of disciples to be faithful even to death, just as Jesus was (Yoder 1972).

Although any workable theological ethics must take moral principles and consequences into account, *virtue ethics* broadens the focus of ethics to look at the person as a whole and deepens its scope by considering the fundamental dynamics of the heart (Porter 1990; Statman 1997). It shifts attention from acting to being, to asking what sort of person we should become in response to God's gracious action in Christ. Action follows from character and in turn reinforces moral identity. This focus on the whole person fits the radical response that Jesus demands at the beginning of Mark's Gospel: "The time is fulfilled, and the kingdom of God has come near; repent, and believe the good news" (Mark 1: 15). Paul expresses this radical conversion in his dramatic claim that baptism has plunged the Christian into the core of Jesus's experience: "Therefore we have been buried with him by baptism into his death, so that, just as Christ was raised from the dead by the glory of the Father, so we too might walk in newness of life" (Rom. 6: 4).

The Pauline letters work out theoretically what the Gospels show narratively: the process of conversion takes a long time and encounters great resistance. The newness of life counteracts the sinful habits and affective dynamics of the old self-centered existence. Through the sanctifying power of the Spirit the convert has to take on a whole new identity, a new heart with a new set of attitudes and motivations that correspond to the dispositions of Jesus. The rivalry and conceit that divided Paul's struggling congregations had to be supplanted by the fruits that the Spirit was trying to cultivate in them: "love, joy, peace, patience, kindness, generosity, faithfulness, gentleness and self-control" (Gal. 6: 22).

Virtue ethics focuses on the commitments, emotionally charged dispositions, and habits that define moral character. When we act on our commitments they become habits of the heart, and so shape the sort of person that we are becoming. Values become embodied as dispositions when we intentionally act on them. Since disvalues become embodied through bad habits, this ethical approach is also concerned about vice. Virtue ethics examines the ways in which moral habits are inculcated and expressed, how they become ways of judging and acting, and how they coalesce into a fundamental orientation to good or evil.

Our deeds have a cumulative effect on our emerging moral self-definition. "Sow an act, reap a habit; sow a habit, reap a character; sow a character, reap a destiny," runs an old saying. Beneath our relatively free choices in particular actions we are exercising the more radical freedom of choosing the kind of person that we will become. Put more simply, we become what we do. Whether I am willing to acknowledge it or not, by telling lies I become a liar, and by telling the truth I become an honest person. At no point do we deliberately choose a character; it is the embedded product of all our deeds and relations.

This focus on virtue and character allows Christian ethics to grasp the new life that is emerging through the action of grace. As the moral commitments and dispositions of Jesus take root, the disciple ought to become more like the master. Every virtue gives practical expression to "God's love [that] has been poured into our hearts through the Holy Spirit that has been given to us" (Rom. 5: 5). A theological virtue ethics also focuses on the ways that humans cooperate with the sanctifying work of the Spirit by attending to individual and communal spiritual practices. We become what we do in cooperation with grace. More radically, the focus on character looks at the whole of life as a response to God. Humans do not say "yes" or "no" to the mystery of God directly, but through the ways they affirm or deny the humanity of their neighbors over a lifetime (Rahner 1974). Love of neighbor is integrated with love of God in the Love Commandment (Mark 12: 28–34). Because ethics and spirituality are inseparable, God is loved in and through loving the neighbor. The practices of spirituality strive to relate human interactions to this fundamental orientation to God. Although virtue ethics has been criticized for perfectionism and preoccupation with personal moral development, these tendencies can be corrected by locating the virtuous life within love of neighbor and God (Meilaender 1984)).

Spiritual Practices

Christian spirituality becomes embodied in the lives of believers through intentional disciplines called "spiritual practices." Every way of life is constituted by a set of practices, and Christianity is no exception. Robert Wuthnow distinguishes devotional practices, those aimed at enriching one's spiritual life, practices that express spirituality, and those that derive from one's relationship to the sacred (2001: 313). I will use the term for that core of intentional activities that carry faith into life and that deepen belief through faithful living. In Reformation traditions they have been called "means of grace," since God communicates salvation through these practices and they are "crucial embodiments of this communication and mediation" (Hutter 2002: 206).

The family resemblance of authentic Christian spiritualities is due to their grounding in recurring practices as well as the story of Jesus in the normative biblical text, formal creeds, and the common guidance of the Spirit. Could there be an authentic Christian community without baptism and the Lord's Supper, without preaching the Word and hospitality, without prayer, forgiveness, and generosity toward the poor? When spiritualities are defective it is because they lack one or more of the constitutive practices of the gospel way of life. Although we may debate which practices are necessary and which ought to be given priority, there is a recognizable profile that marks spiritualities as authentically Christian (Murphy et al. 1997). Different communities and eras will stress worship over service or commitment to the poor over preaching the Word, but the core practices should be represented. These practices are the marks of the Body of Christ, its defining characteristics, as Martin Luther taught (Luther 1955).

Virtue ethics shows how spiritual practices are the link between the story of Jesus and the Christian moral life. Practices are the means through which beliefs take root in us by becoming affectively charged dispositions that lead to faithful action. Under the grace of God's Spirit, these embodied convictions of faith become virtues; that is, dynamic habits of the heart to do the right thing with ease and delight. Virtues provide insight as well as motivation. Compassion, for instance, helps us recognize what the suffering need and inclines us to meet that need. Historically, spirituality has insisted that individuals and communities will not be transformed by the Spirit without committed practices. People may shop around for spiritual experiences, but without regular, intentional practices there is no real spirituality. Although peak experiences can make us see the possibility of change, it takes a life of regular spiritual practices in response to grace to yield a new character (Wuthnow 1998; Sedgwick 1999; Spohn 1999).

The notion of practices has recently taken center stage in virtue ethics. The philosopher Alasdair MacIntyre pointed out that every way of life inculcates its characteristic virtues through practices; that is, through socially constituted ways of acting that are worthwhile in themselves and which expand our human capacities (MacIntyre 1981: 175). Virtuous habits are learned from traditions and personal example; they result from acting in certain ways with the right intention. Practices like friendship or writing or playing chess are worthwhile doing in themselves. The saying "virtue is its own reward" means that virtuous practices enhance life in a way that needs no further justification. Most practices, however, can also be used as techniques, as means to something else. So a novelist may write simply for the income, or a salesman may be amiable to cultivate customers.

Practices lead to virtues indirectly since they are not behavioral conditioning that produces good actions automatically. Engaging in a practice exposes one to its inherent values and sharpens the habitual skills that will realize those values. Because virtues have a certain affinity for each other, a practice usually evokes more than one virtue. So, over time, a good friendship will draw us beyond self-concern and defensiveness to be more honest, trustworthy, and compassionate. These marks of a deep friendship also function as its internal norms because violating them would damage or destroy the friendship.

Consider the practice of fidelity as an intrinsic good of marriage and how it becomes an internalized moral standard. Catherine M. Wallace (1998) argues that marital fidelity is not just a prudent investment to ensure the benefits of marriage. More than a commitment to physical exclusivity, fidelity is an intrinsic good and a constitutive ingredient of marriage that allows honest self-disclosure, encourages intimacy, and gives grounds for trust. Without fidelity, these other virtues are unlikely to flourish and the relationship will not be a true marriage. The values inherent in the relationship become the standards for determining whether it is going well or not. Note that these standards are not imposed from outside the marriage; they are ingredients necessary for it to flourish. The commandment against adultery does not make sexual infidelity wrong; rather, it states descriptively that extramarital sex destroys the values at the core of marriage and so dishonors the spouse.

The practice of fidelity is also an instrumental good, in the sense that it does something positive *for* the married. Yet as an intrinsic good of marriage, fidelity does something *to* the married by shaping their characters. Every practice is supported by a series of intentional habits and customs. In a flourishing marriage, regular honest communication, time spent together, good humor, forgiving the spouse for not being like oneself, and the like, support fidelity. By being faithful, the spouses' marriage vows enter into their very sense of self. Wallace states that she writes because she is a writer, not for fun or financial reward:

> So too, I am faithful because I am a wife, because I have committed myself to being a wife . . . not for the sake of getting something in return but as an expression of who I have come to understand that I am, and furthermore who I ought to be, a little more clearly with each passing year. I could not be unfaithful without becoming someone else. (1998: 19)

Over twenty years of marriage, fidelity has become such a central part of Wallace's character that betrayal is unthinkable. The sense of moral obligation does not stem from the moral prohibition against adultery but from virtuous habits that present formidable resistance to betrayal.

Practices are not made up on the spot but have an historical shape. Wallace and her husband learned how to be faithful from their extended families and the Christian tradition that has nourished them despite its ambivalence about sexuality. Biblical stories and symbols give deeper meaning to fidelity for Wallace. The God of Israel is a covenanting Lord who keeps promises from generation to generation. Yahweh's fidelity wears down the infidelity of Israel, just as the prophet Hosea's persistence won back his wandering spouse. Believers discover something about who God is by keeping their own promises, and so come to recognize the Lord in their covenanted relationships. They are not only imitating God's way of loving; they are enacting it in daily life.

Christian spiritual practices go beyond MacIntyre's generic description of practices in two ways. First, not all the norms are internal to Christian practices. The biblical story forms an additional norm since it sets the patterns by which any human practice can be understood as an adequate response to God's love and self-revelation in human experience (Dykstra and Bass 2002). Secondly, spiritual practices are more relational than chess or playing a musical instrument, practices that MacIntyre mentions. No doubt beautiful music and the performance of a chess grand master are socially constructed and involve others, but they can be done well without locating them in an ongoing personal relationship. Friendship is a better analogue for spiritual practices because it necessarily includes another. God is the gracious source and ultimate aim of all Christian practices. Even a solitary practice like contemplation is derived from and flows back into the interdependent social reality of the Body of Christ. Just as fidelity in marriage is practiced for the sake of the relationship, every spiritual practice seeks to deepen the relationship to God and neighbor, not to produce individual spiritual virtuosi.

Practices inculcate virtuous habits through regular, committed exercise that can engage the practitioner at a deep level. Praying only when we feel like it is unlikely to produce a disposition of reverence, and writing the occasional check for the homeless will not instill Christian hospitality as part of our character (Pohl 1999). The commitment persists whether or not any particular exercise of the habit is rewarding. Not every act of worship or hospitality to the poor will be moving, any more than every conversation in a long marriage will be a rich experience of intimacy. What keeps a marriage vital is showing up, being attentive and available to the spouse. Practices like regular worship and service to the poor are not engaged in to win God's favor; that would reduce them to techniques. They are places where the community over time has learned that Christians need to show up, to be available to the work and healing that God will do in and through them.

Affections: The Springs of Action

Practices change the shape of character by educating the affections, the deep emotions of the heart. Through them the Spirit redefines the affections so they increasingly resemble those of Christ. Grace does not merely take natural emotions like courage and generosity and place them in a new context; it reworks them from within to embody the way of Jesus in a new time and place. The visible exercises of discipleship lead first to this interior formation and eventually toward radical transformation of the disciple's character.

No theologian captures the centrality of affections better than Jonathan Edwards, who wrote, "True religion, in great part, consists in holy affections" (1959: 95). The truths of faith are grasped only when they enter the deep affective structure of experience. If people have no experiential appreciation of what God has done for us, can they possibly understand the truths of faith? A life of trusting faith in God, persistent hope in the coming of God's reign, and love that overcomes enmity and death are God's gifts, which must be rooted in abiding dispositions of character. Though at times consciously experienced, faith, hope, and love are not transient feelings or merely entertaining sentiments. Christian virtues are cognitively grounded dispositions that relish God's true beauty and goodness. Appreciation and conviction converge in these character dynamics called affections. Ordinarily they are shaped by practices learned in a community of faith. So Edwards preached hundreds of sermons to detail the specific "means of grace" that allow charity to come to fruition. For example, he taught that honest self-examination was an important way to cultivate the love that "is not puffed up" (1 Cor. 13: 4) and that a generous estimation of others' motives would prevent envy from undermining love (1989: 227).

In order to understand how spiritual practices "tutor" the emotions, we have to realize that emotions can be educated. They are not blind instinctual reactions but learned behaviors. Emotions give us clues about what is happening objectively and how to respond to it. Although emotional impressions and intellectual judgments can be mistaken, in mature people they work together. Emotions are shaped by social conventions, past experience, and other factors. Anger, for example, reacts to a perceived injustice and energetically seeks to rectify it. Although anger may be a universal emotion, it gets scripted since culture teaches what counts as an injustice under what circumstances; culture also conveys the socially acceptable ways of setting things right.

In the Christian way of life, anger is recast, not suppressed. Biblically, righteous anger for holy causes was known as "zeal." The Old Testament attributes this emotion to the Lord, who does not tolerate the rich exploiting the poor. Jesus got angry at his opponents on occasion, most vividly when he drove the money-changers and their animals out of the Temple (Matt. 21: 12–13). Nevertheless, the affection of anger can be a deadly vice, particularly when it goes beyond rectifying the wrong done to punishing the guilty. Jesus's words and example challenge this punitive dimension of anger. The admonition to turn the other cheek, the petulance of the prodigal son's older brother, Jesus's refusal to resist those who came to arrest him, and his final word of forgiveness for those who crucified him all help to rewrite the script for anger. More general convictions also play a role in restructuring it: the belief that God alone judges the merit of human deeds and that humans are not the ones in charge of making the universe turn out right. These convictions combine with the gospel images to make vengeance moot. All the virtues of discipleship are "story-shaped" in the same way (Hauerwas 1981).

James M. Gustafson describes a set of fundamental affections or "senses" that together constitute the basic stance of Christians: radical dependence, gratitude, repentance, obligation, possibility, and direction. Each of these affections is "internally and organically" related to particular aspects of God revealed in Scripture and confirmed in the experience of believers. The sense of radical dependence arises from the experience and belief in God as creator; the sense of gratitude rests on the experience of God as good and beneficent in creation and redemption (1975: 92). Private and liturgical practices of prayer structure these divine qualities into the affections and make a corresponding moral claim: "To speak of God and to address God in the vocative of prayer means to undertake a certain way of existing, and to behave in a certain way toward other persons" (Saliers 1991: 30).

"Organized" religion's traditions, practices, and communities of faith are the media through which Christians become "spiritual." Cognitively, religious traditions give them the language to identify their various experiences of the sacred and recognize the implications that those experiences have for life. Communities convey the stories and assertions of faith that help believers realize who it is they are looking for. As religious affections become part of character, they have a cognitive role in shaping perception and action. So, a truly compassionate person will perceive the needs of others more readily and is likely to recognize how to respond appropriately.

The practices learned in communities of faith testify to the characteristic qualities of God and develop the corresponding affections. There Christians learn to read Scripture prayerfully; hear the Word proclaimed and unpacked; celebrate the Lord's Supper; sing hymns of praise, thanksgiving, and trust; and confess their sins. Through these intentional, repeated activities, God's Spirit works through human processes to develop Christ-like affections. Human dedication does not cause the gift, but the gift enters human hearts through habitual practice. When the mercy and justice witnessed in biblical images and stories are carried into action, they become imprinted on human dispositions, internally rewriting their scripts. This change happens gradually and often fitfully since it encounters resistance from bias, sin, and prejudice, which have written their own scripts onto the affections.

Singing and meditating on the psalms is an ancient biblical practice that reorients the emotions toward God. Let us examine how the process works in a traditional "Negro spiritual" that is often sung in Good Friday services. In a solemn tone and measured cadence the opening line asks: "Were you there when they crucified my Lord?" The second line repeats the first to let it sink in. The third line declares the singer's reaction: "Oh, sometimes it causes me to tremble, tremble, tremble." Finally, it returns to the theme: "Were you there when they crucified my Lord?"

If we are literally minded, the song will not engage us because the literal answer is simply: "No, I wasn't there." Generations of believers, however, have been powerfully engaged by the question as they let their imaginations transcend the literal facts. The hymn presupposes that the crucifixion of Jesus is not a sealed-off past event but is permeable, an event accessible across time and space. Just as Jews remember and relive the Passover in Egypt at the annual Seder meal, Christians remember and enter again the crucifixion on Good Friday. Through ritual that evokes community memory, the crucifixion of Jesus reaches into the present experience of believers, just as it reached into the hard lives of the slaves who first sang the spiritual. "My Lord" articulates a present relation to the One who was crucified – not a bond of memory but a contemporary relation to One who claims the believer. The music and words convey a complex of affections ordered by the gospel narrative. The solemn cadence supports a mood of awe, sorrow, and trembling at mystery. Grief and compassion are at once personal and communal when the spiritual is sung with an assembly that acknowledges a living connection to the One crucified.

The next stanzas of the spiritual deepen the mood by immersing the singers in the specific physical aspects of the event. The second stanza asks: "Were you there when they nailed him to the tree?" And the third: "Were you there when they laid him in the grave?" The repetition of each adds new depth to the sorrow and trembling. These affective responses are not mere sentiments because they make a subtle claim on the singers. The question "Were you there?" asks whether the singers will stand by today's suffering people or flee as Jesus's disciples did. Those who sing the spiritual have a choice to make in the face of such grief and suffering. Finally, the last stanza follows the same mournful cadence but follows the story through: "Were you there when he rose on Easter morn?" The narrative leads grief into hard-won hope, a joy that comes out of sorrow and cannot forget where it came from.

The spiritual has added meaning and depth of impact when sung by a community that commemorates the season of Lent and the entire cycle from Maundy Thursday's washing of the feet to Easter morning's alleluias. Three days of solemn ritual can embed a distinctive pattern into the worshipers' affections. Within that rhythm the mournful hymn first sung by Christians in slavery frames the transition from the quiet but empty commemoration of Good Friday to the cosmic celebration of the Easter vigil. Some Good Friday liturgies acknowledge the gap between the dying and rising of Jesus by ending with the spiritual's third verse. This sets the emotional tone from the end of Friday until the Easter vigil or sunrise service. The period of waiting should convey the realization that it takes time for new life to emerge from suffering and death. Holy Saturday symbolizes the present moral struggle for Christians who are caught between dying to death and living to life. Embedded in liturgical practice, the traditional spiritual teaches that those who do not share in the cross of Christ will not share in his victory (Rom. 6). The Holy Week liturgy inculcates a complex stance of hope in the midst of despair, and confidence that God will keep faith even in the face of death. Even communities that do not celebrate the full rhythm from Thursday to Easter should have their core identity shaped by commemorating the dying and rising of Jesus. Liturgical practice helps them grasp that the cross and resurrection recur through history since God continues to raise the suffering and oppressed from their graves. Because the Body of Christ extends into the world, his suffering and rising are not a one-time event.

When rightly done, liturgical prayer has significant moral consequences. These are not insights drawn by conclusion from theological premises but a reshaping of embodied convictions and attitudes. Expressed in prayer and interpreted through preaching, ritual should help the congregation realize what God is empowering and requiring them to become. The complex affections shaped by Holy Week ought to lead believers to take a definite moral stance toward their own culture and world. The compassion that liturgy evokes should align them with those who suffer, not out of pity, but because they see the oppressed as "the crucified people" of history (Sobrino 1994). Seeing the poor through the lens of Holy Week leads to the imperative to take them down from the crosses to which they have been nailed. A liturgically tutored compassion, therefore, leads to action for justice and solidarity. These affections should also lead Christians to acknowledge their own complicity in the unjust structures of the world and motivate them to take responsibility for the changes they can make (Gilman 2001: 120). Nevertheless, liturgy is not a technique for evoking moral motivations but a grateful response to God's action in Christ that has inescapable consequences for how believers live.

The practice of liturgy can and should engender the full range of affections that are displayed in the story of salvation that is central to the act of worship. "Prayer is giving oneself to the Christian story in such a way that the emotions that characterize that life become the virtues exercised in concrete circumstances" (Saliers 1991: 97). The liturgy of Holy Week holds together a sense of repentance with that of possibility and hope, a sense of gratitude and awe with a sense of responsibility for those who suffer. Anchored in the pattern of the biblical narrative and inscribed on the heart through regular practices, the entire inter-related set of emotions forms the affective norm for Christian conscience. These embedded values can become a moral compass for discerning how to proceed and when to resist. Faithful living should make this internal standard more acute, so that options that conform to the values of Christ will be experienced as harmonious, while those that oppose will clash (Spohn 1999). This developing sensitivity does not exempt Christians from getting the facts straight, consulting with others, considering ethical principles, and thinking through alternative courses of action. Disciples are not called to copy the ways of Jesus but to be both faithful to the demands of the gospel and creative in finding how to act in new situations. Gospel-shaped affections ought to serve as internal guides for all actions, so that whatever a Christian does should express the love, humility, and willingness to serve found in Jesus. Those affections, so clearly displayed in Jesus's washing of his disciples' feet in John 13, are simply irreconcilable with a life of ambition and thirst for power.

Transforming Reality

Christian spirituality envisions a fundamental transformation from self-centered existence to theocentric existence. The trajectory of transformation is clear, even if its realization is eschatological. Jesus proclaimed and inaugurated the Reign of God, a healed
world in right relation to God. The Spirit of Jesus leads disciples beyond personal needs
to set their hearts and actions on that transformation. Although the New Testament
images of growth point to the hidden, steady progress of God's reign, the cross and resurrection of Jesus, which is the central analogy for the path of discipleship, is starkly
disjunctive. Traditional Christian writers emphasized that Christian transformation
took place over a lifetime and happened to only a few (John of the Cross 1973). They
specified different practices of asceticism that were appropriate to the purgative, illuminative, and unitive stages of spiritual development, while emphasizing the apophatic
nature of the process (Coakley 2002). Contemporaries place less emphasis on practices
of self-denial and more on sharing the suffering of others through the demanding practices of solidarity and action for justice (Soelle 1984; Sobrino 1994). An ethics of consequences finds it difficult to understand Christian transformation because its terminus,
union with the mystery of God, defies exact definition.

Analysis of spiritual practices and the affections can address perfectionism and isolation, which are two expressions of self-concern masquerading as genuine transformation. To a degree not matched in contemporary spirituality, traditional writers
appreciated the depth of resistance to radical transformation and the human capacity
for self-deception that are rooted in the abiding influence of sin.

Beyond individualism: practices of the Body of Christ

The first common temptation is a spirituality that seeks experience of God without reference to community. While an estimated 20 percent of adult Americans pursue spiritual experiences apart from organized religion, an increasing number blend devotional
practices from other religions with some allegiance to a Christian denomination (Fuller
2001). When, however, spiritual pursuits are extracted from a community context of
interpretation, they can easily become superficial or distorted.

All the New Testament's metaphors for spiritual change refer to processes that
are primarily social and only derivatively individual: salvation, redemption, justification, sanctification. The Reign of God that Jesus proclaimed was a profoundly social
reality. When he claimed that God was breaking into the world, it signaled that the
collective life of Israel was about to change (Wright 1996). When God reigned, nature
and all human relations would be guided by the divine wisdom and compassion.
The broken world would become the world according to God. In announcing the good
news, therefore, Jesus was calling individuals not primarily to personal renewal but to
enlist in this corporate and cosmic reordering of reality. As the first step to that end,
he called disciples to leave the security of their families to join a new sort of family
under God.

In the next generation, Paul focused on the Body of Christ, the saving social reality that was the beginning of the world according to God. Baptism joins individuals to an organic saving reality where they are as interdependent as the parts of a body. Spiritual practices are salvific only if they are "in Christ," that is, located within the normative saving reality that has theological and social boundaries. From this perspective of the Reign of God or the Body of Christ, therefore, there is no authentic spirituality that is not "religious," that is, connected to a flawed but redeemed community of faith, a social and theological tradition composed of specific people. Contemporary eclectic spiritual seeking arises both from a culture of individualism and from the failure of organized churches to live up to their claims and to transmit vital spiritual practices to their members.

Even spiritual practices that seem solitary are learned in families and churches and sustained by a social history. "Private" meditation on Scripture reflects on biblical texts that were authored by communities and make sense within a history of interpretation. Contemplative Bible reading is a product of "reading in communion" with others over time and space (Fowl and Jones 1991). Even private prayer, the practice of spending time with God alone, is learned from others by word and example. It deepens the friendship with God that is found in and through the social reality of Christ's Body and, like all practices, is measured by whether it builds up that body.

Allen Verhey argues that the practical enterprise of Christian ethics, of determining what we are to do and become, is rooted in the communal spiritual practice of remembering Jesus. Reading the story of Jesus faithfully, Christians "learn to remember, and such remembering is to own a past as one's own and to own it as constitutive of identity and community and as determinative of discernment" (2002: 165). Christian ethics is not first of all an academic enterprise but a communal practice done "by way of reminder" of "the story we love to tell and long to live" (2002: 473). This "remembering" is the intrinsic good at which the practice aims. Verhey specifies three pairs of virtues internal to the practice that determine whether it hits the mark: holiness and sanctification, fidelity and creativity, discipline and discernment. Just as the virtue of fidelity is an internal standard of marriage, these virtues are the criteria that show whether the practice of reading Scripture is authentically Christian. They are not simply the signs of individual spiritual growth but are the virtues that mark the community's collective transformation "in Christ."

Beyond perfectionism: losing oneself

Perfectionism is the second major challenge in moving from self-centered to theocentric existence. It occurs when a spirituality turns practices into techniques for moral growth or personal peace. Such an instrumental approach contradicts the paradox that Jesus laid down: try to save yourself and you will lose yourself; lose yourself for his sake and you will find yourself (Mark 8: 35). As a matter of fact, what is an intrinsic good in one order may be an instrumental good in another order. What is good is always good for someone, but that does not mean that it is pursued primarily for personal benefit. So, the fact that the virtue of justice makes for a richer, deeper human existence does not mean that the individual's primary intention in acting justly is to become a more complete human being. The primary orientation of justice is to redress the rights of the oppressed and seek the common good for all, which usually requires some sacrifice of one's own interests. Or consider the religious practice of contemplation: its intrinsic good is living in the presence of God, which cannot be a totally disinterested pursuit since it meets a fundamental human need. Nevertheless, the inevitable experience of God's absence for extended periods of the spiritual life purifies the heart. The longing for God cannot be reduced to the longing for experience of God. Nor can it be reduced to the pursuit of spiritual perfection or a means to "get to heaven." Even though the intention in starting a devotional exercise like prayer may be instrumental, the intrinsic good of the practice draws the prayerful person to the mystery of God that transcends self-interest.

Spiritual practices are theocentric because they come from God and lead to God. The principal agent in all of them is the Spirit of God, who prays, preaches, sings, and serves in and through believers. Spiritual practices are human actions synergistic with divine grace. Engagement with God progressively takes attention off the self, just as a maturing friendship becomes less about individual satisfaction and more about the goodness of the other person and the union itself. Friendships move beyond the dyad of the friends to causes and values that transcend them. Paul cites his own example: leaving behind all the credentials that once defined him to move single-heartedly to know Christ and the power of his resurrection (Phil. 3).

Edwards held that "Christianity restores an excellent enlargement and extensiveness to the soul" that reverses the contracting self-absorption of sin (1989: 254). He held that the expansive attraction of God's beauty subordinates self-love without eradicating it and redirects personal concern to the moral and religious welfare of the neighbor. Since all genuine religious affections come from love, they should all lead to love. At the same time, Edwards thought that the transforming power of the Spirit acted through believers' intentional and committed use of the "means of grace," such as practices of self-examination, communal worship, charity, generosity, and the like.

In every era, Christian spiritualities mediate between religious tradition and the needs and challenges of a particular society. Authentic spiritualities address major cultural problems and distortions, sometimes adapting traditional practice, and at other times inventing new ones. Today, the practices of justice address the oppression of women and the poor (particularly through solidarity), blending compassion and political action. Response to the environmental crisis adapts practices of conscious unity with creation and calls forth practices of simplicity of life for others. In the developed world, the all-consuming demands of work and productivity have called attention to the ancient practice of keeping Sabbath (Bass 1997: 81). By inculcating intentional practices like these along with the core practices of discipleship, spirituality shapes the affections toward ethical commitment and moral fruitfulness.

References

Barth, K. 1957: *Church Dogmatics*, vol. 2, pt 2. Edinburgh: T. and T. Clark.
Bass, D. C. (ed.) 1997: *Practicing our Faith*. San Francisco: Jossey-Bass.

Coakley, S. 2002: Discerning practices: perspectives from ascetical and mystical theology. In M. Volf and D. C. Bass (eds), *Practicing Theology: Beliefs and Practices in Christian Life*, pp. 78–93. Grand Rapids, MI: Eerdmans.

Dykstra, C. and Bass, D. C. 2002: A theological understanding of Christian practices. In M. Volf and D. C. Bass (eds), *Practicing Theology: Beliefs and Practices in Christian Life*, pp. 13–32. Grand Rapids, MI: Eerdmans.

Edwards, J. 1959: *Religious Affections*. In *The Works of Jonathan Edwards*, vol. 1. New Haven, CT: Yale University Press.

——1989: *Ethical Writings*. In *The Works of Jonathan Edwards*, vol. 8. New Haven, CT: Yale University Press.

Fowl, S. E. and Jones, L. G. 1991: *Reading in Communion: Scripture and Ethics in Christian Life*. Grand Rapids, MI: Eerdmans.

Fuller, R. C. 2001: *Spiritual, but Not Religious: Understanding Unchurched America*. New York: Oxford University Press.

Gilman, J. E. 2001: *Fidelity of Heart: An Ethic of Christian Virtue*. New York: Oxford University Press.

Gustafson, J. G. 1975: *Can Ethics Be Christian?* Chicago: University of Chicago Press.

Hauerwas, S. 1981: *A Community of Character: Toward a Constructive Christian Social Ethic*. Notre Dame, IN: University of Notre Dame Press.

Hutter, R. 2002: Hospitality and truth: the disclosure of practices in worship and doctrine. In M. Volf and D. C. Bass (eds), *Practicing Theology: Beliefs and Practices in Christian Life*, pp. 206–27. Grand Rapids, MI: Eerdmans.

John of the Cross 1973: *Dark Night of the Soul*. In K. Kavanagh and O. Rodriguez (trans.), *The Collected Works of St John of the Cross*. Washington, DC: Institute of Carmelite Studies.

Jones, G. 1995: *Embodying Forgiveness: A Theological Analysis*. Grand Rapids, MI: Eerdmans.

Luther, M. 1955: On the Councils and the Church. In *Luther's Works*, vol. 41, pp. 146–68. Minneapolis, MN: Concordia and Fortress Press.

MacIntyre, A. 1981: *After Virtue: A Study in Moral Theory*. Notre Dame, IN: University of Notre Dame Press.

Meilaender, G. C. 1984: *The Theory and Practice of Virtue*. Notre Dame, IN: University of Notre Dame Press.

Murphy, N., Kallenberg, B. J., and Nation, M. T. 1997: *Virtues and Practices in the Christian Tradition: Christian Ethics after MacIntyre*. Harrisburg, PA: Trinity Press International.

Pohl, C. D. 1999: *Making Room: Recovering Hospitality as a Christian Tradition*. Grand Rapids, MI: Eerdmans.

Porter, J. 1990: *The Recovery of Virtue: The Relevance of Aquinas for Christian Ethics*. Notre Dame, IN: University of Notre Dame Press.

Rahner, K. 1974: Reflections on the unity of the love of God and the love of neighbor. In *Theological Investigations*, vol. 6, pp. 231–49. New York: Seabury.

Saliers, D. 1991: *The Soul in Paraphrase: Prayer and the Religious Affections*, 2nd edn. Akron, Ohio: Order of St Luke Publications.

Sedgwick, T. F. 1999: *The Christian Moral Life: Practices of Piety*. Grand Rapids, MI: Eerdmans.

Sobrino, J. 1994: *The Principle of Mercy: Taking the Crucified People Down from the Cross*. Maryknoll, NY: Orbis.

Soelle, D. 1984: *The Strength of the Weak: Toward a Christian Feminist Identity*. Philadelphia: Westminster.

Spohn, W. C. 1999: *Go and Do Likewise: Jesus and Ethics*. New York: Continuum.

Statman, D. (ed.) 1997: *Virtue Ethics: A Critical Reader*. Washington, DC: Georgetown University Press.

Verhey, Allen. 2002: *Remembering Jesus: Christian Community, Scripture, and the Moral Life*. Grand Rapids, MI: Eerdmans.

Wallace, C. M. 1998: *For Fidelity: How Intimacy and Commitment Enrich our Lives*. New York: Knopf.

Wright, N. T. 1996: *Jesus and the Victory of God*. Minneapolis, MN: Fortress Press.

Wuthnow, R. 1998: *After Heaven: Spirituality in America since the 1950s*. Berkeley, CA: University of California Press.

——2001: Spirituality and spiritual practice. In R. K. Fenn (ed.), *The Blackwell Companion to Sociology of Religion*, pp. 306–20. Oxford: Blackwell.

Yoder, J. H. 1972: *The Politics of Jesus*. Grand Rapids, MI: Eerdmans.

PART V

Interdisciplinary Dialogue Partners for the Study of Christian Spirituality

CHAPTER 17

Social Sciences

John A. Coleman

In the early 1990s, I was invited, along with about eight other social scientists and theologians, to join a faculty discussion group at the University of California, Berkeley. For a span of about two years, we met monthly to discuss what might constitute spirituality from a social science perspective. The catalyst for the group came from Guy E. Swanson, a social-psychologist who headed Berkeley's Institute for Human Development. For decades, since the 1920s, the Institute has carefully tracked two cohorts of people, born in Berkeley and Oakland, throughout their childhood, adolescence, early adulthood, and so on. Swanson discovered, in the rich archival trove of interviews from that famous cohort study, that many of those interviewed at mid-life had re-engaged with religion or, alternately, had turned to a kind of newly found spiritual reflexivity outside of organized religion. Just how, Swanson wondered, could we go about conceptualizing spirituality in social science studies? How is it related to religiosity and how might it be conceived of as a semi-independent conceptual variable?

If one begins – as the theologians present to the seminar all did – with a Catholic schema for spirituality (around key concepts and practices such as "grace," the imitation of Christ, communal and personal discernment, spiritual direction by a mentor, ideals of a calling, meditation and *lectio pia*, the Eucharist, and so on) how might one, *mutatis mutandis*, extract analogous concepts and practices for Jewish, Muslim, Orthodox, Protestant, Buddhist – indeed, even a "secular" – spirituality? The majority of the participants tended to opt for a concept of spirituali*ties* rather than a generic spirituality, although analogous forms of belief, practice, and ritual would be found across the spectrum of differing spiritualities. Religion and spirituality could neither be conflated nor posited as simply in opposition. They could be conceptually differentiated, although in fact the bulk of spiritualities grew out of and were explicitly fostered by religious traditions.

There was little in the social science literature at the time to serve us with much help on these questions. If we take the sociology of religion (my own discipline) as a kind of benchmark, we uncover a history of research on religiosity/spirituality during the second half of the twentieth century which looks much like the following. In the 1940s and 1950s, major studies emphasized *degrees* of religiosity. The focus was mainly on how participation in religious groups (church attendance, other practices such as daily prayer or Bible reading) yielded variable impacts on attitudes about the political order, the economy, work, marriage, gender roles, and other effects. No explicit mention was made of spirituality, which was seen, if at all, as folded into religiosity (Fichter 1951; Lenski 1961). Gordon Allport, however, in a ground-breaking set of studies on religion and prejudice, had postulated a dichotomized *intrinsic* versus *extrinsic* religiosity. The former was reflexive, personalized, individuated, while the latter involved belonging rather than genuine believing and self-appropriation. Intrinsic religiosity correlated highly with tolerance, altruism, and social service, while extrinsic religiosity tended toward authoritarianism and narrow group loyalties. Intrinsic religiosity yielded the lowest levels of prejudice (lower even than non-believers), while extrinsic religiosity tended to produce high out-group prejudices (Allport 1950, 1954). A variant of Allport's categories would re-emerge in the 1990s, with spirituality being closely aligned with his intrinsic religiosity and religion being somewhat caricatured as a species of what Allport called extrinsic religiosity.

In the 1960s and 1970s, the main writers in the sociology of religion – Charles Glock, Rodney Stark, and Peter Berger – also did not explicitly explore spirituality. Glock and Stark, however, began to focus on types of religious involvement and what they called discrete "dimensions" of religiosity (ideological, ritualistic, intellectual, experiential, and consequential) (Glock and Stark 1965). Their categories of experiential and consequential religion provide some overlap with what we would now call spirituality but were seen, then, as sub-sets of the broader category, religiosity. Since religiosity encompassed spirituality, Glock and Stark did not pay much attention to those who are spiritual but not religious. Glenn Vernon, however, showed that one-quarter of those who said they were not religiously affiliated were, nevertheless, believers, and could state that they had experienced God's presence (Vernon 1962). Vernon's was the first sighting of what would later be called the "spiritual but not religious."

For his part, Berger was mainly interested in religion's role as a societal legitimacy system, a "sacred canopy" (Berger 1967). He stressed collective over individual meaning systems. Yet, in his *A Rumor of Angels* (1969), Berger, like Glock and Stark, delved into experiential and individual religion. Berger's quondam colleague, Thomas Luckmann, postulated that overarching societal religious legitimacy systems in modernity no longer prevailed, such that individuals and subcultural groups had to work hard, in a counter-cultural move, to shore up their religious beliefs and practices. Invisible religion lent itself to a kind of eclecticism, since modernity erodes all coherent traditions (Luckmann 1967). Berger echoed much the same theme in his *The Heretical Imperative* (1979). Berger and Luckmann do not treat spirituality as such, but do broach a topic much mined in the 1990s about spirituality being a creative personal appropriation from many traditions, an eclectic bricolage.

If you wanted to find something akin to what is now called spirituality in the sociology of religion literature of the 1960s and 1970s, you might look under other rubrics such as "the individual and his/her religion," "unofficial religion," or "lived religion." None of these, however, had a perfect overlap with spirituality. For some forms of lived religion (for example, family altars, intimate blessings, the use of medals and icons, and so on), while not prescribed by "official religion," do not negate it and are often encouraged by it. Moreover, some forms of lived religion or "unofficial religion" are much more communal (for example, popular religiosity) than the term spirituality has come to embody.

This history of research on religion and spirituality, of course, reflects the *Zeitgeist* of the times in which the researchers were doing their work. In the wake of the Depression, World War II, and the Cold War, the 1940s and 1950s comprised a period of respect for and conformity to religious/social institutions. Americans tended to see religiosity (measured, almost always, by participation in religious groups or engaging in official religious practices) and spirituality (a personal, appropriated relationship with God) as inseparable. A world which could be synthesized by Will Herberg's (1955) classic tripartite America of "Protestant, Catholic, and Jew" seems, in retrospect, quite parochial, in an America which now includes as many or more Moslems, Orthodox Christians, and Buddhists as it does Jews.

The 1960s represented a kind of watershed for the study of religion. All institutions became suspect, including religious ones. New religions abounded, with a major importation of Eastern religions and a consciousness revolution which discovered alternative spiritualities, outside the churches, in New Age networks, a turn to angelology, witch covens, psychological groups that engaged in meditation, and bodily regimes and spiritual practices, such as at Esalen (Needleman 1970; Glock and Bellah 1976; Wuthnow 1976; Cox 1977; Wilson and Cresswell 1999). The earliest books on the psychology of religion, for their part, tended to stress the adjective "religious" and to broach topics very cognate with those of the sociology of religion: beliefs, practices, attitudes, orientations, moral values and coping and problem-solving mechanisms (Grensted 1952; Clark 1958; Pruyser 1968).

Some of the later psychological treatments of religion, like sociology, began, in the 1990s, to veer toward an explicit look at spirituality (Collins 1991). The new religious movements have been assiduously studied (perhaps overly so, given their actual percentages in the population), and accounts of them have noted how their ideas and practices have sometimes percolated back into the churches. As Princeton sociologist, Robert Wuthnow, has claimed: "The larger impact of Eastern spirituality was to popularize practices that could be pursued piecemeal and on one's own" (1998b: 219). Looser ties, new Buddhist and Hindu immigration from Asia after 1965, and the increased mobility of Americans (Wuthnow 1998a; Putnam 2000) made for the now often canonical distinction between spirituality and religion where, frequently, religion is seen as bad/hypocritical/hopelessly formal and spirituality is esteemed good/authentic, as in the consecrated phrase: "I am spiritual but not religious." But any careful social science attention to the category of the spiritual is a phenomenon only of the later 1990s.

Social Scientific Studies of Spirituality since the 1990s

It may help to review some of the major studies addressing the issue of spirituality and religion in the late 1990s. I will then try to generalize about some things students of spiritualities can learn from social science studies, and also about an unfinished agenda in the social sciences in studying spiritualities.

Wade Clark Roof

Without any doubt, Wade Clark Roof's *The Spiritual Marketplace: Baby Boomers and the Remaking of Religion* (1999) is the best single social science monograph on contemporary spirituality and religiosity, although, in places, Roof seems too sanguine and cheery about the religious shifts of the latter part of the twentieth century, too sure that a thoughtful reflexive spirituality will win the day, ultimately, over mere eclectic individualism. But the book remains a kind of *tour de force*. In an earlier study of baby-boomers and their religion, *A Generation of Seekers*, Roof proffered an initial definition of spirituality: "Spirituality gives expression to the being that is in us. It has to do with feelings, with the power that comes from within, with knowing our deepest selves and what is sacred in us, with, as Mathew Fox says, 'heart knowledge'" (1993: 64). This definition is quite flawed by its being skewed toward inwardness and disjointed from any notion of communal rootedness or outward service. It also dis-embeds spirituality from community. Indeed, some critics thought Roof was here exalting that "expressive individualism" that Robert Bellah and his associates, in their much-regarded *Habits of the Heart* (1985), excoriated as eroding republican virtue, American community, and civic mindedness.

Still, in *A Generation of Seekers*, Roof helps us to see the main comparative categories for looking at competing spiritualities in contemporary culture. These are the following five:

1   *Conceptions of the self*: is the self fixed and anchored in community as a settled category, or is it ephemeral, negotiated, and context-fluid? Modern culture, Roof contends, tends to privilege the second notion of the self over the first.
2   *Locus of authority*: is it within or without the individual? The second anchors some traditional spiritualities (Christian or otherwise) which root belief and practice in an objective God, moral truths, revealed practices. The former (authority within) could well appeal to a transcendence that is immanent in nature or a God-head within. As Emerson (1940) once put it, such people see themselves as part and parcel of God dwelling within them.
3   *Meaning system*: is it expressive or authoritative? Does spirituality bring forth and express some real "authentic self" or some hidden meaning within me, or does it link up to a trusted external transcendent authority?
4   *Spiritual styles*: some spiritualities emphasize a kind of "letting go" and allowing some surge of spontaneous energies and creativity to well forth. Others put more focus on asceticism, on mastery and control of errant desires.
5   *Availability of spiritual resources*: is spirituality in rich supply or is it, rather, a scarce and hard-won achievement? Roof notes that an abundant supply-side spirituality thinks "that abundance rather than scarcity, plenty rather than poverty is our true spiritual condition" (1993: 68). For the baby-boomers in the Roof sample, at least,

"the new values emphasize self-fulfillment and self-growth; inner spiritual discovery and exploration; a greater sense of self; appreciation of the body, of gender and spirituality; of reaching out to others and letting go" (1993: 47). In this boomer sample, 86 percent claimed to be religious; 14 percent said they were not religious. Of that latter group, however, 65 percent of the non-religious said they were spiritual. These represented 9 percent of the Roof boomer sample.

Some critics of *Spiritual Marketplace* (1999), a follow-up to the earlier boomer study, felt that Roof overly privileges that 9 percent, whom Roof denominates "intense seekers." Since the overwhelming majority of those who say they are spiritual are also religious, and the overwhelming majority of the religious also say they are spiritual, the carriers of the bromide "I am spiritual but not religious" are a decided minority. In the overall sample for *Spiritual Marketplace*, 74 percent say they are religious; 73 percent claim to be spiritual; 79 percent of those who are religious are also spiritual; 54 percent of those who disclaim the religious label are, nevertheless, spiritual (1999: 173).

The false but emerging dichotomy between religion and spirituality gets canonized in the Roof study. Spirituality is seen to implicate something distinct from religion, and deeply subjective. "Organized religion," in contrast, looks cut and dry, encrusted and culturally bound. Overall, Roof's sample (which includes a majority of adherents to churches as well as the "seekers" who belong to no churches) is amazingly open to spiritual exploration. The percentage open to spiritual exploration in Roof's second study had increased over the earlier boomer study: from 52 to 60 percent. Some 48 percent seemed to wear any loyalties somewhat lightly, claiming that "all the religions of the world are equally true and good"; 54 percent of the sample agreed that "the churches/synagogues have lost the real spiritual part of religion."

Religious identities in contemporary society have become fluid, multi-layered, and, to a considerable extent, personally achieved. Increasingly, people switch out of religious groups in which they were raised. From his multiple interviews with contemporary Americans, Roof essays, in *Spiritual Marketplace*, a definition of spirituality: "The spiritual comprehends but cannot be contained by intellect, cognition, or institutional structure; it reaches out for unity and the ordering of experience; it abhors fixity in the interest of transformation. Both the notion of ordering experience and that of transformation suggest something deeply existential, directed to connections with ultimate meanings, values, and ethical commitment." To be sure, the majority of Americans are both religious and spiritual. But, "as Americans speak of spirituality today, the term may, and most often does, include religion in the sense of tradition, yet for many it is not bound by doctrinal, creedal or ecclesiastical categories" (1999: 34).

Roof undertakes a cultural analysis of what he calls "a quest culture" where, increasingly, spirituality uses a language of journey, walk, growth, the primacy of experience, the legitimacy of doubt and seeking, a resort to the body. To be sure, much of what passes as spirituality in this culture is a mere pastiche or collage – religious pluralism within the individual, a mixing of codes, and an eclectic choice of practices from many traditions; in short: religion à la carte. But Roof envisions an alternative reflexive spirituality which encourages "a more deliberate engaging effort on people's part for their own spiritual formation, both inside and outside religious communities"

(1999: 75). The need for a reflexive spirituality arises from the erosion by modernity of most coherent communities and traditions. A hunger for wholeness is the reverse face to this eroding acid of modernity where all that is solid melts into air. "Modernity severs connections to place and community, alienates people from their natural environments, separates work and life, dilutes ethical values – all of which makes the need for unifying experience so deeply felt" (1999: 62).

The marketplace in Roof's title refers to an expansion of choice in modernity. No religious organization any longer has a monopoly over the symbolization of the sacred or any privileged access to it. An open, deregulated religious market, of course, can encourage a mere spiritual consumerism or a tourism mentality in the realm of the sacred. There are also many new suppliers of spirituality found in bookstores, small groups, new networks and constituencies, even a virtual world of spirituality on the Internet. Three conditions of the modern world call forth this quest for a new spirituality. One is the dissociation of symbols from their referents, allowing for the free play of signifiers. This is often named the condition of postmodernity. It allows for mixed codes, as in the surprising finding of Roof's survey that one-third of boomer Christians believe in reincarnation! Secondly, there has been a de-centering of authority in meaning, discourse, and social forms. We live, increasingly, in a plural world, a sort of supermarket of choices. Finally, the globalization of culture (in media and information), along with consumerization and the information glut, make the sustenance of a stable self increasingly precarious.

Roof provides us with an ideal-type of differing spiritualities:

- Born-again Christians
- Seeker Christian churches
- Mainstream Christians
- Metaphysical believers and seekers who stress a non-personal conception of God (this category, which also includes some feminist spiritualities, shows up in the sample as the group least socially embedded and most optimistic)
- Dogmatists and secularists; the former category includes those who say they are religious but not spiritual (15 percent of the sample) and the latter includes those who say they are neither religious nor spiritual (12 percent of the sample).

But for all the differences in styles of spirituality and emphasis on intrinsic versus extrinsic authority, all the groups, except the last, show a surprising convergence on a set of themes, despite obvious differences: an emphasis on direct experience; physical and emotional healing; personal and social transformation; the democracy of believers and followers; expectation of future change; and a deeply based quest for wholeness (1999: 154). This vocabulary about spirituality pervades yet supersedes life inside the world of organized religion.

In the end, however, one is never quite sure that Roof gives us adequate evidence that a thoughtful and reflexive spirituality actually is pervasive. He makes a clear argument for it as a *desideratum*, even its necessity under conditions of a pluralist world and late modernity. The empirical evidence does indicate that religious identities have become more fluid and multi-layered, more a personal achievement than an ascription.

They may be more heteroglossic, speaking in many voices, dipping into many traditions. But whether the new capacious spirituality mirrors a fragmentation and commodification of the self in late capitalist and consumer societies rather than some remedy and antidote to fragmentation has not yet been adequately demonstrated.

Robert Wuthnow

The multiple books of Princeton sociologist Robert Wuthnow, the doyen of sociologists of religion, have probed the small group movement in America, the transformation of American religion, American evangelicalism, stewardship movements in the church, religion and its confrontation with materialism, and religion and civil society. In recent years, Wuthnow has turned his attention to the nexus between spirituality and religion. His first such book, *After Heaven: Spirituality in America since the 1950s* (1998b), explored much the same terrain as Roof's *Spiritual Marketplace*. The two authors converge on seeing religion now as more private and eclectic, and in claiming that organized religion has less of a monopoly over the sacred. (Wuthnow provides data indicating that a third of his sample state that they have experienced the presence of angels!) Both authors stress increased mobility, looser ties, negotiated identities, the salience of a language of journey and seeking. Both see a renewed interest in the inner self as a way of re-engaging the sacred. The emphasis is more on a God within than a God outside of us. Wuthnow defines spirituality as follows: "At its core, spirituality consists of all the beliefs and activities by which individuals attempt to relate their lives to God or to a divine being or some other conception of the transcendent . . . but spirituality is not just the creation of individuals; it is shaped by larger social circumstances and by the beliefs and values present in the wider culture" (1998b: viii).

Wuthnow postulates a large cultural shift from images of dwelling to images of seeking. Poll data show that among Americans interest in spirituality seems to be growing, while organized forms of religion remain stable. Wuthnow's main thesis is that a subtle reordering of the sacred has taken place in America. "A traditional spirituality of inhabiting sacred places has given way to a new spirituality of seeking. [Americans] negotiate more among competing views of the sacred, seeking partial knowledge and practical wisdom" (1998b: 3). The social universe has so changed that it can no longer be conceived as something fixed and stable, a home. We move in and out of communities, and no longer dwell in them. Earlier notions of the sacred postulated the existence of sacred places, a kind of community in which we could find a secure habitation. Newer notions stress rather the ideas of pilgrimage, journey. A spirituality of seeking or journeying is less likely than traditional church-generated spiritualities to maintain grand conceptions of the universe. It is more likely to invoke a pragmatic attitude that prompts us to try whatever promises to work and proves useful. "The newer pattern emphasizes looser connections, diversity and negotiation; practical activity takes precedence over organizational positions. Rather than rules, symbolic messages prevail" (1998b: 9). This new pattern is found both within and outside churches and transmutes how congregants see their local congregation. Rather than a place of sacred loyalty and a safe haven, congregations are, increasingly, viewed as functional suppliers of spiritual goods and services. Now more people look for practical rules or practices that will sustain and guide them in their daily lives. They seek more inner transformation than a settled creed.

Wuthnow appeals to two notions central to most spiritualities: practice and discipline. He insists that the concept of a practice is essential to understanding authentic spirituality. Practice implies an intentionality and involves a deep reflection about who one is. It entails a cluster of intentional activities that maintain a relation to the sacred. Practice-oriented spiritualities require devoting a significant amount of time and effort to praying, meditating, examining deep desires, and focusing attention in a worshipful manner on one's relationship to God. Spiritual practices, perforce, must be performed individually. They can, to be sure, be performed in the company of others or be enjoined by traditional religions but, ultimately, they involve a self-appropriation. Moreover, spiritual practices need not, inevitably, be embedded in religious traditions and institutions. One virtue of Wuthnow's definition of spiritual practices is that it does not seem to privilege – as Roof appears sometimes to do – either seeker spirituality or religiously grounded spiritualities.

Discipline can have multiple and divergent meanings for contemporaries. For some, it primarily means detachment. For others, it connotes self-control of urgent desires. For still others, it can imply the sustaining of a cheery attitude. For a subsection of Wuthnow's respondents, discipline implies less any sense of inner guidance than a reassurance, through faith, in the ultimate goodness of the world and life. Discipline in the spiritual life, however, has been increasingly taken out of the communal contexts in which generations understood it to be embedded, and left largely now to the discretion of individuals. Moreover, even those who emphasize discipline in the spiritual life remain unlikely to abandon the expressive concern for freedom. Choice, in the end, trumps discipline when they conflict.

Wuthnow is less sanguine that a practice-oriented spirituality will take deep roots in American society. He notes that a spirituality that results from the process of a continuing negotiation about the self is harder for any societal agency to control. But, without deeper institutional rootedness, it may also be harder to sustain. Wuthnow is more jaundiced than Roof about the benevolence of spiritual marketplaces. "But if seekers of the light are often finding little more than spirituality lite, the fault is not entirely theirs. Spirituality has become big business and big business finds many of its best markets by putting them in small, easy to consume packages" (1998b: 132). Moreover, there is very little in the official ideologies or wisdom of public institutions that would validate the sacred except as a personal choice. In the end, Wuthnow sees that if the new spirituality of seeking is suited to the cultural/organizational complexities of American society, "it nevertheless results in a transient spiritual existence characterized more often by dabbling than depth" (1998b: 168). Clearly, Wuthnow argues, there is a continuing but – for a majority of Americans – casual interest in spirituality (1998b: 111). Critics of *After Heaven* fault its overly heavy zero-sum-like dichotomizing of a spirituality of seeking and a spirituality of dwelling.

Wuthnow's *Creative Spirituality: The Way of the Artist* (2001) is much more specialized. In it, Wuthnow interviewed artists for whom, generally, seeking takes precedence over dwelling. His sample of artists included many who were deeply spiritual, but not religious (20 percent of the artist sample had no religious preference, compared to 8 percent of the general public). *Creative Spirituality* also picks up and explicates the meaning of practice and discipline for a serious spiritual life. "If there is a single key to artists' perspectives on the spiritual, it is this: spirituality, like art, must be practiced to be perfected. The way of the artist involves doing, rather than only believing in the possibility of doing. It requires training, discipline and a considerable investment of oneself" (2001: 4).

The artists in Wuthnow's sample were driven to explore. They were not casual shoppers. Their spiritual journeys, as they recount them, involved a kind of pilgrimage. Moreover, "whereas shoppers emphasize their freedom to make changes, these artists generally felt they had no choice." Their spirituality involved mindfulness and attention in order to make sense of themselves. Centeredness rather than eclecticism prevailed. "For these artists exposure to religious diversity has not resulted in an eclectic brew, combining a little of everything but a sharper realization that there is more to spirituality than any individual can understand" (2001: 101).

The majority of the artists used a language that emphasized therapy, healing, spiritual awareness, and the idea of recovery. Many recounted how spiritual practices (for example, meditation, breathing rhythms, chanting) fed into their art. They stressed spending time in practice, having a mentor, and finding a way to move from practice to service. Wuthnow would have people in religion learn two things from the spirituality of artists: their emphasis on the crucial importance of sustained practice, and the importance of creativity. "Too often religion has been viewed as a belief system that necessitates adopting someone else's understanding of who you are. The artistic approach to self-identity builds on insights from religion but includes a place for creativity as well" (2001: 100).

Wuthnow's third monograph on spirituality, *All in Sync: How Music and Art are Revitalizing American Religion* (2003), builds on the work in *Creative Spirituality* and explores a hypothesis that goes deeply against the cultural grain that asserts a dichotomy between religion and spirituality. *All in Sync* mines data to argue, instead, that most of the public's interest in spirituality is being absorbed by organized religion and that most people who develop a serious interest in spirituality wind up pursuing that interest through organized religion. By focusing on those in his national random sample (23 percent) who claim to have devoted a great deal of effort to spiritual growth and to engage regularly in spiritual practice, such as prayer and meditation, as opposed to those who express a more casual interest in spirituality, Wuthnow discovered that those with the highest commitment to spiritual growth are overwhelmingly involved in religious organizations. Of those who value spiritual growth, 80 percent are church members; 71 percent of this group say they attend worship services almost every week and that they admire clergy a great deal. Those who claim to put effort into their spirituality, to work at it, are also more likely to engage in service volunteering. So, argues Wuthnow, far from serious spirituality and religion being in competition, anything that would nudge the public interest in spiritual growth to higher levels (and actual practice rather than mere dabbling) is likely, ultimately, to benefit organized religion. The new bromide suggested by Wuthnow's data runs something like this: "I am serious about spirituality (and practice it regularly and show concern about spiritual growth) and, therefore, I am also religious."

Meredith McGuire

From her early doctoral work on Catholic "underground" house churches, through an award-winning study of Catholic charismatics (1982) and her careful ethnographic study, *Ritual Healing in Suburban America* (1988), sociologist Meredith McGuire has assiduously looked at alternative forms of religion and spirituality both within and outside the church. In *Ritual Healing*, McGuire looks at Christian healing groups; Eastern meditation and human potential groups; metaphysical groups; psychic/occult groups, and healing groups which appeal to non-traditional alternative techniques, such as Shiatsu massage. Her careful ethnography shows that these various groups employ divergent understandings of the source of healing (impersonal power or God) and the role of healers (incidental or truly mediating the meaning and healing). She also shows that alternative healing rituals do not garner recruits mainly from uneducated or desperate people but are firmly anchored in the middle class. Participants see alternative healing rituals as complementary rather than as supplanting the medical model. Alternative rituals provide vehicles for a counter-assertion of power and agency, and alternative understandings of the self in relation to society. But a careful reading of *Ritual Healing* compels us to speak of spiritual*ities* rather than a generic spirituality. Meaning systems, a sense of the moral order, and the notion of the self transmute as one moves across the varying alternative spiritual groups (Albanese 2001).

McGuire has always stayed close, using ethnographic methods, to "lived religion" (Orsi 2003). She also appeals to sources for understanding spirituality from theological and non-sociological sources. In an important essay, written primarily for Christian practitioners of spirituality, McGuire echoes Wuthnow and Roof in stressing new roles for the body and gender in spirituality and a greater mixing of codes across traditions. She portrays a Catholic Hispanic woman who maintains a home altar that includes "amethyst crystals used in healing meditations, oriental incense and a Tibetan prayer bell, a large colorful tryptich of Frida Kahlo and a modern representation of the Virgin of Guadalupe in running shoes" (1997: 4). McGuire (2002) has also explored the salience, interpretation, and role of the body in spiritual disciplines.

McGuire has recently warned sociologists about overly reductive methods for assessing spirituality:

> It is useful for sociologists who claim to be studying spirituality to challenge their own operative definitions of spirituality. For example, would we be able to grasp, with our definitions and methodologies, the intensely interior discipline required to "practice the presence" of the divine? How are practitioners' bodies and minds (as well as spirits) involved in the subtle yet richly complex practice of contemplation? Social scientists must study *all* significant religious practices, not merely the obvious ones like formal prayer. (2003: 301)

McGuire lays down a challenge for future sociological studies of spirituality. "Religious traditions, in different periods, have been predicated on different images of the self. How do contemporary patterns of spirituality get linked with emerging and diverse images of the self today?" (2003: 301).

Don Miller and "engaged spirituality"

Don Miller serves as the Director of the Center for Religion and Civic Culture at the University of Southern California. He has written a monograph (1997) on non-denominational mega-churches that cater to spiritual seekers. In a study co-written with Gregory Stanczak, *Engaged Spirituality: Spirituality and Social Transformation in Mainstream American Religious Traditions* (2002), the authors focus on how to connect spirituality with social service and advocacy, the latter a prime research topic at the Center for Religion and Civic Culture. The authors interviewed sixty-seven social activists or spiritual people who combine spirituality and social service/activism (for example, the Benedictine Joan Chittister; the founder of Sojourners, Jim Wallis).

In their preliminary review of the literature on spirituality, Stanczak and Miller note three main types of academic social science model for spirituality. The therapeutic model (found in psychology and social work) turns to a study of spirituality primarily as a source for meaning and motivation in human lives and tracks different rates of recovery or adjustment from physical ailments, addictions, and psychological and social disorders between those who engage in spiritual practices and those who do not (Joseph 1987; Helminiak 1996; Galanter 1997; Canda 1998; Sheridan 2001). Organizational or business models around the notions of a "spiritual workplace" favor a secular, psychologically based, non-specific spirituality. Elements of this spiritual workplace model favor recognition of the worth and value of people or employee-centered management; a working climate of high integrity, creating trust, faith, justice, respect, and love; and meeting both the economic and individual needs of employees (Burack 1999). A third model focuses on conceptualizing spirituality as a distinct sociological variable (Zinnbauer et al. 1997; Spilka 2003).

Very little attention has been paid, however, in the social science literature to the nexus between spirituality and social service/advocacy. In their interviews, Stanczak and Miller found many social activists who engaged in regular spiritual practices to sustain their motivation and avoid burnout. These respondents seemed startled when asked about their spirituality since it remains a privatized and unthematized topic in their organizational worlds of social service and action.

Engaged Spirituality enumerates six different elements or dimensions to spirituality:

- a holistic sense
- directionality through discernment about actions to be taken
- empowerment by being given new energy and motivation
- a therapeutic or healing dimension
- a unifying dimension which allows spiritual practitioners to link transcendent meaning to their mundane worlds of everyday life
- an experience of transcendence.

The study also postulates a typical developmental pattern which nudges spiritual practitioners into service and action. Its three steps include:

1   *Individual interaction*: significant others serve as mentors in the spiritual path to engagement.
2   *Organizational opportunity*: organizations (even explicitly religious organizations) differ widely in the ways in which they highlight or accentuate spirituality (many draw deeply upon it but leave it relatively unthematized) and service. One telling interview in *Engaged Spirituality* depicts an Assembly of God minister who became convinced of the utter inseparability of spirituality and social justice. He noted, however, that, organizationally, his church rarely accentuated the nexus between the two, so he applied most of his energies on organizational change to provide an impetus for service outreach from the church. Differential organizational resources for spirituality and the nexus of spirituality to service remains a little studied area.
3   *Spiritual revelation*: the third step involves a spiritual revelation, for the practitioner, of the utter inseparability of spirituality and social service and action, and the ways service and action, themselves, constitute a spiritual path.

Stanczak and Miller looked at 193 Christian or Jewish seminaries. They found that only thirty-one of them made spirituality a central curricular focus. Even in these seminaries, however, "Spirituality and spiritual practice are most often presented within the curriculum with reference to private, reflective and personal formation" or in its ministerial applications (2002: 62). The authors conclude their study by noting that, in the majority of cases, spirituality communities do not discuss social transformation, and social action organizations, while sometimes using religious language, do not reflect much on the spirituality practices of their participants. These frequently engage in spiritual practices, but the organization does not lift this up as a conscious theme to serve as a resource for enacting its mission. As a result, some of the unique benefits of spirituality for social transformation (for example, providing purpose, reducing ego through detachment, support for sustainability) have been dissipated.

Marler/Hadaway and Zinnbauer

A final dyad of studies explicitly inspects the dichotomy of the spiritual/religious. Penny Marler and Kirk Hadaway (2002) ask whether the assumption that "spirituality" and "religiousness" are mutually exclusive is warranted. In a national random sample survey, Marler and Hadaway asked respondents whether they considered themselves religious persons; 73.5 percent answered yes. A parallel question sought to know whether respondents considered themselves spiritual persons; 82.4 percent answered yes. Cross-tabulation yielded a subsample of: (a) those both religious and spiritual (64.2 percent); (b) those spiritual only but not religious (18.5 percent); (c) those religious only but not spiritual (8.0 percent); and (d) those neither religious nor spiritual (8.4 percent). Clearly, the majority of respondents see themselves as both religious and spiritual.

In follow-up focus interviews, Marler and Hadaway explored what respondents meant by the terms "being religious" and "being spiritual," and how they related the two. The following pattern emerged: 28 percent saw being religious/being spiritual as the same concept; 8 percent saw being religious/being spiritual as different and independent concepts; 63 percent saw being religious/being spiritual as different but interdependent concepts.

Marler and Hadaway demonstrate that "being religious" and "being spiritual" are not zero-sum propositions. Their data show that "being religious" and "being spiritual" are most often seen as distinct but interdependent concepts. While many of their respondents recognized the possibility of a "naked," religion-less spirituality or an empty, "soul-less" religiosity, spirituality was mainly seen as a connection between the individual and some larger, usually supernatural, reality. Religion is the organized expression of that connection. In the words of some of their respondents, it is "organized spirituality." Moreover, their data – much like Wuthnow's in *All in Sync* – indicate that the most religious are also those most likely to be the most spiritual, and that the most spiritual tend, more than the general population, to maintain religious ties. Indeed, for many in the Marler/Hadaway sample, the choice of "being spiritual but not religious" was a default position.

To be sure, a small contingent of people, who see themselves as "spiritual but not religious," are not church-going. This subsample tends to be agnostic and to have loose social bonds. They are more likely to experiment with New Age or Eastern practices. But the overwhelming majority of Americans tend to express their spirituality in continuity with their religiousness. Marler and Hadaway conclude that most Americans see themselves as both religious and spiritual. Nor do they share Roof's optimism about some surge of "reflexive spirituality":

> In fact, when possible change can be traced through examining successive age cohorts or by comparing more with less churched respondents, the pattern is toward less religiousness *and* less spirituality. The youngest and the most religiously marginalized are much less likely to see themselves as religious and spiritual, slightly more likely to see themselves as spiritual only and much more likely to see themselves as *neither* religious nor spiritual. (Marler and Hadaway 2002: 297–8)

Brian Zinnbauer and his associates probed respondents' actual definitions of spirituality and religiousness (Zinnbauer et al. 1997). They note a growing tendency in the social scientific literature to narrow down definitions of religiousness as something cribbed and institutional and to characterize spirituality as something personal and subjective. They found that their respondents attribute many meanings to the two terms. Spirituality, in ordinary usage, is a fuzzy concept that embraces obscurity with a passion; it is an often obscure concept in need of empirical grounding and operationalization. In point of fact, the Zinnbauer sample found the two concepts to be different but not fully independent. Once again, the most religious were the most spiritual:

> Spirituality was most often described in personal or experiential terms, such as belief in God or a higher power, or having a relationship with God or a higher power. Definitions of religiousness included both personal beliefs, such as belief in God or a higher power, and organizational or institutional beliefs and practices such as church membership, church attendance, and commitment to the belief system of a church or organized religion. (1997: 561)

Zinnbauer et al. fault the implicit endorsement of a dichotomy between spirituality and religion (and a pejorative tint to the latter) in many social scientific accounts of the two. Theorizing about the terms as incompatible opposites and rejecting conventional or traditional expressions of worship simply runs counter to the experience of most believers, who appear to integrate both religiousness and spirituality into their lives. The authors call, instead, for a broadband definition of religion since the religious, in fact, show up as the most spiritual and "the various phenomena associated with spirituality are essential parts of religion; they lie at the core of religious life" (1997: 583). Moreover, attempts to relegate spirituality to the merely personal appropriation of the transcendent neglect systematic organizational analysis of sources of spirituality, mentoring in the spiritual life, social networks, and the ways in which spirituality often eventuates in social service and advocacy.

To be sure, a small proportion of the Zinnbauer sample (19 percent) did denominate themselves as "spiritual but not religious." Certain professions or groups in the sample (New Age groups and mental health professionals) were more likely to dichotomize sharply the two concepts. Compared to the much larger "both spiritual and religious" portion of the sample, this small proportion of "spiritual but not religious" was less likely to evaluate religiousness positively, less likely to engage in traditional forms of worship such as church attendance and prayer, less likely to hold orthodox or traditional Christian beliefs, more likely to be independent from others, more likely to engage in group experiences related to spiritual growth, more likely to be agnostic, more likely to characterize religiousness and spirituality as different and non-overlapping concepts, more likely to hold non-traditional "New Age" beliefs, and more likely to claim to have had mystical experiences. Also, this group was more likely to hold a pejorative definition of religiousness, labeling it as a means to extrinsic ends such as feeling superior to others and avoiding personal responsibility (Zinnbauer et al. 1997: 561). The "spiritual but not religious" may be an interesting small subsector of American society. But they are in no way representative of American religion and spirituality or some vanguard for the future. Why social scientific studies of spirituality have so focused on this small subsample, to posit dichotomies between what are clearly interdependent and overlapping concepts of religiosity and spirituality, is a legitimate question to press.

Robert Fuller

A useful monograph on spiritual but not church-related traditions in American culture, Robert Fuller's *Spiritual but Not Religious: Understanding Unchurched America* (2001) presents an historical and religious-studies perspective. Fuller introduces a new term into our lexicon: the unchurched. Among the 40 percent of Americans who are unchurched, some 8–15 percent (15 percent is, however, a high-end estimate) are neither religious nor spiritual. Ten percent have ambiguous relations and loose ties to churches. They remain both religious and spiritual, but with tenuous bonds to organized religion. Another 19 percent or so are "spiritual but not religious" and frequently draw from resources other than traditional religious sources. Fuller provides a demographic profile of this group: they are more likely than the general population to be college-educated, to hold white-collar professional jobs, to be liberal politically, to have weaker social relations or bonds in society, and to be offspring of parents who were less church-going.

Since there is, palpably, a category of the "spiritual but not religious," we do need a concept of spirituality that reflects this reality without, however, dichotomizing the two concepts or failing to see that, for most Americans, the two are interdependent and intertwined. Fuller defines spirituality as follows: "Spirituality exists wherever we struggle with the issue of how our lives fit into the greater cosmic scheme of things . . . An idea or practice is 'spiritual' when it reveals our personal desire to establish a felt-relationship with the deepest meanings or powers governing life" (2001: 8).

A strong virtue of Fuller's study is that he limns for us the cultural tradition – a long, influential, and unbroken tradition – of unchurched spirituality in America. Just as there were famous religious awakenings, there have been periodic metaphysical awakenings. From the work of Emmanuel Swedenborg, through Transcendentalism, Mesmerism, Spiritualism, Theosophy, New Thought, and Harmonial Religion, various metaphysical movements (often with a linkage to Hindu or Buddhist appropriations or practices) have a long and legitimate subaltern cultural history in American spirituality. Fuller paints a synthesis of the core beliefs in this metaphysical tradition: a pantheistic understanding of God; continuities of the self with this ever-present divine reality; our innate susceptibility to subtle spiritual energies that reinvigorate our physical and emotional systems; experience and personal reflection as crucial criteria for arriving at religious or spiritual beliefs; a personal spiritual outlook that builds on, rather than repudiates, science (2001: 85).

Fuller argues that unchurched spirituality (this metaphysical tradition) has gradually had an impact even on ideas of spirituality in the churches. He contends that church-based religion will not wither away, but that religion, over time, may garner less loyalty among casual attendees, such that those with weak ties will drift off into the realm of the "spiritual but not religious" as a default position. His typification of metaphysical practices and beliefs can alert those in the churches who dabble in practices taken over from New Age or Eastern religious beliefs (although it is possible to borrow ideas and practices from alien traditions and transmute them, as Christianity has abundantly shown with its many borrowings from paganism or Greek philosophy) that such practices are, often, linked to beliefs and ideals of the self and the transcendent that are incompatible with traditional religiosity.

Recent sociological research on the unchurched shows an amazing growth in respondents who claim no religious affiliation. Their proportion of the population has doubled in a decade, from 14 million in 1990 to 29 million in 2001. Sociologists Michael Hout and Claude Fischer argue that this recent rise of religious "nones" has more to do with politics than declining religious piety. "In the 1990s many people who had weak attachment to religion and either moderate or liberal views found themselves at odds with the conservative agenda of the Christian Right and reacted by renouncing their weak attachment to organized religion" (Lattin 2003: 15). Stemming from the evangelical family of churches, these new unchurched Americans are highly unlikely recruits to metaphysical or New Age spiritualities. In sum, a more careful analysis of the unchurched seems needed before we can know, fully, what the claimed status "spiritual but not religious" really means.

Challenges to Christian Spirituality and Social Science Studies of Spirituality

Social scientific studies of spirituality present practitioners of Christian spirituality with both challenges and opportunities.

(1)   There exists a capacious niche among unchurched Americans who, while somewhat chary of the institutional face of organized religion, seek a deeper spirituality. Some of the unchurched will remain unlikely recruits to the world of Christian spirituality and will remain agnostic and secular. A second minority niche will look to the non-Christian, metaphysical, theosophist, or Eastern religions for the spirituality they embrace (sometimes dabbling, sometimes in serious and sustained practice). Sociological data about unchurched religion show that it includes a majority who say that they believe in Christ, pray, and expect an afterlife (Bromley 1988). Just as members switch out of churches to the category of the unchurched, the unchurched is also not a fixed and stable group. Many convert to churches every year from the "nones." Christian churches that reach out to spiritual seekers have been growing apace (Miller 1997). Christian churches need to send out a clear message that spirituality – its promised transformative conversion, its practices, and lived out way of life – is at the core of what it means to be religious.

(2)   As Robert Wuthnow's (2003) data show, Christian churches that emphasize in-depth programs of spiritual growth are well placed to flourish. One of the anomalies of the 1970s and 1980s was that Eastern religious gurus and teachers promised seekers concrete practices – yoga, breathing exercises, mandalas – to abet spiritual transformation (Cox 1977). Frequently, Christian churches in that period espoused spiritual values but seemed unable to provide seekers with concrete practices and spiritual discipline. Thirty years ago the term "spirituality" remained suspect in much of Protestant America, with memories of an earlier sentimental pietism. This situation has changed. As Wuthnow claims, anything that nudges Americans' interest in spirituality to higher levels (and actual practice) is likely, ultimately, to benefit organized religion, since the overwhelming majority of Americans see themselves as both religious and spiritual.

(3)   Sociologists converge on seeing evidence for a new style of spirituality emerging and growing in American culture: one that emphasizes an immanent God, stresses experience and practice, translates the spiritual into everyday affairs and concerns, honors the body, is sensitive to gender differences, and values seeking, residual doubt, and exploration as part of the journey. From Saint Bonaventure's *The Soul's Journey to God* to Bunyan's *Pilgrim's Progress*, Christianity has a long history and multiple resources to engage the journey motif. Discernment and selective appropriation could probably incorporate many of these newly salient cultural themes into an authentic

Christian spirituality. But discernment may also challenge an easy eclectic individualism in spirituality, a feel-good spirituality-lite, or a consumerist attitude toward spiritual practices, which sociological studies show is fairly rampant in contemporary American culture.

(4)   Willy-nilly, many Christian practitioners of spirituality will continue to dip into other traditions, adapting originally non-Christian practices such as yoga, Zen meditation, holistic massage, mandalas, aromatherapies, and so on. Once again, careful discernment seems called for to cull out beliefs (for example, reincarnation, a pantheistic impersonal principle of transcendence, exalted notions of angels) and practices that remain inconsistent with authentic Christian self-understanding. Even here, though, the long experience of Christianity in assimilating and transmuting popular religiosity – for example, pagan shrines and practices, Greek religion – and integrating them into Christian practices can temper exaggerated fears of a hopeless hodge-podge of eclectic bricolage. The danger of an eclectic individualism remains real enough and warrants caution, but it need not be an inevitable outcome of some mixed codes in the spiritual life. A hunger for wholeness and spiritual seeking can be as much opportunity as danger.

(5)   There are also challenges to the social sciences if they would move resolutely to a serious study of spirituality. We need better qualitative inductive approaches to the meanings that "spirituality" and "religion" actually have for people, and to the costs and benefits that accrue to choosing one term to the exclusion of the other. We need to tease out ideal types of self-concepts correlated to seeing the self as "religious" or "spiritual." Right now, social scientists lack clear consensual definitions of the terms, or clear measures for the two terms for survey research. One ought to be chary of definitions that assume either a zero-sum view of the two or their conflation into one category of religiosity, as betraying ideological bias. We still know next to nothing about the social sources of religiosity and spirituality – when taken separately or together. What impacts do age, education, generation, race, ethnicity, parental religiosity/spirituality, peer influence, mentoring, and region have on concepts of religiosity/spirituality? We also need better studies of the social consequences of religiosity/spirituality (for example, for views of the gap between rich and poor; for the nexus between spirituality and engagement in service/advocacy; for social capital). It does seem that an isolated individual spirituality (even if rooted in concerted practices) does not have the impacts that religiosity has on volunteerism, social capital, and broader civic sense (Wuthnow 1991: 325).

"Lived religion" has rarely enacted, simply, the precise scripts of "official religiosity," whether Christian, Buddhist, or metaphysical. What to make, for example, of trinitarian Unitarians (they exist!)? Of those who look equally to Buddha and Jesus? Of New Age metaphysicals who also pray to Jesus for healing? Of Catholics who claim, somehow, to believe in reincarnation? Here the challenge to the social scientist is to go beyond the often crude and simplistic indices of spirituality frequently found in survey research to the deeper ethnographic, "thick descriptions" of lived spirituality to which Meredith McGuire (2003) has called us.

References

Albanese, C. 2001: *American Spiritualities*. Bloomington, IN: University of Indiana Press.

Allport, G. 1950: *The Individual and his Religion: A Psychological Interpretation*. New York: Macmillan.

—— 1954: *The Nature of Prejudice*. Cambridge, MA: Addison-Wesley.

Bellah, R. N., Madsen, R., Sullivan, W. M., et al. 1985: *Habits of the Heart*. Berkeley, CA: University of California Press.

Berger, P. 1967: *The Sacred Canopy*. Garden City, NY: Doubleday.

—— 1969: *A Rumor of Angels*. Garden City, NY: Doubleday.

—— 1979: *The Heretical Imperative*. New York: Anchor Press.

Bromley, D. 1988: *Falling from Faith: Causes and Consequences of Religious Apostasy*. Beverly Hills, CA: Sage.

Burack, E. 1999: Spirituality in the workplace. *Journal of Organizational Change Management* 12 (4), 280–91.

Canda, E. (ed.) 1998: *Spirituality in Social Work*. New Directions, NY: Haworth Pastoral Press.

Clark, W. H. 1958: *The Psychology of Religion: An Introduction to Religious Experience*. New York: Macmillan.

Collins, J. 1991: *Mysticism and the New Paradigm in Psychology*. Savage, MD: Rowman and Littlefield.

Cox, H. 1977: *Turning East: The Promise and Peril of the New Orientalism*. New York: Simon and Schuster.

Emerson, R. W. 1940: On the oversoul. In B. Atkinson (ed.), *The Complete Essays and Other Writings of Ralph Waldo Emerson*, pp. 261–78. New York: Modern Library.

Fichter, J. 1951: *Southern Parish*. Chicago: University of Chicago Press.

Fuller, R. 2001: *Spiritual but Not Religious: Understanding Unchurched America*. New York: Oxford University Press.

Galanter, M. 1997: Spiritual recovery movements and contemporary medical care. *Psychiatry* 60, 211–23.

Glock, C. and Bellah, R. (eds) 1976: *The New Religious Consciousness*. Berkeley, CA: University of California Press.

—— and Stark, R. 1965: *Religion and Society in Tension*. Berkeley, CA: University of California Press.

Grensted, L. W. 1952: *The Psychology of Religion*. New York: Oxford University Press.

Helminiak, D. 1996: *The Human Core of Spirituality: Mind as Psyche and Spirit*. Albany, NY: State University of New York Press.

Herberg, W. 1955: *Protestant, Catholic and Jew: An Essay in American Religious Sociology*. Garden City, NY: Doubleday.

Joseph, M. V. 1987: The religious and spiritual: aspects of clinical practice. A neglected dimension of social work. *Social Thought* 13 (1), 12–24.

Lattin, D. 2003: Living the religious life of a none: growing numbers shed organized church for loose spiritual sensibility. *San Francisco Chronicle* December 4, 15.

Lenski, G. 1961: *The Religious Factor: A Sociological Study of Religion's Impact on Politics, Economics and Family*. Garden City, NY: Doubleday.

Luckmann, T. 1967: *The Invisible Religion*. New York: Macmillan.

McGuire, M. 1982: *Catholic Pentecostals*. Philadelphia: Temple University Press.

—— 1988: *Ritual Healing in Suburban America*. New Brunswick, NJ: Rutgers University Press.

—— 1997: Mapping contemporary American spirituality: a sociological perspective. *Christian Spirituality Bulletin* 5 (1), 1–8.

—— 2002: New-old directions in the social scientific study of religion: ethnography, phenomenology and the human body. In J. Spikard, J. S. Landres, and M. McGuire (eds), *Personal Knowledge and Beyond*, pp. 195–212. New York: New York University Press.

—— 2003: Review of Sarah Coakley, *Powers and Submissions: Spirituality, Philosophy and Gender* (Oxford: Blackwell, 2002). *Journal for the Scientific Study of Religion* 42, 301.

Marler, P. and Hadaway, K. 2002: Being religious and being spiritual in America: a zero-sum proposition? *Journal for the Scientific Study of Religion* 41, 289–300.

Miller, D. 1997: *Reinventing Protestantism*. Berkeley, CA: University of California Press.

Needleman, J. 1970: *The New Religions*. Garden City, NY: Doubleday.

Orsi, R. 2003: Is the study of lived religion irrelevant to the world we live in? *Journal for the Scientific Study of Religion* 42, 171–4.

Pruyser, P. 1968: *A Dynamic Psychology of Religion*. New York: Harper and Row.

Putnam, R. 2000: *Bowling Alone: The Collapse and Revival of American Community*. New York: Simon and Schuster.

Roof, W. C. 1993: *A Generation of Seekers*. San Francisco: Harpers.

—— 1999: *The Spiritual Marketplace: Baby Boomers and the Remaking of Religion*. Princeton, NJ: Princeton University Press.

Sheridan, M. J. 2001: Defining spiritually sensitive social work practice: the heart of helping. *Social Work* 46 (1), 87–92.

Spilka, B. 2003: *Psychology of Religion: An Empirical Approach*. New York: Guilford.

Stanczak, G. and Miller, D. 2002: *Engaged Spirituality: Spirituality and Social Transformation in Mainstream American Religious Traditions*. Los Angeles: The Center for Religion and Civic Culture, University of Southern California.

Vernon, G. 1962: *Sociology of Religion*. New York: McGraw Hill.

Wilson, B. and Cresswell, J. 1999: *New Religious Movements: Challenge and Response*. New York: Routledge.

Wuthnow, R. 1976: *The Consciousness Revolution*. Berkeley, CA: University of California Press.

—— 1991: *Acts of Compassion*. Princeton, NJ: Princeton University Press.

—— 1998a: *Loose Connections*. Cambridge, MA: Harvard University Press.

—— 1998b: *After Heaven: Spirituality in America since the 1950s*. Berkeley, CA: University of California Press.

—— 2001: *Creative Spirituality: The Way of the Artist*. Berkeley, CA: University of California Press.

—— 2003: *All in Sync: How Music and Art are Revitalizing American Religion*. Berkeley, CA: University of California Press.

Zinnbauer, B., Pargament, K., Cole, B., Rye, M., Butter, E., Belavich, T., Hipp, K., and Kader, J. 1997: Religion and spirituality: unfuzzying the fuzzy. *Journal for the Scientific Study of Religion* 76, 549–64.

CHAPTER 18

Personality Sciences

Janet K. Ruffing

The study of Christian spirituality is rapidly developing as an interdisciplinary field. According to Sandra Schneiders, "it seeks to understand [Christian experience] as it actually occurs, as it actually transforms its subject toward fullness of life in Christ, that is, toward self-transcending life-integration within the Christian community of faith" (1998: 3). As such, Christian spirituality is studied within the horizon of meaning and practice created by its specifically Christian content and context. Its interdisciplinary partners will ordinarily include the history of Christian spirituality, Scripture as its foundational source, and the particular history and theological emphases of specific Christian traditions. The particular aspect of spirituality, a given issue or problem constituting a scholar's inquiry, will dictate which additional disciplines the researcher will bring to bear on the particular problem.

Because of the intrinsic inter-relationships between spirituality and psychology – both fields concentrating on human interiority and its patterns of deformation, development, integration, and its relationship to the sacred – this particular dialogue has moved from hostility to rivalry, to mutual cooperation, and to mutual respect. In many schools of psychology today, the significance of spirituality as one aspect of the client's worldview and its importance in contributing to positive or negative therapeutic outcomes have made spirituality a major contemporary research topic. The current interest from the perspective of psychology is so intense that psychology may well become the authoritative discipline in the study of spirituality on the basis of the sheer quantity of studies and practitioners who are rapidly incorporating spirituality into their research and therapeutic work. The vast majority of these researchers and therapists embrace generalized definitions of spirituality that assume the independence of spirituality from religious communities of faith, an eclectic approach to spiritual practices emphasizing Eastern meditation, and frequently a markedly privatized account of spirituality and religious experience detached from commitments to actions of love, compassion, or justice in church and society.

Scholars specifically interested in the study of Christian spirituality will need to be alert to these subtle biases and correct for the way in which Christianity historically specifies spiritual life *vis-à-vis* the triune God revealed in Jesus and the ongoing participation in the paschal mystery in actual communities of faith in and through the gift of the Spirit. This kind of dialogue implies the need to incorporate mutually critical correlations in the use of the personality sciences in the study of Christian spirituality. Despite the need for a critical reading of psychological resources, the explosion of research in the past fifteen years provides a rich starting-point for this dialogue. Specific contributions from psychology include: the development of psychoanalytic theory that is appreciative of spirituality as well as critical of its pathological uses, developmental psychology, cognitive psychology, gender differences, understanding of the neurological and physical benefits of meditation practices, the development of qualitative research methods, and a variety of psychometric scales measuring some aspects of spirituality, as well as a rich source of potential correlations between spiritual practices and physical and psychological wellbeing in health-related research. There is also a host of individual topics, such as consciousness studies, transition theory, sexual issues, therapeutic modalities, forgiveness, and trauma, among other possibilities.

Problems of Definition

Frequently, various psychologies understand spirituality in ways that may be subtly or dramatically at variance with a Christian perspective. Ewert Cousins developed this definition of spirituality for the Crossroad "World Spirituality" series:

> that inner dimension of the person called by certain traditions "the spirit." This spiritual core is the deepest center of the person. It is here that the person is open to the transcendent dimension; it is here that the person experiences ultimate reality. The series explores the discovery of this core, the dynamics of its development, and its journey to the ultimate goal. It deals with prayer, spiritual direction, the various maps of the spiritual journey, and the methods of advancement in the spiritual ascent. (Cousins 1985: xiii)

My own definition further specifies Cousins: Christian spirituality is our way of being, the way we live our lives as a consequence of our experience of God in Jesus. It is how we respond to the "Holy" and how we express the implications of that experience in our relationship with ourselves, with others, with society, with the creation. It is a dynamic love relationship, responsive to the ultimate loving source of our being who desires for us fullness of life. It includes our reciprocation of that love by our being loving, caring, justice-making inhabitants of our world, appreciators of this beauty and life.

The assumptions in these definitions from a theological perspective include the reality of God and the reality of spirit in the human person that has the graced capacity to move toward self-transcendence. Relationship to transcendence imbues life with profound meaning both as belief and as relational experience. Christian tradition offers a horizon of meaning, a community of believers, a way of life, a history of this spiritual quest, and practical means to achieve it. It includes not only a privatized realm of personal religious experiencing, but also actual commitment to love of neighbor as a criterion of our love for God whom we do not see. Implied in these definitions is that this dimension of human life unfolds over time and admits of development.

Depending on the particular psychological theory employed, psychologists often define spirituality functionally as comprising beliefs and values as its meaning-making function and spiritual experiences as its experiential component. Typically, religious practices such as church attendance or affiliation, reading/study, meditation and prayer constitute behavioral dimensions. Less obvious in the psychological definitions are commitment to spiritual practice, a relational context for mystical experience, and criteria for recognized behaviors and attitudes that show continuity between religious experience, worship in a committed faith community, and activities in the world.

Psychoanalytic Theories

Psychoanalytic theory began as hostile to religion/spirituality, framed by Freud as an "illusion" that people would eventually outgrow. Akhtar and Parens summarize two of his points on the origins of religious belief: "1. Religious beliefs derived from the child's earliest experiences of helplessness, which is continued in the adult. 2. 'Religion is comparable to a childhood neurosis' and Freud wondered if 'mankind [can] surmount this . . . neurosis'" (2001: 5). Nevertheless, Freud's discovery of the unconscious, of unconscious conflicts within the psyche and their origins in very early childhood experiences, of the phenomena of transference and counter-transference, and of methods of access to the unconscious through dreams, everyday slips of the tongue, and the therapeutic process of free association have all become part of our understanding of the human. From the perspective of Christian spirituality, Freud's reductionism of religion exclusively to neurosis or pathology must be rejected, although pathological manifestations of spirituality or religious practice can certainly be recognized through his theories.

Freud's drive theory based on the instincts of sex and aggression within a self-contained, autonomous model of the psyche has undergone the greatest amount of revision in the psychoanalytic tradition that developed after him. Freud's emphasis on psychopathology, while continuing to offer considerable insight into what has gone wrong in individual psychic life, was amplified into theories of the psyche accounting for normal growth and development. The ego psychology of Erik Erikson, Margaret Mahler, Anna Freud, and Heinz Hartman might be placed in this category. Mahler's work detailing the singular importance of the mother in normal development modifies Freud's placing the need for protection and dependence on the father, suggesting that God-representations and Freud's "oceanic experience" are more accurately rooted in the maternal. She further developed the idea that dependence is not restricted to childhood experience and that adults continue to be dependent as adults, not necessarily in a regressed form. Akhtar and Parens build on this insight to assert that "religious belief can be a fulfillment of some people's adult dependency needs" (2001: 10). Erikson's "basic trust" established in the maternal matrix also suggests a non-pathological basis for faith, and his developmental schema, which extends through the life-cycle with characteristic tasks and virtues for each stage, has been a frequent dialogue partner for the study of Christian spirituality. Feminist critique points out the male bias of this "normative" schema and requires correction for female development over the life-cycle.

Object relations theory and self-psychology offer rich and complex possibilities for understanding Christian spirituality. Theorists such as Winnicott, Milner, Stern, Mitchell, Kernburg, Bowlby, and, more recently, a number of feminist psychologists at the Stone Center in Massachusetts, have been part of a paradigm shift in psychoanalysis. According to Stephen Mitchell (1988: 17): "mind has been redefined from a set of predetermined structures emerging from inside an individual organism to transactional patterns and internal structures derived from an interactive, interpersonal field." Mitchell describes contributions from these theorists along three main lines: discoveries that humans are relational by design, by intent, and by implication. He summarizes the complexity of this relational matrix:

> human beings are simultaneously self regulating and field regulating. We are concerned with both the creation and maintenance of a relatively stable, coherent sense of self out of the continual ebb and flow of perception, and affect, and the creation and maintenance of dependable, sustaining connections with others, both in actuality and as internal presences. The dialectic between self-definition and connection with others is complex and intricate, with one or the other sometimes being more prominent. Self-regulatory and field regulatory processes sometimes enhance each other and sometimes are at odds with each other, forming the basis for powerful conflicts. The intrapsychic and the interpersonal are continually interpenetrating realms, each with its own set of processes, mechanisms, and concerns. (Mitchell 1988: 35)

Heinz Kohut's self-psychology emphasizes early "narcissistic" functions of the parent's admiring "mirroring" of the child's perfection and the child's "idealizing" this perfect parent. He saw that the sense of self as stable and valuable grows out of these two key experiences. The self object provides an empathic function. In Kohut's theory (1971, 1977), this use of "narcissistic" is developmental rather than a disorder.

D. W. Winnicott (1965, 1971) built his theory on the basis of his observations of mothers with their children. He developed rich theories of these interactions, describing functions among them, such as "facilitating environment," "holding environment," "transitional objects," and "transitional phenomena." The good-enough mother provides an environment in which the child's needs are sufficiently met in an almost invisible way so that the child feels a "subjective omnipotence." Gradually, the child becomes aware of her as a presence, and can both internalize an image of her and maintain symbolically a connection with her through a "transitional object" imbued with her presence, even when she is physically absent. Winnicott also talks about the space between the child and its mother. This space in between the self and an "object" (the actual mother) provides the psychic space for their interaction, a between within which self and other can be differentiated and discovered. In Winnicott's theory, this "space between" grounds the capacity to be alone, which first needs to happen in the presence of another and is also the space in which play unfolds (Winnicott 1965). Winnicott generalizes this transitional kind of experiencing to the realms of creativity and culture in adult life.

William W. Meissner and Michael Eigen both recognized the potential for religious or mystical interpretations of transitional phenomena. Meissner (1987) applied this term to faith, God-representations, symbols, and prayer. Eigen (1998) not only incorporates these transitional phenomena into his understandings of the mystical, but also adopts the sacred "incommunicado core of the self" and the necessary "unintegration" that allows new experiences to emerge and fosters a reworking of the sense of self. Akhtar and Parens (2001: 7) add to the possibilities for the relationship of "transitional phenomena" to religious experience:

> Transitional space, Winnicott suggests, is where the feeling of oneness and vagueness experienced while being nurtured by mother resides. It is experienced as a confluence of reality and unreality but such matters do not form its content. It is the psychic area where imagination is born and paradox reigns supreme. Transitional object is a concrete representative of the experience of being nurtured by mother, whereas the transitional phenomenon is an affective-perceptual psychic state that is transportable into selective experiences. The transitional object can be held, cuddled, sucked on, thrown into a corner, subjected to abuse. The transitional phenomenon is not contained in a concrete structure; it cannot be held or discarded. It is subjectively experienced, enjoyed, and neither questioned nor not questioned for its verity. Religious feelings and belief seem to lie in this realm.

Jones (1991) describes how "In prayer there really is no 'object' that the believer manipulates but rather a psychological 'space' or state of consciousness which s/he enters. From a religious standpoint that may be the most significant referent of the term 'transitional'" (1991: 126).

Object relations theories and self-psychology offer great potential for elucidating the self/other relationship that unfolds over time in Christian faith and mystical experience. Prayer can be understood as entering into a state of consciousness that promotes this mutual influence and discovery of two subjectivities. It can be seen as more than an exercise in projection but something much richer in the interplay between two others. These theories also suggest models for understanding the positive psychological growth and development of the self as a result of encounter with God in prayer, as well as the likely transformation of both self-objects and God-representations (Frohlich 1993; Gillespie 1995). A relational theory of psychological development is more congruent with Christian spirituality's belief in a God who self-reveals and relates. These theories might also suggest compassionate ways of understanding what might have gone wrong in an individual's development that makes it psychologically impossible or unlikely to achieve religious ideals such as a capacity for agapic love.

God-representations

Ana-Maria Rizzuto (1979) pioneered the psychoanalytic study of God-representations, or images of God, in her client population as well as in research with other subjects. Her approach as an analyst to this phenomenon is carefully intrapsychic. In other words, therapists need to explore with a high degree of sophistication the client's subjective experience of God. Rizzuto (2001) notes the way in which most people in American culture form an unconscious and frequently conscious representation of God based on their life history, object relations, narcissistic balance, and defensive structures – all areas to be worked with therapeutically. She asserts that therapists need to explore these representations and their sources as they would any other psychic content. She also claims that therapists should refrain from theological assertions or rejections of the existence of God, which she says lie outside the realm of empirical work. She restricts her consideration to the formation of what she calls a "personal God" that may bear great or little resemblance to the images of God presented within the client's religious tradition. She describes ways in which this internal representation of God develops and changes over time. Finally, she offers accounts of helpful and harmful client relationships with their personal God. "The help or lack of it coming from such a God depends on the relational dynamics between a particular personal God and the conception of oneself in relation to God" (2001: 23). These God-representations contain parental images, but Rizzuto has also discovered that they are usually not purely exalted parental images. When they are, it is often seriously pathological. Rather, these representations are "collages of significant aspects of primary object, significant adults, (grandparents, aunts and uncles, and at times siblings and religious figures) who have created meaningful, real or imagined libidinal ties with the child" (2001: 29). In the course of development, God, as an internally represented object, undergoes modifications as the result of a person's experiences and encounters with others.

Rizzuto also finds that believers engage in a lifelong process of forming and reforming their personal God in relation to the teachings of their tradition, which presents a God who transcends this personal representation, and in relation to events that challenge their representations. She finds that a positive, loving, responsive image of God corresponds to human desires for intimacy and relationship. This God is "always there" – similar to Winnicott's "good-enough mother" in whose presence the child can be comfortable being alone. When parents also believe in God, children can take comfort and hope that their parents' omnipotence can be moderated by a God who is greater than the parents. However, Rizzuto concludes that God-representations may either help the person or be exceedingly persecutory and destructive. It depends on the God-representation through which the person relates to God in prayer, as well as on the person's unconscious dynamics. God-representations may be part of the transference, may be a resistance, or may be used defensively. If a therapist is willing to follow all the ways in which these God-representations offer clues into a client's psychodynamics, the client may "acquire a new mode of believing that is devoid of its old psychological burdens" (2001: 46).

Elsewhere Rizzuto carefully states that for this benefit to be attained:

> it is indispensable that the analyst *never make any pronouncement about God or religion.* Technically, such pronouncement disrupts the working through of the personal representation of God and of personal belief. It also conveys to the patient that the analyst knows God for sure, and has the right to demand that the analysand submits to the authority of the analyst. This goes against the aim of treatment, which is to help the patient find maximal autonomy and internal freedom. It is not the responsibility of the analyst to help

the patient find the "true" God and religion. His responsibility is to help the patient to find God and religion in the context of his past life history and present circumstances. (1996: 429)

Rizzuto suggests that this type of analytic work is very difficult for therapists who have not explored their own development and transformation of their God-representations.

In addition to this psychoanalytic research and reflection on clinical experience, Joseph Ciarrocchi (2000) reports that extensive empirical studies of people's perceptions of God have been done at Loyola College in Maryland. Pointing to a growing body of data that requires further exploration to discover the inter-relationships of various factors, he calls for theologians (and I would add those who study Christian spirituality) to take these findings seriously, critically incorporating them into their own work.

Cognitive Theorists

One of the most common definitions of spirituality in the psychological literature is "the sense of meaning and purpose in life." Developmental psychologists, beginning with Piaget's account of cognitive development, have created a variety of stage theories of development. These are primarily ways of describing the ability to increase cognitive complexity as one progresses through the stages. In relation to spirituality, this means that the worldview and meaning-making approaches of people in each stage of development are distinctive ways of viewing multiple aspects of reality within a comprehensive worldview. Stage theories assume that the stages are sequential, with each requiring the achievement of the preceding stage and including it. Typically, stage change, which is not necessarily achieved by all beyond a conventional level, is facilitated by "pacers" (some kind of challenge that promotes change) combined with an adequate "holding environment" that provides a context for a person undergoing stage change to experience both confirmation and challenge. Ordinarily, persons within a particular stage cannot abstractly recognize the worldview in which they are currently embedded until they progress to the next stage.

Lawrence Kohlberg explored stages of moral development by exploring children's moral reasoning. His colleague and collaborator Carol Gilligan challenged the gender bias of his theory and described a relational ethic of care as more typical of women than Kohlberg's ethic of rules. James Fowler applied the general stage theory to faith development. Robert Kegan (1982, 1994) developed yet another model of cognitive development, giving a progressive account of what constitutes the "self" and what constitutes the "other," noting the affective process of losing the self one knows and reconstituting a new self. Elizabeth Liebert (1992) adopted Kegan's account of process and combined it with Jane Loevinger's (1976) account of ego development based on studies of women. More recently, Fredric Hudson (1999) has proposed a more complex and socially integrated theory of adult development in his theory of self-renewing adulthood. Hudson focuses on life mission as the core around which each new life-chapter is organized. This makes a core sense of meaning the point of stability around which other changes of the self revolve. Both Liebert and Joann Wolski Conn (1989) have shown the applicability of these theories to spiritual development, spiritual direction, and pastoral counseling.

Analytic and Transpersonal Psychology

Even in Freud's own lifetime, Carl Jung broke with him over his exclusively sexual interpretations of libidinal theory and rejected his interpretation of religion as a defensive distortion of individual libido. Jung in 1912 broadened the meaning of libido from sexual need and sexual desire to "passionate desire" (Halligan and Shea 1992). Jung sought to include all dimensions of psychic life as important, and posited that psychological healing could occur through a spiritual dimension which he accessed through dreams and myths. Analytic psychology focused its attention more on psychological developments that tend to take place at midlife or later, and that Jung believed were essentially spiritual issues – questions related to meaning and openness to the unconscious and its collective archetypes, including the numinous archetype of the self. This inherent openness to admit spiritual experience into analysis through dream, symbol, and experiences of the "numinous" made analytic psychology a natural conversation partner for studies in Christian spirituality. Jung himself wrote from considerable familiarity with various mystical traditions, and although the way he posited the possible existence of God or Spirit remained conceptually ambiguous in his scientific writings, this conceptual lack of clarity became an intensive object of focus and stimulated many studies relating the compatibility of this theoretical frame with Christianity. Although feminist scholars have consistently critiqued the patriarchal bias within the Jungian system, his model of the unconscious and the psyche's journey through individuation continues to attract scholarly and practical interest.

As a psychologist, Jung tries to describe the intrapsychic process of relating to multiple aspects of psychic life through conscious assimilation of the personal and collective archetypes activated uniquely in each person's psyche. The primary disadvantage of analytic psychology is its neglect of instinctual and relational life. This intrapsychic exploration can tend to become increasingly intellectualized and abstracted from life, and maintain the analysand's focus on the products of his/her own consciousness within his/herself rather than an actual relatedness to others and activity in the world that revolves around the progressive transformation of the self in relationship to the reality of Godhead. For some, Jungian psychology functionally becomes a gnostic form of spirituality. Nevertheless, analytic psychology opened the way for many rich explorations of Christian symbols, rituals, and images that shape Christian consciousness and organize psychic energy in particular directions.

Roberto Assajoli (1971), one of Jung's followers, developed this symbolic aspect of analytic psychology in quite practical ways through his system of psychosynthesis. This school of transpersonal psychology developed methods of discriminating between the disintegrating and integrating potential of working directly with symbolic material as it emerges from the middle-unconscious, that part of the unconscious ready to emerge into consciousness. These methods and techniques presuppose a higher transpersonal center of consciousness that is not identified with the ego or with any of the partial contents of the unconscious. Using waking imagery guidance, therapeutic interventions can encourage psychic growth integrated around this transpersonal center by safely encountering the disintegrative images and modifying them with alternative images until they transform into a new synthesis. This approach to symbols and how they organize, express, or dissipate psychic energy is particularly helpful for understanding and nurturing these processes within imaginative prayer or as they appear in visionary mystical states. This connection between imagery and psychic and even physical health has produced a voluminous literature.

Transpersonal psychologists have continued to hold as their central concern the "movement and growth of consciousness – its development, vicissitudes, and varied expressions in its divine unfolding" (Cortright 1997: 49). Again according to Cortright, "the ideal would be both great cohesion of the conditioned part of consciousness, that is the self, along with a free, unobstructed connection to the unconditional, spiritual being underlying this surface self" (1997: 48). William James pioneered a religious experience model, while Abraham Maslow focused on self-actualization and peak-experiences. Both tended to privatize their accounts of religious experiencing, deracinating them from specific religious traditions. Yet they gave accounts of healthy spiritual development within these limitations. Transpersonal psychology consistently resists the attempts of psychological theory to reduce the search for God, for self-transcendence – a major human motivation – to the kinds of regressive interpretation favored by early Freudians. Transpersonal psychology takes for granted a worldview that includes and learns from the world's spiritual traditions and that posits multiple rich forms of consciousness. As Cortright says, "the first two decades of writings in the field were largely focused on the 'high end' of human experiencing" (1997: 12). The mission statement of the first *Journal of Transpersonal Psychology* illustrates these concerns:

> publication of theoretical and applied research, original contributions, empirical papers, articles and studies in meta-needs, ultimate values, unitive consciousness, peak experience, ecstasy, mystical experience, B-values, essence, bliss, awe, wonder, self-actualization, ultimate meaning, transcendence of the self, spirit, sacralization of everyday life, oneness, cosmic awareness . . . and related concepts, experiences, and activities. (Sutich 1969: 16)

These particular research interests have contributed considerably to the understanding of altered states of consciousness, the psychology of meditation, and the pleasurable side of spiritual experience.

The work of Cristina and Stanislov Grof (1989) challenged a previous tendency of clinicians to pathologize some "breaktthrough" experiences into unfamiliar states of consciousness as psychotic states requiring medication to eliminate them. The Grofs recognized some confusing altered states of consciousness as "spiritual emergencies" requiring, instead, a safe holding environment enabling the person to understand the emergence of a transpersonal realm in their experience and to integrate it, with or without the help of medication. Transpersonal psychology sought to understand the

kind of personality development needed in order to sustain intense states of consciousness or sensory deprivation without temporary or permanent psychic disinte-
gration and to begin to differentiate when both mystical and psychotic features were
simultaneously present (Lukoff 1985). The ability to recognize that mystical experience
may occur in some people without pathological symptoms once the mystical interlude
has ended validates long-held assumptions within the Christian mystical tradition. Recognizing the simultaneous presence of pathological symptoms and mystical experience
enables researchers to identify pathological symptoms within the life histories of some
mystics (Agosin 1992). Transpersonal psychology frequently attempts to demonstrate
that it is possible to contact a deeper source of wisdom or guidance within than is
available through surface levels of personality, and that this is helpful to psychological
growth. Further, fostering conscious alignment of personal will and desires with
spiritual impulses is a positive life value (Cortright 1997).

As transpersonal psychology has developed, it is now giving more attention to
spirituality and ordinary life, as well as to experiences of suffering, pain, and abuse.
The transpersonal psychologists have contributed to a more general shift in clinical
work toward respect for spirituality and a variety of therapeutic approaches that
work with wounds from early development without denigrating the transpersonal
dimensions of human life. Nevertheless, there remain within the psychological literature, even the transpersonal work, explanatory systems that conceptualize the
"transpersonal" as some part of the unconscious, some aspect of human experience,
some aspect of psychological experience that falls short of the complex interpersonal
relationship with God, a divine Other, not identified with the self but certainly
experienced as affecting the self. It appears as if soul/spirit has so thoroughly collapsed
into psyche that there is little conceptual room left for the mysterious and unaccount-
able spiritual effects of this relationship, which, according to Christian mystics, often
takes place beneath psychological awareness, but nevertheless brings about transformations in both the divine–human relational life and the Christian's day-to-day
experience.

Most of the literature in transpersonal psychology is focused on non-dualistic
Eastern forms of religion or spiritual practice. Many of the "maps" of consciousness,
such as Ken Wilber's spectrum of consciousness and other theories, tend to force the
more theistic, inter-relational forms of religious experience into this overarching framework. Wilber has attempted to delineate various levels of consciousness, each affecting
personal growth, largely in a Buddhist framework (1981). Wilber attempts to relate
psychotherapy to personal growth by showing which levels of personal reality are
addressed by specific therapeutic approaches. His map of consciousness does not
necessarily correspond to the progression of Christian spiritual life. For Wilber, psychological work precedes spiritual development.

Wilber is a creative and original thinker who is currently attempting to form a unified
theory that can join science and spirit, but he frequently fails to correct his earlier constructions on the basis of more recent understandings (1999). His model contributes
the basic insight that psychological therapies of various kinds can only address certain
layers of the psyche. (Early wounds require a psychoanalytic approach, and so on.) His
model of psychological growth preceding spiritual growth, which has been taken up by

many, fails to take into account the possibility that spiritual awakening can and does happen in very young children and can occur at any point in the life-cycle. At the same time, he rightly recognizes that spiritual practices alone do not adequately address psychological deficiencies suffered along the way. His recognition that spiritual levels of consciousness are not addressed by therapeutic means places some limits on psychology – limits psychologists need to pay attention to. Psychological training is not the same as spiritual development within a specific religious tradition. Nor do one's personal religious experiences alone qualify one to facilitate another's spiritual growth. A second important contribution made by Wilber is his concept of the "pre/trans fallacy." He suggests that Western psychotherapy typically made the mistake of associating transpersonal states, Freud's "oceanic feeling," with pre-personal development or regression to that level in a psychosis. Wilber asserts that transpersonal states, rather than being psychotic or regressive, represent a development beyond solid reflexive ego consolidation. They also introduce a non-ego bound way of experiencing reality. It makes a difference whether or not these experiences occur before or after ego development.

An interesting attempt at applying Wilber's framework to an explicitly Christian context is Jim Marion's (2000) account, which sets his personal spiritual journey within this structure. Marion describes this testimony as an account of the "inner work of Christian Spirituality" illustrating his application of Wilber's schema to Christianity. But his assertions of completely non-dual states of consciousness and the restriction of his account exclusively to the inner states he experiences raise critical questions. Is he still within a Christian paradigm? And what has happened to the actual community of believers we understand to be the church? More exemplars will be needed to substantiate his claims.

Finally, among the transpersonalists is Michael Washburn (1994), who integrates a Jungian approach to the mid-life experience with psychoanalytic perspectives in the first half of life. Washburn uses John of the Cross and Teresa of Avila almost exclusively as Western mystics who represent a theistic, more interpersonal mysticism. One of his most valuable insights is his description of "regression in the service of transcendence," which he characterizes as periods in which the ego finds itself alienated or distanced from ordinary preoccupations, combined with the emergence of new experiences from the dynamic ground including both the lifting of repressions and spiritual experience (Washburn 1995). Although his account of the mid-life experience is highly nuanced, he often conflates descriptions of the dark nights with ordinary mid-life deconstruction, without being able to account for the spiritual aspects of this experience, the transformations happening within systems of belief, the experience of faith, and contemplative experiences that are beyond ego control. Although the dark nights can be described in the psychological terms he employs, his schema does not account for the individual quality of these experiences, nor for the ordinarily competent personality functioning in daily life that tends to accompany these passive purifications. Every mid-life experience is not theologically a dark night of either sense or spirit. His account is helpful in appreciating insights from psychoanalysis, especially developments in object relations and self-psychology, and how they play out spiritually. But, again, he does not adequately account for earlier spiritual awakening and development prior to the mid-life experience, nor does he really suggest what happens spiritually or psychologically after mid-life, if both passive purifications are mid-life phenomena.

Transcendence

Of singular importance for the study of Christian spirituality is the goal of human development, regardless of the particular school or theorist scholars work with. As Walter Conn puts it, "Can psychological ideals of self-realization, self-fulfillment, and self-actualization be reconciled with traditional Christian ideals of self-denial, self-surrender, and self-sacrifice?" (1998: 35). Conn affirms that self-realization can be understood as compatible with Christianity if it refers to the fulfillment of our true selves, so that self-denial is understood as the "rejection of any interest, desire, or wish of the self that interferes with the realization of our true selves." The self realizes its authentic being in its drive for meaning, truth, value, and love, and rejects self-centered striving for happiness. Authentic self-realization results from a movement beyond oneself in an effort to bring about the good of others. This can even mean losing one's life in the service of love of another. He concludes his introductory treatment of transcendence with this summary: "Every achievement of creative understanding, realistic judgment, responsible decision, and generous love is an instance of self-transcendence. Such cognitive, moral, and affective self-transcendence to which the gospel calls us in service of the neighbor – and nothing less – is the criterion of authentic self-realization" (1998: 36).

  This movement toward self-transcendence is a repeated spiral of response within a relational matrix. It requires freedom of spirit and of choice-full commitment, so it cannot be coerced. Various psychological understandings of lack of freedom resulting from wounds in the past, visions of life that are inadequate to account for the complexity and ambiguity of graced human existence, an exclusive focus on self apart from the entire interpersonal context of relationship – all of these can impede the process of self-transcendence. To what shall we commit ourselves in love? Psychological understandings of the self and the goal of human development need to be critiqued and appropriated in such a way that they are compatible with this central goal of Christian spiritual life.

The Development of Empirical Measures of Spirituality

A major impetus to the development of reliable measures of spirituality during the past decade emerged from interests in finding relationships between religiosity/spirituality and health (Larson 1993; Matthew et al. 1993; Matthew and Larson 1995; Matthew and Saunders 1997). Early studies on meditation documented some of the physiological effects of primarily Eastern meditation practice. A recent review of the current state of the question, now using MRI and other brain scan technology, offers greater possibility for more significant findings and points to further research. The primary measure of spirituality within Judeo-Christian traditions has been church attendance, which potentially conflates multiple variables related to church affiliation, such as intensity of religiosity, social factors, worship styles, personal prayer practices, values, and beliefs. The meditation studies tend to neglect Judeo-Christian prayer practices and focus on Zen, yoga, and transcendental meditation (Seeman et al. 2003). There are fruitful research opportunities here that will require scholars in Christian spirituality to build on the existing measures and assessment tools to further refine them conceptually and to work with psychologists toward greater context specification.

Hill and Hood (1999) reviewed 125 measures of religion and spirituality, which they placed in seventeen different categories. These included, for example: beliefs, attitudes, religious orientation, faith development, fundamentalism, attitudes toward death, congregational involvement, and satisfaction (Hill and Pargament, 2003). The more specialized Fetzer Institute/National Institute on Aging Working Group (1999) developed a multidimensional measurement of religiousness/spirituality based on twelve domains, which could be used by health researchers without much familiarity with the multiple ways in which religion and spirituality function in people's lives. These twelve domains are: daily spiritual experiences, meaning, values, beliefs, forgiveness, private religious practices, religious/spiritual coping, religious support, religious/spiritual history, commitment, organizational religiousness, and religious preference.

Hill and Pargament identify three conceptual cautions related to the development of these measures as they now exist. They note that the tendency to bifurcate the meanings of religion and spirituality creates greater polarization than is necessary. They point out that *spirituality* is coming to mean "the personal, subjective side of religious experience" in contrast to *religion* as identified with "a fixed system of ideas or ideological commitments" (2003: 64). Thus religion is equated with "an institutional, formal, outward, doctrinal, authoritarian, inhibiting expression" and spirituality with "an individual, subjective, emotional, inward, unsystematic, freeing expression." This split creates different measures for institutional and individual domains. This privatized notion of spirituality neglects the fact that all spiritual expression takes place in larger social contexts, and that organized faith traditions are concerned with both public and private domains of experience. This split assumes that spirituality is generally a positive factor and religion a negative one. This assumption may result in overlooking the negative aspects of spirituality and the positive benefits of religion. Participants in faith traditions experience spirituality within organized religious contexts, although not all persons who espouse spirituality embrace an organized religion. Unnecessary duplication of effort could result from this conceptual trend, instead of the refinement of current measures of religiosity and spirituality. Religion and spirituality are distinct but related constructs and need to be defined in ways that acknowledge their common orientation to the sacred. The same authors note that the empirical research developed by psychologists of religion is not well known by health researchers, and that religion other than religious pathology is not well represented in psychology textbooks.

Nevertheless, Hill and Pargament describe advances already made in developing "spirituality concepts and measures that are functionally related to physical and mental health" (2003: 66–7). They discuss several of these in some detail: perceived closeness to God; orienting, motivating forces; religious support; religious and spiritual struggle. They hope for the development of alternatives to self-report measures, measures of religious and spiritual "outcomes" rather than of "predictors" alone, and measures of religious and spiritual change and transformation. A further area of development is in longitudinal studies rather than the more popular cross-sectional studies that do not chart development over time. The development of these measures that build conceptual bridges between the study of Christian spirituality and this current empirical work of psychologists of religion could open rich areas for more complex study designs. The implications for further studies and for more competent dialogue between empirically based information and understandings of Christian spirituality could be rich, indeed. How do these findings require changing assumptions about spirituality based in theological and historical disciplines? How might researchers in Christian spirituality contribute to the development of measures that are congruent with Christian experience and practice?

Qualitative Research in the Study of Christian Spirituality

Qualitative research is becoming increasingly popular as a research methodology in a variety of fields, including psychology, and offers new avenues of inquiry for Christian spirituality as well. Qualitative research is often the starting-point of projects that begin with a conceptual development of the focus of study and eventually result in quantitative studies that can further test the hypotheses and findings of the smaller-scale interview process usually used in qualitative work. Qualitative work is rich in suggestive detail and fosters an exploration of multiple aspects of the study subjects' experience (Miles and Huberman 1984; Moustakas 1990, 1994; Ruffing 1995; Anderson 1998; Hay 1998). The use of qualitative methodology enables ethnographic, phenomenological, and heuristic forms of research that enable the researcher to go beyond his or her own limited perspective yet draw on the researcher's empathic understanding and insight as they emerge in the process of the study. Although the results of such studies do not yield statistically reliable data, they do produce new insights about a broad range of human experiences which may be infused with the sacred, and are thus an appropriate method of research for scholars in Christian spirituality.

Conclusion

Each approach to the personality sciences presents its own perspectives, insights, and limitations. Therapeutic approaches remain limited to human means. Beneficial interventions can be compared to ascetical means; therapy is a human activity that contributes to self-knowledge, repairs psychic wounds, and contributes to better ego integrity and agency by increasing the client's freedom. It is no longer possible to understand human personhood in its process of choosing some form of self-transcendence, union with the divine, altruistic dedication to others, or even minimally the robust recognition of the claims of others to the same full personhood as one claims for oneself, without appropriating an adequate understanding of depth psychology. Psychological studies that demonstrate the health benefits of certain meditation practices or forms of Christian prayer may help scholars in Christian spirituality make better recommendations about specific means at certain times in people's lives related to both their existential condition and progress in contemplation.

However, the Christian contemplative tradition holds that prayer and meditation have as their primary purpose the fostering of one's personal relationship with God, and that the ongoing transformation of life and consciousness, resulting over time, unfolds in unpredictable and unique ways for each person. The results of the mysterious interaction of God and the human (spirit/psyche, body) can never be limited to what can be empirically measured or expected from human technologies of the self. Prayer during times of spiritual struggle and change may be one of life's stressors rather than a stress-reducer. Practices that promote healing do not prevent mortals from eventually dying. The quest for meaning or achieving a sense of the value of one's life remains a lifelong project, as does the commitment to the practices that sustain the whole web of relationships constituting Christian life. Psychological language, concepts, and therapies are important, but remain only part of the picture. They cannot become the single methodological lens for the study of Christian spirituality. Scholars in this field will need considerable control over the emerging schools and insights of psychology in order to discover which theorists and which studies offer the greatest potential for adequate understanding of the particular phenomenon that forms part of the problematic for each specific study.

References

Agosin, T. 1992: Psychosis, dreams, and mysticism in the clinical domain. In F. Halligan and J. Shea (eds), *The Fires of Desire: Erotic Energies and the Spiritual Quest*, pp. 41–65. New York: Crossroad.

Akhtar, S. and Parens, H. 2001: Is God a subject for psychoanalysis? In S. Akhtar and H. Parens (eds), *Does God Help?: Developmental and Clinical Aspects of Religious Belief*, pp. 1–18. Northvale, NJ: Aronson.

Anderson, R. 1998: Intuitive inquiry: a transpersonal approach. In W. Braud and R. Anderson (eds), *Transpersonal Research Methods for the Social Sciences: Honoring Human Experience*, pp. 69–94. Thousand Oaks, CA: Sage.

Assajoli, R. 1971: *Psychosynthesis*. New York: Viking.

Ciarrocchi, J. 2000: Psychology and theology need each other. *National Catholic Reporter* March 17.

Conn, J. W. 1989: *Spirituality and Personal Maturity*. New York: Paulist Press.

Conn, W. E. 1998: *The Desiring Self: Rooting Pastoral Counseling and Spiritual Direction in Self-transcendence*. Mahwah, NJ: Paulist Press.

Cortright, B. 1997: *Psychotherapy and Spirit: Theory and Practice in Transpersonal Psychotherapy*. Albany, NY: State University of New York Press.

Cousins, E. 1985: Preface to the series. In B. McGinn and J. Meyendorff (eds), *Christian Spirituality: Origins to the Twelfth Century*, pp. xi–xiv. New York: Crossroad.

Eigen, M. 1998: *The Psychoanalytic Mystic*. Binghamton, NY: ESF.

Fetzer Institute Working Group 1999: *Multidimensional Measurement of Religiousness/Spirituality for Use in Health Research: A Report of the Fetzer Institute/National Institute on Aging Working Group*. Kalamazoo MI: Fetzer Institute.

Frohlich, M. 1993: *The Intersubjectivity of the Mystic: A Study of Teresa of Avila's Interior Castle*. Atlanta: Scholars Press.

Gillespie, K. 1995: Listening for grace: self-psychology and spiritual direction. In R. J. Wicks (ed.), *Handbook of Spirituality for Ministers*, pp. 347–65. Mahwah, NJ: Paulist Press.

Grof, C. and Grof, S. 1989: *Spiritual Emergency*. Los Angeles: Tarcher.

Halligan, F. and Shea, J. 1992: *The Fires of Desire: Erotic Energies and the Spiritual Quest*. New York: Crossroad.

Hay, D., with Nye, R. 1998: *The Spirit of the Child*. London: Fount.

Hill, P. C. and Hood, R. W. (eds) 1999: *Measures of Religiosity*. Birmingham, AL.: Religious Education Press.

——and Pargament, K. 2003: Advances in the conceptualization and measurement of religion and spirituality: implications for physical and mental health research. *American Psychologist* 58, 64–74.

Hudson, F. M. 1999: *The Adult Years: Mastering the Art of Self-renewal*. San Francisco: Jossey-Bass.

Jones, J. 1991: The relational self: contemporary psychoanalysis reconsiders religion. *Journal of the American Academy of Religion* 59, 119–35.

Kegan. R. 1982: *The Evolving Self*. San Francisco: Jossey-Bass.

——1994: *In Over our Heads: The Mental Demands of Modern Life*. Cambridge, MA: Harvard University Press.

Kohut, H. 1971: *The Analysis of the Self*. New York: International Universities Press.

——1977: *Restoration of the Self*. Madison, CT: International Universities Press.

Larson, D. 1993: *The Faith Factor: An Annotated Bibliography of Clinical Research on Spiritual Subjects*, vol. 2. Rockville, MD: National Institute for Healthcare Research.

Liebert, E. M. 1992: *Changing Life Patterns: Adult Development in Spiritual Direction*. Mahwah, NJ: Paulist Press.

Loevinger, J. 1976: *Ego Development*. San Francisco: Jossey-Bass.

Lukoff, D. 1985: The diagnosis of mystical experience with psychotic features. *Journal of Transpersonal Psychology* 17, 123–53.

Marion, J. 2000: *Putting on the Mind of Christ: The Inner Work of Christian Spirituality*. Charlottesville, VA: Hampton Roads.

Matthew, D. A. and Larson, D. B. 1995: *The Faith Factor: An Annotated Bibliography of Clinical Research on Spiritual Subjects*, vol. 3: *Enhancing Life Satisfaction*. Rockville, MD: National Institute for Healthcare Research.

——and Saunders, D. 1997: *The Faith Factor: An Annotated Bibliography of Clinical Research on Spiritual Subjects*, vol. 4: *Prevention and Treatment of Illness, Addictions, and Delinquency*. Rockville, MD: National Institute for Healthcare Research.

——, Larson, D., and Barry, C. 1993: *The Faith Factor: An Annotated Bibliography of Clinical Research on Spiritual Subjects*, vol. 1. Rockville, MD: National Institute for Healthcare Research.

Meissner, W. 1987: *Life and Faith: Psychological Perspectives on Religious Experience*. Washington, DC: Georgetown University Press.

Miles, M. B. and Huberman, A. M. 1984: *Qualitative Data Analysis: A Sourcebook of New Methods*. Beverly Hills, CA: Sage.

Mitchell, S. 1988: *Relational Concepts in Psychoanalysis: An Integration*. Cambridge, MA: Harvard University Press.

Moustakas, C. 1990: *Heuristic Research: Design, Methodology, and Applications*. Newbury Park, CA: Sage.

—— 1994: *Phenomenological Research Methods*. Thousand Oaks, CA: Sage.

Rizzuto, A-M. 1979: *The Birth of the Living God: A Psychoanalytic Study*. Chicago: University of Chicago Press.

—— 1996: Psychoanalytic treatment and the religious person. In E. Sahfranske (ed.), *Religion and the Clinical Practice of Psychology*, pp. 409–32. Washington, DC: American Psychological Association.

—— 2001: Does God help? What God? Helping whom? The convolutions of divine help. In S. Akhtar and H. Parens (eds), *Does God Help?: Developmental and Clinical Aspects of Religious Belief*, pp. 21–51. Northvale, NJ: Aronson.

Ruffing, J. K. 1995: The world transfigured: kataphatic religious experience. *Studies in Spirituality* 5, 232–59.

Schneiders, S. M. 1998: The study of Christian spirituality: contours and dynamics of a discipline. *Christian Spirituality Bulletin* 6 (1), 1–12.

Seeman, T., Dubin, L. F., and Seeman, M. 2003: Religiosity/spirituality and health: a critical review of the evidence for biological pathways. *American Psychologist* 58, 53–63.

Sutich, A. J. 1969: Some considerations regarding transpersonal psychology. *Journal of Transpersonal Psychology* 1, 15–16.

Washburn, M. 1994: *Transpersonal Psychology in Psychoanalytic Perspective*. Albany, NY: State University of New York Press.

—— 1995: Regression in the service of transcendence. In *The Ego and the Dynamic Ground: A Transpersonal Theory of Human Development*, pp. 171–202. Albany, NY: State University of New York Press.

Wilber, K. 1979/1981: *No Boundary: Eastern and Western Approaches to Personal Growth*. Boulder, CO: Shambhala.

—— 1999: *The Marriage of Sense and Soul: Integrating Science with Religion*. New York: Broadway.

Winnicott, D. W. 1965: *The Maturational Process and the Facilitating Environment: Studies in the Theory of Emotional Development*. New York: International Universities Press.

—— 1971: *Playing and Reality*. London: Routledge.

CHAPTER 19

Natural Sciences

Robert John Russell

It is the task of this essay to add to the study of Christian spirituality the experience of God in, with, and through the realities of God's creation, the universe, as these realities are discovered and understood by the natural sciences. After considering methodologies for introducing science into Christian spirituality, I will explore various implications that science might have for deepening spirituality and, conversely, suggestions that spirituality might offer for interesting directions in scientific research. Throughout, my style will frequently be to pose issues as questions, both to engage the reader in the excitement and dynamism of the field and to acknowledge that these are, in fact, genuine research questions awaiting future scholarly resolution.

The "Book of Nature" Tradition

In some ways, our most basic spiritual interaction with nature is one in which we experience the world non-reflectively, or at least with a minimum of second-order analysis (Barbour 1974: 51–3). This is the experience of "being in the world," of the sheer, surprising, and compelling taste and touch of the natural world around us and within us. Recall the moment when you first saw a spider web glistening with dew in a dark night or a full moon rising behind flowing clouds at sunset. Was there a sense of "presence," or perhaps a chill of "otherness"? Drift through the satiny warm waters of a luxuriant coral reef teeming with life in a Tahitian atoll; watch clouds forming on the frozen north face of the Matterhorn; soar over the Serengeti plain and its streaming, numberless herds of wildebeests; watch thousands of penguins nesting in the Antarctic; trek slowly through a tropical jungle in Hawaii with the call of parrots in the background; watch with Jane Goodall as gorillas emerge from their forest to stop and look upwards at a tremendous waterfall as though they, too, experienced a tangible moment of sacred space. Feel the rising heat and pounding thirst for "living water" as you stand in the presence of the Australian aboriginal peoples' sacred place, Uluru ("Ayers Rock"), or the sacred spaces of the Western plains for Native Americans. Recall the story of the burning bush on Mt Sinai.

Clearly, the "text" for the spirituality of many people is the "Book of Nature," and for Christians it can serve along with the "Book of Scripture" as a profound source of our experience of God in our life and world, and transcending our life and world. The spirituality born of such immediacy with nature is conveyed in texts ranging from St Francis's *Canticle of Brother Sun* to Teilhard de Chardin's *Hymn of the Universe*. It is found in the contemporary genre of "nature-writing," as the essay by Douglas Burton-Christie discusses in this volume (chapter 27). Spiritualities associated with this immediate experience of nature and its mediating of the divine include the numinous encounter with the Holy in and through nature (a kataphatic spirituality), mystical union with the divine source of nature (an apophatic spirituality), and union with nature-as-community (a relational spirituality).

Still, there is a "second side" to nature that we also experience in daily life, and it leads to fear and dread. We have just pointed to the goodness of creation; this "second side" might well be called "natural evil," and its inevitable role in nature must be acknowledged. Thus the spider web hides the terror of the trapped insect watching the impending jaws of the spider. The full moon rising might cause tidal waves that devastate low-lying villages in the Pacific. The brightly colored coral reef is often the haunt of a reef shark, while the exquisite beauty of the jellyfish distracts us from the poison in its tentacles. Clouds forming on the face of the Matterhorn may actually come from an avalanche taking the lives of climbers. Across the Serengeti plain, wildebeests die in the jaws of lions just as Antarctic penguins are devoured by killer sharks as they leap off an ice shelf into surrounding waters. Indeed, in the predator–prey cycles that mark the history of life on earth most animals die an agonizing death.

How are we to affirm these "polar opposites" that come in the same moment and open us to ultimacy? This question takes us beyond "first-order" phenomena into the analytic tasks of this essay. In his study of world religions, Rudolf Otto (1958) coined the term *mysterium tremendum et fascinans*. By our polar experiences of the natural world, our Christian spirituality, as Otto suggests, will include both radical judgment over good and evil, and radical nearness of the intimate, immanent, and divine source of holiness, beauty, and joy, which is God.

Science and the Prerequisites for the Possibility of Spirituality

In his Introduction to this volume, Arthur Holder offers us a working definition of Christian spirituality: "the study of the lived experience of Christian faith and discipleship." Now a crucial aspect of lived experience is *discernment*: the practice of waiting upon God's "still small voice" within us. Discernment is both a divine gift and a human capacity through which we are completely open to alternatives without letting our personal desires predetermine the outcome. Holder's definition of spirituality also involves *discipleship*: our lived response to God's calling in the world. Over time this becomes an iterative process of listening and acting within a community of Christians gathered as a church.

Starting from Holder's definition of Christian spirituality, we can discover several connections with natural science by exploring what I will call the "prerequisites for the possibility" of discernment and discipleship. It turns out that the world that science discloses is, in fact, the kind of world that fits these prerequisites.

Prerequisites for discernment

Let us focus here on two prerequisites for the possibility of discernment. First, God's hidden action in the world: the epistemic/methodological argument. Discernment presupposes that God's will and action in history and nature are both "hidden" and yet "discernible." God's will and action must not be so "unarguably obvious" from the nature of the world that faith in God would be unnecessary. This means that the world must be *etsi Deus non daretur* ("as if there were no God"). Yet God's will and action cannot be so "hidden" by the world that we can never come to a faith that is intelligible in light of our knowledge of history and nature (*fides quaerens intellectum*). A helpful term for this paradoxical combination of hiddenness and discernibleness is "epistemic distance," a term introduced by John Hick in his analysis of the prerequisites for an environment in which moral growth is possible (1966: 280–91). I would extend Hick's argument by saying that "epistemic distance" is also what must be the case if spiritual discernment is to be possible.

How is science relevant here? The answer lies in the methodological presupposition on which science is based, namely methodological naturalism: scientific theories account for the processes of nature in terms of natural causes and effects. It would violate this methodology to invoke "God" in a scientific theory. Now, we have just seen that epistemic distance as a requirement for both moral growth and Christian spiritual discernment entails that the world must be "as if there were no God." Thus epistemic distance is *also* the prerequisite of methodological naturalism, and thus, in turn, of natural science. The "hiddenness" of God in the world makes possible a scientific understanding of nature, by which we view the world "as if there were no God." Yet the possibility of discerning God in and through nature means that scientific theories, such as Big Bang cosmology or biological evolution, can be given a theological interpretation in terms of God's will and action in nature (and thus "theology and science" is possible). One could conclude that a crucial condition for the possibility of spiritual discernment, for moral growth, and for science, is met in the fact that in creating the universe, God gave epistemic distance.

Second, God's hidden action in the world: the constitutive/ontological argument. For discernment to mean discernment of God's will through God's action in the world, we must presuppose that God really does act in the world. In the growing literature on "divine action" in theology and science such a presupposition is labeled "non-interventionist objective divine action" (Russell et al. 1993, 1995, 1998, 1999, 2001). "Objective" signifies that God really does act in the world. "Non-interventionist" means that God acts without suspending or violating the scientific laws of nature; instead, God's actions are "hidden" from science. Since the "laws of nature" are, ultimately, our description of God's regular, faithful action (i.e., general providence), it makes good theological sense that God's additional, special action (i.e., special providence) should be consistent with these laws even while leading to something radically new. Discernment, then, presupposes that God's will and action are in some ways hidden in natural and historical processes *and* that they nevertheless make an objective difference in the *specific* future course of nature and history.

Once again, contemporary science plays a remarkable role in making these claims intelligible. The mechanistic view of nature inherited from Newtonian physics and Enlightenment philosophy depicted the world as a closed, causal order. In such a view of nature, objective divine action would have to be interventionist, a result that contributed historically to the growing divide between theological conservatives and liberals. But contemporary natural science, including such areas as cosmology, quantum physics, complexity studies, and evolutionary and molecular biology, offers real hope for a new philosophy of nature in which the world is seen as open to both divine and human agency. Working with this interpretation, we can view God as acting together with nature without violating natural processes. In sum, the world God is creating is a world in which Christian discernment is possible.

Prerequisites for the lived experience of faith and discipleship

Discipleship is crucial to spirituality, as Holder points out. Now, a prerequisite for discipleship is that we can respond freely to God's influence in our lives as God's grace heals our sins and sets us free. But freedom to respond to God presupposes that, while we may be predisposed by such factors as genetic inheritance and social conventions, our choices are not fully determined by them. Recent studies in the relation between genetics and psychology, while controversial, tend to support this presupposition. But freedom also presupposes that we can act without physical constraint. As discussed above, while this presupposition was challenged by the mechanistic interpretation of nature, the world is now seen as dynamic, inter-relational, genuinely open and replete with novelty. This view, in turn, is consistent with the presuppositions related to our understanding of Christian discipleship.

Introducing Science into Spirituality

With these more general and preliminary ideas in mind, let us turn to the methodological question: how are we to relate Christian spirituality and the natural sciences? To respond, we first need to expand our working definition of Christian spirituality from the compact one Holder offers. In a pivotal article published over a decade ago, Bernard McGinn (1993) reports on over *thirty-five* different definitions of spirituality. Fortunately for our purposes, he sorts them out into three broad categories or approaches involving both spirituality as a phenomenon (i.e., "first-order" definitions) and the study of this phenomenon (i.e., "second-order" definitions):

1   The theological approach focuses on "second-order" definitions, often treats spirituality exclusively from a theological perspective, and distinguishes generic human striving for transcendence from a specifically Christian response to revelation.

2   The historical-contextual approach focuses on historical exemplars, the particular history of a spiritual community, and the way in which the unity of faith across history is understood in historical terms.

3   The anthropological approach focuses on spirituality as a generic aspect of human experience involving "depth," "authenticity," the "inner dimensions."

How, then, should we proceed in defining spirituality: choose one of the three approaches or look for a combination of them?

McGinn takes the latter route because of the "mutual implication of all three approaches": they focus on the actual accounts of spiritual experience by historical and contemporary figures, the way these accounts were formalized into theology and analyzed for their truth claims, and what these accounts tell us about human nature from both a philosophical and a social-scientific perspective (1993: 7). I think McGinn's suggestion provides a helpful point of departure. The *theological* approach is probably the most natural place to introduce science into Christian spirituality. The "second-order" character of theological language is a "natural fit" to the "second-order" character of theoretical language in the sciences, where the "primary order" is, of course, experimental data. It allows us to take advantage of the tremendous growth in scholarship on the relations between theology and science over the past half-decade. It calls us to reformulate theology in light of the natural sciences, and thus it makes theology a more vigorous and contemporary discipline in its relation to Christian spirituality. Moreover, it does so while guarding against atheistic approaches that attempt to undermine theology (and spirituality) based on a reductionist/materialist reading of science. At the same time, the *historical* and *anthropological* approaches can also offer places for introducing science not only into theology but into spirituality as well.

My concern with McGinn's suggestion is that it does not provide a sufficiently complex analysis of how these three approaches work together. Here the research by Sandra Schneiders is very helpful. Schneiders defines spirituality as "the experience of consciously striving to integrate one's life in terms not of isolation and self-absorption but of self-transcendence toward the ultimate value one perceives" (1989: 684; see also 1994, 1998). She supports an anthropological/hermeneutical approach, which she views as intrinsically "interdisciplinary" since it involves two layers of epistemology: (a) constitutive disciplines that supply the data of Christian spirituality (thus Scripture and Christian history) and (b) problematic disciplines that offer a crucial perspective on Christian spiritual experience (such as psychology and sociology) (1998: 7). What then about theology? Schneiders sees it as belonging to both layers: it functions as a *constitutive* discipline when, through critical reflection on Scripture and the history of Christian experience, it sets out the Christian character of such experience. Still it remains within the scope of the *problematic* disciplines since, while offering critical reflection on experience, it can never supply the actual data of Christian spiritual experience.

I suggest we work with the nuanced methodology that Schneiders offers. Elsewhere, I have explored several ways to relate science and spirituality given Schneiders's methodology (Russell forthcoming). Here, the key contribution to this methodology will be the insight that a theology influenced by a creative interaction with science can, in turn, greatly enhance the interactions between spirituality and theology that

Schneiders describes. To sustain this insight, I must first argue against two widespread assumptions. First, against the assumption that science and theology are mutually irrelevant I will argue that their modes of rationality are analogous. Second, against the assumption that theology, and all other disciplines, can be reduced without remainder to science, I will argue that they all fit within a non-reducible epistemic network. With these arguments in place, I will then suggest that the best relation between science and theology is a "two-way" interaction.

Analogous methods

According to Ian G. Barbour's careful analysis, an analogy exists between the way in which theories are constructed, deployed, and evaluated in science and in theology (read "doctrine" for "theory"). In both fields, paradigms offer an overarching framework of interpretation and include both metaphysical and aesthetic elements. The choice of which data count as relevant reflects the biases of the theory being tested (i.e., "all data are theory-laden"). Imagination plays a key role in the construction of models and theories. Theories (doctrines) are tested by their fruitfulness in interpreting new kinds of data and in their practical consequences for life. Both fields can be given a critical realist interpretation in which knowledge is referential although partial and revisable, and in which both subjective and objective elements are present. Finally, both science and theology rely on metaphorical language: the "expanding universe," the "genetic code," the ecological "web." Often these metaphors are combined in the theology/science dialogue as when Sallie McFague refers to the universe as the "body of God" (1982, 1988, 1993).

I suggest we extend this analogy between scientific and theological methodology to include the discipline of Christian spirituality. The interpretation of data (i.e., Scripture, tradition) within paradigms of spiritual practice shapes the way in which historical communities grow and deepen. The practice of discernment requires an openness to the influence of the Spirit as to what data count and how to integrate them within our "life project," to use Schneiders's wonderful term. The test of this integration is based on the "fruits of the Spirit." Finally, Christian spirituality presupposes that terms like "God" can have some referential meaning, as critical realism entails, even while underscoring their ineffable mystery. Thus the methodology of Christian spirituality as an academic discipline is analogous in many ways to the methodology of science.

Epistemic constraints and irreducible emergence

Given, then, that the methodologies are analogous, how do we "import" the discoveries of science into Christian spirituality? Scholars such as Arthur Peacocke (1993: esp. 217, fig. 3), Nancey Murphy (1997, 1998b), and George Ellis (Murphy and Ellis 1996: esp. 204, fig. 9.3) have developed a complex proposal for interpreting the discoveries of science within Christian theology, and I suggest we generalize their proposal to include the field of spirituality.

These scholars view the sciences and humanities as layered in a holistic epistemic network where the layers are disciplines studying increasingly complex systems. The network starts with physics at the bottom level and works upwards through chemistry, biology, neurophysiology, psychology, linguistics, economics, to the arts, ethics, and theology. In this approach, the lower levels place *epistemic constraints* on the upper levels; yet there are genuinely *new and irreducible properties and processes* that emerge at the upper levels. Thus biology cannot contradict physics; instead, it presupposes physics, but it cannot be reduced to physics. This approach means that theology must take seriously and be affected by all the knowledge of the other disciplines, including the natural sciences, even while it deals with realities, such as divine grace and the *imago Dei*, that cannot be reduced to and explained away by these other disciplines.

We can extend this argument by claiming that spirituality should be included within this network of disciplines. By doing so, spirituality will be affected by all the disciplines that theology deals with, including the natural sciences. At the same time, Christian spirituality includes genuinely new domains of knowledge and experience, such as discernment and discipleship, that can never be reduced away from it. In short, I believe that Christian spirituality, as an academic discipline, can learn from the sciences, while retaining its irreducible character as an academic discipline.

Interaction

Finally, in my own writing I have urged that we make this network genuinely interactive by adding to it the ways in which the upper-level disciplines in the network can have an indirect influence on the lower-level disciplines. An historical example is offered by the role theology played in the rise of modern science. Contemporary examples can be found in the ways in which theological and philosophical beliefs have inspired the construction of new scientific research programs in the twentieth century in such areas as quantum mechanics and physical cosmology. I have called this extended approach the "creative mutual interaction" between theology and science (Russell 2002a). Now we can move one step further and include Christian spirituality in this account, allowing for the possibility that it too could play a constructive heuristic role in the developments of research science.

In sum, I propose that Christian spirituality should now be understood as a part of the holistic epistemic network that includes the natural sciences, and that discourse and fertile exchange flow in a multitude of overlapping directions between all these disciplines. We can now explore this complex interaction by starting with some of the many promising exchanges between theology and science and then pointing to ways in which Christian spirituality can be creatively enhanced by these exchanges as well as contribute to them. Here I will draw on research material in theology and science (Barbour 1990; Peacocke 1993; Polkinghorne 1994); helpful introductory material is readily available as well (Haught 1995; Richardson and Wildman 1996; Barbour 1997; Peters 1997b; Polkinghorne 1998; Southgate et al. 1999; Russell and Wegter-McNelly 2004).

The Mathematical Laws of Nature and the Ascent to God as Transcendent

For many scientists, the laws of physics are approximations of the underlying, fundamental laws of nature and these fundamental laws represent the rationality and intelligibility of nature. This view opens onto several insights for theology and spirituality.

Why is nature intelligible to us? As Albert Einstein remarked so eloquently, "The eternal mystery of the world is its comprehensibility" (1978: 292). One theological response that dates back to Justin Martyr (CE 100–165) is that the rationality and intelligibility of nature is grounded in the *Logos* (which the Gospel of John identifies with Jesus), through which all things are created (John 1: 1–3). This same *Logos* is present to us in our capacity to reason, an aspect of the *imago Dei*. Hence our ability to formulate the laws of nature reflects the divine *Logos* within us (Torrance 1969; Polkinghorne 1994: esp. 74). Our thirst to discover (even to "taste," *gustus*) these laws and our joy in their discovery is rooted in a spirituality of participation in ultimacy through the process of knowing – what could be called an Augustinian/Franciscan spirituality (Tillich 1967: vol. 1, 40–6).

Mark Richardson (2002) has claimed that there are three distinct literary genres in the writings of scientists on science and spirituality: "rationalist-speculative," "affective-holistic," and "critical-historical." Authors who write in the "rationalist-speculative" genre typically view science as an ascent from the world to God. Science starts with controlled experiment, is generalized through the imagination into models and then theories of nature, and then it leads one through a rationalist-speculative ascent beyond the world to the ineffable and transcendent "mind of God" in which the laws of nature are Platonic ideal forms. The doing of theoretical science is thus "thinking God's thoughts after God." Examples include Albert Einstein, who spoke of "cosmic religious feeling," and Paul Davies, who speaks of reading "the mind of God" (1992). This view represents a Platonic spirituality and occasionally a gnostic, world-denying spirituality.

Mathematics has played an intimate role in our exploration of the concept of God. Much of the reasoning about the traditional attributes of God, such as omnipresence, eternity, omniscience, reflects a Greek view of infinity as defined in opposition to the finite. For some scholars, however, advances in mathematics in the nineteenth and twentieth centuries, such as Cantor's transfinite numbers, depict the infinite as including, even while transcending, the finite. These advances in mathematics in turn invite a reconsideration of the traditional concepts of God's attributes and of God's relation to creation such that God is revealed even while God is hidden in the "transfinites" of the world (Russell 1997). Such a theological view could lead to a deepened spiritual experience of the kataphatic within the apophatic.

The Expanded Experience of Nature and the Immanence of God in the World

In his compelling analysis of the "ambiguous" role of nature in the history of Christian theology, Paul Santmire (1985) uses the image of climbing a mountain as the basis of two conflicting metaphors. In one metaphor we climb the mountain in order to move away from nature and closer to God (the "world-denying" metaphor). In the other metaphor we climb the mountain to gain a broader vista on the world (the "world-affirming" metaphor). I suggest we can extend his metaphor to include the way in which science functions as the "mountain" we are climbing. For some, the laws of nature offer an ascent from this world to God, as we have just seen. For others, the instruments of science – the Hubble telescope, electron microscope, infrared spectrometer, the particle accelerator at CERN, the gene sequencers – offer a connection with nature far beyond unaided human sense experience. We can literally "see" and "hear" nature in ways simply unattainable without science in a seemingly endless growth of scope (think light-years) and depth (think subatomic). Through scientific instruments the intricate spider web becomes a thicket of organic molecules, atoms, and elementary particles. A full moon rising becomes a grain of dust in an ever-expanding horizon of galaxies and clusters of galaxies stretching across the visible universe. The teeming terrestrial biology of a Tahitian atoll is a microcosm of the vast splendor of life scattered throughout our galaxy and beyond. Clouds forming on the north face of the Matterhorn resemble iridescent, light-year long streams of interstellar dust, the nurseries of new stars being born as witnessed by the Hubble telescope. Standing beyond gorillas at a waterfall is the galactic community of intelligent life that scientists like Carl Sagan and Frank Drake believe populates our Milky Way – and awaits our "coming of age" to join them.

These vistas can remind us of the God who relishes in the sheer joy of God's creation, delighting in "behemoth" (Ps. 104: 26). They can lead to a kataphatic spirituality, the experience of ultimacy in and through what we know about the world, the immanence of God in the depths of the world. Some experience the universe as pointing beyond itself to the God who is its creator, as Augustine so richly portrayed in the *Confessions* (1991: 183). To others, science serves as a window on the world as intrinsically sacred. In general, Richardson (2002) calls this genre "affective-holistic," and he includes the writings of such scientists as Pauline Rudd, Joel Primack, and Brian Swimme. We now come to the primary literature in "theology and science," or what Richardson calls "critical-historical" writings.

Science and Creation *ex nihilo*

Historians of science have shown that the doctrine of creation *ex nihilo*, with its historical roots in Jewish, Muslim, and Christian theologies, contributed to the intellectual climate in which the natural sciences arose. Its distinctive claim that God created the world *ex nihilo* means that the world is both contingent and rational. Contingency means that the universe need not exist, that its sheer existence is its most profound mystery. It also means that genuine knowledge about nature can only come from empirical methods and not from purely deductive reason. The rationality of the universe means that nature is knowable to reason and our rational knowledge can be represented in mathematics.

These features – contingency and rationality – have tremendous implications for Christian spirituality. We have already discussed the significance of the rationality of the universe *vis-à-vis* the laws of nature. The *contingency* of the universe and all that is within it – including us – means that we are all "creatures." There is no Gnostic "divine spark" within our mortal bodies, nor is the material universe a strategy by which God saves immortal souls from an endless fall into oblivion (as Origen thought). Instead, God's ongoing gift to us is our sheer existence, just as it is to all creatures and to the universe. The spiritual significance here is that our very being as a living creature, that which is presupposed as a condition for the possibility of spiritual experience, is a continuous gift of God.

What, in turn, might Christian spirituality have to offer for consideration by scientists? As just said, the doctrine of creation contributed a conception of nature as rational and contingent to the foundations of science. It also, however, understood nature in axiological and aesthetic terms: all that God created is good and beautiful. Similarly, our spiritual experience of the universe is irreducibly one that finds goodness and beauty in nature. Following the method of "mutual creative interaction" it would be interesting to explore whether these assumptions about axiology and teleology in nature, when properly nuanced and interpreted carefully, could lead to new and fruitful research programs in science.

$t = 0$

When we turn to a specific scientific cosmology, such as Big Bang cosmology, we are led to profound "limit questions," to use David Tracy's phrase, which point beyond cosmology to philosophical and theological issues (discussed in such publications as Peters 1989; Russell et al. 1993; Worthing 1996; Clayton 1997).

Astrophysical evidence portrays the universe as expanding from an initial period of arbitrarily small size and soaring temperatures some 13 billion years ago. This evidence, in turn, indicates that the universe had an absolute temporal origination (symbolized by "$t = 0$"); it provides indirect evidence of the universe's being the creation of God *ex nihilo*. More formally, a temporal beginning of the universe would be one way to concretize the philosophical argument that the universe is contingent, and thus the theological argument that it is created, although an eternally old universe would still be contingent in a strict sense (Russell 1993). Meanwhile, the discovery that all things had a common origin at $t = 0$ can inspire a spirituality of connectedness through a cosmological common origin to all creatures.

Anthropic principle

According to the anthropic principle, the universe is highly "fine-tuned" for life. If the fundamental laws of physics or the values of the physical constants differed by even one part in a billion, life could never have evolved in the universe (Barrow and Tipler 1986; Leslie 1989). Such "fine-tuning" can be taken as further "evidence" for God and for God's intentions in creating *this* universe (Ellis 1993; Murphy 1993; Peacocke 1993: esp. 106–12). Nancey Murphy and George Ellis, in turn, point not just to life but to the capacities for intelligence and moral agency in the human species as placing even stricter physical limits on the fundamental laws and constants (Murphy and Ellis 1996). I would extend their reasoning to suggest that our capacity for spirituality must also be taken seriously in such "fine-tuning" arguments. Creatures capable of entering into a covenant of faith and spiritual discipleship thus provide a crucial "clue" to the meaning of the universe and a special "constraint" on the possible laws and constants that must be realized in the universe if it is to be compatible with our existence. This move is not anthropocentric or anthropomorphic, but simply one that takes with utmost serious-ness the fact of our being physical and biological creatures that have evolved in this universe and that are capable, through divine grace, of entering into covenant with God.

Of course, science changes, and Big Bang cosmology has undergone important modi-fications in the past few decades. In the 1980s, inflationary (or "hot") Big Bang cosmologies challenged the standard Big Bang theory, questioning the scientific status of $t = 0$ and with it the anthropic principle/fine-tuning argument. Current approaches to quantum gravity/quantum cosmology raise further challenges and opportunities for interaction with theology and spirituality: Will these cosmologies also be open to fruit-ful interpretation by Christian spirituality? Conversely, what might such a spirituality offer to the formative process of developing new scientific models for those working from a perspective informed by the academic study of Christian spirituality?

Quantum Mechanics and Special Relativity

We have already seen that an indeterminist interpretation of quantum physics makes possible a "non-interventionist" account of objective divine action in nature. Quantum mechanics also suggests that physical entities at the subatomic level are more complex ontologically than our ordinary world of waves and particles. From the Einstein–Podolski–Rosen arguments of the 1930s to the ground-breaking theorems of John Bell in the 1960s, a compelling case can be made that quantum systems are "non-local": when two particles that had been in a bound state are widely separated, their indivi-dual properties remain correlated in ways that defy a classical explanation. These cor-relations may indicate that the particles, even at a tremendous distance, remain part of a single, "non-separable" system. This perspective might, in turn, suggest a "whole-ness" or "unity" to nature that is much more subtle and ontologically grounded than the "web" or "interaction" models drawn from ecology (Russell et al. 2001).

Quantum non-separability offers a powerful insight into the spiritual experience of intrinsic relationality such as found in the trinitarian perichoretic relations, the *ad extra* work of the triune God, the unity of the church, and the unity of creation (humanity, earth ecology, universe). Conversely, if we look at quantum non-separability through the lens of trinitarian spirituality, what new insights might we discover for further scientific research at the level of fundamental physics? Finally, how would all this change if other interpretations of quantum mechanics replaced quantum non-separability?

According to Einstein's theory of special relativity, space and time are no longer separate dimensions of nature but instead are radically interconnected, leading to such "paradoxes" as time dilation, length contraction, and the result that has changed human history irreversibly: $e = mc^2$. Special relativity, in turn, can be given several competing interpretations (Isham and Polkinghorne 1993). First, according to the standard, Minkowskian view, these interconnections indicate that space and time are part of a single four-dimensional geometry called "spacetime." This interpretation undercuts our fundamental, lived experience of time as "flowing." Instead, we live in a "block universe" in which all events that we call past, present, and future are equally real. Secondly, special relativity can be given a "flowing time" interpretation that is faithful to our lived temporal experience, but it is difficult to reconcile with all aspects of special relativity.

Both interpretations, however, shed light on Christian spiritual experience. The mystical union with God is often experienced as a "timeless" moment, while the passage of time is basic to the category of lived experience, personal agency, and Christian discipleship. Moreover, the conflict between these interpretations might be resolvable through contemporary trinitarian theologies and their treatment of "time and eternity" (Peters 1993). And, as we move from theology to science, this richer, fully temporal view of eternity might shed new light on our understanding of special relativity (Russell 2000).

Biological Evolution and God's Action as Creator

Contemporary biology interprets the evolution of life on earth as a consequence of random genetic and environmental variations together with natural selection (Ayala 1998a). Given the crucial role, then, of "chance" in evolution, can evolution be interpreted theologically as due to the ongoing action of God? Atheists like Richard Dawkins say "no!," but Christians like Arthur Peacocke say "yes!" According to "theistic evolution," God acts through law *and* chance; indeed, God created the universe *ex nihilo* such that it would be compatible with God's continuous creating activity (*creatio continua*) (Peacocke 1979, 1993).

Now we can take theistic evolution one step further. We know that quantum physics is involved in the production of genetic mutations. If we interpret quantum physics as open to God's non-interventionist action, then theists can claim that evolution is indeed the way God creates life, mind, and, in humanity at least, creatures capable of spiritual experience. With this robust view of theistic evolution we may be led to a spirituality of gratitude and trust through understanding the evolutionary processes out of which we, and all life, have evolved as the ongoing gift of the immanent creator.

Still we must respond to the enormous challenge that suffering, disease, death, and extinction in the natural world pose to Christian faith. Life feeds on life: without death, the ecosystems of our world would not be possible, and without extinction, the evolution of complex life would not have occurred. Clearly biological death is not the consequence of "the Fall" (Gen. 3) at the dawn of human history; instead, it is *constitutive* of life. Suffering is concomitant to sentience in complex organisms: most animals die an anguishing death as the food for others. The phenomena of suffering, disease, death, and extinction inevitably raise the problem of "natural evil" and thus "natural theodicy": does God, by creating through evolutionary processes, allow – even cause – natural evil?

In response, scholars such as Ian Barbour, John Haught, and John Polkinghorne have turned to a kenotic theology of God's redemptive suffering as the divine response to "natural evil," extending it to include the whole sweep of life on earth (Barbour 1990; Haught 2000; Polkinghorne 2001; Russell 2004). As Holmes Rolston puts it, nature is "cruciform" (1987: 144–6, 289–92; 2001: 58–65). Now if evolution, and not just humanity, radically expands the scope of Christ's (com)passion, then our experience of the presence of God in and with the suffering of the poor and oppressed should now include all living creatures. But the cross of Christ without his resurrection at Easter would be an unremitting tragedy. Can we then understand the hope offered by Christ's resurrection to include all living creatures? We will return to this crucial question below.

Christian Spirituality in Light of Humanity's Evolutionary Origins

What are some of the implications for Christian spirituality of the biological evolution of *Homo sapiens*?

Adaptive purpose

We now know that the myriad species of life on earth are related more like a shrub than a tree; against our traditional and overweening sense of importance, humanity does not sit at the pinnacle, because there is none. Still, we are at the end of one foliated branch of the shrub, and there is a sense of directionality to the evolution of life. There is also functional purpose (teleonomy) in the way species are adapted to their environment, but it is an evolved purpose produced by a recipe (the genetic code), not by a blueprint, and it requires no external "agent" (*pace* the proponents of "intelligent design"). This more modest, but nevertheless genuine, sense of "purpose" opens our spiritual experience to God as creating "from within" the dynamic history of life on earth, working in and through its ever-changing pathways, responding continually to its varying contours with the eschatological future in mind. This dynamic view of God's purposeful action in evolution resonates with our lived spiritual experience of God's continuing and purpose-filled influence in our lives.

Ethics

In humanity, at least, the evolution of self-consciousness and rationality has proved an adaptive advantage. With them comes the capacity for moral reflection and behavior, but, according to Francisco Ayala (1995, 1998b), only as a surplus capacity: the contents/moral norms of our ethics are left as a "free variable" for culture to determine. This means that ethics cannot be reduced to biology as some sociobiologists claim (Ruse

1995). Instead, it may be understood as our response to the revelation of God. What, then, about the evolution of the "soul" (Murphy 1998a)? The evolution of the capacity for sin? The evolution of the capacity for spirituality?

Genetics

The biochemistry of our genes is shared by all life on earth, leading us to a spirituality of community with nature. Genetic variation, in turn, is a driving factor in evolution and a locus of God's continuous creation in nature. Genetic diversity produces both human diversity, which we celebrate, and human unity as a species which cultural divisions cannot overcome. But genetic variation also gives rise to thousands of diseases and their treatment may require genetic engineering. In most cases, treatment only involves an individual patient, but in rare cases it might involve germ-line genetic engineering, and here the results could affect the human gene pool. Should this be rejected as "playing God" and as a new form of eugenics, or does our ethical mandate to cure disease require us at least to consider such radical approaches to medicine? Closely related to this, the predispositions which our genes impose on every aspect of our personality, including our modes of spirituality, can lead either to a debilitating fatalism ("genetic determinism") or to a dangerous sense of empowerment to alter the future gene pool, a view that Ted Peters calls "Promethean determinism" (1997a). How are we to critically assess and ethically integrate the seemingly contradictory implications of genetics within Christian spirituality? How might such a spirituality address and affect the directions of genetic research?

Food

The common biochemistry of all life makes the food chain possible, and with it the phenomenon of animal suffering. Yet food plays a crucial role in a sacramental spirituality of bread and wine. How does our empathy for suffering in nature reshape our spiritual experience of God's presence in our common and sacred meals?

Neuroscience and the mind/brain problem

If mental states arise from brain states ("bottom-up causality"), how does the mind influence the brain ("top-down causality" and/or "supervenience") (Russell et al. 1999)? How do we understand our experience of Christian spirituality, including discernment and discipleship, if the neurosciences so strongly stress only "bottom-up causality"?

Artificial/computer intelligence

What do advances in artificial intelligence have to tell us about human nature? One way to respond is by asking whether embodiment makes the difference between human intelligence and computers. Another way is to ask, with Noreen Herzfeld (2003), why we project our need for community onto our interactions with computers; and, conversely, do models of the *imago Dei* as the capacity for relationality have something to offer to research in computer science? And what do computers tell us about our capacity for spirituality (Palmer 1997)?

Technology and religious icons

Humankind is *Homo faber*, tool-maker; the making of artifacts is part of our identity as human. The connection to spirituality is profound: we fashion religious icons to mediate our relation to God and to represent the sacred in our midst. We build cathedrals to provide a sanctuary from worldly traffic; their stained glass windows told the biblical story when few could read. At the same time, we are warned by the biblical injunction against idolatry to remember that nothing we create is divine. Indeed, our ethical concerns about the misuse of technology are parallel to our spiritual rejection of worshiping what we create.

Technology and our spiritual relation to nature

Ian Barbour has developed a typology that suggests parallels between human attitudes toward nature and those toward technology (1980: ch. 2). Our attitudes toward technology also reflect our spiritual relation to nature and our understanding of the *imago Dei*. This can be a spirituality of "work as prayer" modeled after St Benedict and invoking the stewardship of nature. It might also be a spirituality of unity with nature whose focus is on our common future, as suggested by Philip Hefner's fascinating interpretation of the *imago Dei* as "created co-creators" (Hefner 1989, 1992, 1993). But technology can also give us brutal "power over" nature when we succumb to the temptation to distort authentic human dominion into sinful domination (White 1967; Barbour 1993: ch. 3). Here the ecofeminist critique (Merchant 1980; Ruether 1992) of science and technology as linked to patriarchal models of the relation between God, humanity, and the earth leads us to a spirituality of confession and repentance.

The Cosmological Far Future and the Experience of Resurrection Faith

Finally, science projects a future for the universe that challenges our experience of hope and meaning. The earth will be destroyed in the eventual nova of the sun some 5 billion years from now. Even if humanity migrates to the stars, earth's cornucopia of life will be lost. Beyond this is the inevitable dissolution of our galaxy and the end to the physical conditions required for life anywhere, leaving the universe to expand and cool forever or recollapse into a fireball (the cosmological "freeze or fry" scenarios).

But Christian hope is based on the eschatological coming of the reign of God, and with it God's transformation of the universe – not just the earth – into the new creation. Such hope is founded on God's proleptic act at Easter: the bodily resurrection of Jesus of Nazareth. Scholars are divided over the meaning of resurrection: is it a "bodily" resurrection, as emphasized by the empty tomb traditions (though certainly far transcending the "resuscitation" accounts in the New Testament such as the raising of Lazarus) and constituting a new event in the continued life and experience of Jesus beyond the grave through the radical act of God? Or is it a "spiritual" resurrection for which the empty tomb traditions are irrelevant, a subjective experience of the disciples in which they gained new hope and confidence after Golgotha? If we take the former approach, it seems most likely to entail an eschatology of "new creation": the coming of Christ in the "future" with the transformation of the world into something radically new (where "transformation" entails continuity within discontinuity versus a totally new creation *ex nihilo* or a mere extension of this creation in a "physical eschatology"). Research in theology and science that engages the challenge of scientific eschatology is truly a "frontier field" (Polkinghorne and Welker 2000; Russell 2002a, b).

Along with it we need a new understanding of Christian spirituality which takes cosmology squarely on board and which points to a universe-transforming eschatology. Teilhard de Chardin moved in this direction, but his writings now seem anthropocentric: nature was redeemed through the hominization of the world and its eschatological fulfillment in the Omega point. Instead, we need a spirituality whose eschatological horizon is the universe and in which all creatures find hope and eternal life in God's new creation. From this perspective we might depict humanity's role as "eschatological companion" (Russell 2003).

Conclusion

In an age in which science and theology are often seen as either mutually irrelevant or in outright conflict, the task of introducing science into the academic study of Christian spirituality is indeed daunting if we are to avoid exacerbating the options – irrelevance or conflict – or of "lowering the bar" by settling for a superficial view of both fields. Instead, in this essay I hope to have shown ways in which the methodologies operative in the academic study of Christian spirituality can be augmented to include a creative interaction with the natural sciences, one in which spirituality, along with theology and science, can benefit. On the one hand, the astonishing scientific discoveries about the expanding universe and the evolution of life on earth can enliven and renew a variety of forms of Christian spirituality. On the other hand, Christian spirituality in its many modes can offer new insights for what could become potentially fruitful scientific research.

Acknowledgments

I would like to thank Nancy Wiens St John for her extensive editorial suggestions on the final manuscript, and Arthur Holder for his support and editorial guidance throughout the project.

References

Augustine of Hippo 1991: *Confessions*, trans. H. Chadwick. Oxford: Oxford University Press.

Ayala, F. J. 1995: The difference of being human: ethical behavior as an evolutionary byproduct. In H. Rolston III (ed.), *Biology, Ethics and the Origins of Life*, pp. 117–35. Boston: Jones and Bartlett.

—— 1998a: The evolution of life: an overview. In R. J. Russell, W. R. Stoeger, and F. J. Ayala (eds), *Evolutionary and Molecular Biology: Scientific Perspectives on Divine Action*, pp. 21–57. Vatican City State: Vatican Observatory Publications.

—— 1998b: Human nature: one evolutionist's view. In W. S. Brown, N. Murphy, and H. N. Malony (eds), *Whatever Happened to the Soul? Scientific and Theological Portraits of Human Nature*, pp. 31–48. Minneapolis, MN: Fortress Press.

Barbour, I. G. 1974: *Myths, Models, and Paradigms: A Comparative Study in Science and Religion*. New York: Harper and Row.

—— 1980: *Technology, Environment, and Human Values*. New York: Praeger.

—— 1990: *Religion in an Age of Science*. Gifford Lectures, 1989–90. San Francisco: Harper and Row.

—— 1993: *Ethics in an Age of Technology*. Gifford Lectures, 1989–91. San Francisco: Harper.

—— 1997: *Religion and Science: Historical and Contemporary Issues*. San Francisco: Harper.

Barrow, J. D. and Tipler, F. J. 1986: *The Anthropic Cosmological Principle*. Oxford: Clarendon Press.

Clayton, P. 1997: *God and Contemporary Science*. Grand Rapids, MI: Eerdmans.

Davies, P. C. 1992: *The Mind of God: The Scientific Basis for a Rational World*. New York: Simon and Schuster.

Einstein, A. 1978: Physics and reality. In *Ideas and Opinions*, pp. 283–315. New York: Dell.

Ellis, G. F. 1993: The theology of the anthropic principle. In R. J. Russell, N. C. Murphy, and C. J. Isham (eds), *Quantum Cosmology and the Laws of Nature: Scientific Perspectives on Divine Action*, pp. 367–406. Vatican City State: Vatican Observatory Publications.

Haught, J. F. 1995: *Science and Religion: From Conflict to Conversion*. New York: Paulist Press.

—— 2000: *God after Darwin: A Theology of Evolution*. Boulder, CO: Westview Press.

Hefner, P. 1989: The evolution of the created co-creator. In T. Peters (ed.), *Cosmos as Creation: Theology and Science in Consonance*, pp. 211–34. Nashville: Abingdon Press.

—— 1992: Nature's history as our history: a proposal for spirituality. In D. T. Hessel (ed.), *After Nature's Revolt: Eco-justice and Theology*, pp. 171–83. Minneapolis, MN: Fortress Press.

—— 1993: *The Human Factor: Evolution, Culture, and Religion*. Minneapolis, MN: Fortress Press.

Herzfeld, N. 2003: *In our Image: Artificial Intelligence and the Human Spirit*. Minneapolis, MN: Fortress Press.

Hick, J. 1966: *Evil and the God of Love*, rev. edn. San Francisco: Harper and Row.

Isham, C. J. and Polkinghorne, J. C. 1993: The debate over the block universe. In R. J. Russell, N. C. Murphy, and C. J. Isham (eds), *Quantum Cosmology and the Laws of Nature: Scientific Perspectives on Divine Action*, pp. 134–44. Vatican City State: Vatican Observatory Publications.

Leslie, J. 1989: *Universes*. London: Routledge.

McFague, S. 1982: *Metaphorical Theology: Models of God in Religious Language*. Philadelphia: Fortress Press.

—— 1988: Models of God for an ecological, evolutionary era: God as mother of the universe. In R. J. Russell, W. R. Stoeger, et al. (eds), *Physics, Philosophy, and Theology: A Common Quest for Understanding*, pp. 249–72. Vatican City State: Vatican Observatory Publications.

—— 1993: *The Body of God: An Ecological Theology*. Minneapolis, MN: Fortress Press.

McGinn, B. 1993: The letter and the spirit: spirituality as an academic discipline. *Christian Spirituality Bulletin* 1 (2), 1, 3–10.

Merchant, C. 1980: *The Death of Nature: Women, Ecology, and the Scientific Revolution*. New York: Harper and Row.

Murphy, N. C. 1993: Evidence of design in the fine-tuning of the universe. In R. J. Russell, N. C. Murphy, and C. J. Isham (eds), *Quantum Cosmology and the Laws of Nature: Scientific Perspectives on Divine Action*, pp. 407–36. Vatican City State: Vatican Observatory Publications.

—— 1997: *Anglo-American Postmodernity: Philosophical Perspectives on Science, Religion, and Ethics*. Boulder, CO: Westview Press.

—— 1998a: Human nature: historical, scientific, and religious issues. In W. S. Brown, N. Murphy, and H. N. Malony (eds), *Whatever Happened to the Soul? Scientific and Theological Portraits of Human Nature*, pp. 1–29. Minneapolis, MN: Fortress Press.

—— 1998b: Nonreductive physicalism: philosophical issues. In W. S. Brown, N. Murphy, and H. N. Malony (eds), *Whatever Happened to the Soul? Scientific and Theological Portraits of Human Nature*, pp. 127–48. Minneapolis, MN: Fortress Press.

—— and Ellis, G. F. 1996: *On the Moral Nature of the Universe: Theology, Cosmology, and Ethics*. Minneapolis, MN: Fortress Press.

Otto, R. 1958: *The Idea of the Holy: An Inquiry into the Non-rational Factor in the Idea of the Divine and its Relation to the Rational*, 2nd edn. London: Oxford University Press.

Palmer, N. W. 1997: Should I baptize my robot? What interviews with some prominent scientists reveal about the spiritual quest. *CTNS Bulletin* 17, 4.

Peacocke, A. R. 1979: *Creation and the World of Science*. The Bampton Lectures, 1979. Oxford: Clarendon Press.

—— 1993: *Theology for a Scientific Age: Being and Becoming – Natural, Divine and Human*, enlarged edn. Minneapolis, MN: Fortress Press.

Peters, T. (ed.) 1989: *Cosmos as Creation: Theology and Science in Consonance*. Nashville: Abingdon Press.

—— 1993: *God as Trinity: Relationality and Temporality in the Divine Life*. Louisville, KY: Westminster/John Knox Press.

—— 1997a: *Playing God? Genetic Determinism and Human Freedom*. New York: Routledge.

—— 1997b: Theology and the natural sciences. In D. F. Ford (ed.), *The Modern Theologians: An Introduction to Christian Theology in the Twentieth Century*, 2nd edn, pp. 649–68. Malden, MA: Blackwell.

Polkinghorne, J. C. 1994: *The Faith of a Physicist: Reflections of a Bottom-up Thinker*. Princeton, NJ: Princeton University Press.

—— 1998: *Science and Theology: An Introduction*. London: SPCK.

—— (ed.) 2001: *The Work of Love: Creation as Kenosis*. Grand Rapids, MI: Eerdmans.

—— and Welker, M. (eds) 2000: *The End of the World and the Ends of God: Science and Theology on Eschatology*. Harrisburg, PA: Trinity Press International.

Richardson, W. M. 2002: Introduction. In W. M. Richardson and R. J. Russell (eds), *Science and the Spiritual Quest: New Essays by Leading Scientists*, pp. 1–20. London: Routledge.

—— and Wildman, W. J. (eds) 1996: *Religion and Science: History, Method, Dialogue*. New York: Routledge.

Rolston, H., III 1987: *Science and Religion: A Critical Survey*. New York: Random House.

—— 2001: Kenosis and nature. In J. Polkinghorne (ed.), *The Work of Love: Creation as Kenosis*, pp. 43–65. Grand Rapids, MI: Eerdmans.

Ruether, R. R. 1992: *Gaia and God: An Ecofeminist Theology of Earth Healing*. San Francisco: HarperCollins.

Ruse, M. 1995: Evolutionary ethics. In H. Rolston III (ed.), *Biology, Ethics and the Origins of Life*, pp. 89–113. Boston: Jones and Bartlett.

Russell, R. J. 1993: Finite creation without a beginning: the doctrine of creation in relation to big bang and quantum cosmologies. In R. J. Russell, N. C. Murphy, and C. J. Isham (eds), *Quantum Cosmology and the Laws of Nature: Scientific Perspectives on Divine Action*, pp. 293–329. Vatican City State: Vatican Observatory Publications.

—— 1997: The God who infinitely transcends infinity: insights from cosmology and mathematics into the greatness of God. In J. M. Templeton and R. L. Herrmann (eds), *How Large is God?*, pp. 137–65. Philadelphia: Templeton Foundation Press.

—— 2000: Time in eternity. *Dialog* 39 (1), 46–55.

—— 2001: Divine action and quantum mechanics: a fresh assessment. In R. J. Russell, P. Clayton, K. Wegter-McNelly, et al. (eds), *Quantum Mechanics: Scientific Perspectives on Divine Action*, pp. 293–328. Vatican City State: Vatican Observatory Publications.

—— 2002a: Bodily resurrection, eschatology and scientific cosmology: the mutual interaction of Christian theology and science. In T. Peters, R. J. Russell, and M. Welker (eds), *Resurrection: Theological and Scientific Assessments*, pp. 3–30. Grand Rapids, MI: Eerdmans.

—— 2002b: Eschatology and physical cosmology: a preliminary reflection. In G. F. R. Ellis (ed.), *The Far Future: Eschatology from a Cosmic Perspective*, pp. 266–315. Philadelphia: Templeton Foundation Press.

—— 2003: Five attitudes towards nature and technology from a Christian perspective. *Theology and Science* 1, 149–59.

—— 2004: Natural theodicy in an evolutionary context: the need for an eschatology of new creation. In B. Barber and D. Neville (eds), *Theodicy and Eschatology*. Task of Theology Today, vol. 4, pp. 121–52. Adelaide, Australia: ATF Press.

—— forthcoming: The importance of the natural sciences to Christian spirituality as an academic discipline. In B. Lescher and E. Liebert (eds), *Festschrift for Sandra M. Schneiders*. New York: Paulist Press.

—— and Wegter-McNelly, K. 2004: Science. In G. Jones (ed.), *The Blackwell Companion to Modern Theology*, pp. 512–56. Oxford: Blackwell.

——, Clayton, P., Wegter-McNelly, K., et al. (eds) 2001: *Quantum Mechanics: Scientific Perspectives on Divine Action*. Vatican City State: Vatican Observatory Publications.

——, Murphy, N. C., and Isham, C. J. (eds) 1993: *Quantum Cosmology and the Laws of Nature: Scientific Perspectives on Divine Action*. Vatican City State: Vatican Observatory Publications.

——, ——, Meyering, T. C., et al. (eds) 1999: *Neuroscience and the Person: Scientific Perspectives on Divine Action*. Vatican City State: Vatican Observatory Publications.

——, ——, and Peacocke, A. R. (eds) 1995: *Chaos and Complexity: Scientific Perspectives on Divine Action*. Vatican City State: Vatican Observatory Publications.

——, Stoeger, W. R., and Ayala, F. J. (eds) 1998: *Evolutionary and Molecular Biology: Scientific Perspectives on Divine Action*. Vatican City State: Vatican Observatory Publications.

Santmire, H. P. 1985: *The Travail of Nature: The Ambiguous Ecological Promise of Christian Theology*. Philadelphia: Fortress Press.

Schneiders, S. M. 1989: Spirituality in the academy. *Theological Studies* 50, 676–97.

—— 1994: A hermeneutical approach to the study of Christian spirituality. *Christian Spirituality Bulletin* 2 (1), 9–14.

—— 1998: The study of Christian spirituality: contours and dynamics of a discipline. *Christian Spirituality Bulletin* 6 (1), 1–12.

Southgate, C., Deane-Drummond, C., Murray, P. D. et al. (eds) 1999: *God, Humanity and the Cosmos: A Textbook in Science and Religion.* Harrisburg, PA: Trinity Press International.

Tillich, P. 1967: *Systematic Theology: Three Volumes in One.* Chicago: University of Chicago Press.

Torrance, T. F. 1969: *Theological Science.* London: Oxford University Press.

White, L., Jr 1967: The historical roots of our ecologic crisis. *Science* 155, 1203–7.

Worthing, M. W. 1996: *God, Creation, and Contemporary Physics.* Minneapolis, MN: Fortress Press.

CHAPTER 20
Aesthetics

Alejandro García-Rivera

How should one speak of the beautiful? Although the beautiful appears obvious when experienced, trying to describe the experience reveals the task to be one of the most difficult ever attempted. Why is it so difficult? Theologians have a ready answer. There is an intrinsic relationship between beauty and the divine. Early in the history of the Christian church, theologians proposed that Beauty is another name for God. In doing so, theologians made an implicit distinction between beauty and the beautiful. While Beauty is another name for God, the beautiful is the human experience of divine beauty. To speak of the beautiful, then, means not only to speak of the divine, but also to speak of the spiritual nature of our humanity. This spiritual nature has two related dimensions. If beauty is divine, then its human experience has a spiritual basis not only in the human ability to experience God, but also in the human ability to create works that are themselves beautiful. In other words, the spiritual dimension in an aesthetics lies in the intrinsic human ability to experience divine beauty as well as the unmistakable human activity of making beautiful works.

The Roots of the Theology and Spirituality of Beauty

The history of the theology and spirituality of beauty could begin with the first cave paintings of the first men and women, but it is more instructive to begin with the Greeks. The Greeks were one of the first to detect an intrinsic religiosity or spirituality in the experience of beauty. The Greeks saw this implicitly in their struggle to name their experience of the beautiful. They had two words for beauty: *kallos*, a noun whose root form means "to call," and *to kalon*, an adjective whose meaning could be translated as "the called." Not only the root meanings of these two words, but also the need for two words to name the experience, speak of two profound religious intuitions into the nature of beauty.

In the pair of words used to denote beauty, the Greeks recognized, albeit mysteriously, a unity between paradoxical pairings. They grasped intuitively that the experience of beauty involved a kind of union between an objective exteriority and an intimate interiority, a seductive otherness and a subjective psychology, an invitation and a response. The fact that the Greeks saw the need to use two words to describe beauty amplifies our understanding of the religious basis at the heart of the beautiful. Beauty will not allow itself to be named too easily. There is something very special about the experience of beauty that cannot be pinned down to a single name. In other words, the Greeks recognized intuitively an intrinsic transcendence to the reality of beauty that they tried to name. Two great Greek philosophers, Plato and Aristotle, gave voice to these profound religious intuitions, but in two very different ways.

Plato

Plato's most influential accounts of the Greek experience of beauty can be found in the *Greater Hippias* and in a later work, the *Symposium*. Plato accounts for the sense of a mysterious pairing and a transcendent reality in the experience of beauty through his notions of an Eternal Beauty, a distinction between this Eternal Beauty and a sensible beauty, and an intrinsic relationship between them. Plato saw Eros or Love guiding the human soul from the realm of sensible beauty in an ever-upward ascent toward the realm of Eternal Beauty. Thus, Plato warned against seeing beauty simply in terms of pleasure or mere sensual experience. A crude summary of Plato's warning might be "All that glitters is not gold." In this aesthetics, Plato gives us the sense that there exists such a thing as a "spiritual intelligence" and that this intelligence comes to the fore when evaluating the experience of beauty.

The experience of beauty has a logic that requires a special kind of intelligence that is more than mere rationality. In order to describe this intelligence, Plato used the metaphor of vision to describe a new aesthetic category, the "Idea" or "Form." Such "Forms" (or "Ideas") exist eternally in a world beyond human experience. Nonetheless, they make themselves manifest in the world of men and women through a myriad of sensible forms in human experience. As such, these experiences are but shadows or mere imitations of the Eternal Forms, so one must discern the Eternal in the mortal and sensible. It is in this way that we ascend from a cave-like existence in which we see only dim shadows of reality to the bright sun of a true spiritual vision of the immortal world of Forms.

Plato applied this amazingly fertile scheme to the beautiful. He identifies an Eternal Beauty as a pure Form or Idea. Eternal Beauty enters the world of human experience by giving rise to a variety of sensible forms which humans experience as beautiful. The experience of beauty, i.e. the beautiful, becomes separated from Eternal Beauty and undergoes a devaluation. The beautiful is not identical with beauty. It comes to us as sensible beauty, a myriad of forms in human experience that are but mere imitations of the one Eternal Form of beauty. Finally, this means that the degree to which something can be said to be beautiful depends on the degree to which sensible beauty participates or subsists in the one Form that is Eternal Beauty.

Plato, of all the Greek philosophers, gives us in his aesthetics the most religious account of the nature of the beautiful. Indeed, Iris Murdoch, in her book *The Fire and the Sun* (1977), argues that Plato saw the beautiful as a purely religious experience in contrast to so much of modern aesthetics, which sees beauty as a purely aesthetic experience. Nonetheless, Plato's account overlooks an important religious dimension of the beautiful. Contemplation of Eternal Beauty does justice to the "calling" dimension of beauty but hardly accounts for beauty's dimension as "the called." In other words, Plato's understanding of beauty completely devalues human-made forms or works of art. Plato saw human works of art as "imitations of imitations." The artist imitates (*mimesis*) an intellectual vision of natural form by making it concrete in some medium. Since the natural form is already an imitation of an Eternal Form, a human-made form is an imitation of an imitation of an Eternal Form. Plato gives us a good account of beauty as an invitation to participate in the Eternal, but no convincing account of beauty as a spiritual response by our humanity.

Aristotle

In contrast, Aristotle, a student of Plato, gives a much better account of beauty as a human spiritual response. He does this by giving us a different account of human intelligence. Key to understanding Aristotle's aesthetics is recognizing his belief in the superiority of the intellect to know and grasp reality. This is due, in part, to Aristotle's different understanding of form. If Plato saw form with a capital "F," Aristotle understood form with a minuscule "f." Unlike Plato, who saw form as residing in a realm beyond experience, Aristotle sees form as the essence of experience itself. In other words, Aristotle believed that form and matter, the two elements of concrete experience, were inextricably related. Form gave "shape" to matter according to some "end" that, in a sense, defined the nature of the concrete reality under consideration. Aristotle's form does not enter the world of experience as a visitor from another world, but as the active shaper and mover of this world.

Aristotle's understanding of form plays a much more active role than Plato's Eternal Forms. The beautiful, for Aristotle as for Plato, manifests itself in experience through form but, unlike for Plato, the experience has more the character of active expression than passive reception. Aristotle's forms enter experience as its shapers and movers, while Plato's Forms enter experience by being imitated and participated in through experience. Plato's aesthetics emphasizes the passive dimension of the experience of beauty (receptivity), while Aristotle's aesthetics emphasizes the active dimension of the experience of beauty (expression or art).

Aristotle's aesthetics can be found in their most developed form in his *Poetics*. If, in nature, form gives shape to matter according to some "end," then human-made forms are nature-like in that they too shape some medium according to an "end" envisioned by an artist. As such, human works of art are seen, as with Plato, as imitations of an imitation, but they are imitations of nature's own active work of shaping and forging the world around us. This insight of Aristotle's is captured in the famous Latin phrase, *ars simiae naturae* or "art imitates nature." Thus, imitation for Aristotle is a much more positive process than for Plato. The human ability to imitate nature's own activity means that humans have the capability to imagine possibilities not yet fully realized by nature's work, yet consistent with it. In other words, human works of art can explore reality even if it is, ultimately, a constructed reality.

As Aristotle tells us in *Poetics 2.5*, human-constructed realities can represent actual realities (past or present), conceptions about the world, or norms of proper behavior or actions. In this way, Aristotle's aesthetics gives an influential account for the arts that continues to live on into our present. Human-constructed realities (i.e. works of art) legitimately allow us to explore a *possible* world that an audience can grasp and evaluate much as they might grasp and evaluate a *real* world. This has an important philosophical implication. Because, in imitating nature's activity, the connection between the imagined world of artistic construction and the real world of natural construction is legitimated, artistic works such as poetry can be more philosophical than a Platonic dialogue.

The connectedness that can exist between constructed and natural worlds is a kind of union. Both worlds consist of a wholeness and completeness. In the real world, wholeness and completeness lie in the coherence and integrity of natural forms shaping the natural world to its intended "ends." In the artistic world, wholeness and completeness lie in the formula given in *Poetics 9* of a work of art consisting of a "beginning, a middle, and an end." Engaging wholeness and completeness, however, is a religious activity. Thus, it could be said that Aristotle gives us a unique account of union that is, like Plato's, essentially religious.

Perhaps the most religious element in Aristotle's aesthetics of union, however, is that the engagement of wholeness and completeness has a unitive, empathetic dimension. It is what the Greeks called *catharsis*. Unfortunately, *catharsis* is a word that had many meanings in Greek culture, and Aristotle did not help us understand what he meant by it, since he only used it once in all of his *Poetics*. Plato is more helpful here. Plato summarizes the many meanings of *catharsis* by telling us in *The Republic* that it amounts to "removing the bad and leaving the good." It does not take a lot of imagination for someone who is familiar with religious studies to discern the religious associations possible in the many meanings of *catharsis*. One possible religious interpretation of what Aristotle meant by *catharsis* would begin with his observation that an audience experiences rich and profound emotions of a moral or altruistic character as response to their experience of an artistic imagined world. This response is pleasurable, but it is a pleasure laced through and through with intelligence and philosophical insight. Nonetheless, this account of *catharsis* corresponds rather well to the religious experience of the spiritual union between the one that calls and the one that is called, the experience denoted by the Greek words *kallos* and *to kalon*.

These two great thinkers, Plato and Aristotle, provided the philosophical soil upon which a faith seeking understanding could explain an astounding revolutionary development in a religion that had as a commandment "You shall not make cast idols" (Exod. 34: 17 NRSV).

The Aesthetics of the Early Christian Church

He could not stop looking at the beautiful mosaic that covered the apse at St Apollinaris's basilica in Ravenna. Its beauty mesmerized his soul and in this ecstasy he made a profound and ironic decision. He would become a monk. Thus, Thomas Matus (1985, 1994) describes St Romuald's discovery of his vocation as the founder of the Camaldolese hermit-monks in tenth-century Tuscany. A profound irony permeates the story, for the very pleasure of the art that he beheld at St Apollinaris inspired him to devote his life to seeking God away from the ordinary pleasures of life. St Romuald's conversion to his monastic vocation highlights one of the great mysteries in art history. How did the Christian church go from embedded Jewish roots in an aversion to images to a sudden explosion of breathtakingly beautiful art in the third and fourth centuries?

Few examples of Christian art exist before the fourth century. In his book *The Clash of Gods* (1993), Thomas Mathews makes an important observation. Although the art in the Basilica of St Apollinaris is rather sophisticated, the art that preceded it was not so. The very earliest Christian art was amateurish and unsophisticated. This raises an important question for Mathews. "What made the ill-knit Christian works of art, conceived in a haphazard, experimental fashion, executed at first in obscurity in graveyards by journeymen artists, more potent than works of a centuries-old tradition of the most sophisticated accomplishment?" (1993: 10).

The received answer was worked out by a great body of German scholars who proposed what Mathews calls the "Emperor Mystique." This view was developed and promulgated by the great iconographer André Grabar, who proposed that before the conversion of Constantine in 312, Christian art was essentially private, restricted to house churches and catacombs (Grabar and Nordenfalk 1957). After the conversion of Constantine, Christian art appropriated the grandeur of imperial art, especially in presenting the person of Christ in emperor's clothing. Thus, Christian art after 312 took on the "living imagery of the court ceremonial," such as Christ surrounded by his saints as the emperor was surrounded by his court. This grand view, however, can be questioned.

As Mathews points out, there was competition: the sophisticated pagan art of the imperial Hellenic pagan culture. Somehow the images at St Apollinaris affected and attracted the people of late antiquity in a way that the received Hellenic cultural images did not. Referring to art that dealt specifically with images or allusions to the miracle stories in the Gospels, Mathews reasoned:

> In miracle imagery, Christ stepped into a void that none of the gods of the ancient world had managed to fill. He showed himself a god of the "little man," a genuine "grass-roots" god. In succinct images, from tableware to sarcophagi, he showed himself a caring god, concerned if you were losing your sight, were bent with arthritis, or suffered menstrual problems. The ancient world, of course, had a host of gods to whom people turned in times of distress; this was nothing new. What was new was the imagery. Now suddenly the God was *seen* walking among his people, touching, stroking, comforting, pressing his warm and life-giving hands on them, and working a very visible magic. This was a radically new imagery of extraordinary power, and the competition had nothing to match it. The images of the pagan gods had failed to show them attending to the needs of mere mortals. (1993: 92)

Mathews's explanation helps us understand what appears to be a paradox in St Romuald's response to the beauty of the mosaic at St Apollinaris. Romuald's decision to become a monk is one with his experience of the beautiful apse at the basilica – to dwell deeper in the presence of God. Romuald's motivation can be seen today in the icons of the Eastern Church. An authentic appreciation of Eastern icons inextricably involves a need to touch and be touched, to see and to be seen, indeed to be healed by the presence inherent in a likeness of Jesus. Indeed, the Christian experience of beauty extends beyond the Eastern icon. From the Christ imaged in the center of the cross of St Apollinaris's basilica to Warner Sallman's *Head of Christ*, the imaging of Christ's like-ness suggests that something more profound is at work than some political or cultural co-opting of Christ's image. This question became the center of a theological storm in what is known as the iconoclastic crisis of the eighth and ninth centuries.

What is this "something more profound"? It should not surprise us that the answers given in the iconoclast debate by St John Damascus and St Theodore the Studite revolve around the very issues that Plato and Aristotle discussed. The decisive difference, however, lies in the fact that Plato and Aristotle found the challenge of explaining the beautiful in its relationship to an impersonal divine presence, while the Christian church found the challenge of explaining the beautiful in its relationship to a *personal* divine presence. The iconoclasts of the eighth and ninth centuries interpreted Plato's and Aristotle's philosophical difficulties in terms of the adequacy of an image to its original prototype. The iconodules (those who defended the veneration of icons) questioned the adequacy of the relationship between image and prototype to describe a personal divine presence.

In a sense, it is the same quarrel as the one between Aristotle and Plato. Are images "imagined worlds" that correspond to a "real world," or mere shadows, "fakes" of an eternal, sacred presence? The iconoclasts put Plato's arguments in a decidedly Christian way. If Christ was both human and divine, how can a graven image of a human Christ circumscribe his divine nature? The philosophical force of this argument depends on Plato's view that Eternal Forms cannot be adequately represented by sensible forms. The iconodules, however, saw through this most religious argument. It did not grasp the significance of the church's experience of the risen Christ. If one, however, is to understand the iconodule response to the iconoclast challenge, then the continuity of Christian use of images with its Jewish heritage needs to be examined.

Perhaps the most common mistake made about Christian art is that it is discon-tinuous with a Jewish belief in the inadequacy of images to represent God. Israel, after all, was not absolutely aniconic. Judaism had its visual art. Though Israel (as well as Christianity) was forbidden to make graven images of God, she was not forbidden to express her experience of God. Following the commandment not to make graven images, the account in Exodus continues with detailed instructions on how to build the Ark of the Covenant which, like the Eastern icon, would make accessible the presence of God to Israel. As the great iconographer of the Old Testament, Othmar Keel, puts it: "[the protest against images] by no means disallows every attempt to lend form and expression to the experience of God. Without that, and without a certain accessibility, a communion of the kind that existed between God and Israel (and between God and individual Israelites) would be inconceivable" (1978: 178).

What was at stake in the command against images, according to Keel, was not the impossibility of representation but the affirmation of Yahweh's full presence with Israel, a presence that cannot be substituted by an image. In other words, it is not the (impossible) representation of the divine by a copy but the substitution of a personal presence by an impersonal image. Images serve the community of belief by helping form a sensibility to the presence of the divine. Israel had a rich store of visual imagery coming from her experience of the presence of an active personal God inviting communion. Seen in this light, early Christian art is not discontinuous with its heritage. Indeed, in one sense, it completes and fulfills it. Christianity, after all, claims the experience of the personal God of Israel in its experience of the presence of Jesus of Nazareth. Just as the Ark of the Covenant gave expression to Israel's experience of the living, personal presence of the God of Abraham, early Christian art lent form to the experience of the presence of the risen Christ.

In a sense, this was the iconodules' answer to the iconoclasts' challenge. A sacred image is more than a representation. It is more than a conceptualization. It is even more than a sacred presence. It is communion with a personal sacred presence. Though an icon only "circumscribes" the human features of Christ, it is the presence of the whole Christ, human and divine, that "calls" the faithful to experience communion with the risen Christ. To see icons as mere images is to idealize or conceptualize the image. For images, especially sacred images, are more than conceptualizations or representations. They are inextricably sensual. The answer that the iconodules gave in the controversy over icons can be put this way: icons are about presence. But this presence is a very special type of presence. It is the presence of God-with-us, Emmanuel, the incarnation.

The early Christian church revolutionized religious art not by discarding its heritage against idols, but by boldly recognizing that a God who wants us to know and love him gave us the means to do so. The wider meaning of the Christian icon is to show us that, whether Christian or not, religious art is more than mere representation. It serves to make the sacred present in such a way that it invites us to touch and to be touched, to see and to be seen, by a divine beauty that, in turn, sees us as beautiful as well.

The Middle Ages

Peter Brown (1999) identifies a noticeable shift in Christian art in the passage from late antiquity into the medieval period. The art of the Middle Ages began to emphasize less the experience of participation than a route to a "higher" spiritual world, less the experience of art as a "window" to the divine than a "bridge" to the spiritually invisible God. Brown suggests that a subtle but important shift began to take place around CE 700 in the church's understanding of aesthetics. The icon's aesthetics of communion with divine presence begins to shift to a more mediated, contemplative aesthetics of divine presence. Brown's suggestion of a decisive shift can be easily affirmed by making a series of instructive contrasts.

If the icon brings to mind the aesthetics of the Eastern, Byzantine Church, then the stained glass window does the same thing for the Western, Roman Catholic Church. If early Christian aesthetics wrestled with the Hellenic culture's love of images, then medieval Christian aesthetics wrestled with the Roman culture's love of powerful rhetoric. The challenge of the Hellenic culture to the early Christian church was an iconoclasm that denied the possibility of God-with-us. The challenge of the Roman culture to the medieval Christian church was an iconoclasm that denied the possibility of Heaven-with-us. Heaven-with-us meant for the medieval church not only the challenge of seeing the spiritually invisible through the materially visible, but also discerning the threshold between this world and the world to come.

In other words, as the Christian church left late antiquity and entered the Middle Ages, its religious art began to take the form of a *porta caeli*, a "gate to heaven," in which the world-to-be intersected the world-that-now-is. These *portae caeli* afforded the medieval believer with a kind of "spiritual vision," the aesthetic sense of a "higher" and a "lower." As such, it was more than vision; it was a sanctifying experience as well. Like the early Christian church, the medieval Christian church came to this insight from a Western-style iconoclast challenge. In the year 600, Bishop Serenus of Marseilles, in a fit of iconoclastic fury, destroyed all the religious images in the churches of his city (or so it was reported). What brought on such fury? One cannot be precisely sure, for Serenus does not tell us directly. It would be a good hypothesis, however, to propose that Serenus felt that images somehow cheapened the sacred words of Scripture and tradition. Serenus, in other words, may have simply been a prophet of the Roman culture's esteem of the power of words to engage the mind (Besançon 2000: 149).

Serenus' action was brought to the attention of Pope Gregory the Great, who articulated in a letter a Western Christian aesthetic principle that would be quoted again and again in the history of the Christian church. Gregory wrote to Serenus:

> It is one thing to worship a painting, and quite another to learn from a scene represented in a painting what ought to be worshiped. For what writing provides for people who read, paintings provide for the illiterate (*idiotis*) who look at them, since these unlearned people see what they must imitate; paintings are books for those who do not know their letters, so that they take the place of books specially among pagans. (quoted in Besançon 2000: 149)

Thus, Pope Gregory articulated the basic aesthetic principle to justify the use of the arts in the church. They are the *libri idiotarum*, the books of the illiterate. In this famous phrase, Pope Gregory revealed three basic aesthetic principles forgotten today in our modern secular aesthetics.

The arts can help not only by teaching spiritual truths but also by keeping those principles ever present before us to remind us of the spiritual dimension in our ordinary lives. Most important, the sensuality of art engages our spirituality much more effectively than words engage the mind. It is this last aesthetic principle that gave an answer to the heirs of Roman culture. Rhetoric may be found in other ways than fiery speeches or elegant prose. As the historian Besançon put it in *The Forbidden Image*:

> The image fortifies, edifies the faithful, it touches their intelligence, their feelings (*componctio*), their memories, that is, their "selves," in the sense the ancients gave that word. The image is rhetorical in the strong sense. It persuades, it instructs, it moves, it pleases, it counsels (deliberative mode), it accuses or defends (legal mode), it praises or blames (epideictic mode): the categories of Ciceronian rhetoric perfectly applied to Gregory's program. (2000: 150)

Pope Gregory had taken an iconoclastic view of Roman rhetoric and transformed it into a powerful aesthetic principle for the Western Christian church. The arts began to take on the dignity of sacred Scripture in the church and shifted the nature of sacred art from being a sacred object (such as an icon) to being akin to sacred Scripture. This had powerful aesthetic implications. The aesthetics of Western Christian art aimed less at faithful representation of a divine presence than at powerful persuasion toward a devoted and virtuous Christian life. Moreover, it meant that just as sacred Scripture must be interpreted, so must sacred art. Such interpretation, however, is not some sort of cerebral analysis, but a matter of discerning how the emotions are engaged through the powerful aesthetics of a work of art.

Thus, medieval aesthetics strove to bring great expressiveness and animation to art, an expressiveness seen most clearly in the gargoyles that adorn many Gothic cathedrals. To achieve such expressiveness, however, required great craftsmanship and skill. Pope Gregory's aesthetic principle of the *libri idiotarum* led to the great period of medieval art whose major characteristic was a marvelous craftsmanship. (One might pause at this point and note that, in a religious aesthetics, craftsmanship is not something apart from the fine arts but can be considered as a spiritual dimension that goes into any truly religious art. It is a point not often made in a secular aesthetics.)

No account of religious medieval aesthetics would be complete, however, if it failed to explore the period's fascination with color and light. In his *Summa theologiae*, Thomas Aquinas tells us that the beautiful consists of *integritas* (the organic unity of the parts to the whole), *consonantia* (the harmonious relationship between proportions), and *claritas* (the luminosity of color or radiance from within a form or, even, the self-expressiveness of an aesthetic form). What is new in this definition is the aesthetic principle of *claritas*. The Greeks acknowledged *consonantia* and *integritas* as aesthetic principles, but *claritas* became distinctive to a Christian aesthetics at least in its religious sense.

The religious sense of *claritas* comes from the church's reflection on the metaphysics of light and the spiritual meaning of certain scriptural passages. Augustine was one of the first theologians to base an aesthetics on such a reflection. In *The Literal Meaning of Genesis*, Augustine (1982) notes that, according to Genesis, light was one of the first creatures made by God ("*fiat lux*") and, moreover, it was made "out of nothing" (1.12.23–4). Thus, Augustine concludes that light is the "first incarnation" of God's Word and, since it is incorporeal, it is the most spiritual of all creatures and the supreme example of God's beauty or form. This conclusion, for Augustine, suggests a spiritual aesthetics of vision.

Augustine acknowledges that we are capable of corporal or physical sight. He also acknowledges, as Plato did, that we are also capable of intellectual vision, the contemplation of idealized forms. Augustine, however, goes on to tell us that since light is essentially spiritual, it can imprint images in our spirit where they are stored in our memory. As such, a special kind of vision is possible to us, a "spiritual vision" that acts as a bridge between the physical, corporal vision of this world and the intellectual vision of the world to come. "Spiritual vision," in other words, allows "heaven" to become present to us.

Besides Aquinas and Augustine, the next great thinker of the medieval period was the monk known cryptically as Pseudo-Dionysius. True to the monastic tradition of "dying to the world," this monk practiced humility by refusing to put his true name to his writings. He simply attributed his very influential works such as *The Divine Names* and *The Celestial Hierarchy* to Dionysius, the Areopagite mentioned in the Book of Acts. Whatever his real name was, Pseudo-Dionysius provided one of the most influential aesthetics of the Western church.

Pseudo-Dionysius, borrowing from Neoplatonic thought but also bringing in an original contribution, reflected on the passage in the prologue of John that speaks of the "light that shines in the darkness." Pseudo-Dionysius saw all being as emanating from God, the One of Neoplatonism. Since all creatures emanate from God and thus participate in some way in the very being of their creator, an analogy can be made. All creatures are images, symbols, or mirrors of God. Light, however, is the principal form or "mirror" of God. This means that all creaturely participation in God must be measured by the degree to which a creature partakes of light. Visualizing such participation draws on the analogy of a light that becomes dimmer the further away it is from its source. Thus, participation of creatures in their creator measured by their participation in the "light that shines in the darkness" amounts to a hierarchy or "ladder" of participation.

Although the idea of a hierarchy or "ladder" of participation has fallen into ill repute in our day, it gives rise, in Pseudo-Dionysius' system, to a powerful aesthetics. All material realities have a corresponding spiritual dimension, a degree of participation in God that becomes visible through their engagement with light. In other words, all that exists in the universe exists as "steps" in an analogical "ladder" that metaphysically leads all the way to God. As such, any physical object can analogically provide the discerning spirit with what Augustine called "spiritual vision." This vision is an "interpretation," for material realities by virtue of their analogical participation in the One are also symbols, and symbols must be interpreted. In this way, Pseudo-Dionysius decisively describes a spiritually based aesthetics. It is an interpretation that is at the same time a vision. Aesthetics is not only a spiritual experience; it is also spiritual insight.

What is the nature of this aesthetic, spiritual insight that is also an experience? It is what Pseudo-Dionysius called "anagogy." Anyone who has entered a quiet church during a lunch break and knelt silently in the soft, blue light from its stained glass windows knows what an anagogical experience is. For anagogy means "to uplift," or "to raise higher." In other words, it is the experience of a "higher" and a "lower," a threshold between this world and the one to come. It is the experience of standing at the *porta caeli*. It is the aesthetic experience of a "Heaven-with-us." As such, Pseudo-Dionysius' thought became the foundation of a powerful spiritual aesthetics of what I have called the "anagogical imagination." The "anagogical imagination" is perhaps the greatest legacy of a religious-oriented aesthetics that comes to us from the Middle Ages. It still serves us well as a companion to spirituality.

The nature of a religious-oriented aesthetics, however, changed dramatically as the Middle Ages entered the modern era (let us say from the Renaissance to the late twentieth century). Although some have seen it as a slow and continuing process of gradual secularization of a grand medieval aesthetic synthesis, I believe there is a kinder perspective. My own understanding is that the modern era begins a new search to understand what the Greeks had detected in the experience of beauty – a paradoxical call to communion of the contingent human spirit with a transcendent divine presence. Although the twists and turns that aesthetics takes in modernity are incredibly complex, I believe that its spiritual journey can be summed up as a new search for what St Thomas Aquinas called *claritas*. What sets the modern era apart from the Middle Ages is that the moderns began to look for beauty's *claritas* not in the divine, but rather in the mystery of human creativity and in the power of the human mind. Hans Urs von Balthasar (1983–91) argued that this modern search ultimately led to a secularization of the transcendent, divine dimension of beauty and the divinization of the contingent human spirit. Although I believe that von Balthasar has correctly characterized the spiritual journey of aesthetics in the modern era, one must not lose sight of the fact that it was, at heart, a spiritual search.

The Modern Era

To see clearly the roots of the modern search for beauty's *claritas*, one must begin with Cardinal Nicolas of Cusa. Like Pseudo-Dionysius, Cusa wished to bring heaven closer to earth. However, he did not see this closeness in terms of a spiritual anagogical "ladder" leading to the divine. Rather, he saw it as a mystical closeness that owes much in its formulation to the writings of Meister Eckhart. This mystical closeness comes from the principle Cusa called the *coincidentia oppositorum*, the coincidence of opposites. Cusa rejected the idea that the infinite could be conceived by means of the finite. In other words, analogy and anagogy did not do justice to the absolute unknowability proper to the Infinite God. This does not make Cusa some sort of theological skeptic. Rather, Cusa sees that the absolute opposition of the infinite and the finite can only be reconciled in a logic that is not traditional but mystical. This mystical logic he calls *docta ignorantia* or ignorant knowing. It relies on a Platonic-like intellectual vision that can see beyond all logical divisions or oppositions to a simple origin where they ultimately become one. This is the coincidence of opposites, and it radically challenged the anagogical aesthetics of the Middle Ages.

Cusa's *coincidentia oppositorum* transformed the spiritual cosmos of Western Christian Europe from a "ladder" of values connecting the earthly to the heavenly, to the co-existence of the heavenly and the earthly. As such, Cusa's cosmos began to influence how moderns saw the subtle spiritual connection between heaven and earth, between God's creation and human creativity, between natural forms and artistic forms, between nature and art. It would transform, for example, the view of art from skillful imitation of natural form to a mysterious expression of an artist's creativity.

Since the cosmos was no longer a "ladder" to heavenly things, the location of the *porta coeli* changed. The door to heavenly and spiritual realities lay within the human soul. The *claritas* of divine beauty would not be sought in the external macrocosmos of nature but in the internal microcosmos of the human spirit and the human mind. The beginnings of this shift can be seen in the way in which artists began to see themselves as the world entered modernity. In the Renaissance, artists begin to see themselves in a different light (Wittkower and Wittkower 1969). Art was more science than skill. Renaissance artists saw themselves rather as professors, or even educated clergy, than medieval craftsmen. Leonardo da Vinci, for example, was fascinated, like medieval theologians, in the spiritual nature of light. Unlike medieval artists and theologians, however, he loved light not because it would give him a "higher" vision but for its ability to let him see the extraordinary in the ordinary forms of nature. For da Vinci, precise observation of the ordinary was the means to achieve spiritual vision of the extraordinary. Thus, an artist's rendition of a natural object became more than mere imitation of a natural form; it was a new kind of *porta coeli*, a door into the spiritual reality that co-exists in the world of natural reality. Thus, art as a science began to see nature as more than to be imitated; it was rather the door to a new vision of spiritual reality, the mathematical laws that govern natural form.

The view that transcendent spiritual beauty consisted of mathematical forms is not particularly modern. It is as old as Pythagoras and his followers. It also has a rich Christian heritage. Theologians such as Augustine put much weight on the passage from Wisdom 11: 20: "You, however, ordered all things by measure, number and weight." In the modern era, however, the mathematical realities present in nature became identified more and more as the very essence of nature rather than as the artistic activity of God. Moreover, these mathematical realities go counter to our experience of nature. They are what Amos Funkenstein calls in *Theology and the Scientific Imagination* (1986) "counter-factual conditional" realities. In other words, these mathematical realities are not perceived by ordinary experience but only by an act of the imagination that can grasp mathematical form. As such, the beautiful is not perceived primarily through the senses. In the New Science, the door to transcendent spiritual beauty was to be found in the mind's eye of the scientific imagination.

This idea, however, has an important corollary. Art was more than skillful craftsmanship or the rendering of sacred stories. Art was the product of the creative activity of an artist's soul. Leone Battista Alberti, for example, began to introduce the notion of *invenzione*, or invention. Alberti was seeking a formula for the beautiful. He sought absolute, perfect beauty in the very principles of art itself. He thought he found it in the idea that there exists an ultimate element in a painting that gives pleasure "even by itself." This was the artist's ability to express something new, i.e. *invenzione*. In the notion of *invenzione*, Alberti begins a new type of aesthetic reflection on the spiritual nature of the artist and how that spirituality is expressed on the canvas or the marble. Though the Renaissance had no name for this process, it is known today by the term "creativity." It signals a shift from an aesthetics concerned with the divine transcendent to an aesthetics that is concerned with human self-transcendence. The quest now becomes to explain not the "call" of beauty but the "calling" of the artist. It is this "calling" that the next generation will begin to explore.

Kant and Hegel

These new developments that began with Cusa and continued in the Renaissance were given philosophical articulation by Alexander Baumgarten in 1735. It was he who coined the term "aesthetics." Derived from the Greek word for the senses (*aisthesis*), Baumgarten saw it as the science of "sensory cognition." In other words, Baumgarten felt that the senses brought us their own special kind of knowing and such knowing was accessible to rational thought. In this conviction, one can detect Cusa's call for a new kind of knowing that does not depend on the analogical or the anagogical. Unlike Cusa, however, Baumgarten has little patience with any notion of mystical knowing. Baumgarten is interested in rational knowing, even that of the beautiful.

As such, the beautiful, in Baumgarten's new science of aesthetics, undergoes a secularization. Aesthetics begins to concentrate more and more on the nature of knowing the beautiful rather than in experiencing divine beauty. In other words, Baumgarten's new science of aesthetics leads to an emphasis on knowing rather than experiencing. The effect is to locate the spiritual dimension of the beautiful in the workings of the human mind. This secularization can be seen most clearly in the two thinkers who are heirs to Baumgarten's aesthetics and who have most influenced a secular understanding of aesthetics in the modern era: Kant and Hegel.

Kant developed two terms that were in much discussion in his day: *genius* and the *sublime*. In doing so, Kant gave voice to a set of aesthetic intuitions that shaped a modern aesthetics and continue to have influence today. These two terms, "genius" and "the sublime," continue the aesthetic insights developed in the Renaissance but in a decidedly secular way. Such secularization may be seen as the attitude of seeing the world of nature and the world of the human spirit as discontinuous. More importantly, such secularization may be seen in the location of the transcendent dimension of beauty within the workings of the human mind.

Kant, for example, posited the notion of the sublime as distinct from the beautiful. As Kant put it, the sublime is the experience of being "drawn gradually by the quiet stillness of a summer evening as the shimmering light of the stars breaks through the brown shadows of night and the lonely moon rises into view into high feelings of friendship, of disdain for the world, of eternity" (1960: 47). Finite beauty leads to an "awakening" of some super-sensible faculty within us that is able to "detect" the infinite. This faculty involves a kind of judgment that joins the vital, intimate feeling of pleasure with the nature of the object that is the source of that pleasure. In other words, it is a judgment that allows us to say "This rose is beautiful." It is a judgment of taste rather than of reason.

Such judgments, however, allow for two possibilities. One is judging the pleasure an object gives because of its boundedness, or form. The other is judging the pleasure an object gives due to its unboundedness, or resistance to being given form. The pleasure of the former is what Kant called the "beautiful"; the pleasure of the latter he called the "sublime." It is this latter sense of the judgment of taste that allows Kant to define the sublime as the "absolutely great." In this distinction, Kant sets up a contrast between the "beautiful" and the "sublime" that many have identified as having serious consequences in the spiritual journey of aesthetics.

The other term developed by Kant is "genius." It is not a new term and was discussed at great length in the literature of the seventeenth and eighteenth centuries by thinkers such as Edmund Burke. As developed in Kant's time, the term "genius" finds analogy in the mystical state described in the spiritual literature of his day. Mystical experience was discussed in Kant's day as a gift and a special grace that is given to certain individuals. As such, it cannot be described, for it is highly original and its principles are intrinsically mysterious. This mystical state was applied by philosophers of Kant's day to the creative inspiration of the artist. Kant took the analogy one step further by seeing "genius" as that which makes the sublime fully conceivable. "Genius" makes possible the capacity to think of the infinite, the "absolutely great," without contradiction. The curious mark of Kant's aesthetics is how little it says about works of art. In developing the notions of "genius" and "the sublime," Kant had little to say about art itself.

While Kant says precious little about works of art, Hegel founds his aesthetics in the historical process in which the beautiful makes itself known through the work of art (see Hegel 1998). In this system, Hegel introduced two ideas that have also been influential in modern aesthetics. Hegel, for example, introduced the idea that art has a history. Moreover, this history is an evolutionary one. Art, for Hegel, was a manifestation of spirit rather than a competitor for natural beauty. Art's history is the history of spirit sensibly realizing itself through an historical process as "a spiritualized sensible appearance or a sensible appearance of the spiritual" (Besançon 2000: 205). Hegel saw God as Absolute Spirit working historically in this world. Indeed, the historical process of art corresponds to the historical engagement of Absolute Spirit in the world. The artist captures part of this spiritual activity in the work of art as a concrete image that is historically conditioned yet, nonetheless, makes present this divine, spiritual activity. Thus, Hegel begins a new chapter in the history of aesthetics by setting the grounds for the new fields of art criticism and art history.

Within this idea, however, lies another, even more influential aesthetic. What does Hegel mean by spirit? Hegel refers to spirit by the German word, *Geist*, which can also mean "mind." Spirit, for Hegel, was the activity of thought making its consciousness felt concretely in the conflicts and resolutions of human history. Art, for Hegel, is the most direct means by which this spiritual consciousness makes itself concrete in the historical process. Thus, the spiritual nature of art becomes associated with the nature of mind and the absolutely transcendent divine becomes associated with absolute knowledge. Absolute knowledge, however, cannot be represented. As art progresses in the unveiling of the unrepresentable *Geist*, its representations of the spiritual become more and more abstract. Finally, the time comes when art exhausts its resources to represent the unrepresentable and comes to an end. Thus, the beautiful evolves historically into the sublime.

The theological aesthetics of Hans Urs von Balthasar

The consequences of Kant's and Hegel's aesthetics on the perceived relationship between art and the spiritual cannot be overestimated. For many, the implications of the philosophizing of aesthetics by Kant and Hegel were liberating. It freed the artist from church discipline or dogmatic intervention. The artist was now free to explore the human spirit with unprecedented authority and force. It freed, as well, lay participation in the criticism of art. One need not be a theologian to speak with authority about the merits of a work of art. A work of art could be judged on its own merits. For others, however, it represented a kind of "fall." Art changed from being a source of great spiritual power to a mere commodity in the marketplace of wealthy art collectors. Art lost its connection to a community of faith. Instead of hanging on church walls where a devout community would kneel in deep contemplation, art now hangs on isolated and mute museum walls which have never heard a single prayer.

This "fall" has been articulated in the literature. From early works like John Dewey's *Art as Experience* (1959) and Yanagi and Leach's *The Unknown Craftsman* (1972) to more recent works like Elaine Scarry's *On Beauty and Being Just* (1999) and J. M. Bernstein's *The Fate of Art* (1992), a certain unease with art's spiritual vitality is powerfully expressed. To this growing number of voices, theologians have also begun to add their own perspectives. The most forceful exposition of this "fall" has been by the Swiss theologian Hans Urs von Balthasar. In his seven-volume work *The Glory of the Lord* (1983–91), von Balthasar identifies the "fall" of aesthetics in two tendencies that have their roots in the Greek classics.

The first tendency corresponds to the acts of the Greek hero, Prometheus, who seized the secret of fire from the gods. This Promethean tendency finds its highest realization in the philosophy of Kant and Hegel where the human "I" or mind is made to coincide with the divine "I" or mind. It is the exaltation of the human spirit that can, like Prometheus, transcend its own humanity by learning what God knows. The other tendency corresponds to the Greek god Dionysius. The Dionysian tendency of modern humanity lies in the ambitiousness of its aspirations toward self-transcendence. It is, however, a transcendence seeking to escape the limitations of its own existence rather than, like Prometheus, seeking to dominate them. Such transcendence, however, is followed by disenchantment, and the modern-day Dionysius becomes filled with a sense of the absurdity of existence (von Balthasar 1937).

For von Balthasar, these two aesthetic tendencies, the unfettered optimism of Prometheus and the disenchanted nihilism of Dionysius, arise because modernity has forgotten the "primal phenomenon" of the beautiful. Beauty, von Balthasar says, confronts us "simultaneously with the figure and that which shines forth from the figure, making it into a worthy, a love-worthy thing" (Steck 2001: 15). In terms of the Greek distinction between the "call" and the "called" of beauty, von Balthasar identifies the theological element in this tension, namely, love. This love is represented on God's side of the "call" by the biblical notion of "glory." The beauty of creation is not only a gift to us, but it is also "given" to us; not only a "datum," but also a "donatum." This means that the forms of natural beauty are imbued by the love of the One who created them. This love is the splendor that shines forth from within the forms Kant saw in the "starry skies" above.

Our response to this love, on the other hand, is also love but in the nature of an *ekstasis*, a being pulled out of ourselves. It is this *ekstasis* that defines human self-transcendence. Such transcendence, however, is not absolutely autonomous but relies on God's grace. Von Balthasar makes this claim by an interesting analogy. The more the human spirit participates in the divine Spirit, the more the human becomes aware of how disproportionately distant the human is from the divine. As Aidan Nichols puts it in *The Word Has Been Abroad*, in this fruitful analogy von Balthasar combines "the mind of St Thomas with the heart of St Augustine, all in the spirit of St Ignatius Loyola" (1998: xiv). This analogy sets up what von Balthasar calls a "theological aesthetics."

A theological aesthetics recognizes that it is God's glory that is the transcendent dimension of worldly beauty. God's glory is expressed through God's love for us. Such love constitutes an aesthetics in that God takes up worldly and cultural forms in order to shine forth his glory from within. The nature of transcendent beauty is the very use of forms in order to break them from within and thus allow God's glory to seize us and delight us. The model for all such forms is the ultimate form of Jesus Christ. Thus, von Balthasar sets up a series of discussions in which he contrasts worldly beauty and divine glory (theological aesthetics), finite freedom and infinite freedom (theo-drama), and created truth with uncreated truth (theo-logic). These contrasts correspond to the three transcendentals of medieval philosophy: the beautiful, the good, and the true.

Von Balthasar has laid the foundations for theology once again to take up its natural relationship to aesthetics. Nonetheless, there is much left to do toward a theological aesthetics that truly engages the challenges and possibilities hinted at in today's world, a world many see as postmodern. Indeed, a new generation of theologians has begun to explore the possibilities of a theological aesthetics. Frank Burch Brown's *Good Taste, Bad Taste, and Christian Taste* (2000), Richard Viladesau's *Theological Aesthetics* (1999), Jeremy Begbie's *Voicing Creation's Praise* (1991) and *Theology, Music, and Time* (2000), and my own *The Community of the Beautiful* (1999) and *A Wounded Innocence* (2003) all mark a real shift in theological sensibilities toward its intrinsic relationship to the beautiful. After a very long dry spell, it appears that aesthetics is about to become, once again, a companion to spirituality.

References

Augustine of Hippo 1982: *St Augustine: The Literal Meaning of Genesis*, 2 vols, trans. J. H. Taylor, Jr. New York: Newman Press.

von Balthasar, H. Urs 1937: *Apokalypse der Deutschen Seele*. Salzburg and Leipzig: Anton Pustet.

—— 1983–91: *The Glory of the Lord*, 7 vols. San Francisco: Ignatius Press.

Barasch, M. *Theories of Art: From Plato to Winckelmann*. New York: New York University Press.

Beardsley, M. C. 1975: *Aesthetics from Classical Greece to the Present: A Short History*. Tuscaloosa: University of Alabama Press.

Begbie, J. 1991: *Voicing Creation's Praise: Towards a Theology of the Arts*. Edinburgh: T. and T. Clark.

—— 2000: *Theology, Music, and Time*. Cambridge: Cambridge University Press.

Bernstein, J. M. 1992: *The Fate of Art: Aesthetic Alienation from Kant to Derrida and Adorno*. University Park, PA: Pennsylvania State University Press.

Besançon, A. 2000: *The Forbidden Image: An Intellectual History of Iconoclasm*. Chicago: University of Chicago Press.

Brown, F. B. 2000: *Good Taste, Bad Taste, and Christian Taste: Aesthetics in Religious Life*. Oxford: Oxford University Press.

Brown, P. 1999: Images as substitute for writing. In E. K. Chrysos and I. N. Wood (eds), *East and West: Modes of Communication. Proceedings of the First Plenary Conference at Merida*, pp. 15–34. Leiden: Brill.

Cassirer, E. 1964: *The Individual and the Cosmos in Renaissance Philosophy*. New York: Harper and Row.

Dewey, J. 1959: *Art as Experience*. New York: Capricorn.

Dupré, L. 1988: Hans Urs von Balthasar's theology of aesthetic form. *Theological Studies* 49, 299–318.

Finney, P. C. 1994: *The Invisible God: The Earliest Christians on Art*. New York: Oxford University Press.

Freedberg, D. 1989: *The Power of Images: Studies in the History and Theory of Response*. Chicago: University of Chicago Press.

Funkenstein, A. 1986: *Theology and the Scientific Imagination from the Middle Ages to the Seventeenth Century*. Princeton, NJ: Princeton University Press.

García-Rivera, A. 1996: Creator of the visible and the invisible: liberation theology, post-modernism and the spiritual. *Journal of Hispanic/Latino Theology* 3, 35–56.

—— 1999: *The Community of the Beautiful: A Theological Aesthetics*. Collegeville, MN: Liturgical Press.

—— 2003: *A Wounded Innocence: Sketches for a Theology of Art*. Collegeville, MN: Liturgical Press.

Grabar, A. and Nordenfalk, C. A. J. 1957: *Early Medieval Painting from the Fourth to the Eleventh Century: Mosaics and Mural Painting*. New York: Skira.

Harrison, C. 1992: *Beauty and Revelation in the Thought of Saint Augustine*. Oxford: Clarendon Press.

Hegel, G. W. F. 1998: *Aesthetics: Lectures on Fine Art*, trans. T. M. Knox. Oxford: Clarendon Press.

Jolley, N. 1995: *The Cambridge Companion to Leibniz*. Cambridge: Cambridge University Press.

Kant, I. 1960: *Observations on the Feeling of the Beautiful and Sublime*, trans. J. T. Goldthwait. Berkeley, CA: University of California Press.

Keel, O. 1978: *The Symbolism of the Biblical World: Ancient Near Eastern Iconography and the Book of Psalms*. New York: Seabury Press.

Kessler, H. L. 2000: *Spiritual Seeing: Picturing God's Invisibility in Medieval Art*. Philadelphia: University of Pennsylvania Press.

Lindberg, D. C. 1976: *Theories of Vision from al-Kindi to Kepler*. Chicago: University of Chicago Press.

Mathews, T. F. 1993: *The Clash of Gods: A Reinterpretation of Early Christian Art*. Princeton, NJ: Princeton University Press.

Matus, T. 1985: *". . . And I Will be your God": The Monastic Life of the Camaldolese Benedictines*. Big Sur, CA: Hermitage Books.

—— 1994: *The Mystery of Romuald and the Five Brothers: Stories from the Benedictines and Camaldolese*. Trabuco Canyon, CA: Source Books.

Miles, M. R. 1979: *Augustine on the Body*. Missoula, MT: Scholars Press.

—— 1989: *Carnal Knowing: Female Nakedness and Religious Meaning in the Christian West*. Boston: Beacon Press.

Murdoch, I. 1977: *The Fire and the Sun: Why Plato Banished the Artists*. Oxford: Clarendon Press.

Nichols, A. 1998: *The Word Has Been Abroad: A Guide through Balthasar's Aesthetics*. Edinburgh: T. and T. Clark.

Rorem, P. 1993: *Pseudo-Dionysius: A Commentary on the Texts and an Introduction to their Influence*. New York: Oxford University Press.

Scarry, E. 1999: *On Beauty and Being Just*. Princeton, NJ: Princeton University Press.

Sendler, E. 1988: *The Icon, Image of the Invisible: Elements of Theology, Aesthetics, and Technique*. Redondo Beach, CA: Oakwood.

Steck, C. W. 2001: *The Ethical Thought of Hans Urs von Balthasar*. New York: Crossroad.

Tatarkiewicz, W. 1980: Beauty: history of the concept. In *A History of Six Ideas: An Essay in Aesthetics*, pp. 121–52. The Hague: Nijhoff.

Theodore the Studite 1981: *On the Holy Icons*, trans. C. P. Roth. Crestwood, NY: St Vladimir's Seminary Press.

Viladesau, R. 1999: *Theological Aesthetics: God in Imagination, Beauty, and Art*. New York: Oxford University Press.

362   ALEJANDRO GARCÍA-RIVERA

Wittkower, R. and Wittkower, M. 1969: *Born under Saturn: The Character and Conduct of Artists. A Documented History from Antiquity to the French Revolution.* New York: Norton.

Wolfson, S. J. 2001: *The Cambridge Companion to Keats.* Cambridge: Cambridge University Press.

Yanagi, M. and Leach, B. 1972: *The Unknown Craftsman: A Japanese Insight into Beauty.* Tokyo and Palo Alto, CA: Kodansha International.

Zajonc, A. 1993: *Catching the Light: The Entwined History of Light and Mind.* New York: Bantam Books.

CHAPTER 21
Feminist Studies

Amy Hollywood

In an important essay on the study of spirituality as an academic discipline, Bernard McGinn tells a story about the inception of Paulist Press's "Classics of Western Spirituality" series:

> A Long Island commuter stands on a platform watching trains speeding past each other east and west in their rush towards what seem to be opposite goals. This particular commuter happens to be a religious editor who suddenly grasps this as an image of the mutual ignorance and lack of connection between Eastern and Western spiritual traditions. If only something could be done to get the trains to slow down, he thinks, to stop, to converse window-to-window, might they not realize that their opposition is not as great as it seems? (1993: 21)

McGinn reads the editor's moment of insight as akin to what Augustine calls intellectual vision, thereby suggesting some of the ways in which "the efforts of believing teachers and educators relate to first-order spirituality" (1993: 21). My interest in the story diverges from McGinn's, however, for the editor's insight speaks in compelling ways to a perhaps unforeseen achievement of the "Classics of Western Spirituality" series.

As McGinn notes in telling the anecdote, the series was initially planned to be one half of two parts, the whole to be called the "Classics of Eastern and Western Spirituality." Arguably, in the absence of its westbound train, the series fails to live up to its inspiring vision. Yet there is another conversation between apparent opposites in which it has, since its inception, participated. The first volume published in the series was Edmund Colledge and James Walsh's translation of the fourteenth- and early fifteenth-century anchorite Julian of Norwich's *Showings*, in both its short and long versions (Julian of Norwich 1978). Many of the subsequent volumes published in the series included texts by women, texts from spiritual traditions within Christianity (and on its edges) in which women have played a crucial role (for example, the medieval

English anchorite movement), or texts that show men and women in conversation, debate, and sometimes intense conflict (for example, Francis de Sales and Jane de Chantal). Of course, the "Classics" series has not been alone in making available in English texts by and about Christian women and their spirituality. Among a host of important publications, I will mention only the ground-breaking anthologies by Katharina Wilson (1984) and Elizabeth Alvilda Petroff (1986), and Margot King's imprint devoted specifically to early and medieval Christian women's spiritual writing, Peregrina Publishing.

There are some good reasons why a series dedicated to Christian spirituality might, from the outset, be compelled to include texts by both women and men. To get at these reasons, we need first to dip into the vexed question of how to define spirituality. Although scholars have rightly questioned the generality of the various conventional definitions, there is good reason to follow McGinn in understanding spirituality as the lived experience of belief or the striving after such experience (McGinn et al. 1985: xv; for one criticism, see Eire 1990). If nothing else, this seems to be how the term is most often used in scholarly and other contexts. At the core of most colloquial uses is an insistence, moreover, familiar to theologians since Schleiermacher: that what is essential to religion is neither doctrine nor practice, but "feeling." The difficulties in defining "feeling" and "experience," together with the related questions of the relationship between experience and belief and between experience and action, are at the center of debates about what constitutes spirituality. (On spirituality and practice, see Hadot 1995; on spirituality and theology, see McIntosh 1998.)

So, what does all this have to do with men and women on trains seemingly going in opposite directions, slowing down to talk through their respective windows? In other words, why might a series in Western spirituality be a place in which men and women speak and in which, as I will show, issues of sexual difference, gender, and sexuality almost inevitably come to the forefront, whether explicitly or implicitly, simply through the choice of texts to be translated? The first and most obvious answer is that within the Christian tradition, at least, some of the most important texts dealing with the lived experience of belief have been written – and continue to be written – by women. This, despite the fact that for most of the history of the Christian tradition, misogynist assumptions have precluded women from holding most church offices, from serving as preachers and teachers to mixed audiences of men and women except on very rare occasions, and from attending the elite educational institutions in which theology is taught. Loopholes, however, could always be found and women (and the men who often supported them) discovered, fairly early on in the Christian tradition, how to use them. A key issue was the presumption, supported by biblical texts, that women might receive special graces: within the early and medieval period and modern Roman Catholicism especially (but by no means only) those women who dedicated themselves to God as virgins (Aspegren 1990; Newman 1995). If God chose to give women visions, to bestow prophecies on them, or to render himself one with them in a union of the spirit or a union without distinction, then might they also not be permitted – indeed, even called on – to speak and write of these things? As a result, women's lived experience of Christian truth became one of the primary means through which they were empowered to speak, teach, and write (Petroff 1986; Newman 1987; Weber 1990; Lochrie

1991; Mack 1992; Connor 1994; Hollywood 1995; Watt 1997; Kienzle and Walker 1998; McGinn 1998; Harris 1999; Hilkert 2001; Bell and Mazzoni 2003).

Yet even if women had not themselves written, any study of the spirituality of a tradition that purports to include women within it will speak, in some way, to women and issues of gender difference. Liturgical and prayer books, hagiographical texts, and guidebooks for the pursuit of the Christian life (or that of any other tradition) are key to the study of spirituality (Newman 1995: 19–45; Mews 2001). Almost every religious tradition known to scholars, furthermore, argues that the religious life be lived in ways that are clearly marked by gender. Hence, gender differentiation and spirituality go hand in hand. In addition, almost all religious traditions use gender as a way to think through important spiritual issues. Thus, as Kate Cooper (1996) shows in the case of early Christianity, femininity becomes a crucial category through which male religious identity and spirituality is thought and enacted. What is remarkable about the Christian tradition is the extent to which women were able to participate in the written expression of spirituality, hence providing a rare glimpse into the ways in which men's understanding of how women should live and women's own self-conceptions and experience differ, as well as insight into how women "think with" gender in ways like or unlike men.

So as it turns out, within the history of Christianity, men and women have always been talking about spirituality (McGinn 1998). These conversations have taken many different forms. Sometimes men have taken women as their guides and models, at other times they appear as equals (Coakley 1991a, b; Ranft 1998, 2000), and – perhaps most often – men have guided, commanded, even coerced women into particular forms of spiritual life (Newman 1998; Hamburger, 1998: esp. 35–109, 197–232; Voaden 1999). (For arguments that in the Christian Middle Ages clerical insistence on developing rules for the discernment of spirits led to greater clerical control over women and may have contributed to the mentality and practice of the late medieval and early modern witch hunts, see Kieckhefer 1994; Dinzelbacher 1995; Elliott 1998, 1999: 127–63, 2003; Caciola 2000.) Despite the near ubiquity of these conversations, however, the historical tendency to consign women's writings and lives to oblivion – either through the effacement of their stories and texts or through a refusal to see the connections between women and men and between women across time – renders it necessary once again to slow down the trains and to show the wealth of women's contributions to Christian spiritual traditions, as well as the central differences gender has made to the constructions of these traditions.

Feminist scholars of Christian spirituality have been pursuing this work of reclamation, commentary, and analysis for over twenty years (with important precursors in the late nineteenth and early twentieth centuries). It would be impossible adequately to summarize the wealth of resources that have been discovered or rediscovered, the subtlety of commentary and analysis, and the plethora of exciting new questions being asked of this material within the contemporary academy. What I will try to do is map out the terrain shaped by scholars in the 1980s and some of the most important questions inspired by their ground-breaking scholarship. The work of Caroline Walker Bynum must stand at the center of this discussion, for no other scholar has done so much to shape feminist work on Christian spirituality. After careful attention to the main lines of Bynum's arguments about female spirituality within the Christian Middle

Ages, I will turn to some of the most important questions raised about her work. Attention to these critiques, refinements, and extensions of Bynum's ground-breaking scholarship will in turn lead to discussion of new directions in the feminist study of spirituality. (It should be noted that feminist interventions in the study of Christian spirituality also take the form of analysis of texts, writings, and images by men produced without a female or mixed audience explicitly in mind. For an early example of such work, see Massey 1985.)

Caroline Walker Bynum and the History of Medieval Women's Spirituality

Second-wave American feminism was from its outset tied to Christianity and had an immediate impact on Christian theology and spirituality (Braude forthcoming). Critique of male-dominant institutional structures and theological visions went hand in hand with attempts to reclaim aspects of the Christian tradition for women (for recent accounts of this work, see Schneider 1998; Armour 1999; Parsons 2002). Caroline Walker Bynum, in a series of pivotal studies produced during the 1980s, both furthered feminist studies of Christian spirituality and raised central questions about the assumptions under which much feminist theology and work in religion then operated. Bynum's work challenged two key premises of second-wave feminist theology and thealogy. First, most of this feminist scholarship on religion presumes that the mainstream traditions of Christianity, with their male-governed institutional structures, male deities, and emphases on virginity, asceticism, chastity, and obedience as primary modes of access to leadership for women, were and are inherently disempowering for women. The second and related point of Bynum's critique questions the presumption that theological language and imagery reflects and sustains social structures, so that a male God empowers men and/or reflects men's power and that, as a consequence, the only way for women to achieve power is through the advent of gender neutral or feminine language for the divine. (For the continuing appeal of such arguments, see Irigaray 1985 and Raphael 2000. For intelligent discussion of the goddess movement in the United States and its theoretical and historical limitations, see Eller 1995, 2000. Two nuanced and historically grounded arguments for the necessity of gender parity in religious symbolism can be found in Keller 2000 and Newman 2003).

In *Jesus as Mother: Studies in the Spirituality of the High Middle Ages* (1982), Bynum engages in a detailed reading of key images and metaphors within the writings of twelfth- and thirteenth-century religious writers in order to show that there is little evidence for men's greater attraction to masculine language and symbols or women's greater attraction to feminine language and symbols. In fact, Bynum argues, the image of Jesus as mother is found in texts by both men and women, albeit deployed in different ways. Moreover, devotion to the Virgin Mary arguably plays a greater role in texts written by men (and so perhaps within their religious lives) than in those written by women. (On feminist studies of Mariology, see Warner 1976; Johnson 1987; Fulton 2002; Newman 2003: 245–90.) In addition, Bynum shows that the particular forms of life adopted by both men and women (monks versus canons or beguines versus nuns) had as much impact on the nature of an individual's spirituality as did gender. At the same time, Bynum argues that there *is* a change in female patterns of sanctity around 1200, although historical explanations of this phenomenon in terms of "some kind of inherent female 'emotionalism' or some kind of affinity between women and female imagery . . . will not do." As Bynum pointedly asks, "if women become mystics because they are intrinsically more emotional, imaginative, religious, or hysterical than men, why did it take centuries for this to emerge?" (1982: 172–3)

Bynum gives programmatic form to these historical insights in the introduction to a volume she co-edited with Stevan Harrell and Paula Richman, *Gender and Religion: On the Complexity of Symbols* (1986). At the same time, she more explicitly situates her work and that of the other contributors to the volume in relation to feminist critiques of Christianity and other male-dominant religions. Bynum follows feminist scholars in insisting "that all human beings are 'gendered' – that is, that there is no such thing as generic *Homo religiosus*." Yet, unlike those feminist critics of religion who presume that religious symbols "prescribe and transcribe reality," Bynum insists on the "polysemic" nature of religious symbols – on the varieties of ways in which symbols mean and in which they can be used:

> Gender-related symbols, in their full complexity, may refer to gender in ways that affirm or reverse it, support or question it; or they may, in their basic meaning, have little at all to do with male and female roles. Thus our analysis admits that gender-related symbols are sometimes "about" values other than gender. But our analysis also assumes that all people are "gendered." It therefore suggests, at another level, that not only gender-related symbols but all symbols arise out of the experience of "gendered" users. It is not possible ever to ask How does a symbol – *any* symbol – mean? without asking For whom does it mean? (Bynum et al. 1986: 2–3)

Bynum's argument works to untether gendered symbols from easy presumptions about their social effects and meanings. Yet, at the same time, she insists on the possibility that men and women may use symbols in radically different ways.

Her contribution to the volume, "'. . . And Woman His Humanity': Female Imagery in the Religious Writing of the Later Middle Ages," together with essays by John Hawley and John Toews, make just such a case. As Bynum summarizes their conclusions, she, Hawley, and Toews do not find that medieval Christian mystics, Hindi poets, and twentieth-century psychoanalysts operate with the same concepts of gender, but:

> they do find that men and women of a single tradition – when working with the same symbols and myths, writing in the same genre, and living in the same religious or professional circumstances – display certain consistent male/female differences in using symbols. Women's symbols and myths tend to build from social and biological experiences; men's symbols and myths tend to invert them. Women's mode of using symbols seems given to the muting of opposition, whether through paradox or through synthesis; men's mode seems characterized by emphasis on opposition, contradiction, inversion, and conversion. Women's myths and rituals tend to explore a state of being; men's tend to build elaborate and discrete stages between self and other. (1986: 13)

Thus, even as Bynum engages in the project of uncovering women's previously neglected history within Christian spirituality, she at the same time makes bold claims about the particularity of women's writings and women's spirituality.

Bynum's overriding thesis, articulated in both *Holy Feast and Holy Fast* (1987) and *Fragmentation and Redemption* (1991), is that women's spirituality in the late Middle Ages differed in significant ways from men's. Perhaps the most succinct formulation appears in an oft-cited passage from "The Female Body and Religious Practice in the Later Middle Ages":

> Thus, as many recent scholars have argued, the spiritualities of male and female mystics were different, and this difference has something to do with the body. Women were more apt to somatize religious experience and to write in intense bodily metaphors; women mystics were more likely than men to receive graphically physical visions of God; both men and women were inclined to attribute to women and encourage in them intense asceticisms and ecstasies. Moreover, the most bizarre bodily occurrences associated with women (e.g., stigmata, incorruptibility of the cadaver in death, mystical lactations and pregnancies, catatonic trances, ecstatic nosebleeds, miraculous anorexia, eating and drinking pus, visions of bleeding hosts) either first appear in the twelfth and thirteenth centuries or increase significantly in frequency at that time. (1991: 194)

Bynum's concern in this passage is to suggest that bodies – in this case women's bodies – have a history and that they "begin to behave in new ways at a particular moment in the European past" (1991: 195). Her answer to the question of why this should be so has been as influential on scholarship about medieval women's spirituality as has her depiction of the change itself.

Bynum suggests a number of overlapping explanations for the distinctive nature of female piety in the High and Late Middle Ages. We can broadly characterize these as: (a) ecclesiastical and social; (b) psychological and biological; and (c) ideological and theological. In the first instance, the particular constraints placed on women in the pursuit of the religious life and religious leadership render their appeal to experiences of the divine a central form of legitimation (Bynum 1982, 1987, 1991; Bynum et al. 1986; Petroff 1986; Newman 1987; McGinn 1998). Moreover, women's relatively limited access to Latin education plays a role in their pursuit of the vernacular (Bynum 1982: 170–1, 1991: 196; see also Grundmann 1936; and now Blumenfeld-Kosinksi et al. 2002 and the work cited there). Bynum also shows that male religious leaders actively encouraged women's bodily forms of piety as a useful instrument in the fight against dualist heresies (Bynum 1991: 195; see also Hollywood 2002a: 253–7 and the scholarship cited there).

In *Holy Feast and Holy Fast*, which argues for the centrality of food to medieval women's piety, Bynum points to women's roles within the larger society as formative of their religiosity. Hence in the medieval world, Bynum argues, food preparation was one of the few domains over which women had control. The regulation of food intake, the distribution of food as alms, and an emphasis on Christ's body as food thus emerge as key aspects of female spirituality in part because of the particularities of women's social situation (1987: 189–244). Similarly, the broader argument about the bodily nature of women's piety made in *Fragmentation and Redemption* can be tied to social roles. As Bynum argues, "to some extent, women simply took . . . ordinary nurturing over into their most profound religious experience" (1991: 198; see also McNamara 1991).

Bynum is more hesitant to ascribe the differences between men's and women's spirituality to psychological and biological differences, although the move from an emphasis on women's role as nurturers in late medieval culture to one based on a claim for men's and women's different psychological development is relatively easy to make (and many readers of Bynum have presumed just such an argument). In *Holy Feast and Holy Fast*, moreover, Bynum does appeal to the work of Nancy Chodorow and Carol Gilligan in order to suggest that women's role as nurturers and caregivers might give rise to particular psychological formations in women and men (1987: 282–96). The move to biology does not necessarily follow, of course, and Bynum alludes to the possibility of biological differences between men and women as an explanation for their differing spiritualities only with great hesitation. "It is possible," she writes, "that there is a biological element in women's predisposition to certain kinds of bodily experience. The fact that, in many cultures, women seem more given to spirit possession and more apt to somatize their inner emotional and spiritual states suggests a physiological explanation" (1991: 200). (Note the tension between Bynum's argument here and her categorical rejection of similar hypotheses in *Jesus as Mother*.) At the same time, she argues, biology and culture are notoriously difficult to disentangle. "The various cultures in which women are more inclined than men to fast, to mutilate themselves, to experience the gift of tongues and to somatize spiritual states are all societies that associate the female with self-sacrifice and service" (1991: 200).

Ultimately, the decisive explanations for Bynum are ideological and theological. Hence, she shows that in the Christian Middle Ages women were associated with body, whereas men were associated with mind. Women, however, used these misogynist assumptions to their advantage by focusing on the central role that Christ's suffering flesh – representative of his suffering humanity – played in redemption. By using the identification of women with the body (and hence with humanity) as a justification for their identification with Christ in his suffering human body, women were able to make their lowly social and ontological status the means of their participation in the salvific work of Christ. Seen from this perspective, women's extreme asceticism and bodily piety are not simply or even primarily expressions or outcroppings of medieval misogyny and anti-body dualism. Rather, as Bynum movingly argues,

> late medieval asceticism was an effort to plumb and to realize all the possibilities of the flesh. It was a profound expression of the doctrine of the Incarnation: the doctrine that Christ, by becoming human, saves *all* that the human being is . . . Thus Francis of Assisi telling his disciples that beatings are "perfect happiness," Beatrice of Ornacieux driving nails through her palms, Dorothy of Montau and Lukardis of Oberweimar wrenching their bodies into bizarre pantomimes of the moment of Crucifixion, and Serafina of San Gimignano, revered *because* she was paralyzed, were to their own contemporaries not depressing or horrifying, but glorious. They were not rebelling against or torturing their flesh out of guilt over its capabilities so much as using the possibilities of its full sensual and affective range to soar ever closer to God. (1987: 294–5)

Bynum here pinpoints what is arguably the central theological explanation for much medieval women's spirituality, perhaps best encapsulated in the words of the thirteenth-century beguine, Hadewijch of Brabant: "We all indeed wish to be God with God, but God knows there are few of us who want to live as men with his Humanity, or want to carry the cross with him, or want to hang on the cross with him and pay humanity's debt to the full" (1980: 61). This, however, is what Hadewijch and many other devout women believed was necessary for those desirous of pursuing the heights of spiritual perfection.

Questioning the Paradigm

I write in some detail about Bynum's work on women's spirituality because of both its importance and its enormous influence on subsequent scholarship. Bynum's scholarship has not only been instrumental in introducing a new generation of readers to a body of hagiographical and mystical literature previously little known in English, but also provides a powerful paradigm through which that literature can be understood. (See also Dronke 1984; Kieckhefer 1984; Lagorio 1984; Bell 1985; Dinzelbacher and Bauer 1985, 1988; Petroff 1986; Newman 1987; Nichols and Shank 1987; Peters 1988; for some of the key early twentieth-century European scholarship, see Ancelet-Hustache 1926; Grundmann 1995 [1935]; Roisin 1943, 1947.) Much writing on Christian women's spirituality over the past twenty years has worked within or struggled against that paradigm – and often both at the same time.

One of the primary difficulties with Bynum's claims, particularly in *Holy Feast and Holy Fast* and *Fragmentation and Redemption*, is their grounding in two very different types of source. She distinguishes, as the passage cited above shows, between women's and men's spirituality in three ways: with regard to women's harsh asceticism, the proliferation in their lives of paramystical bodily phenomena, and their use of bodily metaphors to describe their encounter and union with the divine. (For some very different accounts of how to read these bodily metaphors, see Robertson 1991, 1993; Milhaven 1993; Hale 1995; Hollywood 1999; Rudy 2002; Poor 2004.) Yet, until about 1300, only the last of these three claims holds for mystical texts authored by women. Before 1300, claims for women's harsh asceticism and paramystical bodily phenomena occur in the primarily male-authored hagiographies of religious women (Hollywood 1995: 27–39, 1999).

Particularly in *Holy Feast and Holy Fast*, Bynum emphasizes the necessity for care in treating sources (1987: 6–9, following Ringler 1985) and she divides her presentation of the evidence within that study in terms of hagiographical and mystical writings. Yet when she turns to the women mystics at the center of her analysis, in three of the four cases (Beatrice of Nazareth, Catherine of Siena, and Catherine of Genoa) she cites both their own writings and those of hagiographers (although it must be noted that at times this distinction is difficult to make, particularly with regard to Catherine of Genoa). Similarly, in her desire to provide a picture of the sweep of medieval women's spirituality, she does not look for or note differences that occur over time, leading from the relative lack of emphasis on the bodily asceticism and paramystical phenomena in women's mystical writings before 1300 and the development, after 1300, of what Richard Kieckhefer and Kate Greenspan term "autohagiography" (Kieckhefer 1984: 6; Greenspan 1991, 1996).

Of course, we cannot move from the absence of accounts of extreme asceticism in women's texts before 1300 to an assertion that women did not engage in these practices. Nor can we take the appellation "autohagiography" as a dismissal of later accounts as pious fictions (Hamburger 2001: 152). Yet careful attention to the different ways in which men write about women and women write about themselves demonstrates that, although women often internalize and enact predominant views, they also resist them (Mooney 1999). Moreover, when men's and women's religious writings are looked at together, we see that men and women engage in often intense relationships of mutual influence, debate, and appropriation. As a result, any clearly marked distinction between men's and women's spirituality almost immediately breaks down (although the tendency for men to *want* women's spirituality to take certain forms remains constant at least throughout the Middle Ages and no doubt well into the modern period). (For the beguine influence on the thirteenth- and early fourteenth-century Dominican, Meister Eckhart, for example, which breaks down both older claims about women's affective spirituality versus men's speculative mysticism as well as Bynum's slightly different thesis, see McGinn 1994; Hollywood 1995, 1999. Nicholas Watson [1991] makes similar arguments with regard to Richard Rolle.)

The methodological problem in Bynum's work is tied to larger historiographical issues about power, agency, and resistance. Thus David Aers (Aers and Staley 1996) and Kathleen Biddick (1993), albeit in quite different ways, question what Aers refers to as Bynum's "empowerment thesis." Once again, Bynum herself provides suggestions that lead to the critique itself. Aers notes that in the 1989 essay cited previously, "The Female Body and Religious Practice in the Later Middle Ages," Bynum suggests the limitations of the idea that identification with Christ's suffering flesh and humanity empowers women. As Bynum writes,

> This argument must also recognize that the clergy themselves encouraged such female behavior both because female asceticism, eucharistic devotion and mystical trances brought women more closely under the supervision of spiritual directors and because women's visions functioned for males, too, as means of learning the will of God. Moreover, theologians and prelates found women's experiential piety useful in the thirteenth-century fight against heresy. The increased emphasis on bodily miracles and indeed the appearance of new miracles of bodily transformation came at exactly the time of the campaign against Cathar dualism. (Bynum 1987: 195; cited by Aers and Staley, although with notable ellipses, 1996: 34)

The problem for Aers is that Bynum does not push these insights further, thereby missing an opportunity to explore the ways in which the feminized body of Christ and the suffering female saint or mystic "are produced within specific discursive regimes with specific technologies of power" (1996: 34–5). In describing a dominant ideology and arguing that it was empowering for women, Bynum does not ask whether this ideology in fact fed male power and male fantasies of femininity and whether anyone – male or female – resisted them (1996: 35). Moreover, as Julie Miller (1999) forcefully argues, Bynum provides no standpoint from which one might question the valorization of violence found within the model of sanctity she describes.

Bynum might read this as an anachronistic demand, yet there is significant evidence for women's resistance to male conceptions of female sanctity, especially before 1300. As I said, women's writings before that time show little concern for intense bodily asceticism and paramystical phenomena. This suggests, at the very least, that women refused to describe themselves within the paradigms provided by primarily male-authored hagiography. The beginning of the fourteenth century saw the partial condemnation of semi-religious women, known as beguines, as well as forms of spirituality associated with women, suggesting that the turn to autohagiography may mark women's capitulation to male-prescribed conceptions of sanctity in the face of increased scrutiny by religious leaders (Hollywood 1995, 1999, 2002a; Elliott 1999; Erler and Kowaleski 2003).

Although I argue for added nuance to Bynum's account, I think that Aers posits an antithesis between empowerment and domination far too simple to handle the complexity of the materials under discussion. Bynum is right that women often received – and arguably still today receive – religious recognition, ecstatic pleasure, and leadership opportunities on the basis of their adoption of male-prescribed modes of female sanctity. There still remains Kathleen Biddick's (1993) question – implicit also in Aers – about who was suppressed by these extraordinary women's accession to power. Only careful attention to the vexed interplay of power and domination within Christian spiritual traditions can begin to enable us to discern the answers to these complex questions. (For a sophisticated feminist reading of Michel Foucault, Judith Butler, and Hannah Arendt on power that might aid such an enterprise, see Allen 1999.)

Just as importantly, to get at the complexities of domination and empowerment within the history of spirituality, we need to remember that gender is not the only – and at times not the most salient – category of difference operative within the Christian Middle Ages or any other society. As the essays recently collected by Sharon Farmer and Carol Braun Pasternack in *Gender and Difference in the Middle Ages* (2003) show, medieval identities were shaped by shifting and intersecting differences – of gender, but also of social status, sexuality, and religion. (Again, Bynum herself points in this direction in *Jesus as Mother*.) In an earlier essay, Farmer questions scholarly assertions that in the Middle Ages women were associated with bodiliness and physicality while men were associated with rationality. Looking at material from the thirteenth century that describes the different kinds of work appropriate to different members of Christian society, Farmer finds that "poor men, as well as poor women, were very much associated with the body" (2000: 170). Without denying that "at various points along the hierarchy of social status" we do find "that medieval clerical authors . . . make statements that drew stronger associations between women and the body than between men and the body," Farmer convincingly demonstrates that attention to the differences between servants and elites renders easy generalizations about gender difficult (2000: 171).

Despite Bynum's arguments for the association of women with the body in the late Middle Ages, so aptly nuanced by Farmer and others, Bynum consistently argues against what she sees as a modern tendency to equate the body too quickly with sexuality (1987, 1995a, b). Her explicit aim throughout her work on the body is to expand the meanings we ascribe to corporeality in medieval texts and practices. Yet Karma Lochrie and Richard Rambuss show that Bynum "herself can be quick to delimit the erotic – and especially the homoerotic – potentialities of her own devotional polysemy of the medieval body" (Rambuss 1998: 48; see also Lochrie 1997). When Catherine of Siena writes of "putting on the nuptial garment," Bynum argues that "the phrase means suffering" and so is "extremely unerotic." She goes on to argue that in Catherine's

> repeated descriptions of climbing Christ's body from foot to side to mouth, the body is either a female body that nurses or a piece of flesh that one puts on oneself or sinks into . . . Catherine understood union with Christ not as an erotic fusing with a male figure but as a taking in and taking on – a becoming – of Christ's flesh itself. (1987: 178)

Bynum's assumptions here about sexuality and erotic desire – most crucially that erotic desire can be clearly distinguished from suffering, the maternal, and identification – are, at the least, subject to debate (Hollywood forthcoming).

As Rambuss (1998) suggests, however, perhaps the most salient point is Bynum's refusal to see same-sex desire as potentially sexual. If Christ's body is feminized (and so becomes a point of identification for women), Bynum assumes that it cannot also be the object of female sexual desire (or even of a desire for the divine *analogous* to sexual desire). In insisting on the feminization of Christ's body on the cross, Bynum provides a locus for female identification with the divine and protects the divine–human relationship from even metaphorical sexualization. Rambuss not only takes issue with Bynum's assumption that identification and desire cannot accrue around the same object, but also questions whether, in its passivity and woundedness, Christ's body is necessarily feminine. In response to Bynum's reading of the blood from Christ's side wound as analogous to mother's milk, he cogently asks, "Are male bodies without their own orifices?" (1998: 38). So when the twelfth-century monk Rupert of Deutz describes himself climbing onto the altar, embracing and kissing Christ on the cross ("I sensed how pleasing he found this gesture of love, when in the midst of the kissing he opened his mouth, so that I could kiss him the more deeply" [cited in Fulton 2002: 310]), Rambuss suggests there we should read this passage – at least on one level – as homoerotic (1998: 47).

As a number of recent scholars show, medieval men and women did use explicitly erotic language to discuss their relationship with Christ, and they did so in ways that often challenged the prescriptive heterosexuality of the culture in which they lived (Holsinger 1993; Lavezzo 1996; Lochrie 1997; Dinshaw 1999; Moore 2000; Epps 2001; Wiethaus 2003). The challenge occurs not only through women's feminization of Christ's body or of the divine, or through men's relationship with the male Christ, but also through the intense, hyperbolic deployment of apparently heterosexual imagery (Lochrie 1997). Among the beguines of Northern Europe, for example, arguably most well known for their so-called bridal mysticism (and hence, it would seem, for a resolutely heterosexual, non-queer sexual imaginary), we find accounts of insane love and endless desire in which gender becomes so radically fluid that it is not clear what kind of sexuality – within the heterosexual/homosexual dichotomy most readily available to modern readers – is being metaphorically deployed to evoke the relationship between the human and the divine.

Although the three beguine mystics Hadewijch, Mechthild of Magdeburg, and Marguerite Porete focus on an erotic relationship between the soul and God, one legitimated in part by early and medieval Christian readings of the Song of Songs, as Bynum recognized over twenty years ago, "bridal mysticism" cannot encapsulate the full range of gendered positions occupied by the believer and God within their texts. (For the limitations of the characterization of thirteenth-century women's religious writing as "bridal mysticism," see Bynum 1982: 171–2 and Newman 1995: 137–67. For a sophisticated argument about the use of bridal imagery in women's texts when it does appear, see Keller 2000). Sometimes the female soul meets a male deity, at other times the soul is male in relationship to a female divine, and at yet other moments both the soul and God are female. As Rambuss argues with regard to early modern male-authored religious poetry, the absence in these texts "of a polarizing system of sexual types tends to open these works in the direction of greater plasticity of erotic possibilities, possibilities not entirely containable by our own (often only suppositiously coherent) sexual dichotomies" (1998: 58). We cannot contain medieval religious eroticism within modern sexual categories. This does not de-sexualize medieval men's and women's texts and practices, but instead demonstrates their queerness in relation to modern conceptions of heteronormativity.

New Directions in Feminist Scholarship on Christian Spirituality

Much of the critical work pushing Bynum's thesis in new and ever-more subtle directions depends on distinguishing between male-authored and female-authored texts or between texts written within a clerical context and those written on its fringes, even in its shadows. Yet recent scholarship shows that there are dangers in assuming any clear-cut distinction between male-authored and female-authored texts – or even in thinking about medieval religious texts in terms of individual authorship (Peters 1988; Mooney 1994; Dinshaw and Wallace 2003; Summit 2003). There are very few early Christian texts that can be ascribed to women (Clark 1990). Virtually all the medieval women's spiritual texts available to us are mediated in some way, either by scribes, editors, translators, or compilers (Summit 2003). In some cases, women who may not have been able to read or write either in Latin or the vernacular made use of scribes to produce their texts. In others, male confessors or confidants collected and distributed women's work, translated it, or were otherwise instrumental in its dissemination.

These complex patterns of textual production do not end for women with the introduction of print. In the early modern period, women's writing continues to be imagined as textual and treated in ways similar to that produced within a manuscript culture (Summit 2000). Religious teachings or visionary reports were often transcribed by others or written down on the basis of conversations with the holy woman. Well into the twentieth century there are examples of holy women whose rapturous utterances are transcribed by those with whom they live (in the case of Gemma Galgani, without her knowledge or permission [Bell and Mazzoni 2003]; for an earlier example of this phenomenon, see Maggi 1998).

The vagaries of women's authorship within the medieval period, then, are not simply tied to their production within a manuscript culture, but have to do with the twin demands often placed on religious women's writing: that they be grounded in experience (often, although not always, extraordinary experiences of God's presence) and that the religious woman herself display absolute humility. (The same problems are visible in some men's lives and writings, particularly those who lack clerical authority or base their religious claims on something other than that authority. Most exemplary for the medieval period is Rupert of Deutz; see Fulton 2002: 309–50.) Although the particular shape and dynamics of these twin demands change over time, the discussions around medieval women's texts are instructive for the broader study of women's spirituality.

At the center of many discussions of medieval religious women's authorship and authority lie texts ascribed to the late thirteenth- and early fourteenth-century Umbrian laywoman Angela of Foligno and to the fifteenth-century English laywoman Margery Kempe. In both instances, scholars have debated at great length the extent to which we can take their texts as their own. Jacques Dalarun (1995) takes historical skepticism to an extreme, asking if Angela might not have been a fiction created by her Franciscan scribe. At the other end of the spectrum, Lynn Staley (1991, 1994) argues with regard to Margery Kempe that her use of scribes does not decrease but rather increases her authorial status. As Jennifer Summit puts it, by "collating Margery Kempe with an existing canon, the scribe establishes Kempe's authority by showing precisely that she is not an original creator, but rather one who upholds pre-existing models of *traditio* and *auctoritas*" (2003: 98). Because medieval views of authorship and authority differ so substantially from our own, what modern readers might take as a mark of inauthenticity becomes, according to Staley and Summit, the means of legitimating Kempe – a pious laywoman – as part of an authoritative tradition of visionary spirituality.

What interests Staley, Summit, and others is the way in which medieval and early modern women pursued their spiritual lives in the context of complex communities. (For the influential idea of "textual communities," see Stock 1983.) Women did write what we think of as original works with their own hands, but they also dictated, compiled, translated, and commissioned spiritual texts, and all of these diverse forms of writing must be attended to in any attempt to describe women's contributions to Christian spirituality and the possible contours of a specifically women's spirituality. (On women's use of scribes, see Ferrante 1998. For women as scribes, see D'Avray 1985: 2; Smith 1996. For women as producers of books and images, see Taylor and Smith 1996; Hamburger 1997; Hult 2003. For women as readers and commissioners of spiritual works, see S. Bell 1982; Hamburger 1990, 2001; Robertson 1990; Meale 1993; Bartlett 1995; D. Bell 1995; Smith and Taylor 1995; McCash 1996; Suydam 1999; Erler 2002.)

Carolyn Dinshaw perhaps summarizes the state of current scholarship most succinctly when she reminds us that, on the one hand, "it would be naïve . . . to try and separate authentic female voices from masculine textual operations." Yet at the same time, we must remember "the tendency of masculine mediators to accentuate the importance of their own roles, or to occlude female involvement" (Dinshaw and Wallace 2003: 5). Moreover, as we have seen, men tend to read the women whose work they mediate in terms of male-prescribed forms of female sanctity. Even as we question simplistic conceptions of agency and authorship within writings by, to, and about women, we need to attend to the power dynamics that shape the communities in which these texts are formed, disseminated, and re-formed. Most importantly, we need to recognize that these textual communities were often – although not always – made up of men and women, working with, for, and at times against each other. (For the claim that some women's textual production was relatively independent of male authority, see Lewis 1996; Garber 2003.)

Seen from the perspective of spiritual and textual communities, the afterlife of religious writings by and about women and the history of manuscripts and books used by women become prime areas for research. Attention to the dissemination, disappearance, and reappearance of manuscripts and books by, about, and for women yields important insights into changing conceptions of gender, authorship, and sanctity (Voaden 1996; Winstead 1997; Summit 2000; Hamburger 2001; Poor 2004). In addition, a host of scholars is now asking what happens to medieval conceptions of spirituality and sanctity when taken into the modern world. Although the commonalities between late medieval and modern prescriptions for female spirituality suggest that we may find standard periodizations inadequate to the history of women's (and perhaps also men's) spirituality, many scholars suggest that common conceptions of spirituality must always be read against the background of changing social, political, and economic realities (Blackbourn 1994; Christian 1996; Harris 1999; Taves 1999; Schmidt 2000; Dinan and Meyers 2001; Greer and Bilinkoff 2003).

Scholars have sought in numerous ways to break down the putative divide between male-authored and female-authored religious texts, not least by recognizing women's spiritual writings as works of theology in conversation with those of male theologians. I noted earlier the thesis that women actively participated in the development of what Bernard McGinn and Nicholas Watson call "vernacular theology"(McGinn 1994; Watson 1995). Barbara Newman has made another important proposal for breaking down the distinction between men's and women's religious texts with her introduction of the term "imaginative theology." According to Newman, "the hallmark of imaginative theology is that it 'thinks with' images, rather than propositions or scriptural texts or rarified inner experiences – although none of these need be excluded. The devices of literature – metaphor, symbolism, prosopopoeia, allegory, dialogue, and narrative – are its working tools" (2003: 298).

Both dream and waking visions are central to imaginative theology, and Newman's new category enables her to recast traditional distinctions between the two. (Newman here intervenes in a debate, particularly heated within the German scholarship, about the relative transparency or literary quality of vision accounts. For summary of the debate, see Tobin 1995: 115–22.) As a result, Newman reads the writings of the twelfth-century Platonists Dante and Christine of Pizan alongside those of "visionaries" like Mechthild of Magdeburg and Hadewijch, thereby breaking down any clear-cut distinction between the genres of male-authored and female-authored theologies. The category will arguably be of even more salience when turned to early modern and modern texts, in which fiction and poetry often become the domain in which theological positions are rendered. Arguably, some of the most vital, daring, and life-sustaining theological thinking of the modern era occurs in imaginative writing. Newman suggests that this might also be the case, against all presumptions to the contrary, in the twelfth through fifteenth centuries.

As I wrote at the outset of this essay, it turns out that within Christian spiritual traditions men and women have been talking all along, although we now have a better sense of the ways in which feminist scholarship demands attention to the particular power dynamics of these conversations. The further question remains: do these conversations speak to us? Much of the criticism of Bynum centers on an uneasiness with what Dominic LaCapra calls her "redemptive view" of history (1994: 178–83; and in a different and more sympathetic light, Watson 1999). Yet, even as she attempts always to read the past empathically – in ways, some argue, that allow insufficient space for critique – Bynum also insists on our distance from the past. "We write the best history," she argues,

> when the specificity, the novelty, the awe-fulness, of what our sources render up bowls us over with its complexity and its significance. Our research is better when we move only cautiously to understanding, when the fear that we may appropriate the "other" leads us not so much to writing about ourselves and our fears as to crafting our stories with attentive, wondering care . . . We must rear a new generation of students who will gaze in wonder at texts and artifacts, quick to puzzle over a translation, slow to project or to appropriate, quick to assume there is a significance, slow to generalize about it. (2001: 74)

Empathy, in other words, demands time, patience, and a refusal too quickly to collapse our concerns with those of the past. Yet, as Bynum repeatedly demonstrates in her own work, this does not preclude conversation between the past and the present.

The problem, of course, is how to recognize the theoretically and theologically vibrant insights offered by the past without abrogating our responsibility to history. Christian spiritual traditions – in all of their variety – speak in compelling ways to issues at the heart of the human situation and often also at the heart of specifically feminist concerns. Can we maintain sight of this fact without losing sight of the difference that history makes? (For a compelling account of the value of women's mystical writings for contemporary feminism, see Jantzen 1995. In a review of that book, however, I argue that Jantzen gives too little attention to precisely the kind of historical detail about which Bynum so rightly cares; see Hollywood 1996.)

Contemporary feminist investments in Christian spirituality take many forms, but let me speak here of one unlikely site of appropriation in order to get at the historiographical, theoretical, and theological issues. The putative division between men's and women's forms of spirituality arises already in the Middle Ages and is picked up in various ways by modern scholarship (most recently, as we have seen, by Bynum). The distinction does not bear up to careful scrutiny, yet it continues to wield tremendous power. In addition, the female forms of spirituality, generally defined in terms of their greater emotionalism, affectivity, and visionary quality (as opposed to the intellectual, speculative, and abstract mysticism associated with men) are routinely denigrated both in the later Middle Ages and in modern scholarship. One of Bynum's great – although also, I will suggest, potentially dangerous – accomplishments is to have reversed this trend.

As I argue in *Sensible Ecstasy: Mysticism, Sexual Difference, and the Demands of History*, fascination with affective, visionary, and ecstatic forms of Christian spirituality appears much earlier in the twentieth century, and in a rather unlikely place. For certain French secular intellectuals, most importantly Georges Bataille, Simone de Beauvoir, Jacques Lacan, and Luce Irigaray, affective, bodily, and ecstatic forms of spirituality serve as a central model for their thinking and practice (Hollywood 2002a; see also Mazzoni 1996). At the heart of this fascination, I argue, lies a confrontation with the reality of human limitation, disease, and death. Critically following my French subjects, I contend that attention to the Christian mystical tradition can help us think about how to deal with the traumatic effects of illness, mortality, and loss (2002a: 19–21, 274–8). At the same time, women like Angela of Foligno and Teresa of Avila, with whom Bataille, Beauvoir, Lacan, and Irigaray are fascinated, "struggled to maintain interpretative control over [their] experience against the continual encroachment of male clerical elites." Similarly, I argue, "medieval women's texts proleptically resist" modern appropriations in that they contest the cultural roles prescribed for women in the Middle Ages (2002a: 6). More particularly, a number of thirteenth-century women mystics actively resist the association of women with the body so central to hagiographical accounts of female sanctity. Similarly, I argue, we must resist any too easy identification of women with the body (and hence with disease, limitation, and death), even as we attempt to find ways to recognize the embodied nature of all human subjectivity.

Even as scholars question the widespread association of women with bodiliness, another recent research trend turns attention to the role played by the body within Christian mystical traditions. One of the ways in which many of the twentieth- and twenty-first-century theoretical and theological projects invested in Christian spiritual writings differ most radically from these texts is in the place given to ritual or practice. Hence many historians and theologians follow colloquial uses of the term "spirituality" in assuming that pursuit of the spiritual life has little to do with the body and action. Important recent scholarship, however, demonstrates the centrality of bodily and mental practices, ritual, and action to the development of the spiritual life in the Christian Middle Ages and beyond (Despres 1989; Asad 1993; Hadot 1995; Carruthers 1998; Suydam and Ziegler 1999; Mahmood 2001a, b; Fulton 2002; Hollywood 2002a, b, 2003). Jeffrey Hamburger, for example, shows that previously denigrated forms of devotional art made for – and at times by – medieval women were key to their meditative practice and hence central to their spirituality (Hamburger 1990, 1997, 1998). Attention to images and practices, moreover, opens the door to investigation of the spirituality of men and women who do not write and are generally not written about – Christians who pursue the divine through their engagement with the ritual life of the church, paraliturgical events, and personal devotions often centered on devotional objects and images.

The attempt to uncover and understand spiritualities hitherto visible only indirectly within texts and artifacts opens up a host of methodological challenges. How do we read liturgies, prayer manuals, and guide books for religious and laity in the absence of first-person accounts of how such texts were used (Beckwith 1994; Bestul 1996; Hollywood 1999; Mews 2001)? How do we understand devotional images and objects, often in the absence of textual explanations of their significance and use (Hamburger 1990, 1997, 1998)? In approaching living traditions, what methodological principles will yield best access to and understanding of spiritual communities, their beliefs and practices (Orsi 1985, 1996; Griffiths 1997; Castelli 2001)? Careful attention to such methodological issues, drawing on the resources of historiography, anthropology, sociology, art history, performance studies, philosophy, theology, history of religion – and no doubt other fields – is essential if we hope to bring new voices (and bodies) onto the train and to develop nuanced understandings of the conversations in which they are engaged.

References

Aers, D. and Staley, L. 1996: *The Powers of the Holy: Religion, Politics, and Gender in Late Medieval English Culture*. University Park, PA: Penn State University Press.

Allen, A. 1999: *The Power of Feminist Theory: Domination, Resistance, Solidarity*. Boulder, CO: Westview Press.

Ancelet-Hustache, J. 1926: *Mechthilde de Magdebourg (1207–1282): Étude de Psychologie Religieuse*. Paris: Champion.

Armour, E. 1999: *Deconstruction, Feminist Theology, and the Problem of Difference: Subverting the Race/Gender Divide*. Chicago: University of Chicago Press.

Asad, T. 1993: *Genealogies of Religion: Disciplines and Reasons of Power in Christianity and Islam*. Baltimore, MD: The Johns Hopkins University Press.

Aspegren, K. 1990: *The Male Woman: A Feminine Ideal in the Early Church*. Uppsala: Almqvist and Wiksell.

Bartlett, A. C. 1995: *Male Authors, Female Readers: Representation and Subjectivity in Middle English Devotional Literature*. Ithaca, NY: Cornell University Press.

Beckwith, S. 1994: Passionate regulation: enclosure, ascesis, and the feminist imaginary. *South Atlantic Quarterly* 93, 803–24.

Bell, D. 1995: *What Nuns Read: Books and Libraries in Medieval English Nunneries*. Kalamazoo, MI: Cistercian Publications.

Bell, R. 1985: *Holy Anorexia*. Chicago: University of Chicago Press.

——and Mazzoni, C. 2003: *The Voices of Gemma Galgani: The Life and Afterlife of a Modern Saint*. Chicago: University of Chicago Press.

Bell, S. 1982: Medieval women book owners: arbiters of lay piety and ambassadors of culture. *Signs* 7, 742–68. Reprinted in M. Erler and M. Kowaleski (eds) 1988: *Women and Power in the Middle Ages*, pp. 149–87. Athens: University of Georgia Press.

Bestul, T. 1996: *Texts of the Passion: Latin Devotional Literature and Medieval Society*. Philadelphia: University of Pennsylvania Press.

Biddick, K. 1993: Genders, bodies, borders: technologies of the visible. *Speculum* 68, 389–418. Reprinted in K. Biddick 1999: *The Shock of Medievalism*, pp. 135–62. Durham, NC: Duke University Press.

Blackbourn, D. 1994: *Marpingen: Apparitions of the Virgin Mary in Nineteenth-century Germany.* New York: Knopf.

Blumenfeld-Kosinksi, R., Robertson, D., and Warren, N. (eds) 2002: *The Vernacular Spirit: Essays on Medieval Religious Literature.* New York: Palgrave.

Braude, A. forthcoming: Christianity, feminism, and women's history. *History of Religions.*

Bynum, C. W. 1982: *Jesus as Mother: Studies in the Spirituality of the High Middle Ages.* Berkeley, CA: University of California Press.

——1987: *Holy Feast and Holy Fast: The Religious Significance of Food to Medieval Women.* Berkeley, CA: University of California Press.

——1991: *Fragmentation and Redemption: Essays on Gender and the Human Body in Medieval Religion.* New York: Zone Books.

——1995a: *The Resurrection of the Body in Western Christianity, 200–1336.* New York: Columbia University Press.

——1995b: Why all the fuss about the body? A medievalist's perspective. *Critical Inquiry* 22, 1–33.

——2001: *Metamorphosis and Identity.* New York: Zone Books.

——, Harrell, S., and Richman, P. (eds) 1986: *Gender and Religion: On the Complexity of Symbols.* Boston: Beacon Press.

Caciola, N. 2000: Mystics, demoniacs, and the physiology of spirit possession in medieval Europe. *Comparative Study of Society and History* 42, 268–306.

Carruthers, M. 1998: *The Craft of Thought: Meditation, Rhetoric, and the Making of Images, 400–1200.* Cambridge: Cambridge University Press.

Castelli, E. (ed.) 2001: *Women, Gender, Religion: A Reader.* New York: Palgrave.

Christian, W. 1996: *Visionaries: The Spanish Republic and the Reign of Christ.* Berkeley, CA: University of California Press.

Clark, E. 1990: Early Christian women: sources and interpretations. In L. L. Coon, K. J. Haldane, and E. W. Sommer (eds), *That Gentle Strength: Historical Perspectives on Women in Christianity,* pp. 19–35. Charlottesville, VA: University of Virginia Press.

Coakley, J. 1991a: Friars as confidants of holy women in medieval Dominican hagiography. In R. Blumenfeld-Kosinski and T. Szell (eds), *Images of Sainthood in Medieval Europe,* pp. 222–46. Ithaca, NY: Cornell University Press.

——1991b: Gender and the authority of friars: the significance of holy women for thirteenth-century Franciscans and Dominicans. *Church History* 60, 445–60.

Connor, K. R. 1994: *Conversions and Visions in the Writing of African-American Women.* Knoxville: University of Tennessee Press.

Cooper, K. 1996: *The Virgin and the Bride: Idealized Womanhood in Late Antiquity.* Cambridge, MA: Harvard University Press.

Dalarun, J. 1995: Angèle de Foligno a-t-elle existé? In *Alla Signoria: Mélanges offerts à Noëlle de la Blanchardière,* pp. 59–97. Rome: École Française de Rome.

D'Avray, D. L. 1985: *The Preaching of the Friars: Sermons Diffused from Paris before 1300.* Oxford: Oxford University Press.

Despres, D. 1989: *Ghostly Sights: Visual Meditation in Late-Medieval Literature.* Norman, OK: Pilgrim Press.

Dinan, S. E. and Meyers, D. (eds) 2001: *Women and Religion in Old and New Worlds.* New York: Routledge.

Dinshaw, C. 1999: *Getting Medieval: Sexualities and Communities, Pre- and Postmodern.* Durham, NC: Duke University Press.

——and Wallace, D. (eds) 2003: *The Cambridge Companion to Medieval Women's Writing.* Cambridge: Cambridge University Press.

Dinzelbacher, P. 1995: *Heilige oder Hexen? Schicksale auffälliger Frauen in Mittelalter und Frühneuzeit*. Zurich: Artemis and Winkler.

——and Bauer, D. (eds) 1985: *Frauenmystic im Mittelalter*. Ostfildern: Schwabenverlag.

——and —— (eds) 1988: *Religiöse Frauenbewegung und mystische Frömmigkeit im Mittalter*. Cologne: Böhlau.

Dronke, P. 1984: *Women Writers of the Middle Ages: A Critical Study of Texts from Perpetua (d. 203) to Marguerite Porete (d. 1310)*. Cambridge: Cambridge University Press.

Eire, C. 1990: Major problems in the definition of spirituality as an academic discipline. In B. C. Hansen (ed.), *Modern Christian Spirituality: Methodological and Historical Essays*, pp. 53–61. Atlanta: Scholars Press.

Eller, C. 1995: *Living in the Lap of the Goddess: The Feminist Spirituality Movement in America*. Boston: Beacon Press.

——2000: *The Myth of Patriarchal Prehistory: Why an Invented Past Won't Give Women a Future*. Boston: Beacon Press.

Elliott, D. 1997: The physiology of rapture and female spirituality. In P. Biller and A. Minnis (eds), *Medieval Theology and the Natural Body*, pp. 141–73. Woodbridge: York Medieval Press.

——1998: *Dominae* or *dominatae*? Female mystics and the trauma of textuality. In C. Rousseau and J. Rosenthal (eds), *Women, Marriage, and Family in Medieval Christendom: Essays in Memory of Michael M. Sheehan, CSB*, pp. 47–77. Kalamazoo, MI: Medieval Institute.

——1999: *Fallen Bodies: Pollution, Sexuality, and Demonology in the Middle Ages*. Philadelphia: University of Pennsylvania Press.

——2003: Women and confession: from empowerment to pathology. In M. Erler and M. Kowaleski (eds), *Gendering the Master Narrative: Women and Power in the Middle Ages*, pp. 31–51. Ithaca, NY: Cornell University Press.

Epps, G. P. J. 2001: *Ecce homo*. In G. Burger and S. F. Kruger (eds), *Queering the Middle Ages*, pp. 236–51. Minneapolis, MN: University of Minnesota Press.

Erler, M. 2002: *Women, Reading, and Piety in Late Medieval England*. Cambridge: Cambridge University Press.

——and Kowaleski, M. (eds) 1988: *Women and Power in the Middle Ages*. Athens: University of Georgia Press.

——and —— (eds) 2003: *Gendering the Master Narrative: Women and Power in the Middle Ages*. Ithaca, NY: Cornell University Press.

Farmer, S. 2000: The beggar's body: intersections of gender and social status in high medieval Paris. In S. Farmer and B. Rosenwein (eds), *Monks and Nuns, Outcasts and Saints: Religion in Medieval Society*, pp. 153–71. Ithaca, NY: Cornell University Press.

——and Pasternack, C. B. (eds) 2003: *Gender and Difference in the Middle Ages*. Minneapolis, MN: University of Minnesota Press.

Ferrante, J. 1998: "*Scribe quae vides et audis*": Hildegard, her language and her secretaries. In D. Townsend and A. Taylor (eds), *The Tongue of the Fathers: Gender and Ideology in Twelfth-century Latin*, pp. 12–35. Philadelphia: University of Pennsylvania Press.

Fulton, R. 2002: *From Judgment to Passion: Devotion to Christ and the Virgin Mary, 800–1200*. New York: Columbia University Press.

Garber, R. L. R. 2003: *Feminine Figurae: Representations of Gender in Religious Texts by Medieval German Women Writers, 1100–1375*. New York: Routledge.

Greenspan, K. 1991: The autohagiographical tradition in medieval women's devotional writing. *A/B: Auto/Biographical Studies* 6, 157–68.

——1996: Autohagiography and medieval women's spiritual autobiography. In J. Chance (ed.), *Gender and Text in the Later Middle Ages*, pp. 216–36. Gainesville: University Press of Florida.

Greer, A. and Bilinkoff, J. (eds) 2003: *Colonial Saints: Discovering the Holy in the Americas*. New York: Routledge.

Griffiths, R. M. 1997: *God's Daughters: Evangelical Women and the Power of Submission*. Berkeley, CA: University of California Press.

Grundmann, H. 1936: Die Frauen und die Literatur im Mittelalter: Ein Beitrag zur Frage nach der Enstehung des Schrifttumsin der Volksprache. *Archiv für Kulturgeschichte* 26, 129–61.

—— 1995: *Religious Movements in the Middle Ages: The Historical Links between Heresy, the Mendicant Orders, and the Women's Religious Movement in the Twelfth and Thirteenth Century with the Historical Foundation of German Mysticism*, trans. S. Rowan. Notre Dame, IN: Notre Dame University Press (orig. pub. 1935, rev. edn 1961).

Hadewijch 1980: *The Complete Works*, trans. C. Hart. New York: Paulist Press.

Hadot, P. 1995: *Philosophy as a Way of Life: Spiritual Exercises from Socrates to Foucault*, trans. M. Chase. Cambridge: Cambridge University Press.

Hale, R. D. 1995: "Taste and see for God is sweet": sensory perception and memory in medieval Christian mystical experience. In A. C. Bartlett, T. Bestul, J. Goebel, et al. (eds), *Vox Mystica: Essays for Valerie M. Lagorio*, pp. 3–14. Cambridge: D. S. Brewer.

Hamburger, J. 1990: *The Rothschild Canticles: Art and Mysticism in Flanders and the Rhineland circa 1300*. New Haven, CT: Yale University Press.

—— 1997: *Nuns as Artists: The Visual Culture of a Medieval Convent*. Berkeley, CA: University of California Press.

—— 1998: *The Visual and the Visionary: Art and Female Spirituality in Late Medieval Germany*. New York: Zone Books.

—— 2001: Women and the written word in medieval Switzerland. In S. Bieri and W. Fuchs (eds), *Bibliotheken Bauen: Tradition und Vision/Building for Books: Traditions and Visions*, pp. 112–63. Basel: Birkhäuser.

Harris, R. 1999: *Lourdes: Body and Spirit in the Secular Age*. New York: Viking.

Hilkert, M. C. 2001: *Speaking with Authority: Catherine of Siena and the Voices of Women Today*. New York: Paulist Press.

Hollywood, A. 1995: *The Soul as Virgin Wife: Mechthild of Magdeburg, Marguerite Porete, and Meister Eckhart*. Notre Dame, IN: University of Notre Dame Press.

—— 1996: Justice and gender in mysticism. Review of Grace Jantzen, *Power, Gender and Christian Mysticism*. *Christian Spirituality Bulletin* 4 (1), 28–9.

—— 1999: Inside out: Beatrice of Nazareth and her hagiographer. In C. Mooney (ed.), *Gendered Voices: Medieval Saints and their Interpreters*, pp. 78–98. Philadelphia: University of Pennsylvania Press.

—— 2002a: *Sensible Ecstasy: Mysticism, Sexual Difference, and the Demands of History*. Chicago: University of Chicago Press.

—— 2002b: Performativity, citationality, ritualization. *History of Religions* 42, 93–115.

—— 2003: Practice, belief, and feminist philosophy of religion. In P. S. Anderson and B. Clack (eds), *Feminist Philosophy of Religion: Critical Readings*, pp. 218–33. London: Routledge.

—— forthcoming: Sexual desire, divine desire: or queering the beguines. In Gerard Loughlin (ed.), *Queer Theology: New Perspectives on Sex and Gender*. Oxford: Blackwell.

Holsinger, B. 1993: The flesh of the voice: embodiment and homoerotics of devotion in Hildegard of Bingen (1098–1179). *Signs* 19, 92–125.

—— 2001: *Music, Body, and Desire in Medieval Culture: Hildegard of Bingen to Chaucer*. Stanford: Stanford University Press.

Hult, D. 2003: The *Roman de la Rose*, Christine de Pizan, and the *querelle des femmes*. In C. Dinshaw and D. Wallace (eds), *The Cambridge Companion to Medieval Women's Writing*, pp. 184–94. Cambridge: University of Cambridge Press.

Irigaray, L. 1985: *Speculum of the Other Woman*, trans. G. C. Gill. Ithaca, NY: Cornell University Press.

Jantzen, G. 1995: *Power, Gender and Christian Mysticism*. Cambridge: Cambridge University Press.

Johnson, E. 1987: Marian devotion in the Western church. In J. Raitt, with B. McGinn and J. Meyendorff (eds), *Christian Spirituality: High Middle Ages and Reformation*, pp. 392–414. New York: Crossroad.

Julian of Norwich 1978: *Showings*, trans. E. Colledge and J. Walsh. New York: Paulist Press.

Keller, H. 2000: *My Secret is Mine: Studies on Religion and Eros in the German Middle Ages*. Leuven: Peters.

Kieckhefer, R. 1984: *Unquiet Souls: Fourteenth-century Saints and their Religious Milieu*. Chicago: University of Chicago Press.

——1994: The holy and the unholy: sainthood, witchcraft, and magic in late medieval Europe. *Journal of Medieval and Renaissance Studies* 24, 355–85.

Kienzle, B. M. and Walker, P. J. (eds) 1998: *Women Preachers and Prophets through Two Millennia of Christianity*. Berkeley, CA: University of California Press.

LaCapra, D. 1994: *Representing the Holocaust: History, Theory, Trauma*. Ithaca, NY: Cornell University Press.

Lagorio, V. M. 1984: The medieval continental women mystics: an introduction. In P. Szarmach (ed.), *An Introduction to the Medieval Mystics of Europe*, pp. 161–93. Albany, NY: State University of New York Press.

Lavezzo, K. 1996: Sobs and sighs between women: the homoerotics of compassion in *The Book of Margery Kempe*. In L. O. Fradenburg and C. Freccero (eds), *Premodern Sexualities*, pp. 175–98. New York: Routledge.

Lewis, G. J. 1996: *By Women, for Women, about Women: The Sister-books of Fourteenth-century Germany*. Toronto: Pontifical Institute of Medieval Studies.

Lochrie, K. 1991: *Margery Kempe and the Translations of the Flesh*. Philadelphia: University of Pennsylvania Press.

——1997: Mystical acts, queer tendencies. In K. Lochrie, P. McCracken, and J. A. Schultz (eds), *Constructing Medieval Sexuality*, pp. 180–200. Minneapolis, MN: University of Minnesota Press.

McCash, J. H. (ed.) 1996: *The Cultural Patronage of Medieval Women*. Athens: University of Georgia Press.

McGinn, B. 1993: The letter and the spirit: spirituality as an academic discipline. *The Cresset: A Review of Literature, Art and Public Affairs* 56 (7b), 13–22.

——(ed.) 1994: *Meister Eckhart and the Beguine Mystics: Hadewijch of Brabant, Mechthild of Magdeburg, and Marguerite Porete*. New York: Continuum.

——1998: *The Flowering of Mysticism: Men and Women in the New Mysticism, 1200–1350*. New York: Crossroad.

——, Meyendorff, J., and Leclerq, J. (eds) 1985: *Christian Spirituality: Origins to the Twelfth Century*. New York: Crossroad.

McIntosh, M. 1998: *Mystical Theology*. Oxford: Blackwell.

Mack, P. 1992: *Visionary Women: Ecstatic Prophecy in Seventeenth-century England*. Berkeley, CA: University of California Press.

McNamara, J. A. 1991: The need to give: suffering and female sanctity in the Middle Ages. In R. Blumenfeld-Kosinski and T. Szell (eds), *Images of Sainthood in Medieval Europe*, pp. 199–221. Ithaca, NY: Cornell University Press.

Maggi, A. 1998: *Uttering the Word: The Mystical Performances of Maria Maddalena de' Pazzi, a Renaissance Visionary*. Albany, NY: State University of New York Press.

Mahmood, S. 2001a: Rehearsed spontaneity and the conventionality of ritual: disciplines of *salat*. *American Ethnologist* 28, 827–54.

——2001b: Feminist theory, embodiment, and the docile subject: some reflections on the Egyptian Islamic revival. *Cultural Anthropology* 16, 202–36.

Massey, M. C. 1985: *The Feminine Soul: The Fate of an Ideal*. Boston: Beacon Press.

Mazzoni, C. 1996: *Saint Hysteria: Neurosis, Mysticism, and Gender in European Culture*. Ithaca, NY: Cornell University Press.

Meale, C. M. (ed.) 1993: *Women and Literature in Britain, 1150–1500*. Cambridge: Cambridge University Press.

Mews C. (ed.) 2001: *Listen, Daughter: The Speculum Virginum and the Formation of Religious Women in the Middle Ages*. New York: Palgrave.

Milhaven, G. 1993: *Hadewijch and her Sisters: Other Ways of Loving and Knowing*. Albany, NY: State University of New York Press.

Miller, J. 1999: Eroticized violence in medieval women's mystical literature: a call for feminist critique. *Journal of Feminist Studies in Religion* 15, 25–49.

Mooney, C. 1994: The authorial role of Brother A in the composition of Angela of Foligno's revelations. In E. A. Matter and J. Coakley (eds), *Creative Women in Medieval and Early Modern Italy: A Religious and Artistic Renaissance*, pp. 34–63. Philadelphia: University of Pennsylvania Press.

——(ed.) 1999: *Gendered Voices: Medieval Saints and their Interpreters*. Philadelphia: University of Pennsylvania Press.

Moore, S. 2000: The Song of Songs in the history of sexuality. *Church History* 69, 328–49.

Newman, B. 1987: *Sister of Wisdom: Saint Hildegard's Theology of the Feminine*. Berkeley, CA: University of California Press.

——1995: *From Virile Woman to Woman Christ: Studies in Medieval Religion and Literature*. Philadelphia: University of Pennsylvania Press.

——1998: Possessed by the Spirit: devout women, demoniacs, and the apostolic life in the thirteenth century. *Speculum* 73, 733–70.

——2003: *God and the Goddesses: Vision, Poetry, and Belief in the Middle Ages*. Philadelphia: University of Pennsylvania Press.

Nichols, J. A. and Shank, L. T. (eds) 1987: *Peace Weavers: Medieval Religious Women*. Kalamazoo, MI: Cistercian Publications.

Orsi, R. A. 1985: *The Madonna of 115th Street: Faith and Community in Italian Harlem, 1880–1950*. New Haven, CT: Yale University Press.

——1996: *Thank You Saint Jude: Women's Devotion to the Patron Saint of Hopeless Causes*. New Haven, CT: Yale University Press.

Parsons, S. F. (ed.) 2002: *The Cambridge Companion to Feminist Theology*. Cambridge: Cambridge University Press.

Peters, U. 1988: *Religiöse Erfahrung als literarisches Faktum: Zur Vorgeschichte und Genese frauenmysticher Texte des 13 und 14 Jahrhunderts*. Tubingen: Niemeyer.

Petroff, E. A. (ed.) 1986: *Medieval Women's Visionary Literature*. Oxford: Oxford University Press.

Poor, S. 2004: *Mechthild of Magdeburg and her Book: Gender and the Making of Textual Authority*. Philadelphia: University of Pennsylvania Press.

Rambuss, R. 1998: *Closet Devotions*. Durham, NC: Duke University Press.

Ranft, P. 1998: *Women and Spiritual Equality in Christian Tradition*. New York: Palgrave.

——2000: *The Forgotten History of Women Spiritual Directors: A Woman's Way*. New York: Palgrave.

Raphael, M. 2000: *Introducing Thealogy: Discourses on the Goddess*. Cleveland, OH: Pilgrim Press.

Ringler, S. 1985: Die Rezeption mittelalterlicher Frauenmystik als wissenschaftliches Problem, dargestellt am Werk der Christine Ebner. In P. Dinzelbacher and D. Bauer (eds), *Frauenmystik im Mittelater*, pp. 178–200. Ostfildern bei Stuttgart: Schwabenverlag.

Robertson, E. 1990: *Early English Devotional Prose and the Female Audience*. Knoxville: University of Tennessee Press.

—— 1991: The corporeality of female sanctity in *The Life of Saint Margaret*. In R. Blumenfeld-Kosinski and T. Szell (eds), *Images of Sainthood in Medieval Europe*, pp. 268–87. Ithaca, NY: Cornell University Press.

—— 1993: Medieval medical views of women and female spirituality in the *Ancrene Wisse* and Julian of Norwich's *Showings*. In L. Lomperis and S. Stanbury (eds), *Feminist Approaches to the Body in Medieval Literature*, pp. 142–67. Philadelphia: University of Pennsylvania Press.

Roisin, S. 1943: L'efflorescence cistercienne et le courant féminin de piété au XIIIe siècle. *Revue d'Histoire Ecclésiastique* 39, 342–78.

—— 1947: *L'hagiographie cistercienne dans le diocèse de Liège au XIIIe siècle*. Louvain: Bibliothèque de l'Université.

Rudy, G. 2002: *Mystical Language of Sensation in the Later Middle Ages*. New York: Routledge.

Schmidt, L. E. 2000: *Hearing Things: Religion, Illusion, and the American Enlightenment*. Cambridge, MA: Harvard University Press.

Schneider, L. C. 1998: *Re-imagining the Divine: Confronting the Backlash against Feminist Theology*. Cleveland, OH: The Pilgrim Press.

Smith, L. 1996: *Scriba, femina*: medieval depictions of women writing. In J. H. M. Taylor and L. Smith (eds), *Women and the Book: Assessing the Visual Evidence*, pp. 21–44. London: The British Library.

—— and Taylor, J. H. M. (eds) 1995: *Women, the Book and the Godly*. Cambridge: D. S. Brewer.

Staley, L. 1991: The trope of the scribe and the question of literary authority in the works of Julian of Norwich and Margery Kempe. *Speculum* 66, 820–38.

—— 1994: *Margery Kempe's Dissenting Fictions*. University Park, PA: Penn State University Press.

Stock, B. 1983: *The Implications of Literacy: Written Language and Models of Interpretation in the Eleventh and Twelfth Centuries*. Princeton, NJ: Princeton University Press.

Summit, J. 2000: *Lost Property: The Woman Writer and English Literary History, 1380–1589*. Chicago: University of Chicago Press.

—— 2003: Women and authorship. In C. Dinshaw and D. Wallace (eds), *The Cambridge Companion to Medieval Women's Writing*, pp. 91–108. Cambridge: Cambridge University Press.

Suydam, M. A. 1999: Beguine textuality: sacred performances. In M. A. Suydam and J. Ziegler (eds), *Performance and Transformation: New Approaches to Late Medieval Spirituality*, pp. 169–210. New York: St Martin's Press.

—— and Ziegler, J. (eds) 1999: *Performance and Transformation: New Approaches to Late Medieval Spirituality*. New York: St Martin's Press.

Taves, A. 1999: *Fits, Trances, and Visions: Experiencing Religion and Explaining Experience from Wesley to James*. Princeton, NJ: Princeton University Press.

Taylor, J. H. M. and Smith, L. (eds) 1996: *Women and the Book: Assessing the Visual Evidence*. London: The British Library.

Teresa of Avila 1979: *The Interior Castle*, trans. K. Kavanaugh and O. Rodriguez. New York: Paulist Press.

Tobin, F. 1995: *Mechthild of Magdeburg: A Medieval Mystic in Modern Eyes*. Columbia, SC: Camden House.

Voaden, R. (ed.) 1996: *Prophets Abroad: The Reception of Continental Holy Women in Late-Medieval England*. Cambridge: D. S. Brewer.

—— 1999: *God's Words, Women's Voices: The Discernment of Spirits in the Writing of Late-Medieval Women's Visionaries*. Woodbridge: York Medieval Press.

Warner, M. 1976: *Alone of All her Sex: The Myth and Cult of the Virgin Mary*. New York: Knopf.

Watson, N. 1991: *Richard Rolle and the Invention of Authority*. Cambridge: Cambridge University Press.

—— 1995: Censorship and cultural change in late-medieval England: vernacular theology, the Oxford translation debate, and Arundel's Constitutions of 1409. *Speculum* 70, 822–63.

—— 1999: Desire for the past. *Studies in the Age of Chaucer* 21, 59–97.

Watt, D. 1997: *Secretaries of God*. Cambridge: D. S. Brewer.

Weber, A. 1990: *Teresa of Avila and the Rhetoric of Femininity*. Princeton, NJ: Princeton University Press.

Wiethaus, U. 2003: Female homoerotic discourse and religion in medieval Germanic culture. In S. Farmer and C. B. Pasternack (eds), *Gender and Difference in the Middle Ages*, pp. 288–322. Ithaca, NY: Cornell University Press.

Wilson, K. M. (ed.) 1984: *Medieval Women Writers*. Athens: University of Georgia Press.

Winstead, K. 1997: *Virgin Martyrs: Legends of Sainthood in Late Medieval England*. Ithaca, NY: Cornell University Press.

CHAPTER 22
Ritual Studies

Susan J. White

Over the past several decades, the study of ritual has increasingly engaged the imagination and interest of those asking a number of different questions about the nature of human beings and human communities. It has also become big business, as innumerable marriage counselors, motivation experts, and self-help gurus offer "ritual workshops" which claim to produce intense experiences of interpersonal bonding and insight. But the claims of those who study ritual in a more serious, academic way are almost as extravagant. To understand ritualization is to understand the inner workings of culture, religious worship, human psychology, and community formation, as well as the ways in which people construct their individual and social worlds.

The roots of ritual studies lie in the rise of the human sciences in the late 1800s. Soon the structured analysis of ritualization lodged itself within the fields of psychology, sociology, and cultural anthropology. During the last quarter of the twentieth century, however, there was a clarification of the methods and goals of the discipline to the point that it developed into a discrete field of study in its own right. Because human ritual behavior is thought to play an important role in meaning-making and in the forging of inter-relationships among human beings and between human beings and the transcendent, many students of Christianity (and particularly those concerned with Christian praxis, including liturgy, sacramental theology, and, more recently, pastoral care and counseling) have entered into a fruitful dialogue with the field of ritual studies. The dialogue between ritual studies and Christian spirituality is admittedly less advanced, but there is little doubt that the study of human ritualization can be a significant tool for the study of the spiritual formation of individuals and groups.

Definition of the Field

Ritual can be defined as a culturally constructed system of symbolic communication, consisting of patterned repetitions of words and actions. Most ritologists (students of ritual), whether they approach ritual from an anthropological, a sociological, or a religious-studies perspective, are agreed on this most basic definition of the subject of their scholarly attention. Opinions vary widely, however, on the interpretations, sources, characteristics, and outcomes of human ritual behavior. Can there be individual rituals, or are they always only a collective act? Is ritual always invariable and formal, or can it be inventive? Is the ritualizer a passive or active agent in the process of ritualizing? Is ritual necessarily meaningful, or are its functions primarily affective and psycho-social? The history of ritual studies as a discipline, including its contemporary history, is the story of the attempts to clarify these questions and to apply insights from the investigation of human ritualization to various other questions of human identity.

Even before the development of ritual studies as a scholarly discipline, the power of ritual, which has both constructive and destructive potential, has been widely understood, and has led religious leaders throughout the centuries to superintend carefully the ritual behavior of adherents. This has resulted in a wide variety of institutional responses: the imposition or promotion of official rites, sanctions on participation in unauthorized ritual activities, and the elimination of certain specified ritual and symbolic elements from worship and devotional life. For many communities of faith, religious ritual is understood to have divine origins, laid out in varying degrees of specificity in sacred texts or handed down by oral tradition. As such, the ultimate test of one's theological conformity is often adherence to prevailing ritual norms, and penalties for non-compliance can be quite severe. But, at the same time, scrupulous attention to religious ritual is also understood to move believers toward spiritual maturity and a heightened sensitivity to transcendent reality. The connection between the contemporary field of ritual studies and the study of Christian spirituality is rooted in these basic understandings, as well as in questions raised within ritology about the role of ritual behavior in the formation of religious identity, insight, and integration.

The History of Ritual Studies as a Discipline

Although the establishment of ritual studies as a distinct discipline is relatively recent, one can trace its foundations to a number of prominent contributors to twentieth-century intellectual life. But they come at the subject from a number of different perspectives. Among the first to give serious scholarly attention to ritual were those who specialized in the study of world religions, including historians, comparativists, and philosophers, who became interested in the ways in which myth, ritual, and symbolization operate within the various world religious traditions. One of the earliest of these was philosopher of religion Rudolf Otto (1869–1937), whose book *The Idea of the Holy* (1917) introduced the idea of "numinosity" as a key religious category, one which could be applied to all religious traditions, both theist (such as Christianity, Judaism, and Islam) and non-theist (such as some forms of Buddhism). This helped to move many scholars away from the idea that the only meaningful religious categories are those connected with the cognitive and rational, i.e., what people believe or value. Although Otto treated ritual only tangentially, his insights helped open the way for the study of ritual as a non-rational form of connecting with the numinous.

At about the same time, anthropologist and ethnographer Arnold van Gennep (1873–1957) became interested in comparative ceremonial in the African tribal religions with which he was working. He insisted, unlike many of his contemporaries, that ritual could not be understood apart from the social and religious context within which it was set; that it was part of an organic whole with a multiplicity of functions and meanings. His primary contribution to the study of ritual was the identification and analysis of what he called "rites of passage" (Van Gennep 1960), which, he argued, enabled people to negotiate various significant life crises and helped societies maintain equilibrium. He distinguished several stages in these rites which accomplished the shift from one social state of being to another: for example, from child to adult, single to married, living to dead. In the "separation" stage, the person is disengaged from his or her old social status; in the "transition" stage, conditions are set up that will allow the person to gain insight into the nature of life and into the new role she or he will take up; and in the "incorporation" stage, the person is integrated into the new social state. Although he did not specifically use the language of spirituality, van Gennep's work has allowed students of spirituality to understand the importance of ritual in the spiritual growth and maturity of individuals.

In the turbulent years leading up to and following World War II, interest in the field of comparative religious ritual burgeoned. Although some scholars continued to focus on the critical differences among the various religious traditions, most endeavored to uncover their underlying commonalities in the context of a Western society brought to the brink of destruction by deeply rooted divisions and conflicts. One of the most significant voices during this time was the Romanian scholar of comparative religion Mircea Eliade (1907–86), who taught for many years at the University of Chicago. In a number of influential books and monographs, Eliade attempted to identify the archetypal symbolic constructs that operated deep within the human imagination across all cultural and religious boundaries (see Eliade 1961). Influenced by both Indian philosophy and the depth psychology of Carl Jung, Eliade argued that contemporary human beings have lost their connection with the cycles of nature, and that the prevailing linear view of history was at the root of all modern conflict. While most of his research lay in the ethnographic exploration of mythology and symbolism, his attention to the place of ritual as a means of revealing the inherent sacredness of the world allows his work to be seen as a critical link between the field of ritual studies (although not then clearly defined) and Christian spirituality.

Other anthropologists and ethnographers, although not ritologists in the strict sense of the term, have also been deeply interested in ritual as a mode of religious communication, and in its place in the spiritual development of persons. Victor Turner (1920–83) and Mary Douglas (b. 1921), both of whom spent much of their professional lives studying tribal religions in Africa, are perhaps the best known by students of Christianity, who have made use of their insights into the ways in which religious significance is established and maintained. Douglas's work revealed the ways in which people classify material objects (good/bad, clean/dirty, pure/impure, for example), and the symbolic significance they give to these classifications (Douglas 1982, 2002). For his part, Turner advanced van Gennep's analysis of rites of passage, and particularly initiation rituals. But perhaps of more immediate importance, Turner established the boundaries for the study of ritual as a separate discipline, introducing terms such as "liminality," "ritual process," "social drama," and "communitas" as key concepts in the discipline (see Turner 1969, 1974). At the same time, psychologists such as Bruno Bettleheim (1903–90) and Erik Erikson (1902–94) were highlighting the importance of ritual in the early stages of human psycho-social development, and especially its role in alleviating primal anxieties, in making sense of ambiguous experiences, and in negotiating the disjuncture between instinctive desires and social acceptability (what has come to be called the "body/culture dialectic") (see Bettelheim 1966, 1975; Erikson 1977). Each of these people can be seen as bridging the gap between the work of the early human scientists and what would become the field of ritual studies.

By the late 1970s, the study of ritual had begun to establish itself as a discrete academic discipline, taking its place as a subspecialty not only in departments of anthropology and sociology, but of religious studies, philosophy, and theology as well. Among the first of those to define themselves as "ritologists" was Stanley J. Tambiah, whose seminal article "A Performance Approach to Ritual" appeared in the *Proceedings of the British Academy* in 1979, and Jonathan Z. Smith, who was among the first to develop a comprehensive model for ritual studies in his 1987 book *To Take Place: Toward a Theory of Ritual*. Ronald L. Grimes, Professor of Religion and Culture at Wilfred Laurier University in Canada, has been influential not only in writing specifically on the topic of religious ritual, in which he always takes spirituality seriously as a form of religiosity, but also in founding the *Journal of Ritual Studies* in 1987. The establishment of this journal can be seen as the "Declaration of Independence" for ritual studies as a free-standing academic discipline.

Three Approaches to Studies in Ritual

In the relatively short time since its inception, the field of ritual studies has developed not as a single monolithic academic discipline, but as a field which accommodates many different approaches. While these approaches are not mutually exclusive, each one does carry its own particular set of presuppositions and methodologies, and each has a particular contribution to make to the study of Christian spirituality. The diversity of connection points between the disciplines of ritual studies and Christian spirituality is the direct result of the multiplicity of paradigms within both fields of study, and should be seen as a strength, not as a weakness, in the dialogue. But this situation also makes the conversation between the two less than straightforward, and much of what follows will be an attempt to look at each of the main approaches to the field of ritual studies and at the specific contribution it might make to the advancement of the study of Christian spirituality.

Performance theory

The term "performance" has a number of specific meanings within ritual studies, but all are rooted in the idea that words and gestures have the power to alter reality, i.e., that they can "make things happen." With regard to language, the use of the term can be traced back to an extremely important series of lectures delivered in 1955 by philosopher J. L. Austin (1911–60) at Harvard University and later published under the title *How to Do Things with Words* (1961). Austin's thesis was that words do not simply describe states of being, but when used declaratively in ritual formulas they can bring about the state of affairs they assert. The examples which he uses are such things as "I pronounce you husband and wife," uttered in the context of the marriage rite, and "I christen this ship the Queen Mary," at the launching of a vessel. There are, of course, certain necessary conditions that must be met in order for the performative power of language to be released, including the enactment of appropriate gestures and the concurrence of the community on the meaning of the act. But when these preconditions are in place, words can indeed effect what they signify, and the question then becomes not "Is what is being said true or false?" but rather "Is what is being said successful or unsuccessful?"

Others who approach the study of ritual from the perspective of performance look to drama theory as their primary interpretive lens. In an influential little book entitled *The Empty Space* (1968), Peter Brook (b. 1927), theater director and acting teacher, argued for the subversive power of theater and for its ability to transform human perception and perspective. Ronald Grimes (b. 1954), carrying forward Brook's description of "holy theater," is particularly interested in religious rituals, which he defines broadly as any ritual with an ultimate frame of reference and which is seen to be of cosmic necessity. Grimes understands such ritual as having the power all good drama possesses to lead the actors toward self-abandonment, and claims that ritual drama can allow us (as actors) to *create* what in the traditional terms of religion has been only understood to be passively "discoverable" (see Grimes 1982, 1993). Another director and drama theorist, Jerzy Grotowski (1933–99), head of the Polish Theater Laboratory in the 1960s and 1970s, also made a significant impact on students of ritual. With his attention to the transformative power of "holy play" for both actor and audience, and his clarion call for actors to transcend themselves and to internalize mythic themes, Grotowski speaks persuasively to students of ritual and religiosity alike (see Grotowski 1968).

Semiotics

At the same time, there are those who tend to approach the study of ritual from the perspective of semiotics. The field of semiotics, which grew up at about the same time as the field of ritual studies, focuses on the ways in which signs (Greek = *semion*) and systems of signs operate within the lives of individuals and communities. Semiotics began as, and in some ways remains, a subdiscipline within literary theory, linguistics, and philosophy which is primarily concerned with the interaction between text and reader, and especially with questions of meaning. Who determines what something means? And by what processes is symbolic meaning decided? Since the beginnings of semiotics in the work of its earliest proponents, Mikhail Bakhtin, Hans-Georg Gadamer, and Roland Barthes, literary texts have been the primary concern of the semioticists (see Barthes 1972; Bakhtin 1981; Gadamer 1999). But ritologists who have been influenced by this school of thought attempt to read human ritual behavior as a kind of "text," with ceremonial gestures and words the "signs" to be analyzed. Influenced by the work of the "father of modern semiotics," Charles S. Pierce, many of those concerned with human ritualization wish to claim that not only do ritual symbols help people express their innate religiosity, but indeed that people cannot be religious at all without the use of ritual signs and symbols (see Pierce 1992–8).

Semiotics tends to represent itself as a universal key to the understanding of reality, but it has presented a number of problems for those wishing to apply its theoretical foundations to questions of ritual studies. The first difficulty is the tendency of the field of semiotics toward dualism, with the conviction that only in seeing the world in terms of binary opposites can we understand the nature of things. The second difficulty, which poses a particular problem for students of Christian spirituality who may wish to apply the insights from semiotics to their work, is that semiotics is not particularly interested in the underlying reality behind the signs it studies, claiming indeed in some cases that no reality exists but the signs themselves. At the very least, the semioticists argue, no direct apprehension of reality is possible without the mediation of the sign.

Human sciences

Those who come to the study of ritual from the human sciences perspective, including psychoanalytical, anthropological, sociological, and neurobiological approaches, have remained close to the intellectual roots of ritual studies as a discipline. Anthropological studies continue to exert a strong influence on ritual studies, and ethnographic research in the field is of persistent interest to those concerned with human ritual- and symbol-making. The expansion of the field of anthropological and ethnographical ritology to include not only tribal religious ritual, but also the ritualization, both religious and social, that takes place in industrialized societies as well, has given students of ritual behavior among Western Christians much useful data. Many who work from the anthropological side of ritual studies continue to be interested in comparative ritology, asking questions which apply to all ritual-making activity. How is the power of the past brought into the present through ritual? How are ritual "outsiders" transformed into ritual "insiders?" How are ritual boundaries established, and what makes ritual places "holy?" Does ritual activity change the structures of human neural circuitry? How does ritualization consolidate belief and faith? Attempts to answer these questions by careful observation of the lives of real people across a wide spectrum of cultural and religious situations allow us to identify the deep structures of our religious praxis.

Erving Goffman (1922–82), who attended to ritual as a sociologist, can be seen to have been especially significant to the forging of a relationship between ritual studies and the study of Christian belief and practice. His concern with how social worlds are created, and how people construct their sense of self within those worlds, was articulated in a number of important books, including *The Presentation of Self in Everyday Life* (1959), *Behavior in Public Places* (1963), and *Strategic Interaction* (1969). Called an "ethnographer of the self," Goffman made the case that ritual both reflects and shapes human identity, and as such is indispensable to the full realization of human person-hood. More recently, Catherine M. Bell, who is also concerned with the formation of the self, has highlighted the place of ritual in the maintenance (and also the disruption) of power structures in human societies. In her important book *Ritual Theory – Ritual Prac-tice* (1992), she claims that the ultimate purpose of ritualization is not to advance the stated purposes of the ritual, nor even the stated purposes of the ritualizers, but to produce *ritual agents*, people whose instinctive knowledge of how to perform the ritual empowers them in complex social situations. Other ritologists have taken up this theme of ritual and power, and insights from the field of ritual studies have become useful in the postcolonial analysis of culture and in understanding the place of ritual in the maintenance of and resistance to structures of authority.

If any one area of Christian studies has been most open to appropriating the insights of these various facets of ritual studies, it has been the field of liturgiology: the study of the history, theology, and practice of Christian worship. This has led to the widen-ing of liturgists' field-of-vision in a number of important areas. The early work of Otto and Eliade on the interplay between ritual and enlightenment helped students of liturgy articulate the ways in which Christian ritual acts as a mediator of transcendence; the ethnographic work of van Gennep and Turner on initiation practices helped them iden-tify the underlying structures of the rites of baptism and confirmation. And ritologists' investigations into the complex relationship between ritual and power has allowed litur-gists to see that Christian ritual has the potential both to maintain and to subvert struc-tures of social control. But other areas are only beginning to be explored by worship specialists, particularly the philosophical and semiological underpinnings of Christian ritual and the neurobiology of ritual behavior. It is likely, though, that wherever bridges are made between ritual studies and the study of Christian spirituality, the field of litur-giology will be a significant connector.

Challenges in the Dialogue between Ritual Studies and Christian Spirituality

As even this briefest of descriptions of the field of ritology suggests, the dialogue between ritual studies and the study of Christian spirituality will not be an easy one. Several presuppositions that are held by proponents of one or another strategy in ritual studies might seem to guarantee a failure of the discussion at an early stage. (The claim by some of the semioticists that no ultimate reality lies beneath the sign is a good example.) But, as a whole, the multi-faceted discipline of ritual studies provides a rich feast of insights which, employed carefully, can be of enormous value to the advance-ment of the entire spectrum of studies in Christian spirituality – historical, phenom-enological, and practical. Certainly, the basic notion that the noetic, the affective, and the experiential are worthy subjects of scholarly attention is at the heart of both studies in ritual and studies in Christian spirituality, and the more highly developed arguments for that proposition that have been advanced in ritual studies can be applied equally by those working in the field of Christian spirituality.

But even at its most congenial, ritology also provides serious challenges to the study of Christian spirituality as it is currently undertaken. For example, the ritologists' general approach to texts, both ancient and modern, is a complex one, and few students of ritual are willing to give a great deal of weight to the "intended" meanings of the authors of texts, nor to the interpretive significance of the historical context in which they are written. Most ritologists insist that the meaning of a text is highly dependent upon the hermeneutic encounter between reader and text; that reader and text interact to *make* meaning. This will certainly have serious implications for the understanding of the textual deposit of spirituality. If texts cannot be considered simply and straightforwardly as accurate accounts of the spiritual experience of individuals and groups, business-as-usual for many scholars of Christian piety will likely be disrupted.

The same holds true for the way in which students of ritual approach verbal, first-person accounts of the shape of a person's experience. In the same way that the meaning of texts is changed by the act of reading, so too is the meaning of reportage changed by the act of hearing. The importance of this for students of Christian piety is clear, especially for spiritual directors but also those who wish to undertake field studies in Christian spirituality. If the direct and immediate link between the description of a person's interior life and the theological meaning that can be derived from that description is broken by the ritologists' insistence on the mediating function of the reader/hearer, then intense scrutiny of both the interpreter and that which is being interpreted will be necessary in every case.

The prevailing understanding of the self among ritologists is another area of potential difficulty in the conversation with students of Christian spirituality. If, as many in the field of ritual studies suggest, human identity is always a "work-in-progress," and is continually being "constructed" in and through interaction with other persons and with the world of experience, then questions about the essential nature of the human soul are likely to arise. The fact that "soul-talk" is so prevalent in the discipline of Christian spirituality and virtually absent from the discipline of ritology will mean that some common ground will have to be found in this area in order for the discourse to be fruitful. Equally challenging will be the ritologists' reinterpretation of the notion of "traditions," which has become the prevailing principle of organization for much of the field of Christian spirituality, especially in historical studies, within which traditions are understood primarily as identifiable patterns of shared thought and belief. Ritologists, on the other hand, have encouraged us to consider that "traditions" might not be patterns of *cognition*, but rather patterns of *behavior* within which the underlying narrative is embedded and by which it is transmitted. Understanding the term "tradition" in this wider sense, while it may challenge the internal geography of the study of Christian spirituality, may also uncover links with other forms of spirituality which have hitherto remained hidden.

Potentially Fruitful Areas of Inquiry

Although there will be serious challenges to the dialogue between spirituality and ritual studies, they should not discourage those who are seeking deeper understanding of the

Christian devotional life. A forthright engagement with what could easily be seen as a sister discipline to Christian spirituality will surely provoke a host of insights in a number of areas of inquiry, four of which will be considered below as a suggestion of the outlines of a discussion that will surely be fruitful for both disciplines.

Power and efficacy

Christian spiritual mentors and scholars of the devotional life have always talked with genuine conviction about the "power of prayer," and have been able to articulate the ways and means of devotional potency in theological categories as a function of the God–human relationship. They have been less successful, however, in arguing for the efficacy of prayer in other terms, terms understood across interfaith lines and among those who wish to speak of prayer within the wider context of human linguistic activity. J. L. Austin's notion of the performativity of language, i.e., the ability of language to create, under certain specified conditions, a new reality, deserves serious attention by those who wish to push more deeply into the philosophical underpinnings of our language about the power of words directed to God. More recently, those who consider the nature of performativity have begun to consider the question of whether the performance of ritual words might not be an end in itself, rather than a means of achieving some further result. To take seriously prayer as a thing in itself rather than as simply a means to produce some effect or state of being external to itself, might elicit startling new theological insights, as well as new approaches to spiritual praxis and mentoring.

At the same time, however, it has all too often been the case that students of spirituality have concentrated very heavily on the verbal aspects of Christian piety, while tending to downplay the somatic aspects. Such things as kneeling for prayer, walking the labyrinth, counting the beads of a rosary, beating the breast, or making the sign of the cross have been given far less scholarly attention than the words of prayer or written descriptions of the interior landscape. This is in part because, although we have had relatively reliable hermeneutic tools with which to interpret the textual record of the spiritual lives of men and women, we have had only rudimentary methods for analyzing ritual behavior. Examining the efficacy of ritual, and the ways in which ritual can reveal deeper (and perhaps contradictory) meanings in the words that accompany the actions, will be necessary for those who wish to gain a full picture of the variety of spiritual experience.

Students of spirituality have always noted the persistence of piety, which tends to remain relatively stable even when the larger structures of belief and values within which it is embedded fluctuate. Ritual studies can help to explain this relative stability. Research into the psychology and neurobiology of ritual has shown that the combination of narrative (myth) and patterned action (ritual) results in the deep internalization of both the narrative and the relationships among ritual participants. And when accompanied with forms of song or chant this internalization is strengthened further. This will have implications not only for those who engage in field research in spirituality, and for historians of the changing geography of Christian piety, but also for spiritual directors who wish to understand more fully the nature of their clients' adherence to certain patterns of devotion.

The mind/body connection

Many of those who study human ritualization are intensely interested in what ritual behavior can tell them about the relationship between the mind and the body. Although they may approach this question from a variety of perspectives – anthropology, philosophy, neuroscience – there is the prevailing belief among ritologists that while there is indeed a mind-centered form of knowledge, cognition is not the only way people can be said to "know" things. The primary question for both students of ritual and students of spirituality is: "Is there a way of knowing that is non-mental?" Or, to put it another way: "Is there a 'body-knowledge?'" Many contemporary scholars of ritual, and especially feminist scholars, have been trying to understand how the lived experience of the body can absorb and encode a logic that is beyond the level of consciousness or articulation. In *Ritual Theory – Ritual Practice*, Catherine M. Bell uses the example of the relationship between submission to God and the act of kneeling for prayer. Kneeling, she says, does not "merely communicate subordination to the kneeler" but rather "produces a subordinated kneeler" (1992: 100) in and through performing the act itself. The idea that there might be a non-cognitive way of knowing is surely congenial to students of Christian spirituality, but our ability to explicate the ways in which this takes place could perhaps be advanced by a dialogue with the literature of ritology.

Those who approach human ritual behavior from the performance perspective have their own insights to add to this question of the relationship between mind and body, in this case between human utterance and human behavior. In *How to Do Things with Words*, J. L. Austin suggests that much of the kind of language students of spirituality usually rely upon for the interpretation of the interior life is not descriptive at all but rather performative. In other words, statements such as "I believe," "I know," "I desire" do not simply report on particular mental states, but are best understood as announcing the intention to *act as if* I believe, know, or desire. This linguistic connection between being and doing can not only be employed by students of the Christian devotional life as a check on the accuracy of accounts of an individual's spiritual state, but also as a way of forging a link between Christian spirituality and Christian ethics. To see that many of the statements people make about their spiritual state are not merely reflexive or introspective but also have a strong ritual character may open us to understanding their potency in producing meaningful behavior.

Another aspect of this conversation about the relationship between mind and body is concerned with the category of "enplacement," and with questions of how we human beings attempt to find our place in a complex and chaotic world through the establishment of ritual space and time. Through ritualization, the ritologists argue, differences between places and times are asserted and the incongruence between "what is" and "what should be" is illuminated. As the ritual is performed, the past and the present are freed from their precise historical locations to form what Jonathan Z. Smith

(1987) calls "fused temporality." In this situation, the ritualizer is able to perceive the essentially a-temporal nature of reality. The same sort of thing happens within ritual space where, by putting bodies (and things) in their "proper places" through the performance of the rite, ritual agents are able to re-align themselves with both the spiritual and the physical world which they inhabit. Although some ritologists argue that these are primarily (if not exclusively) psycho-social processes, many others, such as anthropologist Roy Rappaport (1999), assert the absolute necessity of the numinous in the perception of sacred place and time, and this integral relationship between spirituality and ritual emplacement in time and space opens the way for students of Christian spirituality to expand their own understanding of the importance of "location" in Christian piety.

Method

The social-scientific approach of ritology has tended to be attentive to questions of research methodology, and there is much in this discussion of method which should be of value to students of Christian piety. The matter of "objectivity" in observing and recording human behavior is taken up not only as a practical, but also as a philosophical issue in much of the ritual studies literature, and this discussion raises serious questions for those involved in field research in spirituality. In a now-famous 1983 article entitled "From the Native's Point of View," anthropologist Clifford Geertz challenged the then-prevailing dichotomies of "insider" versus "outsider," and "objective" versus "subjective" in field research, arguing persuasively that the researcher into any sort of human behavior is always both an insider and an outsider, both subjective and objective. It was argued that both distance and involvement were not only necessary to research in the various human studies disciplines, but inevitable, and that it is possible to arrive at real comprehension of human behavior because of the quality of "reflexivity" which we all possess, the ability to reflect on our own thoughts and actions. The student of Christian spirituality must surely consider the implications of this discussion carefully. What, for example, are the ontological dimensions and consequences of being both an "insider" and an "outsider" when observing, recording, and analyzing Christian spiritual praxis?

At the same time, the techniques by which ritological field research is undertaken, and the scholarly critique of those techniques, deserve to be considered by those who study Christian devotional life. Ritologists are clear that people "speak" of their religious experience in multiple modes, including somatically, and that different sorts of people speak in different modes. The particular processes by which students of ritual "read" the various forms of symbolic communication are determined by their particular approaches to the discipline, but all assume that it can indeed be decoded for its underlying meanings. Perhaps students of Christian spirituality need to become "bilingual," able to interpret both human gesture *and* spoken word for their spiritual significance. As the previous discussion on the nature of objectivity suggests, the contribution of the participant-observer in field research is an increasingly accepted method for studying spirituality in the field. But we can also understand how researchers in the history of spirituality can be described as "participant-observers," and how reflecting on that status can be a valuable exercise.

For ritologists, the boundary between social and religious ritual is not at all clearly drawn, and social ritualizing merits the same degree of scholarly attention that is accorded to formal religious rites. Gestures of greeting and showing respect, rituals of mourning and celebration, symbolic markers of social status, and the sign-systems operative in the fields of law, medicine, and politics are all grist for the scholarly mill of ritual studies. This raises the question about the way we set up boundaries within the field of Christian spirituality, and what information about the operative spirituality of individuals and groups we might gain from a serious look at their non-religious ritual behavior.

Ritual and spiritual health and wellbeing

Students of Christian spirituality who are particularly concerned with the promotion of spiritual health and wellbeing, including spiritual directors and pastoral caregivers, have spoken of the importance of the integration of the various aspects of human personhood: spiritual, emotional, social, psychological, physical. Many ritual studies theorists are convinced that that kind of wholesome integration happens primarily in and through participation in ritual. The role of ritual in therapeutic processes, for example in psychotherapy and medicine, is beginning to be explored, and many practitioners claim that, while ritual can be an aspect of psychological illness, it can also be a key element in whatever personal transformation takes place in the process of therapy. Ritual becomes a means by which painful memories can be safely encountered and contained, catharsis can be promoted, emotional consciousness can be raised, meaning can be created out of disparate experiences, and empowerment can be achieved. In some cases, healing is promoted by substituting healthy rituals for ritual behaviors that have proved to be destructive.

Very few writers have explored the place of ritual in spiritual direction and spiritual formation. Those who take a penitential/sacramental approach to spiritual direction certainly value the acts of confession and absolution, the receiving of communion, and the renewal of baptismal vows, for example. But there is a great deal of work yet to be done in the area of formal reflection on ritual in the process of growth toward spiritual maturity, on the process of spiritual direction itself as a ritual with real potency, and on the possibility of creating rituals that might engender a deepening of insight.

The place of communal ritual in the process of spiritual formation has also had little visibility in the spirituality literature, partly because of the individualist tendency in the field as a whole, and partly because communities are simply more difficult to study than individuals. In any basic course in the history of Christian spirituality, one is far more likely to study notable persons (Francis of Assisi, John Wesley, George Fox, for example) than notable communities of faith (the Franciscans, the Methodists, the Quakers), and the communal experience of these notable individuals is often treated as incidental to their spiritual formation. But a close reading of the work of the ritologists makes it immediately clear that this tendency toward individualism is likely to lead us away from a deep understanding of human spiritual experience, and that to introduce the category of community at each and every point of the discussion will get us closer to the true nature of Christian piety. Ritual is at the center of the bonded community of belonging, where values, worldviews, and identity are formed in and through ritual activity. Ritologists suggest that even when religious ritual is performed in solitary – the saying of a rosary or the lighting of a candle – it always implies a community, a community which has transmitted the technique of the ritual to the individual, and within which the meaning of the rite is held. Those who approach the field of ritual studies from an ethnographic or anthropological perspective point to the sociological stability of ritual communities; semioticists point to the sign value of the community itself; those who understand ritual from the perspective of drama theory understand the mutual relationship between the community of ritual actors and the empowerment of the individual as an actor in the world. The communal basis for all Christian life and thought, including spirituality, also has theological grounding, forcing us to take seriously what Karl Rahner (1971) called the "social horizon" of human existence.

Conclusion

There is little doubt that an engagement with ritual studies in any of its manifestations will complicate the work of students of Christian spirituality. Historians will find their hermeneutic task made more complex by the slipperiness of meaning and interpretation; observers of contemporary praxis will find themselves challenged by the ambiguity of their role as participant-observers; spiritual directors will be forced to evaluate both the constructive and destructive aspects of ritual behavior in their clients. All of us will find that the clear boundaries we have set for and within our discipline are not as clear as we have thought them to be. But, at the same time, those who wish accurately and sensitively to interpret the spiritual life of individuals and communities will find it rewarding to meet these challenges, and to incorporate the insights of this rich field of ritual study into their work. No crystal ball exists to tell us what the future of the dialogue between ritual studies and studies in Christian spirituality holds. In these pages, we have only been able to consider some of the possible changes that might take place in the field of Christian spirituality as a result of this dialogue.

But surely the interaction between the two disciplines, if undertaken with genuine commitment, will precipitate a change in both fields. Ritual studies may be called upon to reconsider its stance on the social construction of the self and on the infinite mutability of meaning. And those who see communal ritual behavior only as an aspect of group social-psychology may have to consider the idea that some real transcendent encounter must be included in any explanation of events. But the future of the field of ritual studies is not in our hands. Suffice it to say that the dissolving of boundaries between disciplines, and the move to a more holistic view of human personhood, cannot but transform the quest for understanding of the spiritual lives of Christian people.

References

Austin, J. L. [1961] 1975: *How to Do Things with Words*, 2nd edn. Cambridge, MA: Harvard University Press.

Bakhtin, M. 1981: *The Dialogic Imagination: Four Essays*. Austin, TX: University of Texas Press.

Barthes, R. 1972: *Mythologies*. New York: Farrar, Strauss, Giroux.

Bell, C. M. 1992: *Ritual Theory – Ritual Practice*. Oxford: Oxford University Press.

Bettelheim, B. 1966: *The Empty Fortress*. New York: Macmillan.

——1975: *The Uses of Enchantment: The Meaning and Importance of Fairy Tales*. New York: Alfred Knopf.

Brook, P. [1968] 1982: *The Empty Space*. Harmondsworth: Pelican.

Douglas, M. 1982: *Natural Symbols: Explorations in Cosmology*. New York: Knopf.

——2002: *Purity and Danger: An Analysis of the Concepts of Pollution and Taboo*. New York: Routledge.

Eliade, M. 1961: *Images and Symbols: Studies in Religious Symbolism*. London: Harvill Press.

Erikson, E. 1977: *Toys and Reasons: Stages in the Ritualization of Experience*. New York: W. W. Norton.

Gadamer, H-G. 1999: *Hermeneutics, Religion, and Ethics*. New Haven, CT: Yale University Press.

Geertz, C. 1977: *Interpretation of Cultures*. New York: Basic Books.

——1983: "From the native's point of view": on the nature of anthropological understanding. In *Local Knowledge: Further Essays in Interpretive Anthropology*, pp. 55–70. New York: Basic Books.

Goffman, E. 1959: *The Presentation of Self in Everyday Life*. Garden City, NY: Doubleday.

——1963: *Behavior in Public Places: Notes on the Social Organization of Gatherings*. Glencoe, NY: The Free Press.

——1967: *Interaction Ritual: Essays on Face-to-face Behavior*. New York: Doubleday/Anchor.

——1969: *Strategic Interaction*. Philadelphia: University of Pennsylvania Press.

——1974: *Frame Analysis: An Essay on the Organization of Experience*. New York: Harper and Row.

Grimes, R. L. 1982: *Beginnings in Ritual Studies*. Lanham, MD: University Press of America.

——1993: *Reading, Writing, and Ritualizing: Ritual in Fictive, Liturgical and Public Places*. Washington, DC: Pastoral Press.

Grotowski, J. 1968: *Towards a Poor Theater*. New York: Simon and Schuster.

Otto, R. [1917] 1950: *The Idea of the Holy*, 2nd edn. Oxford: Oxford University Press.

Pierce, C. S. 1992–8: *The Essential Pierce*, 2 vols. Bloomington, IN: Indiana University Press.

Rahner, K. 1971: *Theological Investigations*, vol. 8: *Further Theology of the Spiritual Life*. New York: Herder and Herder.

Rappaport, R. 1999: *Ritual and Religion in the Making of Humanity*. Cambridge: Cambridge University Press.

Ricoeur, P. 1971: A model of the text: meaningful action considered as a text. *Social Research* 8, 529–62.

Smith, J. Z. 1987: *To Take Place: Toward a Theory of Ritual*. Chicago: University of Chicago Press.

Tambiah, S. J. 1979: A performance approach to ritual. *Proceedings of the British Academy* 65, 113–69.

——1981: *A Performance Approach to Ritual*. New York: State Mutual Book and Periodical Service.

Turner, V. W. 1969: *The Ritual Process: Structure and Anti-structure*. Chicago: Aldine.

——1974: *Dramas, Fields and Metaphors: Symbolic Action in Human Society*. Ithaca, NY: Cornell University Press.

Van Gennep, A. 1960: *The Rites of Passage*. Chicago: University of Chicago Press.

CHAPTER 23

Theology of Religions

Michael Barnes

Even a couple of decades ago, the interface between Christian spirituality and the great religions would have been lightly patronized as a fringe activity. Now it is treated with a good deal more seriousness. The scholarly discipline of spirituality has emerged as an important complement to theology, as many chapters in this volume testify. While the other side of the interface may be more problematic and diffuse, it still raises questions which are as fundamental to Christian spirituality as they are to the more familiar realms of theology and philosophy. What is the nature and source of that extraordinary energy that is human religiosity? How does Christianity relate to the great world religions? And what do those ancient traditions and ever-changing practices of faith have to say about Christian discipleship and the Christian account of human destiny?

With its provenance set deep in nineteenth-century positivist accounts of historical development, the portentously named "history of religions" seems too monochrome and limiting a term to cope adequately with the dangerously fragmented world of contemporary religion. Its successor discipline, religious studies, is made up of a number of forms and methods of investigation. In recent years, two have achieved some prominence: first, an approach which begins with typically "religious" phenomena, such as myth, ritual, prayer, canon, creed, and relates them to fairly well-defined, discrete "religious traditions" such as Hinduism, Islam, and Christianity; secondly, an approach which is less concerned with the various traditions as such than with religion in relation to wider society, culture, and politics (Woodhead 2002). In practice, however, the two work together. What has changed is less the subject matter itself than the broader context or overlapping backgrounds that have to be taken into account. Today, scholarly interest in religion seeks to combine anthropological, psychological, and sociological with "purely" historical and philological readings. Not only has scholarship made available a wide range of texts and commentaries, the *living* tradition of contemporary practice adds a new complexity to the quest for understanding what will always remain a complex and elusive subject.

As with history of religions, religious studies seeks to understand religion through objective observation, a process which clearly begs awkward questions not just about the nature and essence of religion but, more subtly, about what in "the religious" is *available* for study (Byrne 1988: 20). It may not be necessary to be an active believer in order to understand a tradition; indeed, a degree of disinterested scholarly scrutiny is as necessary to theology as it is to anthropology or psychology of religion. But the religious imagination is a curious beast and not even the most hard-nosed of positivist historians would deny that a degree of empathetic engagement is needed if religious phenomena are to be appreciated not just as human institutions patent of academic investigation like any other but as what their practitioners claim them to be: windows into ultimate reality and sources of human transformation. Clearly, a range of responses is possible, but the once hard-and-fast distinction between the committed communication of a tradition proper to theology and the more detached methods of religious studies cannot be one of them. If the former has recovered its roots in the liturgical practice and doxology of the Christian church, the latter has begun to find a tentative role for normative as well as purely descriptive accounts of the different world religions. A decade ago, a book entitled *Buddhist Theology* (Jackson and Makransky 2000) would have been unthinkable; even today it raises a quizzical eyebrow. But its authors only claim to be doing what Christian theology has done for centuries: applying the wisdom of the tradition to the questions that a complex multicultural society raises for human living.

To some extent, of course, the academy is only responding to what is happening at the interface of church and society – Vatican II's "church in the modern world." Judaism has long been a familiar, if distinctly problematic, part of the Western religious scene. Now there are Hindu, Sikh, and Buddhist diasporas throughout Europe and North America, while Islam is arguably the fastest growing and most diverse of all the new immigrant communities. Vatican II did more than rubber-stamp the growing interest in inter-religious dialogue. *Nostra aetate*, the declaration on the relationship of the church to non-Christian religions, stated explicitly that the Christian church rejects "nothing that is true and holy in these religions" and calls on Christians to "recognize, preserve and encourage the spiritual and moral good things" found among people of other faiths (para. 2). This revolutionary shift in attitude, setting out a new trajectory for Christian self-understanding, began with the painful retrieval of a sense of the church's intrinsic relationship with its "primary other," the Jews, the people of the covenant which has never been revoked, and setting that defining relationship within a whole series of dialogues with "other others." Since then, a great deal of practical wisdom has been learned and a whole new genre of theological literature has developed – the "theology of religions." The old chestnut about the salvation of the non-Christian has ceased to be an issue. Implicit in the work of Karl Rahner – what makes his celebrated theory of the Anonymous Christian much more than an exercise in Christian imperialism – is a question about the *means* of salvation. If, as Rahner argues, people of other faiths are saved not *despite* their ancient traditions of faith but precisely *through* them, then this must mean that such religions have a positive role to play in the unfolding of God's providential purposes for humankind (see Rahner 1978).

This is not a position that has acquired universal acceptance in church circles, but it does raise an unavoidable issue for Christian theologians and historians of religion alike: the *theological significance* of other religions. Wilfred Cantwell Smith (1976: 16) once famously remarked: "we explain the fact that the Milky Way is there by the doctrine of creation, but how do we explain the fact that the *Bhagavad Gita* is there?" The same question might be raised about the Qu'rān, about Gotama the Buddha, about the Sikh tradition, about Zoroastrianism and the Jains. Or even about Torah. What are they all *for*? Purely contingent phenomena that invite Christians to redouble the missionary effort? Or are they saying something important to Christians about what God is doing in a multi-faith world?

These are, of course, theological questions and in raising them I hope it is clear that I am less interested in chronicling an engagement between the academic disciplines of Christian spirituality and religious studies than in describing the broader context which a whole spectrum of engagements, from theology to political relations, brings to any account of "the religions." That may sound like an excuse for muddying the waters. But, if Christian spirituality is concerned with the lived experience of Christian faith and discipleship, then context – the "edges" of a life which is always lived under the influence of the Spirit of Christ – becomes crucially significant. To anticipate the argument of this chapter: the formative experience of Christian faith, the *kenosis* of Christ who submits in faithful obedience to the will of the Father, necessarily places Christians on the borders of an engagement with what is always "other." In elucidating this point, my first task is to expand further on the rapprochement between theology and the multi-faceted world of religious pluralism which has led to the emergence of a new theological discipline, the theology of religions. There is no space to do more than allude to the wider social and political dimensions of this context here. But it is important at least to raise it in order to give adequate attention to the nature of religion and the challenge that the plurality of religions raises for Christian living and spirituality.

Theology of Religions: Paradigms and Beyond

The theological debate about the religions has centered largely around versions of a "threefold paradigm" – exclusivism, inclusivism, and pluralism. This attempt to map the development of the theology of religions has its origins in the work of Alan Race (1983), who takes his inspiration from John Hick (1973, 1989). As a survey of a decidedly intractable area of study, this approach has been highly influential. Unfortunately, as Gavin D'Costa remarks, it also has the disadvantage of forcing "diverse material into easily controlled locations" (1997: 637). Suggestions for a way forward through reorganizing the original map or drawing up further paradigms (see especially Dupuis 1997) have not met with general approval. The weakness of an approach through theological "types" is that it actually stifles debate by favoring a pluralist agenda; the three positions are linked in a sort of hierarchy, ranked according to their openness to the other. What this misses is any attention to the *theological significance of the other* which is revealed in the process of dialogue. Hence, the distinction I advocate between a "theology *for* dialogue" and a "theology *of* dialogue" (Barnes 1989, 2002). The former, including the various approaches categorized in the threefold paradigm, is mainly concerned with the justification of certain *a priori* theories about religion or the relationship of religions. A theology *of* dialogue commends a different starting-point. Here theology emerges from reflection not on the *results* of dialogue but on the implications for Christian faith of the experience of being *in dialogue*, in relationship with the other. This does not mean, however, that a theology of dialogue is merely an alternative to, or extension of, the threefold paradigm – a further "fourth model." Rather, a theology of dialogue has a different logical status: not a theoretical exercise which attempts to situate the other in a Christianity-centered world, but a *prior* exercise of responsible attention to the role that the other – what is "not-self" – in all its forms, plays in the formation of Christian faith. What theological significance does the inter-personal encounter hold for Christian faith and living?

In addressing this question, it is important to note that, to use Panikkar's terms, the "dialogical dialogue" cannot be neatly separated from the "dialectical dialogue" (1984). People need the particular languages of faith if they are to make themselves understood. In other words, faith is shaped by textual traditions. But the time is long past when such traditions occupied separate cultural spaces. The *Bhagavad Gita* is more familiar than the Old Testament to many Indian Christians; compendiums of religious wisdom are freely available in the West, from the poetry of Rumi to the sayings of the desert fathers. Both within the academy and in the more free-wheeling world of popular spirituality, it is possible to think in terms of a different and more creative approach to inter-religious relations than is allowed by the prescriptions of the paradigm approach. The recent development of "comparative theology," for instance, pioneered most successfully by Francis Clooney, is best understood as an exercise in imaginative dialogue in which the hymns, prayers, and commentaries of one religious tradition are allowed to speak to similar texts from another (Clooney 1993, 1996, 2001). What such a cross-textual reading assumes, however, is the faith that expects meaning to emerge from the engagement. For many people in the multicultural West, it is a short step from encountering the "textual other" to the more open-ended inter-personal dialogue of faith.

If the availability of canonical texts and scriptures has created a mood of familiarity with other religions, it has also sensitized Christians to the political and ethical dimensions of what are very much living and changing traditions of faith. David Tracy has accustomed us to think of theology as addressing three "publics" – the academy, the church, and society at large (Tracy 1982: 6ff). I would want to argue that the religions make a fourth. This is not to say that there is some discrete essence of religion which it is the joint task of theologians and historians of religion to uncover. Nor is it to deny that society includes religion. My point is that the very complexity of "the religious" cannot be subsumed within any neat theoretical framework; it is an irreducible dimension of the context within which contemporary Christian theology and spirituality are to be pursued. Although this essay is not concerned with inter-religious dialogue as such, some degree of overlap is inevitable. When "the religions" existed in the Western consciousness as systems of belief, dialogue took place at a fairly abstract level;

"comparative religion" identified the continuities and analogies between Christianity and other religions, usually to the detriment of the latter. That somewhat romantic view of inter-religious relations has long given way to a more hard-headed political version which confronts all societies today. A history of pogroms and excommunications, crusades and *jihad* continues to affect inter-religious relations. Violence thousands of miles away – riots in Gujerat, terrorist outrages in Kashmir, war in Iraq – all have their repercussions in the inner-cities of Europe and North America where large immigrant communities have established themselves. It is a truism expressed in that curious term "globalization," which suggests that the world is connected by intricate webs of political and economic power. What is often ignored, however, is the role that religion, culture, and the traditional forms of self-identification have to play in the preservation – and demolition – of such structures.

This is not a "9/11 issue" – though it has undoubtedly gained in public awareness through the appalling attacks on the World Trade Center and the Pentagon on September 11, 2001. Nor is it just a question arising from the Christian–Muslim encounter and the perplexity with which "the West" confronts the vast yet fragmented civilization that is Islam. In some degree, all the major religions in today's world are experiencing a sense of weakness. A deep-seated insecurity often results in retreat into a self-defining religious enclave. What is all too easily denounced as fundamentalism cannot, of course, be reduced to a few all-embracing universals. Nevertheless, it is arguable that it represents the other face of globalization, a reaction to homogenizing forces which seeks solace and support within carefully defined religious enclaves. An inward-looking nostalgia then seeks a scapegoat, a target, both within and without, which must feel the force of a deeply felt anger. The ultra-nationalist *hindutva* movement in India, for instance, has constructed a very specific myth of origins which manipulates the broad Hindu tradition into a virulent anti-Muslim and anti-Christian polemic. But it also targets less obvious scapegoats, such as *dalit* groups regarded as subverting the caste-system that gives the ruling elite its power. Other examples could be chosen; it would be a melancholy task to catalogue them all. Human religiosity is an ambiguous phenomenon, capable of both the most sublime creations of the human spirit and of deeply corrupt deformations. Whether in traditional rural villages which have been suddenly "globalized" by modern communications, or on the multi-faith streets of modern cities in the West, where immigrant communities have to adapt to a thoroughly pluralist environment, problems arise when the undoubted power of religious creeds and ideas gets turned into ideology and manipulated for political ends.

Hans Küng insists that there can be no peace between the nations without peace between the religions (see Küng and Kuschel 1993). In an obvious sense he is right; religion is a complicating issue in so many of the conflicts and wars in today's world. At another level, he begs a question about the relationship between religion and whatever it is that makes for nationhood. Not only is the complex ecology of history, religion, and culture always a matter of considerable obscurity, it is impossible to extract some agreed minimum of ethical values from the world's religions without doing violence to the delicate patterns of human meaning that sustain them. Before "religion" is defined away as a set of different traditions, it is an *energy*, a source of motivation.

Nevertheless, Küng's "global ethic" project does point to an issue of ever-growing significance. If the dividing line between religion and politics is breaking down, then theology of religions cannot rest content with adjusting the old Christianity-centered map of religious relations or even with drawing up a new one. A more intractable agenda is appearing – one for which there is as yet no map. No doubt the boundaries between peoples have been breaking down ever since our earliest ancestors started moving from warfare to subsistence economies. But today's religious fragmentation only makes more acute questions about why boundaries are there in the first place, how particular local interests are to be maintained in face of the power of overarching centralizing global interests – and, most awkwardly, about what contribution religion can make to whatever people understand by the "common good." Very quickly, the encounter of religions – whether conducted in the academic seminar or in more intimate dialogue between individuals sharing their experience of faith – penetrates beneath the superficial exchange of commonalities to confront a vast number of unruly factors that cannot be constrained by the benign pluralism of liberal modernity, still less by the *diktat* of ecclesial authority.

In summary, theology of religions cannot rest content with some sort of "fourth paradigm." That would be to compound the original problem, erecting a further *a priori* scheme which fails to account for the theological significance of all manner of "otherness" for Christian faith. Rather, the theological "types" need to be taken back to their origins and rooted in practice. This is the approach advocated by Charles Mathewes who, in a remarkably fresh and insightful article (1998), associates the three types not with theological schools as such but with the three theological virtues. In these terms, "exclusivism" witnesses to that faith which speaks of what it knows through the specificity of tradition; "inclusivism" looks forward in hope to the fulfillment of all authentically religious truth and value; "pluralism" itself expresses that love which seeks always to affirm the values of faith and hope in the present. This shift of attention – from consideration of the specific *objects* of theological study to the nature of the theological *subject*, the community of faith that exists in irreducible relationship with "the other" – makes for a more ethically as well as theologically nuanced account of the rich complexity of inter-religious relations than is allowed by a prescriptive or "normative pluralism."

Elsewhere, I have myself attempted to sketch the terms of a theology of religions which makes a deliberate point of working out of the "dimension of otherness within which *all* Christian theology is to be done" (Barnes 2002: 28). My argument is that a theology which takes seriously the many dimensions of today's multi-faith reality can no longer be conceived as a strategy for disarming a troublesome other. The crucial question is not how Christians are to develop theories of religious meaning, but how they are to shift attention from theory altogether to the skills and dispositions which sustain people in their pursuit of meaning. What may be termed the Christian *habitus* is learned in the living out of the tradition, beginning with the liturgical celebration of memories and the transmission and re-imagining of life-giving stories, and continuing with the various practices of faithful discipleship which they support, from commitment to justice and peace issues to the relationship with other persons of faith. In the final chapter of that book (Barnes 2002), therefore, I deliberately return to the practice of inter-religious engagement and to the ethical and political demands that it makes on Christian living. Understood as the "negotiation of the middle," the dialogue with the other is never complete and always provisional. It takes time and cannot be reduced to a few rules and precepts, still less to a programmatic theological scheme. In this process of open-ended and unpredictable negotiation is implied a Christian *spirituality* of religions.

Spirituality and the Religions: "Schools of the Spirit"

I shall leave it to other chapters in this present volume to unpick the unruly strands of the symbiosis between theology and spirituality. But that discussion cannot be entirely avoided here, if only because the tension between theology and dialogue, so lucidly illustrated by Race (2001), raises questions about the significance of the relationship with the other for Christian faith and practice. Race's point is that the "twin tracks" of theology and dialogue can only be brought into a creative alignment through religious practice and experience, by individuals and communities being prepared to enter sympathetically into the spiritual life of the other. In this he is expressing a common experience, almost an interfaith cliché, that dialogue begins when people, not systems, meet. The question for Christian spirituality is clear. How is the Christian life to be lived in such a way that the relationship with the other becomes not an awkward problem to be theorized away but *an intrinsic dimension of that transformative vision of Christian personhood which is revealed in the paschal mystery of the death and resurrection of Christ?* To put it in more explicitly theological terms, how can the many dimensions of Christian engagement with other persons of faith – from neighborly concern to more formal theological dialogue – be said to reveal something of *the* Other, of God?

When used within the broader frame of religious studies, "spirituality" often assumes an almost iconic status to account for the significance of "the religious" in a post-secular age. At stake here is the relation between tradition and religious experience. If organized religion in its traditional form is on the decline, what Paul Heelas calls "spiritualities of life" or "self-spirituality," an eclectic mix which acknowledges only the authority of personal concern or conviction, has become a guiding concept (in Woodhead 2002: 362). All too often the term "spirituality" is used as a general designation for "the spiritual" or "the sacralization of life" or, even more vaguely, as some sort of cross-religious sense of personal connectedness. Following in the footsteps of Hick's normative pluralism, Race strangely subverts his perceptive analysis by opting for a version of Wayne Teasdale's tautological concept of "interspirituality." The danger here is that the "inter" of interfaith is given such uncritical prominence that a syncretistic hybrid is unwittingly constructed which fails to engage with the particular languages and symbol-systems that make up the various traditions of faith. But it is precisely the force of the "inter" of spirituality, the experience of existing "between," in irreducible relationship with the other, that needs more philosophical analysis than ill-defined generalities like "vital connection" and "universal responsibility" allow (Teasdale 1999: 27–8). Although philosophers of religion like Hick have stressed the ethical element of the encounter of religions and brought theology and the data of religious studies into a dialogue, surprisingly little attention is ever paid to the nature of theology as *intrinsically* related to spirituality, the broad context of religious living. The pluralist agenda, both in its account of the history of religions and in its rewriting of the history of Christian engagement with the other, masks a model of theology as a largely theoretical exercise in the ordering of human experience of the divine. The fallacy of such an approach is obvious: God is ultimate mystery, not the "metaphysical object" of some speculative quest. However the relationship between theology and spirituality is to be conceived, some sort of *aufhebung* (elevation) of the dialectic into a supposedly universal spiritual wisdom simply will not do. Christian theology is not an intellectualist vision "above the action" but a rooting *in* the action, a response to the God who is always incarnate as "Emmanuel," a prophetic presence in the mysterious "between" which defines all human living. *A fortiori* is this true of a theology which would seek to explore the complex world of religious faith. To put it another way, theology is less about exploring the nature of God than about *communicating*, through practices as diverse as prayer and inter-religious encounter, the implications for human living of what God says about God.

The problem, however, lies not just with the "speculative model" of theology and its problematic modes of relating to "the other." If theology of religions is to recover a sense of its roots in the practice of faith, in prayer and spirituality, then it is necessary also to question an account of "the religions" as different versions of some generalized spiritual belief and practice. Such an account fails to make adequate reference to the particular processes of historical and cultural formation that make them unique. It is, of course, possible to posit some sort of common foundation or essence for the religions, to seek out and build on the "family resemblances" between religious traditions: the mythical, the devotional, the scriptural, the ethical, and so on. Religions are built out of particular fabrics of scripture and story, belief and custom, prayer and devotion, which yet overlap with each other. On closer examination, however, the terms of any analogy or comparison are often put into question. Holy founders, for instance, do not fulfill the same role in all religions; nor do apparently common features such as sacred books and symbolic representation. The problem with an account of religion conceived in global terms is that it subordinates what are essentially fluid processes of interpersonal teaching and learning to the demands of the ideal conceptual scheme. There is, in other words, much more to "religion" than a generic term for an infinitely adaptable variation on some universal spiritual theme.

It is now taken for granted that the great world religions are not discrete versions of some transhistorical essence but complex historical constructions. It is a peculiarly modern idea that religions stand *above* culture; whatever truth there may be in this, first and foremost religions are products *of* culture. This is not to say that they do not remain significant and unique visions of an ultimate truth, only that there is no vision that has not been refracted through the perspectives and prejudices of centuries of human interaction. Hinduism is only the most obvious example. The religion of India – more exactly, of course, a whole series of philosophies, devotions, practices, and ways of life associated with the sub-continent – was invented by missionaries and colonial administrators through analogy with the deism of the Enlightenment *philosophes* (Halbfass 1988). More recent accounts stress the strangely integrative capacity of the Sanskritic tradition to hold together a number of seemingly disparate strands of religious practice (Lipner 1994). Buddhism too has benefited not just from the scholarship that has flowed from the dissemination of hitherto esoteric material in the West, but also from a more nuanced notion of the origins of the *Buddhadharma* in the brahmanical tradition (Williams 1989). This is where history provides an important corrective to anthropological abstractions about the nature of religion. "There cannot be a universal definition of religion," says Talal Asad, "not only because its constituent elements and relationships are historically specific, but because that definition is itself the historical product of discursive processes" (1993: 29). In other words, religion as a configuration of symbolic forms cannot be separated from the practices and disciplines of faith which give it a particular form.

This suggests a more evocative model of religion than the "map" image noted earlier. Given Wilfred Cantwell Smith's retrieval of the concept of faith as forming "cumulative traditions," an idea which has received powerful expression in Christian theological terms by Nicholas Lash (1996), it makes better sense to understand religions as rather like centers of teaching and learning which seek to form and educate a particular group of people by introducing them to the collective wisdom of the group. Such a school seeks to encourage an imaginative dialogue between an ancient wisdom and the traditions that it seeks to enhance and preserve, on the one hand, and the wider world beyond the group which it encounters and by which it is challenged, on the other. In this sense, a Christian might want to describe religions as "schools of the Spirit," insofar as they reflect the work of the Spirit which activates and enlivens the memory of the past, while at the same time giving concrete expression to the virtue of hope, anticipating new and unexpected forms of God's providential action in the world.

Such a "school of the Spirit" model of religion encourages precisely that creative engagement with the other that is at the heart of good spirituality. If this is correct, then it raises the question: how can Christian spirituality both support the integrity of commitment that is demanded by the discipleship of Christ *and* build virtues – not just faith, hope and love, but also patience, hospitality and generosity – which are appropriate expressions of that discipleship in today's multi-faith world? Shortly I shall examine a concept of spirituality which quite consciously attempts to cross religious boundaries – that associated with the work of Raimon Panikkar. Prior to that, however, it is necessary to stay for a moment with the questions noted above and to link them with the assertion that religions are processes of learning before they are institutionalized as complexes of belief.

Given that this essay takes as its theme the experience of Christian faith engaged with "the other," let me expand briefly on Mark McIntosh's understanding of spirituality as a "discovery of the true 'self' precisely in *encountering* the divine and human other" (1998: 5). McIntosh is not concerned with inter-religious issues as such, but he does preface his study with the hope that analogies between spiritual practices will emerge as the dialogue continues. He thus reminds us that Christian spirituality and theology begin not with the isolation of some supposed religious universal but with the articulation of the historical particularity of faith. In challenging the popular notion that spirituality is concerned with identifying a core of "inner" experience which in some mysterious way grounds all religious traditions, his definition roots spirituality not in interiority as such but in the more complex experience of relationality – an experience which, I want to argue, is intrinsic to Christian life, discipleship, and prayer.

Spirituality and the Spirit: The Dimensions of Practice

In these terms Christian spirituality is not a "thing" but a task, the task faced by every believer: to respond to that question which emerges from the experience of loss and transformation which is the paschal mystery. In what is arguably the foundational narrative for all Christian spirituality, the appearance on the road to Emmaus, a shattered world is unexpectedly put back together by the encounter with the stranger on the road. The two disciples recognize the risen Lord over a meal, in a borderline between ordinary and extraordinary experience, between the prosaic sharing of bread and the moment in which the broken pattern mends itself and forms again. In Lucan terms, the passage looks forward to the experience of the church in Acts where the disciples are continually led by the Spirit into new ways of exploring and explaining to others what is always *God's* mission. Paul before the Areopagus is in some ways the story of failure; many of the Athenians laughed when Paul mentioned God raising Jesus from the dead. But it is also the first example of what has come to be called "inculturation," the experiment of speaking the truth in a new language. Paul was not just translating Jewish terminology, finding word equivalents in another language. More obviously, he was acting like the Jesus of the Emmaus story – bringing the conviction that the Spirit always goes ahead of the church, inspiring new encounters, into line with the "given story," the concrete historical form or memory of the Christ-event.

Success or failure is immaterial. What this practice of faith builds is what I called above the Christian *habitus*: a sensitivity and a critical generosity which is prepared to learn how the mystery of God's self-revealing love – Father and Son united in the Spirit of love – is often to be discerned in the engagement with persons of different faiths. I may well learn something about the other which points me back to my own faith and to what I know of the "Spirit of Christ." To that extent I may also learn more about my own faith. But to say that I "learn more" is only to stress that I enter more deeply into the trinitarian mystery; I become more sensitive to the way in which the Spirit always seeks to impart the form – the form revealed in Christ – taken by God's self-revealing love. This is what Christians will always seek to do – to seek to relate the strange, unknown, and unexpected to what is revealed in Christ. But this is – to be more exact – the work of the Spirit. The Spirit enables Christians to look in *two directions* at once. As the ultimate agent of God's self-revelation, the Spirit is always unseen and therefore beyond human imaginings. But as the "Spirit of Christ" the Spirit always points back to Christ, reminding the church of the shape that Christian living and discipleship takes – the following of Jesus of Nazareth. In bringing the two movements together, the Spirit inspires Christians not just to imagine new ways in which the Kingdom which Jesus proclaimed can be made present in our contemporary world, but also to discern the "seeds of the Word" which through the ever-creative Spirit of God are *already* there. However, if Christians are to respond generously to that vision and to speak the words of prophecy that witness to everything the Spirit teaches, they still need to ask how that vision is to be born and how it is to grow. That is the task of a spirituality which would teach a vision of the Christian life lived in that ambiguous and sometimes threatening world that crosses religious boundaries.

If the particular school of the Spirit that is Christianity can be described in some such terms, how are we to relate it to other analogous schools? How does the vision of Christian life and spirituality which this school teaches become genuinely open to the other and not just a covert form of Christian imperialism? One of the few attempts that have been made to mend the divide between Christianity-centered readings of other religions and the more bland pluralist mappings of the universe of faiths is that of Raimon Panikkar, particularly in his brilliant meditation on the Trinity (1973). Panikkar begins that work by defining "any given spirituality" as "one typical way of handling the human condition . . . [which] represents man's basic attitude *vis-à-vis* his ultimate end" (1973: 9). He wants some way of crossing religious boundaries, some term which expresses the similarities between religions without simply reducing them to a few abstractions. Spirituality he considers a broader and more flexible term than religion. "One religion, in fact, may include several spiritualities, because spirituality is not directly bound up with any dogma or institution. It is rather an attitude of mind which one may ascribe to different religions" (1973: 9). That is to say that, while it can never be separated from particular religious phenomena, such as ritual and myth and dogmatic beliefs, spirituality somehow manages to transcend them. Where the term religion is largely conterminous with the belief system of a group or community, spirituality crosses cultural and religious boundaries because it focuses on practice, especially on the different forms of prayer which provide the inner energy or motivation for action. To that extent, a spirituality is almost by definition cross-religious. Where religions often divide, spirituality – as described by Panikkar – unites.

Panikkar uses this concept to expound his own typology of three fundamental forms of cross-religious spirituality. This he takes from the Hindu *trimarga*, three ways of spiritual practice, *karma*, *bhakti*, and *jñana*. Literally, these are the way of "work," the way of "devotion" or "loyalty," and the way of "gnosis" or mystical knowing. They can be translated as ritual, devotion, and – less happily – meditation. In Panikkar's terms: *iconolatry*, *personalism*, and *advaita*. The history of Indian religions, Panikkar's immediate inspiration, would order the *trimarga* according to the Vedic, Upanisadic, and Puranic phases of development. Putting it all too briefly, the formality and magical esotericism of the sacrificial cult inspired first the pursuit of interior certainty through yogic and other ascetic practices and then various forms of love mysticism, beginning with the intellectualist devotion of the *Bhagavad Gita* and culminating in more intensely affective not to say erotic texts such as the *Bhagavata Purana*. It would, no doubt, be possible to trace similar developments within other religious traditions.

The formality of Islamic *jum'a* prayer, for instance, is complemented by the love mysticism of the Sufi *tariqas*, while there is an argument for seeing in Buddhist meditation, a version of the *jñanamarga*, an intensification of the ritual of the taking of the refuges. Panikkar's interest, however, is less phenomenological and analytic than theological. Ultimately, he sees three forms of spirituality or three dimensions of authentic human living as reflecting the inner life of the Trinity: the spirituality of the Father supported by the virtue of obedience which ritual commands, that of the Son by the love inspired by God's self-revelation, that of the Spirit by "the supra-rational experience of a 'Reality' which in some way 'inhales' us into himself" (1973: 29). But the three spiritualities are only three in the sense that they are discernible stages or aspects of a single process. Panikkar's key point is that the three forms are interconnected and interdependent, with one leading to and, as it were, inspiring another in a never-ending movement of giving and receiving. Any mature account of the spiritual life demands that a balance be maintained among the three. The task, in other words, is to integrate the practices of faith and the virtues they form. Otherwise, he implies, a purely ritual spirituality will develop an excessive formalism or even idolatry; a spirituality fixated on personal devotion risks an anthropomorphism which is little different from a vaguely "spiritualized" humanism; a purely meditative spirituality, with its pursuit of an inner gnosis, may lead to what he calls "angelism," a disembodied pantheism. Only in the Trinity and, therefore, in what Panikkar calls the "theandric mystery" is a resolution to be found.

Integration and Interdependence

Panikkar's approach is persuasive but still problematic. How is spirituality as an "attitude of mind" any more than a collusion in the cultural status quo? How can it avoid the obsession with interior states of consciousness that characterizes so much of contemporary spirituality, especially those that are often cultivated through the "dialogue of religious experience" with forms of Eastern meditation? More awkwardly, can the Christian doctrine of the Trinity ever become the basis of interfaith relations?

These questions cannot be addressed at any depth here. I want to focus on one key point: Panikkar's conviction that a balanced spiritual life must seek to integrate different spiritualities into a single life. In this, Panikkar follows in the footsteps of the Jewish personalist philosopher, Franz Rosenzweig, whose magisterial philosophical study *Star of Redemption* (1970) is a brilliant apologetic for a Judaism whose destiny is to be found in its intrinsic relationship with Christianity. The key to understanding his dialogical philosophy lies with the complex inter-relation of three elements, God, World, and Man, and the relations which unfold between them – Creation, Revelation, and Redemption. In this process, Rosenzweig argues that Jews and Christians have equally necessary and complementary roles to play. There is a curious anticipation here of Panikkar's "theandric mystery," particularly with regard to the mutual dependence or indwelling (*perichoresis*, perhaps, to allow Panikkar his trinitarian vocabulary) of a threefold spirituality and the three-personed God of which it is a distant trace. Panikkar finishes with a rhetorical flourish in commending a:

spirituality which combines in an authentic synthesis the three dimensions of our life on earth as well as in heaven. In it are to be found *contemplation* that is something more than thought, *action* which does not limit its purview to a building of the earthly city . . . [I]n short, a sense of the Spirit that is not discarnate combined with a sense of Incarnation that does not neglect the Spirit, an *affirmation* that is not exclusive and a *negation* that is not closed in upon itself. (1973: 82)

Panikkar's infuriatingly allusive essay is a unique example of a Christian theology of religions based on spirituality and religious practice. The objection is that he too easily takes for granted an *a priori* triadic pattern in the forms of human meaning-making which is supposed to mirror the triune life within the Godhead. As an account of "the religions," or even of spirituality, his essay remains highly schematic and doubtfully coherent. And his tendency to assimilate the supposedly cross-religious spiritualities to particular religions – Buddhism, for instance, as typically the "spirituality of the Father," Vedantic Hinduism the "spirituality of the Spirit" – while in many ways brilliantly illuminating, does rather take away from the openness and fluidity of the "attitudes of mind" with which he begins. Rowan Williams's careful critique, which finds Panikkar "sketchy on origins" (2000: 171), is an important reminder of a point noted above that no practice of faith takes place in some cultural and historical vacuum. Spirituality is tradition-specific, Christian or Buddhist or Hindu, at least in the sense that practices of self-transformation are dependent on the living out of the tradition which has formed a community in a particular way. Panikkar's universal and invariant "attitudes of mind," which cross the religious boundaries, cannot properly be understood without attending to important questions about how practices of faith are developed in the first place, and how *historically* they relate to each other. There is, to repeat, no "view from nowhere," no vantage point "above the action" which enables persons of faith to pontificate about spiritual verities in splendid isolation from the particular practice of faith. As McIntosh insists, spirituality and theology do not exist "apart from concrete historical life" (1998: 5).

This is where Christian spirituality and the various disciplines that make up the study of religions begin to converge. If the term "spirituality" is to have any purchase on the unhappily diffuse interfaith world of conflicting religious languages, then the *specific* context of myth, ritual, and devotion which shapes interiority has to be borne in mind. Thus historians of religion will always be at pains to uncover those historical and cultural processes that have led to the development of particular religious practices. Considerable light has been shone on the origins of Christianity by setting them within the cultural matrix of Second Temple Judaism; that relationship formed Christian faith and practice in a very particular way. But something analogous can be said for other inter-religious relationships. Early Buddhism, for instance, emerged from the "renouncer culture" which reacted against the Upanisadic traditions of Vedic Hinduism. And Islam, so often represented in monolithic terms, betrays variations of practice and belief that can be traced back to the early years of its formation – and particularly to its volatile relationship with its semitic predecessors. What are often stereotyped as separate traditions frequently reveal, on closer inspection, less obvious borders and distinctions than might once have been imagined.

A Matter for Discernment: Word and Spirit

The interface between Christian spirituality and the religions, as I have sought to describe it, is not about how to spice up Christian prayer and liturgy with a few esoteric touches of "Oriental mysticism." Nor is it about the sharing of some dimly perceived spiritual essence. My argument has been that, if Christian spirituality is about *lived* experience, then the very ambiguity of religion – its capacity to create and destroy – can be a source of growth and the radicalizing of faith. So often there is discovered on the borders of inter-religious relations a lack of completeness, a disarming sense of radical otherness, which demands a return and yet further engagement. In Christian terms, the "seeds of the Word" take time to discern. The question raised by Panikkar's analysis is not, then, the comparatively straightforward matter of how to trace points of comparison between forms of religious practice but, much more painfully, *how to live with the tension that makes discernment possible*; that is to say, with the never-ending dialectic between form or *Logos* and the inexhaustible life of Spirit. Word and Spirit *together* speak out of the silence of the Father and unfold the inner life of the Godhead. Such a vision of God unfolding the purposes of God in the never-ending negotiation of a space shared with the other is surely why it makes sense to describe "the religions" by analogy with Christian faith as living "schools of the Spirit." The form of an ancient wisdom is preserved yet constantly finds new power and meaning by responding to new questions raised by "the other." Although very clearly distinct and different, the great religions are communities of struggling human beings before they become hardened into discrete systems of belief. What holds them all together is what holds all human beings together – the dimly sensed reality of the infinite at the heart of human existence.

Perhaps in the end the most effective criterion of discernment is that willingness to explore the ambiguity of human religiosity in the conviction that it is precisely here, on the edges of the human struggle, that *God* is at work. Christian spirituality nurtures a life of discipleship lived across religious boundaries which builds the virtues of inter-faith engagement in all its forms, a sensitivity to what God may be doing in the "schools of the Spirit," the religions of the world. The Spirit leads Christians into the truth by reminding them of the prophetic Word which goes on being spoken even in times and places of deep darkness. And the Spirit goes before the church, drawing its attention to all manner of ways and forms of God's loving presence, the "seeds of the Word," which the church does not know. This suggests an alternative to a model of the Spirit's role in the salvific economy as the communication of a power which is essentially vested in the Word of God. The danger with this way of thinking is that everything the church experiences is referred back to the Word as the normative self-revelation of God, *the* example of what God is like. It follows that other scriptures or other persons of faith only become valid insofar as they reflect what is to be found in Christian Scripture; other persons of faith have their own integrity only insofar as they conform to a model which is set by Christ. This, however, is to make the Spirit a sort of "secondary mediator" whose work is subordinated to that of the Word. It then becomes difficult to give other faiths a substantive role within the wider providential unfolding of God's purposes.

Another model, more sensitive to the church as itself a "school of the Spirit," living and working alongside other such schools, would recognize that *before* the Spirit points to what God is doing in Christ, the Spirit is at work within the paschal mystery itself. Here the Spirit does not continue the work of Christ in some more or less "linear" pattern (the Lucan emphasis) but points back, in more Johannine terms, to the mutual witness of Father and Son. In other words, the Spirit does not just inspire Christians to see the world in Christ and to speak words of prophecy in the name of Christ; *the Spirit brings to birth in Christians that relationship of trusting faith in God which the Spirit brings to birth in Christ.* The Spirit's role is to recreate in the hearts of believers the life-giving relationship of love that unites Father and Son. Put like that, it might seem as if the economy of salvation is more Christianity-centered not less. But that would be to mistake the role of the Spirit and to underplay the dimension of inexhaustible life that the Spirit represents. The Spirit makes possible what Rowan Williams calls the "translatability" of the mystery of Christ into the diversity of history (2000: 125), giving that mystery a freedom and unpredictability which can only be a source of wonder, not an excuse for overweening triumphalism. So, far from pressing the whole of religious experience into some sort of sub-ecclesial totality, an emphasis on spirituality, on the formative practice of Christian living and discipleship, gives "the other" a proper place within the providential unfolding of God's purposes.

References

Barnes, M. 1989: *Religions in Conversation*. London: SPCK.

―――2002: *Theology and the Dialogue of Religions*. Cambridge: Cambridge University Press.

Byrne, P. 1988: Religion and the religions. In S. Sutherland, L. Houlden, P. Clarke, et al. (eds), *The World's Religions*, pp. 3–28. London: Routledge.

Clooney, F. X. 1993: *Theology after Vedanta*. Albany, NY: State University of New York Press.

―――1996: *Seeing through Texts*. Albany, NY: State University of New York Press.

―――2001: *Hindu God, Christian God*. Oxford: Oxford University Press.

D'Costa, G. 1997: Theology of religions. In D. Ford (ed.), *The Modern Theologians*, 2nd edn, pp. 626–44. Oxford: Blackwell.

Dupuis, J. 1997: *Toward a Christian Theology of Religious Pluralism*. Maryknoll, NY: Orbis.

Halbfass, W. 1988: *India and Europe*. Albany, NY: State University of New York Press.

Hick, J. 1973: *God and the Universe of Faiths*. London: Macmillan.

―――1989: *The Interpretation of Religion*. London: Macmillan.

Jackson, R. and Makransky, J. 2000: *Buddhist Theology*. London: Curzon.

Küng, H. and Kuschel, K-J. (eds) 1993: *A Global Ethic*. London: SCM.

Lash, N. 1996: *The Beginning and the End of "Religion"*. Cambridge: Cambridge University Press.

Lipner, J. 1994: *Hindus*. London: Routledge.

McIntosh, M. 1998: *Mystical Theology*. Oxford: Blackwell.

Mathewes, C. T. 1998: Pluralism, otherness, and the Augustinian tradition. *Modern Theology* 14, 83–112.

Panikkar, R. 1973: *The Trinity and the Religious Experience of Man*. Maryland, NY: Orbis.

―――1984: The dialectical dialogue. In F. Whaling (ed.), *The World's Religious Traditions*, pp. 201–21. Edinburgh: T. and T. Clark.

Race, A. 1983: *Christians and Religious Pluralism*. London: SCM.

——2001: *Interfaith Encounter*. London: SCM.

Rahner, K. 1978: *Foundations of Christian Faith*. London: Darton, Longman, and Todd.

Rosenzweig, F. 1970: *Star of Redemption*. London: Routledge.

Smith, W. C. 1976: The Christian in a religiously plural world. In W. G. Oxtoby (ed.), *Religious Diversity: Essays by Wilfred Cantwell Smith*, pp. 3–21. New York: Harper and Row.

Talal Asad 1993: *Genealogies of Religion*. Baltimore, MD: The Johns Hopkins University Press.

Teasdale, W. 1999: *The Mystic Heart*. Novato, CA: New World Library.

Tracy, D. 1982: *The Analogical Imagination*. London: SCM.

Williams, P. 1989: *Mahayana Buddhism*. London: Routledge.

Williams, R. 2000: *On Christian Theology*. Oxford: Blackwell.

Woodhead, Linda (ed.) 2002: *Religions in the Modern World*. London: Routledge.

PART VI

Special Topics in Contemporary Christian Spirituality

CHAPTER 24

Experience

David Hay

7 April 1791. *My mind sweetly drawn this morning into silence, where I was favoured to experience that "They that wait upon the Lord shall renew their strength; they shall mount up with wings as eagles; they shall run, and not weary; they shall walk and not faint." O to be enabled to hold on my way.*

1 June. *No time for retirement to-day; yet in my solitary walk met with the beloved of souls, who sweetly attracted me, and melted me into tears under a sense of his goodness and my own nothingness: feeling at that time that all good proceeded from him, and that it is only as we receive ability from him, that we can do any thing aright.*

Mary Waring (1809)

The Historical Context of Modern Empirical Research

Christians have always recognized that there are special moments in the life of believers when they have the experience of being strongly aware of the presence of God. This is borne out by innumerable passages in the Bible, ranging across Moses' encounter with the burning bush, the calling of the boy Samuel when he was asleep in the temple, the meeting of the disciples with the risen Christ on the road to Emmaus, and the celebrated moment when St Paul was stricken to the ground on the road to Damascus. Nevertheless, the specific term "religious experience" did not come into common use until long after biblical times. It arose in connection with doctrinal developments within Calvinist and Pietist circles in Europe during the seventeenth and eighteenth centuries (Weber 1930; Stoeffler 1970; Erb 1983). Still later (according to the *Oxford English Dictionary*), the first English book to use the term in its title, *A Diary of the Religious Experience of Mary Waring*, was not published until 1809. It is therefore important to note that, though Mary was culturally and historically remote from biblical times, she did not see her use of language as an innovation. Her biblical quotations and syntax demonstrate that "religious experience" had for her a direct and unmistakable reference to Holy Scripture.

In seventeenth-century English Puritanism, the salience of religious experience was exemplified by a characteristic emphasis on the need for conversion and repentance (Breward 1970). An influential precursor of this view was William Perkins (1558–1602). Michael Watts, in his review of the complex and obscure history of English dissent, singles Perkins out, claiming that "the process of conversion as outlined by Perkins was upheld by English evangelicals for three centuries as the normative Christian experience" (1978: 173). In Perkins's writing we see coming into being the idea of conversion as a tangible *bodily* experience. The normal route by which this experience comes about is by hearing the preaching of divine law. At the same time, preaching offers a way of escape from the despair induced by repentance, and the discovery of the love of Christ: "Herein stands the power and pith of true religion, when a man *by observation and experience in himself,* knows the love of God in Christ towards him" (Perkins, quoted in Breward 1970: 31, emphasis added). It is not an accident that almost all modern empirical research into religious experience was initiated by people with this Protestant background, many of them from New England. The influx of Puritans into the east coast of North America in the seventeenth century and their consequent geographical isolation from England meant that they came to a position of social and political dominance unequalled in the Europe they had left behind. This supremacy gave the conversion experience a highly significant cultural role in the mainstream of society (Miller 1975; Cohen 1986), one that was to be reflected upon with considerable insight by the Congregationalist minister Jonathan Edwards (1703–58).

Apart from being famed as a hellfire preacher, Edwards has also been called the founding father of American psychology because of the incisiveness of his thoughts on the nature of what he called *The Religious Affections* (1746). His ideas were based on an adaptation of John Locke's philosophy of perception (Miller 1948; Lee 1988). For Edwards, spiritual understanding is never merely intellectual or theoretical; it derives from a direct first-hand encounter with sacred reality. He proposed that there exists what might be called a supernatural yet quasi-empirical "sense of the heart" that comes into play in the course of conversion:

> For if there be in the saints a kind of apprehension or perception, which is in its nature perfectly diverse from all that natural men have . . . it must consist of their having a certain kind of ideas or sensations of mind which are simply diverse from all that is or can be in the minds of natural men. And that is the same thing as to say that it consists in the sensations of a new spiritual sense which the souls of natural men have not. (1746: 196)

According to Edwards, it is the "infinite excellency of God" that is perceived, and he goes on to claim (in spite of what his contemporary David Hume would have to say about these matters) that this is not simply a perception of a fact; it is also a perception of meaning and value. In summary, faith is not an admission of ignorance; it is based on a kind of empirical evidence.

The Beginnings of Modern Research

The Harvard psychologist William James (1842–1910) is often credited with initiating the modern currency of the term "religious experience" via his Gifford Lectures in

Edinburgh University, published in 1902 as *The Varieties of Religious Experience*. He was not the only American psychologist to have this interest – other contemporary figures included Edwin Starbuck (1899), Stanley Hall (1904), George Coe (1916), and James Leuba (1925) – but he was certainly the most gifted. Like Jonathan Edwards, he was of Calvinist stock, though his father became a follower of Emmanuel Swedenborg. James's debt to the investigations that had been begun by Edwards 150 years earlier is manifest in his writing. He quotes from or refers to him, sometimes extensively, in numerous passages in the *Varieties*. The Victorian context of James's reflections may have been more skeptical than that of Edwards's day, but it nevertheless drew from him a not dissimilar form of argument. In a letter to a friend he outlined the underlying purposes of his Gifford Lectures:

> first, to defend (against all the prejudices of my "class") experience against philosophy as being the real backbone of the world's religious life – I mean prayer, guidance and all that sort of thing immediately and privately felt, as against high and noble and general views of our destiny and the world's meaning; and *second*, to make the reader or hearer to believe, what I myself invincibly do believe, that, although all the special manifestations of religion may have been absurd (I mean its creeds and theories) yet the life of it as a whole is mankind's most important function. (1920, vol. 2: 127)

In spite of his empirical stance, James himself did no practical research in preparation for his lectures. He drew many of his illustrative examples of religious experience from data collected by Edwin Starbuck (1866–1947), who at that time was a student in the Harvard Divinity School. Starbuck attended James's classes in psychology and lent him the materials from his doctoral research, consisting of large numbers of descriptions of their conversion solicited from New England Protestants.

From the moment of its inception, empirical research into religious experience proved to be controversial. During the winter of 1894–5, Starbuck gave a seminar in the Divinity School to a group of graduate students of the philosophy of religion. After discussing his initial findings in a straightforward factual manner, he invited discussion:

> Some quite hot water was poured into the baptismal font. The first douse of it came from Edward Bornkamp, who rose, his face white with emotion. His first sentence, fervid with the warmth of deep conviction, was, "It's all a lie!" . . . Of course the attempted damnation of the infant by the first speaker was because its swaddling clothes were only the filthy rags of earthly psychology, ill-becoming the sacredness of religion. (Starbuck 1937: 226)

When Starbuck asked his psychology tutor Hugo Münsterberg for advice about studying religion, Münsterberg was "antagonistic and finally explosive." "He declared that his problems were those of psychology, while mine belonged to theology, and that they had absolutely nothing to do with each other" (Starbuck 1937: 225). William James's view, which he put in a preface to Starbuck's 1899 book about his research, was that:

> Rightly interpreted, the whole tendency of Dr Starbuck's patient labour is to bring compromise and conciliation into the longstanding feud of Science and Religion. Your "evangelical" extremist will have it that conversion is an absolutely supernatural event, with

nothing cognate to it in ordinary psychology. Your "scientist" sectary, on the other hand, sees nothing in it but hysterics and emotionalism, an absolutely pathological disturbance. For Dr Starbuck it is not necessarily either of these things. (Starbuck 1899: ix)

Conversion experiences may have been James's starting-point, but his Enlightenment assumptions about universality meant that his lectures soon outstripped the bounds of the data studied by Starbuck. As Cushing Strout remarks, his enthusiasm led him to conflate an extraordinarily wide range of accounts of experience from "saints, philosophers, artists and ordinary people, from Protestants and Catholics, Jews, Buddhists, Christian Scientists, Transcendentalists, Quakers, Mormons, Mohammedans, Melanesian cannibals, drug takers, atheists and neurotics, including himself in the guise of an anonymous Frenchman" (1971: 135).

Strout and numerous subsequent critics have been in no doubt that James's conflation was illegitimate. Nevertheless, on this basis, in his final Gifford Lecture James attempted a generalization about religion, couched in psychological terms. In spite of the variety and contradictoriness of the world's religions, there is, he claimed, an experiential common core or nucleus, which involves:

1   An uneasiness; and
2   Its solution.

1   The uneasiness, reduced to its simplest terms, is a sense that there is *something wrong about us* as we naturally stand.
2   The solution is that *we are saved from the wrongness* by making proper connection with the higher powers. (James 1902: 400)

Self-surrender is the key, and James quotes Starbuck with approval: " 'Man's extremity is God's opportunity' is the theological way of putting this fact of the need of self-surrender; whilst the physiological way of stating it would be, 'Let one do all in one's power, and one's nervous system will do the rest.' *Both statements acknowledge the same fact*" (1902: 173). Here we see James drawing upon the psycho-physical parallelism (or more accurately "bio-theological" parallelism) that he had previously developed in his *Principles of Psychology* (1890). Starbuck followed his mentor in this respect, even offering a sketch of the specific neurological events accompanying the experience of conversion (1899: 100–17).

James was also impressed by the idea of "subliminal consciousness" put forward by F. W. H. Myers (Gurney et al. 1886) to try to account for telepathic phenomena. Accordingly, "Let me then propose, as an hypothesis, that whatever it may be on its *farther* side, the 'more' with which in religious experience we feel ourselves connected is on its *hither* side the subconscious continuation of our conscious life" (James 1902: 487). And as to "truth," James the pragmatist says, "we have *in the fact that the conscious person is continuous with a wider self through which saving experiences come,* a positive content of religious experience which, it seems to me, is *literally and objectively true as far as it goes*" (1902: 405).

That final "as far as it goes" is a get-out clause that continues to trouble contemporary discussions of religious experience. By turning to biology for at least a partial explanation of such experience, James was emphatically suggesting that what he was examining is something at least potentially present in all human beings. Hence this must include not only adherents of every sort of religious belief apart from Christianity, but also those who think that religious ideas are mistaken or nonsensical. If this is so, can such experience legitimately be called "religious?" Might it not be more appropriate to seek a naturalistic explanation for it based entirely on physiology, or some other discipline within the physical and social sciences? In a letter written to James in 1902, commenting on the *Varieties*, James Ward refers perceptively to his notion of religious experience originating in the "subliminal consciousness": "The only people to feel at home with your theory would be the thoroughgoing Calvinists, but you are far too Pelagian to suit them in other respects" (quoted in Perry 1935, vol. 2: 649).

The small group of students of religion that had developed in New England around the end of the nineteenth century had sufficient energy to generate (briefly) an academic periodical, the *Journal of the Psychology of Religion*, edited by Stanley Hall. But the conflicting religious or secular commitments of the participants created tensions that were too great for the movement to survive (Beit-Hallahmi 1974; Hay 1999). In 1909. Hall, in his role as first President of Clark University in Massachusetts, invited Freud, Jung, and other leading psychoanalysts to take part in the twentieth-anniversary celebrations of the new institution. He thereby precipitated psychoanalysis into the public eye in the United States, and with it Freud's interpretation of religious experience as symptomatic of neurosis or temporary psychosis (Freud 1928b; Reik 1940). The ease with which Freudian ideas entered the American consciousness has been interpreted by Howard Feinstein (1970) as being due to congruencies between the Puritan procedure for the preparation of the heart for conversion and the techniques of psychoanalysis.

A second debilitating factor was the arrival of behaviorism under the aegis of J. B. Watson in his 1914 book *Behavior: An Introduction to Comparative Psychology*. Watson's position that human behavior could be explained entirely in terms of reflexes, stimulus–response associations, and the effects of reinforcers upon them, thereby excluding all "mental" terms, further reduced the likelihood of research on religious experience being taken seriously (except when seen as pathological). By the 1930s, the empirical study of religious experience had lost most of its plausibility, as signaled by Abraham Cronbach's exasperated review of books on the subject, the final one to be given space in the *Psychological Bulletin*:

> From the analysis of a psychotic Buddhist, Pfister comes to pronounce Buddhism a flight from life's conflicts . . . In various ancient vows and sacrifices, Reik is struck by their resemblance to modern insurance schemes . . . For Selbie the defense of religion consists in discrediting every psychological pronouncement that seems at variance . . . with current or traditional theological views . . . The widespread admixture of the non-scientific in works supposed to be scientific or in works that otherwise are scientific has made the construction of this list no easy matter. (1933: 327)

I need to mention briefly a European parallel to the American empirical approach. Friedrich Schleiermacher's (1768–1834) famous definition of religion as "the feeling of absolute dependence" influenced numerous subsequent students of religious experience including Karl Girgensohn, Rudolf Otto, Ernst Troeltsch, Freidrich Heiler, Gerardus van der Leeuw, Joachim Wach and, more remotely, Mircea Eliade. All but one of these men were first and foremost phenomenologists or historians of religion (McKenzie 1994), and Schleiermacher's influence on empirical research has primarily been indirect. But the Lutheran theologian Karl Girgensohn (1875–1925) did make a serious attempt to do a practical investigation of Schleiermacher's understanding of religious experience. He founded a school of research at the University of Dorpat (Tartu in modern Estonia) which used a method of experimental introspection to study what he called "the traces left by religious experiences" in selected volunteers who gave their immediate feeling responses to carefully chosen religious texts (Girgensohn 1921). Girgensohn's approach and assumptions have been severely criticized (Wulff 1985; Nase 2000), mainly for the inadequacy of the introspectionist methodology. Unfortunately, the activities of the school founded by Girgensohn, and continued by Werner Gruehn, lost any chance to develop a more adequate method. They were brought to an abrupt halt in 1940 when Estonia was absorbed into the Soviet Union and all theological activity was banned.

The Empirical Study of Religious or Spiritual Experience after 1960

William James's claim that he was studying a human "universal" made it inevitable that some of his followers would draw a distinction between "spiritual awareness" as an innate human capacity common to all members of the species *Homo sapiens*, and "religious experience" as its expression within the terminology of a particular religious culture. This is a matter that is currently much debated, and in feeling free from now on to refer to "religious or spiritual experience" I am recognizing the unresolved state of the argument.

During the 1960s, scientific curiosity about such experience was re-energized. Why interest re-emerged is not entirely clear. Perhaps the cultural changes that ushered in New Age ideas gave more legitimation to that universe of discourse. Certainly the plausibility of behaviorism became more questionable as cognitive psychology gained ground, and sustained critiques of certain aspects of psychoanalysis began to appear (cf. Eysenck 1985). In recent years, the subject has attracted the increasing attention of anthropologists, biologists, medical researchers, physicists, psychologists, neurologists, and sociologists to such an extent that it cannot be reviewed comprehensively in a brief essay. To give some shape to the succeeding discussion I shall therefore concentrate on the biological perspective, whilst making allusions to other disciplines where appropriate.

Some conceptual issues relating to empirical research

Almost ninety years after James's lectures, Alasdair MacIntyre made the focus of his 1988 Edinburgh Gifford Lectures the fact that there is no longer any agreement about the starting-point in the investigation of religion from a naturalistic perspective. In his bequest of 1885 Lord Gifford had required the lecturers to treat their subject (natural theology) "as a strictly natural science . . . just as astronomy or chemistry is." James's lectures had approximated to that ideal, but there is now "no set of first premises or principles upon which there is any consensus. Hence even when the arguments proceed, each from their own particular starting point, with some rigour, their conclusions are such as to compel rational assent only from those who were already in agreement upon where to begin" (MacIntyre 1990: 10).

Legitimacy

On what grounds, then, might it be acceptable to proceed with an empirical investigation of spiritual experience? One of the most notable contemporary critics of the way in which scientific research has been applied to the field of religion is John Milbank. In his book *Theology and Social Theory* (1990) Milbank makes the point that "secular reason" (he specifies sociological reasoning, but the argument is probably generalizable to the entire scientific study of religion) is seldom recognized as a domain that "had to be instituted or *imagined*." It employs a metaphor in relation to Christianity of "the removal of the superfluous and additional to leave a residue of the human, the natural and the self-sufficient" (1990: 1).

The major naturalistic theories of religious or spiritual experience that are currently taught in universities certainly do have this characteristic, at least in their origins. Traditional accounts of the development of a detached and critical view of religion and religious experience (cf. Preus 1987) assume that the mainstream of intellectual history has led to a progressive emancipation from religious belief. They entail the necessity to offer explanations of how the religious mistake came to be so widespread. I am thinking here of Marxist, Freudian, and Durkheimian interpretations of religious experience that in their initial form clearly had this purpose, though admittedly, post-Ricoeur, they have been taken up via the hermeneutics of suspicion as, so to speak, purifications of religion (see, for example, William Meissner [1984] and André Godin's [1985] use of psychoanalysis in the interpretation of religious experience, and perhaps Ana-Maria Rizzuto's [1979] psychoanalytic study of the formation of the God representation).

Milbank's critique implies that scientists as a body, even though they may feel benignly toward religion, are simply unaware of the closed circuit of secular argument in which they are caught. No doubt this is true of many, perhaps a majority in the scientific profession, but it is not necessarily the case for all. One could conceive of scientists who are also committed Christians using empirical methods to ask such questions as "What is it about our God-given biological makeup that enables us to be religiously aware?" I contend that this is a perfectly legitimate stance that does not detract from, and might even strengthen, the perspectives that characterize Milbank's work.

The local and the universal

Closely associated and overlapping with the problem of legitimacy is the question of universality. Unfortunately, this leads us into the heart of an unresolved contemporary debate about the relationship between culturally separate universes of discourse. James's universalism has been repeatedly criticized (cf. Katz 1978; Lindbeck 1984; Proudfoot 1985; Lash 1988; Bagger 1999; Taylor 2002) on the grounds that he fails to take account of the social context in which our experiences are constructed, quite often in ways that make them incommensurable. Thus Steven Katz (1978) has wondered what common ground there could be between a Jewish and a Buddhist mystic. The Jewish mystic has a conception of God

> as the sort of being who is in some sense personal and even more, is ethically and evalu-atively personal, i.e. a God who is affected by good deeds and acts of obedience . . . the Jewish conditioning pattern so strongly impresses the tradition's mystics (as all Jews) with the fact that one does not have mystical experiences of God in which one loses one's iden-tity in ecstatic moments of unity, that the Jewish mystic rarely, if ever, has such experi-ences. (1978: 34)

On the other hand, the young Buddhist is taught that:

> His goal, "Nirvana" is not a relationship state in which the finite self encounters a saving or loving transcendental being – God . . . that there is no encounter of any sort, results from the fact that he is taught there is no real self and no transcendental other self . . . There is no intelligible way that anyone can legitimately argue that a "no-self" experience of "empty calm" is the same experience as the experience of an intense loving relationship between two substantial selves, one of whom is conceived of as the personal God of Western religion and all that this entails. (1978: 38)

A second difficulty is due to the development of studies of "altered states of conscious-ness" (ASCs), many of them associated with religious or spiritual experience across a wide variety of cultures. In an effort to aid cross-cultural analysis, Locke and Kelly (1985) offered a formidably complex summary of the factors involved in the induction of ASCs. Could such a diverse range of human experience be credibly subsumed under the single category of "religious experience?"

I have discussed these questions in detail elsewhere (Hay 1988). In summary, much theoretical analysis of experience in different religious cultures has been done by exam-ining the language of historical scriptures that, almost by definition, are concerned with maintaining an orthodoxy. Our modern understanding of the function of language in the construction of reality certainly explains how these texts operate to generate cultural differences in experience. In spite of that, *practical* inter-religious encounter, for example between Christian and Buddhist practitioners of meditation, at least as culturally remote as Katz's hypothetical Jewish and Buddhist mystics, has often uncovered common ground. Close parallels exist in the ethical prerequisites, the methodology used to enter into meditation, and the physiological correlates of that state; there is even a high degree of reported similarity in terms of phenomenology (cf. Suzuki 1957; Merton 1968; Graham 1971; Johnston 1974; Kadowaki 1980).

Those who assert that religious or spiritual experience is no more than the result of an interaction between physiology and social construction place it in a realm of absolute subjectivity remote from the empirical process of perceiving a given reality.

The assertion more or less colludes with secular reason by implying that the experience is a culturally constructed delusion. In contrast, people who choose to talk about their religious or spiritual experience usually strongly deny that it resembles subjective imaginings and say that it is much more like a direct perception. In the case of ASCs, we need not suppose that because different kinds of practices (trance, the use of drugs, contemplation, and so on) are used in the production of, or less reductively, "opening the awareness to" such states, that these states are necessarily physiologically different from each other. Research using modern brain-scanning techniques may help to clarify this question.

Asking questions

The problems discussed above become crucial at the point where one starts to construct questions that can be used in empirical research. Researchers in this field have often asked direct questions (cf. Glock and Stark 1965; Back and Bourque 1970; Greeley 1975; Unger 1976; Wuthnow 1976; Hay and Morisy 1978; Hay 1979; Hay and Heald 1987). Below I present some examples of the kinds of questions that have been used in surveys in Britain and the United States up to about the middle of the 1980s:

> Have you ever as an adult had the feeling that you were somehow in the presence of God? (Glock and Stark 1965)

> Have you ever felt as though you were very close to a powerful spiritual force that seemed to lift you out of yourself? (Greeley 1975)

> Have you ever felt that you were in close contact with something holy or sacred? (Wuthnow 1976)

> Would you say that you have ever had a "religious or mystical experience" – that is, a moment of sudden religious insight and awakening? (1978 Gallup Poll)

> Have you ever been aware of or influenced by a presence or a power, whether you call it God or not, that is different from your everyday self? (Hardy, adapted by Hay and Morisy 1978)

The range of wording of these questions is very wide, to the point where one might wonder to what degree their meanings overlap. My own experience of field-testing a number of different forms of wording with pilot samples within a British population suggests that there is a considerable degree of recognition that they do refer to a common universe of discourse. In the case of the Greeley and Hardy questions, their use in a single National Opinion Poll omnibus survey in Britain in 1976 showed a very high level of concordance (>0.9) between the populations answering "yes" to either query.

There are, however, doubts remaining about the validity of comparisons between positive respondents to these different questions. The difficulty is vividly demonstrated where a question is quite clearly drawn from a particular subculture within Christianity, as in the case of Glock and Stark's (1965) well-known study of Northern

Californian church members. They asked respondents whether they had ever had "a sense of being saved in Christ." This is such a familiar part of evangelical Protestant rhetoric that it was no surprise to find that Protestants were much more likely than Catholics to respond positively to the question. There are no quick solutions to these problems, although Michael Mason (1988) has drawn up criteria for the valid use of particular wordings, including the necessity to identify the major symbolic universes within the various religious communities before attempting to create questions.

Another approach has been to present extracts of accounts of experience and invite respondents to state whether they resemble anything in their own lives. Ralph Hood (1975) devised a scale for measuring reported religious experience using such extracts. Others have used them in a less structured way to elicit responses from the general public (Paffard 1973; Hardy 1979) or as part of a larger survey (Robinson and Jackson 1985), whilst I have used the major categories emerging from a classification of the archives of the Religious Experience Research Centre to make enquiries in two national surveys in Britain (Hay and Heald 1987; Hay and Hunt 2000).

A third method of eliciting responses has been to show pictures of people in situations where they might be expected to become spiritually aware and ask them to comment on what is happening. This has proved useful in studying the spirituality of children where more formal methods are inappropriate (Hay et al. 1996). In a very large study of the religious and spiritual life of children and young people in Finland, Kalevi Tamminen (1991) presented photographs of children in religious settings with captions that invited a projective response (for example, a picture of two children looking at a crucifix, with the caption "Lisbeth and Henry saw a crucifix. They stopped to look at it. They thought . . ."). More recently, Rebecca Nye (Hay, with Nye 1998) used similar pictures, whilst intentionally avoiding overt religious content, in her fieldwork with six-year-old and ten-year-old children. This was because she was attempting to investigate spirituality that might extend beyond formally religious contexts or interpretations.

A Biological Perspective

I now turn to a specific example of an empirical approach to the study of spiritual experience. My intention is to illustrate how such research may contribute in a positive way to an understanding of Christian spirituality.

During the academic sessions of 1963–4 and 1964–5, the Oxford zoologist Alister Hardy delivered the Gifford Lectures at Aberdeen University. Published as *The Living Stream* (1965) and *The Divine Flame* (1966), the lectures proposed that religious awareness is biologically structured into the human species and has evolved through the process of natural selection because it has survival value. Hardy's presuppositions were those typical of an empirical scientist and committed evolutionist (Hay 2004); that is to say, he was a critical realist. He understood religious experience as loosely relating to Rudolph Otto's (1950) account of "numinous" awareness, but he believed that it is much commoner than the overwhelming experience of the *mysterium tremendum et fascinans* that Otto describes.

Hardy defended his conjecture by appealing to the fields of psychology, animal behavior, anthropology, and, more controversially, psychical research. Referring to the work of social anthropologists (in particular, Émile Durkheim and R. R. Marrett), he attempted to demonstrate that some awareness of the sacred is more or less universally reported in the human species. With regard to survival value, he was particularly impressed by the thesis proposed by Durkheim in *The Elementary Forms of the Religious Life* (1915). Durkheim had noted that for believers,

> the real function of religion is not to make us think, to enrich our knowledge, nor to add to the conceptions which we owe to science others of another origin and another character, but rather, it is to make us act, to aid us to live. *The believer, who has communicated with his God, is not merely a man who sees new truths of which the unbeliever is ignorant; he is a man who is stronger.* (1915: 416, emphasis added)

Shortly after his Gifford Lectures, in 1969, Hardy founded the Religious Experience Research Unit in Manchester College, Oxford, with the purpose of exploring his hypothesis. He began by employing the method most natural to him as a zoologist, that of the natural historian. Primarily through the British national press, he invited responses from the general public. That and succeeding appeals have resulted in the accumulation of nearly 6,000 written responses which are held in the Alister Hardy Centre for the Study of Religious and Spiritual Experience (now based in St David's College, Lampeter). Detailed qualitative discussions relating to this material have been given by Beardsworth (1977), Cohen and Phipps (1979), Hardy (1979), Robinson (1983), Hay (1987, 1990), Ahern (1990), and Maxwell and Tschudin (1990).

In preparation for a national survey in Britain, I made a study of previous attempts to classify the contents of the archive and identified eight major types of experience reported in order of frequency, as:

1   A patterning of events in a person's life that convinces them that in some strange way they were meant to happen.
2   An awareness of the presence of God.
3   An awareness of receiving help in answer to prayer.
4   An awareness of being looked after or guided by a presence not called God.
5   An awareness of being in the presence of someone who has died.
6   An awareness of a sacred presence in nature.
7   An awareness of an evil presence.
8   Experiencing in an extraordinary way that all things are "One."

The next step was to discover the frequency of reports of experience in a general population and compare them with other findings. Table 24.1 shows the positive response rates for a series of national surveys (using the various questions already mentioned) conducted in the United States, Britain, and Australia and reported between 1970 and 2000. Inspection shows that the rates of report range from 20.5 percent in the case of the 1962 Gallup survey in the United States (commissioned by Back and

Table 24.1 Positive responses to questions about religious experience in twelve national surveys, 1970–2000

Survey	Publication date	Country	Sample size	Percentage claiming experience
Back and Bourque	1970[a]	United States		
(Gallup)	(1962)		3,232	20.5
	(1966)		3,518	32.0
	(1967)		3,168	41.0
Greeley (NORC)	1975	United States	1,467	35.0
Hay and Morisy (NOP)	1978	Britain	1,865	36.0
Gallup	1978	United States	3,000	31.0
PRRC	1978	United States	3,062	35.0
Morgan Research[b]	1983	Australia	1,228	44.0
RERC/Gallup	1985	Britain	1,030	33.0
RERC/Gallup	1985	United States	1,525	43.0
Hay and Heald (Gallup)	1987	Britain	985	48.0
Hay and Hunt (ORB)	2000	Britain	1,000	76.0

[a] The article published in 1970 reviewed surveys in 1962, 1966, and 1967.
[b] An Australian affiliate of Gallup Poll.
NORC, National Opinion Research Center, Chicago; NOP, National Opinion Polls Ltd, London; PRRC, Princeton Religion Research Center; RERC, Religious Experience Research Centre, Oxford; ORB, Opinion Research Business, London.

Bourque 1970) to 76 percent in the national survey conducted by ORB in the millennium year (Hay and Hunt 2000).

Table 24.2 gives the comparative frequencies of report of six types of religious or spiritual experience for the British surveys by Hay and Heald (1987) and Hay and Hunt (2000). Where the same form of questioning has been used in successive pieces of research – for example, in the 1987 and 2000 British national surveys – the trend of the figures over time is upwards. Whilst 48 percent of the sample claimed experience in 1987, the figure had risen to 76 percent in 2000, an increase of almost two-thirds over a thirteen-year period. The data from table 24.2 show that there has been a steep rise in all six categories measured. In contrast, during approximately the same period, regular church attendance in the mainstream Christian denominations in Britain declined by 20 percent (Brierley 2000) and currently stands at just over 7 percent, leading some sociologists (Brown 2001; Bruce 2002) to announce the demise of formal religion in the United Kingdom. It seems that, in some paradoxical way, the rapid decline in the power of the institution has given more social permission for people to admit to experience that has always been there but in the past has been kept secret because of embarrassment (Hay 2003).

According to the most recent statistics gathered by the European Study of Values (ESV), this divergence has a counterpart in several other countries in Europe, especially amongst young people (Y. Lambert, personal communication 2003). The radical gulf

Table 24.2   Frequency of report of religious or spiritual experience in Britain for the years 1987 and 2000

Religious or spiritual experience	1987 (%)	2000 (%)	Change (%)
A patterning of events	29	55	+90
Awareness of the presence of God	27	38	+41
Awareness of prayer being answered	25	37	+40
Awareness of a sacred presence in nature	16	29	+81
Awareness of the presence of the dead	18	25	+38
Awareness of an evil presence	12	25	+107
Cumulative total	(48)[a]	76	+58

[a] This includes totals for respondents to two additional questions asked in 1987 about "awareness of a presence not called God" (22%) and "awareness that all things are 'One'" (5%), i.e. the cumulative total of 76% for the year 2000 is quite likely to be, relatively speaking, an underestimate.
Sources: Hay and Heald (1987); Hay and Hunt (2000)

appearing in British people's minds between institutional religion and spirituality also seems to have some echoes in the United States. Research by Zinnbauer et al. (1997) has shown that, even though the Christian churches are much stronger in the United States, there is a parallel increasing tendency to make a distinction between "spirituality" and "religion." The feeling that we may be observing a large-scale trend is further supported by a number of small-scale researches in Australia which have reported findings very similar to those in Britain (Tacey 2003).

Testing the Biological Hypothesis against Alternative Naturalistic Hypotheses

How much confidence can be placed on an interpretation of spiritual experience based on the biological hypothesis? This, of course, depends on one's theological stance, a point I will return to later. More immediately, the question relates to the resilience of the hypothesis when tested against the currently dominant naturalistic speculations of Marx, Durkheim, and Freud.

The "opium" hypothesis

Marx's most famous statement on the subject of religion is in the introduction to his *Contribution to the Critique of Hegel's Philosophy of Right* (1844) where he describes it as "the opium of the people." The implication is that the opiate (in its extreme form, productive of religious delusions) will be most necessary as a painkiller amongst the poorest and most oppressed sectors of class society. This is a testable hypothesis. Table 24.3 gives the data for four national surveys in which figures are available for social

Table 24.3 Report of experience compared with social class for four national surveys, 1978–1985

Social class	UK 1978 (%)	USA 1978 (%)	Australia 1983 (%)	USA 1985 (%)
Upper middle class	47	–	–	–
Professional middle class	49	39	50	44
Lower middle class/white collar	41	33	42	35
Skilled working class	31	31	31	29
Unskilled/subsistence	32	29	49	28

Sources: UK, Hay and Morisy (1978); USA, Gallup (1978, 1985); Australia, Morgan Research (1983)

class. The overall trend toward increasing reports of religious/spiritual experience as one moves up the social scale is the reverse of what would be predicted on the basis of Marx's assertion, but fits with predictions that could be made on the basis of the biological hypothesis. That is to say, lack of religious or spiritual awareness could be construed as a deficit analogous to and caused by other forms of poverty. However, it is important to note that the one clearly anomalous figure, the high positive response from the Australian "unskilled" group, may imply plausibility to Marx's thesis in at least some as-yet-unclear circumstances. Alternatively, since this group probably includes a large proportion of the Aboriginal population, we may be looking primarily at a cultural difference between Europeans and native Australians.

The "effervescence" hypothesis

Durkheim's interpretation of religious experience as the "effervescence" generated in the context of large religious gatherings appears in *The Elementary Forms of the Religious Life* (1915). There have been two pieces of research testing this hypothesis. In Hay and Morisy's (1985) British study of a stratified random sample of citizens of Nottingham, over 60 percent reporting spiritual experience said they were completely alone at the time. In a British national survey conducted by Gallup Poll (Hay and Heald 1987), the percentage of people reporting the experience as taking place when they were alone varied from 61 to 76 percent according to the type of experience (table 24.4). The data are the reverse of what would be expected from Durkheim's prediction. They coincide with what might be expected on the basis of an interpretation of religious awareness as natural to individuals, rather than socially generated.

The "neurosis" hypothesis

I have noted that Freud believed religion to be symptomatic of neurosis (1928a) and religious experience to be perhaps a temporary psychosis (Reik 1940). Very few studies

Table 24.4   Percentage of people saying "no" in answer to the question: "Have you told anyone else about your experience?"

Religious or spiritual experience	%
Awareness of prayer being answered	76
Awareness of the presence of the dead	75
Awareness that all things are "One"	69
Awareness of a presence not called God	68
A patterning of events	66
Awareness of the presence of God	64
Awareness of a sacred presence in nature	64
Awareness of an evil presence	61

Source: Hay and Heald (1987)

using independent measures of religious/spiritual experience have looked directly at its links with mental health. Those that do, show either no association (Lindskoog and Kirk 1975) or suggest, on the whole, a positive relation with mental health (cf. Hood 1974; Thomas and Cooper 1980; Jackson and Fulford 1997). The common assumption that such experience is particularly strongly associated with temporal lobe epilepsy also appears to be unfounded, according to one of the few carefully designed studies on the subject (Sensky et al. 1984).

There have been two large-scale surveys that have investigated the relationship between report of religious experience and "psychological wellbeing" as measured by the Bradburn Balanced Affect Scale (Bradburn 1969). The validity of this scale was reviewed by Bowling (1991), and whilst scores on the scale do not necessarily equate to an individual's level of mental health, Berkman (1971) demonstrated that the scale is an adequate indicator of mental health in a large sample. Andrew Greeley (1975) used the Bradburn scale in an American national survey and found a significant relationship between report of religious experience and psychological wellbeing. In a subgroup of "mystics" more tightly defined, the association with positive affect was at that time the highest correlation recorded for any group measured by Bradburn's scale. Hay and Morisy (1978), in their national survey in Britain, found a similar positive relationship between report of experience and positive scores on the Bradburn scale, though not as high as in the case of Greeley's American sample.

These findings, which are what one would expect if the biological hypothesis is correct, would seem to contradict Freud, although the picture is not straightforward. According to Freud (1928b), religion, as the universal but unrecognized neurosis, constitutes a "crooked cure" with the paradoxical consequence that religious people *appear* to be less neurotic than other people. On Freud's reading of religion, those reporting religious experience are hallucinating and thus are deeply caught in that universal neurosis. But I contend that there is a defect in a view that implies that the populations discussed above, scoring as they do on the dimensions measured, must be defined as neurotic with temporary psychotic hallucinations because they claim to have had a religious experience. It depends on a prior belief that religion is nonsensical. Although that is a widely canvassed perspective, the question goes beyond science, since it involves philosophical or theological issues, hence making Freud's scientific argument circular.

Looking Ahead

From the time of William James up to the present day, empirical research on religious or spiritual experience has operated under the shadow of an intellectual critique of religion that has had several centuries to become sedimented into everyday consciousness. Moreover, it seems that theologians have at times colluded with this critique. In his book *At the Origins of Modern Atheism*, Michael Buckley (1987) suggests that during the seventeenth century numerous mainstream Christian theologians (Protestant and Catholic) had a failure of nerve in relation to experience. Unlike their Puritan and Pietist co-religionists, they no longer felt that Christianity could be defended by reference to our ordinary experience of God. Hence they turned to an indirect apologetic based on the argument from design and gave over the defense of religion to cosmologists like Isaac Newton. But this giving up of spiritual experience eventually generated the destruction of religion that it was meant to avoid:

> For if religion itself has no inherent ground upon which to base its assertion, it is only a question of time until its inner emptiness emerges as positive denial . . . Eventually the self-denial of religion becomes the more radical but consistent denial that is atheism. If religion has no intrinsic justification, it cannot be justified from the outside. (Buckley 1987: 360)

The legacy is a widespread uneasiness about the possible relationship of religious or spiritual experience with illusion or mental instability. As recently as 1987, in the third edition of the *Diagnostic and Statistical Manual* of the American Psychiatric Association (DSM III), professionals in the field of psychiatry were advised to consider diagnosing mental illness on the basis of claims to such experience ("sensing a presence," "feeling that God has given you a mission"). Some professionals, as well as widely read popular scientific writers, continue to assert that it is symptomatic of pathology or illusion (cf. Persinger 1997; Dawkins 1998; Alper 2001; Boyer 2001). The taboo that assumptions of this kind have created is extremely powerful, as my own most recent research demonstrates (Hay 2003).

Apart from the considerable volume of data I have cited which contradicts the negative assessment of spiritual experience, there are signs of a more open attitude in other sectors of the scientific community. Recent neurophysiological research has been accompanied by interpretative commentary which has much less of a reductionist bias (cf. Ramachandran and Blakeslee 1998; Newberg et al. 2001). There has also been much more scientific debate on the possibility that spiritual experience has positive functions (cf. Jackson and Fulford 1997; Pargament 1997; Koenig 1998; Koenig et al. 2001; Swinton 2001).

Another development is the recent research evidence suggesting that spiritual experience has an important role in underpinning a social coherence that is not based on political coercion. Rebecca Nye's qualitative study of the spirituality of six-year-old and ten-year-old children in two large industrial cities in England identified "relational consciousness" as the precursor of all the children's spiritual talk. Nye describes it as having two components:

> An unusual level of *consciousness* or perceptiveness, relative to other passages of conversation spoken by that child.
>
> Conversation expressed in a context of how the child *related* to things, other people, him/herself, and God. (Hay, with Nye 1998: 113)

The biologically inbuilt nature of relational consciousness has been given strong empirical support by pioneering research in Hungary (Nagy and Molnar 1994) and the United Kingdom (Trevarthen 2002) on intersubjectivity in young and newborn infants. These findings also cohere with the data emerging from the investigation of the biophilia hypothesis (Wilson 1984; Kellert and Wilson 1993). This conjecture asserts the existence of a fundamental, genetically based human need to affiliate with life and lifelike processes, and, in an extensive review, Peter Kahn (1997) provides data on work with children in the United States and the Brazilian Amazon that support the plausibility of the hypothesis. In concordance with these findings, studies with adults (Greeley 1975; Wuthnow 1976; Hay and Morisy 1978; Hay 1979) show overwhelmingly that the commonest response to spiritual experience is a desire to live a more ethical and less materialistic life.

The suggestion that relational consciousness is the structural underpinning of both spirituality and ethical sensitivity offers an empirical basis for those theologians who seek to argue beyond the constraints of social construction to a foundational awareness of self and God (cf. Rahner 1983; Kelly 2002). Recent empirical investigators seem to be encountering a pre-verbal knowingness, pre-dating the potent analytical emphasis of language and encompassing an awareness of our indissoluble link with the seamless robe of reality. This knowingness appears to inspire the altruistic impulse and to be cognate with Martin Buber's reflections in *I and Thou* (1937). It may also relate to what Emmanuel Levinas has to say about responsibility for the "other" as pre-existing any self-conscious reflection, and his insistence on ethics as "first philosophy" (Levinas 1984; Bernasconi and Wood 1988).

The centrality of the relational dimension of spiritual experience also sheds light on the tension that exists between spirituality and Western individualism. In *The Political Theory of Possessive Individualism* (1962), C. B. Macpherson explored the way in which individualism has become fundamentally structured into the operation of the marketplace. He traced its influence back to the seventeenth century, showing how the individualism of Thomas Hobbes initiated and continues to supply the basic assumptions on which the market operates. Albert Hirschman's magisterial *The Passions and the Interests* (1977) develops this theme as it relates to the elevation of self-interest to the status of a virtue (at one time it was labeled "avarice" and, according to Dante, consigned its perpetrators to the fourth level of Hell). Probably the most influential vehicle for this view is Adam Smith's masterpiece, *The Wealth of Nations* (1776), since that book makes self-interest the pivot of its doctrine and forms the basis of almost all subsequent economic theory. There are powerfully conflicting interests at stake here. The difficulties of religion in the Western world are perhaps not surprising when there is such a large economic investment in an understanding of human nature that is at odds with the insights of spiritual experience. There are obvious temptations to collude with such a view because it appears to bolster the economic system.

The good news is that the morally ambivalent phenomenon of globalization (Held and McGrew 2002; Stiglitz 2003) has itself raised questions about the adequacy of individualism as a basis for the management of the economy. Students of globalization have begun to use the metaphor of the "global brain," thought of as a "synaptic network," the relevance of which lies in its endless interconnections. During the 1991 Gulf War, politicians talked of "linkages," tracing out, as best they could, the causes, effects, and consequences of the Middle East conflict (Duffield 2001). The linkages proliferated never-endingly, eventually re-igniting the conflict in 2003. Multitudes of such linkages are constantly forming and re-forming synaptic networks that reach into every corner of world politics, economics, and ecology.

Awareness of these changes is making traditional individualism less appropriate and, to an increasing degree, outdated in the field of management and in the global market. A spiritual understanding of the way in which human beings relate to one another is beginning to seem the most fitting model for the global village. Unfortunately, from the perspective of the Christian institution, the empirical evidence I have presented also shows that there is a rapidly increasing gap in the public imagination between spirituality and religion. This is a distinction that has haunted this essay in the form of my discomfort over whether to speak of "religious" or "spiritual" experience. A major intellectual and pastoral task for the Christian church is to learn how to engage in communication across that gulf.

References

Ahern, G. 1990: *Spiritual/Religious Experience in Modern Society: A Pilot Study*. Oxford: Alister Hardy Research Centre.

Alper, M. 2001: *The "God" Part of the Brain: A Scientific Interpretation of Human Spirituality and God*. New York: Rogue Press.

American Psychiatric Association 1987: *Diagnostic and Statistical Manual of Mental Disorders*, 3rd rev. edn (DSM III). Washington DC: American Psychiatric Association.

Back, K. and Bourque, L. B. 1970: Can feelings be enumerated? *Behavioral Science* 15, 487–96.

Bagger, M. C. 1999: *Religious Experience, Justification and History*. Cambridge: Cambridge University Press.

Beardsworth, T. 1977: *A Sense of Presence*. Oxford: RERU.

Beit-Hallahmi, B. 1974: Psychology of religion 1880–1930: the rise and fall of a psychological movement. *Journal of the History of the Behavioral Sciences* 10, 84–90.

Berkman, P. 1971: Measurement of mental health in a general population survey. *American Journal of Epidemiology* 94, 105–11.

Bernasconi, R. and Wood, D. (eds) 1988: *The Provocation of Levinas: Rethinking the Other*. London: Routledge.

Bowling, A. 1991: *Measuring Health: A Review of Quality of Life Measurement Scales.* Buckingham: Open University Press.

Boyer, P. 2001: *Religion Explained: The Human Instincts that Fashion Gods, Spirits and Ancestors.* London: William Heinemann.

Bradburn, N. M. 1969: *The Structure of Psychological Wellbeing.* Chicago: Aldine Press.

Breward, I. (ed.) 1970: *The Work of William Perkins.* Appleford: Sampford Courteney Press.

Brierley, P. 2000: *UK Christian Handbook: Religious Trends.* Carlisle: Paternoster.

Brown, C. G. 2001: *The Death of Christian Britain.* London: Routledge.

Bruce, S. 2002: *God is Dead: Secularization in the West.* Oxford: Blackwell.

Buber, M. 1937: *I and Thou,* trans. R. G. Smith. Edinburgh: T. and T. Clark.

Buckley, M. 1987: *At the Origins of Modern Atheism.* New Haven, CT: Yale University Press.

Coe, G. A. 1916: *The Psychology of Religion.* Chicago: University of Chicago Press.

Cohen, C. L. 1986: *God's Caress: The Psychology of Puritan Religious Experience.* New York: Oxford University Press.

Cohen, J. M. and Phipps, J-F. 1979: *The Common Experience.* London: Rider.

Cronbach, A. 1933: The psychology of religion: a bibliographical survey. *Psychological Bulletin* 30, 327–61.

Dawkins, R. 1998: *Unweaving the Rainbow: Science, Delusion and the Appetite for Wonder.* London: Penguin.

Duffield, M. 2001: *Global Governance and the New Wars.* London: Zed Books.

Durkheim, É. 1915: *The Elementary Forms of the Religious Life,* trans. J. W. Swain. London: George Allen and Unwin.

Edwards, J. [1746] 1961: *The Religious Affections.* Edinburgh: Banner of Truth Trust.

Erb, P. C. (ed.) 1983: *Pietists: Selected Writings.* London: SPCK.

Eysenck, H. 1985: *Decline and Fall of the Freudian Empire.* London: Penguin.

Feinstein, H. 1970: The prepared heart: a comparative study of Puritan theology and psycho-analysis. *American Quarterly* 22 (2), 166–76.

——1984: *Becoming William James.* Ithaca, NY: Cornell University Press.

Freud, S. 1928a: *The Future of an Illusion.* London: Hogarth Press.

——[1928b] 1961: A religious experience. In *Standard Edition of the Works of Sigmund Freud,* vol. 9. London: Hogarth Press.

Girgensohn, K. [1921] 1930: *Der seelische Aufbau des religiösen Erlebnis: Eine religionspsychologis-che Untersuchung auf experimenteller Grundlage,* corrected and supplemented by W. Gruehn. Gütersloh: C. Bertelsmann.

Glock, C. Y. and Stark, R. 1965: *Religion and Society in Tension.* Chicago: Rand McNally.

Godin, A. 1985: *The Psychological Dynamics of Religious Experience.* Birmingham, AL: Religious Education Press.

Graham, A. 1971: *The End of Religion: Autobiographical Explorations.* New York: Harcourt Brace Jovanovich.

Greeley, A. M. 1975: *The Sociology of the Paranormal: A Reconnaissance.* Beverly Hills, CA: Sage.

Gurney, E., Myers, F. W. H., and Podmore, F. 1886: *Phantasms of the Living,* 2 vols. New York: Trubner.

Hall, G. S. 1904: *The Psychology of Adolescence,* 2 vols. New York: D. Appleton.

Hardy, A. 1965: *The Living Stream.* London: Collins.

——1966: *The Divine Flame.* London: Collins.

——1975: *The Biology of God.* London: Jonathan Cape.

——1979: *The Spiritual Nature of Man.* Oxford: Clarendon Press.

——1984: *Darwin and the Spirit of Man.* London: Collins.

Hay, D. 1979: Religious experience amongst a group of postgraduate students: a qualitative study. *Journal for the Scientific Study of Religion* 18, 164–82.

—— 1985: Religious experience and its induction. In L. B. Brown (ed.), *Advances in the Psychology of Religion*, pp. 135–50. Oxford: Pergamon Press.

—— 1987: *Exploring Inner Space: Scientists and Religious Experience*, 2nd edn. London: Mowbrays.

—— 1988: Asking questions about religious experience. *Religion* 18, 217–29.

—— 1990: *Religious Experience Today: Studying the Facts*. London: Mowbrays.

—— 1994: "The biology of God": what is the current status of Hardy's hypothesis? *International Journal for the Psychology of Religion* 4, 1–23.

—— 1999: Psychologists interpreting conversion: two American forerunners of the hermeneutics of suspicion. *History of the Human Sciences* 12, 55–72.

—— 2003: Why is implicit religion implicit? *Implicit Religion* 6, 17–41.

—— 2004: A biologist of God: Alister Hardy in Aberdeen. *Aberdeen University Review* 60 (3), 208–21.

—— and Heald, G. 1987: Religion is good for you. *New Society*, April 17.

—— and Hunt, K. 2000: *The Spirituality of People who Don't Go to Church*. Final Report, Adult Spirituality Project, Nottingham University.

—— and Morisy, A. 1978: Reports of ecstatic, paranormal or religious experience in Great Britain and the United States: a comparison of trends. *Journal for the Scientific Study of Religion* 17, 255–77.

—— and—— 1985: Secular society/religious meanings: a contemporary paradox. *Review of Religious Research* 26, 213–27.

—— with Nye, R. 1998: *The Spirit of the Child*. London: HarperCollins.

—— Nye, R., and Murphy, R. 1996: Thinking about childhood spirituality: review of research and current directions. In L. J. Francis, W. K. Kay, and W. S. Campbell (eds.), *Research in Religious Education*, pp. 47–72. Leominster: Gracewing.

Held, D. and McGrew, A. 2002: *Globalization/Anti-globalization*. Cambridge: Polity Press.

Hirschman, A. O. [1977] 1997: *The Passions and the Interests*, 20th Anniversary Edition. Princeton, NJ: Princeton University Press.

Hood, R. W. 1974: Psychological strength and the report of intense religious experience. *Journal for the Scientific Study of Religion* 13, 65–71.

—— 1975: The construction and preliminary validation of a measure of reported religious experience. *Journal for the Scientific Study of Religion* 17, 179–88.

—— (ed.) 1995: *Handbook of Religious Experience*. Birmingham, AL: Religious Education Press.

—— 2001: *Dimensions of Mystical Experiences: Empirical Studies and Psychological Links*. Amsterdam: Editions Rodopi B.V.

Jackson, M. and Fulford, K. W. M. 1997: Spiritual experience and psychopathology. *Philosophy, Psychiatry and Psychology* 4, 41–66.

James, W. [1890] 1950: *The Principles of Psychology*, 2 vols. New York: Dover.

—— [1902] 1985: *The Varieties of Religious Experience*. Cambridge, MA: Harvard University Press.

—— 1920: *The Letters of William James*, ed. Henry James, 2 vols. Boston: Atlantic Monthly Press.

Johnston, W. 1974: *Silent Music: The Science of Meditation*. London: Collins.

Kadowaki, J. K. 1980: *Zen and the Bible: A Priest's Experience*. London: Routledge and Kegan Paul.

Kahn, P. H. 1997: Developmental psychology and the biophilia hypothesis: children's affiliation with nature. *Developmental Review* 17, 1–61.

Katz, S. T. (ed.) 1978: *Mysticism and Philosophical Analysis*. New York: Oxford University Press.

Kellert, S. R. and Wilson, E. O. (eds) 1993: *The Biophilia Hypothesis*. Washington, DC: Island Press.

Kelly, T. M. 2002: *Theology at the Void: The Retrieval of Experience*. Notre Dame, IN: University of Notre Dame Press.

Koenig, H. G. (ed.) 1998: *Handbook of Religion and Mental Health*. San Diego: Academic Press.

——McCullough, M. E., and Larson, D. B. 2001: *Handbook of Religion and Health*. Oxford: Oxford University Press.

Lash, N. 1988: *Easter in Ordinary: Reflections on Human Experience and the Knowledge of God*. Notre Dame, IN: University of Notre Dame Press.

Lee, S. H. 1988: *The Philosophical Theology of Jonathan Edwards*. Princeton, NJ: Princeton University Press.

Leuba, J. H. 1925: *The Psychology of Religious Mysticism*. London: Kegan Paul, Trench, Trubner and Co.

Levinas, E. 1984: Ethics as first philosophy. In S. Hand (ed.), *The Levinas Reader*. Oxford: Blackwell.

Levinson, H. S. 1981: *The Religious Investigations of William James*. Chapel Hill, NC: University of North Carolina Press.

Lindbeck, G. A. 1984: *The Nature of Doctrine: Religion and Theology in a Postliberal Age*. Philadelphia: The Westminster Press.

Lindskoog, D. and Kirk, R. E. 1975: Some life-history and attitudinal correlates of self-actualization among evangelical seminary students. *Journal for the Scientific Study of Religion* 14, 51–5.

Locke, R. G. and Kelly, E. F. 1985: A preliminary model for the cross-cultural analysis of altered states of consciousness. *Ethos* 13, 3–55.

MacIntyre, A. 1990: *Three Rival Versions of Moral Enquiry*. London: Duckworth.

McKenzie, P. 1994: Otto, Wach and Heiler: towards a systematic phenomenology of religion. *Diskus* 2, 29–44.

MacPherson, C. B. 1962: *The Political Theory of Possessive Individualism: From Hobbes to Locke*. Oxford: Clarendon Press.

Marrett, R. R. 1920: *Psychology and Folklore*. London: Methuen.

Marx, K. [1844] 1957: Introduction to the contribution to the critique of Hegel's philosophy of right. In K. Marx and F. Engels, *On Religion*. Moscow: Progress.

Mason, M. 1988: Toward further research on religious experience. Unpublished paper.

Maxwell, M. and Tschudin, V. 1990: *Seeing the Invisible: Modern Religious and Other Transcendent Experiences*. London: Arkana/Penguin.

Meissner, W. W. 1984: *Psychoanalysis and Religious Experience*. New Haven, CT: Yale University Press.

Merton, T. 1968: *Zen and the Birds of Appetite*. New York: New Directions.

Milbank, J. 1990: *Theology and Social Theory: Beyond Secular Reasoning*. Oxford: Blackwell.

Miller, P. 1948: Jonathan Edwards on the sense of the heart. *Harvard Theological Review* 41, 123–45.

——1975: *Errand into the Wilderness*. Cambridge, MA: Harvard University Press.

Nagy, E. and Molnar, P. 1994: *Homo imitans* or *Homo provocans*? In search of the mechanism of inborn social competence. *International Journal of Psychophysiology* 18, 128.

Nase, E. 2000: The psychology of religion at the crossroads: Oskar Pfister's challenge to psychology of religion in the twenties. In J. A. Belzen (ed.), *Aspects in Contexts: Studies in the History of Psychology of Religion*, pp. 45–89. Amsterdam: Editions Rodopi B.V.

Newberg, A., d'Aquili, E., and Rause, V. 2001: *Why God Won't Go Away: Brain Science and the Biology of Belief*. New York: Ballantine.

Otto, R. 1950: *The Idea of the Holy*, trans. J. W. Harvey, 2nd edn. Oxford: Oxford University Press.

Paffard, M. 1973: *Inglorious Wordsworths*. London: Hodder and Stoughton.

Pargament, K. I. 1997: *The Psychology of Religion and Coping: Theory, Research, Practice*. New York: Guilford.

Perry, R. B. 1935: *The Thought and Character of William James as Revealed in Unpublished Correspondence and Notes, Together with his Published Writings*, 2 vols. Boston: Little, Brown.

Persinger, M. A. 1997: *Neuropsychological Bases of God Beliefs*. New York: Praeger Press.

Preus, S. 1987: *Explaining Religion: Criticism and Theory from Bodin to Freud*. New Haven, CT: Yale University Press.

Proudfoot, W. 1985: *Religious Experience*. Berkeley, CA: University of California Press.

Rahner, K. 1983: *Foundations of Christian Faith*, trans. W. C. Dych. New York: Crossroad.

Ramachandran, V. S. and Blakeslee, S. 1998: *Phantoms of the Brain*. London: Fourth Estate.

Reik, T. 1940: *From Thirty Years with Freud*. New York: Farrar and Rinehart.

Rizzuto, A-M. 1979: *The Birth of the Living God*. Chicago: University of Chicago Press.

Robinson, E. 1983: *The Original Vision*. New York: Seabury Press.

——and Jackson, M. 1985: *Religion and Values at 16+*. Oxford: Alister Hardy Research Centre/Christian Education Movement.

Sensky, T., Wilson, A., Petty, R., et al. 1984: The interictal personality traits of temporal lobe epileptics: religious belief and its association with reported mystical experiences. In R. J. Porter et al. (eds), *Advances in Epileptology: 15th Epilepsy International Symposium*, pp. 545–9. New York: Raven Press.

Smith, A. [1776] 1999: *The Wealth of Nations*, ed. A. Skinner, 2 vols. London: Penguin.

Starbuck, E. D. 1899: *The Psychology of Religion: An Empirical Study of the Growth of Religious Consciousness*. New York: Walter Scott.

——1937: Religion's use of me. In V. Ferm (ed.), *Religion in Transition*, pp. 222–7. London: George Allen and Unwin.

Stiglitz, J. E. 2003: *Globalization and its Discontents*. London: Penguin.

Stoeffler, F. E. 1970: *The Rise of Evangelical Pietism*. Leiden: E. J. Brill.

Strout, C. 1971: The pluralistic identity of William James. *American Quarterly* 23, 135–52.

Suzuki, D. T. 1957: *Mysticism, Christian and Buddhist*. London: George Allen and Unwin.

Swinton, J. 2001: *Spirituality and Mental Health Care: Rediscovering a Forgotten Dimension*. London: Jessica Kingsley.

Tacey, D. 2003: *The Spirituality Revolution*. Sydney: HarperCollins.

Tamminen, K. 1991: *Religious Development in Childhood and Youth: An Empirical Study*. Helsinki: Suomalainen Tiedakatemia.

Taylor, C. 2002: *Varieties of Religion Today: William James Revisited*. Cambridge, MA: Harvard University Press.

Thomas, L. E. and Cooper, P. E. 1980: Incidence and correlates of intense spiritual experiences. *Journal of Transpersonal Psychology* 12, 75–85.

Trevarthen, C. 2002: Proof of sympathy: scientific evidence on the co-operative personality of the infant, and evaluation of John Macmurray's "Mother and Child." In D. Fergusson and N. Dower (eds), *John Macmurray: Critical Perspectives*, pp. 77–118. New York: Peter Lang.

Unger, J. 1976: *On Religious Experience: A Psychological Study*. Stockholm: Almquist and Wiksell.

Waring, M. 1809: *A Diary of the Religious Experience of Mary Waring, Daughter of Elijah and Sarah Waring; late of Godalming*. London: William Phillips.

Watson, J. B. 1914: *Behavior: An Introduction to Comparative Psychology*. London: Kegan Paul, Trench, Trubner.

Watts, M. 1978: *The Dissenters*, vol. 1. Oxford: Clarendon Press.

Weber, M. 1930: *The Protestant Ethic and the Spirit of Capitalism*, trans. Talcott Parsons. London: George Allen and Unwin.

Wilson, E. O. 1984: *Biophilia*. Cambridge, MA: Harvard University Press.

Wulff, D. M. 1985: Experimental introspection and religious experience: the Dorpat School of Religious Psychology. *Journal of the History of the Behavioral Sciences* 21, 131–50.

—— 1997: *Psychology of Religion: Classic and Contemporary*, 2nd edn. New York: John Wiley.

Wuthnow, R. 1976: *The Consciousness Reformation*. Berkeley, CA: University of California Press.

Zinnbauer, B., Pargament, K., Cole, B., et al. 1997: Religion and spirituality: unfuzzying the fuzzy. *Journal for the Scientific Study of Religion* 76, 549–64.

CHAPTER 25

Mysticism

David B. Perrin

Mysticism is a phenomenon known to all religions and religious systems. A definition of mysticism, however, even from within the same religious tradition, is no easy task to accomplish, if possible at all. In a now classic study by Dom Cuthbert Butler, first published in 1922, the problem of defining mysticism is clearly stated:

> There is probably no more misused word in these our days than "mysticism." It has come to be applied to many things of many kinds: to theosophy and Christian science; to spiritualism and clairvoyance; to demonology and witchcraft; to occultism and magic; to weird psychical experiences, if only they have some religious color; to revelations and visions; to other-worldliness . . . (1966: 3)

More recently, Bernard McGinn, in a lengthy appendix titled "Theoretical Foundations: The Modern Study of Mysticism" in *Foundations of Mysticism* (1991), affirms the same position as he cites a variety of authors who have likewise acknowledged the lack of agreement on the meaning of the term "mysticism" and the near impossibility of coming to a consensus on its precise definition or its relationship to institutional religion, prayer, or dogmatic belief.

What is acknowledged, however, is that how one defines mysticism depends on one's perspective, and, as Grace Jantzen makes clear in her study *Power, Gender, and Christian Mysticism* (1995), also depends on one's gender. Jantzen further argues, and rather convincingly, that the definition of mysticism is a social construction and is tied closely to knowledge, power, and politics. Thus, it would be the work of an entire essay to review and sift through the various meanings of the word "mysticism" in a way that would do justice to it. Thankfully, these studies, such as those by Cuthbert Butler, Bernard McGinn, and Grace Jantzen cited above, are already available to the reader. Nonetheless, it is important to suggest at least a working definition for mysticism that will get the current reflection on mysticism started without limiting ourselves exclusively to it. But note, by the end of this essay we will have reason to abandon even our working definition!

By way of a disclaimer, it must be acknowledged that the working definition of mysticism that structures this essay is focused on a Western, theistic approach to mysticism, perhaps more easily identified with the Islamic, Jewish, or Christian traditions. The perspective of this essay holds that mystical experiences are "religiously specific experiences: Buddhists have Buddhist mystical experiences; Jews Jewish ones; and Christians have mystical experiences relating to Christ" (McGinn 1991: 322). Thus, while acknowledging that mysticism is "known to all religions and religious systems," such as Buddhism, Sufism, Hinduism, Judaism, or Islam, the treatment of mysticism in this essay presumes a theistic backdrop characteristic of monotheistic religions.

The modern approach to mysticism, especially in the Christian West, is often identified with those individuals who have been gifted with ecstatic or extraordinary intimate experiences of the divine or numinous Other, in whatever way that Other is named. The experience of *oneness or intimacy with some absolute divine reality* is at the heart of what has come to be commonly identified as mysticism. From within our working definition of mysticism these experiences are not usually considered "ordinary" everyday experiences occurring in the flux and flow of our lives, although there is a way of understanding "everyday mysticism" which will be taken up below. However, our definition for mysticism at the beginning of this essay presumes this personal, intense, extraordinary experience in which the boundaries of one's own self become somewhat blurred in the movement of self-transcendence in communion with some absolute divine reality.

These experiences are sometimes described in colorful and vivid terms. For example, visions, auditory occurrences, bodily levitations, and out-of-body experiences have been recounted by men and women who have come to be known as mystics both in the Eastern and Western religious traditions. But to reduce mysticism to these outwardly appearances would render a great disservice to the phenomenon that has come to be known as mysticism. This is not to deny the occurrence of these phenomena, for they have been documented in the history of mysticism. However, to go no further than an exploration of these surface and private phenomena would barely be a beginning in the study of the human experiences known as mysticism. Mystical experiences do not necessarily include extraordinary phenomena; rather, the depth of the mystical experience is the encounter of the Other in the delight of being loved and loving. Here I am proposing that a theistic love-mysticism lies at the core of mystical experiences, but I also acknowledge that not all mystics, nor interpreters of mysticism, would affirm this position, as McGinn's survey reveals (1991: 263–343).

I suggest that the core of mysticism is the radical surrender of self to the loving embrace of the Other who is at the foundation of all life, the One to whom we owe our very existence. This acute awareness may occur with or without the extraordinary phenomena mentioned above. Thus, to enter into the depth of the human experience known as mysticism is to enter into the story of the passionate love affair between humanity and the divine. This outpouring of love has resulted in the transformation of individuals, society, and the church in very many different ways. Some examples will show how this is true.

Francis of Assisi, an Italian Roman Catholic who lived in the thirteenth century, sensitized us to the sacredness of nature and of the entire cosmos. His example continues to inspire many today, especially those involved in various ecological movements. In the fourteenth century, Catherine of Siena, also an Italian Roman Catholic, spoke against the abuses of power by clergy, bishops, and even the pope at the time. Her forthrightness led to church reforms and a return to Rome of the pope who was then living in Avignon, France. Vladimir Solovyov, an Orthodox layman living in the nineteenth century, stressed God's immanence *and* transcendence in sublime unity with all creation. This placed God's presence dead-center in the heart of human life and not in some "other world" out of reach of humanity. The consequences of this led Solovyov to defend oppressed groups and work for the equality of all people. Simone Weil, a French Jewish woman who died in 1943, was radical in her social and political outlook. Her struggle for justice and peace amidst the anti-Semitism of Nazi Germany gave witness to the radical empowering presence of God in her life. Dag Hammarskjöld, the Swedish secretary-general of the United Nations, strived relentlessly for peace and was awarded the Nobel Peace Prize posthumously shortly after his death in 1961.

All these men and women are identified as mystics today. From these few examples we can easily notice two things. First, through the mystical experiences of all these men and women we come to a realization that God's profound love, as experienced in mystical encounter, is not to be locked up within the confines of a monastic cell, or be reserved for subtle expressions in academic treatises or even romantic poetry. Rather, mysticism expresses the deepest aspects of our humanity and the truth about the way that God is alive in the world. Not reserved for the elite or "the holy," mystical experiences are the fuel behind some of the most radical transformations in church and society. Mysticism can be politically dangerous! However, it must be noted, according to Gershom Scholem (1967), that the social effect of mystical experience can go two ways: prophetic critique, or an affirmation of the status quo. What is emphasized here is the positive reformative potentiality that resides in the mystical encounter. Second, though we may imagine that mysticism was largely a "love-affair" of later medieval Europe in the great flowering of mysticism in the twelfth to fourteenth centuries, and subsequently during the intense mysticism of sixteenth-century Spain, we see that mysticism is alive and well in our own times. There continue to rise up among us today men and women who profess intimate and loving encounters with the divine Other. This spurs them on to social, political, and ecclesial involvement on very many different levels.

Although all the examples cited above come from within the Christian tradition, the same is true of mysticism erupting in other faiths. This is to say that mysticism is not added onto what might be otherwise described as the "ordinariness" of a religious culture. Instead, mysticism is an inseparable part of any religious system. Mysticism lies at the core of what helps shape the praxis and beliefs of the world's religious systems, whether shamanism or Buddhism, Catholicism or Islam. The paradox arises, however, that often the mystics are not part of the mainstream within their own religious systems. Rather, they are men and women who, in some ways, stand on the periphery of them; the mystics often lie at "the edge" of the established structures of belief systems. It is *because* they have pitched their tent on "the edge" of these systems that they can be prophetic. This is part of the charism of the mystic; a gift the mystic brings to others. At the foundation of this impetus, for theistic religions, is a profound and intimate experience of the love of the divine Other. Intimate, compelling love is what pulls the theistic mystic forward to face daunting challenges in church and society. But what is even more significant than this is the witness they bear to the profound and intimate love of God.

Historical Sources of Christian Mysticism

The Christian Scriptures do not identify very easily, or very clearly, what has come to be known as mysticism, strictly speaking, in the Christian East and West. The adjective "mystical" (Greek *mystikos*) does not even occur in the New Testament. If we use the rough definition of mysticism alluded to above, that is, "the experience of oneness with some absolute divine reality," then we could tease out certain biblical stories that might be referring to mystical experience as it has been described so far in this essay. Ezekiel 1: 28 – 2: 2, which describes the Lord Yahweh speaking directly to Ezekiel, may qualify as an experience of "direct encounter" with God. Paul of Tarsus's intense experience that results in his conversion on the road to Damascus (Acts 9: 3–9) is easily described as a mystical experience. Paul also appears to be having mystical experiences which he relates in 2 Corinthians 12: 1–4. This text describes "visions and revelations" which he has had "from the Lord." Of course, Jesus himself is portrayed "as a mystic" in his various and many intimate experiences with God.

Whatever might be said of attempting to identify mystical strands in biblical litera-ture that describe intimate encounters or experiences of oneness with the Christian God, later mystics will use biblical texts abundantly to describe and narrate their own mystical experiences. The way mystics draw on the Song of Songs is an apt example of this phenomenon. Bernard of Clairvaux, who lived in the twelfth century, wrote eighty-six sermons on this one scriptural text. Thus, by implication, mystics endow the bibli-cal texts with mystical interpretations, albeit with rather wide amplitude at times, even though the biblical passages might not be explicitly relating mystical experiences.

The biblical witness is essential to understanding the experience of mysticism throughout Christianity, especially in how it relates the description of the profound love of God for humanity and the world. But, from an historical perspective, so is it neces-sary to acknowledge the powerful influence of Hellenistic thought on the development and description of Christian mysticism. The early Christians lived within a Greco-Roman world that had appropriated Plato's philosophy from the fourth century BCE. Christian writers, in turn, used the language, concepts, and categories of Greek thought patterns to articulate their own doctrine of the Christian God and the spiritual quest.

These concepts included the superiority of the uncreated soul to the created mater-ial body and the emanation of the singular soul from the divine One in order to take up "temporary residence" in the body, only to return to union with the One through contemplation. These concepts, among many others, affirmed a dualistic worldview that separated the body from the soul and reinforced a kind of bodily asceticism that would serve as the foundation for aspirants to mystical experiences right up to our own times. That is, in order for the soul to "get to God" one had to "get rid of" the body through severe fasting, corporal flagellation, and extreme isolation. Greek thought, as presented in Neoplatonism, taught that humanity lived in two worlds. Not only is one isolated from the other, but one (the physical world) must be overcome in order to enter the other (the spiritual world). This worldview fed the Christian movement of men and women going to the desert in the second and third centuries.

Later on, it was an anonymous Christian mystic who wrote in the sixth century under the pseudonym of Dionysius the Areopagite, the convert and apostle of Paul mentioned in Acts 17: 34, who would draw on these various ideas and articulate a language of mysticism that was to be the foundation for the future of mysticism up until our own times. This mystic attempted to Christianize Neoplatonist thought in a series of treatises he wrote in Greek in which he developed a highly speculative form of mysticism. The Neoplatonic framework, as appropriated by Christians, aimed at deification (*theosis*) of body *and* soul. This is an important balance to its extremely hierarchical and ascetical emphasis in the purely Greek tradition.

Dionysius was actually thought to be the disciple of Paul from the first century when his writings were uncovered in the ninth century and translated into Latin. Because he was thought to be the disciple of Paul, his writings were given great authority by medieval theologians such as Thomas Aquinas who, in the thirteenth century, incorporated Dionysian ideas into his own writings. The writings of eminent theologians such as Thomas Aquinas went on to make their own place in Christian thought. Thus the "mystical Trojan horse," containing the language and concepts of Greek philosophy, found its way into mainstream Christian teachings.

Following the teachings of Pseudo-Dionysius, many writers, especially from the twelfth century on, set out to describe the stages through which one must pass in order to achieve true mystical enlightenment. Based on the threefold ascending spiritual itinerary of the purgative, illuminative, and unitive way to God mentioned in the writings of Pseudo-Dionysius, there developed a preoccupation with degrees of perfection, and what "must be done" in order to climb the mystical pathway. This "ladder" approach to mysticism was to be the preoccupation of the Christian West for many centuries to come. Somehow the biblical witness of the gratuitous and liberating grace of God at the foundation of all mysticism was cemented over by prescriptive formulas, methods of prayer, and regulating doctrines that were designed by theoreticians in order to achieve progress along the mystical threefold way.

Of course, there were many exceptions to this tendency to view the spiritual life as a linear path following predetermined stages. True mystics, and not theoreticians, continued to rise up both in the East and the West. These mystics did not always fit into the mold of what had become the accepted teachings and practices of the institutional church. For example, in the latter part of the twelfth century a group of laywomen known as the beguines, some of whom were clearly mystics, developed a profound spirituality that focused on active involvement in "worldly" social affairs such as teaching, health care, and care for the poor. These women did not live in monasteries, but did share a communal life together. One of the beguines, Marguerite Porete, was burned at the stake in 1310 because of her teaching of the radical freedom of the individual soul from ecclesiastical disciplines, teachings, and even the sacraments. Instead, Marguerite taught that the individual soul was only dependent on the love and enlightenment of God. The mystic Meister Eckhart (1260–1327) was condemned, but not put to death, for his radical views which stemmed from intense mystical experiences of God. Eckhart's teachings were based on the Neoplatonism mentioned above, and thus were sometimes dualistic in nature, but he also espoused the highest oneness with God in the here and now. Eckhart's teaching on the human soul and God becoming one, not only in mystical rapture, but substantively, was officially condemned in 1329, after his death. As we can see, despite what the theorists were saying, mysticism was alive and well in the dung-laden streets and back-alleys of medieval Europe.

The relationship of themes commonly found in mystical writings ("being one with God," the nature of God, and the dynamics of spiritual development) to the corpus of established dogmatic teachings continues to be a major issue in the reception and study of mysticism today. The Neoplatonism of Pseudo-Dionysius took such root in Western culture, as well as the culture of the Christian East, that we continue to struggle with recognizing the prophetic voice of the mystic that might radically alter some of our thoughts on these issues and many like them.

Where does all this leave us? Essentially, up until modern times (for our purposes, up until the mid-seventeenth century), mysticism was viewed as a largely deconstructive element in mainstream religions. Mystics frequently brought forth challenging new perspectives to view the world, self, God, institutional religion, and society in general. But the paradox was, and still is, that the mystics' insights, albeit founded in the dynamics of being loved and loving, were held with the highest skepticism if their "room with a view" did not fit into the "established household." However, this was to shift in the period between 1890 and 1970, according to the report of Don Cupitt in his intriguing (even if at times somewhat exaggerated) analysis titled *Mysticism after Modernity* (1998).

The Mystical Return: Pre-modern, Modern, Postmodern

Don Cupitt claims that, starting at the end of the nineteenth century, the modern concept and language of mysticism were solidified (1998: 23–7). Essentially, at this time, the mystics were *rediscovered* as men and women who confirmed *the truth* of orthodoxy through their experiential appropriation of the same. Before this time, however, especially during the seventeenth and eighteenth centuries, the word "mysticism," which had originated in France, was used to refer to extravagant and wild spiritual impulses. Mysticism, referring not to "the mystics," but rather to the unbridled expressions of religiosity such as that found in the Quakers (and others too), was the subject of ridicule in "serious" religious conversations by high-ranking churchmen in France during the seventeenth and eighteenth centuries. This changed in the period between 1890 and 1970, the time in which the major books *about* Christian mysticism were published. In particular, at the turn of the century, there was an intense renewal in the academic study of mysticism.

Thanks to the academic interests of those such as William Inge, *Christian Mysticism* (1899), William James, *The Varieties of Religious Experience* (1902), Friedrich von Hügel, *The Mystical Element of Religion* (1908), and Evelyn Underhill, *Mysticism* (1911), as well as many others, the academic study of mysticism received renewed and serious attention from many different perspectives. What is important to underline here is the fact that these writers attempted to analyze critically the phenomenon of mysticism in order to unearth its true nature and value. Beginning, in fact, even earlier, in the early part of the seventeenth century in France, the first attempts were made to compile lists of those known as mystics and identify their writings. The fabrication of a body of texts that would be identified as "mystical literature" came into being at this time. The writings identified as mystical literature, however, would undergo a radical shift in the way in which they were received by academic and practitioner alike as we move toward the twentieth century. Starting in the latter part of the nineteenth century, well-known mystics were "repackaged" into mainstream advocates of the status quo: because of their own "witness" mystics were perceived to be able to make truth claims that were consistent with highly orthodox religious beliefs. This "repackaging," as Cupitt (1998) points out, caused the mystics of the past to be canonized by the same religious systems that had previously ridiculed and even harshly persecuted them. Why was this the case?

Beginning roughly in the mid-seventeenth century, there was a tendency to search for and establish a unified worldview from the perspective of the introspective human subject, and not from the perspective of divine revelation based on God's self-revelation. The radical beginning of this approach to truth and reality is easily pinpointed to the philosophical analysis of René Descartes who, in 1637, published his *Meditations* in which he arrived at his famous *cogito*: "I think, therefore I am." Accompanying this, we have the rise of psychology and its further emphasis on the "interior landscape" pioneered, for example, by Carl Jung and Sigmund Freud in the latter part of the nineteenth century and beginning of the twentieth century. Psychology's emphasis on the non-linguistic and introvertive nature of humanity fed mysticism's interest in the same.

As we move into the twentieth century, mystics were believed to have gifted insight into the depths of reality, and thus mystical experiences, as a subset of religious experience in general, were seen to have a certain noetic value. Through suspension of normal cognitive capacities, the mystic was appreciated as being able to "get behind" reality in order to "get at" its foundations and bring these truths back to this world. This ability of the mystics was harnessed in order to undergird the theoretical systems currently in place. From subjective experiential knowledge of the transcendental subject (the divine or numinous Other) there was a hoped-for objectification of religious truths. This experiential witness became (and continues to be) the authenticating principle of the modernist period. But what the institution retained from the mystics was highly selective in nature. Those insights that did not fit into the system were quietly brushed aside.

However, Cupitt (1998) claims that we are currently involved in a return to the earlier, pre-modern role of mysticism within our religious systems as reflected in a preoccupation with God's loving self-giving. This shift coincides with the entry into what has become known as the postmodern period. The publication by Steven Katz of *Mysticism and Religious Traditions* (1983) marks this in a particular way. Katz argues, and rather successfully, that religious experiences are always described within the "locally available symbolic vocabulary." Culture forms and shapes experience; the experience itself is not independent of the cultural tools (including linguistic ones) available for its expression. For Cupitt, the postmodernist concept of mysticism, developed from the 1970s onward, appreciates the more subtle and radical content of mysticism that is based on the readily available symbolic system of the everyday world and not on the esoteric world of private introspection. Cupitt describes this as a "mysticism of secondariness" (1998: 6). Mysticism of secondariness claims that there is no privileged starting-point from which all subsequent knowledge and ideas can be deduced; that is, there is no absolute primary substance that is fixed in time and place, merely waiting to be "discovered." Cupitt claims that we are always in secondariness, observing and experiencing from this point, then from that, correcting this insight with a latter realization or revisiting a previous one, and so on.

This perspective fits neatly into what is happening on many levels in postmodernist thought. The notion of piecing together a super-narrative that explains and accounts for all aspects of human becoming – whether political, theological, sociological, and so on – has fallen by the wayside. Furthermore, postmodernist thought has abandoned the ambitious project of authenticating everything from the perspective of the experiencing self, for the fulfillment of the self. Indeed, the quest for personal fulfillment was seen, in itself, as the spiritual quest of the modern soul.

With respect to mysticism, what Cupitt is suggesting is that we must search for a kind of mysticism that makes no truth claims based on a privileged access of the self to things "out of this world" in order to attempt to explain things "of this world." Cupitt suggests that we develop our thinking about a mysticism that makes no truth claims associated with mystical experience; that is, drop the noetic from the mystical. This means that we must not turn away from the *multiplicity* of this world to the *oneness* of the "other" world in order to delve into the depths of life. Rather, he claims, meaningful existence is precisely achieved in the mediated, the secondary things of this world, and not in the embrace of the ultimate and primary in some other.

It is *this* world – the living of it and in it – that holds the key to the mystical embrace of the love affair between the divine and the human. This world, with all its symbolic meanings, its capacity for enormous outpouring of joy, love, and reconciliation, its capacity to birth the divine in an endless display of grandeur, is the mysticism to which Cupitt points. Accompanied with the dissolution of the independent, self-affirming subject, this form of mysticism places us back into the world of relationality and connectedness from which the modern period had dissociated the human subject; the touchstone of truth is no longer located within human subjectivity.

The optimism of what the independent and disconnected human could accomplish is sharply questioned in the postmodernist approach. The mysticism of secondariness points to the death of the notion that the world is fully formed by God and merely waiting to be discovered, charted, and then exploited for the benefit of the human subject. This passive, and at the same time domineering, relationship to the world espoused by modernism appears to be coming to an end. The modern pragmatic use of mysticism and its "altered states of consciousness" in order to gird up and authenticate beliefs about God and dogmatic theology is no longer tenable. Furthermore, the modern attempt to make theoretical use of supposedly value-free and culture-free pre-linguistic states of mind in the uncontaminated interior self leads us to a dead end and has forced us to search for a "new" appreciation of mysticism.

Mysticism of Everyday Life

Cupitt's teachings on the "mysticism of secondariness" can be joined to Karl Rahner's (1904–84) teachings on "everyday mysticism" in order to achieve an appreciation of what the study of mysticism might look like in the future. Rahner's most in-depth writings on mysticism are to be found in *The Practice of Faith* (1983).

Rahner holds that the entire world originates from, and is sustained by, the mysterious Other we refer to as God, whether we are consciously aware of this reality or not; or whether we have connected the transcendental truths of life to God (or some other transcendental Other) or not. For example, the transcendental human capacity to "hope against all odds" may or may not be sustained by the belief in a caring and loving God who wills good for the world and who lies at the core of human hope. Or the belief that we are connected to our loved ones, even in death, may not be sustained by a belief in the Christian resurrection. What Rahner is saying is that we have built within our human nature a capacity to live beyond our phenomenal world, even though we may not adhere to any faith system that gives shape and structure to this capacity.

However, Rahner holds that from time to time there emerges within the consciousness of some people a radical awareness of the intimate connection to the transcendental Other who sustains all life. This "awakening" is but an intensification of what already exists in the everyday life of the individual, and thus is not seen as a special gift given to the privileged few. Thus Rahner places mystical experience within the flux and flow of everyday life and the objects of that life (whether they be cultural things, objects, relationships, particular experiences, and so on).

What is key here is the fact that Rahner places the experience of mysticism within the movement of the self-revelation, or better, the self-giving of God. God's loving self-giving is not predicated on particular beliefs or practices of the individual. God's free and gratuitous self-giving, as mediated in the events of everyday life, is at the core of Rahner's notion of "everyday mysticism." Rahner insists that "the real basic phenomenon of mystical experience of transcendence is present as innermost sustaining ground (even though unnoticed) in the simple act itself of Christian living in faith, hope, and love" (1983: 70).

This being said, Rahner does hold a place for what he calls "radical mysticism," which is more closely related to our working definition of mysticism in this essay: direct, immediate, and conscious experiences of God's love (1983: 75). This is an explicit form of mysticism whereby the Christian, *as a Christian*, undergoes a radical experience of God's loving intimacy and names this as such. Aware in a direct and clear fashion that the ground of one's being *is* the Being of God, he or she has a radical experience of such. We might associate this experience with what is often referred to as "infused contemplation," or "the unitive way," that is, the experience of oneness with the divine Other. Yet, Rahner insists, "radical mysticism" is not a higher state of affairs that is more salvific than "everyday mysticism." Radical mysticism is not a higher level of holiness than that given in the ordinariness of the mediated presence of God's self-giving in the occurrences and objects of everyday life. What differentiates "everyday mysticism" from "radical mysticism" is the capacity explicitly to name the origin of the experience within the parameters of the language and religious culture to which one adheres.

The above is a very generalized presentation of Rahner's appreciation of mysticism. Many questions could be asked of Rahner as to how he is able to account theologically and psychologically for the relationship of mysticism to ordinary religious experience; or what role mysticism plays (again theologically as well as psychologically) in the development and growth of one's spiritual life. These questions, and many others like them, must be left for the interested reader to pursue elsewhere. What we want to hold on to here is Rahner's firm belief in the sameness-in-kind of the "ordinary" and "extra-ordinary" way of Christian life. Rahner contends that mysticism, the basic and foundational unity and oneness with God, is at the basis of all human faith, hope, and love, whether or not we name it explicitly as such. What Rahner is addressing is the basic continuity and similar path that all Christian pilgrims are invited to pursue.

Don Cupitt joins Rahner on this point. Cupitt's movement away from the fearful modern God of omnipotence and judicial authority, to a God who is inserted into the relationships of one's everyday life, shifts the emphasis from a mysticism of the extraordinary to a mysticism of the ordinary. After all, Christianity purports to be the religion of the incarnation. A God intimately inserted into the complexity of everyday life, its burdens and joys, failures and successes, is the God of everyday mysticism and the mysticism of secondariness. This is the God of the great Spanish mystic John of the Cross (1542–91) and Thérèse of Lisieux (1873–97), as well as many other mystics down the ages. It is a God who calls us forth *from behind*! God *pushes us* along the pilgrim path rather than calls us forth from some distant future. This is to say that mysticism precedes asceticism. It is because we are intimately bound to God through the event of the incarnation, a relationship that calls us beyond ourselves, that we are able to respond to ascetic practices that deepen the relationship to the mysterious Other we name God.

The Role of Language and Text

Paul Ricoeur, a French philosopher, helps us understand the role of language in human becoming in his extensive work on writing, reading, and interpretation theory. Ricoeur (1981) notes that the critical moment introduced by the mediatory capacity of "languaging" works to expose the illusions of false consciousness and concealed motives both within one's own life and in the dogmatic systems to which one may adhere. It is the *distance* created between the writing subject and subsequent reception of that text through reading that opens the way for new (and potentially dangerous) meaning to emerge. Ricoeur (1991) understands text in its widest meaning, as including cultural traces such as music, painting, sculpture, and so on. It is the moment of critical reflection introduced by the text, and subsequent reception of it in various and different worlds through time, that contributes to a greater sense of historical consciousness and appropriation of selfhood.

This position brings serious consequences to our appreciation of mysticism understood as a kind of "otherworld ecstasy," which is the way mysticism was appreciated in the modern period. The modern thinker on mysticism held that the mystics had ineffable experiences outside of language and then, in a second step, worded these experiences in language always held to be inadequate. Cupitt's position, to which we can join Ricoeur's, holds that the mind does not transcend language at any stage of the cognitive process. Religious experience, even in its most ecstatic state, is not autonomous from language, and therefore mystical texts cannot be made to hold the burden of attempting to bear witness to something experienced "beyond" in another world. Rather, language, from within a particular cultural and linguistic perspective, gives the experience itself and is capable, in subsequent linguistic encounters, of working to appropriate and deepen the experience.

With each textual encounter thereafter emerges the possibility that the self is again enlarged, so the self is not static or fixed, but undergoes continual transformation in order to achieve the project of one's humanity. Similarly, the mystical text is subversive inasmuch as it challenges the status quo of any ideology that would claim to be a completed system and thus not open to further precision and enlargement of meaning. The self, as any belief system, is always rooted in the mysterious loving Other, and therefore eludes any totalizing description. Mysticism, understood as a phenomenon that occurs in the flux and flow of everyday life and not some reach-of-the-mind into otherworldly bliss, is therefore very dangerous indeed. A return to this appreciation of mysticism, and a re-reading of mystical texts from the past with these sensitivities, points us into the future with all its concomitant consequences.

Mystical Texts

Based on the linguistic theory of Ricoeur, the way in which we read what have been identified as mystical texts needs to change. Instead of reading mystical texts from a realist perspective in order to describe states of union or degrees of perfection in relationship to an absolute reality analogous to the way we know ourselves to exist, we need to read them as narratives produced within various literary traditions using differing genres. According to Paul Ricoeur (1975), genre is not so much a description of the classification of a kind of text but rather describes "rules of production" that guide subsequent meaning-events as the texts are taken back up again into living speech. Mystical texts are not so much descriptive in response to the need to identify mystics as orthodox apologists as they are potent configurations of meaningful worlds yet to be constructed and explored. The mystics' use of strong metaphors and oftentimes erotic language resists the containment of their texts to singular interpretations.

This being the case, mystical texts, because of their surplus of meaning, resist the kind of categories and conclusions arrived at from the heavy emphasis placed on onto-theology in the modern period. As Merold Westphal states, "the onto-theological project commits the fallacy of misplaced concreteness. It abstracts the cognitive dimension of the religious life and gives it essential primacy . . . [I]n its more overtly theological modes, onto-theology finds that it has cut itself off from the modes of appropriation, singing and dancing, for example, that constitute living faith" (1999: 157). The author of the *Cloud of Unknowing*, a fourteenth-century mystic, knew this to be the case. His emphasis on the non-Being of God, similar to the *nada* of John of the Cross, refuses to accept a God of absolute reality that would cut God off from the flux and flow of living faith.

Meaning is encoded in textual form and awaits the possibility of being joined back to meaning through the act of reading. But this reading is not a mere "unpacking" of what exists in the text; that is, the search for some absolute truth. Rather, texts, and in a special way the heavily poetic mystical texts, work in conjunction with the life experience of the reader in order to construct new meaning that may be quite independent of the original intention of the author. Again, to emphasize, mystical texts are not the mere communication of objective information but are the means of constructing new possibilities for living in the face of truths that may have become too solid. In this way they can serve as a severe corrective to current understandings and ways of conducting our political and ecclesial affairs. Through them we can discover new existential possibilities for the self and the way we live in the world.

The mystical text allows us to objectify the dynamics of human life without attempting to limit those dynamics to a singular, finite expression. There is a creative tension in the mystical text that holds together our daily expression of the ethical and the mystical, and therefore works to renew our humanity. Through an openness to mystical texts as "purveyors of the not yet" we are liberated from the limitations of descriptive reference and opened up to access reality in the mode of fiction and feeling. We thus are freed from slavery to ontological certainties that would prevent us from further creation and exploration of our world.

The Future of Mysticism

Given the very brief reflection on mysticism above, we can draw together a number of propositions that might suggest the future landscape of how mysticism might be situated and appreciated in our postmodern world with its developing spiritualities. It is the postmodern world that has, surprisingly, turned toward the mystics in a favorable fashion and has expressed a renewed interest in negative or apophatic theology. We can recall Rahner's often-cited dictum: "The Christian of the future will be a mystic or he or she will not exist at all" (1983: 22). Or to quote David Tracy: "postmodern visions seek out religion most often in its most transgressive and excessive forms – such as the Christian love mystics; the Kabbalists; the Sufis; the apophatic thinkers like Pseudo-Dionysius, Marguerite Porete, or Meister Eckhart; or the uncontainable force of a religious phenomenon like Joan of Arc" (1999: 177). Both these well-known scholars bring into focus what might be summarized by way of conclusion in the following points:

Radical embodiment

Spiritual practice is always "local" and "embodied." Mysticism needs to include the acknowledgment that it involves the integration of all elements of the person, and thus let go of the preoccupation with the disembodied experience of unity with some transcendent Other. This emphasis includes the need to recognize that the self only exists in relationship to a larger community, beyond the confines of one's own skin. The "nature of human nature" is undergoing serious reassessment as a result of the way we are returning to a pre-modern appreciation of what the mystics bring to discussions concerning human anthropology and epistemology. The paradigm of inter-relatedness is the norm. Recognizing this can assist us to overcome our religious alienation of the self from others and from God by acknowledging that we all live in the one world that the human and the divine continually construct as a common project. Mysticism is not so much about finding ways to "name God" as allowing God to "name *us*" as a *we*. This can only lead to the construction of liberating social, political, and ecclesial systems for the community as a whole, and not for the exclusive enjoyment (or holiness) of the singular person.

Prophetic nature

We are currently undergoing a retrieval of the appreciation of mysticism and mystical literature with its focus on the prophetic and charismatic rather than the priestly and institutional. This sensitivity will assist us to acknowledge the intimate connection between knowledge and power (the domain of the modernist mystic) in order to move away from the political model of the God of domination. Furthermore, it will assist us to move away from the social construction of mysticism that has favored male dominance (male religious experience) to the exclusion of that of women. An open "listening" to the mystics will allow us to make God more lovable and loving for all; it will allow us to return to the earliest emphasis (in the Christian tradition) of the God of Absolute Graciousness *for all people*, rather than the sterile Absolute God of Being of the philosophers. The study of mysticism is not about the abandonment of theism; rather, it is a move away from the enslavement of a God who is expected to respond to our whims and transitory desires, or be used to protect the private interests of some segments of society or faith groups. "What to believe" and "what to practice" are questions that must always be kept open for all persons. Sensitivity to the ecumenical and interfaith dimensions of mysticism will be especially important here, since in them we are especially challenged to confront difference in ways that are reconciliatory and productive of wellbeing for all.

Chosen subservience

The mystical tradition has never been the dominant part of the tradition in religious systems. From this place of "chosen subservience," it will continue to deconstruct the classical realistic, philosophical idea of God and human nature in order to place the emphasis on the God of extravagant self-giving love. This will place an emphasis on the horizontal immanence of God instead of vertical metaphysical structures and beliefs that result in alienation – from ourselves and from God. A quiet culture of "protest" has always been alive in the mystical tradition and will continue to be so from this place of subservience in order to assist us to redefine orthodoxy when it falls short of what we currently know about our relationship to God, self, and our world.

Departure from dualisms

Mysticism of the future will need to continually work (and work hard) to overcome the harmful dualisms that have been implanted in it from Greek thought, even as adapted and brought to us through Neoplatonism. Metaphysical discussions on, for example, "things changing" and "things unchanging," or the disconnectedness between the "spiritual" and the "material," must be questioned as to their helpfulness in being sensitive to the "embodied mystic." The way in which we understand terms such as the human mind, spirit, body, and soul will be challenged by a deconstruction of dualistic approaches to our world. We are increasingly coming to understand that things like location, place, perspective, bias, and gender all play a far greater role in mystical construction than the philosophical categories of the speculative mind.

Language

A greater appreciation of the intended irrationality of the language of the mystic and a greater acceptance of the "wild card" played by the mystic in language need to take place. We need to acknowledge that the mystic is not describing reality, but rather works through metaphors (sometimes highly erotic ones), in order to create new, unthought-of worlds of human becoming. Sensitivity to this "poetic play" would make all the difference to the way in which we receive mystical texts. We blind ourselves if we continue to insist on reading the great mystics of the past with an eye to turning them into orthodox apologists. This is to say that we need to set aside the tendency to put speculative truth first. Putting speculative truth first tends to reinforce theological realism – something that the mystics were not about at all. Contemporary hermeneutical theory offers invaluable tools in this regard.

Ineffability

Is ineffability really one of the main hallmarks of mysticism? Given the discussion above, especially the realization that it is the language of one's culture that *gives* the "mystical experience," we need to ask ourselves what we really mean by ineffable, and subsequently the consequences of that understanding. "Mystical experience" is not some voiceless, disembodied moment. We are led, therefore, to question any focus on the introverted, privatized self that first experiences and then, in a subsequent step, "attempts" to bring this experience to language. Questioning the notion of ineffability also raises the specter of the self-validating nature of mysticism, hotly sought after in the modernist quest.

Sacred and profane

The approach to mysticism presented in this essay risks leading toward a secularization of religion; that is, it takes religion into the marketplace of life and out of the institution. Mircea Eliade (1959) has long advocated such a breakdown between the sacred and the profane. This is not a bad thing. The tension between the institution that (falsely) represents the sacred, and the individual in society that (falsely) represents the profane, will most likely always exist. However, the mystic is not about this kind of duality and we, as a whole, need to move beyond it. Furthermore, a breakdown of the sacred/profane duality will require a re-evaluation of what have come to be known as "classical spiritual texts." Mysticism of the future may very well identify a different corpus of "mystical texts" from the past, thereby redefining who counts as a mystic. As well, new forms (genres) of mystical texts, understood in the broadest way *à la Ricoeur*, may be produced and recognized as such in the future. For example, different kinds of written texts, as well as paintings, sculptures, or graphics, may be recognized as the way in which the mystical tradition is received and passed along.

Theocentrism v. Christocentrism

There is some question as to whether the Christian mysticism of the future will be more closely tied to our theistic beliefs, or more closely focused on the life, ministry, death, and resurrection of Jesus. This is to ask the question: is the core of Christian mysticism tied more closely to God, God's Being, attributes, and names? Or, rather, is it to be more closely aligned with the humanity of Jesus, his healing ministry, the way he died, and the ultimate confession of his resurrection by those who believe? What is of concern for the future is not a world-denying mysticism that has little interest in the social and political dimensions of life; rather, the mysticism of the future will emphasize its interpersonal dimension as well as its transformative relationship to social justice and political structures.

Fragments

David Tracy makes a plea that we must let go of any totalizing system whatsoever. We must, he says, "Focus instead on the explosive, marginal, saturated, and at times, auratic fragments of our heritage" (1999: 178–80). Without burdening the mystic with being the singular carrier of such an agenda, we can affirm that the mystic does have a particular role to play in this vision. For it is precisely in the "explosive" and "marginal" that the mystic lives. The mystics have not left behind systems in their writings; rather, they have left behind something far more valuable: "concentrated reflections, saturated images – fragments." In the fragments, the mystics have learned to explore the mysterious wonder of the cosmos, of God, and of our humanity, and to live joyfully in the exploration and construction of these realities. This challenges us with a new way of living and believing, with a sense of hope against all hope. In this hope we can become comfortable living in a rich mosaic of religious experiences and spiritualities that do not necessarily need to be connected to a common ontological foundation.

Our task for the future is to identify the spiritual fragments given to us by the mystics such as Pseudo-Dionysius, Nicholas of Cusa, Julian of Norwich, Hildegard of Bingen, Meister Eckhart, Marguerite Porete, and John of the Cross, whether they fit into "the system" or not, and allow these fragments to continue their hope-filled work of breaking open our current world to new possibilities for life and love. The task is not to construct a new totalizing system, but rather to piece together a "new constellation of fragments" such that our love relationship with God and our world is constantly renewed.

References

Butler, C. 1966: *Western Mysticism: The Teaching of Augustine, Gregory and Bernard on Contemplation and the Contemplative Life*, 2nd edn. New York: Harper Torchbooks.

Cupitt, D. 1998: *Mysticism after Modernity*. Malden, MA: Blackwell.

Eliade, M. 1959: *The Sacred and the Profane: The Nature of Religion*, trans. W. R. Trask. New York: Harcourt, Brace.

Ellwood, R. 1980: *Mysticism and Religion*. Englewood Cliffs, NJ: Prentice-Hall.

Frohlich, M. 2001: Christian mysticism in postmodernity: Thérèse of Lisieux as a case study. In D. Perrin (ed.), *Women Christian Mystics Speak to our Times*, pp. 157–71. Franklin, WI: Sheed and Ward.

Inge, W. 1899: *Christian Mysticism: Considered in Eight Lectures Delivered before the University of Oxford*. London: Methuen.

James, W. 1902: *The Varieties of Religious Experience: A Study in Human Nature*. New York: Longmans, Green and Co.

Jantzen, G. 1995: *Power, Gender, and Christian Mysticism*. Cambridge: Cambridge University Press.

Kaplan, N. and Katsaros, T. 1969: *The Western Mystical Tradition: An Intellectual History of Western Civilization*. New Haven, CT: College and University Press.

Katz, S. 1983: *Mysticism and Religious Traditions*. Oxford: Oxford University Press.

Lewis Furse, M. 1977: *Mysticism: Window on a World View*. Nashville: Abingdon.

McGinn, B. 1991: *Foundations of Mysticism: Origins to the Fifth Century*. London: SCM.

Perrin, D. B. 1996: Mysticism and art: the importance of affective reception. *Église et Théologie* 27, 47–70.

Rahner, K. 1983: *The Practice of Faith: A Handbook of Contemporary Spirituality*. New York: Crossroad.

Ricoeur, P. 1975: Biblical hermeneutics. *Semeia: Experimental Journal for Biblical Criticism* 4, 27–148.

——1978: The language of faith. In C. Reagan and D. Stewart (eds), *The Philosophy of Paul Ricoeur: An Anthology of his Work*, pp. 223–38. Boston: Beacon Press.

——1979: Naming God. *Union Seminary Quarterly Review* 34, 215–27.

——1981: The hermeneutical function of distanciation. In J. B. Thompson (ed. and trans.), *Hermeneutics and the Human Sciences*, pp. 131–44. Cambridge: Cambridge University Press.

——1991: What is a text? Explanation and understanding. In K. Blamey and J. B. Thompson (eds and trans.), *From Text to Action: Essays in Hermeneutics II*, pp. 105–24. Evanston, IL: Northwestern University Press.

Scholem, G. 1967: Mysticism and society. *Diogenes* 58, 1–24.

Sells, M. A. 1994: *Mystical Languages of Unsaying*. Chicago: University of Chicago Press.

Tracy, D. 1999: Fragments: the spiritual situation of our times. In J. D. Caputo and M. J. Scanlon (eds), *God, the Gift, and Postmodernism*, pp. 170–84. Bloomington, IN: Indiana University Press.

Underhill, E. 1911: *Mysticism: A Study in the Nature and Development of Man's Spiritual Consciousness*. New York: Dutton.

von Hügel, F. 1908: *The Mystical Element of Religion as Studied in Saint Catherine of Genoa and her Friends*. London: J. M. Dent.

Westphal, M. 1999: Overcoming onto-theology. In J. D. Caputo and M. J. Scanlon (eds), *God, the Gift, and Postmodernism*, pp. 146–69. Bloomington, IN: Indiana University Press.

CHAPTER 26

Interpretation

Philip F. Sheldrake

The study of Christian spirituality involves critical issues of interpretation both of spiritual traditions as a whole and of specific texts. In this context, the word "texts" may refer to the Scriptures, viewed as spiritual wisdom documents, to other written works in the tradition, or it may be understood more broadly. While biblical texts are obviously accorded a special "revelatory" status, to approach other texts as bearers of spiritual wisdom raises similar interpretative issues. I take interpretation to be essentially a quest for understanding. This is a complex matter as understanding is associated with "meaning" rather than purely with gathering factual information and data.

The fundamentals of Christian spirituality as a field of study, its object and methods, are considered in detail elsewhere in this volume. At this point I merely wish to summarize some key points that relate to the question of "interpretation." First of all, I am going to assume, rather than develop, the widely accepted notion that spirituality is a self-implicating discipline. This suggests that the study of spirituality is not only *informative* but also *transformative*. When we approach particular traditions or texts, we clearly seek *information*. This is likely to include historical data, a detailed analysis of texts, an understanding of theological frameworks, and a determination of the kind of spiritual wisdom or practice that is being represented. However, beyond *information* lies a quest for the "truth" or wisdom embodied in a tradition or text and how this may be accessed. This aspect of coming to understand a tradition or text confronts us with the questions "What difference does this make?" and "What could or should our response be?" This is the *transformative* dimension of the study of spirituality and involves *judgment* (this makes sense, is important, and of value) and *appropriation* (we seek to make this wisdom our own). I will return to this point later.

This rich approach to "understanding" in the field of Christian spirituality inevitably means that the Enlightenment ideal of a single method, appropriate to a free-standing field of study, has to be abandoned. Indeed, in the academic world more broadly, the notion of internally consistent but mutually exclusive disciplines separated by hard boundaries is breaking down. The identity of an area of study is no longer to be found in maintaining sharp distinctions of method. This shift has been characterized as "a centrifugal, rather than centripetal sense of disciplinary identity" (Scott and Simpson-Housley 1991: 178). In this context, Christian spirituality is generally agreed to be an *interdisciplinary* field (albeit with a special relationship to theology) that draws on a range of methods and thus demands a sophisticated rather than simple approach to interpretation.

In the first instance, an interdisciplinary approach expands the disciplines on which the process of interpretation draws. Depending on the nature of the tradition or text under consideration, the classical approach drew on historical, linguistic, and literary methods. Because of the religious nature of what is being interpreted, theological tools were also necessary as aids to analysis and evaluation (Sheldrake 1998: 88–93). To these must now be added an engagement with the methods of modern philosophy, social sciences, and psychology, along with critical fields such as feminist or liberationist theory.

However, the more complex approach to interpretation nowadays implies more than a mere expansion of the methods employed. Precisely because the spiritual traditions and texts to be interpreted are viewed as likely sources of *wisdom*, interpretation has shifted beyond which methods might provide the best data to hermeneutical theory – in other words, to a much deeper consideration of the very nature of interpretation itself. This approach asks what "world of meaning" is presented in a tradition or text and what kind of wisdom is available. Such an approach to interpretation recognizes that what is present in spiritual wisdom texts and traditions is not reducible to what we can know cognitively. Because such wisdom is profoundly challenging and is likely to change us if we pursue it, a contemplative approach must be added to an intellectual one (Schneiders 1999a: 11–25).

Is There Wisdom in History?

Many of the texts and traditions we seek to interpret are strange to us because of historical and cultural distance. Consequently, in approaching the question of interpretation, one fundamental factor is how we view the nature or importance of "history" itself. We exist in a time of cultural change in the West when people often ask whether history any longer has a point. Are Western cultures rapidly becoming history-less and memory-less? If this is the case, then in the long term it will surely have a serious impact on our spiritualities. It is possible to detect in Western cultures a weariness with history and with the notion of being involved in a tradition or in a stream of continuities through time. To base one's life on tradition or to hark back to the past appears to be a distraction. It is much more common these days for people to believe that "history" only signifies the past. The past is what has happened rather than something that enables our present to come into being or that invites us to reflect on the future and on what we aspire to. Yet, tradition (Latin *traditio*) is not merely to hand on an historical story, but also to *hand it over*, so that it may be freely and creatively re-expressed by each generation as part of its own self-identification.

This weariness with history relates to a number of probable factors. Rapid social changes and the decline of traditional communities have broken many people's sense of a living connection with the past. "History" and its sibling, "tradition," are also perceived by some people as conservative forces from which we need to break free if we are to live a more mature and rational existence. The power of "history" (or, more accurately, of history-as-myth) to sustain entrenched social, religious, and political divisions tends to reinforce this negative view. Beyond this, there is a desire for immediacy sustained by consumerism (and reinforced by aspects of information technology) that tends to encourage a memory-less culture without a sense of historical identity. Perhaps the most powerful factor of all during the course of the twentieth century was the death of a notion of "history-as-destiny." This notion was based on faith in the inevitability of progress after a century of industrial growth and imperialistic expansion. Such a belief in "history" as a progressive force evaporated in the face of the mass slaughter of the 1914–18 war, the brutality of mid-century totalitarianism, and the horrors of the Holocaust and Hiroshima.

Despite these contemporary misgivings, historical consciousness is a basic element in the interpretation of religious texts. Apart from anything else, it reminds us of the irreducibly contextual nature, and therefore particularity, of spirituality and spiritual values. Serious consideration of the complexities of history has been a major development in the academic study of spirituality over the past thirty years or so. Before that time, the study of spirituality tended to pay little attention to context, whether the historical context of spiritual texts and traditions or the context of the contemporary interpreter. Studies of historical traditions did not reflect on the contingency of their theological or cultural presuppositions. In the case of classical spiritual writings, problems of interpretation were not a major issue in a world where Christians had little sense of historical distance from the perspective and even the language of ancient authors. The tendency, therefore, was to assume that the meaning of a text was confined to the literal sense of the words, which were not thought to change much over time, and to the intentions of the original author which were assumed to be both transparent and paramount.

The Importance of Context and Culture

One important reason why the study of spirituality in theological circles now pays greater attention to the complexity of historical interpretation lies in an important shift provoked by a significant change of language associated with the Second Vatican Council in the early 1960s. The use of the phrase "signs of the times" by Pope John XXIII, and its repetition in the Council documents, was effectively a recognition that history was not incidental to, but the context for, God's redemptive work. Every historical moment (and the texts and traditions that develop within it) has a dynamic of its own where the presence and power of God may be perceived. Consequently, faith is not opposed to history, and no separation is possible between religious history and world history (Ruggieri 1987: 92–5).

Thus, spiritualities do not exist on some ideal plane outside the limitations of history. The origins and development of spiritual traditions reflect the specific circumstances of time and place, as well as the psychological state of the people involved. They consequently embody values that are socially conditioned. To take merely one example, the emphasis on radical poverty in the spirituality of the mendicant movement of the thirteenth century (not least in Francis and Clare of Assisi) was not the result of spiritual insight detached from the general social and cultural context. "Poverty" was both a spiritual and social reaction to particular conditions in society and the church at the time – not least to what were seen as their prevailing sins (Le Goff 1981).

This does not imply that spiritual traditions and texts have no value beyond their original contexts. However, it does mean that to appreciate their riches fully we must take context seriously. While scriptural values clearly play an explicit role in the development of all Christian spiritualities, critical investigation inevitably reveals two things. First, these values are appropriated in different ways in different contexts. Second, other forces also control the development of traditions and the ways in which they are recorded.

The concept of "context" was originally imported from the fields of history and the social sciences. It has become a primary framework of interpretation in the study of spiritual traditions. All spiritual experience is determined to some degree by culture. By "culture," I imply a system of meaning or a worldview in the sense used originally by anthropology but now borrowed by other disciplines. Culture "denotes an historically transmitted pattern of meanings embodied in symbols, a system of inherited conceptions expressed in symbolic forms by means of which men [sic] communicate, perpetuate, and develop their knowledge about and attitudes toward life" (Geertz 1973: 89). This approach emphasizes that culture itself is a "text," potentially with many layers of meaning. It demands sophisticated interpretation rather than straightforward classification and explanation. The symbols, rituals, attitudes, and perspectives about life that constitute a "culture" enable human societies to cohere and function. Culture regulates how people assign meaning and allocate value in terms of the key elements of human living. It defines their social, economic, political, and religious behavior. Spiritual traditions, and the texts that are their "products," are cultural expressions (Flanagan 1999; Gallagher 1999).

Spirituality is thus never pure in form. "Context" is not really a "something" that may be added to or subtracted from spiritual experience or practice, but is the very element within which these find expression. Even though religions claim a transcendent dimension, all faiths throughout history have been embedded in specific cultures (de Certeau 1966; Sheldrake 1995: 58, 84–6, 167–8). This contradicts an older conception of Christian spirituality as a stream of enduring truth in which the same theories or images are simply repeated in different guises. Even spiritual theologians as sophisticated as Karl Rahner and his brother Hugo appeared at times to place a figure like Ignatius of Loyola essentially outside the limitations of history. His spirituality was "not really an event in the history of ideas that could be inserted, if we were so to choose, in the 'Tridentine' or 'Baroque' periods . . . It is something of exemplary value in a quite fundamental way, for an age that is only just starting." In a footnote, Karl Rahner developed this thought further by suggesting that "Ignatius has something almost of the archaic and archetypal about him . . . He has nothing that really belongs to the Baroque or the Renaissance about him" (1964: 85–7). The writings of the Rahner brothers led the British historians of the Catholic Reformation, Outram Evennett and John Bossy, to point out the danger of making spiritual experience or teaching "a region of certainty transcending any historical or psychological conditions"(Evennett 1968: 55–6, 126–32; see also Bossy 1975).

These comments about culture and context in relation to spirituality would now be widely accepted. However, the way in which contextual studies have developed raises serious questions for people who are concerned with the specifically religious themes of spirituality. For example, the history of spirituality has come to mean the study of how religious attitudes and values are conditioned by surrounding culture and society. This brings historical spirituality close to the study of *mentalités*, or worldviews, so beloved of French historians in the second half of the twentieth century. This "social" version of history is informed by anthropology and religious sociology. The limitation of such an approach to spirituality, if it is exclusive, is that it tends to abandon theological sources and the questions raised by theological theory. We need a middle way between the older (exclusively theological) approach to spirituality and the newer stress on changing social contexts (Bynum 1982: 3–6).

A case study is provided by recent treatments of early Christian asceticism and monasticism. A contextual approach tends to re-situate asceticism in a broader world than that of monasticism or even of patristic Christianity, and approaches its history with questions drawn from a wide range of disciplines. This raises many new and interesting questions. The problem is that such an approach *in isolation* often leaves little or no room for the theological goals that were the active horizons of Christian asceticism (Stewart 1996).

Context and Choices

Because of the contextual nature of spiritual traditions in their origins and in the ways in which they are transmitted, any process of interpretation must address a number of critical questions (Sheldrake 1995: chs 3, 4, and 7). First, in any given period or text how was holiness conceived? Which categories of people were thought of as holy? What places or things were deemed to be particularly sacred – or, negatively, who or what was excluded from the category "holy" or "sacred"? For example, close association with sexual activity (marriage) or with physical reality (manual labor) was for many centuries difficult to connect with ideas of holiness. Secondly, who creates or controls spirituality? For example, to what degree does the language of spirituality reflect the interests and experience of minority groups (who nevertheless controlled spiritual resources) such as clergy or monastic personnel? Thirdly, what directions were not taken? In other words, to what degree has it been assumed that the choices made were in some absolute way superior to those that were rejected? For example, what were the real motives for the condemnation as heretics of the medieval women's spiritual movement, the beguines? Was it a genuine concern for the spiritual welfare of lay people or a suspicion of lay people not sufficiently under clerical control (Murk-Jansen 1998)?

Finally, where are the groups that did not fit? For example, why was it that, within the Western Catholic tradition, the experience of lay Christians, and women especially, was largely ignored until recently in the formulation of spiritual theory?

All historical studies involve choices, and this affects our interpretation of spiritual traditions. First, *time limits* are chosen. In other words, writers decide on the appropriate boundaries within which to date spiritual movements and thus to understand them. For example, our sense of the continuity or discontinuity between the spirituality of the Middle Ages and that of the Protestant Reformation will be affected by an apparently simple matter of how and where authors choose to divide a multi-volume history (Raitt 1987: introduction). Secondly, traditional histories reveal a *geographical bias*. We make assumptions about where "the center" and "the margins" are in the history of spiritual traditions. For example, until recently, the spirituality of Celtic Christianity was usually treated in terms of its absorption into a homogenized Latin tradition around the eleventh and twelfth centuries rather than on its own terms. Thirdly, we choose *certain evidence as significant*. So, for example, if studies concentrate exclusively on mystical texts or monastic rules, the impression is given that spirituality is essentially literary, is to be found exclusively in privileged contexts, and may be distinguished from the mere devotions of "popular religion."

Interpretation and Commitment

The question of choices, even in the context of purely historical study, already suggests that every act of interpretation is value-laden and involves various kinds of commitment that are far from simple. Because, for many Christians, certain important spiritual texts (or "classics") have been accorded the status of wisdom documents, there is a particular edge to the scholarly question of interpretation. With both scriptural texts and spiritual wisdom documents, similar basic questions arise. If our interest in such texts is not purely literary or antiquarian, the questions of *why* we read such texts and what we read them *for* are particularly central. How we proceed to read texts is thus intimately related to why we read them. Fundamentally, we cannot unlock the depths of a spiritual wisdom document, any more than the depths of a scriptural text, except through a process of interpretation that draws the reader into a particular world of meaning.

In this context, a number of scholars now refer to what has been called an "appropriative method" in relation to interpreting Christian traditions and texts, whether scriptural or spiritual. By this, scholars mean that the purpose of interpretation is not merely accurate knowledge but *application* and the purpose of application is *appropriation*. That is, "understanding" a spiritual text fully is transformative rather than purely informative (Downey 1997: 126–31; Schneiders 1999b; Williams 2000: ch. 4). Understanding is concerned with meanings, but also with purpose and values. To be appropriated, texts need to be understood from the inside out, as it were.

In his introduction to a collection of essays on the theological interpretation of Scripture (but with considerable relevance to reading texts of spirituality), Stephen Fowl outlines such an approach. Both the fragmentation of theological disciplines and the separation of theology from praxis are, he argues, products of modernity, with its particular understanding of the process of knowing and the content of knowledge (Fowl 1997: xii–xvii). The modern era promoted historical-critical methods that tended to separate a way of reading directed at historical reconstruction from the theological purpose that a Christian reading of Scripture was intended to serve. However, throughout Christian history it has been normal for the majority of Christians to read the Scripture *theologically*, at least implicitly. That is, they read Scripture "to guide, correct, and edify their faith, worship and practice as part of their ongoing struggle to live faithfully before the triune God" (Fowl 1997: xiii). This same understanding of textual reading may be applied to spiritual "classics." The transformative approach to interpretation and knowledge has also been endorsed in recent decades by philosophical theologians such as the Roman Catholic David Tracy (1991: 77–8) and the Anglican Rowan Williams (1991: ch. 5).

The Nature of Spiritual "Classics"

The presentation of the history of spirituality and the interpretation of texts are of general as well as scholarly concern. Many people associate themselves with historic spiritual traditions in ways that affect their present sense of identity. Equally, other people seek spiritual wisdom through the medium of classical texts. Even those people who have departed from conventional religious traditions paradoxically draw upon the traditional wisdom of such classic Christian mystical figures as Hildegard of Bingen, Meister Eckhart, and the anonymous author of *The Cloud of Unknowing*. The interpretation of classic texts for contemporary use is therefore a live and critical one.

While spiritual texts are historically conditioned, some cross the boundaries of time or place and retain their popularity and importance in contexts very different from their own. This is what is implied by the term "classics" (Tracy 1991: ch. 3). Such texts disclose something that remains compelling. They continue to challenge readers and bring them into transforming contact with what is enduring and vital in the Christian tradition. The nature of a text's literary genre often influences its popularity and effectiveness (Sheldrake 1995: 172–3). In general, the strength of the classics is that they do not merely offer information but are capable of persuading and moving a reader to a response.

A vital aspect of the special power of spiritual classics is the fact that they are *committed texts*. Spiritual classics, rather like scriptural texts, offer a particular interpretation of events, people, or teachings. Every spiritual classic has a specific "take" on the tradition it promotes. In interpreting a spiritual classic, we unavoidably engage with this commitment. We cannot bypass the claims to wisdom – indeed, to a vision of "truth" – embodied in such texts. David Tracy suggests the following in exploring the notion of what he calls a "classic text":

> First, there exists a qualitative difference between a classic and a period piece; second, there exists an assumption that a classic, by definition, will always be in need of further interpretation in view of its need for renewed application to a particular situation; third, a

classic, again by definition, is assumed to be any text that always has the power to transform the horizon of the interpreter and thereby disclose new meaning and experiential
possibilities. (1994: 115)

In a genuine classic there is always what Tracy calls a paradoxical tension between its
particularity and its universality. The "universality" of the classic is its capacity to disclose a world of meaning and to evoke transformation in a potentially infinite succession of readers. Interestingly, for Tracy the category of "a classic" is not limited to
written texts but may be extended beyond books to events and persons that have some
form of revelatory status (Tracy 1994: 118). As we will see later, I would add to this
list artifacts and buildings. Thus, a personality such as Francis of Assisi or a Gothic
cathedral may be as much a "classic text" as the *Showings* of Julian of Norwich.

The Process of Interpretation

We are inevitably aware of different cultural and theological perspectives when we read
a classic spiritual text from another time or place. If interpretation is meant to serve
appropriation, we cannot avoid the question of how far to respect a text's conceptual
framework, structure, or dynamic in relation to contemporary practice. Certain
responses would be naïve. We may ignore the author's intention and the text's structure entirely and simply pick and choose from the text as it suits us. The opposite danger
is to assume that only the author's intention is normative. Even assuming that we can
accurately reconstruct this intention, such an approach subordinates our present horizons to the past and ignores entirely the context of the contemporary reader. Both
approaches assume that the "meaning" of a text is a straightforward matter. A more
fruitful, while more complex, approach to interpretation is to engage in a receptive yet
critical *dialogue* with the text. Such a dialogue allows the wisdom of a text to challenge
us, while at the same time according our own horizons their proper place (Gadamer
1979).

If there is to be a dialogue between the horizons of a text and our own, the text's
historical context is certainly an important starting-point. Spiritual classics were
written for clearly identified audiences and addressed specific concerns. The insights of
literary criticism also remind us that, however familiar words may seem to be in the
first instance, the experiences and assumptions that lie behind them are different from
our own and consequently give particular words a new significance. We also need to
recall that, in reading a text, we are not dealing with two quite disconnected moments
(our own and that of the author), but also with what comes between: that is, how a
text has been transmitted from its origins to the present and the history of its interpretation. The tradition of interpretation and use of a text over centuries affects our
own moment of reading. I will return later to the question of how we are to define the
"community of capable readers" across time.

While historical knowledge has to some extent a normative role in interpreting texts,
there are limits to its value. For example, what we encounter in a text is not direct experience of another time but what the text *claims* about it, for all texts employ the con-

ventional categories of their age. In other words, all texts are themselves interpretations of experience, not merely records of it. Some, such as the Long Text of the *Showings* of Julian of Norwich (the fourteenth-century English woman mystic), were written many years after the experiences that gave rise to them and are explicitly based on hindsight. However, to allow for the interpreted nature of texts is not to reject the value of the results. Indeed, subsequent reflections by the author may be more relevant to those who seek to *use* a text than the original unique experience on its own. For example, *the* classical Christian texts, the Gospels, are creative re-workings of earlier oral or written traditions about Jesus of Nazareth that the Gospel writers allowed to interact with the contexts and needs of their audiences. This creative approach is part of the value of the Gospels for readers in subsequent ages.

However, the conventional approach to textual interpretation inherited from the nineteenth century, and current until fairly recently, had as its basic principle that the values or experiences that a modern reader brings to a classic text are a problem for correct understanding (Sheldrake 1995: ch. 1). Recent developments in hermeneutics seek a broader approach where the possibilities of a text, beyond the author's original conception, may be evoked in a creative way by the new religious world in which such a text finds itself.

While Sandra Schneiders's approach to a scriptural text "as locus of revelatory encounter" (Schneiders 1999b: 10) may be extended to spiritual classics, we should bear in mind certain cautions expressed by Rowan Williams. For example, in his *On Christian Theology* (2000: 147), Williams takes the French philosopher and theologian Paul Ricoeur to task for concentrating too much on the revelatory nature of a *text* in isolation without giving sufficient weight to the revelatory character of the process of interpretation. Thus "God 'speaks' in the response as in the primary utterance." Or, as he puts it elsewhere, "the locus of *revelation* is the text as it stands *in interaction with the reader*" (2000: 124). Implicitly at least, both Schneiders and Williams understand the interpretation of religious texts to be best served by a process that is personally engaged as well as intellectually rigorous. Interpretation in the fullest sense creates a world of meaning in which people come to see and act differently.

The interpretation of spiritual classics is not the preserve of scholars, but also takes place (usually implicitly and occasionally ignorantly) in the practical *use* of texts (for example, Ignatius of Loyola's *Spiritual Exercises* in retreat work). Therefore, the example of the performing arts is helpful in understanding the new approach to interpretation. Musicians interpret a text, the score. They may be technically faultless in reproducing the notes and the composer's instructions. A "good" performance is certainly true to the score because performers cannot do simply anything with a score and still call it a Beethoven symphony. Yet, a "good" performance is *more* than this. It will also be creative because the composer did not merely describe how to produce sounds but sought to shape an experience. Thus, there is no single, definitive interpretation of a text, as new aspects are revealed whenever the text confronts new horizons and questions (Lash 1986: ch. 3).

This image of performance leads us to the core of the interpretative process. Without ignoring the original historical context of a text, or the intention of the original author(s), every time we read it, we reveal new and ever-richer meanings that the author never knew. The pursuit of meaning undoubtedly demands that we understand something about the technicalities of a text. However, a real conversation with it expands our vision rather than merely extending the pool of data. We interrogate the text, but our questions are, in turn, reshaped by the text itself. This process is what is sometimes referred to as the "hermeneutical circle." One of the most influential figures in the development in religious circles of a broader interpretation theory has been the German philosopher Hans-Georg Gadamer. He stressed that a text must "break the spell" of the reader's presuppositions which initially gave the reader an entry point. The text corrects and revises our preliminary understanding (1979: 324–5).

Gadamer's theory of interpretation assumes that texts have an "excess of meaning" beyond the subjective intentions of the author. This is what enables a spiritual classic to come alive in the present. The present situation, as experienced by the reader, affects the meaning of the text, and a text alters the reader's understanding of the present. Gadamer further concluded that understanding, interpretation, and application were not self-contained "moments" but a unified process. In Gadamer's view, the weakness of earlier theories of interpretation was that they detached the practical application of a text (for example, in preaching) from technical analysis. In fact, we come to a deep understanding of a text *only* by applying it to the present (1979: 274–5). In the dialogue between text and reader the aim is to fuse the horizons of both in an interpretation that is always new. A classic may allow a genuinely new interpretation, yet the reader is also provoked (sometimes by what is initially strange or even shocking) into new self-understanding because of the encounter. Thus a spiritual classic is not a timeless artifact that demands mere repetition. Understanding the text implies a constant reinterpretation by people who question and listen from within their own historical circumstances. A concrete example would be the way in which the Rule of St Benedict has, over the centuries, regularly inspired reforms in monastic community which, while retaining a common core, have produced strikingly different lifestyles.

Gadamer's theory is complemented by the somewhat different approach of the equally influential Paul Ricoeur (1976), who emphasizes that once wisdom has been fixed in a written text there follows a radical "distanciation" of the discourse from its original production. First, the text is distanced from its author who effectively "loses control." The text takes on a life of its own as a medium of meaning. Second, the text is distanced from the original audience. A written text inherently becomes available to whoever cares to read it. Third, the text is distanced from its original context (decontextualization) which makes the text able to function in relation to later and different situations (recontextualization). In summary, Ricoeur's emphasis on "distanciation" enables the text to transcend the limitations of its origins in order to function potentially in any context.

What Kind of Meaning?

What kind of meaning is reached through this process of interpretation? From a theological point of view, "interpretation" does not, indeed cannot, produce a form of discourse that offers a definitive and total perspective. In practice, religious accounts operate less as an "exhaustive interpretation" of how the universe operates and more as, in the words of Rowan Williams, "*strategies* [his emphasis] for responding consistently and intelligibly to the world's complexity" (2000: 6). Interpretation is not "an exploratory reduction, but the gradual formation of a 'world' in which realities can be seen and endured without illusion" (2000: 163).

Contemporary approaches to interpretation suggest the need for what are nowadays referred to as a "hermeneutics of consent" and a "hermeneutics of suspicion." In the first case, we "consent" to a text in the sense that its origins, the author's intention, and the consensus of interpretation over time within the "community of capable readers" continue to exert some kind of normative role that prevents us from exploiting the text ruthlessly for our own ends (for example, Gadamer 1979: 325–41). However, in the second case, we recognize that the questions provoked by our contemporary situation may well be critical of aspects of the text and its theological or cultural assumptions. For example, we are nowadays more aware of the *social* conditioning of texts and of the need to expose the hidden biases against certain ideas or groups of people within the Christian tradition, not least the history of spirituality, particularly ones that continue to influence us (for example, Schüssler Fiorenza 1983; John 1988). We need to examine not merely the surface of the "text" but its "silences" – what lies behind the text, what is assumed, what is not said, what is excluded (Downey 1997: 129).

For some theologians, all interpretations of Christian texts or history are radically interrupted by the Holocaust. Thus David Tracy suggests that the very historicity of Christianity inevitably involves "a frightening disclosure of the real history within which we have lived" (1994: 64). Every attempt to retrieve the tradition "must today include a radical hermeneutics of suspicion on the whole of Christian history" (1994: 65). The same judgment, it may be argued, applies with more or less force to other painful elements of the "real history" of Christianity, and of Christian spirituality in particular. I am thinking especially of various forms of Eurocentrism or theological colonialism, the undermining of women's spiritual wisdom, and the dominance of clerical forms of spirituality over an everyday spirituality of work and of sexuality.

What Lies Behind the Text

After addressing important general aspects of the theory and process of interpretation, I want to turn attention to a number of specific issues concerning the contemporary interpretation of texts and traditions. The first concerns the importance of appreciating what lies behind the surface of the texts we see. The second concerns a wider understanding of the word "texts" beyond purely written forms. The third concerns whether classic texts may in principle become unusable. The final issue concerns the related questions of who constitutes a "community of capable readers" and who has the right to access the wisdom of spiritual texts.

The text we see and seek to use sometimes shields a hidden text that is critical to our interpretation. This may apply, for example, to related written texts. If we were to examine the *Constitutions* of the Jesuit Order, they appear on cursory reading to be essentially a practical and legal document (see Ganss 1970). However, contemporary scholars agree that the intelligibility of the text depends heavily on the more foundational text that lies behind the *Constitutions*, that is *The Spiritual Exercises*. In the light of this hidden text, the *Constitutions* are revealed not so much as a legal document but as a flexible attempt to offer a way of living out the experience of the Ignatian Exercises in a communitarian and ministerial form (Gray 1988; Veale 1988). Reciprocally, the *Constitutions* then become of interest to people seeking to deepen their understanding of the Ignatian Exercises but without any particular interest in male clerical community.

The famous *Canticle of the Sun* by Francis of Assisi provides a different example of how the interpretation of a written document vitally depends on understanding something behind the text. On its own, it is possible to reduce the sentiments of the *Canticle* to a bland, romantic love of the natural world. However, the underlying meaning of the *Canticle* is more radical. The key to it is that all our fellow creatures (animate or inanimate) are brothers and sisters and reflect the face of Christ. Francis of Assisi experienced each particular element of creation, not merely Creation in the abstract, as arising from the same source, the Trinity revealed in the incarnate Jesus. The corollary is that each created particularity is a revelation of God. The foundation of Franciscan respect for all created things is that God, through whom everything was created, has come among us to be a creature.

The first nine verses of the *Canticle* speak of the cosmic fraternity of all elements of creation. For example,

> Let everything you have made
> Be a song of praise to you,
> Above all, His Excellency the Sun (our brother);
> Through him you flood our days with light.
> He is so beautiful, so radiant, so splendid,
> O Most High, he reminds us of you.

This uplifting doctrine of cosmic fraternity, however, conceals a sharp prophetic message. For one thing, the text does not simply celebrate God's goodness expressed in the world as God's gift. Verses 10–11 celebrate the peace that comes from mutual pardon or reconciliation. It is generally thought that the verses were written as part of a campaign to settle a dispute between the mayor and bishop of Assisi.

> Be praised, my Lord,
> Through those who forgive for your love,
> Through those who are weak,
> In pain, in struggle,
> Who endure with peace,
> For you will make them Kings and Queens,
> O Lord Most High. (Downing 1993: 129)

Thus the created world shifts from being merely a beautiful place to a "reconciled space" because of the fraternity of all things in Christ. There is no room for violence, contention, or rejection of the "other."

Here we face a critical question. What did Francis understand by the "other?" For this we have to recall one of Francis's foundational experiences. The "other" for Francis had a particular meaning. Behind the text of the *Canticle*, and underlying his whole theology of creation and incarnation, is another "text" – Francis's early encounter with a leper that changed his life. In the first three verses of *The Testament*, dictated shortly before his death in 1226, Francis actually identified the first moment of his spiritual life with his encounter with the leper (Armstrong and Brady 1982: 154). The meeting with the leper was not merely an encounter with human suffering. In medieval terms, Francis was led to embrace the excluded "other." Lepers were not simply infected with a fearful disease. In medieval society they symbolized the dark side of existence onto which medieval people projected a variety of fears, suspicions, and guilt which must be excluded from the community not merely of the physically healthy but also of the spiritually pure. Lepers were outcasts banished from society. They joined the criminals, the mad, the excommunicated, and the Jews (Geremek 1990: 367–9; Moore 1994: 45–63). Through the encounter with the leper, Francis came to see that participation in human experiences of suffering and exclusion was at the heart of God's incarnation as revealed in the face of the crucified Christ.

Buildings as Texts

As we noted earlier, David Tracy, in his description of "a classic," extends the notion beyond written texts. If we have a more inclusive approach to the history of Christian spirituality, we come to realize that, for many people throughout history, spiritual wisdom has not been communicated primarily through literary texts, but through other forms such as religious architecture.

The permanent display that introduces visitors to King's College Chapel in Cambridge begins with the sentence: "We exist not only in the world but in an image or picture of the world." In other words, human beings exist within general systems of signs by which they identify themselves and develop a worldview. Concretely, the great medieval churches and cathedrals of Europe express in their architecture and decoration a quite specific vision of the cosmos.

Unfortunately, the meaning of such places is not self-evident. They are "texts" in the broad sense implied by semiotics. We need a key in order to "read" their sign systems and thus interpret their meaning. Medieval cathedrals were constructed with certain levels of "meaning" built into the stonework, as it were. Because a medieval religious building may be understood as an act of worship in itself, as well as a space for liturgy, it is not unreasonable to say that its art and architecture are directly at the service of theology. The Gothic style of architecture is a bearer of religious ideas – not least about the nature of God (Wilson 1990: 64–6, 219–20, 262–3).

Gothic "space" can be characterized as, among other things, dematerialized and spiritualized. It thereby expresses the limitless quality of an infinite God through the soaring verticality of arches and vaults, which are a deliberate antithesis to human scale. The medieval fascination with the symbolism of numbers cannot be ignored either. The basic three-story elevation of Gothic form (main arcade, triforium, and clerestory) cannot be explained purely by progress in engineering. Both Rupert of Deutz and Abbot Suger in the twelfth century drew explicit attention to the trinitarian symbolism of three-story elevation. Another typically Gothic characteristic is that the stone walls were increasingly pared down compared to earlier Romanesque and replaced by expanses of glass. The stories in the windows might teach the worshiper much about the doctrine of God and of salvation, but there was also a sense in which glass expressed a "metaphysics of light." God was proclaimed as the one who dwelt in inaccessible light, yet whose salvific light illuminated the world.

Until recently, there has been an unbalanced concentration on a "metaphysics of light" derived from the sixth-century writer Pseudo-Dionysius. In fact, it is now considered that Augustinian aesthetics played at least as important a part in monastic theology as Pseudo-Dionysius. And the Dionysian elements are often affected by Augustine's thought (McGinn 1995). Hence *harmonia* or a fitting order established by God is a central theme. This fitting order refers both to the building and to the worshiping community that it contains. Abbot Suger, the great twelfth-century theorist of the birth of Gothic architecture at Saint Denis, referred to "perspicacious order" as the key to his vision for the building – and *ordo* is the characteristic word in Augustine for the harmonious beauty of the cosmos (Suger 1979: 100–1). There may be various ways of understanding "integration" when it comes to architectural style and buildings. An Augustinian approach would certainly begin with the fundamental understanding of the church as a community of people, of the faithful who make up the Body of Christ. This is the *tabernaculum admirabile*, the "wonderful tabernacle" of Augustine's sermon on Psalm 41 (in the Vulgate) within which one attains to God. "See how great wonders I admire in the tabernacle! For God's tabernacle on earth is the faithful" (Augustine 1996: 134).

However, this *tabernaculum admirabile* has a *locus*, a place where it is both shown forth and continually reinforced. This "place" is, first, the liturgy (particularly the Eucharist) and then the building that contains this action. Thus the building in the mind of someone like Suger should evoke wonder, be adequate to its purpose of worship, and point beyond itself to the eternal, transcendent "house of God." As a text, the building is a doorway or access point to this, and its harmony is represented not simply by geometry or architectural coherence but by the degree to which it fulfills this function.

Can Texts Become Unusable?

Precisely because many people approach spiritual texts or traditions in search of wisdom, we face the problem that the language and some of the presuppositions present in a classic are not only strange but positively alien to anyone seeking to appropriate the wisdom in the twenty-first century. An interesting example is the fourteenth-century English mystical text, *The Cloud of Unknowing*. This has become amazingly popular in recent times; in fact, it has been reprinted almost annually since its initial publication by Penguin Classics in the mid-1960s. Yet what are we to make, for example, of the statement that we are to view the self as a "foul, stinking lump of sin" (Walsh 1981: ch. 40)? More detailed study reveals that the text appears more gener-

ally suspicious of the body and of the material world. It also seems to be highly individualistic compared to contemporary spiritual sensibilities. It clearly assumes that
contemplation is only open to a small elite.

It may be possible to argue that in a contemporary re-reading of the text apparent
clashes of culture can be understood differently or interpreted as of merely secondary
importance compared to the fundamental spiritual wisdom of the text (Sheldrake
1995: 184–92). Yet the question remains. In principle, may people eventually be forced
to say that a text is now practically speaking unusable because it is riddled with assumptions radically out of tune with modern knowledge or values?

Any, even tentative, answer depends on the foundations I have already described.
The first is that "meaning" does not reside solely in a fixed text but is also established
in the dynamic conversation between the text and the contemporary reader. As I see it,
the very notion of the "classic text," as put forward by theorists such as David Tracy,
presupposes that certain wisdom documents have shown a capacity to break free from
the constraints of their original contexts. This means that they can no longer be seen
as tied absolutely to the assumptions and horizons of the original author or of his or
her anticipated audience. Such texts have thus already proved capable of being persis-
tently reinterpreted in every act of reading.

In the case of a text that explicitly exists to be *performed*, such as Ignatius of Loyola's
The Spiritual Exercises, the imperative of adaptation to the needs of retreatants is
built into the text itself and is reinforced in the earliest practical interpretations of it
(Ganss 1991: 126–8). Thus the meaning of the Exercises is according to the text's
own logic – not simply the written document, but also what emerges in every use of
the Exercises as a medium of spiritual development (and every use is a unique reinterpretation).

In reference to buildings as texts, we face the same questions. One refreshing aspect
of recent scholarship on medieval cathedrals is the way in which it seeks to integrate
art history and medieval studies with theology and spirituality. The result is a move
away from the idea that buildings are simply fixed monuments of pure architecture.
The spirituality implicit in cathedrals is *not* based on a purely abstract notion of "sacred
place." It is critical to their theological interpretation that cathedrals are places of social
connection and of community definition. To put it another way, a building without performance is merely a piece of abstract styling and, whatever else is true, that is not the
"meaning" of Gothic space. Cathedrals are repositories for the memory and the aspirations of the community, which are constantly renewed and changed across time.
Indeed, the moment a building like a cathedral becomes *fixed*, rather than continually
mobile and changing, it is a museum rather than a living symbol of human community living.

Today, medieval religious buildings are experienced by an audience completely different from their original one. There is no way back to "real" cathedrals or a "real"
medieval audience. Nor should we try artificially to recreate the ambience of a past age.
An historic religious building is a text whose meaning is forever revealed anew as it is
interpreted and reinterpreted through shifting patterns of usage. However fixed such
buildings appear, there seems to be little evidence that their ability to transmit spiritual
wisdom has come to an end, even in a relatively post-religious age.

Thus the "meaning" of classic texts is never definitively *fixed*. In this sense, it does not seem likely, *at least in principle*, that we will reach the limits of possible interpretations and therefore of the "usefulness" of a classic text. Obviously, there are changes of taste that result in certain texts receding into the background, perhaps to be rediscovered in another age. However, in itself this does not imply the loss of classic status. I may well believe, following David Tracy once again, that texts can be judged according to "criteria of adequacy" – that is, the text meets the basic demands of human living – and "criteria of appropriateness" – that is, the text is faithful to a specifically Christian understanding of existence (1975: 72–9). However, the precise way in which these criteria are interpreted is also a matter of context. We can only apply them within the limits of our present time, but we also have to admit that our judgments are not eternally conclusive.

What is a Community of Capable Readers?

The fluidity of "texts" and their capacity to reveal new levels of meaning relate closely to the question of *who* is assumed to be capable of interpretation. In practice, what is sometimes referred to technically as "the community of capable readers" necessarily changes across time. For example, in the case of the Ignatian Exercises, interpretation is no longer understood to be limited to the perspectives of a male, Roman Catholic clerical religious order, the Jesuits. Women, not least religious communities of sisters founded in the same tradition, are no longer passive recipients of an interpretation established elsewhere, but are inherent to the very process of interpretation and the establishment of meaning (Lonsdale 2000: introduction and ch. 10). The same point can be made of vast numbers of lay people more generally. Even more radically, given the Reformation origins of the Exercises, the "community of capable readers" nowadays includes people beyond the boundaries of Roman Catholic Christianity who have benefited from making the Exercises and have joined the ranks of those who guide others through the process (Sheldrake 1990).

In the case of religious buildings, does a hermeneutical process of "conversation" leave open the possibility that today's visitors to a medieval cathedral may, in principle at least, become part of an expanded community of capable readers? Such a thought is deeply problematic for those who believe that cathedrals only exist for the Christian worshiper. Today's visitor may just as easily be a tourist with no sense of what cathedrals originally expressed and how they are used liturgically today. My point is that this does not necessarily imply an inevitable abandonment of cathedrals as social and spiritual texts by the non-Christian majority. If true, this raises interesting issues when there are plans to reorder a medieval cathedral for contemporary use. Whose needs take priority? What understanding of spirituality is modeled in the changes: a purely liturgical one or one that invites a much broader range of people to gain access to spiritual wisdom in and through the building? Are non-worshiping visitors merely an "add on" from the heritage industry? Are they perhaps passive targets for new strategies of Christian evangelism? Or, potentially, may they become active participants in a new hermeneutical conversation that is in process of exploring previously unanticipated layers of meaning in buildings such as cathedrals?

Conclusion

Much of this essay has been concerned with the role of historical consciousness and the *process* of interpreting texts and traditions. However, our last question reminds us that the nature of the "community of capable readers" – in other words, *who* interprets and offers authoritative readings of texts and traditions – is at least as interesting and important a question, theologically and spiritually.

What this final question also illustrates is that the history of interpretation, even in the field of spirituality, involves issues of power (see a discussion of the issues in Ricoeur 1981). Of course, power is not inherently a bad thing or we would not speak of the *empowerment* of people, for example, through a more equitable distribution of skills and information. Within the context of Christian spirituality, the reality of power cannot be avoided in how it is defined, who merits a place in its "official" history, and who is enabled to become an effective interpreter of texts and traditions.

It may seem that the emphasis in this essay on the complexity of the issues surrounding interpretation and appropriation involves a kind of mystification or an elitism that denies access to spiritual wisdom to the non-scholar. My response is that the reverse should become the case. It is vitally important to offer as wide an audience as possible a slice of the hermeneutical cake. Scholars or others with technical knowledge of traditions and texts are not "stewards of private mysteries," neo-gnostics with privileged access to understanding. The task of translation is a theological *duty*. This point touches both on our philosophy of education and on our theology of Christian and human communion. My belief is that even popular courses and workshops on spirituality are severely limited in value if they confine themselves to practical questions rather than seek to mediate a deeper understanding of spiritual texts and traditions in a way that is not only practically relevant but also accurate and intelligible.

References

Armstrong, R. and Brady, I. (eds) 1982: *Francis and Clare: The Complete Works*. New York: Paulist Press.

Augustine 1996: *Expositions on the Book of Psalms*. In P. Schaff (ed.), *A Select Library of the Nicene and Post-Nicene Fathers of the Christian Church*, 1st ser., vol. 8. Grand Rapids, MI: Eerdmans.

Bossy, J. 1975: *The English Catholic Community: 1570–1850*. London: Darton, Longman, and Todd.

Bynum, C. W. 1982: *Jesus as Mother: Studies in the Spirituality of the High Middle Ages*. Berkeley, CA: University of California Press.

de Certeau, M. 1966: Culture and spiritual experience. *Concilium* 19, 3–16.

Downey, M. 1997: *Understanding Christian Spirituality*. New York: Paulist Press.

Downing, F. T. 1993: *Living the Incarnation: Praying with Francis and Clare of Assisi*. London: Darton, Longman, and Todd.

Evennett, H. O. 1968: *The Spirit of the Counter-Reformation*. Cambridge: Cambridge University Press.

Flanagan, K. 1999: *The Enchantment of Sociology: A Study of Theology and Culture*. London: Macmillan.

Fowl, S. (ed.) 1997: *The Theological Interpretation of Scripture*. Oxford: Blackwell.

Gadamer, H-G. 1979: *Truth and Method*, 2nd edn. London: Sheed and Ward.

Gallagher, M. P. 1999: *Clashing Symbols: An Introduction to Faith and Culture*. London: Darton, Longman, and Todd.

Ganss, G. (trans. and ed.) 1970: *The Constitutions of the Society of Jesus*. St Louis: Institute of Jesuit Sources.

——(trans. and ed.) 1991: *Ignatius of Loyola: Spiritual Exercises and Selected Works*. New York: Paulist Press.

Geertz, C. 1973: *The Interpretation of Cultures*. New York: Basic Books.

Geremek, B. 1990: The marginal man. In J. Le Goff (ed.), *The Medieval World*, trans. L. G. Cochrane, pp. 346–73. London: Collins and Brown.

Gray, H. J. 1988: What kind of document? *The Way Supplement* 61, 21–34.

John, O. 1988: The tradition of the oppressed as the main topic of theological hermeneutics. *Concilium* 200, 143–55.

Lash, N. 1986: *Theology on the Way to Emmaus*. London: SCM Press.

Le Goff, J. 1981: Francis of Assisi between the renewals and restraints of feudal society. *Concilium* 149, 3–10.

Lonsdale, D. 2000: *Eyes to See, Ears to Hear: An Introduction to Ignatian Spirituality*, rev. edn. London: Darton, Longman, and Todd.

McGinn, B. 1995: From admirable tabernacle to the house of God: some theological reflections on medieval architectural integration. In V. C. Raguin, K. Brush, and P. Draper (eds), *Artistic Integration in Gothic Buildings*, pp. 41–56. Toronto: University of Toronto Press.

Moore, R. I. 1994: *The Formation of a Persecuting Society*. Oxford: Blackwell.

Murk-Jansen, S. 1998: *Brides in the Desert: The Spirituality of the Beguines*. London: Darton Longman, and Todd.

Rahner, K. 1964: *The Dynamic Element in the Church*. London: Burns and Oates.

Raitt, J. (ed.) 1987: *Christian Spirituality: High Middle Ages and Reformation*. New York: Crossroad.

Ricoeur, P. 1976: *Interpretation Theory: Discourse and the Surplus of Meaning*. Fort Worth: Texas Christian University Press.

——1981: Hermeneutics and the critique of ideology. In J. B. Thompson (ed.), *Hermeneutics and the Human Sciences*, pp. 63–100. Cambridge: Cambridge University Press.

Ruggieri, G. 1987: Faith and history. In G. Alberigo, J-P. Jossua, and J. A. Komonchak (eds), *The Reception of Vatican II*, pp. 91–114. Washington, DC: Catholic University of America Press.

Schneiders, S. 1999a: *The Revelatory Text: Interpreting the New Testament as Sacred Scripture*. Collegeville, MN: The Liturgical Press.

——1999b: *Written that You May Believe: Encountering Jesus in the Fourth Gospel*. New York: Crossroad.

Schüssler Fiorenza, E. 1983: *In Memory of Her: A Feminist Theological Reconstruction of Christian Origins*. New York: Crossroad.

Scott, J. and Simpson-Housley, P. (eds) 1991: *Sacred Places and Profane Spaces: Essays in the Geographics of Judaism, Christianity and Islam*. Westport, CT: Greenwood.

Sheldrake, P. (ed.) 1990: *Ignatian Spirituality in Ecumenical Context. The Way Supplement* 68 (summer).

—— 1995: *Spirituality and History: Questions of Interpretation and Method*, rev. edn. London: SPCK.

—— 1998: *Spirituality and Theology: Christian Living and the Doctrine of God*. London: Darton Longman, and Todd.

Stewart, C. 1996: Asceticism and spirituality in late antiquity: new vision, impasse or hiatus? *Christian Spirituality Bulletin* 4 (1), 11–15.

Suger 1979: *Libellus alter de consecratione ecclesiae Sancti Dionysii* 4, trans. in E. Panofsky, *Abbot Suger on the Abbey Church of St Denis and its Art Treasures*. Princeton, NJ: Princeton University Press.

Tracy, D. 1975: *Blessed Rage for Order*. New York: Seabury Press.

—— 1991: *The Analogical Imagination: Christian Theology and the Culture of Pluralism*. New York: Crossroad.

—— 1994: *On Naming the Present: God, Hermeneutics and Church*. Maryknoll, NY: Orbis.

Veale, J. 1988: How the *Constitutions* work. *The Way Supplement* 61, 3–20.

Walsh, J. (trans.) 1981: *The Cloud of Unknowing*. New York: Paulist Press.

Williams, R. 1991: *Teresa of Avila*. London: Geoffrey Chapman.

—— 2000: *On Christian Theology*. Oxford: Blackwell.

Wilson, C. 1990: *The Gothic Cathedral*. London: Thames and Hudson.

CHAPTER 27

Nature

Douglas Burton-Christie

In the Mausoleum of the Galla Placidia in Ravenna, Italy, there exists one of the earliest and most beautiful expressions of the Christian idea of nature. A simple cross is etched onto a shallow, dark blue dome in the midst of stars arranged in concentric circles, an image whose diminishing size toward the center gives one the impression of gazing into a heavenly vault. The message is clear: the entire cosmos shimmers with the presence of God. Indeed, the ultimate meaning of the cosmos is cruciform. For the earliest Christians, this was neither a vague nor an abstract idea, but a bedrock principle of faith, an expression of how they experienced God. It arose directly from the conviction that God's incarnation in the person of Jesus, the Word made flesh (John 1: 14), resulted in the sanctification of all matter, the entire cosmos. Irenaeus of Lyons gave expression to this ancient belief this way: "because [Christ] is Himself the Word of God . . . who in His invisible form pervades us universally in the whole world, and encompasses its length and breadth and height and depth . . . the Son of God was also crucified in these, imprinted in the form of a cross on the universe" (Ladner 1995: 99).

Here in its simplest form is the ancient and enduring Christian conviction about the meaning of "nature": that the entire cosmos has been brought into being and is sustained by the enlivening power of God's Word, who also redeems and makes whole all who believe and live in that Word. Christ is the key to the cosmos. It is a beautiful image, rich with theological insight, and with implications for how to live in the physical world with an awareness of its deep goodness and value. Yet, reflecting on this image at the dawn of the twenty-first century, in a time of rapidly escalating ecological degradation, also brings with it new and undeniable challenges. Not least of these is the question of whether members of the Christian community are prepared to believe in – and live as though they believe in – the idea of a cosmos brought into being and sustained by the Word of God.

Too often throughout its history, the Christian community has not taken seriously this elemental aspect of its own faith in Christ. To reflect upon that image in the Galla Placidia, then, means not only opening ourselves in a new way to the cosmological reach of Christian faith. It also means reckoning seriously with our many failures to do so and the effect of these failures upon the world we inhabit. This, perhaps, is one of the meanings of that image of the cross floating amidst the stars in the present context, its radically ambiguous symbolic language pointing to the redemptive possibilities inherent in a truly cosmological Christian faith, but also serving as a sober reminder of our endless capacity to destroy and kill. Christians today face the immense challenge of reimagining our faith in terms that will help us cherish and preserve the world.

At the heart of the challenge for contemporary Christians is the need for a serious, critical re-examination of our own spiritual traditions, our spirituality. This will require something more than a narrow, inward-looking examination of conscience; it will also require careful attention on the part of the Christian community to the "signs of the times," especially the signs of ecological degradation that are contributing to an acute unraveling of the ecological, political, social, and spiritual fabric of our world. Attending to these signs and learning how to respond to them in light of faith constitute a hugely demanding and complex task. It means coming to terms with intricate relationships that exist among a range of chronic ecological threats such as global warming, deforestation and desertification, massive erosion of topsoil, diminishment of fossil fuels, and growing scarcity of water. It also means reckoning with the relationships between the cultural, social, economic, and political dimensions of these ecological threats; the myriad ways in which realities such as poverty and over-consumption contribute to ecological degradation; and the ways in which social, political, and economic instability often occur as a result of it (Brown et al. 2002). For contemporary Christians, the work of reflecting on the spiritual significance of these devastating developments has become a crucial expression of faith, a necessary signal of willingness on the part of the Christian community to participate in the larger, communal effort to respond to the assault upon the earth.

This work has taken many forms, including: official church pronouncement articulating the theological, spiritual, and moral rationale for Christian engagement with ecological concerns (Commission for Racial Justice, United Church of Christ 1987; Catholic Bishops' Conference of the Philippines 1988; Dimitrios, the Ecumenical Patriarch 1990; John Paul II 1990; US Conference of Catholic Bishops 1991; Presbyterian Advisory Committee on Social Witness Policy 1996; Catholic Bishops of the Pacific Northwest 2001); critical *historical* work examining the ambiguous role of nature within Scripture and the unfolding Christian tradition (for example, Merchant 1980; Santmire 1985; Cohen 1989; Albanese 1990; Gregory 1992; Harrison 1992; Ladner 1995; Hiebert 1996; Bergant 1998; Hütterman 1999); *theological* examinations of the shifting awareness of God in light of the ecological crisis, with particularly significant contributions coming from eco-feminist theologians (for example, Moltmann 1985; McFague 1987; Cobb 1992; Ruether 1992; Johnson 1993; Bouma-Prediger 1995; Edwards 1995; Fowler 1995; Wallace 1996; Boff 1997; Scharper 1997; Baker-Fletcher 1998; Kwok 1999; Hayes 2001; Hessel and Ruether 2001; Toolan 2001; Eaton 2003; Scott 2003); *ethical* reflections on the range and depth of Christian responsibility for the living world (for example, Nash 1991; Oelschlaeger 1994; Rasmussen 1996); investigations of traditions of *spirituality* (for example, Fox 1983; Gregorios 1987; Louth 1991; Kinsley 1994; McFague 1997; Lane 1998, 2001; Sheldrake 2001);

experiments in living that promise a new way of being in the world (for example, Fritsch 1987; Lefevere 2003). These are expressions of real vitality within the Christian community, examples of the kind of "critical correlation" that David Tracy (1975) has long argued is the *sine qua non* of authentic theological work – the creative juxtaposition and mutual interrogation of classic Christian texts (in this case, extended to include far more than simply texts) and contemporary human experience.

Another important instance of critical correlation that the Christian community is called to is the work of attending carefully and thoughtfully to those expressions of spiritual longing that arise outside the Christian tradition. Here, I mean to include not only the spiritualities of the major world religions, but also the many, often hidden, expressions of such spirituality that fall outside the conventional boundaries that we normally think of when we are evaluating the locus and meaning of religious practice and consciousness. There has been growing attention to this "non-religious" or "secular" spirituality in recent years (Schneiders 1994, 2003; Torrance 1994; Van Ness 1996; McGuire 1997; Taves 2003). Gradually, we are beginning to understand the myriad ways in which both Christians and non-Christians improvise their spiritualities, drawing freely and eclectically upon a range of spiritual traditions, often with relatively little attention to the way in which the established traditions set the terms of belief. Concern has grown over what some see as a tendency toward the erosion of coherent belief and practice capable of being transmitted from one generation to the next. However, these developments surely signal something else, which is undeniably positive and creative: the desire to discover spiritual meaning in spite of the perceived inability of established religious traditions to provide it. It suggests a vitality and elasticity to the human capacity for transcendence which must, after all, lie at the very root of any meaningful understanding of spirituality.

The "greening of spirituality," if we may call it this, has arisen out of the broader social and cultural context in which human beings are searching for ways to cultivate an intimate and meaningful spirituality rooted in a feeling for the living world. Some, including many Christians, are finding this spirituality within their own established religious traditions. Others are searching for it, and finding it, at the margins, in new places that have yet to be adequately mapped or integrated into the world of religious discourse as it has been classically articulated. Christians have an obligation, I believe, to attend carefully to this new quest. Not only is this an act of respect that we owe to anyone embarked upon a serious quest for the transcendent. But it is a quest that has much to teach Christians about their own search for a spirituality that takes the living world seriously.

In the discussion that follows, I want to examine the question of how Christian spirituality might benefit from and be deepened by a sustained conversation with contemporary writers and poets on the spiritual significance of nature (Burton-Christie 1993, 1994a, b, 1999, 2000, 2003a, b). In particular, I want to reflect upon a crucial issue that has come to occupy the very center of this discourse: *the pervasive experience of loss.* The experience of loss in relation to the natural world has many faces: it includes and is often focused upon extreme and devastating losses – of species, of wild places, and of human communities, especially poor communities who suffer disproportionately as ecosystems become diminished. Within this reality lie other losses, just as profound, but less easy to articulate: the loss of beauty, intimacy, the loss of the sacred. Reflection on loss in contemporary writing includes all of this and more. Such reflection is not simply about mourning all that has been lost; it is connected to and often serves as the starting-point for a larger reflective, ethical, and spiritual project of renewal and healing. Fundamental to this project is the work of coming to an awareness of our current predicament, along with our culpability for it – an awareness not unlike that which Christians have long identified with the experience of repentance. Such an awareness is a necessary starting-point in order to arrive at a new realization of the transcendent spiritual value of the natural world, a realization that may well prove necessary if we are to sustain the long-term ethical-spiritual project of renewal and healing that is so urgently needed in the present moment.

The Poetics of Loss

I was sitting around a large table with a group of colleagues who had come to Vassar College in upstate New York to spend six weeks thinking and reflecting about the meaning of the natural world in our scholarship and teaching. Our time together had nearly come to an end and, perhaps in response to our impending departure, we found ourselves talking more intimately and personally about the places in the natural world that had meant something to us in our lives. Stories came tumbling out about childhood places, wild places, ordinary backyard places, places where some intimate sense of connection with the living world had been born in us. There was such delight, even joy, in naming and describing these places. But gradually the conversation turned to the feelings of loss that we also carried within us. Many of these places no longer existed. They had been paved over, plowed under, razed for one form of development or another. The mood in the room darkened. We found ourselves speaking to one another through tears, through an immense grief that, until that moment, had been moving beneath the surface of our conversations. But now it showed itself and it was strong and fierce. There was not a single person in that room who had not been touched by it. In that moment, our sense of shared loss became palpable, dense, and sharp. It was like coming to an awareness of the enduring presence of an old wound.

It is hardly surprising, given the scale at which life-forms are becoming extinct in the world, natural resources are being depleted, places are being destroyed, and entire communities are becoming impoverished as a result, that contemporary reflections on nature so often begin with loss. At the heart of this contemporary experience of loss is a growing awareness that we are presently experiencing a catastrophe of such astounding proportions that we may not be able to undo or repair it. The mass extinction of species is not the only sign of all that we are losing. But it is emblematic of how extreme the estrangement, the loss of intimacy between the human species and other species, has become. Species are becoming extinct at a rate unsurpassed since the end of the age of the dinosaurs sixty-five million years ago (Wilson 1989: 26). Instances of mass extinction have occurred before in the history of the earth, many of them completely unrelated to human causes. However, all that has begun to change. Up until the eighteenth century, the overall rate of extinction remained relatively low (0.25 species per year). By the nineteenth century, the rate of extinction had risen to approximately one species per year. By 1975, species had begun to disappear from the earth at a rate of 1,000 per year. During the 1990s, the rate rose past ten thousand species a year (one species per hour). Since the year 2000, the rate of extinction has increased even more dramatically, to over 40,000 species per year. During the next thirty years, 25 percent of the known species on earth could be erased (Wilson 1984: 122; BBC News Online, May 19, 2003).

Such astonishing statistics are hard to fathom. We struggle to make sense of a phenomenon for which there is no real precedence in human history, and for which our conceptual, imaginative tools often feel inadequate.

> Extinction is a difficult concept to grasp. It is an eternal concept. It's not at all like the killing of individual life-forms that can be renewed through normal processes of reproduction. Nor is it simply diminishing numbers. Nor is it damage that can somehow be remedied or for which some substitute can be found. Nor is it something that simply affects our own generation. Nor is it something that could be remedied by some supernatural power. It is rather an absolute and final act for which there is no remedy on earth or in heaven. A species once extinct is gone forever. (Berry 1988: 9)

When viewed in such stark terms, the extinction of large numbers of species appears as an awful, catastrophic prospect. This is how *we* experience it anyway, as the prospect of an undoing of everything we hold dear, something that might have been avoided if we had only known how to act and to live with real feeling and responsibility for the world and one another. However, the reality of such massive extinction of life-forms cannot and must not be reduced to a subjective experience of loss on our part. It speaks of something immense and ominous threatening the very possibility of life on the planet as a whole. Edward O. Wilson has expressed a concern felt by many that the rapidly increasing rate of extinction is a dark harbinger of the extinction of life itself. "We now have a sense that we are bringing life to a close. I mean, we're destroying life; we're reducing the natural world out there in an irreversible way" (Wilson 1989: 26). Or, to put this catastrophe in slightly different terms: "Death is one thing, an end to *birth* is something else" (Soule and Wilcox 1980: 8).

The prospect of such staggering loss raises an important question: is it possible to translate extinction from a mere abstraction into meaningful terms so that a response becomes possible? One of the ways to bridge this gap is by raising questions of value, by asking what, if anything, is at stake for *us* in all of this? Is the eradication of species and the impoverishment of the world an unfortunate but necessary consequence of social and economic progress? Must we sacrifice the world, or large parts of it anyway, to ensure human thriving? Or do we feel that something essential about the human experience, about ourselves, about the world itself, is diminished when extinction on this scale is allowed to unfold? To put the question another way: to what extent do we feel that our destiny and the wellbeing of *our* species are bound up with, even dependent upon, the survival of these other species? To raise these questions is not to suggest that we are the only, or even the most important, actors in this drama. Clearly, hubris on the part of the human species is responsible for much of the present debacle, and the issue of the intrinsic value of species must be faced honestly. Still, it seems clear that the only way forward is to probe our relationship with other species and with the living world as a whole – including the places in which, and the means by which, that relationship has been broken, where we have experienced displacement and loss.

This is the poet's task: naming and describing loss in all its particularity. In doing so, the poet can and often does help give us imaginative and emotional access to all that we are losing. Such work can help us understand how the distinct and very particular losses we experience – broken relationships, degraded landscapes, historical genocide – are related to one another, how they sometimes coalesce unexpectedly into a single complex and devastating sense of loss. It can help us wake up to the sources of the "fundamental, catastrophic anxiety" that we carry around within us, an anxiety so profound that we often associate it unconsciously with a feeling that "the end of the world" is near (Nicholson 2002: 137). Bringing such apocalyptic anxiety to language can be a first and liberating step out of the debilitating silence that so often paralyzes us. It can be a means of naming not only loss, but also the enduring desire for intimacy and relationship that runs like a strong current within our sense of loss.

These are the issues that Robert Hass raises with such penetrating honesty in his collection of poems, *Sun under Wood* (1996). Here, the most personal and intimate losses touch upon, provide a way into, and are in turn shaped by a much larger landscape of loss. The poet asks what language he can find to describe the loss of his mother, through alcoholism and mental illness, to some far distant place he cannot now reach. Or to account for that tangled web of other losses that seem bound, as if by invisible threads, to this original one. Like the loss of a cherished mountain meadow, "the deep-rooted bunchgrass / and the wet alkali-scented earth . . . pushed aside / or trucked someplace out of the way" (1996: 12), replaced by concrete slabs for a housing development. Or the disappearance of all those indigenous peoples, decimated by influenza and syphilis, who inhabited this land before us, and who "also loved these high meadows on summer mornings" (1996: 6).

How are we to understand the cumulative effect of such losses upon the soul, upon the human community, upon the natural world? They are at once personal (the loss of one's mother), ecological (the loss of those mountain meadows) and historical-cultural (the loss of indigenous peoples through genocide and disease). To hold them together as part of a single, whole reality requires a supple and bold imagination. And, yet, they are so clearly part of a whole. They participate in and express, each in a different way, the loss of relationship, in some cases the violent suppression of relationship. And yet, in each case, there is a memory of some intimacy, some deep connection that lingers in our emotional, spiritual lives. Is there an underlying "something" that helps to account for both the joy we associate with the intimacy we experience and the devastation that comes with the loss of such intimacy?

Susan Griffin, in her book *The Eros of Everyday Life* (1995), helpfully names this "something" as eros. Drawing on Hesiod's ancient cosmogenic sense of the word, she speaks of eros as that which draws us toward those highly charged meetings, encounters with the "other"; that which makes possible the fluid, dynamic exchanges that take place in such encounters; and the very life that emerges from them. Such meetings are, Griffin notes, inclusive of the biological, the emotional, the linguistic, the socio-political, and the spiritual dimensions of our lives. To inhabit the world of eros means recognizing that borders – between oneself and another, between human beings and the more-than-human world, between matter and spirit – are permeable, that life emerges nowhere else so fully and deeply as it does in the exchange across these borders.

Yet we create and inhabit a world of impermeable borders, a world marked by divisions and obstructions, a world where such exchanges become unimaginable. Much of the loss we experience, argues Griffin, arises from the deep memory we carry within us of this rich, relational world. We know that the world we now inhabit, where eros is thin and weak, is not the only world available to us. Consider, says Griffin, our earliest encounters with the world. "Groping with cheeks and mouth, the infant burrows over the mother's breast in search of her nipple. Finding this, her tiny lips must explore at the same time both the contours of the mother's nipple and their own movement, new, uncharted. With his first small acts the child finds nourishment, knowledge and love all in the same efforts." It is only later that the child learns from culture to divide these things. "Eating, he is no longer aware of taking life into his body. Even if she takes sensual pleasure in a meal, she has lost the memory of the mouth as an instrument of intelligence. He has forgone a deeper knowledge of his own existence as part of a continual process of transubstantiation, *bodies becoming bodies*; she loses the eros at the heart of becoming." Yet, such a division, claims Griffin, "is not really possible." It is not, ultimately, sustainable. "All that is severed returns" (Griffin 1995: 69).

Yet Griffin knows, as Robert Hass does, that such a "return" is anything but simple or routine. Retrieving the lost parts of ourselves, the sense of "the eros at the heart of becoming," involves a long, difficult struggle, a willingness to probe the gaps and rifts as well as the possible avenues of return. In Hass's case, this means facing up to and giving careful attention to the effects of his mother's alcoholism and emotional instability upon his own emerging feeling for the world. It means describing the particular shape and texture of his displacement.

In the poem "My Mother's Nipples," Hass describes coming home from school one day, finding his mother missing, and going to the park to look for her.

> She had passed out under an orange tree, curled up. Her face, flushed, eyelids swollen, was a ruin. Though I needed urgently to know whatever was in it, I could hardly bear to look. When I couldn't wake her, I decided to sit with her until she woke up. I must have been ten years old: I suppose I wanted for us to look like a son and mother who had been picnicking, like a mother who had fallen asleep in the warm light and scent of orange blossoms and a boy who was sitting beside her daydreaming, not thinking about anything in particular. (1996: 21–2)

It is difficult to imagine a deeper, more painful, more pervasive displacement than this. It is utterly personal, and yet encompasses the young boy's entire cosmos which in this very moment is rent from end to end. He himself is divided. He cannot bear to look. But he cannot look away – even though he is afraid to look, has always been afraid: "Mothers in the nineteen forties didn't nurse. / I never saw her naked. Oh! yes, I did, / once, but I can't remember. I remember / not wanting to" (1996: 15). But now he looks, gazing upon her ruined face, needing urgently to know where she has gone, hoping he might yet get her back. And he looks away, pretending she has fallen asleep, struggling to create a make-believe world less brutal than the one he actually inhabits, trying to find a way to fill the longing created by her absence.

"They're where all displacement begins." Hass gives this fundamental displacement from his mother's breasts the attention it deserves, probing it like a surgeon searching out the boundaries of a tumor. But he also looks beyond it, or rather to all that is included within it. For there are so many other losses, so many other holes to fill, all bound mysteriously to this primordial loss. There is the gap created by the bulldozing of the upper meadow at Squaw Valley, which the poet remembers as a place: "where horses from the stable, two chestnuts, one white, / grazed in the mist and the scent of wet grass on summer mornings / and moonrise threw the owl's shadow on voles and wood rats / crouched in the sage smell the earth gave back after dark / with the day's heat to the night air" (1996: 12). It is all gone now. So are "The people who lived here before us," whom Hass recalls in the poem "Dragonflies Mating." They "also loved these high mountain meadows on summer mornings. / They made their way up here in easy stages / when heat began to dry the valleys out, / following the berry harvest probably and the pine buds: / climbing and making camp and gathering, / then breaking camp and climbing and making camp and gathering." Of course, there is more to the story. There were also: "The Franciscan priests who brought their faith in God / across the Atlantic, brought with the baroque statues and / metalwork crosses / and elaborately embroidered cloaks, influenza and syphilis and the coughing disease.// Which is why we settled an almost empty California" (Hass 1996: 6, 8).

What conflicted, confused eros created this emptiness? Hass does not even attempt an answer. Still, the juxtaposition of these images itself suggests a pattern. The silence of that eviscerated California landscape also haunts the meadow destroyed by the bulldozer and the heart of that young boy under the orange tree. The accumulation of loss creates its own pattern.

But these poems are not only about loss. They are also about the longing that stretches across the empty spaces created by loss. They are about the possibility of recovering what has been lost, of rediscovering our capacity for intimacy with the living world. Chickasaw writer Linda Hogan suggests that we remember that part of us that is still "deep and intimate with the world" by "feel." "We experience it," she says, "as a murmur in the night, a longing and restlessness we can't name, a yearning that tugs at us" (1995: 83). One senses this longing, this "feel" for the world, in the very language that Hass uses to describe life unfolding before him. There is this careful recollection of the intricate life of that lost meadow: "So many grasses – / reedgrass, the bentgrass and timothy, little quaking grass, / dogtail, rip-gut brome – the seeds flaring from the stalks / in tight chevrons of green and purple-green / but loosening." Or the "rainbow perch / . . . reeled in gleaming from the cliffs, the black rockbass, / scales like polished carbon, in beds of kelp / along the coast," the memory of which helped pull a friend back from the brink of suicide (Hass 1996: 18–22).

Loss and the Sacred

The tenderness, delicacy, and precision of this language are striking. It suggests a feeling for the living world that Christians would describe as sacramental: the capacity to see in the life of ordinary things a larger, transcendent reality. Not a transcendent reality that is somehow detached or separate from those things, but rather one that rises up from within them, that is part of their life and character. In the present context, this "larger reality" may or may not be appropriately named "God." It might be better described as a "whole and integral world." Or as a moral-spiritual posture – say "hope" or "affection" – that helps make such a world possible. Whatever name we may choose to give it, this larger reality to which these particular life-forms give us access is, in the present moment, always and in every way encompassed by the threat of loss, even irrevocable loss. This, it seems, has simply become part of the climate of our contemporary experience of the sacred in the natural world.

Freeman House, whose book *Totem Salmon* (1999) chronicles the painstaking efforts among communities in Northern California to restore the Pacific salmon run in their rivers and streams, reminds us what it feels like to draw close to such beautiful, mysterious, and increasingly rare beings.

> King salmon and I are together in the water. The basic bone-felt nature of this encounter never changes, even though I have spent parts of a lifetime seeking the meeting and puzzling over its meaning, trying to find for myself the right place in it. It is a *large* experience, and it has never failed to contain these elements, at once separate and combined: empty-minded awe; an uneasiness about my own active role both as a person and as a creature of my species; and a looming existential dread that sometimes attains the physicality of a lump in the throat, a knot in the abdomen, a constriction around the temples. (House 1999: 13)

It is a *large* experience, he says, for which one must struggle (and in all likelihood fail) to find adequate language. But the language House does find is revealing. It is analogous to the language often used to describe a defining religious experience. He calls it an "encounter," a "meeting," a "large experience," whose immensity evokes in him a deep sense of humility as he struggles to find his "right place in it." It pervades his entire being. Later, at some remove from the immediacy of this experience, he reflects on its meaning: "Each fish brought up from the deep carries with it implications of the Other, the great life of the sea that lies permanently beyond anyone's feeble strivings to control or understand it . . . True immersion in a system larger than oneself carries with it exposure to a vast complexity wherein joy and terror are complementary parts" (1999: 70).

Who is this Other whom we meet in such moments? Is it the "world" of these luminous beings ("a system larger than oneself . . . a vast complexity" – a world that will forever elude our understanding and because of this remains fundamentally mysterious and alluring)? The beings themselves? God? An encounter with salmon, or any living species, invites us to consider all of these possibilities, to open ourselves and respond to the mysterious Other with honesty and imagination and, perhaps, faith.

To open ourselves in this way to the mysterious Other, without prejudice or constraint, may well be one of the keys to rediscovering a sense of intimacy with other living beings that was once a common and accepted part of human experience. Here is a kind of "archaic spirituality," rooted in the rhythms of the natural world, which still exists, if in a much diminished form, among certain indigenous peoples and still pulses in our veins. Paul Shepard describes it as:

> the way of life to which our ontogeny was fitted by natural selection, fostering a calendar of mental growth, cooperation, leadership, and the study of a mysterious and beautiful world where the clues to the meaning of life were embodied in natural things, where everyday life was inextricable from spiritual significance and encounter, and where the members of the group celebrated individual stages and passages as ritual participation in the first creation. (1982: 6)

It is still possible, he argues, to waken to this dimension of experience, to absorb it into our consciousness, our lived reality. But to do so will entail accepting what amounts to a revolution in consciousness as we learn to open ourselves to the inescapably biological-carnal dimension of our spirituality, a dimension for which animals and the entire non-human natural world are crucial.

This is the idea that stands at the heart of Shepard's great masterpiece of ecological-spiritual thought, *The Others: How Animals Made Us Human* (1996b). We will never arrive at an adequate understanding of human consciousness or the human capacity for transcendence, argues Shepard, unless we reckon with our sixty-million-year-old relationship with the non-human animal world. For our ancestors, a whole range of activities associated with the hunt served to shape human consciousness in a fundamental way. It was here, in the search for food, that we came to develop mental maps and the capacity to read animal and vegetational signs in the landscape. It was here that we learned to develop our capacity for playful imitation of animals that even now at a great remove from that Pleistocene world informs the way in which we form metaphors for the self. Shepard notes the irresistible appeal for children of crab walks, duck waddles, song games like "farmer in the dell," "piggy back" rides, "chicken fights," and the like. Here one catches glimpses of the necessary role of animals in shaping human imagination and language at an early age. But the power of such beings to form us continues long after childhood, suggests Shepard:

> Each of us is an ocean of motives, emotions and ideas. Each animal in play reveals a certain trait or feeling exhibited in its behavior. Each kind of animal gives concrete representation to an ephemeral and intangible element of the human self such as assertion, intimidation, affection, doubt, determination, kindness, anger, hope, irritation, yearning, wisdom, cunning, anticipation, fear, and initiative. Only when these feelings are discovered outside the self and then performed can such intense but elusive "things" be made one's own. (1996a: 83)

To come to terms with such a rich web of relationality, between ourselves and the non-human world and within ourselves – with what Shepard calls "the diverse zoology of the self" – is to find ourselves living in a rich and dense world of reciprocity. Here, the non-human "others" are seen and cherished for who they are, subjects in a rich, intersubjective reality (Abram 1996: 38). The consequences of not accepting this invitation are severe. "We enjoy animals so much," suggests Shepard, "because we are laying up the basis for a language of analogy, the terms for the abstractions of cosmology and poetry . . . failure to nurture childhood enthusiasm for animals produces adults bereft of diverse living forms as the metaphorical basis of religious conceptions and values" (1996a: 88–9).

Seen in this light, the increasingly rapid disappearance of animal and plant species from our world signals not only an irreversible and potentially fatal reduction of biological life, but also an impoverishment of spiritual experience. We are creating a barren landscape, uninhabitable for humans, animals, or God. The loss of the wild world and the loss of the sacred cannot be separated (Burton-Christie 2003b). It is this sense that leads Thomas Berry to conclude: "We are losing splendid and intimate modes of divine presence. We are, perhaps, losing ourselves" (1988: 8).

Loss and the Renewal of Hope

There is an astonishing paradox here: as an increasing number of living beings disappear from the world forever, we are awakening to the enormity of what is being lost to us, for which the only adequate language is God, the Other, the sacred. The world is dying and so is God. A question inevitably arises: can the sense of loss that is increasingly woven into our experience of the natural world (and our experience of God) serve us in our efforts to renew and heal the world? Can we move beyond, or through, the personal sense of loss and remorse that afflicts us to create a new ethic, a new politics, a new spirituality? There is a growing consensus among contemporary writers that unless we can find a means of articulating a political vision of nature that is rooted in a sense of the natural world as sacred, our efforts to preserve and renew the world will be neither effective nor sustainable. So, too, unless we find a way of expressing our personal experience of the sacred in nature within a larger, communal effort to take responsibility for the natural world, the world, along with our experience of it, will die.

The losses we experience are *communal* and *inclusive*. So too must our efforts to arrive at a new and sustainable vision of the natural world be communal and inclusive. The destruction of the natural world we are currently experiencing arises from a collective refusal to confront and address our complicity in the systematic erosion of life all around us. Thus it is not enough to speak of the need for a personal awakening, or a personal change of heart, though of course these are necessary. Such personal awakening must open out onto and inform every dimension of our shared life together; our social, political, and economic arrangements; our cultural values, and yes, our sense of the sacred. It is when this personal transformation takes root in and becomes part of a larger, communal vision that real and lasting change becomes possible.

There are some telling instances of this in the history of the environmental movement. One of the most compelling involves Aldo Leopold, one of the most influential figures in the North American conservation movement in the twentieth century. A story he relates about an experience he had as a young man became emblematic of the kind of change of consciousness needed to inform a sustained political effort. This story has taken its place as part of a growing body of testimony, what might be called a "politics of witness," whereby a new spiritual-ecological-political vision emerges from and is grounded in personal experience. Such testimony, long recognized as crucial to the growth and development of religious communities, is increasingly coming to be seen as necessary to the task of forging a new vision of hope for the earth.

Leopold was a young man when he set off traveling through the canyon lands of Arizona. He and his companions stopped one day to eat lunch on a high rimrock and, gazing into the canyon below, they suddenly caught sight of what appeared to be a doe fording the river. Only when she had crossed the river and had begun climbing toward them did they realize their error: they were watching a wolf. Following behind her were half a dozen others, grown pups who "sprang from the willows and . . . joined in a welcoming mêlée of wagging tails and playful maulings. What was literally a pile of wolves writhed and tumbled in the center of an open flat at the foot of our rimrock." Leopold and his friends did not hesitate: "in a second we were pumping lead into the pack," he says, bringing the old wolf down and scattering the others. He reached the wolf in time "to watch the fierce green fire dying in her eyes. I realized then, and have known ever since, that there was something new to me in those eyes – something known only to her and to the mountain."

Reflecting on this bloody encounter many years later, Leopold noted with chagrin how disjointed his own relationship with the natural world had been at the time, how shallow his judgment and perspective. Not only had he callously assumed the right to kill the wolf, but he had completely misunderstood the delicate ecological balance he was disturbing: "I thought that fewer wolves meant more deer, that no wolves would mean hunters' paradise." The systematic application of this principle during subsequent years in state after state throughout the American West had caused deer populations to explode and vegetation to be decimated. The result? "Starved bones of the hoped-for deer herd, dead of its own too much . . . dustbowls, and rivers washing the future into the sea" (Leopold 1949: 129–32). All this was because we had not learned, as Leopold put it, to "think like a mountain," that is, to consider the implications of our actions from a deep sense of empathy and understanding of the rhythms of the natural world. The birth of Leopold's new sense of relationship with the natural world, and the land ethic he helped to articulate, emerged from that chilling moment when he glimpsed "the fierce green fire" dying in the eyes of the old wolf. This unexpected epiphany removed a veil from his understanding and revealed to him a previously unimagined dimension of reality.

Leopold never ventured to name what it was he encountered that day. But it is clear from his subsequent actions and writings that his encounter with the wolf had touched him at his depths and altered radically and permanently his sense of himself in relation to the living world. Among other things, it opened up within him a new way of understanding "value," in particular the value we ascribe to non-human beings. Toward the end of his now-classic *A Sand County Almanac*, he notes: "It is inconceivable to me that an ethical relation to land can exist without love, respect, and admiration for land, and a high regard for its value. By value, I of course mean something far broader than mere economic value." Such reflection on value, Leopold felt, was crucial if we were to have any chance at freeing ourselves from the tyranny and myopia of judging all our actions in the natural world in accordance with the short-term economic value they might yield. He was convinced that reflecting on our feeling for the land (our love, respect, and admiration for it) would help lead us to a more authentic and sustainable understanding of its value. And this deeper assessment of value would help us to articulate the true meaning of ecological integrity. Leopold himself came to understand and articulate it in these terms: "A thing is right when it tends to preserve the integrity, stability, and beauty of the biotic community. It is wrong when it tends otherwise" (1949: 223–5).

It would be difficult to overestimate the significance of this simple declaration to the growth and deepening of the contemporary ecological movement. Leopold's careful scientific work grounded his "land ethic" in the imperatives of ecological reality. Yet by expanding the circle of moral responsibility to include the non-human world, he also sharpened the challenge of thinking and acting ecologically. Our decisions, heretofore judged solely in terms of their effects upon *us*, would now need to be assessed within a more complex and demanding moral (and political) framework. Not only that, but Leopold's own experience suggested another crucial element to the emerging picture: we would need to take seriously our own experience of the natural world, its effect upon us, its capacity to move us at the depth of our beings. Here, both Leopold's work and his personal witness suggest the necessity of integrating the spiritual, the ecological, and the political into a coherent vision.

Leopold's integral vision of the human place in the natural world has had a profound effect on subsequent generations of writers who have continued the work of deepening and extending the spiritual-ecological-political vision that he outlined. One of the intriguing and hopeful aspects of this discourse is the extent to which articulation of spiritual experience and values informs the deeper concerns of the writers, including their political commitments. It is difficult at the moment to judge the significance or the lasting effect of these new expressions of eco-political spirituality. Whether or not such improvised and personal expressions of spiritual longing can contribute to the formation of communities of shared value that will endure remains to be seen. Still, the vitality of this discourse and its growing significance as a cultural and political fact of life is undeniable. For many of these writers, participation with particular communities in specific geographical locales in the struggle to stem the tide of ecological degradation is crucial. It informs their work and enables their articulation of a spiritual and moral vision to speak with real authority to the deeper concerns of those engaged in the ecological-political struggle.

Conclusion

The work of Montana writer William Kittredge, himself a person standing on the margins of traditional religious practice and discourse (he describes himself as "irreligious as a stone"), gives exemplary expression to this emerging ecological-political-spiritual synthesis. For Kittredge, the primary question we must ask ourselves is: what kind of paradise are we hoping for?

> Not long ago in the American West, it was easy to think we were living in harmony with an inexhaustible paradise. That became, for many, a habit of mind, hard to shake.
>
> But aspects of our paradise have been worked to death. The old-growth timber has been mostly logged; the great salmon runs have vanished; cattle and sheep tromp streamsides to dust and dust again; hard metals percolating up from mine shafts abandoned decades ago poison our mountain waters. (Kittredge 1996: 4)

We have done this. We have inflicted these wounds upon the landscape. We need look no further than this for a contemporary image of paradise squandered, lost. It may or may not be too late to undo what we have done, to preserve the world from its ultimate demise. But, in the present moment, the work of the Spirit demands that we face up to the immensity of the damage we have already inflicted upon the world and search out a new way of being in the world. This will, of course, involve a critical re-examination of our social, political, and economic arrangements, which have contributed so much to the exhaustion of the earth's life-forms. It will also require an honest re-examination of our spirituality, our capacity for living in the world with real feeling, with love. As Kittredge says:

> It's time we gave something back to the natural systems of order that have supported us, some care and tenderness, which is the most operative notion, I think – tenderness. Our isolations are gone, in the West and everywhere. We need to give some time to the arts of cherishing the things we adore, before they simply vanish. Maybe it will be like learning a skill: how to live in paradise. (1996: 35)

Here, perhaps, is where we need to begin if we hope to cultivate a new ethic, a new politics, a new spirituality capable of helping us love and sustain the earth: re-learning the arts of cherishing the things we adore.

But what, whom, do we adore? The image of the cross hanging amidst the immensity of eternity, found in the Mausoleum of the Galla Placidia in Ravenna, suggests the beginning of an answer for Christians. We adore God woven into the very fabric of the universe, into every living being, every place, every person. We adore God hidden amidst the displaced, the broken, and the bereft. We adore God who promises, in "the fullness of time, to gather up all things in [Christ], things in heaven and things on earth" (Eph. 1: 10).

References

Abram, D. 1996: *The Spell of the Sensuous: Perception and Language in a More-than-human World*. New York: Pantheon.

Albanese, C. 1990: *Nature Religion in America: From the Algonkian Indians to the New Age*. Chicago: University of Chicago Press.

Baker-Fletcher, K. 1998: *Sisters of Dust, Sisters of Spirit: Womanist Wordings on God and Creation*. Minneapolis, MN: Fortress Press.

Bergant, D. 1998: *The Earth is the Lord's: The Bible, Ecology and Worship*. Collegeville, MN: Liturgical Press.

Berry, T. 1988: *The Dream of the Earth*. San Francisco: Sierra Club.

Berry, W. 1993: Christianity and the survival of creation. In *Sex, Economy, Freedom, and Community: Eight Essays*, pp. 93–116. New York: Pantheon.

Boff, L. 1997: *Cry of the Earth, Cry of the Poor*, trans. P. Berryman. Maryknoll, NY: Orbis.

Bouma-Prediger, S. 1995: *The Greening of Theology: The Ecological Models of Rosemary Radford Ruether, Joseph Sittleter, and Jürgen Moltmann*. Atlanta: Scholars Press.

Brown, L. R., Larsen, J., and Fischlowitz-Roberts, B. 2002: *The Earth Policy Reader*. New York: W. W. Norton.

Burton-Christie, D. 1993: A feeling for the natural world: spirituality and the appeal to the heart in contemporary nature writing. *Continuum* 2, 229–52.

——1994a: The literature of nature and the quest for the sacred. *The Way Supplement* 81, 4–14.

——1994b: Mapping the sacred landscape: spirituality and the contemporary literature of nature. *Horizons* 21, 22–47.

——1999: Into the body of another: *eros*, embodiment and intimacy with the natural world. *Anglican Theological Review* 81, 13–37.

——2000: Words beneath the water: logos, cosmos and the spirit of place. In D. T. Hessel and R. R. Ruether (eds), *Christianity and Ecology*, pp. 317–36. Cambridge, MA: Harvard University Press.

——2003a: The spirit of place: the Columbia River watershed letter and the meaning of community. *Horizons* 30, 7–24.

——2003b: The wild and the sacred. *Anglican Theological Review* 85, 493–510.

Catholic Bishops' Conference of the Philippines 1988: What is happening to our beautiful land? A pastoral letter on ecology from the Catholic bishops of the Philippines. *SEDOS* 4, 112–15.

Catholic Bishops of the Pacific Northwest 2001: The Columbia River watershed: caring for creation and the common good. An international pastoral letter by the Catholic bishops of the region. Seattle: Columbia River Pastoral Letter Project.

Cobb, J. 1992: *Sustainability: Economics, Ecology, and Justice*. Maryknoll, NY: Orbis.

Cohen, J. 1989: *"Be Fertile, Fill the Earth and Master It": The Ancient and Medieval Career of a Biblical Text*. Ithaca, NY: Cornell University Press.

Commission for Racial Justice, United Church of Christ 1987: *Toxic Wastes and Race in the United States: A National Report on the Racial and Socio-economic Characteristics of Communities with Hazardous Waste Sites*. New York: United Church of Christ.

Dimitrios, the Ecumenical Patriarch 1990: *Orthodoxy and the Ecological Crisis*. Gland, Switzerland: World Wildlife Fund.

Eaton, H. (ed.) 2003: *Ecofeminism and Globalization: Exploring Culture, Context, and Religion*. Lanham, MD: Rowman and Littlefield.

Edwards, D. 1995: *Jesus the Wisdom of God: An Ecological Theology*. Maryknoll, NY: Orbis.

Fowler, R. B. 1995: *The Greening of Protestant Thought*. Chapel Hill, NC: University of North Carolina Press.

Fox, M. 1983: *Original Blessing: A Primer in Creation Spirituality Presented in Four Paths, Twenty-six Themes, and Two Questions*. Santa Fe: Bear and Company.

Fritsch, A. J. 1987: *Renew the Face of the Earth*. Chicago: Loyola University Press.

Galvin, J. 1992: *The Meadow*. New York: Henry Holt.

Goodenough, U. 1998: *The Sacred Depths of Nature*. New York: Oxford University Press.

Gottlieb, R. S. (ed.) 1996: *The Sacred Earth: Religion, Nature, Environment*. New York: Routledge.

—— 1999: *A Spirituality of Resistance: Finding a Peaceful Heart and Protecting the Earth*. New York: Crossroad.

Gregorios, P. M. 1987: *The Human Presence: Ecological Spirituality and the Age of the Spirit*. New York: Amity.

Gregory, F. 1992: *Nature Lost? Natural Science and the German Theological Traditions of the Nineteenth Century*. Cambridge, MA: Harvard University Press.

Griffin, S. 1995: *The Eros of Everyday Life: Essays on Ecology, Gender and Society*. New York: Doubleday.

Harrison, R. P. 1992: *Forests: The Shadow of Civilization*. Chicago: University of Chicago Press.

Hass, R. 1996: *Sun under Wood*. New York: Ecco.

Hayes, Z. 2001: *The Gift of Being: A Theology of Creation*. Collegeville, MN: Liturgical Press.

Hessel, D. T. and Ruether, R. R. (eds) 2001: *Christianity and Ecology: Seeking the Well-being of Earth and Humans*. Cambridge, MA: Harvard University Press.

Hiebert, T. 1996: *The Yahwist's Landscape: Nature and Religion in Early Israel*. New York: Oxford University Press.

Hogan, L. 1995: *Dwellings: A Spiritual History of the Living World*. New York: Norton.

House, F. 1999: *Totem Salmon: Life Lessons from Another Species*. Boston: Beacon.

Hütterman, A. 1999: *The Ecological Message of the Torah: Knowledge, Concepts and Laws which Made Survival in a Land of "Milk and Honey" Possible*. Atlanta: Scholars Press.

John Paul II 1990: Peace with God the Creator – peace with all of creation. World Day of Peace Message, January 1, 1990. *Origins: CNS Documentary Service* 19 (December 14), 465–8.

Johnson, E. 1993: *Woman, Earth, and Creator Spirit*. New York: Paulist Press.

Kinsley, D. 1994: *Ecology and Religion: Ecological Spirituality in Cross-cultural Perspective*. Englewood Cliffs, NJ: Prentice Hall.

Kittredge, W. 1992: *Hole in the Sky: A Memoir*. New York: Knopf.

—— 1996: *Who Owns the West?* San Francisco: Mercury House.

Kwok, Pui-Lan 1999: *Christology for an Ecological Age*. New York: Continuum.

Ladner, G. B. 1995: *God, Cosmos, and Humankind: The World of Early Christian Symbolism*, trans. Thomas Dunlap. Berkeley, CA: University of California Press.

Lane, B. 1998: *The Solace of Fierce Landscapes: Exploring Desert and Mountain Spirituality*. New York: Oxford University Press.

—— 2001: *Landscapes of the Sacred: Geography and Narrative in American Spirituality*. Baltimore, MD: The Johns Hopkins University Press.

Lefevere, P. 2003: Protecting the planet: "green nuns" put land ethic into action. *National Catholic Reporter*, September 19.

Leopold, A. 1949: *A Sand County Almanac and Sketches Here and There*. New York: Oxford University Press.

Lopez, B. 1990: *The Rediscovery of North America*. New York: Vintage.

Louth, A. 1991: *The Wilderness of God*. Nashville: Abingdon.

McFague, S. 1987: *The Body of God: An Ecological Theology*. Minneapolis, MN: Fortress Press.

—— 1997: *Super, Natural Christians: How We Should Love Nature*. Minneapolis, MN: Fortress Press.

McGinn, B. 1993: The letter and the spirit: spirituality as an academic discipline. *Christian Spirituality Bulletin* 1 (2), 1–10.

McGuire, M. 1997: Mapping contemporary American spirituality: a sociological perspective. *Christian Spirituality Bulletin* 5 (1), 1–8.

McKibben, B. 1989: *The End of Nature*. New York: Random House.

Merchant, C. 1980: *The Death of Nature: Woman, Ecology, and the Scientific Revolution*. San Francisco: Harper and Row.

Moltmann, J. 1985: *God in Creation: A New Theology of Creation and the Spirit of God*, trans. M. Kohl. San Francisco: Harper and Row.

Nash, J. A. 1991: *Loving Nature: Ecological Integrity and Christian Responsibility*. Nashville: Abingdon.

Nelson, R. 1991: *The Island Within*. New York: Vintage.

Nicholson, S. W. 2002: *The Love of Nature and the End of the World: The Unspoken Dimensions of Environmental Concern*. Cambridge, MA: MIT Press.

Oelschlaeger, M. 1994: *Caring for Creation: An Ecumenical Approach to the Environmental Crisis*. New Haven, CT: Yale University Press.

Presbyterian Advisory Committee on Social Witness Policy 1996: *Hope for a Global Future: Toward Just and Sustainable Human Development*. Louisville, KY: Office of the General Assembly, Presbyterian Church (USA).

Quammen, D. 1996: *The Song of the Dodo: Island Biogeography in an Age of Extinction*. New York: Scribner.

Rasmussen, L. L. 1996: *Earth Community, Earth Ethics*. Maryknoll, NY: Orbis.

Raymo, C. 1999: *Natural Prayers*. St Paul, MN: Ruminator Books.

Ruether, R. 1992: *Gaia and God: An Ecofeminist Theology of Earth Healing*. San Francisco: Harper.

Santmire, P. 1985: *The Travail of Nature: The Ambiguous Ecological Promise of Christian Theology*. Philadelphia: Fortress Press.

Scharper, S. B. 1997: *Redeeming the Time: A Political Theology of the Environment*. New York: Continuum.

Schneiders, S. M. 1994: A hermeneutical approach to the study of Christian spirituality. *Christian Spirituality Bulletin* 2 (1), 9–14.

——2003: Religion vs. spirituality: a contemporary conundrum. *Spiritus* 3, 163–85.

Scott, P. 2003: *A Political Theology of Nature*. Cambridge: Cambridge University Press.

Sheldrake, P. 2001: *Spaces for the Sacred: Place, Memory, and Identity*. Baltimore, MD: The Johns Hopkins University Press.

Shepard, P. 1982: *Nature and Madness*. San Francisco: Sierra Club.

——1996a: *The Only World We've Got: A Paul Shepard Reader*. San Francisco: Sierra Club.

——1996b: *The Others: How Animals Made Us Human*. Washington, DC: Island Press.

Soule, M. and Wilcox, B. A. (eds) 1980: *Conservation Biology*. Sunderland, MA: Sinauer.

Taves, A. 2003: Detachment and engagement in the study of "lived experience." *Spiritus* 3, 186–208.

Toolan, D. 2001: *At Home in the Universe*. Maryknoll, NY: Orbis.

Torrance, R. M. 1994: *The Spiritual Quest: Transcendence in Myth, Religion and Science*. Berkeley, CA: University of California Press.

Tracy, D. 1975: *Blessed Rage for Order: The New Pluralism in Theology*. Minneapolis, MN: Seabury Press.

US Conference of Catholic Bishops 1991: Renewing the earth. *Origins* 21 (December 12), 425–32.

Van Ness, P. H. (ed.) 1996: *Spirituality and the Secular Quest*. New York: Crossroad.

Wallace, M. I. 1996: *Fragments of the Spirit: Nature, Violence and the Renewal of Creation*. New York: Continuum.

Wilson, E. O. 1984: *Biophilia*. Cambridge, MA: Harvard University Press.

—— 1989: Ecology and the human imagination: dialogue between E. O. Wilson and Barry Lopez. In E. Lueders (ed.), *Writing Natural History: Dialogues with Authors*, pp. 8–35. Salt Lake City: University of Utah Press.

World Council of Churches 1990: *Now is the Time: The Final Document and Other Texts from the World Convocation on Justice, Peace, and the Integrity of Creation, Seoul, Republic of Korea, 5–12 March 1990*. Geneva: World Council of Churches.

CHAPTER 28
Practice

Elizabeth Liebert

"'Right (communal) doing' seems in some sense a precondition for right understanding," claims Miroslav Volf (2002: 251). This statement raises a number of intriguing questions about what constitutes understanding and how we arrive at it, questions that have particular significance for those engaged in scholarly reflection upon spiritual experience. Some of the questions are epistemological. What does it mean to know? Are there different "knowings" for theory and practice? Or might they be figure and ground of the same reality? What particular kind of knowing constitutes "scholarship?" Other questions have to do with perspective. What is the nature of the perspective taken by the scholar *vis-à-vis* the object of study and between the scholar and the scholar's audience? Where, in fact, is scholarship best pursued? And still other questions are of a pastoral character. How can one come to understand the other, be it the other in the professor's office or in the neighborhood, or the socio-economic, racial, ethnic, and gendered other, the ecumenical or interfaith other, or even the non-human other?

In this essay, I will reflect on Volf's first phrase, "right (communal) doing," and ask what it might look like in a particular case: that of the academic study of Christian spirituality. I propose that a particular kind of doing, which I shall call "practice," when employed by the scholar in the study of spirituality, is not merely something useful, but is a *constitutive* dimension of the discipline. Because of this dimension, spirituality offers a useful and necessary perspective to other theological disciplines. Furthermore, when used in conjunction with appropriate scholarly methods, "practice" advances the content of the study itself.

This argument proceeds in three interlocking steps. First, by examining the recent history and development of another young discipline, pastoral theology, I will note some comparisons and contrasts between this discipline and the academic study of spirituality. Second, I will address one of the commitments shared by both disciplines, namely, to "experience." Finally, using the notion of "experience" as the launching point, I will propose the constructive suggestion for the academic study of spirituality concerning "practice."

Pastoral Theology and Spirituality

In their report on "Teaching Christian Spirituality in Seminaries Today," Arthur Holder and Lisa Dahill (1999) note that theology and history dominate the degrees of special- ization among those teaching the introductory course in Christian spirituality (together, 50 percent of their sample). They wonder: "Given the preponderance of historians and theologians among those who teach introductory courses in Christian Spirituality, it is not surprising that these courses tend to stress history and theology, with very little attention to social scientific or aesthetic or practical theological or even biblical per- spectives" (1999: 11). What would happen if we were to pay attention to the insights and methodologies of these other disciplines? In reflecting on my personal history as a pastoral theologian, it occurred to me that the vicissitudes in the development of pas- toral theology as an academic discipline offer interesting similarities and contrasts to the development of the academic discipline of Christian spirituality. Taking my lead from Holder and Dahill's observation, I will examine the discipline of pastoral theology for the insights it may provoke concerning the matter of "right (communal) doing."

Pastoral theology traces its formation to such psychologists of religion as G. Stanley Hall (1904), William James (1908), and James Leuba (1909) in the early years of the twentieth century, Anton Boisen (1936), Richard Cabot, and Russell Dicks (Cabot and Dicks 1936; Dicks 1939) in the 1930s, and such systematizers as Carroll Wise (1942, 1951), Seward Hiltner (1949, 1958), Daniel Day Williams (1961), Wayne Oates (1962), Howard Clinebell (1966), and Paul Johnson (1967), in the 1950s, 1960s, and 1970s. These scholar-practitioners employed various biblical, theological, philosoph- ical, and psychological systems to ground their work. In the late 1970s, as I began my own study in the field, pastoral theology as an academic discipline was not quite sure if it was supposed to prepare clinicians, pastors, theologians, or a hybrid of all three. Consequently, students in various doctoral programs tried on all three personae. But all used, to a greater or lesser degree, a series of practices, both clinical and reflective, to ground the emerging discipline.

According to Burck and Hunter (1990), pastoral theology in its widest sense attempts to relate the meanings and requirements of faith to concrete human problems and situations, using human experience to come to a more profound understanding of God. In this endeavor, it deals inescapably in concreteness, with *this* event, *this* rela- tionship, *this* liturgy, *this* life-crisis, asking the following questions: What does it mean? What does it ask of me, of others? How does it affect an understanding of and rela- tionship to God? Similarly, the correlation proceeds in the other direction. How does my understanding of and relationship to God affect the interpretation of this particular experience? If God/Christ/church/world is like this, then what can I make of this child's death, for example? The dynamic nature of pastoral theology appears in figure 28.1. To read this diagram, begin at the lower right, with the sphere marked "Case," then move to the left, to the sphere marked "Tradition," and finally to the three fruits emer- ging from their dialectical interaction.

Pastoral theology, as this illustration reveals, is the task of prayerfully holding in tension the *particular event or case* in all its concreteness (that is, the individual's experi-

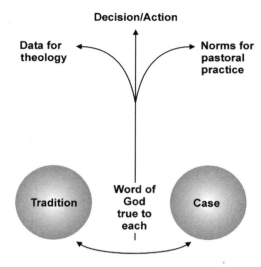

Figure 28.1   The dynamic nature of pastoral theology.

ence; the minister's experience; the community's experience; the sociological, cultural, psychological, economic, and other dynamic realities) with the *tradition* in all its richness and plurality (that is, the texts of the Christian community, particularly the Scriptures and the foundational documents of the given faith community; the history of the praxis of the community; the *sensus fidelium*) until we can hear the word of God that is true to each simultaneously. Once that word of God has become evident, however provisional and specific to the particular situation, it provides threefold direction: it *suggests appropriate responses* to the situation; it *provides touchstones for evaluating the resulting pastoral praxis*; and it *contributes data* to the larger theological enterprise and its development. This holding-in-tension may not be comfortable; its resolution may not be speedy. It may not be generalizable to other situations, yielding a way forward only for this particular situation. The data that it contributes to theology, then, are incremental and inductive.

This description focuses on the moment of doing of pastoral theology. It leaves assumed the prior step of careful description of the case. So, a more complete illustration might look like figure 28.2. By focusing on the process rather than the content, the description begins to look quite like the pastoral circle of liberation theology, which illuminates the dynamic, repetitive nature of a process for determining focused intentional action in a given setting (figure 28.3). All three of these figures illuminate the experience upon which the doing of pastoral theology is based, and without which it becomes disassociated from its source.

Today, in the field of pastoral theology, just as in the academic study of spirituality, there is an explosion of dialogue partners. Groups of scholars from both disciplines are asking "What are the boundaries of our discipline?" Both disciplines attempt to focus their scope in two ways: by crafting a definition that delimits the discipline and by selecting appropriate methods with which to address the subject matter. The definitional

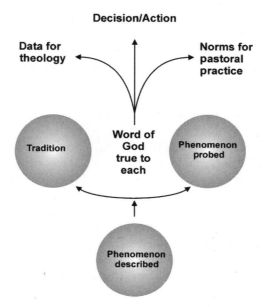

Figure 28.2   A more complete representation of pastoral theology, including the description of the case.

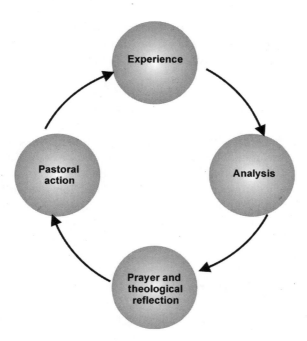

Figure 28.3   Pastoral circle, illuminating the dynamic, repetitive nature of the process.

issues in the field of spirituality have received a great deal of attention in the literature (Cousins 1990; Eire 1990; Hanson 1990; Schneiders 1990, 1993; McGinn 1993) so I will not dwell on these here. As for methodological parameters, pastoral theologians are guided by a particular case, or situation, in determining the critical discipline employed; this discipline, in turn, determines the range of appropriate methodologies by which to correlate theory and practice in a given situation. Analogously, in the academic study of spirituality, the particular research question determines the dialogue partners and methodology (Schneiders 1990: 32).

For pastoral theologians, as for scholars of Christian spirituality, the particular case is itself intrinsically challenging and worthy of critical reflection. It is the "stuff" – the contents – that the discipline studies. Likewise, the "problematic disciplines" of both communities of scholars, to use Sandra Schneiders's language (1998: 3–4), are precisely those that will assist one better to understand the experience (case) at hand with greater knowledge, accuracy, and empathy, and, more importantly, to help the persons or group themselves to understand their own experience and that of others more deeply. In these respects, pastoral theology and Christian spirituality are close cousins. The term "pastoral theology," like the term "Christian spirituality," can refer, at different moments, to the phenomenon (experience/case) in the round, the in-depth reflection on the case (the actual doing of pastoral theology), and to the academic study of the history, methods, and philosophy of the field. Different degrees of abstraction occur when speaking at these levels: one uses first-order religious language to describe the initial, immediate experience; second-order religious language for the explication and critical evaluation or appropriation of the basic meaning; and third-order religious language if the process continues to reflect on the way in which such judgments are made and give a critical evaluation of the procedures (Jennings 1990: 862; Schneiders 1990: 17; Waaijman 2002).

Obviously, there also exist inconsistencies between these two realms of discourse. Perhaps because pastoral theology arose primarily in Protestant theological and ecclesial contexts, it has tended to dwell on the human person in crisis and the appropriate helping acts taken by a representative of the church on behalf of and accompanying the person in crisis, including helping him or her to connect with faith where possible. The angle of entry and the goal of the enterprise differ from the academic study of spirituality, which focuses more on the experience of the Holy as manifested in various theaters of personal and communal life. Yet, while there are significant differences in these disciplines, the common emphasis on experience is important for the purposes of this discussion.

The Common Ground: Experience

Pastoral theology reveals this shared predilection for critical reflection on experience in its consistent use of the particular event or situation, the case. Christian spirituality shows it in its careful attention to Christian religious experience as such, in the self-implicating nature of the study, and in the insistence by those following the "anthropological approach" (Schneiders 1986; McGinn 1993; Downey 1997; Frohlich 2001) that the study of Christian spirituality must be grounded in the lived spiritual life of the one studying as well as the person, movement, text, or event studied. But what exactly do we mean by "experience?" Conversations in the Christian spirituality guild usually assume that the meaning is self-evident. In fact, it is a complex issue. Following my disciplinary roots, I will use resources from pastoral theology to tease out, however briefly, the meaning of this slippery term.

Experience, says pastoral theologian Brian Childs (1990), is "participation in or encounter with reality." The term may also refer to "the practical knowledge gained through such participation or encounter." It is "whatever we have undergone and done, and the ways in which we have *learned* something from what we did and underwent" (Lash 1988: 91). When opposing experience and reflection, an unfortunate dichotomy we would do well to avoid, experience stresses the immediacy of the occurrence as opposed to reflection on that experience. But, Childs insists, experience actually includes reflection as well as the original immediacy. This more holistic sense of experience grounds wisdom and practical knowledge. Furthermore, human experience develops within a web of relationships. These relationships provide the contents, the objects, the environment, and the context of our experience. They provide the material from which our memories, thoughts, images, feelings, and decisions are formed. They comprise the world upon which we act. These "others" can be variously grouped: nature, self, other humans, socio-political structures, and the transcendent (Wiens St John 1998; Howard 2000). Thus, what enhances and makes conscious the web of relationships in, for example, the doctoral classroom makes possible enhanced experience.

Were we to examine the long trail of texts that comprises the history of Christian spirituality, we would quickly determine that these texts appear in a variety of literary forms, including biblical commentary, biography, autobiography, hagiography, letters, prayers, and liturgies. We would also recognize that they were written from the author's own experience of and commitment to particular values and lifestyles and were intended to invite, persuade, encourage, and guide others into their own experiencing, valuing, and reproducing these same values and lifestyles. Only in the contemporary culture of the academy has this grounding in the lived experience of the author come to be seen as suspect and the source of potential distortion on the part of the scholar. Given the subject matter of Christian spirituality, Diana Villegas (2001) argues that participatory knowledge is an important component of knowledge about spirituality, and therefore important as well for the academic study of Christian spirituality.

"Practice" in the Academic Study of Spirituality

Experience, then, provides a bridge between the disciplines of pastoral theology and Christian spirituality. We stay close to experience through actions in which we review, repeat, and reflect on our experiences – practice. In *Honoring the Body: Meditations on a Christian Practice* (2002), Stephanie Paulsell tells a simple story about the foot washing that accompanied the quarterly services of the Lord's Supper in the Free Will Baptist churches of her friends, a story that points clearly to the difference that practice can make in our interpretation:

One woman would sit in a chair, take off her shoes, and place her feet in the basin. The other woman would kneel down in front of her, wash her feet in the water, and then dry them off with the ends of the towel. To me, the drying seemed more intimate than the washing. The washing was simply a matter of swirling water around the top of the foot that rested in the basin. To dry this foot, however, you had to take it in both your hands, prop it on your knee, and rub it, top and bottom, with the towel.

Unlike the Free Will Baptists, most churches have not made the washing of feet a sacrament to be enacted regularly within the community. The lesson of the act, exemplified by the story of Jesus washing the feet of his followers in the thirteenth chapter of John's Gospel, is emphasized instead. And certainly, it is not in ritually washing the nice clean feet of our best friends that we most truly follow Jesus, but in doing justice and seeking to live compassionately among all people.

But when we focus on the interpretation of the act without participating in the practice of it, we miss some important things. We miss, for instance, the startling, excessively intimate experience of handling the feet of another and putting our own feet in another's hands . . .

[O]ur attempts to have clean, sweet-smelling feet to offer betray the many ways we are rendered vulnerable by our bodies. When you offer your feet to another to be washed and gently dried, it is impossible not to notice the difficult relationship between our bodies and our identities. And when you kneel to wash the feet of another, you glimpse the vulnerabilities that attention to the body can evoke. I have only participated in foot washing three or four times in my life. But I can imagine that, practiced over a lifetime, this ritual might nourish a new vision of the relationship between the sacredness and the vulnerability of the body. (Paulsell 2002: 29–31)

What is "practice?" Is it admissible in the study of Christian spirituality? In the doctoral classroom? In general terms, according to theologian Rebecca Chopp, practices are:

Socially shared forms of behavior that mediate between what are often called subjective and objective dimensions. A practice is a pattern of meaning and action that is both culturally constructed and individually instantiated. The notion of practice draws us to inquire into the shared activities of groups of persons that provide meaning and orientation to the world, and that guide action. (1995: 15)

The notions of scope and duration divide the scholarship into two groups. One cluster of scholars takes its impetus from Alasdair MacIntyre's treatment in *After Virtue* (1984) and focuses on large-scale communal practices over considerable periods of time that address fundamental human needs and that together constitute a way of life. Representative of this group is David Kelsey's definition of practice as "any form of socially established cooperative human activity that is complex and internally coherent, is subject to standards of excellence that partly define it, and is done to some end but does not necessarily have a product" (1992: 118). Cooperative human behaviors that Kelsey has in mind are bodily, social, and interactive; share rule-like regularities; contain standards of excellence; and thus necessitate self-critical reflection as part of a larger communal discourse. Dykstra (1991), Bass (1999), and Volf and Bass (2002) also follow this basic notion of practice.

The second cluster of definitions springs from the social sciences. In these disciplines, "practice" can refer to any socially meaningful action, and therefore can include smaller and more discrete actions than would be included under the McIntyre-influenced definition. Sociologist of religion Meredith McGuire illustrates this perspective in an essay about the importance of the body in the study of Christian spirituality: "Lived religion is constituted by the practices by which people remember, share, enact, adapt, and create the stories out of which they live. And it is constituted through the practices by which people turn these stories into everyday action. Ordinary material existence – especially the human body – is the very stuff of these meaningful practices" (McGuire 2003: 15). In this perspective, virtually any action that has a shared meaning can function as a "practice."

In terms of Christian spirituality, and following this latter option, I propose to use the term "practice" as follows: *"Practice" is the intentional and repeated bringing of one's lived spirituality into the various theaters of one's scholarly work and attending to what happens when one does.* I have deliberately chosen the word "practice" because it exists as both a noun and a verb. To many, the word "practice" connotes a particular spiritual discipline. But, as I am using it, "practice" stands for the activity of continually bringing – practicing – lived spirituality into our scholarship. Lived spirituality is, as Mary Frohlich says, "attending with as much authenticity as one can muster to the truth of one's own experience" (2001: 68), including the truth of the other that challenges and de-centers us. As we do our scholarship, we attend to this basic experiential level intentionally, repeatedly, publicly, and self-critically toward some goal beyond itself. Lived spirituality, Frohlich insists, remains the focus of engagement for any study of spirituality. Thus, scholars of Christian spirituality practice reflecting together on the truth of our experience until it becomes second nature to us. We practice until our whole way of approaching a text or a figure or an event is informed by it. We practice attending to our lived spirituality in front of students and we give them opportunities to practice in the very learning of the discipline. That is, we develop a particular *habitus*, or unconscious regulator, that both reproduces and adjusts our response to self-evident-appearing social institutions and that leads to growth in understanding (Bourdieu 1977; Kelsey 1992; Chopp 1995). It is a matter of *doing always* what it is that we *study* (as well as studying what we do). This shared and self-critically reflective experience of lived spirituality is, in shorthand terms, what I mean by "practice."

I can well imagine the kind of objections to these assertions that will inevitably arise: "*But* how will the necessary scholarly rigor be maintained?" "That might work in a seminary classroom, *but* you can't do it in the university, especially a public university." "That may work with some contemporary or more existential topics, *but* it won't work for ancient or classical texts." "*But* I don't do that kind of work." "*But . . .*" Sandra Schneiders has stated the problem most cogently in her presidential address to the Society for the Study of Christian Spirituality:

> How to integrate a holistic approach to research with full accountability to the standards of criticism, personal commitment to what one is studying with appropriate methodological perspective, and practical involvement with theoretical integrity is, in my view, one

of the major challenges the discipline of spirituality faces as it develops its identity in the academy. (1998: 10)

She has also stated the objections most forcefully in her essay, "A Hermeneutical Approach to the Study of Christian Spirituality":

> In the research sphere, however, I would have very serious reservations about the inclusion of any kind of mandatory practice or the direct use of such personal practice in the construction or prosecution of research projects. In the research arena the purpose of the study is, as in any research field, the expansion of knowledge in the field. (1994: 13)

In the same essay, Schneiders does make room for experience in the study of Christian spirituality in several important ways, namely by controlled introspection to access one's own internal processes, and the practicum to get in touch with the lived spirituality of others. She also recognizes that our own thoughtful and passionate work in the discipline of spirituality transforms us: the work of the scholar is inevitably self-implicating, and its disciplined prosecution is itself a form of spiritual practice. Yet, she also insists on bracketing any form of mandatory practice designed to foster the spiritual life of the student, and to restrict such practice to ministerial formation programs. Leaving aside the problem of making any given discipline mandatory for all persons, it still may be that the situation is not this clear and distinct.

I believe that in most situations it is *not* clear that one and only one of these realities, namely "mandatory practice intended to foster the spiritual life of students" versus a scholarly investigation of the material at hand, is occurring at a given moment. For example, one might teach *lectio divina* to divinity students simultaneously as a form of personal prayer that they may find conducive in their own personal spiritual life, as a means of enhancing and deepening the various ways they access biblical texts in sermon preparation, and as a method of group prayer useful in many congregational settings. But if I were teaching Benedictine spirituality in a strictly academic setting such as a doctoral seminar, I might still invite all of us to immerse ourselves for a time in both *lectio divina* and the Divine Office. My primary intent in this situation is not the personal spiritual formation of the student (though I will not object if that occurs), but helping the students understand more deeply aspects of Benedictine spirituality. Even in the doctoral seminar, one means might be to invite immersion in some of the methods that took root in and were transmitted to the wider church through Benedict and Benedictine spirituality. I actually have a second goal that is straightforwardly pedagogical: to involve the student in a variety of avenues for appropriating the material *as suggested by the material itself*. I want to offer many avenues where students can really grasp and be grasped by the material we are together investigating. That is, I want to create a space where the self-implicating and transformative nature of the academic discipline of Christian spirituality can potentially take root. I maintain that when experience "comes into the room," it makes the study of the experience immediate and compelling.

Insights from Educational Theory

Favazza and Glennon (2000) discuss a recent pedagogical strategy in religious studies that bears on the role of practice in Christian spirituality, namely using service projects as a primary means for the learning of the course to occur. Proponents of service learning see the desire to base the study of religion solely on an objective, scientific approach as both epistemologically and pedagogically unsatisfactory. It is epistemologically unsatisfactory because it distances the topic of study from the subjects, professors, and students in the name of neutrality and objectivity. These advocates of service learning claim, with Parker Palmer (1998: 19, 51, 98), that there is an intricate connection between epistemology, pedagogy, and ethics. The relationship of the knower to the known becomes the basis for the relationship of the actor to the world. Thus, an objective, arms-length study of religion or spirituality keeps the teachers and students disconnected from what they know and what they want to know, and may also inhibit appropriate action in relation to what they know. Spirituality, like religion, is precisely about the way in which people generate order and meaning in their lives in relationship to themselves, others, and God. Distancing oneself from the nature of spirituality in order to study it may actually prevent one from fully grasping the essence of various spiritualities and their vitality.

Pedagogically, Favazza and Glennon's (2000) argument can be stated as follows. As we have come to realize in this postmodern era, there are no neutral starting-points or standing-points. What one believes and what one has experienced inevitably influence what one knows (and how one teaches). Better not to try to banish the unbanishable, but to bring it self-consciously but critically into the discussion and dialogue with the study of spirituality in a way that is inclusive, respectful, and productive of greater insight and understanding.

Educational theory offers further insight into the pedagogical aspects of the thesis that the disciplined reflection on lived spirituality is constitutive of the discipline of Christian spirituality. Howard Gardner's work on multiple intelligences brings home the need for multiple entry points to the same material. In *The Disciplined Mind* (2000: 185–99), Gardner offers three important general strategies.

(1)   *Provide multiple points of entry.* How to engage students initially in the topic at hand is an important pedagogical decision. Different students will find various entry points conducive to involving them in the study, and there is no reason why all students should even engage the same one at the same time. In our hypothetical class on Benedict and Benedictine spirituality, one person might enter through the careful exegesis of the text of the Rule, another through the practice of *lectio divina*, another through a narrative of the life of Benedict and the spread of Benedictine spirituality throughout Europe, a fourth through the Benedictine patronage of the arts, and still another through the recent struggle of the Prioress of the Benedictines of Erie (Pennsylvania) to define the scope of Benedictine obedience in the face of Vatican demands.

(2) *Offer apt analogies.* The educator's crucial task consists in conveying the power of the analogy, but, equally important, conveying the limitations as well. The pedagogical challenge consists in figuring out which entry points hold promise for particular understandings, trying them out and evaluating them, and making explicit the assumptions, contexts, possibilities, and limits of the analogies employed. The example of asking doctoral students to engage for some time in *lectio divina* is illuminative. Uncritically appropriated, such a practice can obscure even as it illuminates. Just because we have employed *lectio divina*, do we then know what *lectio divina* was like in Benedict's time? Not necessarily.

Mary Frohlich offers a welcome move beyond the morass we can get ourselves into by bringing experience and practice into the doing of academic spirituality. She recognizes that simply asserting that we begin from "lived spirituality" will not fully answer our most important questions at either the personal or academic levels. She notes:

> A first methodological principle, then, will be to ask the questions, What are we doing with the experiential dimension? What sort of implicit or explicit appeal are we making on its basis? By what steps do we move from the place of living to the place of speaking, writing, and making claims? Are the forms of appeal and the steps we make appropriate to the actual context in which we are living, studying and/or teaching spirituality? (Frohlich 2001: 69)

Thus, it is not merely importing lived experience into our scholarship and teaching that by itself constitutes effective "practice." We must also develop skills and nuance and critical awareness about the way in which experience functions in our scholarship and pedagogy. We must "practice our practice," so to speak, in order that it develops into an intentional methodological perspective on the materials with which we engage.

(3) *Provide multiple representations of the central or core ideas.* Powerful and effective educators can represent the issue in several sets of language, and can evaluate and teach others to evaluate new attempts to express the same topic. An impressive example from the field of Christian spirituality of both multiple entry points and multiple representations of core ideas is Belden Lane's *The Solace of Fierce Landscapes: Exploring Desert and Mountain Spirituality* (1998). Its power lies, I believe, precisely in Lane's decision to juxtapose three different entry points: his own experiences of loss and grief, his immersion into particular places of desert and mountain, and the spiritual tradition of the *via negativa*, creating a brilliant and evocative treatment of desert spirituality. This kind of multiple-leveled engagement, including "practice," is exactly what I am proposing we continue to develop as a self-conscious strategy in our scholarly writing and teaching.

The Importance of Practice in Spirituality

The argument thus far has established that studying the human experience of the transcendent, while carefully excluding many of the possible avenues for experiencing the transcendent offered by Christian spirituality, is pedagogically unwarranted. There is no guarantee that doing so will preserve the investigator from bias, and it may, at least subliminally, perpetuate a seriously truncated notion of spirituality. But the constructive goal lies beyond simply useful pedagogy or even pedagogy that takes seriously the nature of spirituality. In its fullest form, it is this: not only should the practice of spirituality not be banned from the academic study of Christian spirituality (and therefore from the classroom where such academic study takes place), but practice provides one of the constitutive elements of our discipline's approach, and, because of it, spirituality offers both a useful and necessary perspective to other theological disciplines, such as systematic theology and history, that may focus on the same content. Practice offers a possible context for access to the immediate experience of the spiritual life, the subject matter of the discipline. When experience "comes into the room," it makes the study of the experience of the Christian life immediate and compelling. But, more importantly for the development of the discipline, it advances the content of the study itself.

Many scholars of Christian spirituality work almost exclusively with texts: biblical texts, texts of various literary forms that have been recognized as part of our Christian heritage, texts left by important Christian thinkers, pastors, and spiritual guides. The key questions that the academic study of Christian spirituality poses to texts of all kinds and eras include: what is the lived spiritual experience of this text? The experience that gave rise to it? The experience that it met in its first hearers or readers, as much as this can be reclaimed, and its experience in me and in my students today? In light of this discussion, we can now further ask: what new experience is created in the act of investigating this text and wrestling with its provenance, interpretation, and existential usefulness? What experiences of my own would help me enter faithfully into the world of this text? What shared practices would help us come to understand this text and its world and ourselves as interpreters?

The thesis posed here does *not* mean that one can simply read one's own self into the text. All the appropriate exegetical moves must occur, including establishing the accuracy of the text as it exists, the adequacy of any translation employed, the serious study of the context, the author, the author's community, the literary form, the reason that the author is writing this text as far as it can be ascertained, and the position and frame of reference of those to whom the text was addressed. We must also try to become aware of our own assumptions and biases and attempt to set them aside during the investigative phase of our work with the text. But when that foundational work has been done, what are we faced with? A text that in its otherness is struggling to communicate with us across vast gulfs in cultures, languages, worldviews. Do we allow ourselves to be transformed by the disciplined practice of uncovering all the levels of experience present in the encounter, the ones the text brought and the ones we brought? Do we allow the disciplined practice of lived spirituality to help us to rethink the text? What scholars of Christian spirituality do, I believe, is "to interpret the experience it studies in order to make it understandable and meaningful in the present without violating its historical reality" (Schneiders 1998: 3). We make the experience meaningful and understandable in the present, that is, by engaging it *in the present* but *on its own terms.*

The careful work of the scholar, Wendy Wright insists (1996: 21), can be both self-implicating and transformative precisely in the way it brings us face to face with the radical otherness of what it is we study. And, in the very wrestling with this otherness, we might even be transformed. That is, not only might our scholarly opinions and conclusions be revised, but also the very ways in which we pray, act, and live might change.

Diana Villegas, following Robert C. Neville, argues convincingly that such participatory knowledge as we have been addressing under the rubric of "practice" is, in fact, radically objective for two reasons. First, scholars who study through personally distancing methods may succeed merely in projecting the categories and assumptions in the theories and methods they employ – and will likely not be conscious that this has happened. Second, assuming the truth of a spirituality's claim that personal involvement will be personally transformative, then a scholar who engages in this path becomes vulnerable to such a transformation. If it occurs in a disciplined manner, over time and according to the network of meanings of the tradition, it can prevent or correct critical analysis that remains personally distant and the scholar can come to understand through experience precisely the claim that is being made by this spirituality (Villegas 2001: 259).

One of the reasons scholars of Christian spirituality banish practice from the academic study of spirituality is, I suspect, because the immediacy of direct experience can make critical perspectives more difficult. But I do believe it is possible that both can occur simultaneously. It does require careful attention to the need for and process of holding in tension the experience/case, one's own lived spirituality and experience with the spirituality under investigation, and the canons of good scholarship. However, maintaining this tension has substantial benefits for one's scholarly work as well as for one's person.

The Practice of Spirituality

What might this notion of practice as the intentional and repeated bringing of one's lived spirituality into one's scholarly work look like concretely? First, let me offer an example of research and writing and then one of teaching.

The process that my two co-authors and I entered into as we wrote *The Spiritual Exercises Reclaimed: Uncovering Liberating Possibilities for Women* (Dyckman et al. 2001) provides an example of this kind of practice. We had several goals for this work. We wanted to advance the scholarship on the *Spiritual Exercises*, to offer a feminist perspective, and to make the *Exercises* available to contemporary women, thereby advancing their practice. One of our first decisions committed us to a way of being together that would support the vocation of scholarship, but we only gradually learned what that meant in practice. For more than a year, we talked together about our experiences of the *Exercises*, what worked and did not work for us. We talked to contemporary women who have completed the *Spiritual Exercises* and served as directors for others. We conversed and argued back and forth with the text, trying to let it say what it said, not what we thought it said or wanted it to say. We reviewed the history of interpretation of the *Spiritual Exercises* and of the period and context in which they were written.

We tried to pay attention to the anger, the energy, the disjunction, the frustration, and every other experience that arose in all these conversation partners and in ourselves. We frequently disagreed on substance or emphasis and often had to hold our different perspectives in tension for a long time before the way through appeared. We began writing. All the writing came back to the three of us, often numerous times, for comment, critique, and, finally, celebration.

Since we were working with a text that gives directions for prayer, we realized that our appropriation of the text would be incomplete if we stood outside the prayer to which the text invites. We had all previously completed the *Spiritual Exercises* in the thirty-day retreat form and all had directed and taught the *Exercises* in our various settings. But we needed to engage the *Exercises* together and on their own terms if our collective interpretation process was to move into new ground. So, every day that we worked together, one of us took the responsibility to prepare some kind of common prayer related to the aspect of the *Spiritual Exercises* that we were presently struggling with. Sometimes the struggle resolved itself. Sometimes it did not. But our *scholarship* advanced through this common prayer. We gleaned perspectives that we might never have seen without this practice as an integral part of our writing.

There are some predictable pitfalls to this kind of work. One is that publishers may not know what to do with the result. It does not look quite like the typical scholarly book. Our experience suggests that it will take a while to learn to write and publish a new kind of scholarship for a developing discipline. For example, we had included a contemporary re-writing of the dynamics of the *Spiritual Exercises* in the form of a modern morality play. We had to justify its presence in the manuscript not once but several times. We prevailed in the end, but the play is relegated to an appendix, no longer central to the flow of the argument, as we had envisaged. For us, the play offered a way not only to summarize our insights, but also to draw others into their own experiences of the *Spiritual Exercises* and to enhance the learning through their common experience of "readers' theater." We had observed that "practicing" the *Spiritual Exercises* in this non-traditional, communal form against the background of each person's own experience of the *Exercises* served as a kind of Ignatian repetition, with all the benefits that Ignatius suggests for repetition. We wanted to do what we were writing about; we wanted the form to follow the function.

The other venue for our scholarship is the classroom. How can scholars of Christian spirituality practice intentionally and critically bringing lived spirituality into the classroom dedicated to the academic study of spirituality? One of my colleagues, John Endres, has made some interesting discoveries about practice while teaching Psalms to various constituencies over time. These discoveries have changed the way he teaches at a basic level. The impetus for his using practice as an intentional strategy came from students preparing for ministry. "If psalms are sung prayer, can't we sing them in class?" some students asked. Little by little and across introductory and advanced versions of courses on Psalms, he began to recognize that something different happens when students and other interpreters *perform* a text than when they simply read it. This difference appears on several levels. First, performance helps internalize the text; like *lectio divina*, it draws attention to certain words, motifs, and repetitions that may not be noticed otherwise. Students learn these texts from the inside out, and remember and connect them to other texts as they increase their exegetical range. Second, performance allows an immediate understanding of how different people interpret the same text, and reconfirms the position that there is no absolutely correct interpretation. Third, this approach embodies the belief that both synchronic and diachronic approaches to biblical texts are important and necessary in order for the interpreter to complete the task of interpretation. In light of my colleague's discoveries about performing sacred texts, Belden Lane's (2001) description of spirituality as "the performance of desire" is striking.

Granted, the psalms could be seen as a special case of our address to God rather than God's address to us. However, the principles garnered in this special case have wider application. In my colleague's other biblical courses, he now tends to ask: "Does approaching the text inductively, through such practices as singing, listening to or performing musical renditions of a text, looking at artistic interpretations, or allowing movement or dramatic interpretation or response, help to solidify learning about this text?" His criteria for appropriate practices grew out of his commitment to the learning gleaned through performance: "Does the activity we are engaged in help us to become more deeply immersed in the text, to know and understand what is in the text, to grasp various ways to interpret it, and to command something of the history of interpretation?"

Not only are Psalms a special case within the biblical canon, but, in one sense, the biblical canon is a special case within Christian literature: Christians understand it as a record of God's word to humankind and a living text. But what about other Christian texts? Any text with which one interacts deeply and personally and at a transformative level, including intellectually and critically, *becomes* a living text in that very interaction. Thus, any text that offers us contents for the study of Christian spirituality benefits from critical reflection on the lived spirituality of the interpreter. "Practice" is thus constitutive of the academic discipline of Christian spirituality.

Before leaving the classroom context, it is worth noting a style of teaching called "phenomenological." Phenomenology involves reflecting on experience and letting conclusions emerge from these reflections. It assumes that experience is accessible to the inquirer and seeks to understand the intentionality of both the experiencing subject and the experienced other. Mary Elizabeth Moore (1998: 120) describes this method. First, identify the experience that is the focal point of the study. Second, identify and bracket one's own prejudgments and assumptions about the experience. Next, observe and describe the experience. One or more appropriate critical disciplines is brought to bear on the description in order to understand the experience from a variety of perspectives; these disciplines are engaged prior to or along with theological reflection. The final step involves decision about and implementation of an appropriate action. Decisions about actions are related to the reality under study, the one studying, and the various communities where these realities intersect. Phenomenological teaching always takes experience seriously, including the experience of lived spirituality that I have been calling "practice."

Can there be too much practice in the classroom? The question arises readily if practices are used as a means of enticing students into the material the teacher wishes to communicate. But when the rationale for practice shifts to the critical reflection on lived spirituality, then practice becomes intrinsic to the learning process. At this point the question evaporates.

But what of the spirituality research itself, prior to teaching and writing? In his massive exposition of the forms, foundations, and methods of spirituality, Kees Waaijman (2002) isolates four types of spirituality research, all of which he believes are appropriately scientific, but which differ due to the type of phenomenon studied, the purpose of the study, the type of learning community, and so on. His study suggests that different "practices" fit different types of spirituality research. Interestingly, the "blueprint" for Waaijman's method is itself a "practice," discernment, which he defines as the form of critical reflection that developed within lived spirituality to recognize the direction of the way, to discover the deeper motives beneath the surface, to test the soundness of the end and the means, and to describe God's possibilities in the course of life (2002: 305).

The first research methodology is form-descriptive; it describes and analyses the forms of spirituality. Here the appropriate practices might center on phenomenological description of the inner transformative process. Because practices involve a person somatically, psychologically, socially, and spiritually, the practice of the researcher clearly matters. John Cassian says in the Prologue to the *Conferences 1–10*: "If anyone wants to give a true opinion about this life form . . . let him first take their chosen vocation upon himself with a similar zeal" (Waaijman 2002: 610). That is, the best way to gain insight into the phenomenon is by participation in the very phenomenon.

The second research strategy is hermeneutical, focused on the interpretation of spiritual texts. Here the spiritual practices might center on spiritual reading and the hermeneutical process of understanding one's reading stance, what happens in the performance of the text, and the discerning of meaning. Friedrich Schleiermacher's statement, "I very often catch myself in doing hermeneutic operations in the midst of a friendly conversation" (cited in Waaijman 2002: 738), reveals the significance of one's attempts to understand how meaning is made in the process of reading and speaking.

The third strategy is systematic research. A key practice here is communal: *collatio*, or critical study in a community in which the personal positions of the participants-in-discussion are respected but which seeks to examine the phenomenon from many viewpoints. In the dialectical tension between the various positions, not only meaning in the ordinary sense but also revelation in the spiritual sense appear.

Waaijman's final research strategy is mystagogical, in which the main lines of the spiritual journey are elucidated. Here, important practices are spiritual autobiography in its various forms, on the one hand, and the practice of empathy or "contemplative listening," on the other. If we follow John of the Cross on the matter of the qualities of a spiritual guide, key among them is that the guide has already traversed the terrain, and knows from experience what the spiritual phenomenon actually means. These suggestions are necessarily brief. The contours of systematic reflection on different types of "practice" in the academic study of spirituality still lie ahead.

Throughout this essay, I have assumed that the scholar of Christian spirituality is Christian, and works from within this tradition. Is this perspective on practice valid for the scholar who studies Christian spirituality but as an adherent of another spiritual tradition? Likewise, what of the Christian scholar who looks at another spiritual tradition? Can these scholars still employ practices as constitutive of their scholarly work? Although I work from within the Christian tradition, almost exclusively examining aspects of that same tradition, I believe that this understanding of practice as constitutive of the work of scholars of Christian spirituality still extends to these other situations. Both emic and etic perspectives benefit from critical reflection on lived spiritual practice. When one is an outsider to a tradition, however, one must exercise particular sensitivity to the practices selected and the interpretations rendered, giving priority to interpretations from within the tradition where these are available, and taking care not to assume easy correspondences in apparently similar practices from different traditions. Important insights can come from both perspectives (Plantinga Pauw 2002).

It is, I believe, time to quit being so timid about practice as a constitutive aspect of our discipline. We "have a tiger by the tail," and are not quite sure what to do with it, how to tame it sufficiently to allow it into the study and the classroom. But we also have something uniquely useful to offer scholars in other disciplines. When lived spiritual experience comes into the room, it makes the study of Christian spirituality immediate, transformative, compelling, self-implicating, and life changing.

Acknowledgment

An earlier version of this essay was delivered as the Presidential Address to the Society for the Study of Christian Spirituality, November 2001. It was subsequently published in *Spiritus: A Journal of Christian Spirituality* 2 (Spring 2002), 30–49, and is used with permission as the basis of this revision.

References

Bass, D. (ed.) 1999: *Practicing our Faith*. San Francisco: Jossey-Bass.
Boisen, A. 1936: *The Exploration of the Inner World*. Chicago: Willett, Clark.
Bourdieu, P. 1977: *Outline of a Theory of Practice*, trans. R. Nice. Cambridge: Cambridge University Press.
Burck, J. R. and Hunter, R. J. 1990: Pastoral theology, Protestant. In R. Hunter (ed.), *Dictionary of Pastoral Care and Counseling*, pp. 867–72. Nashville: Abingdon.
Cabot, R. and Dicks, R. 1936: *The Art of Ministering to the Sick*. New York: Macmillan.
Childs, B. 1990: Experience. In R. Hunter (ed.), *Dictionary of Pastoral Care and Counseling*, pp. 388–9. Nashville: Abingdon.
Chopp, R. 1995: *Saving Work: Feminist Practices in Theological Education*. Louisville, KY: Westminster/John Knox.
Clinebell, H. 1966: *Basic Types of Pastoral Counseling*. Nashville: Abingdon.
Cousins, E. 1990: What is Christian spirituality? In B. Hanson (ed.), *Modern Christian Spirituality: Methodological and Historical Essays*, pp. 39–44. Atlanta: Scholars Press.
Dicks, R. 1939: *And Ye Visited Me*. New York: Harper.
Downey, M. 1997: *Understanding Christian Spirituality*. New York: Paulist Press.
Dyckman, K., Garvin, M., and Liebert, E. 2001: *The Spiritual Exercises Reclaimed: Uncovering Liberating Possibilities for Women*. New York: Paulist Press.

Dykstra, C. 1991: Reconceiving practice. In B. Wheeler and E. Farley (eds), *Shifting Boundaries: Contextual Approaches to the Structure of Theological Education*, pp. 35–66. Louisville, KY: Westminster/John Knox.

Eire, C. 1990: Major problems in the definition of spirituality as an academic discipline. In B. Hanson (ed.), *Modern Christian Spirituality: Methodological and Historical Essays*, pp. 53–61. Atlanta: Scholars Press.

Favazza, J. and Glennon, F. 2000: Service learning and religious studies: propaganda or pedagogy. *Religious Studies News* 29, 105–7.

Frohlich, M. 2001: Spiritual discipline, discipline of spirituality: revisiting questions of definition and method. *Spiritus* 1, 65–78.

Gardner, H. 2000: *The Disciplined Mind*. New York: Penguin.

Hall, G. S. 1904: *Adolescence: Its Psychology and its Relations to Physiology, Anthropology, Sociology, Sex, Crime, Religion and Education*, 2 vols. New York: Appleton.

Hanson, B. 1990: Spirituality as spiritual theology. In B. Hanson (ed.), *Modern Christian Spirituality: Methodological and Historical Essays*, pp. 45–51. Atlanta: Scholars Press.

Hiltner, S. 1949: *Pastoral Counseling*. New York: Abingdon-Cokesbury.

—— 1958: *Preface to Pastoral Counseling*. Nashville: Abingdon.

Holder, A. and Dahill, L. 1999: Teaching Christian spirituality in seminaries today. *Christian Spirituality Bulletin* 7 (2), 9–12.

Howard, E. 2000: *The Affirming Touch of God: A Psychological and Philosophical Exploration of Christian Discernment*. Lanham, MD: University Press of America.

James, W. 1908: *Varieties of Religious Experience*. Edinburgh: Edinburgh University Press.

Jennings, T. 1990: Pastoral theological methodology. In R. Hunter (ed.), *Dictionary of Pastoral Care and Counseling*, pp. 862–4. Nashville: Abingdon.

Johnson, P. 1967: *Person and Counselor*. Nashville, Abingdon.

Kelsey, D. 1992: *To Understand God Truly: What's Theological about a Theological School?* Louisville, KY: Westminster/John Knox.

Lane, B. 1998: *The Solace of Fierce Landscapes: Exploring Desert and Mountain Spirituality*. New York: Oxford University Press.

—— 2001: Spirituality as the performance of desire: Calvin on the world as a theatre of God's glory. *Spiritus* 1, 1–30.

Lash, N. 1988: *Easter in Ordinary: Reflections on Human Experience and the Knowledge of God*. Notre Dame, IN: University of Notre Dame Press.

Leuba, J. 1909: *The Psychological Origin and the Nature of Religion*. London: Constable.

McGinn, B. 1993: The letter and the spirit: spirituality as an academic discipline. *Christian Spirituality Bulletin* 1 (2): 1, 3–10.

McGuire, M. 2003: Why bodies matter: a sociological reflection on spirituality and materiality. *Spiritus* 3, 1–18.

MacIntyre, A. 1984: *After Virtue*, 2nd edn. Notre Dame, IN: University of Notre Dame Press.

Moore, M. E. 1998: *Teaching from the Heart: Theology and Educational Method*. Harrisburg, PA: Trinity Press International.

Oates, W. 1962: *Protestant Pastoral Counseling*. Philadelphia: Westminster.

Palmer, P. 1998: *The Courage to Teach*. San Francisco: Jossey-Bass.

Paulsell, S. 2002: *Honoring the Body: Meditations on a Christian Practice*. San Francisco: Jossey-Bass.

Plantinga Pauw, A. 2002: Attending to the gaps between beliefs and practices. In M. Volf and D. Bass (eds), *Practicing Theology: Beliefs and Practices in Christian Life*, pp. 33–41. Grand Rapids, MI: Eerdmans.

Schneiders, S. M. 1986: Theology and spirituality: strangers, rivals or partners? *Horizons* 13, 253–74.

—— 1990: Spirituality in the academy. In B. Hanson (ed.), *Modern Christian Spirituality: Methodological and Historical Essays*, pp. 15–37. Atlanta: Scholars Press.

—— 1993: Spirituality as an academic discipline. *Christian Spirituality Bulletin* 1 (2), 10–15.

—— 1994: A hermeneutical approach to the study of Christian spirituality. *Christian Spirituality Bulletin* 2 (1), 9–14.

—— 1998: The study of Christian spirituality: contours and dynamics of a discipline. *Christian Spirituality Bulletin* 6 (1): 1, 3–12.

Villegas, D. 2001: Personal engagement: constructive source of knowledge or problem for scholarship in Christian spirituality? *Horizons* 28, 237–54.

Volf, M. 2002: Theology for a way of life. In M. Volf and D. Bass (eds), *Practicing Theology: Beliefs and Practices in Christian Life*, pp. 245–62. Grand Rapids, MI: Eerdmans.

—— and Bass, D. 2002: *Practicing Theology: Beliefs and Practices in Christian Life*. Grand Rapids, MI: Eerdmans.

Waaijman, K. 2002: *Spirituality: Forms, Foundations, Methods*, trans. J. Vriend. Leuven: Peeters.

Wiens St John, N. 1998: The definition and role of environment in Christian spiritual discernment. Unpublished paper, Graduate Theological Union.

Williams. D. D. 1961: *The Minister and the Cure of Souls*. New York: Harper.

Wise, C. 1942: *Religion in Illness and Health*. New York: Harper.

—— 1951: *Pastoral Counseling: Its Theory and Practice*. New York: Harper.

Wright, W. 1996: Keeping one's distance: presence and absence in the history of Christian spirituality. *Christian Spirituality Bulletin* 4 (1), 20–1.

CHAPTER 29
Liberation

Michael Battle

What does a Christian spirituality of liberation look like, especially in light of seemingly conflicting identities today (for example, black, white, gay, lesbian, straight, rich, poor, women, men, and so on)? I argue that a Christian spirituality of liberation offers movement beyond the limiting definitions of human beings as objects and victims. The ultimate beauty of such a spirituality is that it can liberate human societies from the destructive dialectic of oppressed and oppressor caught in perpetual deadlock, as if this were all we were meant to be. Through the spirituality of Jesus, human societies are taught to see diversity not as the enemy but as the genius of God's creation of community. What does it mean to live within Jesus's spirituality? Two key characteristics of Jesus's spirituality come to mind: poverty and detachment.

Poverty

The crucial claim of liberation theologians is that to live within Jesus's spirituality requires pursuit of the fundamental way in which Jesus was poor. This can be seen through the poor of the Bible, the *anawim*, those humble before God. The *anawim* accept themselves as poor in response to the poverty of being. As they face their inner and outer emptiness they look to God as their source of life. Also important to liberation sensibilities is the understanding of a violent world in which God becomes the refuge and shield of the poor. The poor of the Bible surrender themselves to total dependence on God. Jesus teaches his followers (most of whom were poor) the ability to welcome the stranger and outcast and thereby welcome God. This hermeneutic of the poor in the Bible becomes a willingness to be used by God to restore justice and peace in the world. People who have this quality of Jesus are the "poor in spirit." These are they whom Jesus calls happy or blessed in the Sermon on the Mount (Matt. 5: 3). The New English Bible makes this clear in its translation of this verse: "How blest are those who know their need of God!"

The spirituality of poverty that Jesus teaches, however, does not come automatically to either rich or poor people. In addition, Latin American theology opens us up to many cultural and political theologies that contain the view of Jesus's spirituality among the poor of the earth. Individuals in power can easily impose a worldview instead of co-create one. Both wealth and deprivation can provide a blinding reality that blocks out all other realities. From the perspective of Asian liberation theology, Aloysius Pieris is helpful in this discussion as he points out that Jesus experienced real humiliation and suffered recurrent conflicts and temptations (1988: 16). The tide of Jesus's early popularity changed; instead, forces gathered against him. His following fell away. On Palm Sunday across the world, churches rehearse the story that what awaited Jesus in Jerusalem was not triumph, but a cross. And the church's ultimate atonement theory is that only by Jesus being himself the bloody victim of the unjust social order could God's new order dawn.

Jesus took on poverty and suffered the injustice of the cross not to glorify it, but to overcome it. Poverty was an option he chose, not as a passive state, but as a struggle to create community out of chaos. Jesus's discipleship is invitation into this struggle. This displays the importance of the second part of Jesus's advice to the rich young man. When he had sold what he had, he was to give it to the poor (Matt. 19: 21). The point of becoming poor is to reduce the poverty of others – to join in the struggle to form a new way of being. But who are the poor? Many will say that poverty does not just concern material and exterior resources. There is also the notion of inner poverty. Perhaps the current connotation of the word "depression" comes closest to this meaning of inner poverty. The meaning of interior poverty is only fulfilled if it also has exterior orientation. Pieris is helpful again through his insight in which "the struggle to be poor must aim . . . to follow Jesus who was poor then and to serve Christ who is in the poor now" (1988: 21).

Detachment

Jesus's kind of poverty teaches the difficult lesson that it is detachment *for*, not just detachment *from*, that matters most. Detachment needs an accompanying orientation. "You have made us for yourself," Augustine of Hippo cried to God in his *Confessions* (1991: 3), "and our heart is restless until it rests in you." In his *Spiritual Exercises*, Ignatius of Loyola, the founder of the Jesuit Order, proposes that detachment should be the fundamental attitude of a Christian. He recognizes the danger of people being owned by what they own. A Christian must ultimately be committed to participating in the new reality of Christ who teaches his followers to sit loosely in relationship to the cares of this world (Matt. 6: 19). The value of all things depends on whether or not they serve the goal of Christ. Ignatius states: "For our part, we should not prefer health to sickness, riches to poverty, honor to dishonor, a long life to a short one, and so in all things we should desire and choose only those things which will best help us attain the end for which we were created" (1964: 47–8).

Jesus's detachment is the precise path in this world in which individuals must learn what is in fact valuable and lasting. To struggle to be poor is to walk an uncharted road of discovering what will last forever. In one way or another, opting to follow Jesus in his poverty is to refuse to have more than enough when others have less than enough, so that life's treasures become universal and of ultimate value. It is not to deny that prosperity is God's blessing, but to insist that God's blessing is to be shared. Though this may seem life-denying, it is in fact the opposite. To be the *anawim*, those happy because they know their need of God, is precisely what it means to "choose life," as Moses urged on the Israelites shortly before he died (Deut. 30: 19). The Christian faith is a faith of paradox: it is in giving that we receive, in dying that we know rebirth (cf. the famous prayer often attributed to Francis of Assisi). It is only when we unclench the fist raised against the poverty of being, that our hands can open to the greater good that God would offer us. As Pieris concludes, "bread eaten when others go hungry is an evil; but bread shared becomes a sacrament" (1988: 20).

Lastly, detachment is not only from wealth but also from power. Power does not come only from "above"; it also comes from "below." Although formally subordinate to Pilate, the chief priests were able to maneuver him into doing just what they wanted. Even Jesus, having stayed quiet, responds not to Pilate's power but to his weakness, his fear, as he reassures him: "You would have no power over me unless it had been given you from above; therefore the one who handed me over to you is guilty of a greater sin" (John 19: 11). To be detached for Christ provides the insight that power is not just negative but also involves creativity, healing, and resolution. The exercise of Jesus's kind of power inevitably makes more of the other. A Christian spirituality of liberation worries with the difficult issue of pluralism and how it relates to particularity, especially that of the particular claims of diverse people. A Christian spirituality of liberation seeks to be consistent by showing that pluralism and particularity are necessarily dependent on the other for the definition of each. The very history of the spirituality of the Christian church becomes based upon this mystery of trusting the plurality and particularity of God in Jesus to show us more, not less, of the other.

The Problem of Liberation

What I have presented so far is a spirituality of Jesus who teaches the world that the other, especially poor and oppressed otherness, is to be embraced and healed. There are challenges to this perceived spirituality of Jesus's kind of liberation. Drawing upon Marxist analysis, another liberational paradigm sees society as based not in harmony, but in conflict. The dialectic is constant: where one gains, the other loses. Power is thus seen as fundamental to the constitution of all human societies. It is a controverted question in liberation ideologies today whether or not liberation (i.e., making more of the other) should occur through violent means. The following brief discussion of liberation theology in Latin America will illustrate this problem.

The popular roots of liberation theology lie in the Latin American revolt against corrupt uses of power in the 1950s, 1960s, and 1970s. The problem of liberation was that the populist governments of the 1950s and 1960s – especially those of Perón in Argentina, Vargas in Brazil, and Cárdenas in Mexico – inspired nationalistic consciousness and significant industrial development. This benefited the middle classes and urban proletariat but threw huge sectors of poor people into deeper rural marginalization but sprawling urban shantytowns. This process led to the creation of strong popular movements seeking profound changes in the socio-economic structure of their countries. These movements in turn provoked the rise of military dictatorships, which sought to safeguard or promote the interests of capital, associated with a high level of national security achieved through political repression and police control of all public demonstrations (Boff and Boff 1987).

A theological movement also emerged during these times. The first theological reflections that were to lead to liberation theology had their origins in a context of dialogue between a church and a society in which the longings for transformation and liberation would arise from the people. The Second Vatican Council produced a theological atmosphere characterized by great freedom and creativity. This gave Latin American theologians the courage to think for themselves about pastoral problems affecting their countries. There were frequent meetings between Catholic and Protestant theologians who intensified reflection on the relationship between faith and poverty, the gospel and social justice.

At a meeting of Latin American theologians held in Petrópolis (Rio de Janeiro) in March 1964, Gustavo Gutiérrez described theology as critical reflection on praxis. This line of thought was further developed into what is the core of liberation theology today – a theology of praxis. In December 1971, Gustavo Gutiérrez published his seminal work, *Teología de la liberación* (*A Theology of Liberation*). The door was opened for the development of a theology from the poor dealing with the concerns of those living on the periphery of society, concerns that presented and still present an immense challenge to the evangelizing mission of the church. Besides the important writings of Gustavo Gutiérrez (see, for example, 1988, 1993), other outstanding works were produced by Latin American theologians such as Leonardo Boff (1988a, b, 1989, 1991, 1993, 1995), Juan Luis Segundo (1973–4, 1976, 1984–7, 1985, 1993), and Jon Sobrino (1978, 1984, 1987, 1990, 1993, 1994).

With the process of theological reflection well advanced, the need was seen for a dual process of settling in if the theology of liberation were to become firmly established. The method for theological reflection within liberation theology involves four major stages. The first stage deals with authentic context and the coherent expression within a given context of the themes arising from original spiritual experience. The second stage is called the analytical (*seeing*) stage in which reflection on experience is done. The third stage moves toward discernment of proper action, especially action against injustice. And the fourth stage is the crucial pastoral action stage in which action begins to heal and transform society. In short, liberation theology presupposes the art of linking its theories with the explicit inclusion of practice. More and more theologians became pastors too, militant agents of inspiration for the life of the church at its grassroots and those of society. It became common to see theologians taking part in involved epistemological discussions in learned congresses, then leaving to go back to their bases among the people to become involved in matters of catechesis, trade union politics, and community organization.

In short, the struggle with oppression produced liberation theologians who responded to the jagged economic growth and spiraling inequality. Political systems in the Latin American world were similarly unstable, alternating between promises of wide-reaching reform, government-sponsored mass organizations to harness popular support, and violent military repression. During this time, levels of religious belief and practice were high in the Roman Catholic Church in Latin America; institutionally, however. the Catholic Church was weak. Huge parishes were served by small numbers of clergy, which meant that poor people might not see a priest from one year's end to another. As David Lehmann (1990: 102) remarks with irony, this institutional weakness may have meant that the church hierarchy was less able to neutralize the potential radicalism of its own message.

From within the hierarchy, however, there were moves toward change. The early 1960s saw the global Second Vatican Council in the Catholic Church. This marked a new openness, a vision of the church as a "pilgrim people" ready to re-think tradition and question established patterns of authority. Intense political repression added urgency to these tendencies. In some countries, church buildings became virtually the only places where people could gather without risking arrest. As the state took on totalitarian form and human rights were routinely abused, the liberal division between spiritual and political, church and state, was thrown into question. Could the church just stand by as her people suffered? What theology would serve as the oppressed took up arms against injustice?

The historical roots of liberation theology are to be found in the prophetic tradition of evangelists and missionaries from the earliest colonial days in Latin America, early Christian converts who questioned the type of presence adopted by the church and the way in which indigenous peoples, blacks, mestizos, and the poor rural and urban masses were treated. Others joined in solidarity against oppression of indigenous peoples. Bartolomé de Las Casas (1474–1566) and others represented European Christians who also did not tolerate such oppression (Gutiérrez 1993). It is from such early protests against colonial rule that we gain an understanding of liberation theology that may inform Christian spirituality today.

The past few decades have seen a great extension of situations in which the church has become involved with the oppressed, with a very large number of pastoral workers involved. Many movements have come into being under the tutelage, to a large extent, of liberation theology; these, in turn, have posed new challenges to liberation theology. In Brazil alone, there are movements or centers for black unity and black consciousness, human rights, defense of slum-dwellers, marginalized women, mission to Amerindians, rural pastoral strategy, and so forth – all concerned in one way or another with the poorest of the poor seeking liberation.

Crucial to the emergence of liberation theology was the notion that neutrality is impossible in a world that is so divided and violent. So-called objectivity is a mask for specific interests; knowledge is always from a particular point of view. Instead of being something to hide or apologize for, subjectivity is to be embraced. This makes clear the role of context in shaping views: "where you stand depends on where you sit." It also makes it possible for the poor to reclaim their role as subjects of their own destiny, rather than being objects of others' plans and policies. Thus, liberation theology rejects the European, liberal stance of disinterested observer in favor of the liberational paradigm that urges the importance of "making an option" for those in need. This "preferential option" is to start from the standpoint of the poor and the marginalized. Those who seek God's will in the world must do so quite explicitly from a view "from below" in which God incarnate effected resurrection. To make such an option is not open only to the poor, but also to the non-poor, as an act of solidarity. The stress on subjectivity, however, has led to a strong tendency for identities to become politicized. This means that theologies are often described by reference to the people who produce them (black, Dalit, Asian, or feminist theology), rather than with impersonal terms such as systematic, contextual, or fundamentalist.

Tutu: A Contemporary Exemplar

So far, I have presented a liberational spirituality of Jesus who teaches the world that the other, especially poor and oppressed otherness, is to be embraced and healed. The recent challenges to this perceived spirituality of Jesus's kind of liberation have been articulated by liberation and contextual theology, especially by Latin American, African American and African theologians. It is to this latter vision of African theology that I now turn. In the remaining portion of this essay I focus on Archbishop Desmond Tutu as a contemporary representative (and also critic) of liberation spirituality. In light of the miraculous spiritual practices of reconciliation in South Africa, it seems natural to view Tutu's theology and work as a way forward beyond the liberation hermeneutic of violence and identity politics. It is also natural for me to be an advocate for Tutu's spirituality, since I was deeply influenced by my experiences of living with him from 1993 to 1994 (Battle 1997).

Tutu becomes a contemporary exemplar through his work of explaining the complexity of human identity, in which particular persons may view liberation differently but always need to aim toward the goal of relational spirituality. This goal, however, has not always existed, even among prominent theologians. For example, one of the architects of black theology, James Cone (1969), struggled against the dehumanizing forces of theologies derived from European rationalism, and refused to accept white identity. Tutu understood Cone's articulate voice, but always maintained the goal toward relationality. Tutu states: "I myself believe I am an exponent of Black Theology coming as I do from South Africa. I also believe I am an exponent of African theology coming as I do from Africa. I contend that Black Theology is like the inner and smaller circle in a series of concentric circles" (1993a: 391).

While Tutu recognized himself in Cone's account of a similar struggle against dehumanizing forces, he rejected Cone's black/white dialectic in favor of a complementary solution of human identities in the South African context. Although Tutu deeply respected Cone's heroic theology, the problem he faced in South Africa was that there were many black identities (for example, Zulu, Xhosa) and even multiple white identities (for example, Afrikaner and British). Tutu offers these observations concerning the problem of racial identity within Christianity:

Until fairly recently, the African Christian has suffered from a form of religious schizophrenia. With part of himself he has been compelled to pay lip service to Christianity as understood, expressed and preached by the white man. But with an ever greater part of himself, a part he has been often ashamed to acknowledge openly and which he has struggled to repress, he has felt that his Africanness was being violated. The white man's largely cerebral religion was hardly touching the depths of his African soul; he was being redeemed from sins he did not believe he had committed; he was being given answers, and often splendid answers, to questions he had not asked. (1978: 366)

Countering this "religious schizophrenia," a Christian spirituality becomes a crucial means by which to overcome this incessant ambivalence of being in one of the oppressed groups in need of liberation. For example, in the historically colonial church of Anglicanism, Africans found themselves more and more ambivalent in their encounter with European material culture alongside their search for the spiritual side of African personality. In this light, I proceed to show how Christian spirituality emphasizes the discipline of Christian personality to discern the deeper realities of liberation.

Christian spirituality does not naïvely assume that its goal of community has been achieved. For example, only when all African communities achieve their full share in determining policies in South Africa, thinks Tutu, will the possibility exist for true liberation among all races and cultures. Therefore, through a Christian spirituality of liberation enacted in the South African context, Tutu seeks the correct relational complement of black and white liberation because no one is a person in South Africa until blacks attain the freedom to open their God-given personhood and humanity. In order to frame the following discussion of Tutu's spirituality, it is important to attend to his own self-understanding.

If I am so important, if I am so valuable, then it must mean then that every other human being is of equal worth, of equal value. How wonderful. This is why an authentic Christian spirituality is utterly subversive of any system that would treat a child of God as if he or she were less than this. It is the consequence of my prayers. It is the consequence of my faith. It is the consequence of my spirituality. It has nothing to do with ideology or politics. Every praying Christian, every person who has an encounter with this God, this triune God, must have a passionate concern for his or her brother or sister, his or her neighbor, because to treat anyone of these as if they were less than the children of God is to deny the validity of one's spiritual experience. It is not merely wrong to do so, it is not merely painful to the victim of our injustice, our oppression, our exploitation which it often manifestly is. It is fundamentally blasphemous for this other is destined for fellowship with God. This other is created in God's image. This other is a God carrier, a tabernacle of the Holy Spirit. To treat this person unjustly is to desecrate the dwelling of God, is to dishonor one I should not just respect but indeed revere . . .

Division, disharmony, hostility, alienation and separation are the pernicious results of sin. Any policies that make it a matter of principle to separate God's children into mutually opposing groups is evil, immoral and unchristian. To oppose such a policy is an obligation placed on us by our faith, by our encounter with God . . . It is dangerous to pray, for an authentic spirituality is subversive of injustice. Oppression and unjust governments should stop people praying to a Christian God . . . (1987a)

Tutu rejects radical theologies incapable of reconciliation because they do not fit his understanding of subversive spirituality, which I think offers a creative model in discerning human personality as interpersonality. The goal of interpersonality is Jesus's liberational spirituality, in which he teaches the world that the other, especially poor and oppressed otherness, is to be embraced and healed into one's own personality. I have described Tutu's unique approach to spirituality as interpersonality through the South African concept of *ubuntu*, which means that a person discovers personhood only through other persons (Battle, 1997).

In *Hope in Crisis: SACC National Conference Report: 1986* (Jacob 1986), Tutu devises a relational approach to theology by refusing the common either/or hermeneutic of juxtaposing contextual theologies against each other. For instance, Tutu refuses to separate black, African, and liberation theology. Again, Tutu is able to do this based on his strong emphasis upon the narrative of a catholic church in which all Christians are called to work in order one day to experience a reconciled creation. The church is to live within the reality of reconciled creation through the interpersonality of people; therefore, the church is never allowed to lose consciousness of the reconciling work already accomplished in Christ (2 Cor. 5: 11–21). The church's work is to stay awake to Jesus's spirituality of liberation in which we are no longer slaves to violence and oppression. Thus, Tutu is an African and black theologian, and yet, based on possessing both of these characteristics, he is a liberation theologian who struggles with theodicy questions of how people at war may live harmoniously in a violent world. How does Tutu's spirituality allow him to be Anglican, African, and black all successfully? This essay proceeds to answer this question on the basis of Tutu's theological conviction against privileging the identity of race as determinative of people or nations.

Communal Christian Spirituality

Christian spirituality is often criticized as being atomistic and "navel-gazing," providing little recourse to social action due to Western individualism. However, as many Christians from the Latin American and African contexts have demonstrated, Christian spirituality need not be obsessed with self-fulfillment or the domination of the self over the other. In Tutu's spirituality, the emphasis of the spiritual life should not be so much on self-fulfillment as on the relational fulfillment between God and the world. Liberational spiritualities have always sought to hold on to relational fulfillment as the goal of the Christian life. Such relational fulfillment is not unique to contemporary expressions of the Christian faith. For example, in the early church, the desert tradition was about the communal formation of a radical Christian witness in relation to the corrupted forms of power relations in the world. Ascetical figures like Antony fought against those forces seeking to destroy God's community, whether such forces be found within the church or the secular order. The goal of the desert fathers and mothers was not to create anything new, but to return to the relationality set forth by God's paradise given in the beginning of creation.

The identity of the monastic did not preclude the larger goal of the radical redefining of society through the convictions of Christian identity. For example, Antony gave his contemporary society an opportunity to join an "elite" group of individuals; and yet, unlike the late Greco-Roman society of which Antony was a part, the desert tradition barred no one on the basis of social pedigree. For an ascetic, one's social identity was gained both through contemplation of God's flourishing creation and through action against demonic principalities and powers that were ransacking human institutions. The thrust of the ascetical movement was to access supernatural power through the rigorous training of Christian character in which the ascetic discovered and practiced a disciplined self in order to move beyond the ambiguities of self-definition in this earthly realm. Antony exhorts:

> let us all the more exert ourselves in the discipline that opposes [the demons], for a great weapon against them is a just life and trust in God. They are afraid of the ascetics on several counts – for their fasting, the vigils, the prayers, the meekness and gentleness, the contempt for money, the lack of vanity, the humility, the love of the poor, the almsgiving, the freedom from wrath, and most of all for their devotion to Christ. It is for this reason that they do all they do – in order not to have those monks trampling them underfoot. (Athanasius 1980: 30)

In the early church the line was not clearly drawn between contemplation and action. In light of this ambiguous line, prayer and social witness often became indistinguishable for early Christians like Antony. This is vital in understanding the Christian spiritual tradition, because in order to avoid anachronistic church-against-world typologies we need to read ancients like Antony who followed a Jesus who gave up security, status, dominance, and reputation for the sake of building community. Due to this emphasis on stripping false identities, the desert tradition offered Tutu a profound resource through which to show his South African context that human beings are more than racial classifications defined by an oppressive government. The Anglican anchorite Maggie Ross became Tutu's spiritual director at one time. Her description of those in the early church deeply inspired Tutu's contemporary witness to articulate a spirituality of liberation. Ross is especially helpful in explaining the need to redefine human personhood in light of God:

> We need to read the ancients again and again. We need their wisdom. We need their signposts and road maps. We need the light they left behind as we follow them in this divine spelunking.
>   But we need most of all to recover what they most wanted to teach: that the whole point of the journey into the fiery love of God is self-forgetfulness, a self-forgetfulness evolving from a self-awareness that gradually drops away as we become ever more found in the adoration of God in whom we find our true selves. This movement toward completion no longer needs self-reflection, but needs to be aware only of God. (1987: 23)

The discovery of human identity in relation to God was the primary focus of the desert tradition. This tradition, from which the monastic movement originated, focused primarily upon the achievement of a Christian character that serves as a *martyr* (i.e., witness) to the salvation of the world. But how is this done? The answer is prayer. In the desert tradition, prayer involves *anachoresis*, the art of disengagement. This ascetical concept is applied both individually and socially. On an individual level, *anachoresis* is the art of solitude. Tutu explains:

> Prayer is the physical necessity to shut up. It is being in the presence of God which has to do with a relationship of love . . . We often think of silence as a negative thing or the absence of noise. But it is a positive dynamic. You cannot do creative thinking if you are surrounded by distracting noise . . . Recollected calm and reserved persons [are impressive then]. Jesus called His disciples to come away by themselves for a while . . . Relax, think of yourself in a scene with Jesus in the synagogue when He heals the man with a withered arm. You are there. You smell the dusty, sweaty crowd. Is the synagogue full? Look at the Pharisees, some with shifty eyes watching to catch Jesus out. Can you hear Jesus calling out in anger/compassion for the man with the withered arm? You are there. What does Jesus say to the man? to the congregation of religious leaders? to you? What then does Jesus ask you to do? (1987b)

On a social level, *anachoresis* allows the individual to challenge the oppressive ways of the world. While in church, Antony heard the Gospel passage in which the Lord tells the rich man that, in order to be perfect, he must sell what he possesses and give it to the poor, so that he will have treasure in heaven (Matt. 19: 21). Upon hearing this language of disengagement, Antony gained the courage to engage an oppressive society of Late Roman Egypt by undergoing a period of dark and isolated endurance in the desert (Athanasius 1980: 31). This was no doubt caused by a society of economic insecurity in which there were severe tax burdens and competition among village landowners. Therefore, on a social level, *anachoresis* involved political withdrawal from the increased weight of taxation on communal living.

The act of *anachoresis* itself, rather than any exceptional supernatural powers, was what the early church appreciated about the desert tradition. Christians living in severe states of oppression saw through ascetical figures that power and prestige were redefined through acting out, heroically, how one might truly live in freedom. Monastic spiritual practices were not irrelevant to a social witness against corrupted forms of government. A more positive way of stating this is that the spiritual practices of the desert tradition helped to train people in community to see a truer form of the *imago Dei*. Tutu affirms:

> As an African and as a Christian, I need to contribute to the emergence of a relevant spirituality. The spiritual, it goes without saying, is central to all that we do. The God we worship is an extraordinary God, who dwells in light unapproachable, He is high and lifted up, and His train fills the temple. The angels and archangels and whole host of heaven do not cease to worship and adore Him. Heaven and earth are full of His glory. He is the transcendent one who fills us with awe – the *mysterium tremendum et fascinans*. But He does not allow those who worship Him to remain in an exclusive spiritual ghetto. Our encounter with Him launches us into the world, to work together with this God for the establishment of his kingdom. This is a kingdom of justice, peace, righteousness, compassion, caring and sharing. We become agents of transfiguration, transformation and radical change. (1985: 161)

Another resource offered by the desert tradition is its excellent assessment of *anachoresis* as an explanation of social "death," which implies that the ascetic is attempting to construct a new identity despite the lack of any normal social support. In this regard, the ascetic tradition offers Tutu an invaluable resource to resolve the incoherences of human identity in relation to a corrupted society. And such a resource will continue to offer support in post-apartheid South Africa. Tutu explains the need for such deep reflection of the spiritual life for the future of South Africa:

> There is going to be increasing leisure time as technology and machines take over from humans. We are going to have to learn how to spend that leisure time creatively. We are going to have to be taught how to enjoy our own company; we are going to have to grow more contemplative, to be still at the core of our being, to be in touch with our real selves and with God. We have a God-hunger, and only God can ultimately satisfy that hunger. We must make space for transcendence, for prayer, for meditation and so our democratic state will be determined in ensuring freedom of worship and belief and even the lack of it. (1993b: 318)

The ascetical tradition is important to Tutu's liberational spirituality because it explains how one may see Tutu himself as a political priest, a tradition most associated with Latin American spirituality. From spiritualities that seek human liberation we learn that the goal must always be the restoration of relationality. Christian spirituality guards against becoming an impotent abstraction of Western individualism by modeling the divine life of relationality to the world. In short, this is Tutu's theological strategy: to model the divine life to the corrupt society of apartheid. The ascetical tradition provides Tutu with a resource by which the *telos* of people is no longer racial identity, but a community, expressed in the particular witness of the religious order known as the Community of the Resurrection (COR) or the Mirfield Brothers. It was a monk, Trevor Huddleston, who influenced Tutu's understanding of the Christian vocation as one of reconciliation and the restoration of relationality. The ascetical model of sacrifice and commitment in religious communities offers a contrast to secular power structures. The aim of Tutu's liberational spirituality is always about moving beyond perceived categories of oppressive identity to those of human and divine flourishing.

The COR taught Tutu that what was required was not simply a political program of material improvement or an identity as black or white, but a whole new understanding of society based upon religious community. Tutu states: "It is at this [COR] seminary, St Peter's Rosettenville, Johannesburg, that I learned the nature of an authentic Christian spirituality" (undated address). And this spirituality makes Tutu work from theological commitments based on a deeper and more mystical level than racial classification. On this deeper level, Tutu learned from Trevor Huddleston, perhaps the most famous monk of the COR, whom Tutu describes as follows:

> I came to live in a hostel which the Fathers opened for young men who were working or at high school and had problems with accommodation . . . I made my first real sacramental confession to [Trevor Huddleston] . . . He was so un-English in many ways, being very fond of hugging people, embracing them, and in the way in which he laughed. He did not laugh like many white people, only with their teeth, he laughed with his whole body, his whole being, and that endeared him very much to black people. And if he wore a white cassock it did not remain clean for long, as he trudged the dusty streets of Sophiatown with the little urchins with grubby fingers always wanting to touch him and calling out "Fader" with obvious affection in their little voices . . . (1988: 2)

Through the COR, Tutu realized that the command to love God involved more than the disciplines of democracy; there had to be an understanding of obedience. This would be a different kind of obedience, leading Tutu to escape the identity offered by a corrupt society and to recognize the image of God in all people. For the COR and Tutu, however, the image of God is relationality – an image of *kenosis* (self-emptying) which destroys the false identities that deny God's image of the fullness of relation. Therefore, an ascetical account is necessary in order to understand Tutu's function in South Africa and his own authentic Christian spirituality. Instead of perpetuating practices of racial discrimination, Tutu operates within a spiritual tradition that challenges any force that seduces people toward adopting finite identity as though it were the very image of God.

By focusing on the relational and communal aspects of Tutu's spirituality, I risk incurring the wrath of contextual theologians who surmise that the spirituality espoused above is too weak a concept with which to say anything meaningful about human struggles today, especially the concrete situations in which people suffer. How can Christian spirituality help such people today and in the future? It is with a response to this question that I conclude.

Conclusion: Implications for Liberation Spirituality

How can a liberation spirituality, based on relationality and inclusion, respond to the charge that it is too weak to help oppressed peoples? Based on what I have argued in this essay, I answer the charge of weakness through the tangible formation of human identity that occurs through liberation spirituality. What I mean is this: unlike economic or political ideologies, liberation spirituality provides successful engagement with corrupt human powers (for example, Gandhi's *satyagraha*, Oscar Romero's spirituality, Desmond Tutu's *ubuntu*). Instead of weakness, liberation spirituality has been documented in increasing human community rather than decreasing the dignity of humanity.

More specifically, I have tried to demonstrate through Tutu's spirituality that human identity is primarily defined by God's image through which prayer engages and corrects the abuses of negative determinations of identity. In this way, liberational spirituality resists vapid ideology and instead seeks construction of both individual and community in which particular human identities (for example, racial and cultural) become shaped by a primary identity in Christ. Such primary identity in Christian spirituality offers warring identities practical strategies and exemplary persons who lead toward the fullness of relationality. Such individuals and movements have indeed manifested the strength of the human spirit rather than weakness. They offer the reordering of violent reality toward the sanity of reaching our potential as communities and people.

It is in this reordering of human identity in light of Christ's identity that I answer the charge of weakness. This charge, however, must be taken seriously. Unless one understands this difficult premise on which human identity is shaped in Christ's identity of relationality and peaceableness, Christian spirituality will become self-serving and relativistic. The Christian vision of the liberation of all peoples deepens the mystery of diverse human identity capable of being many and one. Such a vision cannot help but inform healthy politics and economics. And such an image of humanity intimates the deep mystery of God in Christ that refuses the objectification of any person. Herein, the profound strength of Christian spirituality is in its practices of going into all the world in search of this mystery of God's image. Because of what God has shown through relationality in Christ, Christians cannot rest in oppressive structures in which personhood is defiled.

Liberational spirituality focuses on the poor and oppressed because of God's image in Christ. I have shown that liberational spirituality seeks to articulate the need for the poor and the oppressed to rediscover their humanity in light of the image of God. Such a rediscovery is seen only in the liberation of the poor and oppressed and their refusal to repeat the sins of the oppressor. Especially, liberational theologies derived from Latin America and black theology insist upon the rescue of those oppressed and oppressors so that they can see themselves again as God's children. Tutu concludes that this recognition is the insight of being children of God:

> For the oppressed the most vital part of the Christian gospel is its message of liberation from all that would make us less than the children of God – sin, political and economic deprivation, exploitation and injustice. It is also liberation to be people who enjoy the glorious liberty of the children of God, which must include political empowerment to determine the shape of one's destiny. (1985: 163)

But to what extent will those who champion liberational spiritualities go to rescue the oppressed? Could even violence be condoned in such a pursuit? Until a clear Christian spirituality of non-violence accompanies the spirituality of liberation, Christian spirituality will remain ambiguous, relevant only to the one defining its meaning.

My conclusion also deals with the apparent contradiction of Tutu as both an exemplar of liberation spirituality and as a critic of it. This is why I hold up Tutu as a model of a Christian spirituality of liberation: because he provides the inspiration for all of us to maintain the struggle of refusing violence as the normative means by which to rescue the oppressed. Although this may appear to some as weakness, he provides profound strength to look for long-term solutions that refuse violent short-term answers. And yet, Tutu is not a pacifist and could be convinced in certain circumstances to condone so-called "just war." Tutu's theology can be categorized as radical in the rhetorical sense of seeking the root of the Christian faith through the church's practices, but not radical in the sense of juxtaposing political identities of oppression as the hermeneutical key to theology. In other words, he refuses the argument that the essence of human identity is political, and therefore in need of force and coercion.

In the end, Christian liberational spirituality is the work of making spirituality communal. At the heart of this vision for human identity is the life, death, resurrection, and ascension of Jesus, who returns warring identities back to communal being – the triune God. In this vision, violence only becomes blasphemous to the image of God. Christian spirituality becomes communal spirituality in which interdependence of being always refuses violent practice and never turns away from constructive engagement with the poor and rich. Here, I differ in some degree from Tutu's discernment model of when war may be justified. The future of Western Christian spirituality depends upon the discernment of working through how "your" context also becomes "my" context. Western individualism can no longer shape how Christians engage the needs of the world because just-war criteria can no longer be met in the light of weapons of mass destruction.

We must learn from liberational spirituality that there is a plurality of theologies, jostling and competing with each other, but that they can complement and challenge one another at the same time. The *imago Dei* becomes the mystery that informs our spirituality – the divine life of God demands the concert of being. The danger of Western individualism is that it has little incentive to work for interdependent structures. In such a case, the catholic (universal) church becomes unintelligible if there is no consensus of particular identities. The task of Christians then becomes the addressing of specific issues arising from the contexts of particular communities. These particular communities do not become obsolete or irrelevant when their usefulness has burned out because Christian identity has learned to see human identity as eternal, made in the image of God. Christian identity becomes the catalyst in the world to refuse to negate the mystery and gospel that our image of God has been restored in Christ.

Liberational spirituality takes seriously the image of God in the other; so much so that in order for theology to be authentic it needs to be relevant to its particular contexts. Because liberational spirituality focuses upon the context of spirituality, the need for dialogue across contexts becomes essential. Diverse spiritualities are required precisely because Christian spirituality constantly answers different sets of questions by different kinds of people. "So that we now find ourselves," Tutu concludes, "perhaps in a bewildering position of dealing with strange juxtapositions of different theologies, cheek by jowl with one another, complementing or contradicting one another" (1981). Consequently, ecumenical and inter-religious spiritualities of liberation have developed in varying contexts around the world in response to injustice and violence. A great example of this is South Africa's Truth and Reconciliation Commission in which Christians, Muslims, Hindus, Jains, Jews, and many other religious supported the process of reconciliation and truth telling (Tutu 2001).

Expanding the worldview of Western Christianity becomes the great gift of liberational spirituality. Liberational spirituality makes clear that any theology from the position of dispossessed non-Western people must alert Western people that there is no unilateral cultural way of knowing God and neighbor. In the end, Christian spirituality comes from an Eastern religion called Christianity and should not be readily fitted into defined Western interpretations of religion. Much of Western discourse operates within the Enlightenment framework of the rationality of an individual who claims the primacy of identity (race, economic class, gender, or culture) as proper access to expose oppressive structures of thought. In the non-Western world, however, human identity is known more through the socialization processes of communities who teach individuals to discern who they are in light of the community. Much of the non-Western world would distinguish race as different from culture in that the latter is a system of inherited concepts rooted in a way of thinking and acting in light of a community grammar demonstrated through stories and histories that shape peoples in a particular location. What is fundamental to non-Western cultures is the communal way of knowing. The rationale for a liberational spirituality is that only in the particularity of being Latino,

Xhosa, French, Zulu, Portuguese, Yoruba, and so on, may clarity be given to what is true or what is of God.

Christian spirituality has a vital role to play now and in the future to show how interdependence is possible among incommensurate identities. Now, more than ever, Christian spirituality will have to offer discourse in which warring identities may discover alternatives to violence and war. We learn from liberational spirituality, however, to live within the continual need for deconstruction of any claim toward unilateral identity in the effort to expose structures of power, injustice, or surreptitious hegemonic orders. In contrast with an exclusivist, Western hermeneutical methodology, liberational spirituality is based upon theological criteria which seek to reconcile conflicts that naturally arise among all people in their varying contexts and locations.

In summary, a Christian spirituality of liberation develops, thinks through, and practices human interpersonality that flourishes throughout this earth. In the end, attention to how all people flourish will inform a deeper and more systemic form of human liberation beyond humanistic discourse based on violent revolution. A Christian spirituality of liberation comprehends the hermeneutical privilege of oppressed groups, while at the same time holding such claims accountable to the goal of the image of God in the oppressors. The goal, therefore, is for all to discover healthy humanity. God is revealed in the ultimate health of Jesus, who leads us to be on the side of the sinner, the despised, the outcast, and the downtrodden. But this God is not controlled by any such particular group; God remains God. This is important in any context in which many human communities claim the control of God's liberating powers. The story of the Tower of Babel (Gen. 11) illustrates a false unity based on disobedience, a self-securing homogeneity. In such a context, unity is oppressive and gathers people together for the wrong reasons.

Perhaps new to many readers is the understanding that liberation requires ascetical training toward God who calls us to prayer and action amidst human conflict and war. Such training offers a direction out of oppressive realities different from the normal cycles of violence in which today's oppressed end up being tomorrow's oppressor. Jesus's spirituality makes it possible to develop a different kind of history in which a person must leave biological kindred to favor those recreated into kindred by God (Gen. 12: 1; Matt. 12: 46–50). Liberational spirituality is the living testimony of breaking with false forms of relatedness gained through oppressive histories. Rather than promoting warring human identities, Christian spirituality, formed by Jesus, moves us toward God's promise of a new creation instead of toward the lack of a future exemplified by violence and destruction. The end of Christian spirituality then becomes full participation in the mystery of being related in infinite and eternal ways.

References

Athanasius 1980: *The Life of Antony and the Letter to Marcellinus*, trans. R. Gregg. New York: Paulist Press.
Augustine of Hippo 1991: *Confessions*, trans. H. Chadwick. Oxford: Oxford University Press.
Battle, M. 1997: *Reconciliation: The Ubuntu Theology of Desmond Tutu*. Cleveland: Pilgrim Press.

Boff, L. 1988a: *Trinity and Society*. Maryknoll, NY: Orbis.

—— 1988b: *When Theology Listens to the Poor*. San Francisco: Harper and Row.

—— 1989: *Faith on the Edge*. San Francisco: Harper and Row.

—— 1991: *New Evangelization: Good News to the Poor*. Maryknoll, NY: Orbis.

—— 1993: *Path to Hope: Fragments from a Theologian's Journey*. Maryknoll, NY: Orbis.

—— 1995: *Ecology and Liberation: A New Paradigm*. Maryknoll, NY: Orbis.

—— and Boff, C. 1987: *Introducing Liberation Theology*. Maryknoll, NY: Orbis.

Cone, J. H. 1969: *Black Theology and Black Power*. New York: Seabury Press.

Gutiérrez, G. 1988: *A Theology of Liberation: History, Politics, and Salvation*. Maryknoll, NY: Orbis.

—— 1993: *Las Casas: In Search of the Poor of Jesus Christ*. Maryknoll, NY: Orbis.

Ignatius of Loyola 1964: *Spiritual Exercises*, trans. R. W. Gleason. Garden City, NY: Image Books.

Jacob, S. (ed.) 1986: *Hope in Crisis: South African Council of Churches National Conference Report: 1986*. Johannesburg: South African Council of Churches.

Lehmann, D. 1990: *Democracy and Development in Latin America*. Cambridge: Polity Press.

Pieris, A. 1988: *An Asian Theology of Liberation*. Edinburgh: T. and T. Clark.

Ross, M. 1987: *The Fountain and the Furnace: The Way of Tears and Fire*. New York: Paulist Press.

Segundo, J. L. 1973–4: *A Theology for Artisans of a New Humanity*, 5 vols. Maryknoll, NY: Orbis.

—— 1976: *Liberation of Theology*. Maryknoll, NY: Orbis.

—— 1984–7: *Jesus of Nazareth: Yesterday and Today*, 5 vols. Maryknoll, NY: Orbis.

—— 1985: *Theology and the Church: A Response to Cardinal Ratzinger and a Warning to the Whole Church*. Minneapolis, MN: Winston.

—— 1993: *Signs of the Times*, ed. A. T. Hennelly. Maryknoll, NY: Orbis.

Sobrino, J. 1978: *Christology at the Crossroads*. Maryknoll, NY: Orbis.

—— 1984: *The True Church and the Poor*. Maryknoll, NY: Orbis.

—— 1987: *Jesus in Latin America*. Maryknoll, NY: Orbis.

—— 1990: *Companions of Jesus: The Jesuit Martyrs of El Salvador*. Maryknoll, NY: Orbis.

—— 1993: *Jesus the Liberator: An Historical-theological Reading of Jesus of Nazareth*. Maryknoll, NY: Orbis.

—— 1994: *Principle of Mercy: Taking the Crucified People from the Cross*. Maryknoll, NY: Orbis.

Tutu, D. 1978: Whither African theology? In E. Fasholé, R. Gray, A. Hastings, et al. (eds), *Christianity in Independent Africa*, pp. 364–9. London: Rex Collings.

—— 1981: On being the church in the world. Address given at Cape Town, October 13.

—— 1985: Spirituality: Christian and African. In C. Villa-Vicencio and J. de Gruchy (eds), *Resistance and Hope: South African Essays in Honour of Beyers Naude*, pp. 159–64. Cape Town: David Philip.

—— 1987a: Sermon (Pentecost 18), St George's Cathedral, Cape Town, South Africa.

—— 1987b: Quiet day: why be silent? (text: Mark 6: 30ff), Durbanville, January 2.

—— 1988: An appreciation of the Rt Revd Trevor Huddleston, CR. In D. D. Honoré (ed.), *Trevor Huddleston: Essays on his Life and Work*, pp. 1–4. Oxford: Oxford University Press.

—— 1989: Greetings. In M. H. Ellis and O. Maduro (eds), *The Future of Liberation Theology: Essays in Honor of Gustavo Gutiérrez*, pp. 25–6. Maryknoll, NY: Orbis.

—— 1992: The church and human rights in South Africa. Address given at the University of South Africa, Centre for Human Rights, May 18.

—— 1993a: Black theology/African theology – soul mates or antagonists? In J. H. Cone and G. S. Wilmore (eds), *Black Theology: A Documentary History, Volume I: 1966–1979*, 2nd rev. edn, pp. 385–92. Maryknoll, NY: Orbis.

—— 1993b: Postscript: to be human is to be free. In J. Witt, Jr (ed.), *Christianity and Democracy in Global Context*, pp. 311–20. Boulder, CO: Westview Press.

—— 2001: *No Future without Forgiveness*. New York: Doubleday.

—— undated: The centrality of the spiritual. Address given at the General Theological Seminary, New York.

CHAPTER 30
Interfaith Encounter

Kwok Pui-Lan

At the seventh assembly of the World Council of Churches in Canberra, a young female theologian Chung Hyun Kyung (1991) delivered a powerful keynote address on the assembly theme, "Come, Holy Spirit – Renew the Whole Creation." Clad in traditional Korean peasant costume, Chung began with a shamanistic ritual, invoking the spirit of those who died in Hiroshima and Nagasaki, in the Holocaust, in Tiananmen Square, in the Kwang-ju massacre, and other places. Her searing address was accompanied by music, slides, dance, drums, rituals, and two Aboriginal dancers. Chung's presentation created a huge controversy in the global church as some praised her use of shamanistic rituals, Buddhist symbols, and East Asian philosophical ideas to expand our understanding of the work of the Spirit. But others objected that she had gone too far, raising questions of syncretism and the limit of diversity within the Christian church.

Two years afterward, another controversy, stimulated by the Re-imagining Conference in Minneapolis, beset the churches in the United States. The gathering was to celebrate the midpoint of the Ecumenical Decade of Churches in Solidarity with Women, a movement initiated by the World Council of Churches (WCC). Over four thousand Protestant women and some men attended the conference to re-imagine Christianity in fresh ways and to highlight women's struggles in the churches. Bernice Johnson Reagan of the musical group Sweet Honey in the Rock spoke passionately about the heritage of African American music, while Carla DeSola danced the spirit on stage. Liturgical artist Nancy Chinn transformed the lecture hall with banners symbolizing the many cultures that people brought with them. Memorable chants, Native American rites, and Asian blessings enriched the worship services and liturgy. One of the theme songs invoked Blessed Sophia to come and bless the gathering. While many participants felt that this was the most rejuvenating event in years, the conservative wings of the churches denounced the Conference for spreading heresies about Jesus and atonement, using inappropriate liturgies, and paying tributes to goddesses.

These two incidents highlight the diverse understanding of interfaith encounter in the churches, and the potential tensions and misunderstandings that may arise.

The first case emerges from the history of indigenizing the church in Asian cultures shaped by other religious traditions. The second highlights the complex and often unsettling issues of using rituals and spiritual resources from other traditions in Christian worship and gatherings. And both illustrate the dramatic changes brought to Christian worship, liturgy, and spiritual practices by the global women's movement over the past decades.

Sandra Schneiders (1993: 210) defines spirituality as "that dimension of the human subject in virtue of which the person is capable of self-transcending integration in relation to the Ultimate, whatever the Ultimate is for the person in question." She maintains that the study of Christian spirituality must be interdisciplinary, cross-cultural, and inter-religious, giving serious consideration to other forms of spirituality that are not Christian and that may not be literarily articulated and theologically explicated. As she opines: "The world is too small and the stakes are too high to privatize religion or ghettoize spirituality" (1993: 218). In fact, Christianity's encounter with other faith traditions has a long history, which helped to shape Christian identity, worship, and ritual practices from its inception. A brief review of the historical roots of that encounter provides a context for discussing interfaith dialogue and Christian spirituality in our contemporary setting.

Historical Roots

Christian attitudes toward other faith traditions have been strongly influenced by the Bible. Many Christians assume that the Bible teaches that there is only one true monotheistic religion, which prohibits the worship of other gods. But if we look beyond the theological and religious arguments regarding other religions and focus instead on the spiritual and cultic practices of both the Jewish people and the early Christian community, we will discern a much more pluralistic and varied lived experience. For example, as the Hebrew people settled in the land of Canaan, they appropriated many Canaanite rites and ceremonies in the development of the cult and worship of Yahweh. These included the building of sanctuaries and temples, the sacrificial offering of food and drink to the gods, girls dancing in the vineyards during feasts, Canaanite agricultural festivals celebrating new grain and wheat harvests, and the dedication of the first-born to the deity (Fohrer 1973: 106, 157, 202–3, 208).

The Hebrew people lived in a multi-religious environment among the Hittites, Babylonians, Egyptians, and Assyrians, who worshiped many gods and goddesses. Although the prophets repeatedly admonished them not to worship or bow down to foreign gods, these injunctions were obviously not strictly followed. The people of Israel worshiped Baal and Asherah, and equated El with Yahweh, and the religion of El and Yahwism began to coalesce (Fohrer 1973: 104–5). In the past, Christians have often labeled the worship of Baal, Asherah, and Astarte as "fertility cults," but recent scholarship has helped to discern new meaning and vibrancy in some of these traditions. For example, the veneration of Asherah as the goddess who protected the trees had a long history in ancient Israel and Judah (Hadley 2000). And C. S. Song (1993: 7–11), a Taiwanese theologian, has criticized both the prophets' failure to appreciate the "idols" as symbols with religious meaning, and their negative and exclusive attitude toward other religions.

In the New Testament, the early Christian community had to define itself in the pluralistic contexts of Judaism, Greco-Roman traditions, and Near Eastern religions – not only in terms of religious beliefs and ideas, but also more significantly in terms of religious and cultic practices. For example, at the Jerusalem Council, the apostles and elders decided that Gentile believers would not be required to follow Jewish law, after hearing what Paul and Barnabas had done among the Gentiles (Acts 15). As the apostle to the Gentiles, Paul argued vigorously that the Gentiles should not be required to adopt the Jewish practice of circumcision. In his letter to the Corinthian church (1 Cor. 8: 10) Paul exhibited tactfulness and sensitivity in handling the thorny question of whether Christians could eat food sacrificed to the pagan gods (Yeo 1994). The nascent Christian community used baptism as an initiation rite, a practice adopted from Jewish and Near Eastern bathing and cleaning customs, and appropriated Jewish liturgy for its worship service. Gnostic ideas and practices found their way into Pauline and Johannine literature, as well as into the Gospel of Thomas and Gospel of Mary, religious texts that were circulated in the early church period but not included in the canonical Bible. In fact, Rudolf Bultmann (1956: 177–9) has observed that early Christianity was a *syncretistic* movement, which accounted for its success in attracting both Jews and Gentiles into its fold.

The spread of Christianity to other parts of Europe did not completely eliminate indigenous tradition and spirituality, as some of the old ways were absorbed into the Christian church. This is most evident in the case of Celtic Christianity (Joyce 1998). Christianity came to Ireland from Britain, which had in turn received it from Gaul. But at the northern and western edge of Europe, Ireland was too remote from Rome and did not take on many of the organizational attributes of the continental churches that spread with the empire. The Irish were never part of the Roman empire, and many of their own social structures and cultural traditions survived. As a result, many Celtic traits found expression in Celtic Christianity, such as their love of poetry, music, and storytelling, their reverence for nature, and their respect for relationships and kinship. Their non-linear apprehension of time and space and seeing everything as intertwined influenced art, architecture, writing, and decorating. The circle, rather than the straight line, symbolizes Celtic life, and the "spiral knot" signifies the interconnection of all things, with no beginning or end.

But not all "pagan" and folk traditions were welcomed by the church; some practitioners had to continue in secrecy for fear of being condemned and persecuted as heretical. Many of the adherents of folk traditions of Old Europe were women, whose affiliation with these practices made them susceptible to witch hunts in early modern Europe. Interpreting witch hunts with the intention of recovering women's history, Anne Llewellyn Barstow (1994: 109–18) shows that many of the accused witches were healers and diviners, who used spells, potions, and herbs to deliver babies, perform abortions, curse, remove curses, and make peace. Their roles as village healers resembled those of the priests in the church, in which women's leadership was severely limited. Some of these women practiced folk magic and witchcraft, which typically included incantations, the wearing of amulets, and the repeating of charms. Sometimes, these women even cast out demons in the name of the Father, the Son, and Holy Ghost, and recited the Lord's Prayer and Hail Mary when they gathered medicinal herbs. In some cases, women who were brought before the inquisitors belonged to small groups dedicated to the goddesses of Old Europe, such as Diana. These women did not feel that they had committed a sin, as the goddess tradition provided them with a valid alternative to the patriarchal church.

The persecution of the Other within Europe – the heretics, the witches, and the Jews – was linked with European imperialism and racism. Barstow (1994: 12) observes: "The witch hunt took place at the same time as colonial expansion and the Atlantic slave trade, and they were made possible by some of the same ecclesiastical policies and legal changes." Colonial expansion brought the Christian church into contact with many peoples, languages, cultures, and faith traditions. With a Eurocentric mindset, missionaries looked down upon and condemned the religious practices of other peoples as superstitious and idolatrous. At first, the natives were considered pagans and infidels, who could be incorporated into the Christian fold. Salvation of their souls was seen as more important than saving their bodies, an ideology which has justified horrendous genocide and colonial violence. Then, from the late Enlightenment period onward, the difference between colonizers and colonized was increasingly defined by racial difference, and the colonized were denigrated as being backward and inferior (Thomas 1994: 77). Christian mission was recast as a "civilizing mission," bringing not only Christianity, but Western schools and medicine, as well as norms and values, to the colonized world. In terms suggested by the evolutionary theory of the nineteenth century, Christianity was hailed as the highest stage of human religious development.

The political struggles for independence of the colonies of Europe following the Second World War challenged the complicit relation of the church with colonialism, and compelled the church to rethink its mission. At the same time, the mass migration of people into the West as refugees, people in exile or diaspora, and immigrants radically changed the religious landscape in the West, most notably in America. As Diana Eck (2001) has shown, the United States has become the world's most religiously diverse nation, and Los Angeles can claim to be the most complex and diverse Buddhist city in the world. Eck notes that a similar shift toward religious pluralism is seen in other parts of the Western world:

> The dynamic global image of our times is not the so-called clash of civilizations but the marbling of civilizations and peoples. Just as the end of the Cold War brought about a new geopolitical situation, the global movements of people have brought about a new georeligious reality. Hindus, Sikhs, and Muslims are now part of the religious landscape of Britain, mosques appear in Paris and Lyons, Buddhist temples in Toronto, and Sikh gurdwaras in Vancouver. (2001: 4)

As people of many faiths have come to settle in the metropolis, the question for Western Christians is no longer how to missionize non-believers in far-away lands, but how to live among religious neighbors whose children go to the same schools as theirs. Such a situation is by no means new; many Christians in Africa and Asia have been faced with similar questions for a long time. This simply means that people in the Western world are experiencing the pluralistic condition that has defined the religiosity of the majority of the world's population. As religious pluralism has become a global phenomenon, how to live harmoniously together as peoples of faith is a critical key to world peace.

Interfaith Dialogue and Christian Spirituality

With the dismantling of the colonial power and the outcry for cultural autonomy, a triumphal approach to Christian mission became suspect, and dialogue became a catchword (Panikkar 1987: 95). Many people imagine dialogue as people belonging to diverse "religions" coming together to converse with one another. As time went by, however, more and more Christian leaders recognized that their dialogical partners were not members of other "religions," but people of living faiths, with profound spiritual insights and deep personal piety. In his modern classic *The Meaning and End of Religion*, Wilfred Cantwell Smith (1978: 50–1) argues that the concept of "religion" as used in the West has gone through a long process of reification – that is, mentally making it a thing or an objective systematic entity. The continued use of the terms "religion" and "religions," according to Smith, has blocked Western understanding, throughout history and throughout the world, of the vitality of personal faith of people from other traditions. Because of the works of Smith and other religious scholars, the term *interfaith* dialogue is used instead of inter-religious dialogue in some Christian circles.

Since the 1960s, different Christian organizations have explicitly addressed the challenges of other faith traditions. The Second Vatican Council took the unprecedented step of paying serious attention to inter-religious relations, and issued the Declaration on the Relationship of the Church to Non-Christian Religions (*Nostra aetate*), which applauds the "profound religious sense" of other traditions and exhorts all Catholics to "dialogue and collaborate" with other believers (Knitter 2002: 75–6). The Vatican created the Secretariat on Non-Christians, now renamed the Pontifical Council of Inter-religious Dialogue. Meanwhile, the World Council of Churches addressed the question of different religious faiths at the Uppsala assembly in 1968 in the section "Seeking Community: The Common Search of People of Various Faiths, Cultures, and Ideologies." Then, at the following assembly in Nairobi in 1975, dialogue was discussed more broadly, which created quite a stir, as some regarded dialogue as a retreat from Jesus's commission to preach the gospel to the ends of the earth and make disciples of all nations (Eck 1993: 198, 214). In order to help member churches understand the need for interfaith dialogue and to foster a "wider ecumenism" beyond the Christian fold, the World Council of Churches created a subunit called Dialogue with People of Living Faiths.

A former director of the subunit, Wesley Ariarajah from Sri Lanka (1989: 39–47), argues that there are biblical warrants for a wider religious worldview and for interfaith dialogue. He cautions that the stories in the Bible are told primarily from the viewpoint of Israel and may not reflect the understanding of other religious neighbors. He highlights the biblical tradition that stresses God's covenant with all nations and the universal salvation promised by Christ for all people. God is the creator of all humankind, and the universality of Christ provides the foundation for openness, sympathetic understanding, and dialogue with other people. Ariarajah holds up the examples of interfaith encounter of peoples in the Bible as positive models. Jonah, for instance, was at first reluctant to go to Nineveh, the capital of the Assyrian empire. But when he finally went and called the people to repentance, the response was overwhelming and beyond all his expectations. Another example is Peter, who in his vision was exhorted not to consider anything unclean that God has made clean (Acts 10: 9–16). Challenging the custom that Jews were not supposed to mix with Gentiles, Peter met with the Roman centurion, who later became a follower of Jesus. Ariarajah concludes that dialogue does not contradict Christian witness; the early disciples often adopted a dialogical approach before Christianity became institutionalized as a state religion. Paul's mission strategy is a case in point. Respecting the religious backgrounds of his audiences, Paul emphasized Jesus as the Messiah when speaking to the Jews (Acts 17: 2–4), but opted for a more theocentric approach when preaching to the Athenians, acknowledging that they were extremely religious and even worshiped an unknown God (Acts 17: 22–3). Ariarajah convincingly demonstrates that interfaith dialogue is not only a contemporary concern of Christians but was also a challenge to the early church.

While the challenges of interfaith dialogue to Christian theology and mission have been discussed at some length, attention to the issues raised by dialogue in relation to Christian spirituality has been less pronounced. In 1987 the World Council of Churches organized a consultation on "Spirituality in Interfaith Dialogue" in Kyoto, Japan, and began to explore how dialogue changed the spiritual practices of those who had participated in it for a long time (Arai and Ariarajah 1989). In the following I will briefly discuss the implications of interfaith dialogue for Christian spirituality.

First, participation in interfaith dialogue often results in a serious reflection on, or negotiation of, religious identity at both the personal and communal levels. In the Chinese language, dialogue means talking face to face with one another, which implies "mutuality, active listening, and openness to what one's partner has to say" (Kwok 1995: 12). A serious engagement in dialogue deepens our understanding of Christianity as well as the faith traditions of others, and as a result broadens our horizons to see Christianity in radically new ways. A dialogue that is mutual and reciprocal changes both partners involved; the transformation does not signify a weakening of faith, but a maturing of faith, which is constantly open to challenge and enrichment. In the process, Christians recognize that we do not walk the spiritual path alone, but meet many others on the journey; as the statement from the Kyoto Consultation says: "we affirm the great value of dialogue at the level of spirituality in coming to know and understand people of other faiths as people of prayer and spiritual practice, as seekers and pilgrims with us, and as partners with us in working for peace and justice" (Arai and Ariarajah 1989: 2).

Meeting other religious pilgrims raises new questions about our personal and collective understanding of Christian identity. In contemporary theological debates on religious pluralism, there are three distinct positions toward other faith traditions: the exclusivist, inclusivist, and pluralist standpoints (Race 1982: 10–37). But spirituality is more than believing in a set of religious ideas or truth claims, and consequently cannot be easily categorized or put into boxes. Spirituality concerns the shape or mode of Christian living and "being-in-the-world." It involves not just the mind, but the body and the soul as well. Interfaith dialogue pushes us to consider what defines Christian identity. Is it the belief system or the practice? Can we be Buddhist and Christian at the same time, and if so, how? Why do so many people who come from a Christian background say they are spiritual, but not religious, and seldom go to church? Are they post-Christians or latent Christians? We will take up some of these issues below.

Second, interfaith dialogue can deepen and enrich Christian spirituality by exposing Christians to other forms of meditation, prayer, chanting, and religious music. Thomas Merton, the renowned Catholic Trappist monk, expressed great interest in Asian religions in his later years. To work on monastic renewal, he traveled to Asia to converse with Buddhist monastics and Hindu gurus on meditation, mysticism, music, art, and spiritual discipline. Shortly before he died in Bangkok in 1968, Merton met the Dalai Lama, and the two discussed, among other things, meditation techniques, including concrete details such as sitting posture and the position of the hands in order to focus the mind (Burton et al. 1973: 112). In a paper delivered at an interfaith meeting in Calcutta, Merton said: "I think we have now reached a stage of (long-overdue) religious maturity at which it may be possible for someone to remain perfectly faithful to a Christian and Western monastic commitment, and yet to learn in depth from, say, a Buddhist or Hindu discipline and experience" (Burton et al. 1973: 313). Merton considered the Asian monastics kindred spirits, and his Asian journal demonstrated his sincere humility, curiosity, and readiness to learn from others.

While Merton and other Western Christians have found Asian spiritual discipline helpful, some Asian Christians, who had been taught by the church to deny their cultural heritage, are also tapping into their rich indigenous spiritual traditions. For example, Indian theologian Thomas Thangaraj entered the world of Hindu spirituality through his love of music, and as a theological teacher and pastor, he began to incorporate Hindu music and spiritual practices into worship and daily Christian life. Thangaraj testifies: "My whole journey has been one of opening up my spirituality to be inclusive, step by step, and more and more. It has come to be inclusive of Hindu openness, Hindu musical traditions and the spiritual exercises of other faiths" (1989: 22).

Third, genuine interfaith dialogue does not stop at exchanging religious ideas and praying together, but includes working across religious boundaries to promote justice and peace in society. Faith without action is dead, and interfaith dialogue without interfaith solidarity is empty words. Collaborating with others to minimize suffering in the world deepens the Christian conviction that spirituality cannot be divorced from the world of social action and that contemplation and action are inseparable. Many people in the West are inspired by the life and work of the Zen Buddhist Master Thich Nhat Hanh, who first caught the world's attention by his protest against the Vietnam War and his engaged Buddhism, which did not separate being from doing. Among his many followers are Christians who go to church and follow the way of Christ. In his book *Teachings on Love* (1998), Thich Nhat Hanh exhorts Christians and Buddhists alike to cultivate mindfulness and to practice compassion in our words and action so that our love can transform our families, our enemies, and the whole world. Many have come to him to learn about meditation and simplicity of life, with the hope that such spiritual discipline will make a difference in their lives and the world.

An intentional community that seeks to integrate dialogue with action, secular ideology with religious tradition, and liturgy with life is the Devasarana community in Sri Lanka. Living among the village people, the community began as an action-reflection movement based on a Buddhist–Christian dialogue, and subsequently developed into a Buddhist–Christian–Marxist dialogue. The contemplative life at Devasarana drew inspiration from both Eastern and Western traditions, especially those of St Anthony and St Benedict. Concrete social action has involved peasant organization, struggle for land reform, educating the masses, and building a collective farm. It became an experiment of a living dialogue among people of various faiths and ideologies bonded together for a common struggle. Because of disillusionment with traditional forms of worship and to accommodate the diversity of the members, the group developed the New World Liturgy, which drew upon resources from the major religions and ideologies, with the common theme of development, justice, and liberation (Devananda 1989).

Fourth, interfaith dialogue brings into sharp relief the roles of women in religious worship and leadership, women's bodies and sexuality, and women's emerging spirituality. When women of different faiths gather together and compare their situations, they become aware of their marginal position in religious communities, the limits on their access to ritual and liturgical leadership, and the tremendous need for change (Eck and Jain 1987; Abraham et al. 1989). The two examples at the beginning of this essay illustrate the ambivalence of the churches in accepting women's spiritual leadership and their creative exploration of non-traditional forms for expressing their faith. Historically, women have not been at the center of religious institutions, and have less vested interest in protecting doctrinal purity and a hierarchical order that strictly distinguishes the clergy from laity. Chung Hyun Kyung has argued that for women's own survival in this unjust, women-hating world, "poor Asian women have approached many religious sources for sustenance and empowerment . . . Asian women selectively have chosen life-giving elements of their culture and religions and have woven new patterns of religious meaning" (1990: 113). For them, what matters are survival and liberation; neither doctrinal orthodoxy nor ritual purity is high on their list of priorities.

Women's bodies and sexuality have been seen as a threat to spiritual discipline in many traditions in the world (Becher 1991). In some Buddhist traditions, menstruating women cannot approach the altar of the temple, and a woman's body is seen as a barrier for attaining enlightenment. Women have to transform themselves into men through reincarnation and assume a male body in order to attain Buddhahood. In the biblical tradition, the normal functions of menstruation and childbirth were regarded as unclean, and women were exhorted to go through certain purifying rites (Lev. 12: 1–8; 15: 19–30). Some of the church fathers, such as Tertullian, had a very negative view of women's sexuality and considered women the devil's gateway. As the banished children of Eve, women are still being seen as temptresses with insatiable desires, who cannot restrain their own sexual appetite and who have to submit to the control of men.

To counteract these negative stereotypes, women's emerging spirituality seeks to reclaim the body and express itself in creative ways (Webb 1993). The Re-imagining Conference attracted envy and unwarranted criticism partly because it successfully unleashed women's energy and spiritual power through art, music, dance, liturgy, and movement. Today, Christian women who find traditional worship stifling are devising new liturgy and seeking inspiration from other religious resources to express their embodied relation with God and with the earth (Neu 2002). This vibrant and innovative women's spirituality is vividly portrayed by a group of Indian Christians:

> Women's attempts to break through the culture of silence and to transform their pain into political power are a deeply spiritual experience. The attempts to draw on creative expressions – dance, drama, poetry, music, art, story-telling, and folklore – to give expression to the new-found consciousness and energy is spirituality. The longing to reclaim their femininity, as they would define it, and to reclaim their right to control their own reproductive capabilities is spirituality. It is a spirituality that would say "yes" to life and "no" to forces of death. (Indian Preparatory Group 1992: 71)

From the above discussion, we can see that interfaith encounter presents opportunities as well as raises some new issues for Christian spirituality. Two emerging issues that have received some serious attention from the Christian community include multiple religious identity and participation and the use of interfaith resources in worship and congregational life, and these will be discussed below.

Multiple Religious Identity and Participation

Many Christians in interfaith dialogue have no problem accepting that one can learn and adopt spiritual practices from other traditions, such as meditation, prayer, and yoga, to enrich one's spiritual life, while still remaining a faithful Christian. What is more controversial is whether one can have multiple religious identities and participate fully and simultaneously in more than one tradition. The issue of multiple religious participation has surfaced repeatedly in the context of Confucian–Christian dialogue since the late 1980s, when Confucian participants asked if a person can have dual citizenship – that is, belong to two traditions at once. The issue has a much longer history in Hindu–Christian dialogue, dating back to the nineteenth and early twentieth centuries, when the possibility of being a Hindu–Christian was raised. Some scholars believe that multiple religious participation has begun to emerge as an issue for faith and practice in the North Atlantic Christian world (Berthrong 1994: 27, 212). Clearly, this is caused by growing religious pluralism in the West, but the influence of the popularity of New Age spirituality cannot be underestimated.

The question of multiple religious affiliation and participation often causes uneasiness among Christians who live in societies where Christianity is the dominant tradition with exclusive claims. In such contexts, it invariably evokes the fear of syncretism, a taboo in Christian debates, for it implies an indiscriminate mixing of gods and religions. The guidelines on interfaith dialogue published by the World Council of Churches (1979: 14–15) explicitly reject syncretism, for this is precisely the accusation that critics of the dialogue movement have made. But John Berthrong (1994: 177–83), a long-time participant in Confucian–Christian dialogue, cautions us not to reject syncretism with a knee-jerk reaction; he tries to understand its different manifestations from a phenomenological point of view. While some scholars have pointed to Chinese civilization as an example in which syncretism flourishes, Berthrong notes that Christianity has also had a long tradition of absorbing foreign practices, from Judaism and Greco-Roman religiosity to Easter eggs. A living tradition, he surmises, constantly absorbs or rejects new elements it encounters. However, he questions whether there is any stable syncretistic religion, for although a tradition may absorb other ideas and practices, it tends to retain its own core or sense of identity. For example, Christianity was clearly distinguishable from the Judaic and Greco-Roman cultures out of which it emerged. He argues that the same is true for individuals. For while a person may have an interest in more than one religious tradition, he or she usually identifies with one tradition more than others.

In contrast to Berthrong, Judith A. Berling sees the interplay of religious traditions in more dynamic and fluid terms because of her study of how individual Chinese thinkers reconciled the multiple religious strands in their lives (Berling 1980). Her book *A Pilgrim in Chinese Culture* (1997) explores the ways in which Chinese culture has developed strategies for negotiating religious diversity by means of multiple religious participation, and draws implications for her Christian audience. Citing the dynamic interplay among Confucian, Taoist, and Buddhist traditions in Chinese history, she argues that the questions of syncretism and multiple religious participation may look very different from another cultural vantage point. She raises the following questions, which may be helpful to expand the Christian horizon in looking at the religious diversity of humankind:

> What happens if a society starts from the premise that multiple religious affiliations are *normal?*
> What happens if religious organizations are hospitable to one another in order to create and sustain the larger community?
> What happens if a culture develops patterns to create and sustain mutual familiarity and regular interaction among members of various religious groups? (Berling 1997: 38)

Berling recognizes that the Chinese context is very different from that of America, and she does not advocate that Christians should indiscriminately take on other religious identities. Nevertheless, she holds up the Chinese model as a mirror and stresses the importance of hospitality in living with one's religious neighbors and in entering cross-cultural and interfaith dialogue.

Berling would agree with Wilfred Cantwell Smith (1978: 57) when he says that many of the world's cultures have no equivalent term for "religion" as if there are some religious systems that can be externalized and objectified, abstracted from the persons who live them. If we look closely at the spiritual practices of Asian people who grow up in a religiously pluralistic context, we will often see that there is a mixture from many sources, which can hardly be defined by one religious tradition. A Chinese or a Japanese person may go to a Taoist, Buddhist, or Shinto temple, depending on the event and life circumstances. Such fluid and shifting identities challenge the notion of religious identity as rigid and static, and call into question Berthrong's argument that one religious identity tends to dominate over others in an individual. In her candid and lyrical memoir *The Butterfly Healing*, Julia Ching (1998) demonstrates how this fluid identity formation is at work in her life as an expert on Confucian thought and a Catholic. In her pilgrimage between East and West, she embraces the best of Catholic teaching as well as the insights from Buddhist masters, the Taoist Chuang Tzu, and Confucian sages during her long struggle with cancer. For her, the self has many rooms, and she uses the metaphor "the house of self" to express this complexity. Describing her life as a spiritual quest, she writes: "It has been a quest that started in the East and led to the West, only to take me back to the East, culturally speaking" (Ching 1999: 58).

Ching's "passing over and coming back" reflected an in-depth immersion in the multiple traditions she embodied, and a genuine and remarkable reconciliation of the multiple layers of her self. Such spiritual maturity, however, is hard to attain and is the work of a lifetime. Furthermore, her Chinese and Canadian cultures may be more accepting of plurality and multiple religious participation. As John Cobb (2002), a theologian in Buddhist–Christian dialogue, has observed, it is easier to have multiple religious belonging in some contexts than it is in others. While it is possible for a Christian to adopt Buddhist meditation, it is harder for adherents of the monotheistic Abrahamic faiths to cross over. He also thinks that even if a Christian adopts some Buddhist practices, it is difficult to live out both the Christian and Buddhist ways of being and commitments in the fullest sense. Although he supports the experimentation of multiple belonging, which he says may have appeal to those individuals who find it difficult to identify fully with one tradition, he prefers to be rooted in a single tradition, while seeking its constant transformation by the inspiration of others.

Cobb's position is different from that of advocates of the complementarity and convergence of Christianity and other religious traditions. It was for advocating such radical views that Jesuit priest Jacques Dupuis (1997) was investigated by the Congregation for the Doctrine of the Faith of the Vatican. Citing the example of Henri Le Saux (with an Indian name Abhishiktanananda) and the concept of Christ the Omega in Teilhard de Chardin, Dupuis (2002) is open to the possibility that double religious belonging can be a partial anticipation of the full recapitulation in Christ of all religions, which will only be disclosed at the end of time. His fellow Jesuit, Aloysius Pieris of Sri Lanka, shares his view of the complementarity of religious traditions, but does not subscribe to the notion of teleological convergence. A leading voice in Buddhist–Christian dialogue, Pieris says Buddhism and Christianity represent two different poles of experience – gnosis and agape, or wisdom and love – each of which is incomplete without the other:

> What must be borne in mind is that both gnosis and agape are *necessary* precisely because each in itself is *inadequate* as a medium, not only for experiencing but also for expressing our intimate moments with the Ultimate Source of Liberation. They are, in other words, complementary idioms that need each other to mediate the self-transcending experience called "salvation." Any valid spirituality, Buddhist or Christian, as the history of each religion attests, does retain both poles of experience – namely, the gnostic and the agapeic. (1988: 111)

Pieris avoids the terms "convergence," "syncretism," and "synthesis" because they tend to imply the violation of the unique individual identity of each tradition, and because they gloss over differences. Instead, Pieris (1996: 154–61) uses the term "symbiosis," which points to a movement of people of different identities living and working closely with one another and in the process teaching what is important in their own faith. As a Jesuit, Pieris not only received a doctorate in Buddhism, but has also lived among Buddhist monks in a monastery, immersing himself in that tradition and experiencing a true "passing over and coming back," as Julia Ching did.

Any discussion on inter-religious dialogue would not be complete without mentioning Raimon Panikkar, whose erudition and expansive mind has contributed much to the conversation for several decades. Born to a Hindu father and a Catholic mother, Panikkar (1999) has coined the term *intra-religious* dialogue to denote the preparatory process required to enter into deep exchange with one's dialogical partner. If inter-religious dialogue implies a conversation between people of different traditions, intra-religious dialogue means holding two ways of seeing and feeling, thinking and being, within one and the same person. This is the effort of what Panikkar has described as entering into the religious worldview of the other with "com-prehension," and interior "sym-pathy" or "em-pathy." Although Panikkar rejects the eclectic mixing of religions, his own embodiment of multiple religious belonging points to the possibilities of cross-fertilization and the constant expansion of one's own self-understanding.

While the discussion above has focused on interfaith encounter between Christianity and the historical religious traditions, the emergence of a new phenomenon that has been loosely called New Age drastically challenges the old ways of defining religious identity. New Age in America is a very diverse set of phenomena that can include anything from New Age music, self-help spiritual books, tarot cards, crystals, yoga, goddess worship, Buddhist and transcendental meditation, neo-paganism, occult, witchcraft, astrology, and commercialized Native practices. New Age philosophy, in general, draws heavily from the Asian and Native American traditions, with an interest in recovering ancient beliefs and practices. If religious pluralism has changed the *religious* landscape of America, then New Age must be said to have changed its *spiritual* landscape. Fully 20 percent of the American population identify themselves as spiritual, but they do not fit easily with any traditional religion.

In *After Heaven*, Robert Wuthnow surveys the transformation of spirituality in America since the 1950s and characterizes the spiritual shift in this way: "a traditional spirituality of inhabiting sacred spaces has given way to a new spirituality of seeking" (1998: 3). "Habitation spirituality" has a sense of belonging to a home or a dwelling place, inside which one feels protected, secure, and in solidarity with others. It identifies with formal religious structures, traditional religious authority, and remains loyal to religious heritage. Religious boundaries are usually clearly drawn and are based on ethnic and national origins – for example, Irish Catholics, Vietnamese Buddhists, and Indian Hindus. A spirituality of seeking, in contrast, does not have a permanent home, and the nomadic seekers are explorers and sojourners, not dwellers. They exchange certainty and security for the freedom to explore and combine various spiritual practices they deem suitable. They are less likely to accept rigid religious boundaries, authoritarian teachings, and the hypocrisy of religious leadership. They often say they are spiritual, but not religious. "If religion is the channel to pass down a cultural legacy, then spirituality can be seen as the uncharted space to explore personal identity and the fulfillment of life" (Kwok 2002: 4).

As a form of seekers' spirituality, New Age has caught the attention of different Christian groups (Saliba 1999). The evangelical and fundamentalist commentators see New Age as a serious competitor to their traditional Christian values. Their writings reaffirm orthodox Christian doctrines, denounce many of the New Age leaders, and alert Christians to the danger of New Age beliefs. The responses from mainline Protestant churches and writers show a wider spectrum. While some writers stress the incompatibility of New Age with Christian doctrines, others seek to understand the reasons for its appeal and affirm that Christianity and New Age can learn from one another. Among the Catholics, the official response from the church has been largely negative, treating New Age as incompatible with Catholic teachings. The *Catechism of the Catholic Church* (1994) summarily condemned some of the popular practices associated with the New Age movement, such as divinatory practices, horoscopes, astrology, and palmistry. On the other hand, some Catholic writers think that New Age has positive aspects and discern similarities between New Age and the Catholic tradition, such as a positive understanding of creation. They suggest that Catholics can adopt New Age practices that are not at odds with Catholic teachings.

In spite of all these diverse responses, New Age continues to grow unabated. Robert Fuller (2001), a scholar who has studied "unchurched America," argues that New Age meets the psychological and spiritual needs of people who are dissatisfied with the church and other institutional religions. He traces the New Age phenomenon to its historical roots in the nineteenth century, when transcendentalism, Swedenborgianism, theosophy, and spiritualism mushroomed in America. People alienated from the church were attracted to alternative medical paradigms, such as homeopathy, chiropractics, and mesmerism, in seeking other spiritual frameworks to connect the body and the mind. Some of these trends resurfaced in contemporary spiritual quests, especially in practices that integrate the body, mind, and spirit, such as yoga, tai chi, reiki, and therapeutic touch. Scholars who have studied New Age music argue that, by combining ancient traditions and modern ideas, New Age music challenges elitism, the loss of mutuality, and patriarchal control in dominant musical traditions. June Boyce-Tillman (2000: 155–201), who has studied the relation between music and healing, writes that New Age allows mystical traditions and other ancient wisdom suppressed by the dominant culture to re-emerge. She says that the practices of communal music-making, the discovery of "natural sounds," the freedom to express and experiment, and the use of breathing and movement with music to release energy have the potential to connect the soul to the universe and to produce healing at the personal, ecological, and cosmic levels.

The Use of Interfaith Resources in Worship and Congregational Life

While individuals may pursue multiple religious belonging or adopt the eclectic New Age approach, the use of resources from other faith traditions in Christian worship and in congregational life raises more complex questions as it concerns the collective identity and public witness of the church. Different Christian bodies have issued statements or guidelines regarding the use of such resources. In 1989, the Congregation for the Doctrine of the Faith issued a letter to the bishops concerning the use of non-Christian meditation techniques. It says: "proposals to harmonize Christian meditation with Eastern techniques need to have their contents and methods ever subjected to a thoroughgoing examination so as to avoid the danger of falling into syncretism" (para. 12). Then in 2000, the Congregation issued the declaration *Dominus Iesus* to clarify the relation between the Roman Catholic Church and other religions. The document reaffirms the uniqueness of salvation through Christ and says that: "The Church's constant missionary proclamation is endangered today by relativistic theories that seek to justify religious pluralism, not only de facto but also de iure" (para. 4). It explicitly rejects the claim that religions are complementary or converging, and stresses the primacy of the church and the sacraments. Although the document deals primarily with theological arguments, it includes a section on the rituals and practices of other faith traditions:

> Indeed, some prayers and rituals of the other religions may assume a role of preparation for the Gospel, in that they are occasions or pedagogical helps in which the human heart is prompted to be open to the action of God. One cannot attribute to these, however, a divine origin or an *ex opere operato* salvific efficacy, which is proper to the Christian sacraments. Furthermore, it cannot be overlooked that other rituals, insofar as they depend on superstitions or other errors (cf. 1 Cor 10: 20–1), constitute an obstacle to salvation. (para. 21)

The declaration regards other rituals, at their best, as preparing people for the fulfillment of the gospel, and not as having independent salvific efficacy. As the document is not meant to offer practical guidance, it does not spell out how such beneficial rituals and prayers can be used, or how to differentiate them from other rituals that it considers to be based on superstitions and errors.

The Church of England, on the other hand, had to face peoples with diverse religious traditions within the Commonwealth and has discussed interfaith worship since the 1960s. While the statements from the church in the 1960s encouraged dialogue and exchange of visits, they did not encourage interfaith services or the use of local churches for such purposes. But as interfaith worship grew in the late 1980s, creating controversy among the clergy and laity (Braybrooke 1997: 8–13), the Church of England had to offer more practical guidelines on worship in a multi-faith society (Interfaith Consultative Group 1992). These guidelines discuss the questions of using other religious resources while maintaining the integrity of Christian worship, and the danger of trying to fit other religious texts or prayers into the Christian mode, which can be patronizing. They recommend the use of a more neutral place instead of the church building, and when services are held in the church, they have to abide by canon law.

A key issue in using religious resources from other traditions in worship and congregational life is the misappropriation of these traditions. A particularly controversial question is the use of Native American religious resources. While Native American

Christians have reclaimed parts of their heritage such as the symbol of the circle, the four directions, the use of the drum, and purifying rites using cedar, sage, or tobacco in Native American Christian worship (Charleston 2000), the use of Native elements by non-Native people is problematic. Given the history of genocide of Native peoples and their struggle for cultural survival, the use of these elements without the presence of Native people and without accountability to the Native community can be seen as a form of cultural theft. Laura Donaldson (1999), a scholar of Cherokee descent, has particularly warned against the use of Native artifacts such as the feathers, baskets, and blankets as fetishes commodified by New Age, white feminist, and other movements. The misappropriation of Native American religious resources is linked with the global assault on indigenous cultures.

Given the seriousness of the charge of misappropriation, it is important that interfaith worship be conducted with representatives of different faiths present; ideally, the different groups would have formed a multi-faith community before they worship together. It is important to remember that, in adopting other spiritual practices in worship and in church life, we are not merely following some "techniques," but learning from the spiritual traditions of others. All spiritual practices have their specific contexts, religious meanings, and theological or religious roots in a particular community's history. The ethical use of these practices requires us to treat other traditions with respect. As Karen Lebacqz and Joseph Driskill have said: "To be respectful of a tradition is not simply to 'use' it or to use part of it for our own purposes, but to honor its integrity" (2000: 92). It is important for pastors to educate parishioners and warn them of the danger of an easy adaptation.

In addition to interfaith worship in churches, pastors may be called upon to lead interfaith services in hospitals and schools, or in marriages and funerals. Ecumenical leaders have long discussed the need for ministerial formation in a multi-faith milieu (Amirtham and Ariarajah 1986). This is particularly important for churches in Asia, and should be taken seriously for churches in other parts of the world. The existing curriculum of many seminaries and theological schools does not require students to learn about other religious traditions. When spirituality is included in the curriculum, it focuses more on the denomination's tradition, and seldom introduces spiritual practices from a multi-faith perspective. In addition to the training of ministers, those preparing for spiritual direction should also be sensitized to the different cultures and faith traditions that people bring. Lily Quintos (1992), a Catholic religious woman, argues that knowledge of various religious premises and practices will enable a spiritual director to better understand the religious behavior of diverse directees and assist them in seeking integration and spiritual fulfillment.

As interfaith encounter increases, Christian churches have opportunities to rethink their own identity and their mission in a multi-faith environment. To continue its appeal to the religious dwellers and to attract the spiritual seekers, Christian spirituality must be able to address the spiritual crisis of modern times and be open to learning from others. Christians are becoming more aware that other pilgrims can be our dialogical partners and that there are values in different spiritual paths. The ancient Taoist classic *Tao Te Ching* reminds us that the way (Tao) that can be named is not the way. It points to the limits of our language and logic to comprehend the mystery, the way.

Christian spirituality can be enlivened and rejuvenated if we embrace the attitudes of humility, empathy, and inclusiveness in facing the mystery and in encountering the diversity of the human spirit.

References

Abraham, D., Park, S. A. L., and Dahlin, Y. (eds) 1989: *Faith Renewed: A Report on the First Asian Women's Consultation on Interfaith Dialogue*. Hong Kong: Asian Women's Centre for Culture and Theology.

Amirtham, S. and Ariarajah, W. 1986: *Ministerial Formation in a Multi-faith Milieu: Implications of Interfaith Dialogue for Theological Education*. Geneva: World Council of Churches.

Arai, T. and Ariarajah, W. (eds) 1989: *Spirituality in Interfaith Dialogue*. Geneva: World Council of Churches.

Ariarajah, W. 1989: *The Bible and People of Other Faiths*. Maryknoll, NY: Orbis.

Barstow, A. L. 1994: *Witchcraze: A New History of the European Witch Hunts*. San Francisco: Pandora.

Becher, J. (ed.) 1991: *Women, Religion and Sexuality*. Geneva: World Council of Churches.

Berling, J. A. 1980: *The Syncretic Religion of Lin Chao-en*. New York: Columbia University Press.

—— 1997: *A Pilgrim in Chinese Culture: Negotiating Religious Diversity*. Maryknoll, NY: Orbis.

Berthrong, J. H. 1994: *All under Heaven: Transforming Paradigms in Confucian–Christian Dialogue*. Albany, NY: State University of New York Press.

Boyce-Tillman, J. 2000: *Constructing Musical Healing: The Wounds that Sing*. London: Jessica Kingsley.

Braybrooke, M. 1997: The development of interfaith services and a history of the discussion about them. In J. Potter and M. Braybrooke (eds), *All in Good Faith: A Resource Book for Multi-faith Prayer*, pp. 5–25. Oxford: The World Congress of Faiths.

Bultmann, R. 1956: *Primitive Christianity in its Contemporary Setting*. London: Thames and Hudson.

Burton, N., Hart, P., and Laughlin, J. (eds) 1973: *The Asian Journal of Thomas Merton*. New York: New Directions.

Catholic Church 1994: *Catechism of the Catholic Church*. Liguori, Mo.: Liguori Publications.

Charleston, S. 2000: Native American-Christian worship. In J. Beversluis (ed.), *Sourcebook of the World's Religions: An Interfaith Guide to Religion and Spirituality*, 3rd edn, p. 34. Novato, CA: New World Library.

Ching, J. 1998: *The Butterfly Healing: A Life between East and West*. Maryknoll, NY: Orbis.

—— 1999: The house of self. In P. C. Phan and J. Y. Lee (eds), *Journeys at the Margin: Toward an Autobiographical Theology in American-Asian Perspective*, pp. 41–61. Collegeville, MN: Liturgical Press.

Chung H. K. 1990: *Struggle to be the Sun Again: Introducing Asian Women's Theology*. Maryknoll, NY: Orbis.

—— 1991: Come, Holy Spirit – renew the whole creation. In M. Kinnamon (ed.), *Signs of the Spirit, Official Report, Seventh Assembly*, pp. 37–47. Geneva: World Council of Churches.

Cobb, J. B. 2002: Multiple religious belonging and reconciliation. In C. Cornille (ed.), *Many Mansions? Multiple Religious Belonging and Christian Identity*, pp. 20–8. Maryknoll, NY: Orbis.

Congregation for the Doctrine of the Faith 1989: Letter to the bishops of the Catholic Church on some aspects of Christian meditation. *Origins* 19 (28), 492–8.

—— 2000: *Dominus Iesus*: on the unicity and salvific universality of Jesus Christ and the church. *Origins* 30 (14), 1, 211–19.

Devananda, Y. 1989: Living dialogue. In T. Arai and W. Ariarajah (eds), *Spirituality in Interfaith Dialogue*, pp. 67–77. Geneva: World Council of Churches.

Donaldson, L. E. 1999: On medicine women and white shame-ans: New Age Native Americanism and commodity fetishism as pop culture feminism. *Signs* 24 (3), 677–96.

Dupuis, J. 1997: *Toward a Christian Theology of Religious Pluralism*. Maryknoll, NY: Orbis.

—— 2002: Christianity and religions: complementarity and convergence. In C. Cornille (ed.), *Many Mansions? Multiple Religious Belonging and Christian Identity*, pp. 61–75. Maryknoll, NY: Orbis.

Eck, D. 1993: *Encountering God: A Spiritual Journey from Bozeman to Banaras*. Boston: Beacon.

—— 2001: *A New Religious America: How a "Christian Country" Has now Become the World's Most Religiously Diverse Nation*. San Francisco: Harper.

—— and Jain, D. (eds) 1987: *Speaking of Faith: Global Perspectives on Women, Religion, and Social Change*. Philadelphia: New Society.

Fohrer, G. 1973: *History of Israelite Religion*. London: SPCK.

Fuller, R. C. 2001: *Spiritual, but Not Religious: Understanding Unchurched America*. New York: Oxford University Press.

Hadley, J. M. 2000: *The Cult of Asherah in Ancient Israel and Judah: Evidence for a Hebrew Goddess*. Cambridge: Cambridge University Press.

Indian Preparatory Group 1992: An Indian search for a spirituality of liberation. In V. Fabella, P. K. H. Lee, and D. K. S. Suh (eds), *Asian Christian Spirituality: Reclaiming Traditions*, pp. 64–84. Maryknoll, NY: Orbis.

Inter-faith Consultative Group 1992: *"Multi-faith Worship": Questions and Suggestions from the Inter-faith Consultative Group*. London: Church House.

Joyce, T. J. 1998: *Celtic Christianity: A Sacred Tradition, a Vision of Hope*. Maryknoll, NY: Orbis.

Knitter, P. F. 2002: *Introducing Theologies of Religions*. Maryknoll, NY: Orbis.

Kwok P-L. 1995: *Discovering the Bible in the Non-biblical World*. Maryknoll, NY: Orbis.

—— 2002: Spiritual, and also religious? *The Brown Papers* 26 (3), 1–14.

Lebacqz, K. and Driskill, J. D. 2000: *Ethics and Spiritual Care: A Guide for Pastors, Chaplains, and Spiritual Directors*. Nashville: Abingdon Press.

Neu, D. 2002: *Return Blessings: Ecofeminist Liturgies Renewing the Earth*. Cleveland: Pilgrim.

Panikkar, R. 1987: The Jordan, the Tiber, and the Ganges. In J. Hick and P. F. Knitter (eds), *The Myth of Christian Uniqueness: Toward a Pluralistic Theology of Religions*, pp. 89–116. Maryknoll, NY: Orbis.

—— 1999: *The Intrareligious Dialogue*, 2nd edn. New York: Paulist Press.

Pieris, A. 1988: *Love Meets Wisdom: A Christian Experience of Buddhism*. Maryknoll, NY: Orbis.

—— 1996: *Fire and Water: Basic Issues in Asian Buddhism and Christianity*. Maryknoll, NY: Orbis.

Quintos, L. 1992: Experiences of the heart: *The Spiritual Exercises* across cultures. In S. Rakoczy (ed.), *Common Journey, Different Paths: Spiritual Direction in Cross-cultural Perspective*, pp. 89–96. Maryknoll, NY: Orbis.

Race, A. 1982: *Christians and Religious Pluralism: Patterns in the Christian Theology of Religions*. London: SCM.

Saliba, J. A. 1999: *Christian Responses to the New Age Movement: A Critical Assessment*. London: Geoffrey Chapman.

Schneiders, S. M. 1993: Spirituality as an academic discipline: reflections from experience. In M. A. Tilley and S. A. Ross (eds), *Broken and Whole: Essays on Religion and the Body*, pp. 207–18. Lanham, MD: University Press of America.

Smith, W. C. 1978: *The Meaning and End of Religion: A Revolutionary Approach to the Great Religious Traditions.* New York: Harper and Row.

Song, C. S. 1993: Living theology: birth and rebirth. In J. C. England and A. C. C. Lee (eds), *Doing Theology with Asian Resources: Ten Years in the Formation of Living Theology in Asia*, pp. 6–24. Hong Kong: Program for Theology and Culture in Asia.

Thangaraj, M. T. 1989: Journey towards an inclusive spirituality. In T. Arai and W. Ariarajah (eds), *Spirituality in Interfaith Dialogue*, pp. 19–22. Geneva: World Council of Churches.

Thich N. H. 1998: *Teachings on Love.* Berkeley, CA: Parallax.

Thomas, N. 1994: *Colonialism's Culture: Anthropology, Travel, and Government.* Cambridge: Polity Press.

Webb, P. M. 1993: Interfaith and women's spirituality. *The Way Supplement* 78, 23–31.

World Council of Churches 1979: *Guidelines on Dialogue with People of Living Faiths and Ideologies.* Geneva: World Council of Churches.

Wuthnow, R. 1998: *After Heaven: Spirituality in America since the 1950s.* Berkeley, CA: University of California Press.

Yeo, K. K. 1994: The rhetorical hermeneutic of 1 Corinthians 8 and Chinese ancestor worship. *Biblical Interpretation* 2 (3), 294–311.

Index

566 INDEX